The Main Enterprise of the World

WALTER A. STRAUSS LECTURES IN THE HUMANITIES

Series Editor: Peter E. Knox, Eric and Jane Nord Family Professor,
Case Western Reserve University

Sponsored by the Baker-Nord Center for the Humanities at Case Western Reserve University, the Walter A. Strauss Lectures in the Humanities address a broad range of topics across all fields of humanistic research, especially as they intersect with issues that affect the general public.

VOLUMES PUBLISHED IN THE SERIES

The Main Enterprise of the World: Rethinking Education
Philip Kitcher

The Main Enterprise of the World

Rethinking Education

PHILIP KITCHER

OXFORD
UNIVERSITY PRESS

Oxford University Press is a department of the University of Oxford. It furthers the University's objective of excellence in research, scholarship, and education by publishing worldwide. Oxford is a registered trade mark of Oxford University Press in the UK and certain other countries.

Published in the United States of America by Oxford University Press
198 Madison Avenue, New York, NY 10016, United States of America.

© Oxford University Press 2022

First issued as an Oxford University Press paperback, 2024

All rights reserved. No part of this publication may be reproduced, stored in a retrieval system, or transmitted, in any form or by any means, without the prior permission in writing of Oxford University Press, or as expressly permitted by law, by license, or under terms agreed with the appropriate reproduction rights organization. Inquiries concerning reproduction outside the scope of the above should be sent to the Rights Department, Oxford University Press, at the address above.

You must not circulate this work in any other form
and you must impose this same condition on any acquirer.

CIP data is on file at the Library of Congress
ISBN 978–0–19–092897–1 (Hbk.)
ISBN 978–0–19–779933–8 (Pbk.)

DOI: 10.1093/oso/9780190928971.001.0001

Paperback printed by Marquis Book Printing, Canada

For Jorge William and Federico
with love

The main enterprise of the world, for splendor,
for extent, is the upbuilding of a human being.
Adapted from Ralph Waldo Emerson

Contents

Preface	ix
List of Abbreviations	xv
Introduction	1

PART I

1. Overload	23
2. Individuals	49
3. Fulfillment	79
4. Citizens	116
5. Moral Development	153
6. A Role for Religion?	191

PART II

7. The Natural Sciences	227
8. The Arts	256
9. Understanding Ourselves	281

PART III

10. Social Change	323
11. Utopia?	350
Appendix 1	391
Appendix 2	395
Bibliography	397
Index	407

Preface

Nearly two decades ago, shortly after I had begun a serious study of John Dewey's works, I was struck by a characterization of philosophy he offers toward the end of his seminal *Democracy and Education*. According to Dewey, "If we are willing to conceive education as the process of forming fundamental dispositions, intellectual and emotional, toward nature and fellow men, philosophy may even be defined as the general theory of education." From the perspective of my own training in philosophy, and that reigning in Anglophone professional philosophy to this day, that is a bizarre claim. Philosophy of education is viewed not only as a narrowly applied subfield, but also as one in which work is humdrum and unsophisticated. For those capable of probing the central issues of philosophy—the "core problems"—turning to philosophy of education amounts to slumming it.

Intrigued by Dewey's claim, I have spent several years exploring the supposed slum. As I have done so, I have found the orthodox professional judgments to be deeply unfair. Today there are a significant number of scholars in the English-speaking world who are doing work in philosophy of education that meets the highest professional standards. They write clearly, draw on major parts of the philosophical tradition, offer new conclusions and defend them with rigorous arguments—and, unlike some of their snootier colleagues, they address urgent questions. I have learned much from the writings of many people who have contributed to this part of philosophy: a partial list would contain Harry Brighouse, Eamonn Callan, Randall Curren, Catherine Elgin, Amy Gutmann, Meira Levinson, Martha Nussbaum, the late Israel Scheffler, Harvey Siegel, and John White.

Moreover, as I have immersed myself in this part of philosophy, the insight behind Dewey's seemingly outrageous claim has become ever clearer. Dewey was reacting, I believe, to a sentence from Emerson's famous "American Scholar"—the sentence from which I have drawn my title and which I have adapted for my epigraph. Conceiving each human generation as attempting both to foster the development of its successors, and to create for them an improved world, Dewey (and, I think, Emerson) saw the general understanding of education (of "upbuilding" the young) as the central

X PREFACE

philosophical task. To discharge that task is to pose—and answer—some of the oldest and most recurrent philosophical questions. It is to inquire into the most important values and to try to understand how, given the circumstances and knowledge of the age, they might best be promoted.

In arriving at this perspective, I have found myself constantly articulating it in ways shaped by my long interest in historical processes and in evolving systems. The project Emerson attributes to us is one that has had to be undertaken throughout our history as a species. We have been at it for tens, if not hundreds, of thousands of years. The attempted solutions of the past have left their residues in our current situation. Often, educational approaches adapt and re-adapt them. Sometimes, however, it is wise to think more systematically, to take a more distant and abstract view, and to ask whether what are taken as fixed points should be given that status. This book is written in that spirit.

Part I of this book thus tries to construct a general framework for considering concrete educational questions. Part II attempts to consider how and what, in light of this framework, young people today should be taught. Part III asks what broader social changes might be required to implement the educational reforms proposed, and whether there are any serious possibilities of going in the directions I suggest.

The proximate cause of the pages that follow was an invitation from Peter Knox to give a series of Strauss Lectures at Case Western Reserve University. I already had in mind a volume on education and democracy as the second part of a trilogy aimed at elaborating my Deweyan pragmatism. When I proposed to Peter that this might be the topic of my lectures, he approved the idea, and I composed some twenty-five thousand words of draft material. Obviously, since then, some growth has occurred.

The discussions I had in Cleveland, and the many thoughtful and penetrating questions posed by members of the audience, led me to see how the individual lectures needed to be expanded, and how topics toward which I had only gestured (or not mentioned at all) had to be taken up. When the original versions were refereed for Oxford University Press, the readers sympathized with my plans for further development. (I hope that, if or when they see the result, they won't regret doing so.) OUP's wonderful New York philosophy editor, Peter Ohlin, also approved the proposal to extend the lectures, and, as always, offered excellent advice.

PREFACE   xi

I am extremely grateful to Peter Knox for that initial invitation, and to him and his colleagues at the Case Western Center for the Humanities for their warm hospitality and the stimulating conversations I enjoyed during my week in Cleveland. (Indeed, Peter is solely responsible for the existence of one of the chapters in Part II.) Particular thanks are also due to Chris Haufe, with whom I was able to renew the lively discussions of his time at Columbia.

What I have written here has deep roots in exchanges I have had with many people in many places during the past decade. My thinking has been affected by the ideas and reactions of so large a number of generous scholars in so wide a variety of fields that any attempt to name them all would inevitably be incomplete—and for this I must apologize. During the year I spent as a fellow at the Wissenschaftskolleg in Berlin (2011–2012), I learned much from some of my fellow fellows, Jeremy Adler, Monique Borgerhoff Mulder, Alfred Brendel, Ayşe Buğra, Hollis Taylor, and Mark Viney, as well as from Lorraine Daston, Gerd Gigerenzer, Susan Neiman, and Adrian Piper. When I returned to Berlin in 2015, to spend a semester at the American Academy, conversations with Moishe Postone helped me to rein in my tendencies to methodological individualism. Audiences at my Munich Lectures in Ethics raised questions that have helped me in revising this book. I am particularly grateful to my three commentators on that occasion (Rahel Jaeggi, Susan Neiman, and Amia Srinivasan), whose reactions to different material (that of *Moral Progress*, the first part of my projected trilogy) have led me to modify what I otherwise might have written here.

Similarly, in presentations on pragmatist themes in various places, I have learned from the questions and objections of my interlocutors. Many thanks to audiences at my Nordic Pragmatism Lectures in Helsinki, at my Chaire Mercier Lectures at the Université de Louvain, at the Technical University of Delft, at the University of Humanistic Studies Utrecht, at the Erasmus University Rotterdam, and at my 2014 Pentekost Lectures at the University of Bielefeld. A lecture delivered at Indiana University–Purdue University Indianapolis enabled me to try out some of the ideas of Chapter 6; and parts of the material of Chapters 7 and 8 have been presented at the University of Minnesota, at Temple University, at the University of Rochester, as the Jonathan Adler memorial lecture at CUNY, and as the Howison lecture at the University of California at Berkeley. I am particularly grateful for the many insightful comments I received on these occasions.

Participation in the meetings of the Society for Progress—the brainchild of Subrahamian Rangan—has had great influence on the material that follows.

xii PREFACE

The lively discussions among economists, business leaders, and philosophers have left their mark on the whole book, from the change of emphasis I recommend in Chapter 2 to the explorations and arguments of Chapters 10 and 11. David Autor, Julie Batillana, Robert Frank, and Amartya Sen have illuminated my thinking about economic questions. Elizabeth Anderson, Anthony Appiah, Michael Fuerstein, Susan Neiman, and Valerie Tiberius have helped me to refine my views about many of the issues I investigate here. I thank them all.

The community of American pragmatists has been generous in helping a relative newcomer find his feet. Two of my Columbia colleagues (both unfortunately now deceased)—Isaac Levi and Sidney Morgenbesser—taught me that, somewhat in the manner of M. Jourdain, I had been speaking pragmatism all my philosophical life. Richard Bernstein has been extraordinarily generous in sharing with me his store of insights into the pragmatist tradition. Catherine Elgin, Steven Fesmire, and Cheryl Misak have also been wonderful interlocutors, from whom I have learned much.

Closer to home, in the Columbia Philosophy department, I have been aided by many conversations with colleagues. Over the course of the last few years, Bob Gooding-Williams, Michele Moody-Adams, Fred Neuhouser, Christopher Peacocke, and Wayne Proudfoot have, in a variety of ways, shaped the ideas and arguments I try to present here. One of the great revelations—I think for both of us—has been the kinship between my version of Deweyan pragmatism and Axel Honneth's approach to critical theory. Like Rahel Jaeggi, Axel has aided me in seeing how to free myself (so far, I fear, only partially) from the limits of long-standing presuppositions.

The intellectual journey out of which this book has grown has been taken in the company of some truly remarkable graduate students. Over a decade ago, conversations with Michael Fuerstein enabled me (and, I think, Michael as well) to see how to begin a more synthetic treatment of questions on which epistemology, philosophy of science, social philosophy, and political philosophy all bear. More recently, regular conversations with Anuk Arudpragasam, Max Khan Hayward, and Robbie Kubala have opened up new perspectives on Deweyan themes, and have often refined and corrected my first (and second, and . . .) thoughts.

One student, however, must receive the lion's share of credit (or responsibility?) for help in gestating the ideas of this book. When I returned from Berlin at the end of 2015, Natalia Rogach Alexander, then in her first year of graduate school, asked me if I would agree to a directed study to explore philosophical issues about education. From the fall of 2016 on, we have met almost every week of Columbia's term-time, frequently for two hours, reading and discussing principal texts and themes in this area. What I have learned from these conversations, and from her own brilliant dissertation work, is immense. I am enormously grateful to her.

In our complementary projects, both Natalia and I have benefited from the generosity of senior scholars who have devoted large parts of their careers to the philosophy of education. Harvey Siegel spurred me to write in this area by inviting me to contribute to the *Oxford Handbook of Philosophy of Education*. Since then, he has offered me a host of valuable suggestions, including detailed comments on a draft of this entire book. Many changes have resulted from his sensitive and informed reading. Meira Levinson's penetrating questions and suggestions about Chapters 1–4 have led me to recognize the need to clarify many points and to offer more guidance to the reader. Conversations with Ellen Winner, and her comments on Chapter 8, have prompted refinements in my approach to education in the arts. Harry Brighouse's brilliant and incisive reading of Chapters 5 and 6 enabled me to correct misleading formulations, and to make those chapters more precise. For several years now, Randy Curren has offered encouragement, support, and (probing but gentle) criticism. His extensive suggestions about Chapters 1–5 have inspired a large number of improvements.

Two readers of the previous draft deserve special thanks. For two decades, I have enjoyed teaching with two distinguished economists, first with Ronald Findlay, more recently with Dan O'Flaherty. Dan read the penultimate version in its entirety, alerting me to places where more caution was required, and advising me to elaborate some points, and to frame others differently. I can only hope that our interchanges have been half as valuable to him as they have been to me.

Martha Nussbaum offered me a series of questions and suggestions on every chapter of that draft, some general, some specific, all of them remarkably insightful. Her comments have led to the inclusion of new discussions, to the expansion of others, and to a much clearer explanation of the twists and turns of my argument. I am not sure if she will feel that all of her concerns have been adequately addressed, but I hope she will agree that the final version is better for the time she devoted to its predecessor. I am deeply grateful to her.

Finally, I want to thank my family—now a three-generation affair. During the time through which I have been working out these ideas, my life has not

xiv PREFACE

only been enriched by their love and support. I have also learned much from them about the development of the young. Perhaps some progress toward the kind of education for which this book campaigns will be made in time for the little ones to benefit from it. Whether or not that is so, I am confident that the loving parenting they have received provides them with the right kind of start.

List of Abbreviations

The following abbreviations are used for books to which frequent reference is made:

E   Jean-Jacques Rousseau, *Émile*, trans. Allan Bloom (New York: Basic Books, 1979).

LW   *The Later Works of John Dewey*, 17 vols. (Carbondale: University of Southern Illinois Press); references are given by volume number and page number.

MW   *The Middle Works of John Dewey*, 15 vols. (Carbondale: University of Southern Illinois Press); references are given by volume number and page number.

OL   John Stuart Mill, *On Liberty and Other Essays*, ed. John Gray, Oxford World's Classics (Oxford: Oxford University Press, 2008).

PPE   John Stuart Mill, *Principles of Political Economy*, vols. 2 and 3 of *Collected Works of John Stuart Mill*, selected from the University of Toronto's edition of the full set of Mill's works (Indianapolis: Liberty Fund, 2005); the pagination runs continuously through the two volumes.

R   Plato, *Republic*, in *Plato: Complete Works*, ed. John M. Cooper (Indianapolis: Hackett, 1997), 971–1223.

SMC   Steven M. Cahn, ed., *Philosophy of Education: The Essential Texts* (New York: Routledge, 2009).

WN   Adam Smith, *The Wealth of Nations* (New York: Modern Library, 2000).

The Main Enterprise of the World

Introduction

Between two and three million years ago, our forebears started to make stone tools. Around one and three-quarter million years before the present, their technology had progressed, and they began to fashion the "prehistoric Swiss Army Knife"—the hand-axe. Our hominin ancestors continued to make further improvements, and even before our own species, *Homo sapiens*, arrived on the scene, surviving artefacts display accumulated techniques.

Behind the examples in the museum cases lie millennia of education. As we move from the deep past toward the present, it is hard to resist seeing the later tools as more functional. Edges are sharper; points are finer. Older achievements are not lost. Instead they serve later generations as bases on which to build further. Something has been learned and retained—and that means something has been taught.

So the practice of education is extremely old. It antedates the invention of writing, antedates the domestication of animals, even antedates the origin of our own species. Small hominin bands, often struggling to meet the challenges of harsh environments, devised ways of ensuring the survival of useful techniques. During the past tens of thousands of years, from at least fifty thousand years before the present, the task has been more complex. The young have had to learn the approved rules and patterns of group life, absorbing the accomplishments that have made human sociality go more smoothly. A band's continued existence has often depended on its ability to transmit its practical expertise and its social lore to the next generation. The progress of practical skills and of social life has depended on another kind of advance: the adaptation of the system of transmission to meet current needs. Educational progress.

Yet what has been found to work well in overcoming past obstacles may not only provide a basis for tackling those of the present; it may also jeopardize future progress. As with other kinds of evolution, successful ways of solving the problems at hand are retained—and they may subsequently come to constrain the possibilities for addressing today's problems. Locked into a tradition, originally introduced to cope with old difficulties, latecomers struggle

The Main Enterprise of the World. Philip Kitcher, Oxford University Press. © Oxford University Press 2022.
DOI: 10.1093/oso/9780190928971.003.0001

2 THE MAIN ENTERPRISE OF THE WORLD

with new ones. Perhaps they eventually succeed, tacking on some more-or-less clumsy addition to the established arrangements. Over a long sequence of generations, the result can be a ramshackle contraption, a Rube Goldberg device whose functioning is far from perfect. At some point, people may need to strike out in a new direction. They give up the hand-axe, abandon stone tools, opt for a different style of technology. Sometimes, they even need to rethink the ways in which lore is transmitted across the generations.

Much excellent work in the philosophy of education proceeds by leaving the main contours of the *status quo* in place. A problem is taken up, and a solution according with the existing framework is proposed. The value of this kind of work—and there is a significant amount of it—should be evident. The suggested improvement can be adopted quickly (assuming policymakers will listen!) and the education of children can be immediately improved. One very strong reason for objecting to the dismissal of philosophy of education so commonly found in professional philosophy today lies in an important fact: the best work in the field does considerable social good.

This book doesn't attempt philosophy in that vein. Its proposals are more wide-ranging and more radical. The following chapters collectively argue (or campaign?) for an extensive revision of our educational policies and institutions, and for a reconfiguring of society to adapt to the functions education ought to serve today. To think of any rapid translation of my suggestions into reform will—rightly—strike readers as absurd.

Why, then, should anyone read the many pages that follow? Because, from time to time, stock-taking is necessary. Our ways of educating the young have (as I have noted) a very long history. Out of that history *may* have come a grotesque contraption, something so dysfunctional as to foil the advances required to meet human needs in today's world. Isn't it worth taking a look? Doesn't that look require thinking hard about what contemporary education must do? Can we avoid reflecting on large (and difficult) philosophical questions about what makes human lives go well and what makes societies healthy?

Taking that look might buttress confidence in the major features of education as they have developed historically. We might see how there is no need for large-scale revision, either of schools and universities or of the societies in which they are embedded. One useful result of the inspection might be a differential evaluation of facets of our institutions. We could recognize what works well, distinguishing these aspects from others whose success is less

INTRODUCTION 3

evident. Appreciation of such distinctions would assist the piecemeal work of amending the system to improve it.

If I am right, investigation shouldn't generate contented endorsement. Instead, it ought to call for sweeping changes. Yet, even if you come to view my diagnoses and arguments as defective, they may still aid in informing a clearer conception of the virtues you identify in the *status quo*. By provoking, they should lead you to understand *why* what history has bequeathed to us remains useful for our own times. Understanding of that kind helps, when it comes to pursuing further educational progress. It can guide you to see what can be tinkered with, and what must be left intact.

So far, though, I have only gestured, vaguely, at the general tendency of evolutionary processes to constrain and to give rise to jury-rigged solutions to later problems. Beyond that abstract point, there are concrete considerations inviting reflection on our educational inheritance. We are a long way from the world in which schools were introduced to produce scribes, or from that in which universities delivered young men to fill the offices of the Church. We are even distant from the demands of the Industrial Revolution, or of the postwar years in which the importance of scientific research became clearly recognized. In contemporary societies, people from different cultures mingle. Moreover, the human population today faces challenges requiring global coordination. Without widespread cooperation, transcending national boundaries and socioeconomic divisions, our response to the problem of global heating is likely to be inadequate. One legacy we shall almost certainly leave to our descendants is an environment far harsher than that in which we (or our parents) have lived. As I was revising this book, the planet was swept by a pandemic, whose severity was vastly greater than it would have been if the children of the world had been taught to value, and aim at, pan-human cooperation.

Not just an abstract feature of evolving systems, then. Concrete features of our history and of the present suggest a real possibility that current education may be beset with a mess of ill-fitting pieces. Yet the previous paragraph remains too gestural. This book begins (properly begins) with a more precise diagnosis.

My first chapter documents a problem for educational policy—the problem of overload. It arises whenever people step back to ask just what a specific

4 THE MAIN ENTERPRISE OF THE WORLD

educational institution (the elementary school, the secondary school, the university) should offer to those it serves (its victims?). So I begin with the well-motivated catalogue of necessary subjects proposed by one of the most educated and intelligent Englishmen who ever lived. In his inaugural address as rector of St. Andrew's University, John Stuart Mill presented the university curriculum he took his age to require. The speech was long, and the resulting program seems absurdly ambitious. That, I claim, is no accident. It wasn't Mill's fault.

The history of American schools displays just the same tendency—although, this time, educational reflection doesn't combine everything important into one indigestible lump but lurches from one apparently reasonable goal to another, different and equally defensible. In the contemporary world—even in the nineteenth- and twentieth-century worlds—decisions about how to educate the young are dominated by the threat of overload. It comes in two modes: a ludicrous massive conjunction (Mill) or oscillation among different priorities (the twentieth-century American school).

Once the problem is appreciated, an obvious strategy for addressing it suggests itself. Rather than consider curricular or social goals piecemeal, it would seem better to try to identify more general aims, thinking about how young people need to be prepared for life in today's world. Three large capacities seem to be required. First, a capacity for self-maintenance, most obviously directed toward readiness for the work environment. Second, an ability to function as a citizen—and here I focus on participation in democratic social and political life. Third, the ground should be laid so that individuals may be able to pursue lives they find fulfilling. Identifying three capacities rather than a single ability runs an obvious risk. Perhaps, given the circumstances in which people now live, there will be tensions among the broad goals, and thus difficulties in realizing all of them.

In fact, the problem of reconciling aims proves even more tricky than I have so far allowed. Instead of considering what education does (or should do) for the individual, we can ask what it must provide if the interests of a group—the local community, a cultural tradition, or the state—are to be well served. The question arises most obviously when nations arrive at views about the kinds of workers required for success in economic competition. Insisting on the priority of society's needs can easily distort attempts to find a healthy balance of individual capacities. Pursuits potentially promoting someone's fulfillment can become marginalized, or so poorly paid that they make self-maintenance difficult. Developing a community of citizens may be sacrificed to the pressures perceived in the marketplace.

Chapter 1 presents the problem of overload, introduces the most important general aims of education, and identifies some major difficulties in reconciling them. The subsequent chapter then examines a particular source of tension: the demands of the labor market. Even at the dawn of economic theorizing, in the work of Adam Smith and his successors, the potential conflict between the evolution of the workplace and the development of the worker was clearly recognized. It is worth returning to the original recognition of the point to understand the full force of the danger. With that clearly in view, we can turn to the contemporary context, to confront fears of globalization and of automation and to recognize how the measures typically proposed to address the threats accord with an all-too-familiar pattern. Economic constraints are primary. Workers must adapt, or they and their nations must expect to wither and decline.

I suggest a different strategy, that of questioning the alleged economic constraints. Think about giving priority to the aims of citizenship and of personal fulfillment, in the age of globalization and of automation. Instead of lamenting the replacement of factory workers by machines, apparently forcing people into "menial" service jobs, view this as an opportunity for rethinking the conception of meaningful employment. In particular, two generic forms of significant work emerge, once the robots have liberated people from the assembly line: care of the elderly and nurturing of the young. Even under current conditions, when the caregivers and the teachers are poorly paid and often stigmatized, jobs in these sectors are widely viewed as rewarding. Remove the stigmas, offer the compensation this important work deserves, and, I suggest, many people would be able to lead far more fulfilling lives.

Chapter 2 offers some definite proposals—and this is a feature of many subsequent chapters as well. Sometimes what I suggest marks a relatively precise reform of current practice. On other occasions, I intend to indicate a direction in which more specific experiments might be tried. The most important recommendation of this chapter places education at the center of working life. Not only should there be a huge expansion in the class of those who guide the development of the young—properly paid teachers at all levels from infancy on—but all citizens ought to play a part in the nurturing of the next generations. On this conception, the "upbuilding of people" becomes central to all our lives.

6   THE MAIN ENTERPRISE OF THE WORLD

Is this too cavalier? Can economic demands simply be waved away? Those are serious questions, and Part III of this book (Chapters 10 and 11) endeavors to come to terms with them. They must be postponed for a simple reason. Concerns about the feasibility of a scheme for reform can be taken up only when the entire scope and character of the revision has been described. Giving that description will take Parts I and II, the first nine chapters. At that point, it will become possible to ask what general social changes are required to adopt my education-centric position; and, once that first question is answered (Chapter 10), it is possible to explore whether the package of proposals is a utopian fantasy, one whose unfeasibility is exposed once economic constraints are given their due (Chapter 11).

Chapter 2's argument for placing education first, and configuring social and economic life to accord with its priorities, is elaborated further in Chapter 3. Here I attempt to be more precise about the concept of individual fulfillment. My efforts require wrestling with the oldest and most central question of philosophy, posed in the Western tradition by Socrates, when he asked "How to live?" The formulation covers two different issues: "How should *I* live?" and "How should *we* live together?" Anglophone thinkers often accentuate the difference by sharply separating the individual person, with distinctive talents, propensities, and interests, from the ambient society. I attempt to bring the questions closer together by recognizing how, from the very start of life, the self is constituted through relations with others.

In fact, I want to amend the Socratic question in a number of ways. First by understanding how different ways of posing it are pertinent at different stages of human history. We can ask what makes lives happy, good, fully human, meaningful, or fulfilled—and not all of the adjectives may be pertinent to someone's predicament. Appreciating that first point paves the way for a second. Socrates' question is better posed comparatively: given someone's circumstances, we should ask, "How could a life under these conditions be improved—how might it go better than such lives typically do?" The appropriate task is not to look for perfection, but to make progress.

The great liberal tradition of responding to the original question—in which Mill plays an important part—starts from an emphasis on autonomy. The life you live ought to be your own. Its pattern should not be thrust upon you. Thus liberals recognize two conditions on the fulfilled life: you should choose your own "life plan" (although your choice must be consonant with moral principles), and you should have significant success in pursuing it. Many people, including prominent liberals, have taken those two conditions to be insufficient. Something more is required to rule out "life plans" that are harmless but trivial.

A better version of liberalism would add a constraint: your pursuit of your plan ought to make a positive contribution to the lives of others. Yet this addition shouldn't be seen as a patch, something applied after difficulties have been recognized in the original proposal. Better to see the individual's free choice—the heart of the liberal's approach—as itself formed through interactions with others in a specific social milieu. The fulfilled life must be your own, but what counts as "your own" isn't some conformity to and elaboration of a little kernel of a self, present in you at birth. We become who we are through a dialogue in which the growing person learns from and gives back to a broader social group. The autonomy liberals prize is inevitably a matter of degree. The freedom of our choice is improved when the parties in the dialogue are mutually sensitive, when the social interactions through which a person is formed are attentive to the emerging individual, and when the nascent self is similarly sensitive to those who nurture its development. The dialogue goes awry when interlocutors impose, and, equally, when the plan the person makes is insensitive to the needs and aspirations of others.

To view things in these terms deepens the case for the proposals of Chapter 2. Education is the site at which individuals are formed, and thus is rightly central. For the dialogue to go well, individual predilections have to be recognized. The chances of that are increased as more people, who bring varied perspectives, are involved. Moreover, understanding fulfillment through contribution to something larger (and more enduring) than the individual self helps connect the capacity for fulfillment to the capacity for citizenship.

That connection is elaborated in Chapter 4. I begin from a consideration of democracy—and from contemporary perceptions of its troubles. Democracy, I suggest, comes at a number of levels, as well as at various scales. A shallow conception of democracy focuses on elections and votes: democracy is in place whenever there are regular elections, with choice of candidates and opportunities for all adults to vote. A deeper level recognizes the importance of free and open debate, so that citizens have the chance to understand how their votes might best promote their interests. Deeper still lies Dewey's concept of democracy as a "shared way of life" in which regular interactions among citizens promote mutual learning and accommodation.

Although some commentators today worry about defects in the mechanics of voting (as, for example, when questions arise about the ways in

8 THE MAIN ENTERPRISE OF THE WORLD

which the boundaries of electoral districts are drawn), these are not the most fundamental concerns about the health of current democracies. Many would point to the ways in which the conditions of public debate have diverged from the open arena envisaged by Mill and other champions of free speech and discussion. Critics identify the distortions apparently responsible for a misinformed electorate, unable to recognize policies bearing on widely shared concerns (as, for example, in votes for candidates who downplay or scoff at the threat posed by climate change). Worries of this kind probe more deeply than the anxieties about elections, but they do not penetrate far enough. I argue that the problems at the relatively superficial levels cannot be adequately addressed without restoring the conditions central to Dewey's approach to democracy. Deweyan democracy demands educative interactions among citizens, occasions for deliberation together by people with different perspectives.

The core of democracy, I argue, consists in conversations aiming to exemplify three virtues: inclusiveness, informedness, and mutual engagement. Deliberations are more inclusive when more of the perspectives adopted by people affected by the issue at hand are represented. They are better informed to the extent that participants base their contributions on well-established findings and there are barriers to appealing to recognized falsehoods and misinformation. Mutual engagement is promoted the more the discussants are committed to understanding the perspectives of others and to seeking an outcome all those involved can tolerate.

To the extent that deliberations of this sort can be (re)introduced into democracies, we can expect to avoid recurrent reversals of policy that harm all through the instability they generate, and to diminish polarization and fragmentation. Democracy sometimes reigns at small scales—in the family or the local community. The challenge is to build on these models, finding ways to advance democratic deliberations in the political life of large, multicultural states (and, ultimately, across national borders). Answering the challenge is, in part, a matter of constructing social institutions, but it surely requires cultivating a specific kind of citizenship. If young people were accustomed, from their earliest years, to plan together, in ever larger and more diverse groups, they would be more likely to emerge as adults who could transfer their skills and virtues into realizing Deweyan democracy.

Chapter 4 culminates in outlining an educational program for how this might be achieved (and here my proposals are frankly experimental). Deweyan citizens, if they can be reliably reared, would not only overcome some of the pathologies currently diagnosed in democratic societies. They would also learn the kinds of sensitivities to others Chapter 3 viewed as central to personal fulfillment. Hence, an approach appropriate for realizing one of the large aims of education (good citizenship) also contributes to another (fulfillment). Two potentially conflicting goals become more closely aligned, thus helping with the problem of reconciliation (discerned in Chapter 1).

Chapter 5 sets up a further linkage. One traditionally important part of education, broadly conceived, is to foster moral development. Questions arise, of course, about what exactly such fostering requires and how the work should be apportioned between the home and public institutions (like schools). I elaborate an account of morality I have offered in earlier writings[1] and suggest that, from the early years on, schools have an important role to play in children's moral progress.

Whether we reflect on the long history of moral life, extending tens of thousands of years into the past, or consider the episodes in which striking moral advances are made—the abolition of slavery, the expansion of opportunities for women, and the acceptance of same-sex love serve as my three paradigms—the importance of collective deliberation to morality becomes apparent. Progress is made when people engage in an informed and sympathetic manner with all those who are affected by a particular issue. It is retarded when discussions exclude groups with particular perspectives, or when some of the participants are misinformed, or when no serious effort is made to appreciate how the world looks and feels from others' points of view. On my account, morality is a collective affair. No single individual is the final authority. Religious or philosophical texts may supply ideas or tools or stories for thinking through an issue. In the end, however, moral advances are made by societies when they approximate a form of ideal conversation, one in which all "stakeholders" are included, in which the participants deploy the best available information, and in which they listen sympathetically to others, attempting to discover how their lives would be affected if various alternatives came about, and seeking a solution with which everyone could live. Individuals need to acquire capacities for contributing to those kinds of discussions, and for simulating them when they have to make decisions on their own.

---

[1] *The Ethical Project* (Cambridge MA: Harvard University Press, 2011) and *Moral Progress* (New York: Oxford University Press, 2021).

10 THE MAIN ENTERPRISE OF THE WORLD

Fostering moral development is thus closely linked to creating good citizens. In both instances, we require capacities for engaging with others. Moreover, as my earlier discussions of fulfillment have tried to show, capacities of this sort are important in helping individuals find their own path to a fulfilled life. Chapters 3–5 thus combine to construct a framework within which two of the three major educational goals identified in Chapter 1 (in confronting the problem of overload) become reconciled. Further, if the education-first approach to the labor market presented in Chapter 2 proves feasible, we arrive at a framework that promises complete reconciliation.

Part II will attempt to show how that framework might be elaborated as a general curriculum for contemporary young people. Before turning to that task, however, one important concern must be addressed. Although religion is periodically mentioned in some of my discussions in the first five chapters, the status attributed to it is hardly that favored by devout people of various faiths. My stance is resolutely humanistic—not militantly atheistic, consigning religion to the trash can, but also not prepared to give it pride of place in understanding the fulfilled life, or in characterizing citizenship, or as the source of morality. Chapter 5 will surely strike some readers as committing the most glaring sin of omission. Shouldn't religion be included in public education? And what place or role should it be assigned?

These are important questions, and my proposals for reform would ring hollow unless they were addressed. Chapter 6 offers answers, using current debates to elicit and defend my position. Two polar views dominate the contemporary world. One of them, held in several different forms, maintains that a particular religious text or tradition offers authoritative moral guidance: it is the source of all true morality. The other sees all religious doctrines as false, contending that religion should be swept off the face of the earth as quickly and as thoroughly as possible. To my mind, the combination of these positions skews our thinking about the place of religion in society and in the development of the young.

Contending that some favorite piece of scripture settles moral questions is disastrous for the pictures of moral life and of good citizenship I have painted. Conversation should not be stopped by a foot-stamping appeal to the words in a book or the dicta of a religious teacher. More than two millennia ago, Plato confronted the idea of religion as the ultimate authority in moral matters, but my argument turns on Kant's more recent deepening of the point. Before we can accept anything (a text, a contemporary religious teacher) as a guide to what we should do, we must already conduct an

INTRODUCTION 11

appraisal—a *moral* appraisal—of the putative source. Simply gesturing at the power of the supposed authority won't do. For that is to commit the moral error of numerous twentieth-century functionaries who were complicit in evil. Invoking the fact that The Leader commanded you to do it doesn't get you off the hook.

Once this point is fully appreciated, it's easy to recognize important distinctions among kinds of religion. Chapter 6 suggests a rough division, and uses it to sketch an equally rough account of religious progress. Tribal religion (in which gods are viewed as the source of morality and in which the devout serve as their foot soldiers) is the most primitive form. A second stage brings a dose of ecumenicism, as the link between morality and the divine will is retained but the faithful are no longer required to do any "smiting" on the deity's behalf. A more thoroughly ecumenical religion arises when Kant's insight is firmly adopted: even among the unbelievers, there are good people; morality is independent of religion, and properly used to provide independent assessment of the scriptures. At the third stage, the insight remains attached to the thought that the doctrines and practices of a particular faith are uniquely correct; even though unbelievers misunderstand important aspects of the universe—not recognizing the true god, or even not recognizing any god at all—that doesn't prevent some of them from acting just as well their devout counterparts. Finally, at the fourth stage, religions become completely ecumenical when they abandon the assumption of unique correctness. Refined religion takes religious texts to be metaphorical (allegorical, poetic) accounts of a transcendent aspect of the universe, one that cannot be characterized in literal language, but toward which the world's religions gesture.

I argue that the crucial step occurs between the first ecumenical stage and the second, once Kant's insight becomes firmly entrenched. Thus the educational framework and the social structure I envisage cleaves religions into two. Conversation-stopping religions, whose adherents adopt a practice of justifying moral claims by appeal to the authority of a text, cannot be permitted to pursue that practice in public moral, social, or political deliberations. Young people must be shown, at some stage of their education, why that is so. Their schooling should include some comparative understanding of different religions, and it should recognize the important benefits religion (at its best) has conferred. Children should also understand the significance of Kant's insight.

Chapter 6 concludes with some specific proposals for religious education. Those proposals are natural outgrowths of the line of argument just outlined

12   THE MAIN ENTERPRISE OF THE WORLD

(one that the chapter presents in much more detail). They complete my attempt to offer a framework, capable of reconciling the potentially conflicting major aims of Chapter 1, and of placing education at the center of human life. The rest of the book is devoted to explaining in more detail what this might mean for the work of the schools (Part II) and to defending against charges that it is, inevitably, a fantasy (Part III).

Chapters 7–9 fill in the scaffolding erected in Part I by considering the content of a general, pre-university, education, one appropriately shared by all students. Chapter 7 begins with the natural sciences. Public discussions of the institution of science ("science" in the singular) or of the various sciences are frequently distorted by faulty general views—and the early part of the chapter attempts to correct these. I argue that the sciences are diverse, and that individual sciences are inevitably selective. Human inquiry could never attain more than a ludicrously inadequate approximation to "the complete truth about nature," and investigators rightly seek answers to questions meeting human needs and satisfying human aspirations. In consequence, scientific research should be viewed as a socially embedded activity, one that ought to be in dialogue with the people whom the sciences serve.

Educational implications follow. The public must be prepared to play its part in this dialogue, to offer the community of investigators a clear and realistic picture of its own interests and to rely on the outcomes of well-conducted inquiry. Schools and universities do not just have the task of renewing the scientific community, generating new specialists to replace those whose powers have waned. They must also produce citizens able to help set directions for new lines of inquiry, and able to assess how discoveries bear on public policies. All over the world, one of these needs—the need to train the next generation of scientists—is widely appreciated. In reaction to it, many nations, concerned to boost their economies through science-based technologies, have set up programs to encourage (and accelerate) the flow of new researchers.

Blanket attempts to ensure that no potential scientist is overlooked run contrary to the second goal of science education—the cultivation of a scientifically literate public. Force-feeding students as if all were destined for careers in research or in applications of the sciences tends to alienate young people who recognize, from an early age, that this is not a promising direction for them. Dulled by classes in which they are asked to memorize technical

INTRODUCTION 13

vocabulary and to struggle (unsuccessfully) with toy problems, they lose the curiosity of their early school-years, dismissing the sciences as arid, boring, and incomprehensible. As adults—and voters—they are ill equipped to understand the technical issues on which policy questions turn. Even when, as with climate change, such questions are crucial to their own lives, and those of their children and grandchildren.

Chapter 7 proposes a remedy, distinguishing general science education from the forms of rigorous training appropriate for those who come to see a scientific career (perhaps in research, perhaps in some area where work is informed by results of past research) as a real possibility for themselves. Focusing on preserving a sense of wonder and on instilling a capacity for continuing to follow scientific developments, I suggest some concrete ways in which general education in the sciences might be reconfigured. The amended curriculum aims to avoid producing dilettantes, while simultaneously recognizing the deadening effects of treating all students as if they were researchers-in-the-making. Scientific literacy can—and should—be available to all.

If science education is often overemphasized at the secondary level—with the distortions I have noted—training in the arts is typically viewed as a luxury, something dispensable in the competitive contemporary world. Chapter 8 responds to this situation by making the case for continued education in some field (or fields) of the arts (broadly construed). Indeed, I contend that the arts should be awarded a far larger place in the curriculum than they have been given, at least in my lifetime, and quite possibly at any time in the past few centuries.

My case begins with demolishing a myth. Many people believe firmly in the progress of the natural sciences, while denying the progress of the arts. Their judgment rests on a faulty comparison. They recognize, quite correctly, how, in some periods, the works of art produced in a particular genre are superior to those created at later times—perhaps landscape painting has never again achieved the heights attained by the Dutch masters of the Golden Age (the seventeenth century). It's easy to ignore the parallel fact that scientific creativity comes in uneven bursts—Newton's *annus mirabilis* (1665) is aptly named. Natural sciences progress by accumulating resources (statements, equations, graphs, data sets, instruments, and so forth) that can be deployed by subsequent generations. So, too, with respect to the arts. We don't lose van Ruisdael, Hobbema, and Vermeer when we acquire Constable, Turner, and Van Gogh.

14 THE MAIN ENTERPRISE OF THE WORLD

So perhaps the difference between the arts and the sciences consists in the practical applications to which scientific research leads? Advances in biology help (or might help?) us to conserve or improve the environment; landscape paintings don't do anything similar (although they could be sources of inspiration). Nonscientists routinely suppose the importance of investigating the natural world to lie in the practical benefits it ultimately delivers—the agricultural advances, the devices that ease our lives, and above all the medical improvements, the drugs, the treatments, and the vaccines. On that score there is a case for regarding scientific progress as more significant. Yet scientists typically do not view technology as grounding the distinctive importance of their work. Instead, they point to the intrinsic benefits of a deeper and richer understanding of nature. If that is the sphere in which the comparison should be made, then, I maintain, the everyday judgment ought to be reversed. The arts win.

Once the histories of visual art, of music, of literature, drama, dance, and film are seen as amassing resources for the improvement of human lives, it is important to ask just what these alleged resources do for people. I offer a threefold answer. First, encounters with the arts can have a special vitality—they are episodes in which we are most vividly alive. Second, the effects of our engagement with the artworks we love are not transitory; they affect, sometimes profoundly, the course of our subsequent experience. Third, the arts can teach us. Not through any direct inculcation of information, but by showing us the need to revise the concepts and perspectives we have previously brought to our decisions and to our reasoning. Art can modify the framework in which we set our lives, our experiences, and our interactions with others. In the fundamental revisions it generates, it usually has a far more powerful effect on people than do their advances in scientific understanding.

Chapter 8 tries to make a detailed case for the line of reasoning I have sketched. On that basis, I explore ways in which young people's education in the arts should proceed. Here, three points are central. First, it is important to combine receptivity to art with developing abilities to create in some mode. We should take seriously the project of instilling skills sufficient to enable people to enjoy working in the genres of art that appeal to them and to enable them to appreciate and engage with the achievements of others in those genres. Second, we should recognize the diversity of tastes. I defend a moderate egalitarianism. Almost everyone is capable of aesthetic experiences with the three significant benefits I identify. Yet there is significant variation in the genres and works capable of generating those benefits. An important educational task is to guide growing individuals to art able to speak deeply to them. Third, the list of arts often presupposed in thinking about art education (the one I slid in at the beginning of the previous paragraph) is too narrow. For some people, artistic creativity and satisfaction are found in designing a garden, or in sewing, or in cuisine. As in other chapters, I attempt to combine my conclusions in specific proposals for how education in the arts should go.

Chapter 9 continues the lines of thought just developed, by focusing on the humanities and social sciences. Consonant with the framework of Part I, I proceed by exploring how to foster fulfilling lives and capacities for citizenship (concerns about self-maintenance—employment opportunities—are deferred to the end of the chapter). Building on the argument for the importance of the arts, I argue for the power of critical and historical studies to deepen self-understanding: to help young people locate their own distinctive talents and to enter in to the perspectives and lives of others. Achieving these goals is enriched when the humanities and social sciences work in tandem. Geography and anthropology can play an important part from the early school years on. In secondary school, they can be supplemented by introducing students to the approaches, techniques, and findings of psychology, sociology, political theory, and economics.

Conceiving this somewhat unruly collection of subject areas as concerned with understanding oneself—learning what it is to be human, as well as what it is to be a particular individual human being—points to a different educational approach. Throughout the chapter I am concerned with *interactions* among the disciplines I have mentioned. The focus is always on how studies of these kinds can promote the two major goals. In the course of the argument, I reinforce the reconciliation I claimed to achieve in Part I. We see concretely how education advancing fulfillment also contributes to good citizenship and to moral development.

The chapter also builds on my treatment of the natural sciences. Chapter 7 identified the goal of general science education in terms of cultivating scientific literacy. The humanities and social sciences demand analogous forms of literacy. Instead of conceiving them as areas in which students must be introduced to a (potentially vast) corpus of Important Knowledge, they should be seen as providing abilities to read particular kinds of presentations, thus opening the gates to diverse kinds of information and perspectives that can combine to illuminate human life, generally and in individual instances. Successful education provides skills adaptable to the situations in which people find themselves throughout their lives.

16   THE MAIN ENTERPRISE OF THE WORLD

Although I offer specific suggestions about how this might proceed, discussing which kinds of history might be emphasized and which ignored, considering the value of teaching foreign languages, and reflecting on what potential role my own discipline (philosophy) might play, these are, for the most part, intended as illustrative examples. Thus the proposals at the end of the chapter stand back from the particular cases, offering a structure for the humanities and social sciences curriculum. That takes a step toward making the abstract proposals of Part I more concrete, but many details remain to be elaborated.

Yet, in concluding Part II in this way, I may well seem to have intensified concerns about the wide-eyed idealism of my venture. Self-understanding, keyed to fulfillment and citizenship, occupies center stage. Little is said to allay the worry that children educated as I propose will be unable to support themselves in the "real world." Before the end, I offer only a few words to appease the skeptic, pointing back to Chapter 2's vision of a changed labor market in which manufacturing is largely automated and service employment is ever more widespread. Does that do enough to support my focus on two out of the three original large goals? Will educating the young to understand themselves and others better translate into adequate performance in the workplace, not only in the supposedly dominant service positions, but in the many "practical" jobs that inevitably remain?

Skeptical questions of this kind are the entering wedge, provoking much larger worries. If the education outlined in Parts I and II is to succeed, how must society change? And would the reforms prove economically ruinous? Part III will attempt to answer those doubts.

———

First things first. Chapter 10 opens by acknowledging a crucial point. Educational reform this sweeping cannot attain the goals invoked to motivate it if change is confined to the purely educational sphere—seen as a matter of modifying schools and curricula. Features of contemporary societies pose all sorts of readily recognizable problems. Teachers are often seriously underpaid. Schools are often dilapidated and dangerous. Children often live in poverty—and many have no stable homes to leave in the morning and to return to in the afternoon. Parental resources vary widely. Social and economic conditions force students to compete for scarce opportunities. That competition intensifies as they grow older. Stereotypes and biases are everywhere.

If the factors just mentioned were left unchanged, my educational proposals would best be viewed as a joke. Beginning with the simplest problems and

INTRODUCTION 17

proceeding to successively more intricate difficulties, the chapter explores the social changes required to enable the revisionary program for education to succeed. (Here, evidently, I adopt the "education first" stance introduced in Chapter 2.) Out of these investigations emerges the picture of a different society—a *Deweyan Society*—toward which we should strive. The distinctive features of that society are summarized at the end of the chapter.

There are seven of them. First is a validation of all forms of work dedicated toward improving human lives. Here I replace a classical distinction of political economy ("productive" versus "unproductive" labor) with what the arguments of Part I expose as a more fundamental one. Some goods are produced and consumed (and some services provided and compensated) simply because they serve as marks of status. These are (corrupting) luxuries we are better off without. All other types of employment, those advancing the fulfillment of others, should be awarded roughly equal respect.

The second feature of the Deweyan society cashes out the demand for equal respect—literally. Although there may be some differences in wages and salaries, inequalities are sharply reduced. Compensation for any validated form of work must lie within a range. That range is set through the kind of democratic discussion Chapters 4 and 5 recognized as central to political and moral life. Similarly (third feature), the Deweyan society constantly works to decrease inequalities in the performances of educational institutions. Schools, universities, and centers for adult education are free and open to all, with periodic investments to help any that are seen as less successful in promoting the two major educational goals.

Fourthly, as part of its commitment to genuine equality of opportunity, the society fully supports programs for the eradication of prejudices and stereotypes. In particular, throughout lifelong education, it provides funds for people to meet, plan, and deliberate together in heterogeneous groups. Joint decision-making starts in the first school grades, and continues throughout maturity. Adults are encouraged (fifth feature) to take periodic leaves from their regular employment to renew their education, possibly by exploring new interests. They are also expected to participate in the rearing of the next generation, not only within the family, but also in their neighborhood schools. Leaves are fully funded.

Adults who cannot find work are supported at the bottom of the range of allowable income. They are given access to a central clearinghouse, enabling them to seek employment. Finally, any efforts to reintroduce hierarchies of status for different occupations are firmly resisted.

18 THE MAIN ENTERPRISE OF THE WORLD

Some of these features of the Deweyan society involve no direct costs. Others, quite evidently, call for governmental investment in the lives of citizens. The most obvious economic issue is whether, if the society were to be brought into being, it could be sustained. Answering that question is not, however, enough. Skeptics should also wonder if a transition from the *status quo* to a Deweyan society is also economically feasible.

Chapter 11 tries to tackle both questions. It starts by considering gloomy judgments proclaiming the inevitable collapse of societies exemplifying my seven features. Those features depend on a systematic change: once a society has reached a stage of economic comfort, it can increase the time spent away from the workplace instead of striving for ever greater productivity. The crucial move in bringing about the Deweyan society is to declare that enough is enough.

Hence the economic viability of my proposals turns on whether humanity is condemned to pursue economic growth, come what may. Contemporary affluent societies are used to worrying about growth. Newspapers report the ways in which GDP changes, quarter by quarter, with commentators exulting or lamenting depending on the direction. Is this simply a fetish? Something over which informed citizens obsess, with no good reason?

No. Given the arrangements of the world today, keeping track of growth is entirely sensible. Economists see growth as an indicator of the state of the business cycle. Successive periods of falling growth may point to a recession in the offing, with consequent unemployment and hardship. Deweyan societies are organized differently, offering many public goods and services and buffering the conditions under which their citizens live. Their arrangements will continue unless the ability to provide what has proved sufficient is compromised—there is no longer enough. Why should a falling growth rate, or even a state of zero growth, signal that?

Chapter 11 considers three main sources of concern. What has sufficed in the past would do so no longer if productivity failed to meet the needs of a growing population; or if those needs were modified through technological advances, not available within the society at prices it could afford; or if the *relative* growth with respect to trading partners was deficient, so that previously available levels of production could no longer be sustained. Analyses of the three threats uncovers grounds for optimism. Some forms of the challenges can be straightforwardly rebutted. Others conflict with data showing how nations can find their own economic niches, and how they can prosper despite significant reductions in the length of the workweek. At best, the case for thinking Deweyan societies are doomed to collapse is "not proven."

INTRODUCTION 19

Skeptics may offer more general doubts. They may deny, for example, that productivity—today or in the foreseeable future—is enough to support a satisfactory Deweyan society. Or they may question economic regulation, singing familiar anthems to the virtues of the "free market." I offer a response to the first line of argument, by recognizing the enormous waste allowed in our current practices. The second, I suggest, rests on a widespread myth, one that either invokes an impossibility (the completely unregulated market) or else favors a particular style of supposedly "minimal regulation." The latter choice is well suited to reducing the prices of consumer goods. Yet, as wise economists periodically remind us, regulation of markets should be tailored to the goals we intend to achieve. It is not entirely obvious that the lowest possible prices are the *summum bonum* to which everything else we value should be sacrificed.

The chapter concludes by recognizing the difficulty of offering a detailed roadmap showing the route to the Deweyan society. Here, I recommend a pragmatic answer. The conditions distilled at the end of Chapter 10 indicate the directions in which we might advance. Let us head off in these directions, adjust our plans as we go, and see how far we can get.

———

Chapter 1 begins with Mill, and it is fitting that he should return at the close of Chapter 11. A distinctive feature of his approach to economic issues is his willingness to tolerate the "stationary state"—to champion the many-sidedness of human life against the relentless striving to accumulate wealth. That attitude is shared by others, including people from very different traditions—Rabindranath Tagore and John Dewey are notable examples. Despite the dominance of supposed economic constraints in much contemporary thinking about social issues, the attitude still thrives today in the work of socially attuned philosophers—sometimes in the work of thinkers specifically concerned with education, sometimes *en passant* in studies of other facets of our culture.[2]

Perhaps the clearest and most forceful expression of the wish to turn dominance on its head comes in the passage from "The American Scholar" I have adapted as the title and the epigraph for this book. My interpretation of

---

[2] Thus, besides the principal writings of Harry Brighouse, Randall Curren, Meira Levinson, and Harvey Siegel, it pervades Martha Nussbaum's impressive corpus. It is also clearly discernible in Kwame Anthony Appiah's important book, *The Lies That Bind*, New York: W. W. Norton, 2018; see, in particular, 177–79.

20 THE MAIN ENTERPRISE OF THE WORLD

Emerson's words is probably not what he intended.[3] His transcendentalism tends to displace a distant deity, and to view humanity as the *telos* of creation. Emerson was, after all, an odd Lamarckian, one who could write:

> And, striving to be man, the worm
> Mounts through all the spires of form.[4]

Perhaps he thought of the cosmos—or the organic part of it—as having a purpose, the production of the perfect human being ("man"). My use of his phrase is intended differently: the best we humans can do with our lives is to nurture and protect the sentient beings with whom we share the planet; the most striking and effective ways through which that can be done consist in fostering nascent human lives; in that activity, we contribute to something larger than our individual selves, a human project that spans the generations, and that, with our help and with luck, will continue to advance for the remaining duration (inevitably finite) of our species.

In that sense, "the main enterprise of the world is the upbuilding of a human being."

---

[3] I conjecture, however, that his use of the odd word "upbuilding" was an attempt to echo the German "Bildung" (education)—possibly even emphasized in a neologism ("Aufbildung", adding "auf," the German "up," doesn't exist—although "Ausbildung" is an alternative word for education).

[4] "Nature," in *The Complete Writings of Ralph Waldo Emerson* (New York: W. M. Wise, 1929), 913

PART I

1

Overload

In 1867, two years after the students of St. Andrews University had elected him as their rector, John Stuart Mill took a break from his duties as a member of Parliament, and traveled north to Scotland to deliver his Inaugural Address. Mill began by alluding with approval to the custom of using the occasion to offer "a few thoughts" on the subject of liberal education.[1] He continued, somewhat ominously, by remarking that "Education, in its larger sense, is one of the most inexhaustible of all topics."[2] The speech lived up to his advertisement, for, although he spoke quickly, Mill went on for more than three hours.[3] I don't know how his audience reacted, but it seems a safe bet to suppose that the undergraduates found him less entertaining than their successors who listened, just over a century later, to their own choice as rector—the British comedian, and famous silly-walker, John Cleese.

The text of Mill's address might provoke suspicion that, like Topsy, it just growed. Early on, he made it clear how some kinds of education were beyond his intended scope. Professional training has no place in his thoughts. To be sure, there should be schools of law, medicine, and engineering, but these do not belong to the project of general education, to which universities ought to be dedicated.[4] He began with the question, disputed then as now, of the relative roles of the humanities and the sciences in a general education. Mill proposed to settle the quarrel between the ancients and the moderns, the defenders of classical learning and the champions of natural science, by awarding prizes to both sides.[5] The writings of antiquity, in the original Greek and Latin, retain their great importance.[6] Study of them should be

[1] SMC 321.

[2] SMC 321.

[3] See https://news.st-andrews.ac.uk/archive/the-liberal-university-and-its-enemies/.

[4] SMC 322.

[5] SMC 324. This had not always been his position. Some of his earlier writings (e.g., "On Genius" [1832] and "Civilization—Signs of the Times" [1836]) claim distinctive virtues for classical studies. By 1867, he had become more positive about the contributions of modern languages and literature.

[6] SMC 328–33. The special character of the ancients as foils for the understanding of contemporary life and contemporary society features prominently among Mill's reasons. The ancient Greeks and Romans are more unlike (British) students than other modern European peoples, but not totally dissimilar (like the "Orientals"; SMC 329). Classical languages, literature, philosophy, and history

The Main Enterprise of the World. Philip Kitcher, Oxford University Press. © Oxford University Press 2022.
DOI: 10.1093/oso/9780190928971.003.0002

24   THE MAIN ENTERPRISE OF THE WORLD

streamlined[7] to allow a thorough immersion in mathematics and the physical sciences, both mathematical and experimental. Moreover, the understanding of the principal features of astronomy, physics, and chemistry ought to be supplemented with appreciation of the general ways in which the sciences infer their conclusions from the evidence. The rules of deductive logic, and those of non-deductive inference must be studied and assimilated.[8]

At that point, perhaps after some further remarks about how all this could be managed, Mill might have stopped. He didn't. Apparently his parliamentary work had impressed him with the need for public understanding of policies of hygiene. His next step was to extend the scientific curriculum to embrace the study of physiology. Most people, he suggests, "will be required to form an opinion and to take action on sanitary subjects."[9] Moreover, the "science of the laws of organic and animal life" provides a bridge to studies of even greater significance. Following Pope, Mill takes the "proper study of mankind" to be "Man."[10]

The requirements of general education expand further. An encounter with psychology is essential, and here Mill inserts a plug for the ability of philosophy, epistemology in particular, to "sharpen" the "intellectual faculties."[11] Most of all, students need instruction in "the exercise of thought on the great interests of mankind as moral and social beings."[12] Now, subject upon subject come flooding in. History, conceived generally (or "philosophically"), should provide "some incipient conception of the causes and laws of progress."[13] Political science should acquaint the young with the "civil and political institutions" of their own country—and of others as well.[14] Political economy is crucial for understanding the economic constraints on well-intentioned policies.[15] Jurisprudence is "of no less importance," but it should

thus serve as an intended "multicultural" requirement. The social class of Mill's intended audience is made plain by his thought that acquaintance with modern languages and modern cultures is best served through travel and a period of residence in another country.

[7] SMC 325. Here Mill sketches the methods he thinks appropriate in language instruction. Later (SMC 333–34) he castigates the emphasis placed on exercises in writing Greek and Latin verse, pointing out that the important goal is to achieve a reading knowledge of the languages.

[8] SMC 338–40.

[9] SMC 340.

[10] SMC 340–41.

[11] SMC 341, 342.

[12] SMC 343.

[13] SMC 343.

[14] SMC 344.

[15] SMC 344. Here, Mill is at pains to defend the "dismal science" against the charge that it induces insensitivity to others. The significance of this apparent excursion becomes clearer in light of his later interest in the arts as cultivating the emotions.

be supplemented by some study of "International Law."[16] Yet none of these crucial educational domains can be expected to yield its proper fruits unless there is serious attention to ethics. Mill's ideal curriculum requires a thorough and impartial survey of all the "principal systems of moral philosophy," supplemented with a comparative and historical study of the major world religions.[17]

At this point (just past the two-hour mark), Mill announced that he had now said what he had to say on the debate with which he had started,[18] probably arousing the hopes of his audience. But he was not ready to stop. He added a defense of the arts.[19] The "Fine Arts," he suggested, cultivate "exalted feelings,"[20] raising people "above the littlenesses of humanity,"[21] and offering them "insight into subjects larger and far more ennobling than the minutiae of a business or a profession."[22] A deep immersion in the arts complements the other branches of education, thereby helping people to discharge a fundamental human duty. Each of us is "to leave his fellow creatures some little better for the use he has known how to make of his intellect."[23] The promise of education is to provide a "deeper and more varied interest" in life.[24] Unlike other rewards, our sense of making a contribution to the lives of others will not grow "less valuable" as we age. Instead, "it not only endures, but increases."[25] On this high note, Mill ended.

An amusing Victorian pathology? The fantasies of an over-earnest intellectual, force-fed by a father who had started him on Greek at three? The apologia of someone whose brilliance had been clouded by a nervous breakdown in early adulthood, from which he had recovered through reading the poetry of Wordsworth?[26] The demands of this apparently preposterous address are

[16] SMC 344, 345.
[17] SMC 346–49.
[18] SMC 349.
[19] SMC 349–53.
[20] SMC 351.
[21] SMC 352.
[22] SMC 353.
[23] SMC 353. As we shall see, this theme is developed by Dewey.
[24] SMC 354.
[25] SMC 354.
[26] Mill's *Autobiography* provides a detailed account of the curriculum devised for him by his father, James Mill, and gives a poignant account of his breakdown and recovery. Mill senior was a close friend of Bentham's, and intended that his eldest son should be the apostle of Benthamite Utilitarianism for the next generation. The all-too-common interpretation of Mill as a utilitarian who deviated little from Bentham would be corrected if philosophers were to read more widely in Mill's writings—studying the essays "Bentham" and "Coleridge," as well as *Principles of Political Economy, Considerations on Representative Government,* the posthumous chapters on socialism, the *Autobiography,* the literary essays on poetry, and the Inaugural Address. In "Mill, Education, and the Good Life," in *John Stuart Mill and the Art of Living,* ed. Ben Eggleston, Dale Miller, and David

26 THE MAIN ENTERPRISE OF THE WORLD

to be explained away, partly as products of past social conditions, partly as idiosyncrasies of an extraordinarily articulate member of an elite class. So, at least, you might think.

If you are tempted to think that, I hope to convince you that you are wrong. Behind Mill's peroration stands a complex of forces, even more intense today than they were a century and a half ago. The breadth of his understanding of the possibilities of education pushes him to multiply requirements beyond credibility. He is moved by a well-considered conception of what education— "in its larger sense"—is meant to accomplish, for the individual and for the society of which the individual is a part.[27] Anyone who tries to understand and to amend the practice of education by asking after its proper aims will be forced to traverse the ground Mill attempted to cover. The more thoroughly and comprehensively you reflect on the issues, the more demands you will pile up. The end result? Overload.

In the prelude to an aria beloved of bass-baritones, Leporello informs the aggrieved Donna Elvira that she will be "neither the first nor the last" woman seduced by Don Giovanni. Similarly, Mill's exercise in overload has predecessors and descendants. Unlike Leporello, I haven't obsessively constructed a catalogue in which all the exhibits are numbered. But it's worth noting a few high spots.

Plato's *Republic* is rightly recognized not only as a foundational work in metaphysics and political philosophy, but also as the first great discussion of educational issues. The citizens of his ideal society are divided into three classes, the majority who provide the material resources the city needs, a smaller set who defend against potential invasions,[28] and an elite who rule. In the *Republic*, Plato is most interested in the education of this last group. Consequently, the middle books anticipate the form of Mill's

---

Weinstein (New York: Oxford University Press, 2011), 192–211; and in "Mill's Consequentialism," in *The Routledge Companion to Nineteenth-Century Thought*, ed. Dean Moyar (London: Routledge, 2010), 633–57, I have tried to set the record straight.

[27] This conception emerges in Mill's early characterization of the educated person as having a particular specialization set within a broad general knowledge that provides a "map" of the whole (SMC 323), and in the closing picture of human life as increased ("tenfold") in value through contributions to humanity (SMC 353–54).

[28] The military forces Plato envisages are not restricted to defense. Sometimes, apparently, it proves necessary to "seize some of our neighbors' land" (373d; R 1012). As the later *Laws* makes clear, under ideal conditions, no military class would be required. (Thanks to Randy Curren for alerting me to this point.)

OVERLOAD 27

address, enumerating the requirements for proper rulers, and describing the programs through which they can be adequately prepared. Finally, toward the end of Book VII, Socrates is able to add up the time needed to educate someone capable of governing the city. "At the age of fifty," he explains to his interlocutors, "those who've survived the tests" will be ready.[29]

As Rousseau observed, the conception of education developed by Plato looks outward to the public sphere.[30] Concerned to combat the corruption of the individual by the educational practices of his time, Rousseau turned his gaze inward. The detailed program undertaken by Émile's dedicated (overloaded?) tutor aims at harmonizing three factors taken to shape human development.[31] After the necessary exercises have been scrupulously prescribed and strenuously pursued, the pupil will achieve the closest approximation to "happiness on earth."[32] Although the tutor—presumably exhausted—might then be expected to enjoy a contented retirement, that is not to be allowed. Instead he is recruited to supervise and advise Émile and Sophie in their new roles as parents.

Overload is prominent in the two greatest pre-Millian explorations of the aims of education. If it is less evident in the writings of the late nineteenth, twentieth, and twenty-first centuries, that is because, writing, like Rousseau, in reaction to the perceived deficiencies of the times, many[33] subsequent scholars emphasize educational goals they take to have been neglected. Worried about overspecialization and curricula that "favour a particular pursuit," John Henry Newman takes the goal of university education to lie in the "formation of a character."[34] "Liberal Education makes not the Christian, not the Catholic, but the gentleman."[35] Newman's choice of words makes even more vivid the restricted focus of the major historical discussions of education. He differs from Plato and Mill—and even from Rousseau, for

---

[29] 540, R 1154.

[30] "Do you want to get an idea of public education? Read Plato's *Republic.* . . . It is the most beautiful educational treatise ever written." E 40.

[31] E 38. The three "masters" from which each child must learn are "nature, men, and things." I interpret Rousseau as claiming that, in being educated, development is guided by our own individual biological proclivities, by the ambient society, and by the material conditions of our existence.

[32] E 480.

[33] But not all. Systematic attempts to characterize the "aims of education" are sometimes taken up in twentieth-century writings. See, for example, A. N. Whitehead, *The Aims of Education* (New York: Free Press, 1929) and John White, *The Aims of Education Restated* (London: Routledge and Kegan Paul, 1982). It's worth noting that Whitehead is aware of the problem of overload, and reacts to what he regards as its unfortunate effects on the educational regime of his times: "Do not teach too many subjects" is one of his educational "commandments" (Whitehead, 2).

[34] J. H. Newman, *The Idea of a University* (New Haven: Yale University Press, 1996), 77, 85.

[35] Ibid., 89.

28   THE MAIN ENTERPRISE OF THE WORLD

whom Sophie enters at least as an afterthought and an ancillary to Émile—in overlooking women (or "ladies"?). Yet all four concentrate on the education of the privileged:[36] the guardians, the well-to-do, the small minority who qualify for admission to universities. The needs of the masses are of little interest, or possibly of none at all.[37]

From the dawn of the twentieth century on, that changes. Already in 1901, W. E. B. Du Bois questioned the style of education (industrial education) deemed suitable for black Americans.[38] One year later, he explicitly committed himself to securing for at least some "black folk"[39]—the "talented tenth"—university education of the general kind favored by his nineteenth-century predecessors. "I sit with Shakespeare and he winces not," he declares, and later (in 1930), he strips Newman's credo of its limitation to social class: "The object of education is not to make men carpenters but to make carpenters men."[40]

Concerns that education ought to be made more broadly available—and, indeed, to take on new tasks just because some groups have previously been marginalized—are expressed in some of the most significant writings on education of recent decades. Thus Meira Levinson's penetrating study of the educational opportunities available to America's poorest children, typically members of stigmatized minorities, emphasizes the lack of opportunities these young people are given to become active citizens, able to contribute to and shape the supposed democracy in which they will live. She argues cogently for a "civic empowerment gap," documenting its existence and exploring ways of overcoming it.[41] Similarly, like Du Bois before him, Harry

---

[36] Again, Plato's *Laws* offers a different perspective. There Plato considers the educational needs of all citizens.

[37] Pre-twentieth century discussions of questions in other areas sometimes prompt questions about the education of workers. Late in the *Wealth of Nations*, Adam Smith's inquiry into the background conditions required for the market transactions he envisages leads him to consider whether public education should be provided for all. Objecting to the eighteenth-century notion of liberal education on the grounds of its uselessness, he advocates providing those who will implement the division of labor with the ability to "read, write, and account" and perhaps some acquaintance with the "elementary parts of geometry and mechanics" (WN 842, 843). Smith thus defends just the style of education Newman opposes, on exactly the grounds to which Newman objects. As we shall see in the following chapter, Smith's own reflections on his proposal inspire doubts not only in his successors (Marx, Dewey) but also in himself.

[38] "Of Mr. Booker T. Washington and Others," Chapter 3 of *The Souls of Black Folk*, Norton Critical Edition (New York: W. W. Norton, 1999, 34–45).

[39] In later writings, the potential audience for higher education is considerably expanded: "Some day every human being will have college training." "Education and Work," delivered at Howard University in 1930; *The Education of Black People* (New York: Monthly Review Press, 2001), 106.

[40] Ibid., 88.

[41] Meira Levinson, *No Citizen Left Behind* (Cambridge, MA: Harvard University Press, 2014). For her introduction of the idea of the gap, see 33.

OVERLOAD 29

Brighouse identifies the plight of the majority of schoolchildren in the United States and the United Kingdom as one in which education has been distorted. Not, in his view, simply because they are trained for menial tasks, but rather because existing schools fail to provide resources for confronting and overcoming the narrowing effects of a popular culture, dedicated to inculcating "a life-long and unreflective materialism.in as many children as possible."[42]

Others are troubled by different perceived defects. A. S. Neill founded a school dedicated to breaking down children's fears—of teachers and of life—because he saw standard educational regimes as founded on a model of military discipline.[43] Michael Oakeshott harshly dismissed any vision of this kind, taking schools to aim at preparing young people for living in and contributing to a society with settled traditions and conventions; education is to "initiate a newcomer into what was going on and thus enable him to participate in it."[44] Andrew Delbanco and Martha Nussbaum both worry about the decay of American education, Delbanco stressing the importance of community among college students and "lateral learning," Nussbaum offering an eloquent brief for the continued importance of the humanities in contemporary education.[45] Eamonn Callan sees a principal lack in the failure of educational institutions to develop "civic virtue."[46]

So many additions and amendments! My abridged catalogue isn't intended to do justice to the sophisticated thinkers whose ideas I have so cursorily reviewed. Rather, it hopes to show how, beyond Mill's seemingly

[42] Harry Brighouse, *On Education* (Abingdon: Routledge, 2006, 23). The theme of personal development and the cultivation of autonomy runs through this work, as well as Brighouse's other important writings on education. See, in particular, Brighouse, Helen F. Ladd, Susanna Loeb, and Adam Swift, *Educational Goods* (Chicago: University of Chicago Press, 2018).

[43] A. S. Neill, *Summerhill School: A New View of Childhood*, rev. ed. (New York: St. Martin's, 1992). In a similar vein, Rabindranath Tagore (perhaps inspired by Wordsworth's famous "Intimations of Immortality" Ode?) regarded the standard school as a penal institution, in which sensitive young people were encased by "straight walls staring at [them] with the blank stare of the blind." Amiya Chakravarty, ed., *A Tagore Reader* (New York: Macmillan, 1961), 218. For lucid discussion of Tagore's educational ideas, see Martha Nussbaum, "Tagore, Dewey, and the Imminent Demise of Liberal Education," in *The Oxford Handbook of Philosophy of Education*, ed. Harvey Siegel (New York: Oxford University Press, 2009), 52–64.

[44] Timothy Fuller, ed., *Michael Oakeshott on Education* (New Haven: Yale University Press, 1989), 65; the use of the past tense ("was") seems significant. For the critique of those who "affect to believe" that children are "condemned to a prison-like existence in cell-like classrooms," see 73. We might interpret Oakeshott's view as an inversion of Marx's famous thesis on Feuerbach: the point of education is to help children interpret the world and not to change it.

[45] Andrew Delbanco, *College: What It Is, Was, and Should Be* (Princeton: Princeton University Press, 2012). Martha Nussbaum, *Cultivating Humanity* (Cambridge, MA: Harvard University Press, 1997) and especially *Not for Profit* (Princeton, NJ: Princeton University Press, 2011).

[46] Eamonn Callan, *Creating Citizens* (Oxford: Oxford University Press, 1997).

30 THE MAIN ENTERPRISE OF THE WORLD

preposterous assembly of Jobs for Education to Do, there are further attractive ideals and ends. Who could quarrel with extending education to all, to trying to make up for the defects—even the savagery—of the environments in which many children grow up, to trying to cultivate freedom rather than stifling it, to preparing the young to navigate the society and culture of the time and place, to empowering them as citizens, while imbuing the virtues they require to play a constructive role in their social and political lives, to form communities of learners, to develop strong individual characters, and . . . ? In a world like ours, overload seems inevitable. It is the name of the educational game.

And that is no accident. It is, rather, an expectable effect of the cultural evolution of our species. The recent history of education in the United States (and, I suspect, in most other nations of the contemporary world) reveals how failure to confront the problem of overload generates an unstable oscillation among policies designed to remedy the deficiencies of the immediately preceding educational efforts. Today's critical needs prompt a move in particular directions. Without the guidance of a synthetic vision, the result is to overlook other important ends. Hence, tomorrow, new reformers will recognize different features that need to be fixed.

Patricia Albjerg Graham's lucid and wide-ranging history of American schools documents the process of partial adaptation. Her opening sentences describe the gyrations whose rationales and whose developments the ensuing 250 pages will chart in detail:

Schools in America have danced to different drummers during their long history. Sometimes the drumbeat demanded rigidity in all programs; sometimes it wanted academic learning for only a few. Sometimes it encouraged unleashing children's creativity, not teaching them facts. Sometimes it wanted children to solve the social problems, such as racial segregation, adults could not handle. Sometimes it tacitly supported some schools as warehouses, not instructional facilities. Sometimes it sought schooling to be the equalizer in a society in which the gap between rich and poor was growing. Sometimes the principal purpose of schooling seemed to be teaching citizenship and developing habits of work appropriate for a democratic society, while at other times its purpose seemed to be preparation for employment, which needed the same habits of work but also some

OVERLOAD   31

academic skills. Now, the drumbeat demands that all children achieve academically at a high level and the measure of that achievement is tests.[47]

Assimilating new citizens, addressing problems of racial exclusion, promoting equality of opportunity, instilling democratic values, nurturing creativity, providing basic skills, attending to children with learning disabilities, preparing students to compete in a rigorously demanding global economy—it's not hard to understand how *all* of these tasks can seem important, and how, at different times, one among them may appear particularly urgent. Graham's story of the dominant mood of the present reveals how constant worries about "a nation at risk," reinforced by anxious attention to the "league tables" periodically ranking the performances of students from different countries, encourage highlighting some goals at the inevitable expense of others.[48]

Contingent kicks from history often cause the lurch from one partial educational strategy to another. Launching a satellite (Sputnik) prompts startled rival nations to "get serious about science."[49] But these shifts, driven by exogenous factors, changes in other institutions or new technological advances, are not restricted to recent centuries. To ponder the aims of education by taking for granted a matrix of social arrangements and asking how we expect schools and universities to be reformed to adapt to them is already to presuppose too much. For it is to assume that education is rightly pursued in the contemporary world by continuing to have schools and universities, and also that, if the traditional forms of education are somehow at odds with the ambient environments, that it's the schools' and universities' fault; the necessary changes are to occur within the practices of education and not to be directed at pathologies of the enveloping societies. Before we pose Newman's questions about the idea of a university, it is worth pausing to reflect on why universities exist at all. In advance of asking how the school should respond to the demands posed by the modern world, we might consider whether the

---

[47] Patricia Albjerg Graham, *Schooling America: How the Public Schools Meet the Nation's Changing Needs* (New York: Oxford University Press, 2020), 1.

[48] Ronald Reagan's commissioned report, *A Nation at Risk*, published in 1983, has set the tone for subsequent jitters. Graham's fourth chapter explains the rise to dominance of "standards" and the reforms generated in consequence. That chapter, and its successor, should be read in conjunction with Diane Ravitch's sobering account of how the felt need to make American students more competitive gave birth to an emphasis on testing and the sacrifice of important educational values; see *The Death and Life of the Great American School System*, rev. and expanded ed. (New York: Basic Books, 2016).

[49] Graham, *Schooling America*, 106–7 tells the story concisely and accurately.

32   THE MAIN ENTERPRISE OF THE WORLD

pressures that world exerts are harmful and if the wiser course would be to relax them.

Discussions of education often start too late. Fundamental issues go unprobed. Graham's history exposes overload, thus serving as a reminder to think more widely and more deeply. The characters whose actions she so vividly describes struggle with a complex problem, subject to multiple constraints, on whose *raisons d'être* they only have a partial perspective. Her century-long narrative might prompt investigation of a far longer time span and a broader range of cultural contexts. How and why did the particular vision of the American (British, French, German, Japanese, Korean, Brazilian, Finnish, Egyptian, Kenyan, Indian, Indonesian, Chinese, Saudi Arabian, Australian, . . .) school emerge? Genealogy could liberate contemporary educational thinking from the pictures that hold it captive.[50]

The formal educational practices of contemporary societies are recent inventions, emerging from an enterprise extending tens of thousands of years into the past.[51] All human societies, and possibly many hominin societies as well, have fashioned procedures through which younger generations might continue their communal life. The children must acquire the capacities and dispositions required by adults for coping with the physical and social environment. They have to complete the task Oakeshott saw as central. They need to know how to fit in and to carry on.

If you extrapolate from the characteristics of those living peoples whose modes of existence seem closest to those of our prehistoric ancestors, there emerges a simple vision of the educational practice that has dominated all but a minute fragment of our species' history.[52] Call it *basic training*. Once

[50] As I read both Nietzsche and Foucault, they envisage genealogy as a means for pursuing liberatory ends. Through investigating the ways in which an institution or a social practice has come to be, we gain insight into the purposes it was intended to serve and to the ways in which efforts to achieve those ends blocked attainment of rival goals. That can serve as a basis for redesigning the institution or reconceiving the practice. Nietzsche explicitly endorses this view in *The Genealogy of Morality*. My attribution of it to Foucault is aligned with that offered by Gary Gutting in *Michel Foucault's Archeology of Scientific Reason* (Cambridge UK: Cambridge University Press, 1989), but my own espousal of it descends from a lengthy conversation I had with Foucault during the autumn of 1982, when he visited the University of Vermont. Of course, Foucault is famous (notorious?) for having offered different explanations of his projects on different occasions.

[51] Dewey's major work on education, *Democracy and Education*, rightly begins by viewing education within the general context of socializing the young and thus "renewing" society. Formal educational structures grow within this much more general and far older project. See MW 9: 3–12.

[52] Plainly, basing conclusions about Paleolithic education on evidence derived from studies of contemporary hunter-gatherers might misrepresent the actual past. Nonetheless, it is the best available supplement to the sparse social insights available from archeology. The strategy is explicitly endorsed

OVERLOAD 33

infancy has ended, the young are taught to carry out the basic tasks of finding food and water, of constructing and maintaining shelter, and of defending against predation from animals (some of them human). They learn the rules of tribal conduct, and are instructed in the importance of obedience. Insofar as their ambitions transcend the urgent tasks of ensuring their own survival and that of the band, they are likely to focus on being a well-regarded member of the group. Perhaps it is also reasonable to attribute aspirations for relieving communal pain and for spreading communal happiness.[53]

So how did we get from there to here? An important part of human cultural evolution, beginning roughly twenty thousand years before the present, consisted in the agglomeration of human beings into larger groups. The small bands of the Paleolithic started to trade with one another, to form seasonal associations, and finally to merge.[54] Eight thousand years ago, the first cities—containing about a thousand inhabitants—emerged in the near east.[55] Three thousand years later, as the oldest documents we have make

in the most extensive discussion I know of prehistoric education, Frederick Eby and Charles Flinn Arrowood, *The History and Philosophy of Education, Ancient and Medieval* (New York: Prentice-Hall, 1940), 3.

So far as I can tell, the project of offering a large-scale history of education is so out of fashion that I have had to appeal to this dated source (henceforth HPE). Its problematic character is reflected in the terms Eby and Arrowood unselfconsciously use. They talk of "primitive people" and of present-day hunter-gatherers as "culturally retarded." Hence I have tried only to rely on their discussions for the simplest and most basic historical points.

For illuminating studies of the lives of hunter-gatherers, see Christoph Boehm, *Hierarchy in the Forest* (Cambridge MA: Harvard University Press, 1999); Raymond Firth, *We the Tikopia* (Boston: Beacon, 1961); Richard Lee, *The !Kung San* (Cambridge UK: Cambridge University Press, 1979); and Marjorie Shostak, *Nisa* (Cambridge MA: Harvard University Press, 1981).

[53] I thus endorse Mill's judgment in the closing pages of *A System of Logic*. Human history has been dominated by a Benthamite urge to "make human life happy," in "the comparatively humble sense, of pleasure and freedom from pain." As we shall see, Mill aims to go further, beyond this "puerile and insignificant" condition, to a form of life that "human beings with highly developed faculties can care to have." See *Collected Works*, condensed edition (Indianapolis: Liberty Fund, 2006), Volume 8, 952.

[54] See Colin Renfrew and Stephen Shennan, *Ranking, Resource, and Exchange* (Cambridge, UK: Cambridge University Press, 1982), and, for the hypothesis that trade in Africa developed significantly earlier, Sally McBrearty and Andrea Brooks "The Revolution That Wasn't: A New Interpretation of the Evolution of Modern Human Behavior," *Journal of Human Evolution 39* (2000): 453–563. The details are forever lost, shrouded in the mists of the Upper Paleolithic.

[55] The most famous of these are Jericho and Çatal Hüyük. There has been significant debate on whether these settlements should be called "cities" or simply seen as "overgrown villages." According to Ian Hodder, the principal authority on Çatal Hüyük, that question is best abandoned in favor of inquiry into how such settlements functioned. The evidence currently available suggests little differentiation among houses (and thus a relatively egalitarian society), and limited agriculture; see, for example, Hodder, "Çatal Hüyük: The Leopard Changes Its Spots. A Summary of Recent Work," *Anatolian Studies*, 64 (2014): 1–22, especially 5.

34 THE MAIN ENTERPRISE OF THE WORLD

clear, the urban centers of Egypt and Mesopotamia had achieved a significant division of labor, requiring a complex set of ethical and legal rules.[56]

The different functions of the adult citizens demanded specialized forms of training for the young. For much of the population, the necessary skills could be inculcated in the old ways, without the need for any formal institution. The development of writing, however, demanded something distinctive. Scribes needed to learn how to keep the records, setting down information crucial to administering the city's complex of rules.[57] They required a special education, one that passed from the private spheres of family or employment into centralized social control. So the school was born.

In many subsequent societies, writing—often seen as prior to and more significant than reading[58]—has been the province of a small minority. Numerous complex tasks, building and maintaining the canals that brought water to the fields, designing and decorating the temples, embalming the dead, were passed on through lengthy apprenticeships. Inculcation of the skills required could often proceed without literacy. Some societies, like Sparta, emphasized military training, cultivating strong bodies, martial skills, and indifference to pain.[59] Others viewed writing as important not only for the mundane tasks of record-keeping and administration, but primarily in fulfilling the highest purposes of individual citizens and their collective culture. Reading and writing were taught so that the divine message might be thoroughly understood and properly promulgated.

Across cultures and across times, the organization of education, the division between the private and the public spheres, the forms provided by the society, the rules specifying who is to receive training of particular types, the ages at which education begins and at which it ends, all this is enormously variable. Schools are introduced and subsequently adapted in response to perceived social needs (and, to a lesser extent, to views of the healthy development of the young).[60] As tribes and nations interact with

[56] See James B. Pritchard, *Ancient Near-Eastern Texts* (Princeton, NJ: Princeton University Press, 1969). Such documents as the surviving parts of the Lipit-Ishtar code (and the more famous later code of Hammurabi) are plainly codicils to more systematic collections of moral and legal rules, that must have been accumulated over tens of millennia. The same holds of *The Egyptian Book of the Dead* (New York: Dover, 1967).

[57] HPE 63–64.

[58] HPE 72–73, 78–79.

[59] HPE 205–18.

[60] Once schools have been introduced, and attendance at them has become recognized as a gateway to privileged positions, their further evolution is directed by two forces. Not only are they responsive to the perceived needs of the state. They also adapt to the strategies of individuals who seek competitive advantage (for themselves or for their children). Thanks to Randy Curren for drawing this point to my attention.

OVERLOAD 35

one another, sometimes in peaceful trade, sometimes through warfare and conquest, features prominent in one culture are grafted on to the traditional arrangements present in another. Historical contingency is everywhere.

The haphazard character of educational evolution is evident, for example, in the emergence of universities in Western Europe. By the twelfth century, particular cities had attracted groups of scholars concerned with three prominent bodies of learning: medicine, the law, and theology. The first universities, at Bologna and Paris, and, slightly later at Oxford, grew out of the guilds to which these scholars and their pupils belonged.[61] Ironically, the initial impetus arose from groups dedicated to professions Mill set on one side at the beginning of his long address. The faculties of law, medicine, and theology came first. General studies, the *studium generale*, followed, conceived originally as preparing the young men for the important work, their professional studies. Possibly in consequence of a surge of nationalism after the clash between Henry II and Thomas à Becket,[62] Oxford attracted a diverse collection of English scholars. Unlike Paris (focused on theology) or Bologna (centered on law), Oxford—and the breakaway group that migrated to Cambridge—included representatives of all three professions. A shared commitment to the *studium generale*, perhaps intensified by the greater need among the English for preparatory training, led to an emphasis on general studies. So, something more akin to Mill's conception of the university was born.

Its subsequent growth was equally affected by external accidents. The development of the curriculum was fueled by discovery of previously unknown texts. Encounters with the Muslim world led to absorption of the works of Aristotle, seen as providing a valuable synthesis across the disciplines. *If* the Crusades were prompted by a desire to channel the energies of overly boisterous younger sons, sending them off to express their violent urges in distant parts (and with attractive theological goals), from which they brought back manuscripts new to the scholars of the West, then we can trace the rise of classical studies and their prominence in the universities Mill knew to the loutish behavior of landless young nobles in medieval France—and even to far earlier difficulties that had prompted the system of primogeniture and thus left them propertyless.

A tongue-in-cheek historical speculation is a long way short of a serious probing of the origins and development of central educational institutions.

---

[61] HPE 762–66.
[62] HPE 781.

36 THE MAIN ENTERPRISE OF THE WORLD

To the best of my knowledge, there is no available genealogy of central features of educational practice. Yet the simplest and least controversial history reveals a familiar aspect of both biological and cultural evolution. Descendants, whether organisms or social arrangements, retain properties of their ancestors. Although those features are no longer well adapted to the current environment, even if they are maladaptive, they are inherited and they survive.

Their survival is the product of the problem of overload. Once complex societies with intricate division of labor have emerged, synthetic attempts at reviewing all the attractive aims of education generate something so preposterous—or unwieldy or daunting or utopian—as to force a strategy of selection. With so many potential demands on the society's educational practices, the squeakiest doors get oiled. Attempts to stand back and consider how a wide range of important goals might be integrated appear impractical, a time-wasting exercise ill-suited to the urgency of the problems of the moment.

Nevertheless, taking a more abstract, "philosophical," stance can be valuable. Uncovering and scrutinizing presuppositions, and charting tensions among ends can offer guidance for reform. Even a history as cursory as the one I have sketched offers important reminders to people who want discussions of education to offer quick fixes for current ills—and who see that in terms of tinkering with existing structures. The task of preparing the new members of a society for life can easily be undertaken, and adequately discharged, without the kinds of institutions normally studied by educational theory. When schools and universities are present, the question of how to distribute the preparatory effort between them and other spheres arises. How far can basic training go? If only the formal institutions are considered in attempts to address educational problems, that limits the potential options. So I offer a first methodological guideline:

A. *In educational problem-solving consider possibilities of social change outside of the formal system of education, and different ways of distributing educational effort.*

Viewing current educational practices within the frame of a long history, as continuous with basic training, also reminds us that important educational work precedes entry into any formal educational system. By the same token, such work might continue beyond the end of formal education, in principle throughout a person's entire life. The cliché of education as a life-long process might be taken literally and seriously.

B. *Attempts to overcome current educational deficiencies might rethink the distribution of episodes of learning across the human lifespan.*

These two methodological guidelines attempt to enlarge the options for educational theory.

To explore those options, we should step back and ask if there is any general pattern, exemplified in the context-specific responses to the accidents of history. Are there shared features of all the particular aims that redirect education? Common expectations about what educational practice ought to provide for the young?

Many people would start with an obvious answer to those questions. They would emphasize the kinds of preparation Mill self-consciously leaves out—with training for the workaday world. His excision of the skills needed to earn a living, as well as the terms in which he characterizes what doesn't belong in his account—entrée to the "professions"—are easily seen as symptoms of his elitist insensitivity to the predicaments of the vast majority of human beings, in his time as in ours. Our formal systems of education, manifest in schools and (to a lesser extent) in universities, should equip those who pass through them with the ability to earn a living. One common goal of education would seem to be to instill a *capacity for self-maintenance*.

A second obvious goal is to enable those who have been schooled to live together within the ambient society. Education not only makes workers but also citizens. From the perspective of some societies, the crucial capacities may be those of understanding the existing framework of laws and institutions and of being strongly disposed to abide by them.[63] Within others, including both the affluent democracies of today and the nations Mill clearly had in mind, education should acknowledge the possibility of progress, preparing the young to play their part in formulating and implementing policies that

---

[63] This probably applies to most of the human societies there have ever been. In a harsh environment where a society struggles to survive, tinkering with institutions and roles that have worked in the past may appear dangerous or, at best, a luxury. Oakeshott can be read as suggesting that this kind of vulnerability endures into the present.

38   THE MAIN ENTERPRISE OF THE WORLD

would improve on the *status quo*.[64] Citizens need a capacity for *progressive participation in civic life*.

Would achieving these two goals be enough? Mill discerns a further aim. The elevated close of his address views education as directed toward *personal fulfillment*.[65] The school, and perhaps even more the university, should supply the resources for discovering the particular ways in which an individual human being can make a distinctive contribution to human life. For the moment I shall content myself with a simplifying sketch. Elaboration will come later.[66]

Any serious investigation of education must come to terms with the oldest problem of Western philosophy, Socrates' question: What makes a human life go well? The most influential contemporary answer was elaborated by Mill and his predecessors, the Enlightenment thinkers Immanuel Kant and Wilhelm von Humboldt, and it is continued in recent times by many others, including John Rawls, Bernard Williams, and Susan Wolf.[67] It offers what I'll call the *liberal approach*. Liberals suppose that, for a life to go well, its pattern must not be externally imposed. In Mill's famous declaration, the "only freedom worthy of the name" is to choose one's own good and pursue it in one's own way.[68] Those who live well find their own plan of life, a conception of what they aim to do, perhaps explicitly formulated, perhaps implicit in their everyday choices. If they go on to pursue this plan with some measure of success, we count them as having lived well. Not necessarily because they achieve something grand, something that makes a mark across the ages. The person whose life is devoted to nurturing and sustaining a family or a community, and whose efforts are largely rewarded, has had a good life.[69]

But not any old plan will do. Imagine someone who chooses, as freely as anyone ever does, to retreat to a remote region, forswearing all human

---

[64] SMC 340. Dewey articulates the idea in far more detail. See *Experience and Nature* (LW Volume 1), Chapter 6.

[65] SMC 353–54. This Millian theme is explicitly taken up by Brighouse (*On Education*, Chapter 1) and by Nussbaum (*Not for Profit*). Their elaborations of it differ in some respects from Mill's approach, from one another, and from the account I shall propose. Nevertheless, there is broad agreement among the four of us.

[66] Primarily in Chapter 3, below.

[67] John Rawls, *A Theory of Justice*, rev. ed. (Cambridge, MA: Harvard University Press 1999), Bernard Williams, "Persons, Character, and Morality," in *Moral Luck* (Cambridge, UK: Cambridge University Press, 1981), Susan Wolf, *Meaning in Life and Why It Matters* (Princeton, NJ: Princeton University Press, 2010).

[68] Mill OL 17.

[69] For explanation and defense, see Philip Kitcher, *Life after Faith* (New Haven: Yale University Press, 2014), 105–16.

OVERLOAD   39

contact, and dedicating himself to counting and recounting the number of blades of grass it contains.[70] Let the grass-counter be completely successful in accurately numbering the blades and recording his findings. Nevertheless, his project appears pathological, and his pursuit of it pathetic. He has not discovered a hitherto unappreciated answer to the question, "How to live?"

What has gone wrong? In discussing self-sacrifice, Mill provides an important clue. Abnegating personal satisfactions for the sake of bringing good to others, he explains, is rightly praised. To act similarly for any other purpose, however, is no more worthy of admiration than the conduct of "the ascetic mounted on his pillar."[71] To live well is to engage in activities that touch the lives of others, improving the lot of people, some of whom will live on when you have ceased to be. Reflecting on the example of the grass-counter, Rawls writes:

> [T]he conditions for persons respecting themselves and one another would seem to require that their common plans be both rational and complementary: they call upon their educated endowments and arouse in each a sense of mastery, and they fit together into one scheme of activity that all can appreciate and enjoy.[72]

Glossing this proposal in a way Rawls might well reject, I take the notion of *fit* to imply a cooperative contribution to a larger human enterprise, one that spans the generations, something we can envisage each member of our species as potentially contributing to.[73]

The best version of the liberal approach starts with the *Autonomy Condition* (the central project should be freely chosen) and the *Success Condition* (enough of the goals marked out by the central project must be achieved). It adds a *Community Condition*: the central project of a valuable life must be intended to make a positive impact on the lives of others. The choice of central project involves awareness, explicit or at least implicit, of the chooser's community with other people. Community may be expressed

---

[70] The example has become standard in discussions of the good life—although it surely has many relatives. Those who appeal to it continue the ancient tradition of opposing hedonism. Consequently, they invite charges of Puritanism. I favor a more amicable treatment of hedonism, recognizing that *communal hedonism*, which focuses on spreading shared pleasures and ameliorating shared pains, can be assimilated to the liberal approach.

[71] OL 147.

[72] *A Theory of Justice* (rev. ed.), 387.

[73] In the quoted passage, the notion of fit appears to be synchronic. Relating it to the trans-temporal human project introduces a diachronic condition.

40   THE MAIN ENTERPRISE OF THE WORLD

in different ways. Perhaps it consists in providing support or advice when others find themselves in difficult or confusing situations. Or in participating in shared endeavors. Or in preserving and transmitting things the community finds valuable. There are many types of relations binding human communities together.

The vision of living well through contributing to the human project is central to Dewey's philosophy, including his influential writings on education.[74] It is articulated with atypical eloquence near the close of his lectures on religion and humanism:

> We who now live are parts of a humanity that extends into the remote past, a humanity that has interacted with nature. The things in civilization we most prize are not of ourselves. They exist by grace of the doings and sufferings of the continuous human community in which we are a link. Ours is the responsibility of conserving, transmitting, rectifying and expanding the heritage of values we have received that those who come after us may receive it more solid and secure, more widely accessible and more generously shared than we have received it.[75]

Self-fulfillment has an other-directed, a collective, dimension.[76]

A little reflection should now make it evident why the aims of education are so often disputed, why inclusive proposals appear so absurdly ambitious—and why Mill was right to take up so much of his audience's time. Considering education (for the moment) from the perspective of the individuals who are to be educated, there are three different general goals—that can then be specified in a further variety of ways. Individual human beings should develop capacities for sustaining themselves, for civic life and for self-fulfillment. How should the goals be balanced against one another (and with social goals)? Is there some optimal distribution of emphases on each? Ought we to try, as Mill seems to recommend, for the maximal development

---

[74] See, for example, his discussion of the self as socially constituted, an idea that pervades *Democracy and Education*; in a particularly revealing passage, he envisages "a society in which every person shall be occupied in something which makes the lives of others better" (MW 9, 326).

[75] *A Common Faith* (LW 9), 57–58.

[76] As we shall see in Chapter 3, central to the account Dewey endorses—and to the version I derive from him—is the thought of the individual as socially constituted. This thought marks a break with the liberal tradition, and with the notion of autonomy it deploys. Brighouse also appears to diverge from classical liberalism in this way; see *On Education*, 19.

of each capacity? That suggestion founders on the fact that all three capacities are matters of degree. However much an educational system might provide by way of preparation for sustaining people, for inculcating citizenship, or for self-fulfillment, it could always do more. Moreover, the components of self-fulfillment are themselves degreed notions. It's easy to compare the autonomy enjoyed by people who live under different social conditions—think of the differences in women's abilities to make choices across historical time and across contemporary societies. But can we make sense of *perfect* autonomy?[77] Similarly, some of us are more successful than others in pursuing our goals. Given the ways in which achievements typically bring new ends for us to strive for, it is not clear what *complete* success would be. The notion of community is even more complex, since it has so many different dimensions. To the extent that sense can be made of *maximal* other-directedness on any single dimension, the problem of weighing the dimensions against one another remains. The difficulty should be familiar. The counselor, the nurse, the healer, the builder, the judge, and the teacher—as well as the parent, the sibling, and the friend—represent types of other-directedness. Each of us, in our lives, plays many parts. We often struggle to balance different other-directed roles when they tug in different dimensions. And, as a final twist, the autonomy and community conditions are in tension with one another. Societies allowing the richest forms of community typically do better at supporting the projects pursued by their members, but they tend to restrict the range of choice.[78]

As I warned, this is only a first sketch of a complex conceptual landscape. I hope, however, to have said enough to diagnose the conditions whose symptoms present themselves in Mill's long address. The goals I've identified are valuable and important. No utopia realizes all of them. Even in the search for systematic unification of the specific ends toward which educational policies strive, the problem of overload still arises.

---

[77] The difficulties of this notion will be explored in Chapter 3, below.

[78] The more opportunities a community provides for individuals to participate in interactions through which they can positively affect the lives of others, the stronger the tendency to expect uniformities in attitudes and conduct. When individualism is emphasized as a value, there is a tendency to construct separate spheres in which people can pursue their own plans without interference from others. The channels on which agents can then bring benefits to others are correspondingly diminished. Thanks to Randy Curren for urging me to make this explicit.

42 THE MAIN ENTERPRISE OF THE WORLD

And it gets worse. So far, I have focused on what education might provide for the individual. We might instead have begun by asking what nations expect their educational systems to accomplish.

The obvious answers parallel those exposed in taking the individual perspective. Societies sustain themselves through the activities of the citizens. A goal of education is to develop a workforce capable of producing everything needed to support collective life. Societies require at least some degree of internal harmony. A second goal of education is to create a body of citizens who can live together. Finally, contemporary societies, as well as those of the known historical past, have distinctive identities, grounded in their institutions and traditions. They aim to preserve and (sometimes at least) to enrich their distinctive cultures. The educational system must prepare the citizens for that task.

The individual and social perspectives parallel one another. Does that entail a happy harmony? Not necessarily. Consider the task of producing enough for the nation to thrive. You don't need to venture far into history to recognize a wide range of conceptions of what thriving involves. Britain's destiny was once to rule the waves, Germany needed ports on the Baltic, and today (apparently) America needs to become great again. When ambitious goals are set, the workforce has to be reshaped to achieve them.[79] Educational reform along these lines sometimes has happy consequences: I received an extraordinary education in mathematics, thanks to the efforts of Samuel Pepys, Isaac Newton, and other seventeenth-century luminaries, who decided to found the Royal Mathematical School, so that the poor pupils who attended Christ's Hospital might acquire the skills required to navigate the ships of the monarch's navy. But sometimes the emphasis on national productivity clashes with the aspirations of some individuals. In past decades, South Korean children have consistently performed at the highest levels in international assessments of education, particularly in mathematics and the sciences. At Seoul National University, the nation's premier institution of higher education, the space assigned to natural science is comparable to that given to engineering, and both dwarf the buildings housing humanities and the social sciences—even before the many institutes in a wide range of applied sciences are taken into account.[80] In their teens, South Korean adolescents experience an intensifying set of educational demands, as their

---

[79] Indeed, significant shaping of the workforce may be required even to keep the society from perishing. For more on this, see the discussion of global economic pressures in Chapter 2, below.

[80] See http://www.useoul.edu/campus/maps.

OVERLOAD   43

school day extends into the evening, as many of them are enrolled in the "shadow" educational system, and as they prepare for the national university entrance examination—held on a single day—that will determine where they go next. The effects are well-documented. Many young Koreans thrive under the challenges, and receive exceptionally strong training, especially in the sciences.[81] Yet, there are also downsides from the pressure. Alone among the forty nations surveyed, more South Korean teenagers describe themselves as extremely unhappy than those who report being extremely happy.[82] The rates of adolescent suicide are typically higher than in most developed countries.[83]

Clashes between individual and social goals with respect to citizenship and culture initially appear less likely. Yet they are bound to emerge whenever there is disagreement about the character of just political arrangements or about how the national culture should be developed. Sometimes they center on the composition of the student body—as when conservatives decry the forced integration of racial and ethnic groups, and progressives hail integration as essential for political health. Often they surround what should be included in the curriculum and what banished from it—witness controversies over the teaching of religion, of evolution, and of different versions of national history. Participants in these debates typically view their opponents as promoting social interference in the intellectual, moral, social or cultural development of the young. It is hard to see how both sides could be entirely wrong in this judgment. Consequently at least one of the parties must be recommending a kind of interference, and wherever that party is victorious the individual and the social perspectives clash.

My whirlwind review has highlighted two sources of difficulty in identifying the aims of education. One lies in the difficulty of combining plausible ideals, the other in deciding how to interpret the ideals that are widely championed. How are the ideas of social thriving, of civic life, and of sustaining culture properly understood? I now want to propose a pragmatic strategy for addressing the first problem, and then to extend it to help with the second.

---

[81] Although, as Dan O'Flaherty reminded me, some excel in music, dominating East Asian popular culture.

[82] See Figure III.1.1 in the PISA report on students' well-being in OECD countries, available via oecd.org.

[83] See Chin-Yun Yi, ed., *The Psychological Well-Being of East Asian Youth*, Vol. 2 (Dordrecht and New York: Springer, 2013), 272.

44   THE MAIN ENTERPRISE OF THE WORLD

Philosophers often propose ideals. They attempt to say what perfect justice would be, or to state the necessary conditions for living well. Outsiders frequently deride these ventures. As they correctly point out, even when a particular proposal is widely accepted by one generation, it is often discarded by those who come later. Nonetheless, the tendency to mock should be curbed by appreciating the real value of some philosophical efforts.

Appreciation might begin by recognizing the proper role of ideals. Ideals don't single out definite goals, to be realized or at least approximated. Rather, they are diagnostic tools for identifying the problems of the present and the lines along which they might be overcome.[84] As we have seen, it is impossible to combine all the goals Mill ascribes to the educational system into a single end. His various aims conflict with one another. It's perfectly appropriate to respond to the Inaugural Address by exclaiming, "How absurd to imagine any educational system could do all that!"

Yet it isn't so absurd to recognize Mill's laundry list of desiderata as pointing to places where existing educational practices are deficient. Recall the ambitious goals. Education should provide the educated individuals with a capacity for self-maintenance, with a capacity for progressive participation in civic life, and with a capacity for personal self-fulfillment. It should deliver to the society a workforce capable of sustaining that society, a group of citizens who are able to live harmoniously together, and people who can preserve and improve the society's culture. Reflecting on education, as it currently works, here in the United States or, indeed, in most of the world,[85] we can ask how well it performs on each of these dimensions. The answers are sobering. Many young people emerge from their schools—and even from

---

[84] Thus, incompatible ideals are valuable for us in our attempts to improve our current situation. Saddened by the dismal plantings around my house, I may have a number of conflicting ideals that focus my disappointment. I want: a harmonious and colorful display of flowers and shrubs throughout the year, beds that will be easy to maintain even when I shall be absent for significant periods, not to spend a vast amount of money either on initial stocks or on gardeners, a mixture of annuals and perennials, plants that remind me of my childhood, etc., etc. At the beginning of my project, I have no definite idea about how these desiderata are to be ranked against one another or combined—no conception of a final goal state. What I want is something *better than this*, where improvements along various dimensions are marked by my ideals. If I stagger my way to a solution, I shall view the compromise among the ideals as *good enough*—while appreciating that the beds could have turned out in any number of different ways and still left me satisfied. I have made *pragmatic* (non-teleological) progress. For much more discussion of this concept, see "On Progress" (in Subramanian Rangan, ed., *Performance and Progress*, Oxford: Oxford University Press, 2015, 115-133); *Moral Progress*; "Social Progress," *Social Philosophy and Policy 34* (2) (2017): 46–65); and *Homo Quaerens: Progress, Truth, and Values* (in preparation).

[85] Although I shall often appeal to the United States—the society I know best—as an example of problematic features of educational systems, many of my diagnoses are intended to apply far more widely.

places of higher education—lacking the skills for the available jobs. Many of them are ill-equipped to reflect on the principal public issues of the day, or to devote their efforts to progressive social change. For a significant number, the thought of "autonomous choice" of a "life plan" would be an insensitive sick joke. Equally, many lack the social as well as the economic support required to pursue their chosen ends. In an increasingly competitive and atomized society, opportunities for genuine community with others are rare. The citizenry is divided, and our rancorous debates make a mockery of democratic decision-making through "free and open discussion." Polarization extends to the cultural sphere, and to passionate arguments about which features of our traditions should be preserved and which should be modified. Finally, the workforce available is widely taken to be inadequate, incapable of strengthening, or even maintaining, America's foremost position in the global economy.

Even without any sophisticated reflections on the goals of education, the last deficiency has been publicly identified. And a solution has been offered. STEM for the USA![86] *Possibly* a program giving greater emphasis to science, technology, engineering and mathematics would be a promising solution to an urgent problem. But that cannot be determined simply by focusing on *one* of the evident deficiencies of our current educational practice. The proposed remedies might swell the numbers of children who are marginalized by and alienated from the schools they are compelled to attend; it could force others into careers for which they are ill-suited, making even greater mockery of the idea of autonomous choice of life project; it could increase the competitiveness not only of education but of social life, thus attenuating even further the prospects for democracy and for community. I talk here of *possibilities* for negative effects. Neither confidence in STEM nor dismissal of it as educationally counterproductive is warranted. Without a systematic investigation of the aims of education, their interrelations, and their connections to structural features of the world in which we now live, it is impossible to tell whether contemporary American education in science and mathematics is deficient or whether greater emphasis on these subjects would be, overall, a good thing.

---

[86] Beating the drum for more science education is, of course, not restricted to the United States. Many Asian countries, most prominently China, India, and South Korea, have not only emphasized accelerated study of the sciences, but also achieved remarkable successes in producing a significant population of well-trained young people. The American slogan is, in large measure, motivated by viewing this population as an economic threat.

46   THE MAIN ENTERPRISE OF THE WORLD

This example exposes what I view as the main task of the philosophy of education. Formulating ideals, as any venture like Mill's address implicitly or explicitly does, is a prelude toward using those ideals to diagnose the deficiencies of current educational practice, to investigate their entanglements and their causes, with a view to presenting a clear view of the relative urgency of the problems and of some potential ways in which they might be mitigated. Philosophy of education, in my view, involves a synthetic stocktaking, aimed at understanding a stage in the evolution of educational practice, so that that practice is further improved.[87] And, I would add, philosophy generally ought to have this synthetic character, focusing on the major features of the current state of human socio-cultural evolution, so that our progress may be more systematic and more "intelligent" than it has historically been.[88]

Systematically exploring ideals is central to the pragmatism I adopt. Like Dewey I am a meliorist not a perfectionist. The human task is to make valuable things *more* extensive and secure, not to create utopia. And, like Dewey, I see education as a central human institution. If philosophy is not to become "a sentimental indulgence for a few," its "auditing of past experience and its program of values must take effect in conduct"—specifically in the formation of "fundamental dispositions" toward nature and toward other people, that constitutes education in the largest sense.[89]

So the project of the philosophy of education comes into view as a patient confrontation with the problem of overload. Societies *need* the lengthy review Mill offered to the academic community in St. Andrews. And more besides. For Mill omitted vast numbers of people, as well as deliberately ignoring the self-maintenance dimension. What is required would have taken him even longer to describe and would have appeared even more ludicrous. Yet the fuller version he might have offered should be seen not as the specification of utopia but as the first stage of a diagnostic venture. Its importance can thus be appreciated. Elaborating a full range of educational ideals

---

[87] Others would offer an alternative perspective, striking the last clause: Philosophy of education aims at understanding. That alternative reflects an attitude common in discussions of the goals of inquiry (particular with respect to the natural sciences), one that celebrates the value of knowledge "for its own sake." Although I don't want to question the value of such knowledge, I claim that the questions arising for us are shaped by a long history in which practical endeavors play a major role. Pragmatic programs of the past lurk behind the "pure knowledge" viewed as valuable quite independently of the interventions it might enable. For defense of this claim see "Scientific Progress and the Search for Truth" and *Homo Quaerens*. Thanks to Harvey Siegel for prodding me to clarify my views here.

[88] I develop this approach in other places, particularly in "Social Progress" and *Moral Progress*.

[89] Dewey, *Democracy and Education* (MW 9, 338).

isn't the plan of some impossible future, but rather a counter to the myopia that reacts to the largest, closest defect, without considering how tackling it might affect other significant goals. A vision of the whole should be a prelude to finding a practical policy sufficiently responsive to all the ends and values we cherish. Without philosophical stocktaking, "pragmatic" reforms are doomed to lurch from one problem to another.

Which problems are most urgent in our own times? How might they be overcome, or at least mitigated? How might we avoid sacrificing other values in ways our descendants will regret?

Answering these questions is difficult for two separate reasons. First, in our multifaceted society, different groups will rate the gravity of problems differently. Those concerned with a perceived threat to economic security are often troubled by the disinclination of young people to pursue advanced study in the sciences. Parents who send their children to schools that are dilapidated and dangerous, where the teaching staff is constantly changing, and where the most basic equipment is in short supply, are more likely to demand transformation of a system seemingly indifferent to the alienation felt by so many of the young. Other parents, across the socioeconomic continuum, may regret the narrowing of vision they see in the structured, competitive, lives thrust upon their children: with the advent of school, "shades of the prison-house" really do seem "to close upon the growing boy"—and girl.

Understanding and harmonizing the different legitimate priorities is a task for the kind of democratic conversation so sadly lacking in our current polity. One principal task of philosophy is to facilitate such conversation, by clarifying the individual points of view and the considerations motivating them. I'll have much more to say about this later.[90]

The second difficulty, that of addressing the identified problems, results from the lack of any body of systematic theory to guide the work of reform. Attempts at social progress cannot ignore the extent of our ignorance about the causes of complex human phenomena. Nevertheless, the situation is not hopeless. Thanks to research by social psychologists, sociologists, economists, and educational researchers, some things are known—about the role of imaginative play in the development of young children, about differences in children's attitudes across socioeconomic classes, and about

[90] See, in particular, Chapters 4 and 5.

48   THE MAIN ENTERPRISE OF THE WORLD

the effects on later life of early interventions (to stop with three examples).[91] The scraps of information available can be supplemented by educational experiments, potentially on a far broader scale than societies have ever attempted. Surveying the experiments of the past, educational policymakers can try to build on what has worked.

My Deweyan meliorism rests on faith in the possibility of progress. Not, however, the kind of progress suggested by Mill's long address, progress aimed at achieving an ambitious—surely utopian—goal. Teleology gives way to pragmatism.[92] The challenge is to articulate the ideals I have drawn from the lurchings of history, to use them to expose the depth of the difficulties in our educational predicament, and to indicate some possible experiments for tackling them. The following chapters try to take up that challenge, aiming not to draw incontestable conclusions, but to offer some proposals for discussion in the democratic conversation our world so urgently needs.

---

[91] See Paul Harris, *The Work of the Imagination* (Oxford: Blackwell, 2000); Annette Lareau, *Unequal Childhoods* (Berkeley: University of California Press, 2011); and James J. Heckman and Ganesh Karapakula, "Intergenerational and Intragenerational Externalities of the Perry PreSchool Project" (NBER Working Paper No. 25889, https://www.nber.org/papers/w25889).

[92] *Real* pragmatism of a Deweyan stripe—one that appreciates the diagnostic importance of ideals, of systematic philosophical reflection, and of the need for experimentation. Although I have taken Mill's address to suggest a teleological conception of progress, that may well not have been his intention. He may best be understood as a "real pragmatist."

2

Individuals

For my parents, education ended early. My father left school at twelve, my mother at fourteen. The skills they had acquired at that point in their lives were those deemed appropriate for fully grown people of their sex and social class. Entering a local sawmill, officially as a tea boy, my father's main occupation consisted in taking slips of paper back and forth to the nearby (illegal) betting shop. My mother's apprenticeship to a photographer, in which she was trained to color black-and-white pictures ("retouching"), ended in the early 1920s, when she was diagnosed with "juvenile" (Type 1) diabetes. In any event, the development of her artistic talent had always been intended only to tide her over until her marriage, after which she was expected to give up working outside the home.

When, in my middle teens, under the then regnant British educational system, I was wavering between specializing (doing my A-levels) in mathematics and physics or in modern languages and literature, it was hard for my parents to understand how there was anything to decide. Pursuing mathematics and science was "practical." I would be prepared for a life quite different from the ones they had known, able to work in positions inaccessible to them, for a salary far greater than the meager wages on which they struggled along. They were relieved when I chose the practical option. When I was eighteen, however, the same issue re-emerged. Why, they wondered, did I want to go to Cambridge, to spend three years in further study? Given my exam results, I could already "get a good job." I might become an actuary, or an accountant. It took some persuasion before they would sign the forms for me to obtain the Council Grant that would support me. (Yes, in those days, British undergraduates did not have to pay for university education; instead, depending on their needs, they received financial support from the Local Education Authority.)

I was *extraordinarily* lucky. The world has contained millions of related stories far darker than my own. Educational policies have dictated to large numbers of young people how they should maintain themselves. Occupations have been assigned by caste or class or race. Du Bois was another

The Main Enterprise of the World. Philip Kitcher, Oxford University Press. © Oxford University Press 2022.
DOI: 10.1093/oso/9780190928971.003.0003

50 THE MAIN ENTERPRISE OF THE WORLD

of the fortunate ones. His critique of Booker T. Washington rings with the intensity of someone who appreciates the unlikelihood of his own escape. How many of his fellow African Americans, before and since, have seen no option for themselves, except a dreary journey through "industrial education"? (Or, quite possibly, no option at all.) How many factories, mines, and fast food restaurants contain equivalents of the figures buried in the country churchyard, where Thomas Gray imagined alternative lives for them?

> Perhaps in this neglected spot is laid
> Some heart once pregnant with celestial fire;
> Hands, that the rod of empire might have sway'd,
> Or waked to ecstasy the living lyre.
>
> But Knowledge to their eyes her ample page
> Rich with the spoils of time did ne'er unroll;
> Chill Penury repress'd their noble rage,
> And froze the genial current of the soul.
>
> Full many a gem of purest ray serene,
> The dark unfathom'd caves of ocean bear:
> Full many a flow'r is born to blush unseen,
> And waste its sweetness on the desert air.
>
> Some village-Hampden, that with dauntless breast
> The little tyrant of his fields withstood,
> Some mute inglorious Milton here may rest,
> Some Cromwell guiltless of his country's blood.[1]

Gray laments the missed opportunities to act grandly on the world's stage. The vast number of smaller losses are equally poignant. As Mill saw, those denied the chance to "pursue their own good in their own way" have forfeited something of great importance. To the extent that they are forced into a prescribed mold, one that pinches, squeezes, and distorts, human lives are confined and diminished.

Booker T. Washington, however, promised and delivered *something*. Today, in many countries, for many children, the dominant forms of education do less. Officially, they inculcate the skills that will be "needed in the marketplace."

---

[1] Thomas Gray, "Elegy Written in a Country Churchyard," in *The Oxford Book of English Verse*, ed. Sir Arthur Quiller-Couch (Oxford: Clarendon Press, 1957), 531–36, at 533.

Yet they fail, generation after generation, to enable those belonging to some groups—some social classes, some races—to acquire the ability to pursue any but the most menial, unpleasant, and poorly rewarded ways of maintaining themselves. Much has been written about the failures of schools to provide the workers the community, the nation, or the world needs, although whether we should regret this because society is shortchanged or because the ex-pupils struggle to survive is frequently left unclear. In this chapter, I shall focus on a different problem. The attitude shared by Booker T. Washington and my parents has not been abandoned. It has even been voiced by Barack Obama, the most perceptive and most distinguished American president of the last half century. Educational policy must be practical. It must recognize the current state of the market to which workers bring their skills and talents. STEM for the USA!

Should one size fit all? Should one size fit all black children, all minority children, all poor children, all girls, or all children? Of course not. We all agree, at least officially. In practice, however, we recognize the need to be realistic. The young need basic training. That means adapting them, perforce, to the demands of those who supply the jobs. Educational policy must be constrained by economic factors.

Rethinking education might begin by asking: Is that so?[2]

———

The idea that education ought to be shaped to the demands of the workplace descends from the beginning of modern economics.[3] Part of the idea is thoroughly benign (and far older):[4] if some capacities are required for any form of work, then those capacities should be instilled in all those who will need to maintain themselves through their labor. Far darker is the suggestion that *only* what is likely to be useful in the labor market should be taught. Since this suggestion is developed with great force and clarity by Adam Smith, I shall refer to it as *Smith's Principle*.

This chapter is an attempt to free education from the tyranny of Smith's Principle. I shall start by reviewing Smith's original statement and defense of the principle. As we shall see, not only critics but also champions of the principle have worried about the crippling effects of adopting it. These worries are

---

[2] Here I join with many other contemporary writers in the philosophy of education, notably Harry Brighouse, Randy Curren, Martha Nussbaum, Israel Scheffler, and Harvey Siegel.

[3] Although similar ideas were already voiced by Plato in the *Republic*, where different styles of education are to be offered to the three distinct classes.

[4] Essentially part of our prehistoric heritage: the adults of the band convey to its new members all the abilities they will need to sustain the group.

52 THE MAIN ENTERPRISE OF THE WORLD

answered, more or less regretfully, by arguing that failure to abide by Smith's Principle has dire consequences. Any nation committed to a more capacious educational program would lose out in a global competitive economy. Its citizens would suffer reduced wages, and probably significant unemployment.

Champions of liberal education might be tempted to respond to this pessimistic line of reasoning by pointing to factors the appeal to economic efficiency fails to take into account. They might note that the structure of the labor market often changes, new opportunities arise, and new kinds of capacities and skills are called for. Their broader conception of education might then be seen as preparing their citizens for these shifts, thus providing them with the flexibility they need. So, the economic argument for Smith's Principle would be met on its own—economic—terms.

As we shall see, when this rejoinder is analyzed in detail, it fails. There's no way of identifying a proposal for liberal education that would be likely to generate some ability to adapt to changes in labor opportunities. Nevertheless, a more careful consideration of the ways in which the pressures arise in the contemporary global economy points the way toward a reform of education that would abandon Smith's Principle. For the threats to nations violating the principle are twofold: current jobs (for example, in manufacturing) might migrate to parts of the world where cheap qualified labor is plentiful; others might vanish in the wake of increased automation (robotics and other forms of Artificial Intelligence). Despite these potential inroads, certain types of employment are not similarly vulnerable. A large variety of services have to be provided locally.

Because of the enduring possibilities for service work, it is possible to view the shifts in the labor market not as a loss but as an opportunity. When the stigma is removed from service jobs, and when they are reasonably paid, these forms of opportunity prove fulfilling. In light of the approach to fulfillment outlined in the previous chapter (and to be developed further in the next), that should come as no surprise. Fulfillment involves making an individual contribution to the lives of others. In particular, I suggest, societies could respond to losses of some forms of employment by expanding the service sector in two spheres: in the care of the elderly, and, most of all, in enriching the education of the young. The latter expansion, on which this book will concentrate, would yield a double benefit, both by offering fulfilling work to the people recruited to augment education, and by increasing the opportunities for fulfillment to those whose early lives they would help to shape.

INDIVIDUALS 53

The chapter will conclude with some proposals for directions along which the enrichment of education might proceed. Those proposals will be amplified, extended, and defended in the remaining chapters of Part I and in Part II. The task of responding to concerns that the reforms they envisage will bring economic disaster will be postponed to Part III.

So much for an overview of the argument to follow. Now to the details.

———⊶◆⊷———

Characterizing contemporary societies as pursuing a policy of one-size-fits-all can easily appear exaggerated. The intricate division of labor in the modern world provides a wide range of workplace environments requiring varied constellations of abilities. If some skills are necessary for *any* occupation, surely it would be irresponsible not to attempt to instill them. Perhaps there are a few young people for whom that is impossible, or for whom it would be undesirable on some other grounds. In the main, however, it is correct to let the workaday world constrain what occurs in the classroom, specifically to demand that anything required for all forms of self-maintenance should be taught.

How tight should the constraint be? Granted that all students need to learn how to read and write, how to use the elementary parts of mathematics required for everyday transactions, and, perhaps, in these days, how to use a computer, to what extent should the contemporary version of basic training dominate the curriculum? Should everything else be dismissed as mere preparation for "unproductive labor" and thus squeezed out? A long tradition, extending back to Plato's *Republic*, conceives socialization as assigning roles and occupations, and delivering to each new member the appropriate bundle of skills. And no more.

To appraise this conception, it is useful to begin with one of the earliest discussions of mass education, offered by a major Enlightenment thinker whose ideas (variously understood and misunderstood) have shaped the conditions of modern socioeconomic life—a man who celebrated the division of labor, and gave us the concept of unproductive labor. Adam Smith devotes the final Book of *The Wealth of Nations* to reflection on the background conditions required if the market mechanisms he proposes are to work.[5] Besides arguing that the state should provide defense, a system of

---

[5] The discussion of Book V is extensive, WN 747–1028. Many of Smith's vocal champions seem not to have read this part of the work they hail as inspirational. For if they had proceeded that far in it, any glib talk of "free" and "unregulated" markets would have been checked by recognition that some

54   THE MAIN ENTERPRISE OF THE WORLD

justice, and various public goods (roads and canals that enable products to be sold at considerable distances from the places where they are made), Smith reflects on "The Education of Youth."

Dissatisfied with the teaching provided for members of the upper classes, he recommends reform. Universities, he explains, were originally founded with a very specific purpose: they were "ecclesiastical corporations; instituted for the education of churchmen."[6] Accordingly, the curriculum focused on literacy in dead languages, and on ancient philosophical texts (emphasizing such subjects as the "cobweb science of Ontology").[7] Smith tacitly recognizes the ways in which contingent historical events can introduce educational strategies that are retained long after their relevance has vanished.[8] Even though the clientele has changed—universities have come to attract "almost all gentlemen and men of fortune"[9]—the "improvements which, in modern times, have been made in several different branches of philosophy" have rarely been introduced;[10] consequently, upper-class education fails in its proper task.

> No better method, it seems, could be fallen upon of spending, with any advantage, the long interval between infancy and the period of life at which men begin to apply in good earnest to the real business of the world, the business which is to employ them during the remainder of their days. The greater part of what is taught in schools and universities, however, does not seem to be the most proper preparation for that business.[11]

Smith's remedy for the education of those who are to lead the commercial world is to change the incentive structure. Let the recompense of those who teach be proportional to the numbers of students who flock (or fail to flock)

---

structures must be in place before any market can operate. Moreover, they would have understood that hard thinking is required before the appropriate conditions can be identified. For more on this theme, see Karl Polanyi, *The Great Transformation* (Boston: Beacon, 2001) and Charles E. Lindblom, *The Market System* (New Haven: Yale University Press, 2001). In the final chapter, I shall return to some of the issues raised by Book V of WN.

[6] WN 825. Smith's history here is only partially accurate, since he overlooks the importance of the Faculties of Law and Medicine (see Chapter 1, above, 35).

[7] WN 830.

[8] A point about the evolution of cultures I made explicitly in the Introduction and in Chapter 1. See 1–2, 31–36, above.

[9] WN 832.

[10] WN 831. By "philosophy" here, Smith adverts to many branches of learning, including the sciences.

[11] WN 832.

INDIVIDUALS 55

to their classrooms. The result will be that any "science universally believed to be a mere useless and pedantic heap of sophistry and nonsense" will disappear from the curriculum.[12]

The principle at which Smith has arrived—education should be tailored to the demands of the occupations that the pupils will take on—is applied to two large classes of potential students, who are normally left out of educational discussions. Women, he declares, are appropriately trained under the existing conditions:

> They are taught what their parents or guardians judge it necessary or useful for them to learn; and they are taught nothing else. Every part of their education tends evidently to some useful purpose.[13]

They learn, for example, how to make themselves attractive, how to be chaste and modest, how to nurture children, and run a household. A second group of potential pupils requires more extensive discussion. What is to be done for the large mass of men who are to serve in the ranks the captains of industry lead?

The common people are destined to perform simple tasks, reduced, as the division of labor progresses, to some uniform sequence of simple motions. Because their work is "so constant and so severe," they have little opportunity for more abstract reflection.[14] What they need is *really basic* training. Education in accordance with Smith's principle is cheap. For, "the most essential parts of education, . . ., to read, write, and account, can be acquired at so early a period of life, that the greater part even of those who are to bred to the lowest occupations, have time to acquire them before they can be employed in those occupations."[15] Should anything more be offered? Smith reflects: "There is scarce a common trade which does not afford some opportunities of applying to it the principles of geometry and mechanics."[16] So, even abiding by the principle, a little enrichment is in order. No irrelevant study, no "little smattering of Latin." Provide instead "the elementary parts of geometry and mechanics" and "the literary education of this rank

---

[12] WN 838; see also WN 820–21. Smith assumes that students (the potential consumers of educational products) are able to judge correctly what will be relevant to their future occupations.

[13] WN 839.

[14] WN 842.

[15] WN 842.

[16] WN 843.

56 THE MAIN ENTERPRISE OF THE WORLD

of people would be as complete as it can be."[17] Small-scale STEM for the late eighteenth-century workers!

But, famously, Smith wavers. Classically educated, he appreciates the ways in which civic virtues were instilled in the ancient world. Even before he has addressed the proper training of the masses, he has worried about how similar virtues are to develop in a society marked by pronounced division of labor. As he recognizes, with the progress of workplace specialization, "the employment of the far greater part of those who live by labour, that is, of the great body of the people, comes to be confined to a few very simple operations";[18] the worker lacks "occasion to exert his understanding"; he thus "becomes as stupid and ignorant as it is possible for a human creature to become"; the "torpor of his mind" deprives him of any chance to acquire or exercise the "intellectual, social, and martial virtues."[19]

These observations serve as prelude to Smith's consideration of what education workers should receive. The exercise *might* have led him to return to the beginning of his manuscript, and to replace the enthusiastic celebration of the division of labor with a nuanced view. Or, perhaps, to give up the principle tailoring education to the demands of the workplace. They didn't. Smith is surely right to judge that the occupants of the pin factory are not going to be helped by a "smattering of Latin" as they stretch the umpteenth wire to form the umpteenth pin. It's unlikely that, as they do so, lines from the *Aeneid* will resound in their consciousness and uplift them. Equally, it's not obvious what benefits their knowledge of the elementary parts of geometry and mechanics will bring. Some creative application to transform the task at hand? The discussion concludes with some vague gestures toward public competitions that might preserve "martial spirits," and pays no explicit attention to maintaining the intellectual and social virtues. Smith's consideration of education for the workers concludes by lamenting "the gross ignorance and stupidity which, in a civilized society, seem so frequently to benumb the understandings of all the inferior ranks of the people."[20] There are final dim hopes that *some* instruction, in line presumably with the principle, will produce citizens capable of resisting the "delusions of enthusiasm and superstition," who will become "more decent and orderly."[21] With equal

[17] WN 843.
[18] WN 839.
[19] WN 840.
[20] WN 846.
[21] WN 846.

reason, the masses educated along Smithian lines, having graduated to the mind-numbing tedium of the pin factory and its kin, might long for some relief. Wouldn't they be inclined to flock to the gaudy ceremonies of the more flamboyant religions or to join together in a wild and undisciplined spree?

Smith drew his guiding principle from reflections on the deficiencies of education in his times. Schools and universities failed to deliver what the work environment of his age required. Applying an intended corrective, he used the occupational possibilities as a template for educational policy. The position to which he was led was saved from evident implausibility—even from inconsistency—only by its vagueness. Are contemporary educational discussions confined in a similar straitjacket? Do we too fall into the same trap?[22]

Some decades after Smith's masterpiece was published, a young German thinker with a sympathy for radical political ideas decided that he needed to teach himself political economy. In 1844, Karl Marx embarked on a course of reading, making notes as he went. The first three manuscripts he penned essentially summarized the material of the books he read, *The Wealth of Nations* prominent among them. At that point, he plunged into Book V, and was arrested by Smith's discussion of education for the masses. Unlike Smith, he turned back to scrutinize the assumptions from which he had been led to the impasse. Manuscript 4, "Estranged Labor," begins:

> We have proceeded from the premises of political economy. We have accepted its language and its laws. . . . On the basis of political economy itself, in its own words, we have shown that the worker sinks to the level of a commodity and becomes indeed the most wretched of commodities.[23]

[22] Randall Curren offers affirmative answers to these questions in "Peters Redux: The Motivational Power of Inherently Valuable Learning," *Journal of Philosophy of Education* 54 (2020): 731–43. He also shows how opposition to thinking of education as constrained by the demands of the labor market has nineteenth-century roots. Like him, I view an important feature of this problematic constraint as being the intensification of competition from an early age.

[23] Karl Marx, *The Economic and Philosophic Manuscripts of 1844*, ed. Dirk Struik (New York: International Publishers, 1964), 106. These manuscripts were first published (in the original German) in 1932. They are excerpted and translated in a number of anthologies, and the usual English translation of "*Entfremdete Arbeit*" is "Alienated Labor." I have cited Struik's edition because it includes all the manuscripts, and thus shows what lies behind Marx's opening sentence. In teaching himself political economy, he has done exactly what he claims, starting with the first assumptions of the subject—as the first three manuscripts, his reading notes, reveal.

58 THE MAIN ENTERPRISE OF THE WORLD

Unlike Smith, Marx refuses to accept the conclusion and muddle on. Resisting the reduction of workers to commodities, he sets out to diagnose the root cause in the structure of the capitalist economy. And, of course, to change it.

So too did a later writer, more famous as an educational theorist, who, without knowing of Marx's reaction, adopted a similar strategy. From the turn of the twentieth century until the 1930s, an enduring theme in Dewey's writings focuses on the plight of the industrial worker, deprived of any consciousness of the significance of what he does,[24] forced to "take orders" from the machines at which he works.[25] Perhaps a sense of the alienation of the worker partly derived from reading Smith; it could not have come from Marx.[26] Another source lay in Dewey's own experience:

> For some years, I preserved a little piece of cast iron taken from a typical American factory, one of our large agricultural machinery works. I preserved it as a sort of Exhibit A of our social and educational status. The iron came out of the casting with a little roughness upon it which had to be smoothed off before it could become part of the belt for which it was designed. A boy of fifteen or sixteen spent his working day in grinding off this slight roughness—grinding at the rate of one over a minute for every minute of his day.[27]

Like Smith before him, Dewey sees a life passed in this fashion as one of "stupefying monotony," marked by a "total lack of intellectual and imaginative content."[28]

What is to be done to remedy this dismal situation? At times, Dewey attempts to amend Smith's principle. The workplace environment, as it has emerged under early twentieth-century capitalism, is to shape the style of education workers receive. Yet the shaping must attend not only to considerations of economic efficiency, framing the education so as to deliver workers with the skills required for their daily occupations. It must also take into consideration the intellectual development and psychological health of the worker who runs (and is enslaved by) his machine. His "imagination must

---

[24] MW 1, 137; MW 2, 88.
[25] MW 15, 166; LW 3, 124.
[26] The recognition of the worker's estrangement from the labor process is clear in writings of 1900 and 1902 (MW 1, 137; MW 2, 88). Marx's manuscripts appeared (in German) only thirty years later.
[27] MW 3, 288.
[28] MW 3, 288. See also MW 5, 60.

INDIVIDUALS   59

be so stored that in the inevitable monotonous stretches of work, it may have worthy material of art and literature and science on which to feed, instead of being frittered away upon undisciplined dreamings and sensual fancies."[29] At other times, especially when he is concerned with the worker's need to understand the significance of what he does, Dewey calls out for something more radical, a "better social order," one in which the range of opportunities provide everyone with "some kind of productive work which a self-respecting person may engage in with interest and more than mere pecuniary profit."[30] Suggestions of that kind depart more sharply from Smith's Principle. Workers' education and the workplace environment are brought into harmony, not by treating the economic structure as fixed, but sometimes by reforming the opportunities for labor to accord with the human needs of those who engage in it.

The less radical option seems the safer one. The path Marx followed in favoring a (supposedly historically inevitable) economic restructuring is widely viewed as disastrous. Is there any alternative version of the strategy he commended, a strategy which Dewey, in his more ambitious moments, shared?

If anything, the twenty-first century seems even less hospitable than its predecessors to attempts to reject Smith's Principle, or even to venture the more cautious refinements of it envisaged in Dewey's program for stocking the mind of the industrial worker with "worthy material of art and literature and science," suited to relieve the tedium of the working day. Smith's famous argument for free trade depended crucially on the difficulties of supervising and controlling work done in distant places.[31] Unforeseeable advances in communications technology have reduced the problems substantially, allowing for jobs to be outsourced to places where hiring labor is cheap. No wonder that politicians concerned (or those feigning concern) for the nation's workers campaign for the tariffs Smith so vigorously denounced.

---

[29] MW 10, 140. In effect, Dewey turns back here to the kind of solution Smith rejects. But he distinguishes his proposal from orthodox designs of "general education," recommending inquiry into what kinds of studies will provide the envisaged liberation (MW 10, 141). See also MW 15, 166–67. As Randy Curren reminded me, the modern assembly line is not typically a place for "undisciplined dreamings." The worker who indulges in them is likely to fall behind, or, worse, become entangled in the machinery and injured.

[30] MW 11, 83.

[31] WN 484–85.

60   THE MAIN ENTERPRISE OF THE WORLD

Parallel reasons can be advanced to buttress the idea that education must consist in efficient preparation for a demanding global workplace.

To appreciate those reasons, let's begin by considering how Smith might have been led to think that education *only* needs to provide the skills required for the workplace, that it should not attempt to do more. On his account, economic well-being requires continual intensification of the division of labor. As the division becomes more fine-grained, workers must be trained to highly specialized tasks. Any educational time spent on serving other ends, delivering the kinds of rich education educational theorists typically recommend, is time wasted: it would be more efficient, either to inculcate specialized skills more thoroughly or to end training and send the young directly into the workplace. Nations able to train their young people most efficiently will lure entrepreneurs to invest capital. Economic competition among nations thus encourages each state to make its system of public education as efficient as possible—yielding an incentive to accord with Smith's Principle.

From the eighteenth century to the mid-twentieth, the force of this argument would have been mitigated by worries about supervising foreign investments. Difficulties of transmitting information across borders, let alone continents, offset the attractions of setting up your business in distant parts, however wonderfully the workers there have been trained, and however numerous (and thus cheap) they may be to hire. It should be easy to see why Smith's Principle emerges in the context of his reflections on British "gentlemen and men of fortune." Immersed for years in useless studies of Greek hexameters and "cobweb sciences," these men are pathetically ill equipped to *lead* the masses. The ventures they undertake are likely to be less productive than those envisaged by their counterparts in other nations, beneficiaries of a more efficient education.

In our time, however, the principle cannot be restricted to the captains of industry—presumably now reformulated as a directive to select, as early as it can reliably be done, those who have talents for innovation, and to train them, rigorously and efficiently, for the task of discovering new ventures destined to soar across the global economy. For, wherever they are trained, these luminaries of the business world can realize their designs in any place they choose. The costs of labor, and the availability of workers who can reliably perform specialized tasks, will figure prominently in their decisions. Sentimental attachment to the land of their birth or of their education is likely to interfere with their prospects, making them vulnerable to more hardheaded rivals. Competition in the global economy thus generates the

INDIVIDUALS   61

incentive to apply Smith's Principle across the board. "Rich" education is a luxury. There is no time for the frills.

Historically, the line of reasoning I have attributed (fancifully, I confess) to Smith has been resisted in a quite different way. Those who object—or waver, as Smith did—contest the claim that to pursue other educational ends is to waste time.[32] Theorists who emphasize educating for "citizenship" or for "flourishing" often deny that rich education detracts from achieving economic goals. Narrow education, they suggest, fails to prepare young people to adapt to a rapidly changing occupational landscape. Surely there is something to this suggestion. Teaching students to acquire precisely the skills needed in today's job market may turn out to be useless later in life, perhaps even quite soon after they have left school. The engineers who were trained in intricate exercises with slide rules probably regret the hours of their misspent youths. Yet the argument from flexibility is limited. Focusing narrowly on a specific technique, without providing broader knowledge of the field in which the skill is embedded, is almost certainly a misguided quest for efficiency. Friends of Smith's Principle will concede the point. The cure for an overly narrow education in computer science or in biotechnology or in economics is broader engagement with the pertinent science and its close relatives: understanding the mathematical foundations of computer science, deeper embedding of biotechnology in molecular and cell biology, engagement with a broader range of economic ideas and issues. Cultivating flexibility is important, but it should be *useful* flexibility. Working outward from the current set of specialized occupational needs, efficient training stops far short of the rich curriculum that champions of "liberal education" recommend.

———

It is time to present the argument more precisely.[33] As I've already noted, the contemporary economic environment appears to offer a wide variety of types of work. In the familiar tradition of modeling, abstraction can bring order to diversity. Instead of considering two classes of workers (as Smith does), the "men of fortune" who lead and the "mass of the people" who follow

---

[32] Defenders of liberal education, from Mill, Newman, and Du Bois to Brighouse, Delbanco, and Nussbaum, usually emphasize the non-economic benefits, but they also suppose, explicitly or tacitly, that "well-rounded" people will be just as economically productive as the technically trained.

[33] The reasoning I reconstruct in the following paragraphs elaborates an analysis originally proposed in my "Education, Democracy, and Capitalism," chapter 17 in *The Oxford Handbook of Philosophy of Education*, ed. Harvey Siegel (New York: Oxford University Press, 2009), 300–18.

62   THE MAIN ENTERPRISE OF THE WORLD

and toil, I shall divide the laboring population according to the types of skills exercised by different groups. For simplicity I shall also adopt views about the distribution of talents—hypotheses about "native propensities"[34]—that are frequently assumed in discussions of how education should match potential workers to the workplace environment.[35] (These assumptions are at odds with the more egalitarian approach offered in Part III.)

Hence, an idealized model of the labor force. Some abilities are obtainable by many people, perhaps by almost all, and are easily acquired. *Ordinary* work can be carried out by anyone who has these widely shared abilities; besides the factory work, paradigm productive labor, the class includes street-cleaning, mail delivery, retail sales, preparation of simple dishes, and so forth. *Specialized* work demands abilities only acquired after lengthier training, but the abilities in question could be gained by a sizeable fraction of the working population. Plumbers, police officers, nurses, and those who repair appliances all do work of this kind. For the third class, *selective* work, the pool of potential employees is more restricted. Some occupations require people with great strength or with unusual qualities of intellect or character— epidemiologists need to be good at mathematics, orchestral musicians need a good ear, fine carpentry requires good eyes and steady hands, firefighters need to be strong.[36] *Selective* workers must often acquire special abilities to perform the tasks expected of them, but those abilities can only be developed by members of a relatively small percentage of the population.[37] Finally, *innovation* encompasses forms of work that modifies the labor landscape, creating new forms of work. Probably a significant number of people are *would-be* innovators: they have dreams of doing something thoroughly

---

[34] I have expressed skepticism about forms of biological determinism in many places. See, for example, *Vaulting Ambition: Sociobiology and the Quest for Human Nature* (Cambridge MA: MIT Press, 1985); "Battling the Undead: How (and How Not) to Resist Genetic Determinism," in *Thinking about Evolution: Historical, Philosophical and Political Perspectives*, ed. Rama Singh, Costas Krimbas, Diane Paul, and John Beatty (New York: Cambridge University Press, 2001), 396–414.

[35] The assumptions I make will present a line of argument, without the clutter required if they were absent.

[36] With respect to both specialized and selective workers, I have included many kinds that Smith would have labeled forms of unproductive labor (WN 360–62). His distinction has always seemed to me to be myopic. Shouldn't some of the output of the factory hands who are *directly* productive be attributed to the physicians who diagnose their sickness and to the nurses who facilitate their return to the assembly line? Those who maintain and support others who create an obvious product are, in my view, *indirectly* productive. Whether this extends to the orchestral musicians—whose music increases the efficiency of the labor of their refreshed hearers?—is, I admit, more controversial. (I am grateful to Ronald Findlay for many friendly debates about these points.)

[37] As my examples suggest, how small a percentage varies. I suspect that a higher fraction of the population could become firefighters than could become orchestral musicians or neurosurgeons.

INDIVIDUALS 63

new, but are forced to settle in some other form of work hoping that, in time, their proposals will be properly appreciated. The true innovators (who, irrespective of sex or socioeconomic class, play the role Smith assigned to the "gentlemen and men of fortune") are those who realize their visions.

My idealization prepares the way for asking whether rich education, of the kinds popularly envisaged, does anything to promote the economic fortunes of a society. Dividing a wide range of types of work among a manageable number of categories aims to cover all the relevant differences found in a heterogeneous modern workforce. Behind my taxonomy lies the thought that, when conditions change, it is easier to fill some kinds of employment than others. Understanding how changes, especially but not only in technology, can modify the demands made on labor, the crucial question is whether rich education enables workers to adapt quickly and efficiently.

Start with the ordinary workers. Assume, contrary to Smith's pessimistic verdict, that whatever extras rich education would provide for them would not be eroded by the conditions of their employment. When the work environment evolves, the new replacements for now obsolete jobs will either require different skills, easily acquired by most human beings, or they will demand something more. In the former case, the ordinary workers under the old regime will presumably play the same role in the new dispensation. They will quickly acquire the different skills now needed, allowing a smooth and efficient transition. What if the new jobs must be filled by specialized workers, or even by selective workers? Given those circumstances, some members of the workforce will have to receive further training, either to develop the pertinent abilities, or perhaps, to qualify for positions left vacant by specialized workers who have migrated to the new opportunities. Either possibility will involve a lengthy process of society-wide adaptation. Would rich education help to shorten it? It is hard to see how that could be. What the new environment needs isn't liberally educated employees, but people who have a particular style of specialization, one that was not provided, or not provided in sufficient numbers, in advance. If the need could have been predicted, an *economically efficient* educational system would have adjusted its forms of labor-directed training beforehand, introducing novel types of specialized (or selective) education or modifying the distribution of educational effort (more specialized workers, less ordinary workers). Assuming, as is usually the case, that the evolution of the work environment can't be foreseen, there's no reliable policy for any nation to do better than the system that responded efficiently to the old conditions has done. Rich education appears to add

64   THE MAIN ENTERPRISE OF THE WORLD

nothing (except, of course, the non-economic goods on which defenders of liberal education insist).

For the next two classes, the specialized and the selective workers, the prospects for defending the economic benefits of rich education appear brighter. As already conceded, excessively narrow forms of technical education, those dedicated to inculcating the precise skills demanded by current forms of employment, might slow the pace of the transition to the new environment. Educators dedicated to economic efficiency will thus require a broader training, focusing on the fields pertinent to the occupations for which the specialized and selective workers are being prepared. Smith's principle will be broadened to emphasize *technical* education with a wider scope.

Could rich education help in any way? Of course that depends on the kinds of riches offered. We can imagine a large number of variants, drawing different things from Mill's overloaded catalog of subjects of study—and perhaps adding further items gleaned from his liberal successors. Call this envisaged collection the *Rich Possibilities*. It contrasts with the varieties of technical training, centered on the kinds of skills required for the jobs of the present, extended with some degree of immersion in the background fields.

Focus now on a particular kind of employment, requiring specialized training, for example, plumbing, or nursing, or work as a technical assistant in a medical laboratory. Pick any of the plausible varieties of technical training for the occupation in question—a program that combines instilling the skills required by plumbers with some introduction to other forms of repair work, a course in nursing that supplements instruction in medical care with extensions to other situations in which care of different sorts is required, detailed immersion in current laboratory procedures with a broad base in the background biology. From an economic perspective, these programs are assessed by the reliability with which the workers perform their assigned tasks, as well as the amount of effort invested in preparing them and the ease with which they can adapt when the workplace environment evolves. Suppose, then, that a satisfactory average level of performance is fixed, and that we select a program recognized as capable of providing the training required and plausibly delivering flexibility in adaptation. This is the *candidate technical program* (CTP).

What we want to know is whether the Rich Possibilities contains any rival course that could do better, from the standpoint of economic competition, than the CTP. The first task is to select a rival. Given that reliable performance at the tasks currently assigned is crucial, I'll focus on rich forms of education

INDIVIDUALS   65

expected to generate the same average level of performance as the CTP—indeed, for simplicity, let's assume that the CTP figures as the technical part of the rich rival. Any rich rival will thus involve costs of extra investment in the additional training it supplies. So our question is whether these costs are offset by increased power to adapt when the labor environment changes.

Defenders of liberal education would like to find a member of the Rich Possibilities that adds enough elements from Mill's overloaded curriculum to improve flexibility without incurring large expenses through expansions of the training period. How to find just the right "extras"? The extension of technical training supposed that, when changes make some forms of work redundant, the displaced workers migrate to adjacent occupations, demanding similar skills to those already acquired. If rich education is to provide more, that will presumably derive from an ability to adapt more broadly. One way of increasing adaptability would be to require young people to undergo specialized training in more than one field—but that surely doesn't count as rich education. Moreover, if the majority of workers continue to work in a single specialty throughout their lives, or, when they move, do so in the ways facilitated by the extended technical education, the secondary training is wasted. What defenders of rich education seek is a selection from the liberal curriculum that inculcates psychological capacities and character traits enabling people to make transitions more easily and to benefit from the new opportunities that arise.

Perhaps there are such capacities and traits, and perhaps there are courses of education—maybe in literature or history or languages or the arts or anthropology—suited to instill them. The trouble lies in our ignorance. We have no idea what the crucial psychological properties are. Unless they are "all-purpose," fitted to any kind of change, the appropriate characteristics will depend on the changes occurring in the occupational landscape, and those are hard (if not impossible) to predict. Nor do we know which selections from the liberal curriculum would be likely to generate them. If there is a rich rival superior to the CTP, we have no clue about how to find it. Of course, we might resort to experimentation, trying various options on a relatively small scale. But that form of experimentation is problematic, not least because of the difficulties of determining when a successful rival has been found.

Moreover, any review of the diversity within the occupations for which specialized training is required belies the thought of any *single* system of rich education—unless it is comprehensive. If you try to make a manageable selection, one size definitely doesn't fit all. The future adaptability

66 THE MAIN ENTERPRISE OF THE WORLD

of plumbers might be enhanced by increasing their strength (physical exercises) and fine-motor skills (calligraphy, drawing, learning a musical instrument). Nurses might develop greater empathy, on which they could draw in other interpersonal occupations (should they study literature, history, and moral philosophy?).[38] It's not obvious what to recommend to aspiring biotechnicians: perhaps studies that help with data analysis (statistics), or understanding of public health (demography, sociology). The dilemma is obvious. Either the contemporary version of the *studium generale* might deliver added flexibility at the price of becoming vastly expansive (and thus expensive), or it will be suited only to the needs of a small selection of specialized and selective workers, imposing burdens on the rest.

Ironically, the best case for rich education is probably made in fostering innovation—preparing the contemporary successors of the "gentlemen and men of fortune," whom Smith took to be ill-served by the colleges and universities of his time. Whether or not there's firm evidence, we might conjecture that people who are conversant with a wide range of subjects and with the cultures of many societies, past and present, might be stimulated to think in new ways. Interaction with a heterogeneous collection of ideas takes you "outside the box." *Assuming* the possibility of identifying those who are especially imaginative and receptive to novel combinations of thoughts, these potential innovators might be provided with a comprehensive curriculum, drawing lavishly from Mill's catalog, in the hopes that it would inspire them to design new forms of productive work, and thereby swell the nation's wealth. Of course, to do that for all would be enormously costly. Most of the extra effort would be wasted. Hence, the truly creative must be selected in advance.

To sum up: whatever the merits of traditional arguments for the value of general education in advancing non-economic ends (and, as will become clear, if it isn't so already, I appreciate the power of those arguments), attempts to defend that style of education by appealing to its economic dividends prove unsuccessful. The analysis I've offered is, admittedly, by no means conclusive. Comparison of the economic effects of the CTP (whose contours are relatively easy to recognize) with its rich rivals depends on a number of assumptions, and those assumptions might be challenged. Yet, I submit, any articulation of the challenges will lead to precise empirical questions in areas

---

[38] Or, perhaps, they might pursue a curriculum designed to stave off "compassion fatigue." (Thanks to Randy Curren for raising the question.)

INDIVIDUALS 67

where evidence is difficult to acquire. To institute a rich system of education, for many members of a society or for all, would be to *hope* without any sound basis that the economic consequences would not be highly disadvantageous, that the losses would be small and thus tolerable.

Perhaps we should simply plunge ahead hopefully, accepting the risks? Any such recommendation invites an obvious reply. Realistic assessment of the performances of many nations, including affluent countries, in providing a large percentage of their citizens-to-be with the basic skills adapted to the contemporary work environment reveals deficiencies in existing approaches to education. When many students fall short of being fluent readers, or are barely capable of solving simple mathematical problems, or fail to understand basic ideas of well-established sciences, proposals to enrich their education invite a hard-headed riposte: "That's going in the wrong direction. Why think you can do more, introducing ambitious programs, when the results at achieving relatively simple things are so mediocre (at best)? If there's a time for risky experimentation, it should come when the schools learn how to prepare children better for the workaday world. The least they deserve is not to have to spend some of their study time on material that is probably (economically) irrelevant. Better surely to seek ways in which they can be helped to compete better in a global marketplace."

If that updated formulation of Smith's Principle is to be contested, it is hard to see how the challenge can be made on economic grounds.

———⊷———

Yet, as has perhaps already been evident, the preceding analysis omits one obvious threat to existing workers. One species of change in the labor market is eminently predictable. During the next decades, with further progress in artificial intelligence, robots are likely to take over many jobs currently performed by human beings.[39] Omitting this point was not crucial to the arguments just reviewed. Those lines of reasoning were concerned with

---

[39] Estimates of how far AI and robotics will invade vary. One influential study is that of two respected scholars at the Oxford Martin School: C. B. Frey and M. A. Osborne, "The Future of Employment: How Susceptible are Jobs to Computerisation?," available online at https://scholar.google.com/scholar?hl=en&as_sdt=0%2C33&q=frey+osborne+2013&btnG=. A more recent McKinsey report predicts a potential loss of "as many as 375 million" jobs; see https://www.mckinsey.com/featured-insights/future-of-work/jobs-lost-jobs-gained-what-the-future-of-work-will-mean-for-jobs-skills-and-wages. Although some critics have suggested that fears about job loss are overblown, either because AI and robotics will not develop as fast and as far as is hoped or because significant numbers of new occupations will emerge from the replacement of human workers, I shall assume that the threat is serious.

68 THE MAIN ENTERPRISE OF THE WORLD

potential *additions* of opportunities as older jobs became obsolete, and with preparing the displaced workers to adapt to them. The invasion of the robots adds almost nothing; perhaps a handful of maintenance and supervisory positions.[40] It is, first and foremost, simply subtraction—although the gains in productivity may translate into additions in forms of work that resist automation. Most obviously service jobs.

Economists have studied the forces shifting the labor market.[41] Technology already makes it possible for many tasks that used to be performed domestically to be carried out more cheaply in distant places. Artificial intelligence and robotics promise to make many human occupations redundant. Global competition favors a continued flow of employment to countries where labor is plentiful and wages are low. Future national productivity depends on a capacity for training workers who can maintain and refine the existing forms of technology, and perhaps even more important, on preparing young people to devise new ones. Hence the competition extends to systems of education. The winners will be those whose approaches to education are best able to prepare their most talented young people for hi-tech work and for innovation. Everything else is subsidiary.

According to Dewey, the tendency of education in industrial societies was to impoverish children's sense of themselves, of their distinctive talents and capacities, and to weaken democracy.[42] Effectively, the bargains struck in relieving the conditions of the nineteenth-century factory worker constructed an educational system geared to a particular type of work environment, a system that downplayed the significance of citizenship and of individual fulfillment. The resentments expressed by contemporary people in many

---

[40] As Dan O'Flaherty pointed out to me, this is not entirely straightforward. Some kinds of innovations, those that revolutionize a sector, create a vast collection of new forms of employment. To be sure, the invention of the automobile may have affected the work prospects for blacksmiths, carriage-builders, and horse-breeders, but it not only provided vast numbers of jobs for people making cars, but also required road-building, all sorts of devices and systems for controlling and directing traffic, new types of insurance, driving instructors, traffic courts, and on and on. To my mind, the threat posed by automation comes from its potential to revolutionize a large number of sectors in a tightly unified way. The future that worries people consists in a world in which many types of labor are performed by robots and computer-controlled devices, and where the first-level (non-human) workers are built, supervised, and controlled by similar second-level devices, and so on up. At the top of this hierarchy is a greatly reduced human workforce that continues to innovate and to write the programs.

Whether this future is likely is currently unclear. I take some steps in its direction to be sufficiently probable to warrant proceeding on the assumption of coming challenges to full employment in many sectors. (As Daron Acemoglu and Pascual Restrepo point out in "Artificial Intelligence, Automation, and Work," NBER Working Paper 24196, the displacement of workers in some sectors can be countered by an increase elsewhere, particularly in forms of work that cannot be automated. The likely increase is in service work. The paper is available at: https://www.nber.org/papers/w24196).

[41] See the work of Daron Acemoglu, David Autor, and their co-authors.

[42] See, for example, MW 2, 88–93; MW 9, 265–66.

nations as the jobs held by their parents dwindle stem from a sense of not receiving the rewards they expected.[43] Those disgruntled citizens might also wonder about the original bargain. Were the schools always fundamentally directed toward the needs of national productivity, with preparation for community life, autonomy and self-discovery, and democratic participation always seen as optional extras—at least for the masses? At a time of irresistible change in patterns of labor, should there be a serious, even radical, rethinking about what our educational practices ought to do?

What jobs are left when production lines migrate to parts of the world in which people desperate for basic economic support are willing to work for wages citizens from affluent nations would never accept? What can a high school graduate do when local factories are filled with many more robots and many fewer people?

When forms of labor disappear to distant places or are taken over by machines, the remaining jobs are likely to be those that can't efficiently be exported or automated. "Likely" rather than "inevitably," because of the possibility of framing policies to protect domestic employment at economic cost. Yet why isn't this shift cause for celebration? Tasks that resist assignment to machines would appear to be just the ones calling on distinctive human capacities and talents. Whenever sympathy and fellow-feeling are required, artificial intelligence seems to fall short. Moreover, for many of the human contacts people most need, the providers have to be local. It would not be a good idea to run the Cleveland fire department out of Bangladesh, and the machines at your hospital bedside are not—at least not yet—equipped to deliver the relaxing touch or the encouraging smile that keeps you going.

Enthusiasts for AI may believe it to be only a matter of time before the nurses and even the firefighters disappear into the maw of history, joining the blacksmiths, milliners, and bookkeepers—and the assembly-line workers—who have preceded them. Since the late twentieth century, robots have been designed to take over some of the work of caring for the elderly. They can remind old people to eat and to take their prescribed medicines, and encourage

---

[43] Specifically, wages high enough to enable them to live a "middle-class life" and to hope for better opportunities for their children. The rewards of tedious labor are most obviously the ability to buy things that make life outside the workplace go more easily and more enjoyably. To find adequate compensation from this bargain, workers must first be infected with the "life-long and unreflective materialism" that Harry Brighouse sees as a distortion of their genuine interests (*On Education*, 23). Thus they are first offered a bad bargain, and then denied the tawdry goods they were promised.

70 THE MAIN ENTERPRISE OF THE WORLD

them to exercise and contact relatives and friends. Conceived in this way as supplements to traditional forms of nursing, they take over some of the work of human caregivers.[44] Since the late twentieth century, however, robotics engineers have sought to go further. PARO, a robot substitute for therapy animals, was introduced into the market early in the twenty-first century, and its impact on patients with dementia has now been tested.[45] Companies sometimes proclaim an imminent crisis in elder care, caused by a coming shortage of workers able to cope with a massive population of old people. Waypoint Robotics, for example, declares the future to be one in which elder care robots will be necessary on a large scale.[46] Could they take over so many aspects of care that human nurses were no longer needed?

Even if the continued need for firefighters and nurses is conceded, how much consolation does that bring? An obvious retort: to focus on these professions paints a rosy picture of service work. Most jobs in which some people serve others are menial, tedious, and unrewarding (both personally and financially). The workers who regret the loss of opportunities for productive labor, paradigmatically factory jobs, rightly resist being offered only degrading tasks at low pay.

Surveys of job satisfaction among American workers present an interestingly mixed picture.[47] Service positions, including not only nurses and physicians, firefighters and rescuers, but also receptionists, gardeners, flight attendants and teachers, occur high up, even at the top, on the satisfaction scale. At the same time, other service occupations, like janitors and fast food servers, are widely viewed as unsatisfying. Nor should this bifurcation be surprising. If the pay is low and the status accorded to the work is minimal— indeed, if the jobs are seen as suited to people who have little talent and who are only capable of performing the most elementary tasks—those compelled

---

[44] See https://phys.org/news/2018-12-world-culturally-sensitive-robots-elderly.html for an advanced version of this use of AI. The European Union has funded a project (CARESSES) to build robots that will learn and adapt to the habits and culture of individual patients; the acronym stands for Culture Aware Robots and Environmental Sensor Systems for Elderly Support. CARESSES robots are being tested in Japan and the United Kingdom.

[45] See Meritxell Valenti Soler et al., "Social Robots in Aging Dementia," *Frontiers in Aging Neuroscience* 7 (2015), online at https://www.ncbi.nlm.nih.gov/pmc/articles/PMC4558428/; and Sandra Petersen et al., "The Use of Robotic Pets in Dementia Care," online at https://www.ncbi.nlm.nih.gov/pmc/articles/PMC5181659/.

[46] See https://waypointrobotics.com/blog/elder-care-robots/.

[47] For defense of the thesis that many service occupations can be satisfying, see David Autor and Philip Kitcher, "As You Like It: Work, Life, and Satisfaction," chapter 8 of *Capitalism beyond Mutuality*, ed. Subramanian Rangan (New York: Oxford University Press, 2018), 139–60, and the sources cited there. I am grateful to my co-author for his lucid analyses of the empirical data from surveys on job satisfaction.

INDIVIDUALS 71

to make their living in this way are likely to view themselves as condemned to drudgery. Interestingly, some low-paying, low-status jobs are not resented. Those who work at day-care centers often enjoy their work. An occupation can be redeemed by the human contacts it affords, interactions with very young children, say, or the warm gratitude expressed by parents. No human exchange relieves the shift of the caretaker, alone in an office building after hours. For the server at the fast food counter, there are interactions aplenty, but they are typically curt and often unpleasant. Moreover, as the service economy is currently evolving, some sectors have abandoned the protections occupations have traditionally provided. Shop assistants may be "on call," required to come in on short notice, and even turned back once they have answered the summons. The last virtue of work, its underwriting the capacity for self-maintenance, is eroding.

Yet all the negative features of service work are contingent. As George Herbert recognized long ago, sweeping a room could be transfigured by an appropriate motivation and setting—drudgery could become fulfilling. He celebrates work performed for a divine master:

> All may of Thee partake:
> Nothing can be so mean,
> Which with his tincture—"for Thy sake"—
> Will not grow bright and clean.
>
> A servant with this clause
> Makes drudgery divine:
> Who sweeps a room as for Thy laws,
> Makes that and th' action fine.[48]

Of course, those who work in factories and mines cannot view their toil as advancing purposes of any transcendent significance. Perhaps they view themselves as critical to the lives of other human beings. Miners threatening to strike have sometimes emphasized a nation's dependence on their labor, and that may represent a sense of contributing to the welfare of a local community. But, I suspect, more prominent factors offsetting the dangers to health and the stresses of meeting a rigorous imposed schedule are the company of fellows and the material benefits. The workday becomes bearable

---

[48] George Herbert, "The Elixir."

72   THE MAIN ENTERPRISE OF THE WORLD

because of the camaraderie of the pit or the assembly line—and because of the prospect of good pay.

The dignity of factory labor didn't blossom from any intrinsic quality of the work or from appreciation of the merits of the people who undertook it. Higher status was an achievement (largely generated by the labor union movement and lingering even after that movement's decline). It is worth recalling the scathing characterizations of the conditions of work in nineteenth-century Britain.[49] Even by the early twentieth century, the situation of miners and factory hands was barely improved.[50]

Suppose, then, our society were to accept a future in which many, perhaps even most, occupations would be service jobs. Regulations might be introduced to transform the forms of labor at the low end of the satisfaction scales, so that they took on some features of the most satisfying forms of service. That might reasonably start with a living wage and protections to avoid the imperious summoning and dismissal of the "servants."[51] It might continue by introducing space for creativity in problem-solving, by fostering rewarding interactions with those who are served, and emphasizing the importance of the work done and the qualities of those who do it. If some tasks—solitary work in depressing or noxious environments, say—resist these forms of amelioration, they might be combined with other more rewarding positions, through which the workers would rotate. Social and economic reforms could make service labor something to be welcomed. After all, ideology can make "drudgery divine," and social change transformed the subhuman masses of the early Industrial Revolution into the proud productive workers of the pit and the factory.[52] Emphasizing the importance of service work to the lives of others would help in elevating its status. Communities depend on mutual aid—in all its forms.

Suppose, then, that this is the future of labor in our country. How should formal education adapt to it?

---

[49] Friedrich Engels, *The Condition of the Working Class in England*, Oxford World's Classics (Oxford: Oxford University Press, 2009); Karl Marx, *Capital* (New York: Vintage, 1977), chapter 15, 492–639.

[50] George Orwell, *The Road to Wigan Pier* (New York: Houghton Mifflin, 1958).

[51] As I shall argue in Chapter 10, the educational reforms I propose depend on changing many characteristics of the wider social environment. Among the needed modifications is a greatly reduced differential in wages. Many service workers will only feel appropriately appreciated when they are properly paid.

[52] Of course, not all forms of ideology can work the transformation. As Natalia Rogach Alexander reminded me, Stalin's caricature of Marx's ideas generated the idea of the "worker hero" and encouraged new forms of destructive competition.

INDIVIDUALS   73

Domestic automation and global outsourcing will provide the affluent world with a pool of workers whose service could make all our lives go better. Furthermore, the work performed could be central to the lives and to the sense of living meaningfully of those who serve. Among the most rewarding occupations are those centered on relieving the pains of others. Treating and healing respond to adverse situations. Other occupations bring rewards through adding to the well-being of others. Fostering lives is as rewarding as saving them. The teacher stands with the nurse and the doctor.

An aging population would surely benefit from a dedicated army of caregivers, well paid and well respected, who helped the old decline with dignity. (The human caregiver and the therapy robots could continue to serve as partners.) Even more important is the need to nurture our young—all of them. So my first, and most basic, proposal for rethinking education calls for a massive expansion of labor in the field of human growth, conceived as beginning at birth and extending well into adult life.[53]

1. *Education should be viewed as a central mission of society*[54] *(if not the central mission), so that the workforce engaged in it should be dramatically increased. The increase in human investment should be accompanied by the devotion of resources so as to enable the work of the educators.*

This proposal is intended as one obvious way to respond to the problem Smith, Marx, and Dewey all saw: the deadening effects of many contemporary forms of labor. Liberating education from Smith's Principle would open the way to seeing it as directed toward preparing the young for fulfilling lives. At a time when service work is likely to come to dominate the labor market, why not expand the most rewarding forms of service work? As empirical surveys have shown, caring for and nurturing children proves satisfying, even when those who provide the care are appallingly underpaid. I thus see one problem (How to offer opportunities for more fulfilling work?)

---

[53] Anthony Atkinson's brilliant book, *Inequality* (Cambridge, MA: Harvard University Press, 2015), sums up the life's work of a great economist. One of its distinctive features is the distillation of Atkinson's conclusions as numbered proposals. Although I am writing on a different (though related) topic—and with far less expertise—I have followed him in this practice.

[54] Although my proposals are often based on data about the two societies I know best—the United States and the United Kingdom—I take many of them to apply far more broadly.

74   THE MAIN ENTERPRISE OF THE WORLD

as coinciding with another apparent problem (What to do when service work becomes the norm?) to generate an opportunity for social progress.[55]

How great should the increase be? Enough to provide each child with adequate chances of living a fulfilling life, as a democratic citizen, able to sustain herself (or himself) in the ambient environment. If service occupations dominate the labor market, the child will need to acquire the characteristics required not only to engage in these occupations but to fulfill herself through them. As I shall suggest in the next chapters, this requires the development of a kind of other-directedness that promises to bring the three Millian ideals into closer harmony with one another. Maintaining yourself need no longer detract from good citizenship or personal fulfillment.

For the present, however, a proposal for adapting education to a labor environment in which service occupations dominate can be presented in a simple and provocative way.

2. *The task of the education system is to prepare the students to become educators.*

This bald formulation will surely provoke accusations of circularity. How can the function of a system be to replicate itself? But when the question is posed straightforwardly, there's an obvious answer: That's life. Or, to elaborate more philosophically, human lives obtain their meaning through their contributions to something broader, through positive impacts on other lives. It does not matter that those further lives will gain their meaning from contributions of the same kind, or that the chain will ultimately terminate. Emerson appreciates the point in the line I have adapted as my epigraph for this book (and abbreviated in my title): The main enterprise of the world for splendor, for extent, is the upbuilding of a human being.

In case that sounds too highfalutin by half, let me bring it down to earth. A Pew survey on evolving attitudes to the family posed an important question:

> Which of the following statements best describes how important your family is to you at this time: the most important element of my life; one of

---

[55] I don't pretend that the case for this basic proposal is yet complete. The discussions of the chapters to come are intended to make my diagnosis of problems and solutions appear ever more compelling.

the most important elements, but not the most important; not an important element of my life?[56]

Among those surveyed, 76 percent saw the family as the most important element, and a further 22 percent took it to be one of the most important but not the most important. I interpret these results as indicating that only 2 percent of those asked the question thought that the sustained well-being of the people they cared for was not a major determinant of how well their lives were going.

My proposals suggest a direction for finding self-fulfillment in the post-industrial work environment. Extrapolating from the Pew survey, I conjecture that many of those now nostalgic for the labor market of the past are concerned about the financial rewards of a service economy precisely because their lives have been centered on the welfare of their families. The alienation Marx discerned in the industrial conditions of the nineteenth century was not removed by the developments of the twentieth century. Rather, the worker was given a new sense of the welfare of the family, defined in terms of enjoyment of consumer goods and promises of upward mobility and a better future for the children. As wages rose to bring that kind of welfare within reach, trading the workday for a chance to support and advance a family—seen as the most important thing in life—came to seem a good bargain. Service jobs, precarious, low-paying, and demeaning, appear to erode that chance. Remove these features and the threat evaporates. In addition, a service economy might directly reduce Marxian alienation, bringing into the daily work those human aspects of cooperation and mutual benefit that pervade family life, and broadening the communities within which workers are embedded. The bargain is willingly made by many teachers, when they settle for fewer consumer goods in exchange for the ability to exercise "human functions" in the workplace.

How, then, to translate these first two proposals into educational reform? To the extent that systematic theory is available, it can offer guidance; where it is absent, the approach must be experimental. One proposal can draw on empirical research that has already been done.[57]

---

[56] "The Decline of Marriage and the Rise of New Families," Pew Survey, released November 18, 2010.

[57] James J. Heckman and Ganesh Karapakula, "Intergenerational and Intragenerational Externalities of the Perry PreSchool Project" (NBER Working Paper No. 25889, https://www.nber. org/papers/w25889). See also Avi Feller et al., "Compared to What?: Variation in the Impact of Early Child Education by Alternative Care Type," *Annals of Applied Statistics 10* (2016): 1245–85. These important studies show how, even when it doesn't issue in any permanent improvement in academic

76 THE MAIN ENTERPRISE OF THE WORLD

3. *Set up well-designed and well-funded cooperative centers of "Care, play, and instruction," in which children can be enrolled from early infancy until the beginning of school. The staff to child ratio in these centers should be high.*[58] *Parents should have the opportunity for paid release from their regular work, to spend one or two days per week, participating in their children's development at these centers. Each child would be guaranteed a place at zero cost.*

The centers would be modeled on those existing nursery schools which currently receive the highest rates of parental approval. They would, however, explicitly resist attempts to "help children get ahead." Emphasizing cooperation, joint planning, and imaginative play, the staff would take stock of and respond to the development of each child.[59] For children ready to begin learning the formal skills of the school curriculum, help and support would be provided. But acquiring those skills would not be viewed as an overriding goal, to be achieved come what may.

The boundary between elementary school and home would remain permeable. During the early grades, parents should continue to spend one or two days a week participating in the education of their children, with this activity being viewed as a part of their jobs. Moreover, this should be accepted as a norm for *all* parents, not simply for one member of a couple.

4. *The elementary school classroom should contain no more than fifteen students, and at least two teachers. Besides the teachers, at least one other adult assistant, possibly a parent, would be present. The class would also welcome the participation of more parents, and to expect all parents to play a part, as well as visitors able to acquaint children with a variety of arts, studies, and activities. Curriculum would cover reading, writing, and arithmetic (twenty-first-century basic training). Emphasis on*

performance, early education generates many benefits. Children who participated in the Perry program typically pursued their education further, were more likely to obtain steady employment, and were less likely to become involved in crime.

[58] How high? That should be determined empirically. Based on data about the programs parents find most attractive, we might think of ratios of 1:2 for the very early years, and 1:5 later—but those estimates are open to correction by educational experiments, and might reasonably vary for different populations.

[59] As the next chapters will suggest, these emphases accord with trying to move in the directions identified in distilling Mill's ideals for education. But, as Chapter 10 will explain, they require broader social change, specifically the move to a more egalitarian, less competitive society.

cooperative activity and joint planning would continue. Through interac-
tion with adults possessing a wide range of talents and interests, children
would be encouraged to find areas of knowledge, of physical activity, and
of art that especially appealed to them.

The vision of the elementary school behind this proposal is to stimulate curiosity, enabling each child to discover his or her own passions. Autonomy, as
conceived by the liberal approach, turns on self-discovery. You cannot find
your own plan of life without some sense both of who you are and of what
possibilities are available. If members of a diverse collection of adults bring
into the classroom their own deeply felt conceptions of what is valuable and
worth pursuing, the chances that children might find a range of possibilities
for themselves are increased. And through finding a set of initially attractive
options, they are then more likely to arrive at one that retains its charm, that
survives the discipline and the setbacks encountered in its pursuit.[60]

The provocation of Proposal 2 should now take on new significance.
Parents are expected to bring something as educators, not only to their own
children but to a wider community. Moreover, even those without children
of their own may—and should—bring their passions and interests to the elementary classroom. The aim of their own schooling is to help them find something they want to bring to the education of others. Through the leanings
they acquired in their youth, perhaps in the classrooms they attended, they
discovered their own prospective self-fulfillment, and they partially realize
their self-fulfillment by offering it to others.

Yet why should it all happen in those early years? My second methodological guideline[61] recommends thinking of learning as a lifetime activity.
So, in accordance with guideline 1, I envisage a further social change in the
conditions of work.

5. *Workers would have the option of taking a periodic paid leave, to attend*
   a center designed to allow adults to pursue activities to enlarge their intel-
   lectual, artistic, or physical horizons.

While most studies of the value of continuing education focus primarily on
the potential career advantages and secondarily on developing and honing

---

[60] Proposals 3 and 4 will be elaborated further in subsequent chapters.
[61] See Principle B in Chapter 1, 37.

78   THE MAIN ENTERPRISE OF THE WORLD

the traits relevant to economic or social success, my rationale for this proposal looks elsewhere.[62] The patterns of our lives are rarely decided once
and for all in some moment of epiphany in adolescence or young adulthood.
Our educational system should allow for growth and change. People should
have the opportunity to explore new areas, perhaps those they had "always
wanted" to pursue, perhaps others whose attractions have only become clear
once their schooldays are over.

Plainly, there are many specific questions left unaddressed. Some (I hope
the most important ones) will be taken up in the subsequent chapters. For
now, my goal has been to outline ways in which the work environment and
the formal educational system might adapt to one another. Once Smith's
Principle is abandoned, we can begin to explore how to work systematically
toward the most significant types of goals toward which Mill's overloaded
curriculum points. I hope a preliminary sketch is appealing enough to motivate my effort to add some details.[63]

Yet, before I try to add detail, one obvious question has to be posed. How
to pay for so ambitious a commitment to education? That question has an
obvious answer. Through a readjustment of national priorities. We should
end the economic domination of education, opting instead for a thorough
effort to create not only workers, but also citizens and people who can find
fulfillment—and do so, in part, through what they pass on to others. Part III
of this book explores how that might be done.

---

[62] It is a sign of the dominance of Smith's Principle that almost all discussions of the value of continuing education begin with the career benefits. If they go further, it is usually to explain how adult
learning can increase your confidence and your marketing skills. Thoughts of personal development
are sadly neglected.

[63] The argument of this chapter might be viewed as a critique of Smith's Principle, supplemented
by some proposals that respond to foreseeable changes in the labor market—provoking the question,
Why is this the correct way to deny the Principle and react to those changes? My answer will consist
in showing how the approach I have adopted promotes the goals identified in Chapter 1. That will
emerge from the study and articulation of those goals in the next three chapters.

3

Fulfillment

As we have seen, when the tasks amassed for education to discharge are recognized as a monstrous overload, it is no surprise that national policies will try to identify the most important ones. In a world marked by intense economic competition, training the workforce to be as productive as possible and to be prepared for the most lucrative forms of employment is likely to emerge as the top priority. Potential workers will be encouraged by the prospect of economic rewards. As large incomes become prized above all else, and as they are linked to prestige and status, economic competition is further intensified. The screw turns again and yet again. Out of the spiral come purer and purer (or grosser and grosser?) versions of that materialist, consumer culture, whose influence theorists like Harry Brighouse lament.[1]

This dominant perspective is entirely at odds with the great tradition of reflecting on education. From Plato to the present, the Western thinkers who have thought most deeply about how young people should be formed have emphasized quite different values. Mill, recall, began his lengthy address by setting professional training on one side. Preparation for other, more common, forms of work fell below the horizon of his ruminations. Major educational theorists, without exception, would be saddened if they reviewed most of the schooling offered in today's world. They would be appalled by the ways in which, in various parts of the globe, young people are fed into high-pressure educational regimes designed to help their nation's economy. Even more incensed by the dangerous, decaying places to which poor children (not only in America, but perhaps most notably there) are sent to receive inadequate instruction from a rotating cadre of overtaxed, underpaid teachers.[2] But, beyond the kinds of distortion reviewed in the previous chapter, they

---

[1] *On Education*, 23.

[2] See Meira Levinson, *No Citizen Left Behind*; also Jonathan Kozol, *Savage Inequalities* (New York: Crown, 1991) and *The Shame of the Nation* (New York: Crown, 2005). In "Children of the Broken Heartlands" (forthcoming in *Social Theory and Practice*), Randall Curren makes a powerful (and poignant) case for expanding the common vision of educationally underserved children (taking them to be those sent to schools in blighted inner cities). He argues for *rural isolation* as an important source of deprivation.

The Main Enterprise of the World. Philip Kitcher, Oxford University Press. © Oxford University Press 2022.
DOI: 10.1093/oso/9780190928971.003.0004

80 THE MAIN ENTERPRISE OF THE WORLD

should also protest what goes on in the leafy suburbs and in the most prestigious academies of the affluent world. For the screw already turns there, too.

Given the conditions prevailing in many schools in New York City, it would be wrong to shed too many tears for the well-paid professionals who spend harried years jostling to make sure that their children will be "properly educated." Before the baby is born, entry to the "right" preschool must be arranged. The next struggle typically occurs before entry to elementary school—and perhaps after that continuous progress through "appropriate" middle and high schools is assured—or, if not, a new version of the old struggle must be undertaken. Then, of course, comes college preparation, to be undertaken in deadly earnest, so that the well-groomed adolescent can attend one of the most prestigious colleges. Despite the fact that many institutions of higher education in the United States are truly outstanding— plenty of liberal arts colleges, state universities, and technical institutes, as well as the most elite universities, provide outstanding educational opportunities, often in the form of distinctive undergraduate programs[3]—nothing but the "best" will do. Hence, in advance, the credentials must be burnished, the boxes checked. Those destined for admission to the "top colleges" must show how "well-rounded" they are by participating in an appropriate range of activities at an approved schedule.[4] At every stage the growing child must be trained to surmount the next hurdle. The last heat, whether the finish line is an undergraduate degree or an advanced qualification, determines how later life will go after entry to the "real world." For that, the young need to be stamped with the badges of highest repute, and to have associated with others who will lead the competition in the rest of their working lives. Networking counts.

[3] This estimate is based on my visits to many American campuses, particularly during 2016–17, when I had the privilege of serving as a Phi Beta Kappa visiting scholar. The visiting scholar program aims to enable students and faculty at purely undergraduate institutions to interact with scholars from research universities. I went to nine colleges: SUNY Geneseo, North Carolina State University, Washington and Lee, Hofstra University, The College of Wooster, San Francisco State, Randolph College, Albion College, and Wellesley College. Only the last of these would meet the aspirations of the overstressed parents envisaged in the text. And, to be sure, Wellesley provides a superb education, thoroughly deserving its reputation. What struck me, however, was the quality of many of the students I met at each of the other colleges, as well as the excellence and dedication of the professors who taught them. Moreover, each of the eight (non-elite) institutions had designed a distinctive program for its undergraduates, thoughtfully conceived and well administered. I suspect that many students who are pushed toward Harvard or Stanford or MIT or Wellesley would thrive just as well in one of these programs.

[4] See Annette Lareau, *Unequal Childhoods*, for rich descriptions of the micro-organization of many adolescent lives.

To repeat: affluent societies allow many families to suffer worse fates, forcing parents who have already abandoned any dreams they themselves may have had to send their children to schools offering no real chance that those subjected to them will fare any better. We should not cry too much for the overstressed parents who wonder if the local magnet school is "really good enough," or whether attending the flagship state university would condemn their son or daughter to a "second-rate" future. On the other hand, what is visited upon their children merits our sympathy if not an angry protest. They may not suffer the same fate as Smith's "torpid" workers, or experience the even more severe difficulties of those who are denied from their early years any chance to learn, or to find anything other than poorly paid menial work (if that); but they are being shaped to exist on an inadequate diet of values. The consequence will be to diminish their chances of achieving what the educational tradition has seen as a principal benefit. Mill's address rightly crescendos toward a jubilant celebration of that envisaged good: the opportunity for personal fulfillment.

Smith's Principle emerged from reflections on an inevitably competitive world, and it continues to be sustained by them. To move to diminish the competition—as the last chapter did (and as Part III will do more systematically)—is often viewed as dangerously misguided. Economic competition, it is claimed, has delivered important human goods. Thanks to the commercial system set in place in the eighteenth century and refined ever since, billions of people have been lifted out of abject poverty. Technology has transformed lives for the better, making daily tasks easier and enriching leisure opportunities. Yearning for a less competitive future, like nostalgia for an allegedly less competitive past, is a sentimental fantasy from which clearheaded thinkers should free themselves.

Parts of this defense of the economic status quo are entirely reasonable. The statistics tell a story of human progress—in some respects.[5] My tale of two cities, the New York of the impoverished children and the distortions inflicted upon their affluent peers, was intended to draw attention to the losses—for members of both groups. Is it correct to dismiss what has been

---

[5] They are lucidly presented in Angus Deaton, *The Great Escape* (Princeton: Princeton University Press, 2013). Steven Pinker, in *The Better Angels of Our Nature* (New York: Viking, 2011) and *Enlightenment Now* (New York: Viking, 2018), aims to make a more ambitious case, and thus, in my view, overstates what the data show.

82 THE MAIN ENTERPRISE OF THE WORLD

forfeited as insignificant? Would it be possible to combine the gains with restoring the discarded values? As already noted, my final chapter will attempt to rebut a skeptical dismissal of the latter question. For now, my aim is to address the charge implicit in the former: is a plea for personal fulfillment simply an exercise in muddled sentimentality?

Bumper stickers sometimes appear to opt for crass materialism: "He who dies with the most toys wins." But perhaps the joke is on those who take the declaration seriously, rather than as an ironic comment on consumer culture. Whichever reading is apt, most people would probably agree that simply amassing toys—or trophies—is an ultimately unrewarding way to spend your mortal span. Something has gone wrong in the lives of those who dedicate themselves to glory in the rat race. Emily Dickinson offers a poignant diagnosis:[6]

> The World—feels Dusty
> When We stop to Die—
> We want the Dew—then—
> Honors—taste dry—

Yet, even if it's agreed that lives devoted to seeking wealth or prestige, to the exclusion of all else, are *un*fulfilling and *un*fulfilled, claims to provide a positive account of fulfillment or to view formal education as offering guidance about personal fulfillment might nonetheless be rejected. We may recognize the absence of fulfillment when it confronts us, and yet resist theorists who promise to explain how to live well. Schools can help young people acquire the basic capacities they need for life, guiding them toward self-maintenance. Beyond that, the idea of the "meaningful life" or the "fully human life" or the "fulfilled life" is simply too nebulous to have educational implications.

Chapter 1 sketched a response to skepticism of this sort. There I proposed an account of fulfillment—or better a thesis about what makes human lives *more* fulfilling. We find the "Dew" craved by Dickinson's dying protagonist in our contributions to the lives of others, and in their appreciative responses.[7]

> Flags—vex a Dying face—
> But the least Fan

---

[6] R. W. Franklin, ed., *The Poems of Emily Dickinson* (Cambridge MA: Harvard University Press, 1998), Vol. *1*, 501; poem 491.

[7] Ibid.

FULFILLMENT 83

> Stirred by a friend's Hand—
> Cools—like the Rain—

The lines make vivid one way of exemplifying the abstract picture offered by Dewey. Viewing ourselves as small links in an enormous chain extending into the remote past (and, with luck, into a lengthy future) may appear to make daunting demands that only an unusually talented few can aspire to satisfy. How can ordinary lives help in "conserving, transmitting, rectifying and expanding the heritage of values we have received that those who come after us may receive it more solid and secure, more widely accessible and more generously shared than we have received it"?[8] The poets tell us: through the positive differences we make to the lives of others; through the motion of the friendly hand; or, more generally, through "our little nameless, unremembered acts/Of kindness and of love."[9]

According to my Deweyan suggestion, the fulfilled life is one in which a person freely chooses and pursues a project, a life plan, intended to contribute to other human lives, one that succeeds in adding its own increment of value to the vast human project. In the rest of this chapter, I shall try to make this idea less nebulous, and to uncover its import for the formation of the individual, including the role properly assigned to formal education.

There are many respects in which the brief characterization given in Chapter 1 needs to be clarified and extended. I shall start by defending my humanism— the proposal that fulfillment requires contributing to other human lives— against two indictments of narrowness. The first of these protests the neglect of other sentient beings. The other, probably more common, sees a need to answer to some "higher purpose," to participate in some project that transcends finite physical existence—typically through service to a deity. My attempt to disarm both concerns will identify important common ground between humanism and the insights behind the criticisms.

The next task will be to explore the implications of the history of our species. Philosophers often write as if there were a single problem—"How to live?"—arising at all times and places. I shall contest this. What counts as fulfillment, and even whether "fulfillment" is the correct term to focus the

---

[8] John Dewey, *A Common Faith* (LW 9, 58). See Chapter 1, 40.
[9] Wordsworth, *Lines: Composed a Few Miles above Tintern Abbey*, ll. 34–35.

84   THE MAIN ENTERPRISE OF THE WORLD

Socratic question, varies with circumstances. The important form of the question, I shall argue, is always comparative. Rather than seek some ideal form of "the good life," what is of interest is to identify the dimensions along which human lives prove deficient, and thus prepare for ways in which they might be improved.

After these preliminary clarifications, I shall take up issues about fulfill-ment as they have recently been posed and discussed. Two main approaches stand out. One of these, often seen as the legacy of Ancient Greek thought, tries to specify an objective list of features that contribute to the quality of lives. Its rival emphasizes the autonomous choice of the subject, starting from Mill's emphasis on the free choice of a person's "life plan." The grounds of the debate between these two views are evident. Millian liberals regard the list of allegedly objective features as an imposition, narrowing the scope of autonomous choice of a person's "own good." Defenders of such lists reply by pointing to the possibility of trivial life plans and projects, accusing liberals of setting the bar too low. My discussion will attempt to show how to integrate the insights of these views. The best way of doing so, I suggest, abandons the Millian picture of the abstracted subject by recognizing a self who is always socially situated and socially formed.

Even developed in this way, an approach to fulfillment may well seem to inherit the elitism often haunting discussions of "living well." Quite reason-ably, those discussions strike many readers as applying only to relatively priv-ileged people. I shall try to show how to be more democratic and egalitarian, showing how "life plans" can be tacitly present in everyday choices, how there is no necessity for any grand moment of decision, and how fulfilled lives can undergo changes of direction. Further, I'll abandon the Puritanism of many accounts of fulfillment, recognizing how various kinds of pleasures—especially those that are shared—can contribute to the value of a life.

Given all these attempts to make the notion of fulfillment more precise, I shall come to terms with the fact that the factors taken to contribute to fulfillment—autonomous choice, success, and engagement with the lives of others—are all matters of degree. In particular, the degree of freedom any of us can exercise in choosing a pattern for our lives will depend on the char-acter of a dialogue between the growing self and the ambient society. How we are educated matters. This will lead to a conception of education, especially in the early years. The dialogue between society and the nascent individual must be as sensitive as possible. Those who play a role in forming young people should provide enough options to structure a choice, without imposing any

FULFILLMENT   85

definite pattern. Above all, they must listen for the first murmurings of a distinctive personality and character.

So we shall return to education, and to the proposals made in the previous chapter. Those suggestions are, I claim, buttressed by the account of fulfillment as it will be elaborated here. And they will be further supported by the chapters to come.

My proposal starts from an emphasis on the human.[10] It can be questioned in one of two ways, either by pleading for greater inclusiveness—taking account of the well-being of other sentient animals—or by insisting that contributions to something beyond, "higher than," humanity are required to deliver fulfillment. The first clarification of my position will consist in taking up these points in succession.

During the past half century, a significant locus of moral progress has been attitudes toward and treatment of non-human animals.[11] The roots of the current increased awareness of our moral deficiencies in this domain are far older. In many Asian writings and teachings, concerns about other creatures have been voiced for millennia. Among Western thinkers, Jeremy Bentham already claimed in the eighteenth century that sentient animals' capacities for pleasure and pain require that they be included in the moral calculus.[12] Analogous conclusions are easily generated within other ethical frameworks. Consequently, like many other people today, I believe that we have obligations to change our ways toward many non-human animals: that the sports and displays to which we have subjected them are often cruel and always distort their lives, that our practices of raising them for food are barbaric, and that the scientific experiments to which we subject them must meet demanding requirements if the animals involved are not to be the victims of savage violations.[13] How, then, can I view fulfillment in

---

[10] Which might be extended by considering the ways in which our actions impinge on the lives of other sentient animals. For discussion of this possible extension, see Appendix 1.

[11] Classic sources for the upsurge of interest in animal welfare are Peter Singer, *Animal Liberation* (New York: Random House, 1975), and Tom Regan, *The Case for Animal Rights*, 2nd rev. ed. (Berkeley: University of California Press, 2004). Among the many more recent discussions, I recommend Lori Gruen, *Ethics and Animals* (New York: Cambridge University Press, 2011), and Christine Korsgaard, *Fellow Creatures* (New York: Oxford University Press, 2018).

[12] Jeremy Bentham *Introduction to the Principles of Morals and Legislation* (originally published in 1780; repr., London: Methuen, 1980).

[13] For elaboration and defense, see my "Experimental Animals," *Philosophy and Public Affairs 43* (2015: 287–311.)

86   THE MAIN ENTERPRISE OF THE WORLD

terms of our contributions to the lives of other *humans*? How can one see the attempt to transmit values across the generations (as Dewey eloquently conceives it)[14] as a purely "*human* project"? Isn't this to fall guilty to a narrow, speciesist, view, one that ought to be expanded once the moral status of our evolutionary cousins is more fully appreciated?[15]

It's a fair cop. Fulfillment, I claim, comes about through our contributions to a trans-generational project. In *one* sense, that project is aptly recognized as a *human* project—for we, members of our species, are the agents in it, and it is through our efforts that advances are made. In another sense, however, it is not a *merely* human project. People can contribute to it by making the world they leave behind them a better place than the world into which they were born—and that does not require a contribution to other *human* lives. Yet this formulation is dangerous. It suggests that the improved state of the world gains that status independently of the quality of the lives of sentient beings: that is, even if the supposed advances made no positive difference to the life of any animal (human or non-human), there would still be some improvement in the world. That I deny. It would be preferable to say something different: to advance the human project is to change the world in a way that affects the lives of sentient beings for the better.

But that way of talking, too, needs to be properly understood. Unfortunately, it can easily be interpreted as a form of utopianism, one that should be rejected. For, without differentiating the ways in which humans interact with the lives of other sentient beings, it invites us to pursue a goal Darwin should have made obsolete: to think in terms of a "Peaceable Kingdom" where the lives of sentient beings can go maximally well. There is a profound asymmetry in what we can give to one another and what we can provide for our sentient non-human relatives. With respect to other human beings, we can not only avoid doing harm, but can seek to make their lives go better. Perhaps with respect to a small number of animal kinds, the domesticated species with which we live in closest proximity and understand the best, we can sometimes conceive of—and realize—(small) improvements in their lives. The idea of legislating for the entire animal kingdom (or for its sentient provinces), governed as it is by natural selection, dissolves under

---

[14] See above, 40 (text to n.75).
[15] I am deeply grateful to Martha Nussbaum for challenging me on these issues. The paragraphs that follow outline a response to the important questions she raises. More needs to be said to deal fully with them, and I have said *some* of it in the articles referred to in the notes.

serious scrutiny.[16] We can of course interfere in all sorts of ways, favoring some species at cost to others, but, even where our actions can be defended against charges of wanton destruction, there is no standard against which we can measure clear positive improvements. At best, we can intervene in ways that free some animals from dangers and obstacles, without harming others.

To appreciate the point, we should start from a consequence of Darwin's view of life. Natural selection is not the only cause of evolutionary change, nor is it always expressed as "nature red in tooth and claw." Yet, as the *Origin of Species* makes clear, the struggle for existence is central to life. The organic world is organized so that large amounts of conflict are inevitable. A perfect extension of sympathy, in which it flows out evenly across the animal kingdom, is impossible. To sympathize with the predator is to withhold sympathy from the prey, and conversely. Darwin thus disrupts a style of thought that surely permeated earlier religious approaches to the stewardship of creation at their most enlightened and benign, and that continues to linger in the writings of environmentalists and those most committed to animal welfare or to animal rights. He put an end to "Peaceable Kingdom Thinking."

Peaceable Kingdom Thinkers tacitly assume a benign nature, disturbed only through morally problematic human interventions. They see the world through the lens of the Anglican hymn: where "every prospect pleases/And only Man is vile." In consequence, their vision of governance embodies a simple principle—human beings should act only in ways that do not cause any harm or suffering to sentient animals. So they distinguish episodes in which human actions produce animal suffering from those in which very similar suffering is inflicted by non-human animals. It is surely indisputable that members of our species can be very creative in their cruelty, but we do not have a monopoly on actions that prolong pain. Many cat owners have seen their pet toy with a captive mouse. Just as we can try to check our own wanton infliction of suffering on sentient animals, so we can try to restrain the animals over whom we exercise direct control: preventing the cat from torturing the mouse, not training the hounds to hunt foxes. When we venture beyond this narrow sphere, however, we enter moral territory where the terrain is hard, if not impossible, to map. Our efforts to protect some species almost always have costs for others. In pointing to the suffering we prevent, we

---

[16] For defense of this thesis and for a critique of "Peaceable Kingdom Thinking," see my "Governing Darwin's World," in *Animals: Historical Perspectives*, ed. Peter Adamson and G. Faye Edwards (New York: Oxford University Press, 2018), 269–92; and "Experimental Animals." The next paragraphs summarize arguments presented there.

88 THE MAIN ENTERPRISE OF THE WORLD

typically overlook the sufferings our actions cause. We should be honest. We are not legislating to create an overall improvement in the animal kingdom, but to produce a distribution of species that pleases human sensibilities.

In short, the non-human sentient world can be made better through reversing the cruel practices in which human beings have frequently engaged. Beyond that, the indisputably positive impact we can envisage is extremely small. The injunction "First, do no harm!" applies. It is very hard to see, though, what comes second.

Hence, I claim, although the lives of sentient animals are potential targets of our contributions to the human project, the vast majority of such contributions will consist in our refraining from harming them.[17] If we hope to achieve something more positive in our lives, it will usually have to result from what we do for members of our own species. Provided that this is clearly recognized, I have no objection to the more expansive characterization my imagined questioner prefers. But, I submit, the focus on the human, on participation in the "human project," is a reasonable way to approach the search for fulfillment; not only are we the agents in this project, we are, perforce, the main targets.[18]

A final remark on this issue. Our species, too, is subject to natural selection. Why, then, does the Darwinian point not apply in our own case, depriving us of opportunities to contribute positively to the lives of other human beings? Because our cultural evolution has decoupled the things human beings value from the Darwinian "goods" of survival and reproduction. Were our attempts to improve some lives always to bring offsetting costs in the form of losses for other people, we should be in the same bind. In our attempts to advance the "human project," however, we seek ways of helping the targets of our aid that have no bad consequences for others (or bad consequences that are lesser). Although competition for scarce goods sometimes reigns in the human world, thwarting our efforts, it does not always do so by any means. We can escape the "zero-sum" character of the Darwinian struggle for existence in its most typical forms.[19]

---

[17] In essence, the objection's principal insight falls within the *moral* not the *ethical* sphere. Recognizing other sentient beings is profoundly relevant to the question, What should I do? Except in rare cases, it provides little bearing on the question, What kind of person should I be? Life projects seeking to advance understanding of and compliance with our obligations to non-human animals offer opportunities for fulfillment. Attempts to make the world of sentient animals better in further ways are almost always too ambitious.

[18] As I note in Appendix 1, there are some unusual conditions under which a human life could find fulfillment without a positive enhancement of the lives of other human beings.

[19] Since the Darwinian world does allow for cooperation and for mutualisms, there is a limited space in which the would-be legislator of the animal kingdom can act to bring about increased

FULFILLMENT 89

I turn now to the second concern about my humanistic emphasis. Of course, much of the history of Western thought is dominated by a very different approach to questions about the fulfilled life. Christian thinkers, from Augustine on, have supposed our lives to obtain their significance through responding to a larger purpose, promoting the goals identified by a deity. Devout scholars in the Islamic and Judaic traditions have seen the details differently but acquiesced in the fundamental idea. Like Dewey, I have stepped back from any transcendent perspective, replacing the thought of contributing to the project of the deity with that of advancing a collective human endeavor (focused, where possible, on improving the overall state of all sentient animals).

Contemporary religious people, not only those subscribing to the Abrahamic faiths, should appreciate this approach as partially correct—incomplete rather than fundamentally misguided. Viewing the valuable life as one that fulfills the purposes of the favored deity (or deities), devout people would typically include the provision of aid to others as part of the divine plan. The Christian second commandment has counterparts across the major world religions. Hence, from many religious perspectives, despite the imputed significance of aims beyond those concerned with human values, and even though the humanist formulation fails to identify the alleged ultimate significance of the purposes to be fulfilled, using contributions to the human project as a criterion for assessing human lives will often render the correct verdict. To suppose otherwise is to maintain that commitment to the right doctrines washes all sins and shortcomings away, while lack of faith is a deal-breaker. Viewing the secular approach as thoroughly mistaken thus lays a heavy emphasis on doctrine. Even if you accomplish nothing for the human project, espousing the correct credo suffices. Conversely, without faith, the most exemplary conservers and refiners of values fail the divine test. For all their human accomplishments, their lives are worthless.[20]

Ecumenical religions regard those of different faiths as misguided about the character of the transcendent aspect of reality. But they appreciate that people of different faiths—or of none—may live valuable lives, by advancing

overall harmony. The asymmetry to which the argument of the text points is the vastly greater size of this space—and our greater understanding of it—in the human case.

[20] I doubt whether this heavy emphasis on doctrinal belief can be sustained without conceiving the deity as an overweening narcissist—in short, the kind of deity whose purposes should not guide us. For more discussion, see Chapter 6.

90 THE MAIN ENTERPRISE OF THE WORLD

the human good.[21] Ecumenical believers should therefore characterize the humanist answer as an approximation to the truth. It has the right form, but some specific features are wrong. Individual lives do indeed become valuable through their connection to something larger than themselves. What religious people see as a deficiency of secular humanism lies in settling for a *limited* larger project, one that fails to include the transcendence—and the cosmic significance—of the divine plan.

For the time being I shall say no more about the clash between the religious and the secular perspectives. (That debate will come in Chapter 6.) Recognizing the structural kinship between the two approaches—both conceiving the valuable life in terms of contributions to a larger project—helps in understanding how certain obvious concerns about the humanist answer (worries about elitism, for example) cut equally against the religious approach to the good life.

———

Our next step should be to appreciate an important ambiguity underlying the formulations offered so far. In asking "How to live?," Socrates and many of his successors have often elided two questions. Besides the focus on the individual life—How should *I* live?—there is a collective issue—How should *we* live together? The thesis I draw from Dewey bifurcates. First comes a claim about particular human beings: the value of a single human life is assessed by asking how it contributes to the human project. Second is a proposal about human relations and collective human living: the health of a society is evaluated by considering how it advances the accumulation and distribution of values. As the discussion proceeds, it will become clear how these questions are connected. For the present, it is enough to acknowledge their difference and to recognize the relevance of each of them.

To appreciate the difference between the individual question and its collective counterpart only begins the work of disambiguation. Discussions of the Socratic questions are frequently promiscuous in using adjectives. Does the Socratic question concern the *good* life, or the *happy* life, or the

---

[21] As Meira Levinson pointed out to me, people of different faiths will sometimes disagree about what promotes the human good. In consequence, there can be important debates among religious and nonreligious perspectives on whether a life has gone well, even when some hail it as full of contributions to the welfare of other people. Despite the existence of a penumbra of divergence, there is a core of cases on which consensus (or an approximation to it) can be expected. Those who act heroically to save people from danger will almost always receive praise for their efforts, but so too will adults who comfort distressed children or who feed the hungry.

worthwhile life, or the *valuable* life, or the *fully human* life, or the *meaningful* life, or the *significant* life? And my chosen characterizations do not exhaust the possibilities. Sometimes writings in ethics use some or all of these terms as if they were equivalent. Stylistic variation substitutes for monotony, and nothing is supposed to be lost thereby. Yet the adjectives surely vary in their overtones. This is most obvious in the case of happiness. To be sure, there is an (elevated) philosophical concept of happiness, according to which your life cannot be a truly happy one unless it consists of something more than pleasant experiences. Without a structure that gives it meaning, a philosopher might say, it falls short of *genuine* happiness. The philosophical concept is designed to respond to hedonists who are content to view the happy life (even the good life) as one in which pleasures predominate. Yet champions of hedonism may reasonably claim to use "happy" in its everyday sense. Their opponents view a long sequence of physical pleasures—decades spent in the Orgasmatron?[22]—as not attaining happiness "in the *true* sense." Discussions of the quality of human lives, they claim, ought to deploy the "philosophically relevant notion of happiness," for which the happy life must be "fully human" and "meaningful."

The various adjectives orient the Socratic question differently. Just as "happiness" may point toward pleasures, "good" may introduce an ethical or moral tone, "fully human" connect to special ideas about the dignity of our species, and "meaningful" demand self-reflection. So how should the question be phrased? By selecting one term, one spectrum of overtones, and introducing special senses of the others, so equivalence is attained by fiat? The Deweyan proposal offers a better approach. Seeing ourselves as links in a long lineage should remind us of an important truth. "How to live?" ought to be posed differently at different stages of our species' history, and, similarly, for contemporary groups of people who live under very diverse circumstances. All the popular adjectives, in their everyday senses, may have their rationale.

It would be fatuous to gloss "How to live?" for the hunter-gatherers of the Paleolithic, or for the extremely poor inhabitants of the contemporary world, by asking how they might live a meaningful life. Equally, when we reflect on the lives of children who suffer developmental disruptions that

---

[22] Woody Allen depicts a brief visit to the Orgasmatron in *Sleeper*. In *Anarchy, State, and Utopia* (New York: Basic Books, 1974) 42–45, Robert Nozick uses a carefully delineated "Experience Machine" to develop the anti-hedonist point. The general idea extends back at least to Aldous Huxley, and *Brave New World*.

92 THE MAIN ENTERPRISE OF THE WORLD

inhibit their cognitive and emotional capacities, to set standards of dignity and self-awareness would be absurd and insensitive. Yet parents who spend twenty years caring for, protecting, and loving a child whose abilities are sadly reduced might well console themselves after her early death with the reflection that her life had been overall a happy one—and there need be no self-deception in the thought. Even with respect to more severe disruptions, for human beings who must constantly be palliated with drugs to prevent seizures and block pain, the lives may be judged retrospectively: if they do not count as good, they are, at least, as good as they could have been.

The different adjectives are best understood as indicating aspects of human lives it would be valuable to *improve. My Deweyan proposal is comparative.* The values are to become *more* solid and secure, *more* accessible, *more* generously shared. In attempting to explain and defend the importance for education of the ideal of personal fulfillment, I aim to re-pose the Socratic questions. Education should prepare the young to live better—significantly better—than they would otherwise have done. Its central task is not merely to provide individuals with the capacity to maintain themselves, enabling them to survive from day to day, year to year, but to enjoy more rewarding lives. Their world should not feel so dusty when they come to die.

Hand in hand with that goal goes an attempt to improve the societies to which those individuals belong. The idea of ensuring that a particular nation wins in the Contest for Material Wealth—becoming "Great Again"—gives way to efforts to make social life healthier. Through preparing the young for personal fulfillment the path is paved for social progress.

So far, some preliminary clarifications. Instead of aiming at a precise and consistent conception of the good life or of the just society, I have recommended thinking in terms of dimensions along which human lives and human societies might be improved. Concentrate on possibilities of progress, conceived not as steps toward some final perfect state, but as changes that ameliorate or eliminate problematic features of the present. View ideals not as descriptions of states we might ultimately realize but as diagnostic tools for discerning the difficulties of the current situation.[23]

---

[23] Some people understand progress as presupposing an implicit teleology. This strikes me as a mistake for reasons given in n.84 on 44, above, and at greater length in the writings cited there.

The responsibilities Dewey charges us with are to improve the state in which we find ourselves, identifying the factors that limit human lives and human societies, and contributing to the human project by overcoming them. I now want to illustrate this comparative approach by drawing on the two main secular traditions for answering a Socratic question.[24] As I adapt them to my progressivist approach, I hope the concept of fulfillment will come into sharp focus.

Some influential ancient approaches to the good life present a list of features conducive to living well. They point to satisfaction of exacting moral demands, participation in public life, friendships with a special moral character, and contemplation of the most fundamental truths.[25] Because many of the features celebrated in accounts of this sort are difficult for most human beings to aspire to, the proposals are often viewed as elitist, suited to the high-born males of the Greek *polis*, but disparaging the many also-rans. Of course, one can be more generous and inclusive by weakening the requirements, modifying the *objective list* of traits the valuable life should exhibit. Since the end of the eighteenth century, however, many, if not most, philosophical accounts have begun in a different place.

The *liberal approach* takes autonomy to be fundamental. To live well, the life you live must be your own. Any objective list would be an imposition, an external limitation. The subject of a life is to decide on its appropriate contours. As Mill eloquently expresses the theme, the ability to choose our own good and to pursue it in our own way is "the only freedom which deserves the name."[26] Mill's contemporary successors articulate the idea by supposing that those whose lives go well are able to choose a "central project" or a "plan of life."[27] Their choices select a set of goals for them to pursue. If the life is a good (happy? valuable? meaningful? fulfilling?) one, the initial choice is free and the pursuit proves successful, or at least successful enough. When goals are externally imposed, or when there is consistent failure to achieve them, lives do not go well. Liberals are often reluctant to demand more than free choice and successful pursuit, regarding any further constraint as an invasion of individual freedom.

---

[24] The indefinite article is appropriate here, because both traditions concentrate on the individual, typically detached from the ambient society. I shall attempt a more thorough fusion of the two Socratic questions.

[25] The classical presentation of this view is in Aristotle's *Nicomachean Ethics*.

[26] OL 17.

[27] See Chapter 1, 38 above, and the references given there.

94 THE MAIN ENTERPRISE OF THE WORLD

Here we come to the nub of a live debate. Supposing the fulfilling life to be one satisfying a set of objective criteria can be seen as veering too far in the direction of imposing prescribed patterns. Liberal emphasis on autonomy appears to overshoot in the opposite direction. Treating individual choice as sovereign allows for worthless projects to qualify as avenues to fulfillment. Recall the grass-counter of Chapter 1. Pitting the approaches against one another in this way inspires an obvious attempt at compromise. Draw from the ancient approach the idea of an objective list of goods. That supplies a menu for the developing individual. Because the menu is large, and because fulfillment can be found in myriad combinations of the particular values, including some that omit large numbers of good things entirely, there remains plenty of room for personal choice. Fulfillment comes through choosing a plan that freely selects a sufficiently rich set of goals from the objective list and attains enough success in attaining the chosen ends.[28]

Although views of this type are steps in the right direction, they are, in my judgment, flawed in two ways. They neglect history, and they separate individuals from the societies to which they belong: more exactly, they begin by focusing on an individual, without a past and detached from social connections, and, to the extent that such links figure in the account, they are introduced as extraneous, as afterthoughts. The conception of fulfillment I aim to elucidate starts elsewhere. Individual people are socially and historically situated. Their positions matter to what counts as fulfillment for them— or even as to whether "fulfillment" is an apt characterization of what they should aim at as they ask, "How to live?"

The social milieu in which developing individuals are embedded will play a prominent role in later parts of this chapter. For the moment, however, I concentrate on the banal fact that each of us comes into being at a particular historical stage in the human project. Recall my apparent semantic fussiness about the adjectives philosophers employ when they take up Socrates' question(s). At some historical stages, and in some social environments, posing the issue in particular ways is silly—if not insensitive or downright insulting. Anthropologists studying communities in harsh environments,

---

[28] A position of this kind seems to be adopted by Martha Nussbaum and by Harry Brighouse. Nussbaum has been a principal advocate for reconceptualizing the ancient view. See her articulation of the Human Development Approach in *Creating Capabilities* (Cambridge, MA: Harvard University Press, 2011) and her contributions to Nussbaum and Amartya Sen, eds., *The Quality of Life* (Oxford: Oxford University Press, 1993). Brighouse's views are concisely and clearly presented in *Educational Goods,* co-authored with Helen F. Ladd, Susanna Loeb, and Adam Swift (Chicago: University of Chicago Press, 2018).

FULFILLMENT   95

I suspect, rarely find it useful to reconstruct their interlocutors' notion of the "meaningful life" or of the "fulfilled life." A time traveler, arriving on the savannah tens of thousands of years before the present, miraculously equipped with the ability to communicate with a struggling band of hunter-gatherers, might well provoke a hostile reaction, were he to inquire into their lives using translations of the vocabulary routine in a graduate seminar in philosophy. Something like a Socratic question might be posed. But it would be posed in very different terms.

What is valuable for human beings to strive for varies with the circumstances in which they find themselves. Consequently, decisions about how to live are, and should be, made differently at different historical stages. Some thinkers have been tempted to rank the values, supposing human cultural evolution to advance from efforts at satisfying basic needs to aiming at "higher goods."[29] Recognizing diversity does not entail accepting a hierarchy. It is possible to welcome the opportunities for aspiring to ends that have only become available at a later historical stage without supposing that people who lived earlier had lives inferior to our own. Indeed, our predecessors may be seen as helping, in a gradual accumulation of small changes, to expand the range of options bequeathed to us, their fortunate descendants. Part of the point of understanding ourselves as participating in a human project that spans tens of thousands of year is to institute a form of trans-temporal egalitarianism. Ranking the contributions of different historical stages is unnecessary; it also expresses an oblivious ingratitude.

Appreciating the evolution of values undermines the idea of an objective list from which those who live well select their own individual combinations. For, if the list is to be complete, it must contain not only the goods recognized at some particular historical moment—say, our own—but all those that will subsequently emerge. The comprehensive inventory is not available until the end of human history, when it could be assessed from some ahistorical perspective. Historical determinists, those who think human evolution is bound to take a particular course, might suppose the contents of the inventory to

---

[29] Mill succumbs to this temptation. The principal innovation of his *Utilitarianism* lies in the emphasis on the thesis that "some *kinds* of pleasure are more desirable and more valuable than others." See *Collected Works* (Indianapolis: Liberty Fund, 2006), 10:211; also OL 138. In his remarks on the "puerile" condition pervading most of human history (*System of Logic*; *Works*, Vol. 8, 952) and on the "nonage" of some societies that renders them unsuited to full democracy (*Considerations on Representative Government*; OL 225–37, 453–67), Mill explicitly commits himself to judgments that the lives available in some societies are more significant, more valuable, than others. Quite reasonably, many contemporary readers find these remarks both uninformed and offensive. Such passages in his writings often prevent his subtle and important ideas from having the influence they deserve.

96 THE MAIN ENTERPRISE OF THE WORLD

be fixed already. Teleology of this sort is suspect. The things we value have emerged from the contingent efforts of our ancestors, as they struggled to live well by their own lights. Even the goods judged as most central to many human lives, the relationships people typically see as most significant, were shaped by events in the distant past that could easily have gone in different directions.[30] There is no invariant human nature, no set of "fundamental" values giving rise, in different contexts, to different specific versions. To believe in that possibility is either to fail to appreciate the character of human evolution, or to fall victim to the idea that the theory of value can be cast in Euclidean form, admitting of an axiomatic presentation within which different "theorems" about the values appropriate to different ages can be derived. The experiments made by our predecessors in the cultural past—often before the development of written records—have accumulated the values we endeavor to achieve. Rather than viewing the Socratic question as already having an answer, atemporally fixed to guide and constrain our attempts to live well, we should think of ourselves as potential creators, capable, like our ancestors, of finding new patterns from which our descendants may draw inspiration.

Yet the terms in which I have framed questions of fulfillment may still seem to carry a whiff of elitism. Talk of "one's own good" or of a "central project" or of a "plan of life" suggests a kind of choice available only to the privileged, to people who have the leisure and the intellectual resources to reflect on how they hope to leave their mark upon the world. In fact, the high-sounding language is misleading in at least three ways. First, it seems to require some deliberate process of reflecting on the Socratic question. Further, it appears to divide the human lifespan into two stages, an initial one in which we formulate "our own good" and a subsequent one in which we pursue it. Finally, a "project" or "plan of life" sounds like something large and grand. Combining all three resonances, the liberal approach apparently invites us to conceive those who live the good life as if they all play, at an early period in their lives, the part Joyce assigns to the young Stephen Dedalus. After a series of reflective struggles, punctuated by epiphanies,[31] the liver of the good life must go

---

[30] Here I transfer to the general theory of value a point made by Dewey in his discussion of morality (*Human Nature and Conduct*, MW 14, 74, 97). I discuss the issues in more detail in Chapter 3 of *The Ethical Project*, and in *Moral Progress*.

[31] Moments of sudden inspiration, in which the way forward seems clear. Joyce borrowed the concept from Walter Pater.

forth "to forge in the smithy of [his] soul the uncreated conscience of [his] race"—and (unlike Joyce's protagonist) achieve some success in pursuing his lofty goals.[32]

Nothing so dramatic is required. The liberal conception allows for the choice of "one's own good" to be implicit. It may simply emerge from a sequence of responses to everyday options, in which a person expresses her preferences, without any large questions—"What is my life most centrally about?," "What project do I want to pursue?"—ever arising. As she decides to live here rather than there, among these people instead of among those, to engage in some forms of activity and to reject others, a sense of what matters emerges. There may never come a moment at which she specifies her "plan of life" or recognizes her "identity." Indeed, she may find any such language pretentious or repugnant. Yet if a sensitive and comprehending observer were to present her with an articulated version of her "central project," we might expect her to agree—"Yes, that is who I am, and those are the things that matter to me."

Whatever the mixture of large reflection and ordinary small choices, there is no need to divide the lifespan into a period during which the "plan of life" is chosen and a later stage during which it is pursued. Reflective people may change their minds about what is most important in their lives. Those who never formulate a "central project" may make everyday choices that revise their implicit conceptions of who they are and what matters to them.[33] Often the evolution of the "central project" will be judged, explicitly or implicitly, as a process of growth—"My initial direction was a false start, but I eventually figured out the kind of person I wanted to become." When that judgment is sustained throughout the later stages of someone's life, any failures to achieve the goals set earlier are no longer relevant. What counts is the mature conception of the good, endorsed once it has been achieved. Notice, though, that when the liberal idea of a chosen life plan is made more complicated (and more realistic), by recognizing that one conception of the good may metamorphose into or be replaced by another (perhaps, by a sequence of later conceptions), it maintains the emphasis on the subject's autonomy by giving

---

[32] James Joyce, *A Portrait of the Artist as a Young Man*, Norton Critical Edition (New York: W. W. Norton, 2007), 224 (Part V, ll. 2789–90). The opening pages of *Ulysses* reveal that, like Icarus, Stephen has landed with a crash.

[33] It is, however, important that those choices be thoughtful. A plan of life isn't chosen autonomously by simply drifting.

98   THE MAIN ENTERPRISE OF THE WORLD

priority to that conception (or those conceptions) that would be affirmed when the subject had lived under all of them.[34]

A familiar comparison may help to clarify this development of the liberal account. We might imagine people, late in their lives, telling their story, as they understand it, to sympathetic listeners. They offer a narrative to structure what they have been and done. Some autobiographies may accord with a single unified pattern. One conception of the good is chosen early and pursued consistently thereafter. Others may offer their own *Bildungsroman*. A process, perhaps involving false starts, obstacles, and reversals, culminates in a stably affirmed conception of the good. What matters is that everything comes right in the end. There are, of course, other possibilities. An autobiography may chronicle a succession of failed attempts. Or the right way, achieved early on, may subsequently be lost. Nor should the life story be afraid of variety. We can make room for the picaresque life, in which a number of "central projects" succeed one another and none is given priority.

These remarks on the first two versions of the charge of elitism prepare for dealing with the third. Once the possibilities of implicit choice and of evolving plans are appreciated, it is easy to understand how the liberal framework applies to the lives of ordinary people. Very few choose a central project with the aim of writing an epic for the millennia or of discovering the ultimate structure of matter—a good thing, too, since all but an infinitesimal fraction of those who do are doomed to disappointment. For most of us what matters is framed at a far humbler scale. We see ourselves as contributing to the lives of others around us, as nurturing them or helping them to find their own way. Or as participating with neighbors to sustain a community. Or cooperating in the production of something many people will value.

The thought may be phrased in the terms with which I began. Our plans of life aim to contribute to the human project. Not, of course, through some global impact, affecting millions of lives we shall never know. Rather, the effects we hope to produce are local. They are to be felt in lives that overlap and intertwine with our own, some of which will extend beyond our deaths. Because of these effects, and through the effects produced by those whose lives we affect, we become part of something larger than ourselves. The chain of consequences is likely to peter out, and the relative impact of our own actions diminishes as the time horizon recedes. But, to the extent that we

---

[34] Thus echoing Mill's procedure for deciding on whether one pleasure is more significant than another. It is important though that the later judgment not be psychologically distorted in any way—by forgetfulness or depression, for example.

FULFILLMENT 99

are successful in our plans, we achieve not immortality but a kind of endurance. These possibilities underlie the potential for human lives to become meaningful.[35]

My defense against the charge of elitism parallels that offered by religious perspectives on the good life. To view human lives as attaining meaning and value through their contributions to some great project for the cosmos is not to demand that all of us perform miracles, or reshape society in accordance with scripture, or convert large numbers of the heathen. We can advance the grand plan locally, through performing everyday tasks, even, as George Herbert claims, in drudgery.[36] Because the sustaining of other people is an important part of the divine intention, a worthy central project can be focused on those around us.

Yet, even if the liberal approach can be elaborated so as to endorse the projects of the folk, it faces complaints that its abstract, intellectual emphases are too Puritanical, even grim. Doesn't pleasure have any place in the valuable life? Indeed, it does. But many of the most intense pleasures, our moments of joy and rapture, are bound up with the activities and relationships that matter most to us. For many people they are shared with the delight of others—as when parents rejoice in a child's happiness. Pleasures of this sort cohere with and reinforce a person's central project. Others coexist amicably with pursuit of the goals that really matter. On yet other occasions, when pleasant experiences interfere with what someone wants most, a bitter residue remains in their wake.

People with hedonist sympathies should not be satisfied with this response. For them, it will not be enough to start with a serious—over-earnest?—"central project," and then allow pleasure a subordinate place. Isn't there room for people who see life as about "having fun"? The objective lists provided by ancient thinkers often seem designed to counter hedonism. Enlightenment liberalism preserved the disdain for pleasure. Kant and Mill, prominent among its architects, are not obvious candidates for "Fun Lover of All Time." And my earlier gesture at the limitations of life in the Orgasmatron would seem to rank me among the Puritans.

So a whiff of elitism remains. The liberal philosopher over-intellectualizes the question "How to live?," thus condemning the gaiety of the folk, whatever

---

[35] In Chapter 4 of *Life after Faith* (New Haven: Yale University Press, 2014), I argue that our contributions to the lives of people who outlive us provides a secular humanist answer to the challenge that, without belief in the divine, human life is meaningless. See, in particular, 110–16.

[36] See "The Elixir," from which I quoted in Chapter 2 (71 above).

100   THE MAIN ENTERPRISE OF THE WORLD

its form. Like the stern confessors of the church, defenders of the liberal approach enjoin people to fix their eyes on the significant things—where these are no longer viewed as fixed by the divine plan but as the goals adopted (implicitly or explicitly) by an autonomous subject. Once again, the comparison between the liberal approach and its religious counterpart paves the way for providing a more inclusive, less earnest, elaboration.

Distinguish two kinds of hedonist. The first is concerned only with personal pleasures. Seventy years in the Orgasmatron would count, for this person, as an excellent life (although longer would, of course, be better). The second type consists of those for whom the appropriate pleasures are typically shared. Imagine medieval villagers preparing for and participating in spring festivities, decorating the maypole, organizing games for the children, cooking and brewing, feasting and dancing. The grave parish priest may frown on their innocent enjoyment. His liberal philosophical counterpart should find no reason to do so.

In line with my earlier suggestions about implicit "plans of life," hedonists of the second type, people concerned to take pleasure where they can *and* to share it with others, can be vindicated by the liberal approach. These *communal hedonists* (to give them a name) do have a "central project," even though they might look askance at any talk of "identity" or "principal goals" or "accomplishments." They count themselves as members of a community, not always harmonious to be sure, in which cooperative efforts can sustain them all in hard times and provide some occasions of happiness and joy. Pleasure and absence of pain is sought not only for an individual actor, but for others as well. Through their joint efforts, each of these people contributes to the human project, lightening the lives of others, extending and refining the set of customs and traditions, and thus enabling the community to endure, and its descendant generations to enjoy, more "solidly," more "securely," and more "generously shared," the available sources of pleasure.

Most of the human beings who have ever lived have existed under adverse circumstances. They have had very little autonomy, and large features of the patterns of their lives have been thrust upon them. In the limited space remaining for exercises of choice, some of them (how many we shall never know) have shaped their lives as communal hedonists. Among them have been people (again an inevitably unknown fraction) who have succeeded in relieving pain and spreading joy among their neighbors. My elaboration of the liberal approach takes them to be committed to a central project, one they successfully pursue. Their lives count as happy. Given their circumstances,

FULFILLMENT 101

many of them have probably found the best available answer to Socrates' question.[37]

Philosophical distaste for hedonism rests on two insights. First, the life of the *solitary* hedonist, the eager occupant of the Orgasmatron or (slightly more realistically) the completely asocial surfer, however rich in its lonely pleasures, is worthless.[38] Second, when people are equipped with a wider range of options for their lives, when they have opportunities for exploration and reflection, when they are liberated from drudgery and when possibilities of pleasure lie ready to hand, the embrace even of communal hedonism often appears lazy and thoughtless. The points combine in repudiations of crass materialism. The excessively rich, for whom life is about accumulating expensive toys, valued in large measure precisely because so few other people are able to buy them, give an answer to Socrates' question that is not only false but profoundly repugnant. A chasm separates them from my imagined villagers or from the marginalized members of today's affluent societies— people who say "life's all about having a bit of fun," but add "with me mates."[39]

⸺◈⸺

The appeal of the liberal approach lies in its clear recognition of the value of autonomous choice. People should not have the patterns of their lives thrust upon them. Rejecting that type of imposition, whether it comes in the form of a caste system or through the denial of opportunities to women, ethnic minorities, supposed "deviants," or the poor, has been central to my efforts to clarify the concept of personal fulfillment. Individuals are fulfilled through lives that successfully realize life plans they have freely chosen.

---

[37] Thus I take the discussion of communal hedonism to provide a concrete exemplar for the considerations about trans-temporal egalitarianism offered in my earlier discussion of objective list approaches. See above, 95. We should avoid the trap into which Mill falls when he dismisses the forms of existence available to most past members of our species as "puerile."

[38] Communal hedonism requires that the pleasures and ameliorations of suffering recognized as worthwhile be generated through interactions among the participants. A communal Orgasmatron, in which bliss-seekers climaxed side by side, would be little better than the original solitary version. For a more realistic example, I take it to be a reasonable concern of parents, when they regard "shared internet video games" as a second-rate pleasure, when the activity simply consists in separate exchanges with a website. Moreover, with respect both to the Orgasmatron and the video games, one might wonder if the experiences craved and delivered actually undermine the ability to relate to others. (Thanks to Natalia Rogach Alexander for questions that prompted these observations.)

[39] Much depends, however, on the extent of the agents' contributions to the shared enjoyments. Between the creative activities of my imagined medieval villagers and the passivity of a group of drinking companions glued to a mindless television program there is a spectrum of cases. The village festival is less impressive if it simply repeats routines devised for past occasions; the conviviality is improved if Oscar Wilde or Dorothy Parker are of the party, and if others make similar, or complementary, contributions. Thanks to Meira Levinson for prompting me to clarify this point.

102   THE MAIN ENTERPRISE OF THE WORLD

As I already suggested in Chapter 1, the most evident (and most frequently discussed) difficulty of the liberal approach lies in its easygoing attitude toward potential life plans. Many ways in which people could pass their days seem trivial and worthless. The fanatical grass-counter is only one among a vast array of imaginary characters whose pursuits would be a complete waste of a human lifespan. The obvious response to the difficulty would be to add further constraints, requiring the chosen project to aim at realizing specified values. Conceiving those who live well as choosing combinations from a menu of objective goods is a plausible suggestion for remedying the apparent slackness of liberalism.[40] There are other possibilities: perhaps the right constraints are derived from subjective attitudes of the individual, rather than from some supposedly objective values.[41]

My Deweyan proposal—to see life projects as contributions to the lives of others, or, more cosmically, as incremental additions to the human project—might well be framed as an extension of liberalism. Mill offered two conditions on living well. At the center of a fulfilled life must be a freely chosen project (the *Autonomy* Condition); the life must realize enough of the aims demarcated by that project (the *Success* Condition). Apparently I have added a third: the *Community* condition, insisting on positive impact on the lives of others.

To frame things in that way would be to misread Dewey—and to mistake my own intentions.[42] Once the importance of connections to others is fully appreciated, the strangeness of Mill's individualist abstractions becomes evident. Mill removes individuals from their ambient societies, placing them in a space where they can supposedly choose freely what matters most to them.[43] How is this autonomous choice to be understood? As a banal matter of fact, human beings do not spring into the world, equipped with preferences and ideals that can guide their selection of life plans. The horizon bounding their inclinations is set by the possibilities made available by their social milieux. Although they may seek to expand the boundaries, they will inevitably do so

[40] This is the compromise view I attributed to Nussbaum and Brighouse. See n 28 above, 94. Some liberals might propose further that the combination must be novel in order to reflect the creativity or individuality of the subject. It seems to me possible, however, that people might recognize some previously explored pattern for a life as exactly fitting their own talents and predilections.

[41] For an imaginative and careful development of this approach see Susan Wolf, *Meaning in Life and Why It Matters*.

[42] I am grateful to Richard Bernstein, Jay Bernstein, Axel Honneth, and Rahel Jaeggi for forceful criticisms that have led me to be far more explicit about this point.

[43] In fairness to Mill, he does try at times to reintroduce the importance of our connection to others. See OL 70.

FULFILLMENT   103

by beginning from the options they come initially to understand. Moreover, that understanding emerges from their socialization.[44] *The direction of their inclinations is set by the education they receive.* Where, in all this, does the liberal's cherished autonomy fit?

The question strikes at least as deeply as the more familiar concerns about limiting the scope of plans of life, so as to exclude those striking us as worthless. To answer it, we need a more realistic picture of the individual than that enshrined in Mill's influential idealization. The thought of the self as outside (above? prior to?) society must give way to a conception that honors its social constitution.

Late in *Democracy and Education*, Dewey signals his departure from liberal conceptions of the individual by reviewing some mundane facts:

> As matter of fact every individual has grown up, and always must grow up, in a social medium. His responses grow intelligent, or gain meaning, simply because he lives in a world of shared meanings and values. . . . Through social intercourse, through sharing in the activities embodying beliefs, he gradually acquires a mind of his own. The conception of mind as a purely isolated possession of the self is at the very antipodes of the truth.[45]

Crucial to Dewey's social philosophy, however, is the thought that the "world of shared meanings and values" can be reformed, that the ideas and actions of individuals, on their own or in combination with others, can replace existing arrangements with something better, that progress is possible.[46]

Where we start from is not—should not be—where we end. For Dewey, the most important philosophical problem about mind (or minds) concerns how a socially formed mind can critically examine, and then improve, the society that has formed it.[47] His official answer to the question views proper education as directed at "growth," conceived as a process in which the individual

[44] For a clear attempt to show how children's autonomy is to be promoted, while taking account of the profound effects upon them of the background culture, see Harvey Siegel, "'Radical' Pedagogy requires 'Conservative' Epistemology," *Journal of Philosophy of Education* 29 (1995): 33–46.

[45] MW 9, 304.

[46] Most eloquently expressed in the passage I have cited from *A Common Faith*. See above, 40.

[47] When *Experience and Nature* takes up problems connected with our mental lives, the first concern (Chapter 6) is to understand how mind can be "an agency of novel reconstruction of a preexistent order" (LW 1, 168). The mind-body problem, so central to Anglophone philosophy during the past century, is deferred to Chapter 7.

104 THE MAIN ENTERPRISE OF THE WORLD

becomes better equipped to address the challenges and problems inevitably arising in the course of experience.[48] Rather than trying to center an account of personal fulfillment on the (murky) concept of growth, I'll build on the commonplace facts Dewey cites in support of thinking of the self as social.[49]

Grammar sometimes restricts philosophical options. Beguiled by the surface features of a way of talking, people acquire a picture that "holds them captive."[50] So it is, with our use of the noun "mind." If minds are things that young children develop—that is, come to possess—their young lives divide into two periods. Initially, they don't yet have minds; there is no individual self. Later, when the individual self has arrived, they have minds. Yet development is apparently a continuous process, raising embarrassing questions about the moment at which the mind pops into being. One way to avoid embarrassment is to suppose that something like a mind is there from the start. Some embryonic version of the self is present from the moment of birth—or, perhaps, from conception?—growing continuously into the full-fledged mind.

That picture lends itself to a particular view of education. Genuine education is a "leading out" of the self, a process in which the embryonic form is preserved and allowed to grow undistorted. True education, Nietzsche tells us, is a kind of freeing: the seeds of the mature individual are permitted to grow, protected from the weeds, rubbish, and pests that would interfere with their development.[51] When education is properly conducted, we become who we are, finding a life plan that suits us. We discover our individual way of being, and, in following our chosen path (with some success), we are fulfilled.

There is surely something right about the picture. It points to a genuine danger in socialization, to the possibility of distortion, mutilation, alienation. The difficulty that arises, however, concerns how to make sense of this threat. For to talk in terms of distortion seems to presuppose something already present in advance of education, something whose nature does not conform to

---

[48] Problems are often seen as disruptions of a prior equilibrium, and they are overcome by return to equilibrium (although possibly a different equilibrium state). The capacity for addressing challenges more adequately is sometimes tied to an increase in rich and satisfying ("consummatory") experience. I shall not try to probe the difficult issues raised by Dewey's account of growth. By far the best account of which I am aware is that offered by Natalia Rogach Alexander in currently unpublished work.

[49] Dewey's acceptance of the self as social surely descended from his early Hegelianism. By the time he wrote *Democracy and Education*, Darwin had replaced Hegel as his favorite historicist. I shall follow him in his turn to biology.

[50] Ludwig Wittgenstein, *Philosophical Investigations*, 115.

[51] "Schopenhauer as Educator," in *Untimely Meditations*. The early pages of Rousseau's *Émile* present a similar picture.

FULFILLMENT   105

what emerges in the end. Are we compelled to assume the existence of something like a self within the infant, so that the features of this prior entity are preserved and enhanced through a proper educational process or twisted and damaged if socialization goes badly?[52]

Issues about the emergence of mind (or self), whether they arise as phylogenetic or ontogenetic questions, call out for gradualistic treatment. Anyone who studies the history of life should suspect supposedly sharp boundaries. Embarrassment about where to draw lines can be dissolved by abandoning nouns and thinking in terms of adjectives: don't ask when life begins, but focus on the gradual acquisition of the features of living things; don't ask for the boundary between reptiles and mammals, concentrate on tracing the emergence of mammalian traits; don't ask at what stage animals gain minds, but look for the continuous accumulation of the properties associated with mentality.[53] Although ontogeny does not recapitulate phylogeny (as Haeckel mistakenly thought),[54] strategies for coping with general phylogenetic difficulties can be transferred to their ontogenetic relatives. So, I propose, we should think of human development, from the zygote to the adult, as a process in which the properties initially present—physical, chemical, and biological traits—are gradually supplemented with psychological capacities and dispositions, until the set of such features is so rich that we take a mind (or a self) to have been formed.

We think of education—including preschool care, schooling, and (for some) university studies—as playing an important role in this process. Perhaps we should expand the time scale, looking both backward and forward. For the self continues to grow, as Dewey saw, beyond the stage at which schooling ends. Growth also occurs in contexts outside those of formal education. Indeed, we might consider the education of the very young through their interactions with the environments of the crib, the home, and the wider worlds toddlers begin to explore.[55] Maybe we should go even further,

[52] In her important book, *Alienation* (New York: Columbia University Press, 2014), Rahel Jaeggi offers a subtle response to this problem. Although I take a different approach, I have learned much from her discussion.

[53] Dewey's sensible exploration of the relations among the inorganic world, the animate realm, and the beings whom we credit with psychological lives pursues the strategy I endorse here. See *Experience and Nature* (LW, 1) Chapter 7.

[54] See Stephen Jay Gould, *Ontogeny and Phylogeny* (Cambridge, MA: Harvard University Press, 1977).

[55] Some of the writings of Alison Gopnik suggest a conception of this kind. See *The Scientist in the Crib*, co-authored with Andrew Meltzhoff and Patricia Kuhl (New York: William Morrow, 1999) and *The Gardener and the Carpenter* (New York: Farrar, Straus & Giroux, 2016).

106   THE MAIN ENTERPRISE OF THE WORLD

conceiving the ways in which interventions can modify the intrauterine environment as the first potential applications of educational policies. Education would then begin in the womb.

The picture just outlined can be developed to contrast the education through which the self comes to be (drawing out the self in the way Nietzsche emphasizes) from the miseducation that distorts, mutilates, and alienates. Think of education in its most expansive form as a dialogue between the growing organism and the ambient society. Education goes properly when the representatives of society and the institutions within which they work are attentive to the features of the individual, responding to the directions in which they point.[56] By contrast, the educational dialogue goes badly when society fails to listen, insisting on leading in a particular direction whatever signals the developing organism might send.

The idea of a dialogue is, of course, a metaphor. But it is not hard to extend it to offer concrete advice. Even at early stages of a child's life, attentive caregivers can detect properties and tendencies. Some of these, of course, have to be shaped and molded so that the individual-in-the-making will be able to live in community with others. Already, there are dangers of forcing and distortion. Assumptions about the requirements for social life, born of narrow views about what people and societies ought to be, easily constrain future possibilities. Healthy dialogue between society and individual should recognize that current conventions are not the last word. Preparation for moral sensitivity and for relationships with others is essential. Rigid conformity to traditional precepts is not.[57]

For the moment, however, my principal concern is not with the cultivation of moral agency. Instead, I hope to capture the insight in Nietzsche's picture of education as a kind of liberation, while separating his individualism from the elitism that so often infects it.[58] Fostering the moral development

---

[56] Here I echo points lucidly presented in a classic article by Joel Feinberg, "The Child's Right to an Open Future," in Philosophy of Education, ed. Randall Curren (Oxford: Blackwell, 2007), 112–23. As Feinberg's title suggests, he is most concerned with defending against social pressures that would close off opportunities for children—and, in particular, with parents who wish to bring up their children as members of a religious/cultural community. Besides concurring in this point, I also want to emphasize the child's right to a sensitive audience, that is, to a process in which the options presented will be shaped by careful observation of whatever individual tendencies are developing. In the final section of his article (120–23), Feinberg goes in this direction. I suspect I want to go further than he did.

[57] For more on moral education, see Chapter 5, below.

[58] Despite his occasional remarks about the "nonage" of societies and of individuals, Mill typically offers an account of individuality that is free of elitism. Chapter III of On Liberty is exemplary.

FULFILLMENT 107

of individuals is compatible with many potential paths for them to follow.[59] Properly conducted education would guide people to paths that are—in some sense—genuinely their own. It should acquaint them with possibilities that suit them, and prepare them for autonomous selection. They come to see plans of life that resonate with who they are, and the choices they then make are their own.

How does that occur? Through the ways in which those who interact with individuals—with babies, young children, adolescents, and adults of any age—detect the properties of those others, constructing a picture of the predilections, talents, and interests that are emerging. Attentive caregivers spot embryonic tastes, helping their charges to explore them more fully.[60] Long before a child can be credited with a clear sense of self, sympathetic and sensitive observation of distinctive patterns of behavior allows identification of activities that seem likely to prove interesting. Opportunities are offered, not on the basis of what society supposes appropriate for children of that age and sex, but rather because they seem attuned to the ways that individual child is developing. Nothing is forced. Educators listen closely to the particular voice, trying to follow its individual music, and to help it express its own song.

Surely there is much we don't know about how to pursue the healthy dialogues I envisage. Even the most sensitive parents, teachers, and caregivers will likely recall occasions on which they failed to discern the directions indicated by children's behavior. It would be wrong, however, to conclude that the project of attending and responding is hopeless. Across all the contexts in which education is pursued the variation is enormous. Any review of that variation along the dimensions pertinent to the unforced development of the individual will disclose clear contrasts. Some regimes are highly coercive, imposing preordained patterns on human lives. Others attend to individuality, opening up opportunities and fostering choice. Of course, there are

[59] The late Nietzsche might claim that there are no moral constraints at all. My idea of a legitimate social shaping of a moral agent would be seen as an illegitimate invasion of individuality. Although that verdict does not emerge in the *Untimely Meditations*, both *Beyond Good and Evil* and the *Genealogy of Morality* can be interpreted as offering it.

[60] Of course, those caregivers will bring to the situation antecedent conceptions acquired from the ambient culture. Consequently, there is a real danger of their imposing limitations born of prevalent prejudices and stereotypes. The program I envisage must be attuned to this possibility, and that will require the kinds of more extensive social change discussed in Chapter 10. Although awareness of the problem, and resultant efforts to remedy it, are unlikely to eradicate prejudices completely, it is, I suggest, reasonable to hope for piecemeal progress in these respects. Thanks to Meira Levinson for prodding me to acknowledge these difficulties.

108   THE MAIN ENTERPRISE OF THE WORLD

many comparisons about which it is hard to decide. Often, there are genuine doubts about whether responding to individuality would better be served by leading in a particular direction or by stepping back. The message of my Deweyan meliorism is that we should build on the clear cases, and look for further evidence to decide what to do when the comparisons prove difficult.

Mill took autonomous choice of life plan to be central to the good life. On the account I have offered, autonomy is a matter of degree. It is not a property accruing to individuals who are launched into some space outside of (or above?) society. Rather the extent of someone's autonomy is the result of developmental processes in which society is profoundly implicated.[61] The choices we see as autonomous are made possible because our prior socialization has provided opportunities that attentive interlocutors have seen as attuned to the individual features of a person's behavior.[62] Those interlocutors have drawn out embryonic features and instilled capacities for reflective choice. Although they have shaped the self that chooses, they have, nonetheless, cultivated a degree of autonomy . . .

————

. . . and thereby made possible selection of a life plan that will continue the individual's dialogue with the ambient society. For each of us, in our time, plays both parts. As we have received from the fostering of others, so too we grow into beings capable of providing opportunities in our turn. *How* that is done depends on our particular choices, on the project(s) we select and the activities and values they mark out as central.

Life plans satisfying the Community condition are, of course, diverse. A fundamental division is evident in the heterogeneous connections through which some lives make positive impact on others. *Face-to-face* communities contrast with *anonymous* communities. The former connect people who know one another, paradigmatically those who live as neighbors, engaging in frequent interactions. Technology broadens the possibilities. Members of a face-to-face community can be scattered across the globe. They may never find themselves in the same place at the same time. Crucially, however,

---

[61] Here I take myself to be in tune with important voices in contemporary philosophy of education—for example, Brighouse, Curren, and Levinson.

[62] To emphasize sensitivity to the individual is not to conclude that education must be thoroughly individualized. There will often be room for shared curriculum, for common experiences, perhaps to offer the same good to each individual child, possibly to confer distinctive goods on each of them. Thanks again to Meira Levinson for encouraging me to be more explicit here.

each member has the goal of contributing to the lives of identifiable other members.

Valuable lives can also be centered on projects whose goals are to benefit members of an anonymous community. Imagine a recluse who withdraws from all human society to produce something intended to benefit unknown future people. Solitude is to provide the occasion for writing a great epic or for articulating a better code of law or for fathoming some aspect of the physical world or for mapping an area of wilderness so that future generations may be able to appreciate its beauties. Many of the largest and most ambitious projects—the ones that inspire elitists—seem focused on an anonymous community, one that will have members in a distant future (and possibly have *only* such members). Unlike Mill's ascetic, people who choose and pursue projects of this kind can live valuable lives because, despite the lack of a personal link to intended beneficiaries, a different type of human connection remains.[63]

Of course, almost all of those whose central projects aim to improve the lives of members of an anonymous community do not withdraw completely from human society. Typically, they have families, friends, and neighbors, and their projects include goals with a face-to-face dimension. The ambitious novelist or composer hopes to advance the life of a spouse or a lover or a child or a friend—as well as creating something "for the ages." All too often, however, the goals conflict.[64] Far from promoting the lives linked by personal connections, the actions taken to benefit the anonymous community distort, limit, reduce, and even devastate the lives of those for whom the great man claims to care. The lives of Richard Wagner, Thomas Mann, and James Joyce all reveal this pattern,[65] raising hard questions about how to assess their overall worth. Are the forced sacrifices of those who made extraordinary accomplishments possible redeemed by the greatness of what was achieved? Are the lives of the "little people" themselves rendered valuable because the

---

[63] It is even possible for the recluse to resent the contemporary population, and misanthropy to pervade all interactions with others. Lives can be directed toward future people who are imagined as more worthy than the debased denizens of the present. Thanks to Harvey Siegel for a question that has helped me to be more explicit about this point.

[64] These conflicts are often generated by the ways in which social institutions have evolved. Apparently progressive steps in particular domains of human life yield a composite picture that binds some groups of people. This is, I think, most evident in the ways in which purely economic progress locks people in to specific roles, thereby depriving them of opportunities to pursue their most cherished ends. An important part of social policy should be aimed at detecting this "institutional friction" and removing it. Part III attempts to respond to some specific instances of the trouble.

[65] As I have become acutely aware in my studies of these great artists. See, in particular, *Deaths in Venice*, 114–21.

110   THE MAIN ENTERPRISE OF THE WORLD

genius has made so large a mark on human history—and does that enormous contribution vindicate everything? ·

Questions like these are consequences of the measures taken to free the idea of the fulfilling life from elitism. The best answer to Socrates' question, I propose, adopts three constraints on living well: the Autonomy Condition, the Success Condition, and the Community Condition. It recognizes two main ways of attempting to satisfy the Community Condition, corresponding to the division between face-to-face and anonymous communities. Appreciating the many humble ways in which the human project can be locally advanced, it asks whether apparent local disruptions—collateral damage?—can be compensated by the grandeur of what is achieved on a historical scale. Thus the parade of cases of lives that go well, those of the most famous figures in human history, become subjected to critical scrutiny. Is heroism thus subordinated to mediocrity?

I reply: raising such concerns does not impugn the credentials of anti-elitism. Rather, it shows how the Socratic question has typically been addressed in the wrong way. Socrates asked a *practical* question, one looking to the future, not to the past.[66] What is to be made of Wagner or Mann or Joyce is a secondary issue. The point is to improve the prospects of individual lives and of human societies.[67] Our aim should be to facilitate *greater fulfillment*. To achieve that, education in its broadest sense is central. For the education provided, from the cradle to the grave, should be sensitive to the distinctive traits of the individual; it should guide the nascent person toward projects apt for the identifiable inclinations; it should set in place capacities for self-understanding and reflective choice; and, as the decision(s) are made, it should provide support in pursuing the goals the individual has set.

To view the task of education in this way raises important questions about our practices and the background institutions in which they are embedded. Do our programs of early care and training foster enough autonomy, so that the eventual choice of central project—whether made tacitly or explicitly—is

---

[66] In consequence, the standards of appraisal are sensitive to details of context. We ask, for example, how people in circumstances framed by particular social or technological possibilities might live better than we do, and realistic answers must hold fixed things that cannot be changed (or changed sufficiently rapidly to help them). Yet we might also take a longer view, considering ways in which structural conditions affecting their lives might be amended.

[67] As Natalia Rogach Alexander suggested to me, our aim is to nurture the great figures—the Wagners, Manns, and Joyces—while avoiding the "collateral damage." Nietzsche's supposed opposition between a world in which heroes thrive at the expense of "the herd" and a condition of pleasant mediocrity should not be viewed as a forced choice.

autonomous *enough*? Do we provide *enough* in the way of subsequent support and guidance? Are people prepared to forge *enough* positive connections to the lives of others? All three of my conditions involve matters of degree, without specifying any appropriate threshold or even any perfect realization.

Consider autonomy. The condition is motivated by understanding the *lack* of choice in human history. Many of the cultures we know, in the present as well as in the past, formulate and rigorously apply rules assigning individuals to particular roles. Confinement of choice is most evident when the processes of placement focus on sex or race or class or caste. Is autonomy automatically present when those kinds of assignments are abandoned? Surely not. An all-too-familiar feature of the contemporary world is the frequency with which young people, especially but not exclusively the poor, have little opportunity to explore options for their lives and to fathom their own capacities and talents. Although they are formally free, to count them as autonomous in the pertinent sense would embody an insensitive view of their predicaments. Education, within and outside the formal structures of the schools, should open up alternative avenues and offer occasions for discovering which of them might reward the student's further explorations. How deeply should the educational system probe to allow each pupil to learn her distinctive capacities and limitations? How broad should the range of choices be?

With respect to such questions, *comparative* answers are available. Conceiving the educational process in one way, rather than in another, would enable the young to see more clearly what activities best reward their efforts. Introducing a particular modification of the process would increase the range of options for their consideration. But comparative analysis fails both to identify a minimal level or to yield a clear grasp of any optimum. The idea of sufficient autonomy remains unspecified, and the idea of *perfect* autonomy proves elusive. Would the latter involve apprehending all the "experiments of living" human beings might try out? Or all those history has actually witnessed? Is there a point at which the number of options proves overwhelming? In fostering self-understanding, is complete clarity always a virtue? If we think that Socrates' question demands a general theory of the good life, these issues have to be settled. A healthy emphasis on the importance of autonomy is transmogrified into the vain pursuit of an ideal. But my comparative question—How to make lives go better?—avoids the irrelevant commitments. Understanding how some people are much less autonomous than others in choosing the patterns of their lives provides a direction for advancing our approach to education (and, more generally, the human

112   THE MAIN ENTERPRISE OF THE WORLD

project to which it is central). Progress can be made by attempting to remedy a particular feature of the current situation. Discussions of fulfillment aim to provide tools that help us see where lives are *not* going well, and to develop strategies for making those lives go better.

Exactly the same considerations apply to the other two conditions. It is hard to formulate criteria for success in pursuing the goals demarcated by the central project. Even assuming the possibility of drawing up a finite list of the ends pursued, it would be necessary to assign measures of their relative importance, and to decide how the attainment of a smaller number of more significant ends ranks against fulfillment of a larger number of less significant goals. Nor is it realistic to suppose that here we can at least discover a maximum, by thinking of complete success. As already noted, central projects evolve over time, and the goals reached at one stage give rise to new endeavors and new aims. Because life plans are open-ended, the thought of a finite list of ends to be reached is suspect. Consequently, once again, the idea of perfect success proves elusive. Comparisons, however, are available. The success with which people pursue what matters most to them varies. Recognizing the Success Condition should prompt attention to situations in which many people encounter large obstacles in pursuing their goals. It directs us to explore ways of removing those obstacles, and thus enabling human lives to go better.

With respect to the community condition, the difficulties of going beyond comparative judgment are even more severe. For, as I have suggested, community with others may be expressed in very different ways. The notion of community is *multidimensional*. Relations of counsel and mutual support mark out one dimension, participation in common endeavors points to a second, sustaining a set of values or a cultural repertoire indicates a third— and there are others besides. Along each dimension, the strength of the commitments, measured by the frequency and the intensity of the contributory efforts, varies. To the extent to which it is possible to recognize an ideal of other-directedness—exemplified in the conduct of altruists who make the maximum possible effort to contribute to the lives of others—it splits into a large set of candidates that mix commitments on the various dimensions. The counselor, the nurse, the healer, the builder, the judge, and the teacher— as well as the parent, the sibling, and the friend—represent types of other-directedness. Other-directed people typically play several of these roles throughout their lives. Is there an optimal balance at which these altruists should be aiming?

FULFILLMENT 113

Again, comparative judgments are well-grounded.[68] Contemplating the hard-driving entrepreneur, interested solely in greater economic profits, and the dedicated doctor, who spends extra hours with patients and who willingly risks serious infection, few people find it difficult to decide which of them is more pro-social. Comparisons across domains of activity, however, often seem intractable. Moreover, even in considering possible modifications of conduct, perplexities arise. What is "maximum effort" for the doctor? Does it involve taking more risks or less, postponing sleep yet again or allowing time for recuperation?

These are hard questions. Others emerge when the three conditions are considered together. Historically, societies valuing close community relations have tended to offer more support for the projects pursued by their members, but also to restrict, sometimes quite dramatically, the options available for pursuit.[69] Increasing the intensity of community seems likely to generate higher degrees of success but lower degrees of autonomy. Once again, a general answer to Socrates' question would have to explain how the proper balance is struck. By contrast, my proposals about fulfillment are meant to translate into practical questions. How should our educational practices be modified to improve along the dimensions where they seem to be lacking, without sacrificing too much of what we are doing well? A comparative approach doesn't aim at utopia. It hopes to offer tools for making progress.

This chapter has attempted to buttress the specific suggestions offered in its predecessor. Perhaps my recommendation to increase—even dramatically—the number of adults who interact with young children in the preschool environment or in the elementary school classroom appeared odd and unmotivated. Behind it stands the idea of cultivating individuality and autonomy, of improving the delicate dialogue between the nascent person and the surrounding society. If little children observe, and are observed by, gentle and supportive adults, people who differ widely in the ways they have sought (and found) their own fulfillment, the chances of recognizing the incipient

---

[68] Or, at least, they can be. For an account of how justified value judgments might be made, see *Moral Progress*, and the much briefer account provided in Chapter 5, below.

[69] I suspect this comes about because "thick" community, emphasizing connections of a number of distinct kinds, is taken to require a greater degree of agreement. Consequently, possible experiments of living that would diverge from the consensus are excluded, and the range of available options contracts.

114   THE MAIN ENTERPRISE OF THE WORLD

inclinations and of acting to develop them further are likely to be increased.[70] Judgments about a child's talents and predilections are no longer made by a single—overtaxed—teacher, but by a group that adds its counsel to the professional expertise of a team of teachers.[71] There are, of course, many possibilities for setting up a program of this kind. A background approach to fulfillment helps diagnose where the current implementation is problematic, and offer a standard for making progress.

A permeable boundary between the educational environment and the adult world is also valuable in other ways. Those who have found satisfaction in some particular way of living can find further fulfillment in sharing their perspective with others. The lives of the elderly, even of the middle-aged, are sometimes rejuvenated when what they have cherished in their own existences strikes a resonant chord in a much younger person. That kind of encounter can be significant for both. Perhaps we may look forward to the day when such meetings of the mind are no longer left to chance—when someone for whom the contours of life are firmly set receives a message from a teacher in the local school: "There's a student here whom I think you'd enjoy talking to, and who would benefit from a conversation with you." And, of course, when the predictions are strikingly fulfilled.

Before he wrote the *Wealth of Nations*, Adam Smith authored a widely read book on the moral sentiments.[72] In a passage that should surprise those who think of him solely as a champion of rapacious capitalism, he considered the value of worldly success: "If the chief part of human happiness arises from the consciousness of being beloved, as I believe it does, those sudden changes of fortune seldom contribute much to happiness."[73] That holds, Smith believed, insofar as we count ourselves worthy of the love we receive. Thus, he moved towards the thought Emily Dickinson adds at the close of her meditation on what matters, made clear in the moment of dying:

---

[70] But, as noted above (n.59), it will be important that those who engage in the delicate dialogue don't bring to it prevalent prejudices and stereotypes. To prevent that, it may not only be necessary to address directly the biases that can easily be noted, but also to seek out deeper structural features of the society from which they readily emerge. Chapter 10 begins the process of considering how to carry out the broader social changes required.

[71] For this to be profitable, adults who participate in the classroom (ideally, *all* adults) may themselves require some pedagogical training. I shall take up this issue in Chapter 10. Thanks to Dan O'Flaherty for pressing me on the point.

[72] *The Theory of Moral Sentiments* (Indianapolis: Liberty Fund, 1984). Six editions appeared in Smith's lifetime.

[73] Ibid., 41 (Book I, Part ii, Chapter 5). See also 113 (III.ii.1) and 181–85 (IV.i).

> Mine be the Ministry
> When thy Thirst comes—
> Dews of Thessaly to fetch—
> And Hybla Balms—

Dickinson's test for fulfillment[74] emphasizes a reciprocity in relationships. So our title to being loved consists in what we have given. The dusty honors do not matter. Assurance that we have not lived in vain comes from the presence of friends and loved ones. Or, if they are not there, from the tokens and memories they have left us. From the lives that have mutually touched and thereby been changed.

---

[74] The test judges fulfillment by the reflective attitude of the dying. There is obvious kinship to ideas expressed by Tolstoy (*The Death of Ivan Ilyich*), as well as to the criterion for the good life offered by Schopenhauer and developed further by Nietzsche—that one would want to live the same life over again (*The World as Will and Representation*, 1, §§ 54, 59; *The Gay Science*, §341). To the best of my knowledge, Dickinson did not read Schopenhauer, and the formulations by Nietzsche and Tolstoy post-date the poem.

4

Citizens

In 1639, a small group of English Puritans sailed across the Atlantic, seeking to establish a colony where they could live according to their religious convictions. While still at sea, they drew up and signed an agreement to govern their envisaged community. Choosing (and appropriating) a tract of land on the northern shore of Long Island Sound, they settled just to the east of the already existing New Haven Colony. Over three and a half centuries later, the small Connecticut town of Guilford—the outgrowth of their efforts—decided to commemorate its founding by laying a stone slab on which are engraved the words of that original covenant. The first sentence reads:

> We whose names are hereunder written, intending by God's gracious permission to plant ourselves in New England, and as it may be, in the southerly part about Quinnipiack, we do faithfully promise each other, for ourselves and our families and those that belong to us, that we will, the Lord assisting us, sit down and join ourselves together in one entire plantation and to be helpful each to other in any common work, according to every man's ability and as need shall require, and we promise not to desert or leave each other or the plantation, but with the consent of the rest, or the greater part of the company who have entered into this engagement.

There follow the names of twenty-five men (the "heads" of the original households).[1]

Nearly two centuries after those early settlers signed the covenant with one another, Alexis de Tocqueville visited the new republic that had emerged from the original scatter of colonies, and took stock of democracy in America. He was particularly impressed by the town meetings of New England.[2] By the eighteenth century, all across the Northeastern states, in

---

[1] Interestingly, a significant number of the first settlers were unmarried. Some of the older men, including the leader, Henry Whitfield, eventually returned to England.

[2] See *Democracy in America*, Book I, Chapter V.

The Main Enterprise of the World. Philip Kitcher, Oxford University Press. © Oxford University Press 2022.
DOI: 10.1093/oso/9780190928971.003.0005

CITIZENS   117

towns like Guilford, people would come together to discuss the problems of their community. They would express their own perspectives, and listen to those of others. They would seek a solution all could accept—if only because, imbued with the spirit of some original covenant, they appreciated the importance of working together.

Those who "planted" themselves in the inhospitable New World appreciated the challenges they faced. Given the words of the original agreements, and Tocqueville's respect for the local projects in democracy he saw in New England, it is easy to find inspiration in imagining the lives of these communities. We picture all the adults assembling to discuss the difficulties of their situation, bound together in their shared religious convictions and in their sense of the need to face adversity with a single intention. Their deliberations are serious, mutually respectful, and inclusive. Each is concerned not to ride roughshod over the wishes of the neighbors. So, looking back into a misty history, we conjure a vision of the democracy Dewey characterized and advocated: "A democracy is more than a form of government; it is primarily a mode of associated living, of conjoint communicated experience."[3]

Perhaps that is the way things were in Guilford. Yet surely imagination smooths out the wrinkles and hides the blemishes—even the deformities— in those early exchanges.[4] Although it is reasonable to see the deliberations of New England communities as steps *toward* democracy, they fall lamentably short of its perfect expression.[5] Within a small group, perhaps only the male heads of households, cooperation was shaped by discussions among acknowledged equals. Even many local people received lesser status—the women, the young, the indentured servants, and (of course) eventually the slaves.[6] Where joint action with other communities was required, propertied men from other settlements may have had some standing. In many instances, however, outsiders were ignored—beginning, of course, with the indigenous inhabitants of the land, whose previous use of it was casually and callously disregarded.[7]

---

[3] Dewey, MW 9, 93.

[4] The fact that the covenant was signed only by the "heads" of the households ought to raise doubts about whether the women of the community were able to participate on equal terms. We should also wonder about the representation of children's interests.

[5] Thanks to Meira Levinson and Martha Nussbaum for excellent comments that have prompted me to be much more explicit on this point.

[6] It's worth noting an ominous phrase in the sentence I have quoted: "those that belong to us."

[7] As Martha Nussbaum pointed out to me, the unscrupulous seizure of land carried out in Guilford (and other parts of Connecticut) contrasts with the more humane conduct of Roger Williams in Rhode Island.

118   THE MAIN ENTERPRISE OF THE WORLD

What this covenant does reveal is small-scale democracy, accompanied by thoughtless dismissal of any thoughts of applying democratic ideals more broadly. Contemporary societies inherit the failure to scale up—our acute difficulties in facing global challenges stem from a myopic nationalism that mirrors the shortcomings of the Guilford community.[8] Yet we appear to have lost something the New England settlements, for all their severe flaws, achieved—the capacity for a kind of constructive deliberation Tocqueville identified as the core of the American democratic experiment. Today's political systems, even those apparently most deserving the honored title of "Democracy," are riven by disagreements, many of them acrimonious. Even if past communities could conform more closely to Dewey's hopeful description, it is hard to view their customs as pertinent to ourselves. Their lives were pervaded by strong shared religious commitments, and they faced obvious dangers if they failed to stand together. Contemporary societies are diverse and cannot recognize any similar common threat.[9] The supposed model citizens of early New England never existed—and they are a utopian fantasy for the world of today.

All perfectly reasonable as a cautionary reminder. Nevertheless, one of the principal tasks of education is to create—or re-create—the best approximation we can to such citizens.

———————

Democracy is often hailed as the best form of government—or, at least, in a phrase commonly attributed to Winston Churchill,[10] the worst except for all the alternatives. In recent years, however, a significant number of scholars have warned that democracy is in trouble, or even that it is dying.[11] They express a clear sense that, in the contemporary world, democratic government attaining, or even approximating, the virtues typically cited in its favor, is hard, if not impossible, to achieve.

---

[8] This has been most evident in the bickering about climate change. See Philip Kitcher and Evelyn Fox Keller, *The Seasons Alter: How to Save our Planet in Six Acts* (New York: Norton/Liveright, 2017), especially Chapter 6.

[9] As Evelyn Fox Keller and I have argued (*The Seasons Alter*, Chapter 6), humanity today does face a common threat, posed by the changing climate. Even though significant numbers of people, especially young people, recognize the peril, many do not.

[10] Churchill actually alluded to an unidentified source: "it has been said that democracy is the worst form of Government except for all those other forms that have been tried from time to time."

[11] See, for example, Steven Levitsky and Daniel Ziblatt, *How Democracies Die* (New York: Penguin, 2018); David Runciman, *How Democracy Ends* (London: Profile Books, 2018); Susan Jacoby, *The Age of American Unreason in a Culture of Lies*, 2nd ed. (New York: Vintage, 2018). Magazine articles and newspaper editorials on the theme have appeared with great frequency during the past three years.

CITIZENS 119

The grounds for anxiety are quite diverse. Some of those who worry focus on the mechanics of voting. They identify irregularities in recording or tabulating votes, show how the boundaries of districts are cunningly drawn to serve the interests of a particular party, document the ways in which various sectors of the citizenry are disenfranchised or discouraged from going to the polls. Others diagnose a fundamental shortcoming in the ways in which the electorate can express choices; would-be reformers campaign for some system of preferential voting, such as the Condorcet scheme.[12] By and large, discussions along these lines are insightful, and the evils exposed are real.

A different type of concern focuses on the ways in which voters' choices are framed. Many observers lament the role wealth plays in contemporary politics. What shapes the list of candidates among whom the citizens can choose? What structures the cluster of issues around which campaigns are fought?[13] What governs the effectiveness with which a candidate can deliver a message? What influences the ability to ensure that supporters are brought to the voting booths? Money, money, money, and again, money.[14] Cash isn't omnipotent, of course. Enough relatively bare-bones candidacies do sufficiently well to foster the illusion that grass-roots activism can still make a significant difference. The regimes among which we live are still only *statistical* plutocracies: triumph for the interests of the wealthy is not *guaranteed*; the influx of funds merely increases the probability of success—but often decisively.

Yet another species of dissatisfaction stems from the clash between contemporary political life and the principal virtue ascribed to democracy. This system of government is supposed to enhance the freedom of the citizens. Many people view that idea as profoundly mistaken, as overlooking the stupidity of the masses. Natively unintelligent, citizens will select candidates and policies that frustrate their aims. Such hypotheses about the biological determinants of cognitive capacities are dubious: there are no grounds for

---

[12] The Condorcet voting method takes into account the second (third, fourth, etc.) choices of voters. For a clear and precise explanation, see the entry on "Voting Methods" in the *Stanford Encyclopedia of Philosophy*, https://plato.stanford.edu/entries/voting-methods/.

[13] For a magisterial discussion of the virtues and the difficulties of democracy, see Robert Dahl, *On Democracy* (New Haven: Yale University Press, 1998).

[14] The influence of money on American politics has been exacerbated in recent times by two consequential Supreme Court decisions: *Citizens United v. FEC* and the less well-known *McCutcheon v. FEC*. Much debate has swirled around the issue of whether corporations should be favored as "persons" with a right to free speech. Far less attention has been given to the obvious point that air time in presenting ideas is limited, and that allowing indefinite spending by the wealthy crowds out many voices. Thus these decisions, expanding as they do the rights of the wealthy, actually diminish the rights of many citizens. As George Orwell might have noted, all American citizens have equal rights to speech, but some are more equal than others.

120 THE MAIN ENTERPRISE OF THE WORLD

conceiving the electorate as incapable of thinking through issues that bear on voters' interests. Nevertheless, ignorance can be as toxic as stupidity. When voters are deprived of opportunities to learn important facts affecting the consequences of proposed policies, they may troop to the polls and register votes that thwart what they most dearly hope to achieve. Defeating your own ends in the act that allegedly expresses your freedom is one of the bitterest ironies of what we continue to call "democracy." The poison is even more concentrated when the mismatch between preferences and interests results from a cynical campaign of misinformation and disinformation. When, for example, voters are advised not to trust the experts.[15]

Contemporary technology exacerbates the predicament. Idealistic enthusiasts sometimes hail the internet as facilitating democracy. "After all," they tell us, "access to the web is now available widely, giving everyone a voice." An older source of wisdom knew better. In *Henry IV, Part I*, Shakespeare's Owen Glendower announces his powers: "I can call spirits from the vasty deep." Hotspur punctures the boast with a pertinent reply: "Why, so can I, or so can any man;/But will they come, when you do call for them?"[16] Any of us, at any time, can launch words into the air or write on screen or paper. Whether anyone else will pay attention is an entirely different matter. What the internet provides is not a serious opportunity for previously unheard voices to broadcast their views, but for each of us to be confined in echo chambers by search algorithms that, in the commercial interests of unseen advertisers, attend to our prejudices and reinforce them.[17] And, of course, to thrill to the messages borne on bots launched by distant hackers.

These developments are among the causes of a political culture in which trust is eroded.[18] Millions of citizens feel marginalized, lost in a society in which nobody hears their complaints or attends to their needs. Although they do not appreciate the depth of the deception, they are intelligent enough to know that many of the political pronouncements—including those made by figures whom they support—are false. Words become political tools,

---

[15] As, for example, in Michael Gove's famous dismissal of concerns about the economic consequences of Brexit: "I think the people in this country have had enough of experts" (Interview with Sky news, June 3, 2016).

[16] *Henry IV, Part I*, Act 3, Scene 1, 52–54.

[17] As Nicola Mössner and I have argued: "Knowledge, Democracy, and the Internet," *Minerva* 55 (2017): 1–24.

[18] As Randy Curren pointed out to me, there are other factors. The forms of segregation found in online life have often been preceded by recurrent patterns of non-interaction offline (see the work of Levitsky and Ziblatt, referred to in n.11). Withdrawal from any form of civic engagement may also play a role.

spoken to reassure supporters and enrage opponents. All anyone can do is to gravitate to the political figure who seems most closely to approximate some understanding for one's predicament. Once the choice has been made, further support must be given, even when the leader appears to weaken or to demolish some of the traditional democratic institutions. For the alternative is to strengthen the wicked elites, bent as they are on maintaining a society in which the people, the *real* people, have no place.[19]

All the concerns mentioned in this brief review are genuine. All of them discern genuine threats to the health and survival of democracy. Nevertheless, as I have so far characterized them, none identifies the basic cause of democracy's demise. That, I suggest, is the loss of anything remotely resembling the Deweyan ideal. Without the local exchanges Tocqueville saw as the heart of American democracy, democracy at larger scales is undermined.

In what follows I shall try to make this clear by distinguishing three levels of democracy. *Shallow* democracy exists in any society where leaders are elected by the citizens, and where certain other minimal conditions are met: voters have a choice of candidates, they are subject neither to bribery nor coercion, and there are some possibilities of public debate. A deeper level of democracy requires mechanisms to produce an informed electorate, promoting capacities for identifying candidates likely to act in the interests of those who support them. Deeper still lies a level—Deweyan democracy—with institutions for fostering deliberation among people with differing perspectives,[20] and thus for arriving at policies all can tolerate. The health of democracy at any level, I shall argue, rests on the extent to which Deweyan democracy is realized. This conclusion sets the basic educational task. How are citizens to be prepared for Deweyan democracy?

---

[19] Here I follow the incisive analysis offered by Jan-Werner Müller in *What Is Populism?* (Philadelphia: University of Pennsylvania Press, 2016).

[20] Deweyan democracy is a species within what has become a broad genus. During the past thirty years, there has been an upsurge of interest in deliberative democracy, typically emphasizing either the "wisdom of crowds" or the value of assembling people to exchange reasons on disputed issues. Many of the sophisticated proposals owe a debt to the work of John Rawls, and make use of idealizations he made popular. For a sample of the diverse options, see Amy Gutmann and Dennis Thompson, *Democracy and Disagreement* (Cambridge MA: Harvard University Press, 1998), Jürgen Habermas, *Between Facts and Norms* (Cambridge, MA: MIT Press, 1996), Eamonn Callan, *Creating Citizens* (New York: Oxford University Press, 1997), and, for a thorough overview of the alternatives, Andre Bächtiger, John S. Dryzek, Jane Mansbridge, and Mark Warren, eds., *The Oxford Handbook of Deliberative Democracy* (New York: Oxford University Press, 2018).

122 THE MAIN ENTERPRISE OF THE WORLD

The first step will be to consider a simpler and apparently plausible diagnosis of the current troubles. What has gone wrong, it's proposed, is that voters are often misled—indeed, often systematically misled. The root problem is purely cognitive. Societies need better systems of education and better channels through which reliable information can be disseminated. So the would-be diagnostician will try to find ways of teaching the young and of repairing public fora, improving the quality of "free and open" debate, and thus creating (re-creating?) a citizenry whose electoral preferences align with their interests.

I shall argue that this promising suggestion will not do. Focusing on a concrete example, the difficulties of reaching agreement on policies to combat climate change, I'll review well-known obstacles to the proposal. Not only is it too slow, but we also lack any insights about either educating "omnicompetent" citizens[21] or improving the distribution of information to the masses. A much deeper deficiency lies in the need for people to become open to ideas and perspectives they initially view as uncongenial and even threatening. For that to occur, they must lose their sense of vulnerability, gaining confidence that their fellow citizens are committed to protecting them against serious losses. The ability to learn depends on the presence of interpersonal trust— on the affective conditions that small communities sometimes achieve and that today's divided societies have clearly lost.

In this light, Dewey's connection between democracy and education, in which democracy is seen as "a mode of associated living, of conjoint communicated experience,"[22] should no longer seem surprising. Four principal lines of reasoning underlie that linkage. First, as my critique of the popular diagnosis should make clear, enhanced cognitive capacities alone (even if they could be instilled) would not deliver what is required. Second, when the affective conditions are absent, democracies are likely to be dominated by a pathology—the "tyranny of voting"—tending to lead to their fragmentation or demise. Third, the conception of fulfillment developed in the previous chapter depends on the existence of such conditions. Fourth, and perhaps most importantly, the flourishing of democracy at small scales,

---

[21] The phrase stems from Walter Lippmann. See *The Phantom Public* (1927; repr., London: Routledge, 2017), 11. Chapter 2 of this book is a brilliant exposé of "the unattainable ideal" democracy seems to require. Much of the present chapter can be seen as my interpretation of the famous debate between Lippmann and Dewey.

[22] *Democracy and Education*, MW 9, 93.

within families and within some small communities, teaches the central role engagement with the perspectives of others plays.

The chapter will conclude by taking up three further tasks. First, I shall try to respond to concerns about the possibility of Deweyan democracy: specifically, is it too optimistic? Second, I shall elaborate the kinship between my favored version of deliberative democracy and the view of lives as fulfilled through contributions to the lives of others. Finally, I shall draw consequences for education, offering some further proposals, in this case directed toward citizenship, to extend and complement those already provided.

When the troubles of contemporary democracy are reviewed, it's easy to think that a simple explanation is at hand. The root of the trouble lies in the enormous spread of misinformation and the widespread ignorance it causes. Because so many facts are distorted, so many truths disputed, citizens lack any opportunity to identify the causes of their genuine troubles. Instead of condemning those who mislead and exploit them, they blame the wrong people. They gravitate to political candidates who care nothing for their interests, except insofar as the pretense of concern advances their own political ends. Resentment grows, and is misdirected. After sufficient dust has been thrown up, the superficial machinery of democracy can be arranged to suit the agenda of the wealthy. The boundaries of districts can be carefully redrawn, and measures introduced to discourage members of particular groups from voting. Large numbers of citizens applaud these developments, because they hear a story they find plausible. Reforms are needed to address the wicked plans of the forces of darkness, bent as they are on violating the fairness of elections.

The explanation is easily extended. During the twentieth century, technological developments changed the ways in which information was disseminated. Television news provided a substitute for newspapers. For workers, weary after a long day, keeping up with the world by watching and listening came to appear easier than reading long newspaper reports and complex analyses. As the idea that free markets work wonders grew in popularity, new media ventures sprang up. Cable news was born, free of "antiquated" journalistic constraints. In the fierce competition of the marketplace, selection favored those who could best entertain and reassure, while offering the illusion of providing information. Entrepreneurs quickly learned a good strategy. Find a target audience. Tell stories that appeal to people in a particular niche.

124 THE MAIN ENTERPRISE OF THE WORLD

Protect them from "facts" that might disturb their antecedent opinions and challenge their values. The populace easily became fragmented into tightly knit groups, bound by their loyalty to particular sources of information.[23] Alternative visions of the world flourished. Consensus on truth was no longer available. After the arrival of the internet, the whole process was accelerated and intensified.

Once a society has reached a state in which its citizens no longer agree on many important facts, in which those holding rival views are increasingly demonized, it is very hard to see how to go back. Older people, nostalgic for the days of Walter Cronkite or of the BBC, may imagine restoring some impeccable source of news. They envisage a newspaper or television channel or internet site that is universally acknowledged as fair: when the calm voice declares, "And that's the way it is," everyone assents.[24] But how is any voice to be anointed as authoritative? In a world of rival niches, each devoted to the deliverances of one (or some cluster) of the existing sources, any divergence from the favored views will be regarded as undermining the credibility of the supposedly "fair and balanced" alternative. What is hailed as the new BBC will be viewed, at least in some circles, as a revival of *Pravda*.[25]

If this is the diagnosis of what has gone wrong, how can democracy be revived? One of the clichés of social theory identifies appeals to education as a knee-jerk response to major social problems.[26] How should we address poverty or crime or teenage pregnancy or drug addiction or unemployment or . . .? Through education, of course! As might be expected, the habitual turn to adjusting education contributes further to educational overload. Yet, where the trouble arises from cognitive deficiencies, from citizens' inability to gain reliable information, the possibility of a remedy via educational reform seems more promising. Children need to be taught how to navigate in a treacherous informational environment. They must learn how to discern the helpful voices and to ignore the tempting songs of the sirens. Cultivating the ability to assess evidence and to think critically is crucial.[27]

---

[23] As noted above (n.18), tribal politics has other causes, in particular the patterns of non-interaction.

[24] Even during the Vietnam war, when Walter Cronkite ended his broadcast with "And that's the way it is" followed by the date (e.g., Monday, May 4, 1970), people with radically different political views took his word for it. As they went on to argue, they did so on the basis of factual agreement.

[25] In *Science in a Democratic Society* (Amherst, NY: Prometheus Books, 2011), especially Chapter 7, I have previously explored some of the troubles reviewed here, from the perspective of the simple explanation. It now seems to me that the root of the trouble lies deeper than I had supposed.

[26] A response I made in *Science in a Democratic Society*: see 187–92.

[27] Considerable attention has been given to how this might be achieved. See, for example, Harvey Siegel, *Educating Reason* (London: Routledge, 1988), and the useful recent survey by Robert Ennis

CITIZENS 125

Although the account I have sketched could be offered in far more nuanced forms, my brief review of a common response to democracy's troubles exposes the diagnosis it offers and the remedy it proposes. That will be enough to help us recognize how anything along these lines is incomplete. Without attending to the deeper breakdown of democracy, the loss of institutions enabling citizens who disagree, even profoundly, to deliberate together, the attempt to restore some common basis of belief will fail. So, at least, I shall try to show.

First, though, it's important to appreciate a real insight of the simple story. Whatever reasons there are for doubting the idea of a linear regressive history—Was there ever a golden age in which a single cadre of experts was completely trusted?—the account recognizes important factors affecting the abilities of people living at different times to acquire the beliefs they need to pursue their ends. The promise of democracy to enhance the freedom of citizens is violated when the preferences expressed in voting are at odds with the most cherished long-term goals those citizens have.

Harmony between votes and interests is supposed to be preserved through free speech and open debate. The ideal of free speech emerged from recognizing how limitations on liberty were imposed not only through constraints on action but also through mechanisms for shaping belief. Censorship deprives people of the opportunity to appreciate options that would otherwise be open to them. Furthermore, it allows arbitrary conventions to go unchallenged. To those who insist that tradition must be preserved to assure social stability, Milton already offered a classic defense of allowing the public clash of competing ideas. His *Areopagitica* explained how this works:

> And though all the winds of doctrine were let loose to play upon the earth, so Truth be in the field, we do injuriously by licensing and prohibiting to misdoubt her strength. Let her and Falsehood grapple; who ever knew Truth put to the worse, in a free and open encounter.[28]

and David Hitchcock, "Critical Thinking," in Stanford Encyclopedia of Philosophy, https://plato.stanford.edu/entries/critical-thinking/.

[28] *Areopagitica*, in *Milton's Prose: A Selection*, Oxford World's Classics (Oxford: Oxford University Press, 1963), 318–19.

126   THE MAIN ENTERPRISE OF THE WORLD

The theme of truth victorious would later be taken up by Mill and echoed by the readers of his influential essay.[29] But Milton saw something his successors would miss. The triumph of truth depends on particular—fragile—social conditions.

Conditions that have largely disappeared from the world we now inhabit. It is hard to think of the public discussions through which contemporary citizens are supposed to become enlightened about where their interests lie as "free and open encounters" in which Truth will become evident. In part, that results from the technicality of many of the issues on which voters have to decide. Milton and Mill can be forgiven for their optimism about public debate. The questions salient for them—whether to allow divorce or religious diversity, say—could be grasped without any specialized knowledge.[30] Yet this is far from being the only major difference between the circumstances of present exercises in "open debate" and the proceedings imagined by those who have advocated free speech. They envisaged a forum—I shall call it the *Millian arena*, in honor of its most famous champion—in which Truth might be expected to prevail. That arena possesses a number of properties. First, the issues discussed in it are those most pertinent to the aims and projects of the citizens. Second, for any of those issues, all the rival viewpoints are presented and defended. Third, each of the alternatives has adequate opportunity to criticize the claims made by others, and to respond to objections to its own proposals. Fourth, none of the rivals is given a disproportionately long or short period for exposition and defense. Fifth, there is a clear and impartial mechanism for identifying places at which the claims made are at odds with the best available information: fact-checking works! Sixth, in cases where the issues turn on complex technical matters, debate is always preceded by a thorough explanation of the concepts and of the currently supported factual claims. These six conditions combine in a charming Victorian vision. Scrupulously honest, courteous gentlemen in frock coats take their turns at the public microphone, retreating when they have had their say. Attractive though the picture may be, it is hardly the way we live now.

---

[29] OL Section II.

[30] A qualification is in order here. Even though the *questions* raised in the kinds of debates envisaged by the champions of free speech lie closer to everyday experience than many present controversies, that doesn't entail that the *arguments* offered to address those questions would only make use of familiar concepts and easily comprehensible theses. Complex theological ideas were often invoked in discussions of divorce and of religious freedom. Conversely, some contemporary issues—those surrounding the ability of citizens to obtain and carry guns, for example—pose no great demands in terms of technical vocabulary.

The insight of the simple story lies in its clear recognition that retaining the trappings of democracy, the machinery of votes and elections, is not enough. Shallow democracy exists wherever there are elections, protections against coercion of voters, typically several choices of candidates, and (some sort of) public debate of the issues. Shallow democracy has been applauded in images of new voters waving ink-stained fingers in the air. It can be found around the globe, although not in all the nations that advertise themselves as democracies.[31] Frequently it is corrupted through cunningly contrived ways of drawing the boundaries of electoral districts or by introducing measures to discourage certain types of voters from going to the polls. Yet, even if it were perfected, dividing the populace into constituencies with scrupulous fairness and ensuring easy access for all and only those entitled to vote, shallow democracy would not suffice to deliver the freedom heralded as the rationale for this system of government. Something deeper is needed.

If democracy is required to guard against the irony of self-undermining—acting contrary to your interests at the moment when you are supposed to be exercising your freedom—then democracy lapses wherever there is serious danger that large portions of the electorate stand a good chance of being misinformed on issues that affect their central projects and the prospects of attaining their principal ends. The simple story sees that shallow democracy must be supplemented, becoming *Millian democracy*, a state in which voters have good chances of obtaining the knowledge they need to cast their ballots wisely. It also recognizes that, historically, the means through which Millian democracy has been achieved is through the functioning of the Millian arena. Since the conditions of public debate are now (in many places) far from those of the Millian arena, the simple story proposes to rebuild a much closer approximation to the arena. Education is to be the key to this restoration.

How exactly?

Presumably through a two-stage process. At the first stage, through providing young people with the appropriate combination of factual knowledge

---

[31] Some supposed democracies violate the condition on choice of candidates, others go in for bribery and coercion. Even among regimes meeting all the conditions for shallow democracy, some are illiberal, restricting all kinds of freedoms. Moreover, democracies we would classify as liberal can easily decay into illiberalism, retaining all the superficial features needed for shallow democracy. Their decline may go further, leading them to become authoritarian, although the machinery of "elections" enables them to continue to advertise themselves as democratic. I am grateful to Predrag Sustar for prompting me to make these points explicit.

128   THE MAIN ENTERPRISE OF THE WORLD

and abilities in reasoning, an electorate will be created in which deceivers and charlatans will be exposed for what they are.[32] (Evidently, this will take time. Probably one or two generations, and perhaps more.) Once that has been accomplished, the voting public will call for reform, welcoming strict regulation of sources of information in accordance with the requirements for the Millian arena. The resurrections of Cronkite and the BBC will no longer be dismissed as the creation of *Pravda*.

This strategy is almost certainly doomed to fail. First, it is undermined by general considerations about the social character of human knowledge. Second, the more abstract points are reinforced by focusing on a salient contemporary example.

Despite philosophical fascination with the idea of the individual who builds up a vast corpus of knowledge solely through his own efforts, any serious attention to the growth of young children makes evident how deeply dependent they are on the ambient social environment.[33] For most of the history of our species, individual human beings have been able to transcend the body of information they could obtain by themselves through relying on others. Indeed, it's far from obvious, how any human being, at any time, could have acquired any beliefs without being taught a considerable amount. Most societies have enjoyed a clear division of epistemic labor, marking out who is to be believed on what topic. The developmental psychologist Paul Harris has offered an illuminating account of how young children learn whom to trust.[34] Their local strategies—*all our* strategies for identifying the authorities—break down when public dissemination of information becomes driven by considerations of profit, when "market forces" favor finding a niche and feeding the chosen audience news it wants to hear, and when checks on veracity are themselves disputed. Social markers of expertise dissolve, and with their demise vanishes the hope of functional division of epistemic labor. For any such division ultimately requires a decision

---

[32] Eamonn Callan, in *Creating Citizens*, recommends introducing students to the Millian arena during their schooldays. I am sympathetic to this suggestion, and will adapt it at the end of this chapter—although I shall insist on cultivating the affective ties Mill and his successors omit.

[33] Epistemology surely made a critical wrong turn, when it forgot that Descartes' focus on the isolated individual was an idealization. Fortunately, more recent thinkers have restored the obvious embedding of individuals within social networks; see, for example, Alvin Goldman, *Knowledge in a Social World* (New York: Oxford University Press, 1999). As Edward Craig makes clear in a lucid and underappreciated book, *Knowledge and the State of Nature* (Oxford: Clarendon Press, 1990), our concept of knowledge most likely emerged from our need to identify people from whom we could expect to learn.

[34] Paul Harris, *Trusting What You're Told: How Children Learn from Others* (Cambridge, MA: Harvard University Press, 2012).

about where to place your trust. Any educational strategy for bringing a society to a widely shared view about where the problems with the current system of public information lie—for recognizing who the charlatans are—presupposes that radical differences in views about trustworthiness can be overcome. After the appropriate schooling, some (indeed, many) of those who were deceived are supposed to see the light. But why will their antecedent faith not lead them to suspect at least part of what they are taught? How will they accept the whole package as an advance toward enlightenment rather than an attempt at indoctrination?

Enthusiasts for the power of education to restore Millian democracy will likely point to three cognitive capacities they intend to develop. First, and perhaps most obvious, is skill in critical thinking, conceived not simply as having a nose for fallacious reasoning but also as a disposition to find perspectives to expose what is being omitted in a persuasive presentation. Second is a clear understanding of the principal institutions of the society, of the limits prescribed for the occupants of various offices, and of the ways in which benefits flow to people in particular positions.[35] The third cognitive ability, already emphasized in current educational theorizing, consists in some degree of understanding in various technical fields. Training in the natural sciences, people often say, is important for everyone, since so many policy questions turn on scientific facts.

Chapter 7 will have much more to say about education in the sciences, but one preliminary point is pertinent here. The pace of research in the natural sciences, combined with the unpredictable entanglements of science and policy issues over the course of a lifetime, make it hard, if not impossible, to prepare citizens adequately through extensive training in the "relevant" scientific fields. The educators of the 1950s could not have foreseen the future importance of the then-nascent molecular biology; their counterparts in the 1970s had no advance warning of the relevance of climate science. To rely on the third capacity alone is a recipe for helping people think through yesterday's list of disputed questions. Nor, plainly, would it suffice

---

[35] This will enable them to understand when advocates of a particular view would profit from the widespread acceptance of that view. Hence the importance of careful historical studies of how ignorance is disseminated and maintained—studies in "agnotology." For important examples, see Robert Proctor and Linda Schiebinger, eds., *Agnotology: The Making and Unmaking of Ignorance* (Stanford, CA: Stanford University Press, 2008), and Robert N. Proctor, *Cancer Wars: How Politics Shapes What We Know and Don't Know about Cancer* (New York: Basic Books, 1995).

130   THE MAIN ENTERPRISE OF THE WORLD

for preparing citizens to cope with policy questions (and there are many of them) that turn on issues the pertinent domain of inquiry has yet to resolve.[36]

However much time and effort is invested in science education, as it is typically conceived in schools and universities, it seems highly unlikely that it could prepare any large fraction of the electorate to work through the technicalities of the political questions they will encounter.[37] Even if the curriculum succeeds, providentially, in covering just those areas of science involved in the decisions of the coming decades, anything short of specialist training would leave the future citizen vulnerable to bafflement in the face of "competing experts." For, in a fractured polity, disputes about what counts as evidence are likely to arise. The graphs and charts flourished by one set of "experts" will be challenged by others.[38] Very few people, even people with advanced degrees in areas outside the pertinent specialty, are in any position to work through the ways in which a complex mass of data has been collected and analyzed to present a picture of a trend, and to understand exactly why the putative evidence is reliable. In the end, even the scientifically well-educated must decide which of the clashing voices to trust.

To be armed against deception and confusion, citizens need capacities for analyzing and working through complex debates. Part of that requires learning how to identify ways in which conclusions are properly supported by evidence—the province of logic as understood in Mill's Inaugural Address. Instruction in this area should include parts of mathematics typically downplayed in the high school curriculum—some acquaintance with probability, statistics, and decision theory looks far more valuable for participation in civic life than most of the algebra, trigonometry, geometry, and calculus through which adolescents are asked to slog. Yet the development of formal skills is only part of the package. Young people can gain much by studying how past controversies were resolved, within science, in social applications of the sciences, and in the mess of political life. Judgment can be developed by providing a menu of examples with which the debates of the future can be compared.[39]

---

[36] A large number of political questions depend on answers to questions about which social scientists—particularly economists and sociologists—can at best provide tentative answers. I shall have more to say about the social sciences in Chapter 9.

[37] The point was well appreciated by Walter Lippmann; see *The Phantom Public* (repr., London: Routledge, 2017). Lippmann brilliantly mocked the myth of the "sovereign and omnicompetent citizen," 11.

[38] This phenomenon is apparent in debates about climate change. See *The Seasons Alter*, 5–8, 14–19.

[39] For more on these themes, see Chapter 7.

CITIZENS   131

Focusing on these analytic skills isn't enough, however. As already noted, at the end of the day, the citizens have to trust some group of self-described experts when they report on the "evidence." Deciding who is reliable is often more complicated than inspecting a track record of uncontroversial successes and/or failures. Future citizens require an understanding of how the institutions of their societies work, how particular individuals are recruited to particular positions, how their pronouncements are likely to be affected by social or political linkages, and how various segments of the population benefit from the widespread acceptance of particular views. Achieving a reasonable division of epistemic labor requires augmenting our childhood strategies for learning whom to trust with a rich social understanding. Citizens must come to recognize ways in which "expert opinion" can be simulated or distorted.

Leaving government to the ignorant is dangerous. A democratic remedy would educate the citizens so they can learn even in a world awash in "alternative facts," "fake news," and other ventures in misinformation. Unfortunately, perfecting the inculcation of cognitive virtues would not be enough. Unless the future voters are prepared to listen to a wide range of viewpoints, even perspectives they find uncongenial, they are likely to remain trapped in the politically colored vision they have initially acquired. Before you can assess a debate, you must first listen—listen seriously—to the case for the opposition. Without an affective capacity, a willingness to take seriously the ideas and arguments of fellow citizens, no amount of talent for analysis and judgment will solve the problem. However thoroughly the cognitive capacities are emphasized, some version of the mutual regard I attributed to the early settlers in Guilford is needed if education is to restore the Millian arena. And it must be mutual. In opening your mind to the ideas of others, you must be convinced of your interlocutors' willingness to reciprocate—and of their commitment to avoiding any outcome you would experience as devastating.[40] Millian democracy presupposes Deweyan democracy.

An example will illustrate and underscore these general points. In the late twentieth century, the resistance to accepting the reality of climate change demonstrated the extent to which public discussions had departed from the

[40] There's a strong inclination to think of debates involving clashes of values as proceeding in two stages. First the participants settle the facts, and then, on this basis, they can take up the conflicts in values. That tidy picture of an orderly sequence is unrealistic. Before any kind of consensus on factual matters can be sought, inquirers need to be assured of their fellows' commitment to seek an outcome that all can tolerate. Without that, a sense of personal vulnerability will inevitably skew the joint investigation.

132   THE MAIN ENTERPRISE OF THE WORLD

conditions envisaged for the Millian arena. The eloquent warnings presented by eminent climate scientists were widely dismissed, by citizens and by many of their political representatives. Global warming was declared to be "a hoax" or, more mildly, to be an unresolved question. Nor was the refusal to accept the expert testimony confined to the tabloid press or to politically affiliated news media. Major newspapers adopted the craven strategy of "representing both sides" in the "controversy."[41] It took far too long for journalists to announce clearly that the "experts" paraded to deny the consensus of the climate community were scientists from different fields, many of them deriving financial support from fossil fuel companies.[42]

Yet, even a decade after mainstream media recognized that the supposed controversy had long been settled, various forms of climate denial persist.[43] Despite the strenuous efforts of activists—many of them, like Greta Thunberg, young and painfully aware of the perils likely to pervade their later lives—vast numbers of people the world over resist proposals for immediate action to curb the emission of greenhouse gases. Sometimes, in local communities, grass-roots efforts to respond to the gravity of the problem succeed. Very few nations, however, have committed themselves to policies that would adequately address the challenge.[44]

What explains this inaction? Not simply the fact that many people remain ill-informed. Resistance to the kinds of policies for which climate activists campaign stems from entirely reasonable anxieties. For the specific decision problems about climate facing citizens around the world are exceptionally hard. Even when it is understood how failure to curb greenhouse gas emissions will make the future harsher and more dangerous for the generations to come, for cherished children and grandchildren and for any descendants

[41] A prominent example is America's premier newspaper, the *New York Times*, which took more than fifteen years to appreciate the force of the evidence. Even today, the *New York Times* (by contrast with the *Guardian*) tends to understate the urgency of the situation.

[42] Two historians of science, Naomi Oreskes and Erik Conway, played a major role in consciousness-raising with their book *Merchants of Doubt* (New York: Bloomsbury, 2010).

[43] This is perhaps most evident in the Anglophone world. But it is not restricted to the United States, Britain, Canada, Australia, and New Zealand.

[44] The Climate Accord, signed in December 2015 in Paris, was rightly regarded as an encouraging first step, even by those who recognized that the targets set for cutting emissions were too lax. Commentators hoped for a sequence of international agreements, to build on what had been accomplished in Paris and to impose more stringent deadlines. Instead, there has not only been a significant decision to withdraw from the Accord—taken by a US administration seemingly bent on making environmental problems as intractable as possible—but, more significantly, widespread failure to cut emissions at rates commensurate with the (inadequate) schedules previously endorsed in Paris. As temperature records are annually broken and disastrous weather events affect all the major continents, global emissions continue to increase.

CITIZENS   133

they may have, that must be balanced against the burdens added to present lives. How much less perilous can we make the conditions of human existence for those who come after us? How great are the sacrifices that we will have to make? Those questions arise differently for different groups within a nation, as well as for different nations. People who currently lack electricity *reasonably* yearn for the advances that electrification would bring.[45] In affluent societies with pronounced inequality of wealth, those who struggle to survive, or who see their children as likely to sink into poverty, *reasonably* fear the disruptions an energetic climate policy would cause. If they could be presented with a clear plan, one that specified the ways in which their lives would be affected, demonstrating how future relief could be provided while accommodating what they value most, they might well sign on to the call for action. But nobody can provide any such plan.[46] The exact costs and benefits are incalculable. Worse still, because the effects of rival choices—how the future will go given alternative courses of action—are *radically* unpredictable, any attempts to reassure would be irresponsible speculation. All that can be offered is a comparative judgment. The more swiftly we stop emitting greenhouse gases, the less harsh and hostile will be the environment for our descendants.

If this diagnosis is correct, it is easy to see why the proposed educational strategy cannot help to resolve the issue of climate policy (or any other that resembles it). The trouble is not simply that the suggested remedy is too slow (although it is!). However much you enhance citizens' knowledge of science, however astute they become at critical thinking, however deeply they understand the institutions of their society, they will remain uncertain of the consequences of the demands climate action would place on them—and that uncertainty will bring fear in its train. Under these circumstances, it should not be surprising that attitudes toward climate change (and climate policy) are not sensitive to levels of scientific training, but vary strikingly with political affiliation.[47] When you are radically uncertain about some highly consequential issue, it is hardly strange to align yourself with others who share your sympathies, and to resist the attitudes commended by people with whom you sharply disagree.

---

[45] A point made eloquently by Jeffrey Sachs. See *The Age of Sustainable Development* (New York: Columbia University Press, 2015, 155–56).

[46] For a detailed development of this point, see Chapter 4 of *The Seasons Alter*.

[47] See Dan M. Kahan, "Climate-Science Communication and the Measurement Problem," *Political Psychology* 36 (2015): S1, 1–43.

134 THE MAIN ENTERPRISE OF THE WORLD

To address climate change requires coordinated action on a global scale. Since the world lacks any figure or institution powerful enough to bring about the needed cooperation, democracy must be extended across national boundaries. The climate problem demands democracy at a scale our species has not yet achieved, just at the moment when traditionally democratic societies are increasingly polarized and when larger unions are fragmenting. The entire human population finds itself in a vastly expanded version of the predicament faced by those early settlers in Connecticut. *We need a giant analog of the Guilford covenant.* Precisely because of the radical uncertainties, our species requires the mutual assurances that compact provided: promises to "join ourselves together" and "to be helpful to one another in our common work" and "not to desert one another."

Although the general goal is identifiable—a world in which greenhouse gases are maintained at as low a concentration as we can manage—the path to achieve that end is not. We are like a band of hikers, lost in a dark and dangerous wood, who must work together to find a way out before night falls.[48] Cooperation is best achieved under hazardous conditions, if each fearful individual, uncertain and ignorant as all know themselves to be, can rely on the help and protection of the others.

Most people, including philosophers, are inclined to think that agreement on facts is a prerequisite to settling value differences, and thus crafting joint policies. I am suggesting adding an apparent inversion of this piece of everyday wisdom. Sometimes, when a group is at variance over facts *and* values, a commitment to understand and learn from one another, to recognize individual needs and to protect one another against loss, is necessary before any progress can be made. This is our predicament with respect to climate change. But that problem is only the most dramatic illustration of it. Disputes about all kinds of facts and values arise within the world's democracies. Resolving them depends on maintaining a functional community, preserving the democratic culture Tocqueville celebrated. Without Deweyan democracy, Millian democracy and shallow democracy are doomed to wither.

⁂

Dewey maintained that democracy, *deep* democracy, is education. I want to defend this apparently peculiar view, and to use my defense to draw some

---

[48] This image is developed in *The Seasons Alter*, 105–24. It derives from Fitzjames Stephen via William James ("The Will to Believe"). I shall return to it near the end of this book.

concrete proposals for educational experimentation. I'll offer four lines of thought that lead to Dewey's conclusion. Start with the worry just raised in considering education for Millian democracy.

Shallow democracy conceives democratic societies as defined by opportunities to cast votes. Millian democracy adds a condition: the electorate must be informed enough so that the preferences expressed at the ballot box express the voters' interests. Preparing young people to be able to recognize their interests, even in a confusing world, requires inculcating various cognitive skills together with a disposition to engage seriously with the alternative perspectives expressed in sociopolitical debate. Without some tendency to view the proponents of those perspectives as fellow citizens, people whose aspirations and whose ideas should be seriously considered, deployment of the purely cognitive capacities is unlikely.[49] Attaining Millian democracy requires educating a citizenry prepared to open themselves to ideas they initially find wrongheaded and even dangerous. Voters become aware of their interests by working through debates, and the work begins from viewing fellow citizens as people from whom one might learn (and who are genuinely *fellows*—people who will not write off any group of co-citizens as dispensable).

The second of my four lines of thought might be called, with apologies to Tocqueville, *the tyranny of voting*. Suppose that the line of reasoning just rehearsed is flawed. Millian democracy can be attained, and voters can identify their interests, without any attitude of openness to others. The interests in question are understood as the goals most central to their lives, the aims they would reflectively endorse. Presumably, such aims are bound by the law. Beyond that, they are unconstrained. If the result I hope to achieve would make you unhappy, even if it would interfere with your pursuit of what matters most to you, there is no requirement for me to revise my intentions, so long as there are no relevant legal protections to which you might appeal. My judgments about my interests don't have to take you into account. If we are both fortunate enough to have candidates who represent our interests, those candidates will compete for votes. Perhaps yours will win, perhaps mine will win, or maybe we shall both be disappointed. After the victorious candidate has been declared, there is no reason for the winner's supporters

---

[49] This phenomenon is reflected in Dan Kahan's results about the lack of correlation between attitudes toward claims of global warming and level of scientific education, and the impressive correlation between those attitudes and subjects' political affiliations. See n.47, above.

136   THE MAIN ENTERPRISE OF THE WORLD

to regret the predicaments of those who have lost, or even to think further about them. The electorate has decided. And that's that.

Imagine a society in which indifference to others, both in forming preferences and in reflecting on electoral results, prevails. (Perhaps, these days, this isn't so difficult to imagine.)[50] Millian democracy is in place, and all the voters understand where their own interests lie. Moreover, interests repeatedly conflict, and the conflicts affect people's chances of attaining their central goals. Perhaps the political clashes always end in victory for one particular group and defeat for another—some are always in the majority, others always in the minority. Or possibly the fortunes of the groups wax and wane: most people experience periods for which they are ascendant, and other periods when their aspirations are frustrated. Or maybe the shifts in electoral success are so frequent that everyone experiences times of critical reversal—today my triumph permanently scuttles your plans, and tomorrow I am paid back in kind. The first scenario is the tyranny of the majority, feared by Tocqueville and Mill.[51] The second two are potentially worse, leading to outcomes in which *no* member of the society successfully pursues "his own good in his own way."

Whether for all or merely for some, freedom—"the only freedom worthy of the name"—vanishes. Democracy's claim to enhance freedom is thus rendered suspect.[52] The society just imagined is obviously likely to tolerate gross inequalities. But the standard defense of allowing inequalities, to wit, that they are necessary for giving full rein to liberty, collapses. Moreover, the reason for the collapse is evident. The third member of the French revolutionary trinity—fraternity, or, as I would prefer to characterize it, solidarity—is absent.[53] By the assumption of mutual indifference, it is ruled out of the scenario from the beginning. Its departure threatens not only equality (as you might expect) but liberty as well.

Viewing voting as a means to advance your own interests, without consideration for the like interests of other citizens, can generate a form of tyranny no less intrusive than life under a dictatorship bound only by a corpus of

---

[50] Indeed, contemporary politics may be even worse. Part of the satisfaction derived from having triumphed on a particular issue may come from the discomfiture (even the sufferings) inflicted on political opponents. Indifference to the wishes of others may be replaced by spite.

[51] Tocqueville, *Democracy in America* (New York: Library of America, 2004), 288–318; Mill, *Considerations on Representative Government* (in OL).

[52] Of course, both Tocqueville and Mill already worried about the "tyranny of the majority." I'm suggesting that the problem can arise in different forms.

[53] As Konstanty Gebert lucidly pointed out in 2017 in a presentation at the Einstein Forum ("Either Solidarity or Fraternity?"), there are subtle distinctions between these two related concepts.

laws. (The laws prevent only the worst excesses of despotism, while allowing for blocking the aspirations of some or all citizens.) Could Mill's fundamental freedom be restored, even in the absence of solidarity, by appealing to the counsel of prudence? Not obviously. As contemporary politics shows, the interests of groups counted as weak are often disregarded, and there is a recurrent temptation to abrogate supposedly established protections in order to achieve short-term aims.

The scenario of the indifferent society presupposes a popular view of human nature, one that sees us as rational egoists. My third line of thought scrutinizes that idea and its more plausible relatives.

According to the extreme version of the view I have in mind, human beings come to have settled preferences, which, when they reflect on them with maximal clarity, they see as directed toward their most important aims. These constitute their interests. The extent of their well-being depends on how well these interests are satisfied. Social life inevitably involves conflicts of interest. To the extent individual people are rational, they act so as to maximize their well-being. Democracy is a welcome system of political governance because it fosters "treaties of toleration" among citizens, so that conflict gives way to cooperation and each individual member of society can expect to achieve a higher level of well-being than would otherwise be available.[54]

Scenarios involving the tyranny of voting reveal that the idea of society-wide benefit faces some serious challenges. Let's suppose, however, that everything turns out happily. The alliances and the voting yield a sequence of outcomes under which everybody does well. How is that achieved? Apparently through individuals "pursuing [their] own interest," they "promote an end which was no part of [their] intention" (to borrow famous phrases from Adam Smith).[55] Yet, outside the economic contexts Smith had in mind, claiming that our own interests don't involve others is highly implausible. According to an old folk song sung by English children about the "Jolly Miller of Dee": "And this the burden of his song/Forever used to be/I care for nobody, no not I/For nobody cares for me." Misanthropy of so extreme a form is rare. Most of us do care for others. We are incomplete

---

[54] The concept of a treaty of toleration is introduced in David Lewis, "Mill and Milquetoast," *Australasian Journal of Philosophy* 67 (1989): 152–71. Lewis also presents a utilitarian defense of arriving at treaties of toleration. Shallow democracy motivates coming to protective agreements with those who might be inclined to scrap policies or institutions you hope will endure. When deep democracy functions well, such protections become less important, although they may be retained as an extra buffer.

[55] WN 485.

138 THE MAIN ENTERPRISE OF THE WORLD

altruists, wanting to satisfy certain kinds of preferences of particular other people to different degrees.[56] A society is a network in which the welfare of individual citizens connects with the welfare of others with links of various strengths. Potential treaties of toleration are limited, and sometimes overridden, by the ties binding people to particular fellow citizens and to the members of specific groups. When this is recognized, the argument that democracy promotes satisfaction of citizens' interests, and thus realizes "the only freedom worthy of the name," looks suspect.

Political life isn't simply a matter of coordinating the actions of rational egoists. Rather, because people have tendencies to limited altruism, developed in different directions through their early development, it requires shaping, pruning, and extending our variant forms of limited concern for others, so that, in political contexts, all are protected. In the course of our early lives, almost all of us come to give priority to particular other people in the formation of settled preferences—this begins with close family members— and, as we mature, we develop our own idiosyncratic spectrum of altruistic linkages. If we are able to become citizens, capable of participating in a functional democracy, the individual networks must be readjusted to allow for wider forms of cooperative action. Achieving that is the work of education.[57]

How should that be carried out? In principle, it might be achieved in either of two distinct ways. The limited—"natural"—dispositions to be concerned with the welfare of particular sorts of other people might be left unchanged, but emphasis placed on the prudence of tolerating the many who fall outside the scope of individual propensities for altruism. Alternatively, Deweyan engagement with others might be cultivated. Education might be committed to expanding the limited domain of individuals' altruism, through instilling a disposition for seeking out and engaging with fellow citizens. The first strategy accepts the goal of looking out for yourself and your mates, but advises accommodating others in the interests of getting what you want. The second encourages you to expand the circle of those you care about, so it encompasses the entire society.

Teaching young people to get along with those to whom they are indifferent, or whom they even dislike, because it is usually profitable to do so, runs the obvious risk of producing citizens who are prepared to ignore the interests of some (many?) of their fellows if the typical calculus of profits

---

[56] See *The Ethical Project*, 17–35.
[57] As the next chapter will argue, that work is central to the moral development of the individual.

CITIZENS 139

breaks down. Apparently, democracy would be better served if the education system inculcated at least some measure of Deweyan solidarity. Yet the second strategy faces an obvious objection. In attempting to create citizens with a willingness to understand, learn from, and cooperate with people who initially strike them as alien, wrongheaded, and even morally suspect, the education system would mold children into a socially preferred form. It would distort their natural development, thus interfering with their autonomy. Consequently, they would lose the fundamental freedom, whose flourishing democracy is supposed to sustain. To be sure, they might have higher chances of something they might call "well-being," but it would no longer be the realization of their "true interests" (those suited to their "authentic self").

The objection leads to the heart of an important mistake in the popular view, a mistake already diagnosed in the previous chapter. Historically, a varied chorus of educational theorists have sounded the same tune. Education is a drawing out, a liberating of the true self, the authentic individual, who is—somehow—embryonically present in the untutored child. Biological or psychological determinism of this kind is a wild extrapolation from certain mundane facts. Change the social, even the physical, environment as you will, your children or grandchildren are never going to be able to fly solely by flapping their arms. (They will, however, be able to travel through the air in other ways.) Of course there are limits to what human beings can be and do. But that does not mean, as Plato and some of his successors might have thought, that inside every gardener's son there's a little gardener waiting to be grown. Sometimes, it turns out, there's a Gauss.[58]

Suppose, for the moment, the possibility of educational arrangements capable of producing adults who engaged with members of a diverse group of people. Under different circumstances, the very same people would have grown up to reject that kind of engagement. On what basis could you argue for the authenticity of the self produced under the latter regime? What makes the fact that, *as things stand, under the kinds of social arrangements history has mostly seen*, particular kinds of psychological and behavioral characteristics commonly result, evidence for the fact that those particular traits are privileged as *natural*, so that different arrangements, under which they fail to emerge, are distorting?

---

[58] Christian Gauss, the "Prince of Mathematicians," was the son of a gardener. At an early age he stupefied his teacher by finding, in a matter of seconds, a way to add the first hundred numbers.

140   THE MAIN ENTERPRISE OF THE WORLD

The discussion of fulfillment in the previous chapter was intended to free us from the idea of a primitive socially isolated self, awaiting its unfolding. Once the liberating insight is appreciated, we can ask which mode of dialogue would provide greater fulfillment for the individual and greater social health. Dickinson's answer—my answer—is to favor an educational program in which identification with the aspirations of fellow citizens is cultivated. Promoting solidarity should be an aim of education.

This third line of thought should not presuppose our ability to devise a system of education capable of producing citizens inclined to engage with any of their fellows, let alone cosmopolitans who reach out to all humanity. Rather it argues for orienting education toward expanding propensities for understanding and learning from others, seeing that expansion as compatible with a commitment to individual autonomy and as conducive to the aims of Millian democracy.

The three lines of thought just considered underlie the most important defense of the idea of democracy as education. We should begin by correcting an oversimplification, one pervading the reflections just undertaken and many other discussions of democracy as well. There is a common tendency: to talk as if *democracy* were a concept applicable only, or primarily, to whole societies or to nation-states. In fact, democracy can exist at any number of distinct scales. Like charity, it can begin at home. Although patriarchy has been a dominant mode in the history of the family, more democratic forms of decision-making have been practiced, especially recently. Today, nuclear families often settle important matters through exchanges in which the adult members participate on equal terms, and, as the children grow, they are frequently included as well. Extended family councils may have a longer history.

For family democracy—where it exists—voting is a practice of last resort. If people remind their adolescent children (as I sometimes did) that mother has 51 percent of the votes, the remark is a joke. Democratic families value exchange, discussion, conversation. Their members are interested in understanding what others want, and why they want it. They are prepared to adjust their own attitudes in light of what others say. The amusing, but touching, limit of this willingness to listen comes when, once the difference of opinion about what to do is clear, everyone accommodates others by reversing judgment, so that divergence remains.[59] No democratic family would be happy

[59] This actually happens in some families, as I learned from one of the most other-directed people I have ever met, a former graduate student, who described the deliberations occurring in her family.

CITIZENS 141

to resolve its disagreements by having all the members announce what they prefer, and then tallying the votes.

Family democracy is an exercise in mutual learning. Hardly surprising, of course, since kinship is the origin of the ideal of fraternity, from which the more general notion of solidarity springs. Yet, even at a larger scale, similar attitudes can prevail. Within small communities, where people live side by side, working together and sharing times of good fortune and of bad, great effort is made to explore and understand the members' different perspectives and their reasons for holding them. Pursuing a policy that would leave any individual dissatisfied is seen as failure. The councils of the Inuit,[60] like the New England town meetings of the early nineteenth century, exemplify a commit to mutual engagement, conceived as directed toward a solution with which all those in the community can live.[61]

The importance of affective ties among participants is not typically emphasized in theories of deliberative democracy. Yet, as my reference to the Inuit suggests, the need for solidarity is appreciated by many different cultures. Moreover, some theorists from very different traditions—Dewey and Tagore, for example—recognize the crucial role attempts to extend sympathies play in political life. Just as Dewey takes the core of democracy to require mutual communication and learning, Tagore regards sociopolitical life as flawed by our ignorance—and recommends expanding "the limit of our sympathy and imagination."[62] In contrast to the conception of liberty as protection from the interference of others, he offers an eloquent plea for widespread solidarity:

> Only those may attain their freedom from the perspective of an eclipsed life who have the power to cultivate mutual understanding and cooperation. The history of the growth of freedom is the history of the perfection of human relationship.[63]

---

[60] See Jean Briggs, *Never in Anger* (Cambridge, MA: Harvard University Press, 1971).

[61] Although, as noted in my initial discussion of the Guilford covenant, the boundaries of the community may be drawn in troublesome ways. The next paragraphs will address questions about just where boundaries should be fixed.

[62] Rabindranath Tagore, *The Religion of Man* (London: Macmillan, 1931; repr., Martino Publishing, 2013), 130; see also 47, 53, 143–44, 192. I am grateful to Martha Nussbaum for making the kinship between Tagore and Dewey clear to me. In her own discussions of Tagore's defenses of solidarity, she emphasizes his concern to overcome disgust (to my mind easily explicable given the salience for him of the divisions generated from the caste system): see her *Political Emotions* (Cambridge, MA: Harvard University Press, 2013).

[63] Tagore, *The Religion of Man*, 186.

142　THE MAIN ENTERPRISE OF THE WORLD

Perhaps the only amendment Deweyan democracy would offer is the explicit thought that the cooperation should flow from the mutual understanding.

Group decisions might be viewed as lying on a continuum. At one extreme is the deliberative model, realized in the democratic family and the local co-operative community, where anything short of consensus is regarded as a failure. The opposite pole is occupied by groups in which individuals arrive with their preformed views, announce them, count the votes, and resolve the question through some prearranged voting rule (requiring supermajority, majority, plurality, etc.). The contemporary world contains a vast number of decision-making groups, sometimes cutting across national boundaries. The groups come in many sizes, with highly diverse personal and social re-lations among the decision-makers. Often those charged with formulating policies are a tiny subset of a broader group. Participatory democracy within the committee or board is intended to produce representative democracy for the larger association.[64] In principle, all these decision-making bodies could be mapped on the continuum I have imagined. Meliorist pragmatism doesn't propose making all group decisions express the deep democracy of the ideal family or the ideal town meeting—surely a utopian dream. Instead, it suggests thinking of *progress* in democracy as constituted by moving the practice of group decision-making toward the deliberative pole.[65]

Although the proposal, as I've stated it, covers more than political democ-racy, it's reasonable to think of its most important application as within the political sphere. Thinking about families teaches us how deliberations can go awry in three major ways. The participants may be the wrong people—those affected by the outcome may be excluded, and others with no stake in what is decided may be included. Or the discussion can proceed on the basis of faulty factual information. Finally, discussants may not be committed to mu-tual understanding and to finding a solution with which all can live. All three symptoms are apparent in current politics—not only in America but in many other places as well. Like Dewey a century ago, I view the failure of democ-racy in America as residing in the frequency with which these pathologies are found.

---

[64] Examples of small-scale civic organizations with this structure abound: small groups that su-pervise the outreach efforts of churches, trade union locals, the boards set up for the maintenance of condos and other small housing developments, and so forth.

[65] More exactly, correcting certain kinds of faults in deliberation by using a diagnostic ideal. Crucially, that ideal adds to the practices of reason-giving, favored by many champions of deliber-ative democracy, an emphasis on affective relations among deliberators. Failure to seek engagement with the perspectives and predicaments of others is perceived as a vice.

That diagnosis rests on comparing present political life with an ideal of democratic deliberation.

An ideal democratic deliberation is *fully representative*, *fully informed*, and *mutually engaged*. Full representation requires that the perspective of each person who would be affected by the decision be represented, and that the perspectives of those unaffected not be represented. Full information requires that pertinent information bearing on the issue (findings confirmed through rigorous inquiry) be accepted by each discussant, and that no unsupported proposition be used in defending an opinion or proposal. Mutual engagement requires that each participant be committed to understanding the perspectives of each other discussant, and to finding a resolution that all who have engaged in the discussion are willing to accept.

Plainly, these are extremely strong conditions, perhaps impossible to realize even in the most democratic family, let alone in any aspect of political life. But, to repeat, utopia isn't my aim (or Dewey's). Ideals are diagnostic tools, to help us see what is wrong, how we might reduce or resolve the problems, and thus improve the situation.[66]

Making progress depends on understanding what makes realizing the ideal so absurd a fantasy. For many political issues, it is impossible to assemble representatives of all the pertinent perspectives, attending to the fine-grained detail of each. There are too many points of view, and some of those who hold them are unable to speak for themselves: they are too young, too old, too afflicted, or simply not yet born. Representation must often be coarse, lumping together people who would insist on differentiating their views. Excluding the unaffected is, in principle, easier, although, strictly speaking, that would be unnecessary if the condition requiring mutual engagement were perfectly satisfied. (People whose interests were unaffected by the issue but who were ideally mutually engaged would simply excuse themselves and leave.) The full representation condition recognizes the multi-scale character of democracy, and assigns issues to particular political levels. In particular, because some questions, like climate change, affect the human population as a whole (including future generations), the condition points to the need for democratic deliberation on a transnational scale.

---

[66] There's an important residual concern, to be taken up in the final chapter. Diagnoses may be useless in that improving the current state requires changes that are too large to be managed. Piecemeal progress, of the type Dewey and I envisage, will not work. So, according to the challenge, the meliorist promise is empty, and the enterprise remains utopian.

144   THE MAIN ENTERPRISE OF THE WORLD

Plainly, if falsehoods are accepted or truths ignored, the most well-intentioned deliberation can easily produce unfortunate conclusions. Since human beings are not omniscient, it is unhelpful to evaluate the discussions we have by inquiring whether we are using all and only relevant truths. Improving political debate is a matter of trying to ensure that participants don't rely on unsupported conjectures and that they do come to terms with conclusions for which there is convincing evidence. Because people often disagree on what is speculation and what is firmly established, advancing the epistemic quality of deliberation isn't a trivial matter. It is, however, something to which education might contribute. As suggested earlier, developing capacities for critical reasoning and understanding evidence would surely improve some of our urgent political discussions.

Even more evidently, education might develop capacities enabling citizens to engage more fully with others. Indeed, its principal contribution to participation in civic life should lie, not in the inculcation of the cognitive skills for bringing elective preferences closer to genuine interests, but rather in a greater understanding of the diversity of perspectives within our society and a deeper commitment to engaging with and learning from divergent views. (More will be said below about how this might be achieved.)

Yet, even when utopianism gives way to a more modest meliorism, you may still think of the deliberative ideal and of Deweyan solidarity as far too optimistic. For, whatever realistic steps are taken toward making political discussions more representative, better informed, and more deeply mutually engaged, you may well doubt the ability of the reforms to generate consensus. To use a figure popular among the stoics, the practical measures available in contemporary society are equivalent to raising a drowning man, currently ten feet beneath the water's surface, by a foot or two. The achievable progress along the dimensions marked out by the ideal has no effect on the final outcomes of debates. At the end of the day, votes have to be taken, and the losers are bound to go away unsatisfied.

———

People who emphasize the role of deliberation in democracy, as I have done, are often accused of seeing the world through rose-tinted spectacles. They can reasonably retort by pointing to the dangers of failing to achieve consensus. When some members of a society believe themselves to be outvoted, again and again, they come to view their interests as systematically ignored and often campaign for separatism. Sometimes splintering does no harm.

CITIZENS   145

But dividing a large population into groups that no longer deliberate together can have costs. Democracy no longer exists at the scale where it is needed. To return to the example used earlier, one of the deepest problems posed by climate change centers on the need for institutions to govern global cooperation. When the trend is to pursue democracy more locally, the prospects for meeting that need diminish.

Realism requires not only recognizing the difficulties of consensus, but also the costs of abandoning attempts to deliberate. Simple reliance on voting risks one of two pathological outcomes—the fracturing of democracies so that they no longer operate at the appropriate scales or an oscillation of policymaking so that the actions introduced by one transient majority are reversed by its equally transient successor. Instead of viewing optimistic deliberativists as pitted against clear-eyed political realists, it would be better to recognize an important challenge. How can deliberation best work to maintain a cooperative democratic polity, given the difficulties of consensus, especially in heterogeneous societies?

The three conditions of the ideal of democratic deliberation—full representation, full information, and mutual engagement—indicate ways in which, even when an issue is ultimately resolved through voting, those who lose may be able to accept the decision. Living with policies you oppose is never easy. But, to the extent you take your views to have been heard, to the extent you suppose correct and relevant information to have been considered, and the extent to which the discussants are conceived as genuinely concerned to find a solution tolerable by all, you may be moved to reflect on your own prior perspective. Humility should have a place among the civic, democratic virtues.[67] When views have been heard by open-minded, well-informed listeners, the failure of those views to carry the day should provoke some reconsideration among those who hold them.

The ideal of democratic deliberation also allows three mitigating conditions that make consensus more likely. First, the consensus at which it aims is modest. A deliberation would achieve *strong* consensus just in case it concluded with a position ranked by all the participants as the best option. Critics of deliberativist optimism are entirely right to charge that, on many of the issues that arise for contemporary societies, strong consensus is highly improbable. The ideal, however, focuses on a different species of

---

[67] Here I am indebted to presentations by Michele Moody-Adams and to conversations with her.

146 THE MAIN ENTERPRISE OF THE WORLD

consensus. At the end of any discussion, each of the participants will have a collection of options deemed tolerable—the person's *acceptable set*. A deliberation reaches *weak* consensus just in case the conclusion finally adopted belongs to each discussant's acceptable set. Plainly, weak consensus is more likely than its strong counterpart. Its chances can be boosted if the engagement with others tends to expand the options considered tolerable. Although they come to the conversation with commitment to a narrow range of possibilities, the deliberators find themselves including more options as outcomes with which they can live, until ultimately the intersection of their acceptable sets is no longer empty. If the candidates in the final vote all belong to this intersection, weak consensus is achieved.

The second mitigating condition elaborates the idea just sketched. Acceptable sets are most obviously expanded through compromise. Compromise is often seen as a patchwork, in which elements from different perspectives are (more or less clumsily) stitched together. The appropriate concept of compromise for ideal deliberation is shaped by the intended goal, the production of weak consensus. For an option to belong to a deliberator's acceptable set, it must respond to the central needs of the deliberator's perspective, *as that perspective has evolved throughout the discussion*. Apt compromises would not combine elements of the positions with which the deliberators *begin*, but should respond to the changes of perspective produced by learning more about fellow citizens. Nor need those compromises be any kind of patchwork. The evolution of perspectives can allow for a reconceptualization of the issue, and an emergent option that was previously invisible.

The third mitigating condition builds on the thought of compromise by adding a historical dimension. Democratic deliberations are not single events but belong to a sequence of discussions. The past matters. In particular, when weak consensus repeatedly fails, with one group of citizens consistently being confronted with an outcome they deem unacceptable, subsequent deliberations should take account of the fact. Mutual engagement demands attending to perspectives whose central goals have previously been frustrated. Cross-temporal compromise would try to compensate for the past. Just as acceptable sets include the options with which deliberators can live, so *acceptable records* include sequences of decisions holders of different perspectives find tolerable. When democratic deliberations fail to achieve weak consensus, they may yet, in sequence, produce something weaker still, but significant nonetheless. A history of deliberations could be said to *resist partition* just in case the sequence of decisions generated belongs to the acceptable record of each perspective within the polity.

These remarks are only the first stages in a much longer defense of the proposed ideal. For I have not confronted the important objection that compromise is sometimes impossible, and that, for some perspectives, any record containing certain kinds of decisions is unacceptable.[68]

Let's take stock. The tie between education and democracy doesn't simply consist in the need for citizens to be prepared to recognize where their interests lie. Deep democracy, I claim, following Dewey, is a matter of learning from one another. I've offered three lines of thought in defense of that conception. The fourth, the most important, centers on the ideal of democratic deliberation. I've just attempted to respond to charges of wide-eyed optimism. So far, however, no argument for the ideal has been given.

My defense will come in the next chapter. There, I shall try to ground deep democracy in ethics. Given ethical life, as I understand it, the method of democratic deliberation is central. It is the method of ethics.

<hr />

Two tasks remain. The first is to connect the project of deliberating with others to the goal of self-fulfillment discussed in the previous chapter. The second is to consider ways in which formal educational institutions might promote the kinds of deliberations deep democracy requires.

Mill's influential form of liberalism sees joint deliberation as irrelevant to fulfillment. To live well requires only an autonomous choice of your own good and sufficient success in pursuing that good. For that conception of the good life, an ideal version of Millian democracy is enough.

Imagine a society in which the system of education together with the organization of public debate provide all citizens with good chances to discern where their interests lie. The confusions and misinformation so evident in the contemporary world have been removed. Individual citizens are provided with opportunities for choosing their central projects—they are as autonomous as the more fortunate members of any current society. But they are never encouraged either to choose projects that satisfy the community condition or to understand the perspectives of others. Constitutional protections are in place to protect collisions among the individual projects. Mill's Harm

---

[68] The next two chapters will have more to say on these issues. Exploring the potential role of religion, the topic of Chapter 6, is particularly crucial.

148   THE MAIN ENTERPRISE OF THE WORLD

Principle[69] is universally acknowledged. Sensitive to the possibility that patterns of voting might consistently restrict the opportunities for a group of citizens, governments regularly analyze the electoral record and present their findings. Voters are encouraged to correct for a lopsided sequence of policy decisions. In this way, the society attempts to ensure that no segment of the society experiences constant losses and thus becomes disaffected.

This idealized version of Millian democracy adopts a purely external strategy for treating the diverse perspectives of its citizens even-handedly. It doesn't engage the different points of view with one another, but takes note of recurrent disappointments and tries to offer compensation. The society fits well with Mill's official account of the good life. Further, it is scrupulous about *negative* freedom, freedom from the interference of others.

Dewey and I suppose that negative freedom is not enough. Living well requires contributing to the lives of others, and, for that, there must be opportunities to understand how such contributions might be made. Citizens need not only "freedom from" but also "freedom to," specifically, freedom to shape their lives around projects that advance other human lives. Without institutions promoting engagement with others, without entering into alternative perspectives, that second freedom is left to chance. Perhaps my imaginary society might sometimes offer it, at least to some. Yet, in its external strategy for coping with lopsided voting patterns, it treats the need for community as an optional extra.

The current state of many affluent nations reveals what happens when only negative freedom is emphasized. An extreme instance of the pathology occurs when economic freedom is given star or even sole billing. Freedom is reduced to the ability to secure your wealth against the depredations of others, including a government that might want some of it to support public goods. To be sure, so crass a reduction of the concept of freedom has not always dominated during the past decades. Yet, as sociologists like Robert Putnam have documented, those decades have witnessed a steady erosion of community.[70] Even if societies were to move toward the Millian version of democracy, embodied in my imagined society, it seems unlikely that serious

---

[69] The principle that my freedom to choose and pursue my own project is limited by the need to preserve the similar freedom of others: thus I am only constrained when what I propose to do would bring genuine harm to someone else. See OL 17 and especially sections IV and V.

History abounds in debates about how the principle should be applied. The democracy I have in mind is free from the familiar interpretive difficulties.

[70] Robert Putnam, *Bowling Alone* (New York: Simon & Schuster, 2000) and *Our Kids* (New York: Simon & Schuster, 2015). See also Annette Lareau, *Unequal Childhoods*.

CITIZENS   149

engagement with fellow citizens, especially across divergent perspectives, would be restored. Deep democracy, Deweyan democracy, offers greater chances of enabling lives to become meaningful. It promises to harmonize two goals of education—preparing citizens and attaining self-fulfillment.

At last, education re-enters the discussion. The main efforts of this chapter have been directed at finding an appropriate ideal of democracy, one that might be deployed to identify the shortcomings of our current situation, and to indicate ways of overcoming them. If Millian democracy offered an adequate ideal, the project of envisaging educational reform could have extended the themes sounded earlier, concentrating on explaining in more detail how to prepare citizens to recognize their interests when many of the issues they confront are technical and when public pronouncements about them are often misleading. But Millian democracy misses a dimension. An essential task of education today is to help restore the possibilities of community democracy requires.

How? As with Chapter 2, I'll offer some proposals for experiments. Some of these are inspired by practices already tried out in schools (particularly "progressive" schools like Summerhill and the Chicago Lab School).[71]

6. *From early stages, set aside time for children to plan together. Starting perhaps at age three, have daily activities in which groups of children decide what they will do and how they will do it.*
7. *In subsequent years, continue daily planning, gradually increasing the difficulty of the topics, as well as the size and diversity of the groups.*
8. *Periodically, bring together groups of children who have never previously met one another (children who attend different schools in the same region), asking them to solve a problem in joint decision.*
9. *After several years of experience in joint decision-making, supplement the practical activities with studies of differences in human cultures. Integrate these with analyses of the costs of cultural clashes and of the effects of attempts to cooperate.*

[71] See A. S. Neill, *Summerhill School*, and Katherine Camp Mayhew and Anna Camp Edwards, *The Dewey School: The Laboratory School of the University of Chicago, 1896–1903* (New York: Appleton, 1936).

150 THE MAIN ENTERPRISE OF THE WORLD

10. *During adolescence and young adulthood, provide support for extended visits to communities quite different from those in which students have grown up. First to some different region of the country, later to a foreign destination—and, in both instances, the visitors should work with the local inhabitants.*
11. *Encourage adults to take periodic (funded) "sabbaticals," in which they live, plan, and work with people unlike those they have previously encountered.*

Evidently, the proposals could be elaborated in a number of different ways. I don't know (and I don't know whether anyone knows) how to specify the details of promising trials. The hope is that *some* program along these lines might educate citizens for deep democracy.

The intended result is to produce people who are eager to engage with and learn from others, even from those whose perspectives they initially find alien. A very direct way to attempt that would be to use the ideal of democratic deliberation throughout the sequence of stages. From the start, there would be an emphasis on including the perspectives of all who would be affected by the outcome, a serious attempt to obtain and use the best available information, and a constant encouragement to understand and respond to the viewpoints of fellow discussants.

So, at the very beginning, a small group of children might be asked to decide which game they would next like to play. The adult (or adults) present make it clear that the children are to reach agreement if they can. The adult role is to facilitate the conversation, to make sure that each child has the chance to speak, that no child dominates, that everyone knows what the various options require, perhaps to introduce possibilities of compromise (e.g., "You could do this for half the time, and that for the other half"). The discussion only stops when each member of the group is willing to go ahead with the plan.

Assuming that early efforts along these lines produced propensities to include everyone's views, to seek out the pertinent facts, and to be unsatisfied until weak consensus had been reached, adult participation would gradually diminish. The initial propensities would be further developed by tackling harder problems of the same kind, cases involving a greater diversity of perspectives, perhaps demanding more significant sacrifices of some. In line with the recognition of historical patterns in decision-making, the same group might address a sequence of problems, so that its members

CITIZENS   151

would acquire a disposition to compensate those who had previously been disappointed.

The propensities would be further tested—and, with luck, extended—by arranging for joint decision-making with previously unknown children. Is it possible to transfer a talent for "iterated" deliberation to the "one-shot" case? Perhaps. The aim of the first three stages of the program would be to cultivate a sense of satisfaction with the activity itself: planning with others comes to appear enjoyable and rewarding, perhaps especially so when the radically divergent perspectives expressed at the beginning evolve into acceptance of a common solution.

Later stages of the program suggest how an attempt to embody the ideal of democratic deliberation can be combined with more standard aspects of school education. I envisage geography, anthropology, and history as showing their importance in extensive understandings of the relations among groups of people.[72] Examples from the contemporary world and from the past can reveal very clearly the high points of mutual engagement and cooperation, and the sufferings produced when joint deliberation either breaks down or (more commonly) is never undertaken in the first place.

Further, following a hint from Mill's Inaugural Address, it would be valuable to integrate the early discussions with children from different backgrounds with the learning of a second language. Mill's case for studying the classical languages starts from the thought that deep access to a culture requires acquiring the language native to its adherents. Whether or not this is exactly right, any program aimed at fostering engagement across cultures would be aided by fostering the ability to learn foreign languages. Studies indicate that beginning early (even at three years of age) facilitates not only fluency in the second language, but also greater ease in acquiring further languages.[73] I propose a double experiment. First, combine exercises in joint planning with instruction in some language used by children with whom those taught will have repeated opportunities to plan. Thus, in areas of the United States with a substantial Latinx population, introduce Spanish, beginning at age three. Second, pursue longitudinal studies to test whether the long-term effects in ability to acquire new languages are greater or lesser when the first foreign language learned is unrelated to the native language (e.g., when English speakers begin with Arabic or Chinese, rather than Spanish).

---

[72] For more on this, see Chapter 9.
[73] Again, Chapter 9 will offer a more extensive discussion.

152   THE MAIN ENTERPRISE OF THE WORLD

In these studies, too, language-learning should be combined with opportunities for joint planning.

The last two parts of the program are directed toward immersing people in cultures other than their own, with the goals of fostering respect for differences and of developing capacities for engagement under what initially seem the most taxing conditions. If young adults spend a significant period of time working alongside people whose backgrounds differ greatly from their own, and if, every decade or so, that experience is repeated with new groups of strangers, two important consequences may flow. First, for the problems demanding democracy on a global scale, transnational deliberation may go more smoothly. Second, the returning citizens can bring fresh eyes and new perspectives to their own internal debates.

The proposals I've offered reflect two main themes of this chapter and its predecessors. First, education today can only be a lifelong matter. Second, democracy is needed at many scales, from the local contexts at which it comes relatively easily to the global cooperation where the challenges are severe. As the example of climate change reminds us, failure to meet the challenge of crafting international democracy will bequeath to our descendants, to our grandchildren and great-grandchildren, a world in which even the most sublime discussions of education, democracy, or the good life will seem a cruel joke. They will be a biting reminder of the privileges of a bygone age.

5

Moral Development

One of the most popular activities throughout human history is to complain about the behavior of the young. Our own times enthusiastically take up a long-standing tradition. Recent surveys report that American adults take themselves to share few values with their teenage contemporaries.[1] Many people today decry the selfishness and materialism of the "me generation."[2] As did our predecessors. Here is a voice from 1274 CE:

> The world is passing through troublous times. The young people of today think of nothing but themselves. They have no reverence for parents or old age. They are impatient of all restraint. They talk as if they knew everything, and what passes for wisdom with us is foolishness with them. As for the girls, they are forward, immodest and unladylike in speech, behavior and dress.[3]

The Earl of Shaftesbury voiced similar complaints in 1843, in the House of Commons, declaring that "the morals of children are tenfold worse than formerly."[4] Almost a century later, the *Hull Daily Mail* echoed his judgment, lamenting the (further) decline in morality: "We defy anyone who goes about with his eyes open to deny that there is, as never before, an attitude on the part of young folk which is best described as grossly thoughtless, rude, and utterly selfish." Apparently, the Me Generation has always been with us.

Early training is supposed to forestall the bad behavior so conspicuous among young people. Since it invariably fails (to judge by the diatribes ringing down through the ages), educational reform is always needed. As

---

[1] See, for example, "The 1998 National Survey of Americans on Values" (*Washington Post*); cited in "The 21st Century Teen: Public Perception and Teen Reality," available at www.frameworksinstitute. org › assets › files.

[2] Jean Twenge, *Generation Me*, rev. ed. (New York: Simon & Schuster, 2014); also "The Evidence for Generation Me and against Generation We," *Emerging Adulthood* 1 (2013): 11–16.

[3] Translation of a sermon preached by Peter the Hermit. Available at: https://proto-knowledge. blogspot.com/2010/11/what-is-wrong-with-young-people-today.html.

[4] Quoted at https://proto-knowledge.blogspot.com/2010/11/what-is-wrong-with-young-people-today.html.

The Main Enterprise of the World. Philip Kitcher, Oxford University Press. © Oxford University Press 2022.
DOI: 10.1093/oso/9780190928971.003.0006

154 THE MAIN ENTERPRISE OF THE WORLD

the varieties of wickedness emerge in increasingly awful forms, each generation must offer its own diagnosis of what has gone wrong. So, in the moral sphere too, educational efforts have "danced to different drummers during their long history."[5] None of them has gotten it right. Indeed, if the Eeyores of history are to be believed, each venture has only made things worse.

Programs to bring the potentially rebellious young into line have a long past. Tens of thousands of years before the invention of writing, our ancestors taught new members of their social groups the customs—*mores*—they were expected to observe. (In the absence of records, we cannot tell if they, too, were disappointed by the results.) For the past couple of millennia, the available documents reveal a dominant trend. Morality, specifying what people are *required* to do, is distinguished from local conceptions of socially acceptable behavior. Conventional customs can be flouted (albeit often at social cost); moral principles cannot. Inculcation of the moral requirements is intertwined with initiation into the group's religious practices, bound up with rites and ceremonies, interwoven with stories and doctrines about deities. Residues of this trend remain in the present, enduring in many nations. Around the world, when people reflect on moral development, a majority probably think in terms of religious education.

Yet, ever since Plato, a tight link between morality and religion, expressed in viewing moral laws as decreed by the gods, has been suspect.[6] Philosophical reflections on morality often sever the connection. Consequently, when fostering moral development is understood to be crucial for the reproduction of society, a multicultural nation has several options. It may decide that the "majority religion" (or the "traditional religion," the one adopted by the nation's founders) should be the vehicle through which morality is taught. Or it may relegate all moral teaching to the private sphere, leaving families and communities to pursue it as they think best. Or it may introduce into the system of formal education some non-religious approach to morality, one that will best integrate the core themes of all the major religions into some philosophical synthesis. Mill's Inaugural Address veers in the latter directions, when he identifies "the home, the family" as providing the core of moral and religious education, while simultaneously supposing that universities should acquaint

---

[5] Patricia Albjerg Graham, *Schooling America: How the Public Schools Meet the Nation's Changing Needs* (New York: Oxford University Press, 2020), 1. As noted in Chapter 1, Graham is concerned with the diversity of tasks American schools have been supposed to discharge.

[6] Plato, *Euthyphro*.

MORAL DEVELOPMENT   155

students with "the principal systems of moral philosophy," in part to remedy the ignorance that often leads people astray.[7]

Whether or not the long litany of complaints about the defects of young people is correct, it points to failure after failure in the various programs of moral education past societies have tried. For, if the harsh judgments delivered about the young are erroneous, we must blame the elders for their faulty moral vision. *Their* moral training has led to a stunted moral development, rendering them unable to grow beyond the specific perspectives they acquired when they were young. The recurrent intergenerational mismatch between standards of conduct should be troubling. Shouldn't our societies strive to do better?

I suspect that we have been misled by an inadequate understanding of what morality is and does. Because of the importance of guiding the conduct of the young, each generation strives to pass on its favored moral code. That code is often thought of as something rigid, definite, and complete. Consequently, when, as they grow, the younger members of society do things that surprise and shock their elders, they are seen as repudiating what they have been taught. They "violate morality" and are condemned as wicked—or worse. I shall offer a different picture, one that recognizes the articulation, refinement, and revision of moral codes as an intrinsic feature of human life, and that sees preparation for moral inquiry as central to education.

As I have already noted, practices of moral education descend from an enterprise with a long history, extending back into pre-moral attempts to initiate the young into the ways of the social group. Initiation is naturally interpreted as a process of transmission. Societies pass on their code to the next generation. When those societies engage in moral direction of conduct what is transmitted is a *moral* code.

How moral education is conceived will depend on what a moral code is taken to be. Should we view societies as always having a single moral code? What are the elements of the codes? What is the supposed status of those elements? I shall begin by trying to address those questions, and by exposing difficulties with popular answers to them.

The strongest claim about a moral code is that it has a special status: it is true, or correct, or in accordance with properly developed human emotions,

---

[7] SMC 346–47.

156   THE MAIN ENTERPRISE OF THE WORLD

or ultimately justified.[8] Moreover, it is complete, applying to any possible human situation. Consequently, it should never be amended and should always be obeyed. I shall argue that all the constituent parts of this claim are incorrect. History shows clearly how past societies have accepted supposedly moral precepts condoning or even commanding actions now viewed as hideously wrong. Furthermore, the idea of a code applicable to any situation is a myth: new circumstances always require extensions and new moral decisions. Finally, moral conduct cannot be reduced to any simple act of obedience; *applying* the code to your particular situation often requires difficult investigations and reflections.

My diagnosis pinpoints two important tasks for a well-educated moral agent. The code that person has inherited should be considered as a collection of resources for use in directing conduct. People need to be able to use those resources well, to deploy them to solve the moral problems they encounter. They also should be able to play their part in the social process through which their code is progressively changed, so that an improved collection of resources is passed on to their successors.

This picture suggests a different view of what are commonly regarded as the elements of moral codes. Precepts, stories of saints and sinners, tests for decision-making, analogies, claims about virtues and vices, specifications of what is appropriate in particular social roles—all these are best viewed as tools in a toolbox. Those tools are used in particular contexts by drawing on our psychological capacities—and different theorists emphasize reason or sympathy or moral intuition. I shall argue that, in moral life, whether in coping with specific situations or in efforts to improve the toolbox, none of the elements should play an overriding role, nor should any of the capacities be assigned fundamental status. Not every occasion calls for a hammer or requires a talent for accurate swinging.

Moral life is pervaded by moral inquiry, and, just as our ancestors made progress in investigating nature when they began to develop (crude and provisional) methods for scientific inquiry, so too with morality. Moral

---

[8] In what follows, I shall not attempt to resolve how my pragmatist approach to morality and ethics relates to views that deploy a notion of moral truth. The account outlined below views moral life as a collective human construction, in which progressive changes overcome (wholly or partially) the problems of the existing situation. The objectivity of morality is grounded in the stable relation between solutions and the indefinitely extended history in which problems emerge. Consideration of moral education can proceed from that picture without taking any stand on whether the position is "realist" or not. Chapter 3 of *Moral Progress* offers some ideas on that issue, and the successor to the present volume will develop them further.

methodology should be the core of moral philosophy.[9] Much of the chapter that follows consists in a preliminary attempt to articulate methods for moral inquiry. My approach will be to use an account of the genealogy of moral life to identify a recurrent problem faced by our species, to which the invention of morality was—and is—the answer. I shall then show how a natural approach to solving instances of that problem can be traced in the messy and highly contingent processes through which three major instances of moral progress were achieved.

The abolition of chattel slavery, the expansion of opportunities for women, and the increasing acceptance of same-sex love all involved two important changes. First, voices previously excluded from moral conversation began to be recognized. Second, ideals for self-fulfillment, traditionally denied to particular groups of people, came to be seen as possibilities for them. The methodology I shall propose suggests social changes for streamlining progress of these two kinds.

Finally, the account of moral method and moral progress will be used to show how people can make advances in their own individual conduct and in promoting the social changes through which moral codes progressively evolve. On that basis, we can begin to discern the kinds of training moral education should supply. It will become clearer how to help people make better use of the moral tools they are given, and how to play their part in improving the contents of the toolbox.

<hr />

The simplest view of moral education sees it as coming in two parts. One is cognitive. Children must become able to distinguish among potential actions, separating those that are required of them, those that are forbidden, and those that are permissible. Early on this might be achieved through a simple list of "dos and don'ts." Later the list is supplemented by identifying general principles, or by telling stories about exemplary behavior (good or bad), or by explaining virtues and vices. The moral code instilled into young people must be supplemented by shaping them to do what the code requires. Tendencies to pursue selfish goals have to be overcome. The will must be strengthened. A conscience is to be built. As Mill observed, the basic steps in modifying attitudes are taken before formal education begins. Embryonic moral agency begins at home. At most times, and in most places, its origins

---

[9] I argue at length for this (blunt) claim in *Moral Progress*.

158 THE MAIN ENTERPRISE OF THE WORLD

have drawn clear lines and imposed rigid discipline. More subtle types of moral motivation—a desire to serve the Almighty, fellow-feeling, pride in being righteous, respect for the moral law—typically come later (if they come at all).[10]

The simple view sees moral education as providing children with a collection of moral beliefs, ideally corresponding to the deliverances of the prevalent moral code, and with a specific set of psychological dispositions, the "healthy conscience" or the "strong will." In its very simplest form, the precepts transmitted have a special status: they are uniquely correct and they cover the entire field of human conduct. Armed with this moral equipment, the young venture into the world where (with luck) their actions will be generated by the attitudes produced by their training. But, of course, the world is a complicated place, and the situations in which they find themselves differ in ways that would defy comprehensive coverage, no matter how extensive their training had been. Furthermore, the world changes, bringing new kinds of circumstances for which there are no precedents. Nobody should be surprised by the doleful history of complaints about the conduct of the young. For their shocking conduct is not simply a matter of forgetting precepts or being led into temptation by the pressures of the moment. They may be doing the best they can to extend to novel contexts the ideas they have been taught. Dewey saw the point clearly:

[R]igid moral codes that attempt to lay down definite injunctions and prohibitions for every occasion in life turn out in fact loose and slack. Stretch ten commandments or any other number as far as you will by ingenious exegesis, yet acts unprovided for by them will occur. No elaboration of statute law can forestall variant cases and the need of interpretation *ad hoc*.[11]

However successful a society is in instilling its moral precepts, however thoroughly it fortifies the consciences of its children, however perfect they are in remembering what they have been taught and maintaining their strength

[10] In *The Ethical Project* (§13) I suggest that the disposition to follow norms can take a variety of forms. To the extent that conformity is important for human beings, cultural selection can be expected to favor redundancy. If early socialization has inculcated a number of potential sources for following the local code, in situations where one is weakened or undermined, another may come to the rescue. Psychological evidence for a single pattern, followed in all instances of moral development—as famously proposed by Lawrence Kohlberg—is at best inconclusive. Unlike Kohlberg's most well-known critics, Carol Gilligan and Jonathan Haidt for example, I reject the assumption of a monolithic pattern of moral development and a single style of developed moral character.

[11] *Human Nature and Conduct*, MW 14, 74.

MORAL DEVELOPMENT   159

of will, new situations are likely to elicit divergent reactions from different people—and perhaps the variation will correlate with a split between generations.

Examples of the predicament are easy to come by. Many sensitive and well-intentioned people are in doubt about how they should respond to homeless people who beg for money, about whether opposition to violent oppression should make use of violence, about how to respond to the demands of people who claim discrimination, about how to apportion the burdens between present and future generations, about the extent of their responsibilities to remedy social inequality—and about how to balance the distribution of scarce resources among different kinds of children in reshaping their local schools.[12] If moral education is to help them, it must do more than the simple picture suggests. It must provide some sort of capacity for going on from a moral code that should be acknowledged as incomplete.

Indeed, not only incomplete, but potentially revisable. Although there have been many societies in human history—possibly even a majority—that have taken their moral codes to contain the complete and final truth about how people should act, contemporary communities should have been jarred out of any similar false security. We ought to be fully aware of the gross errors of the past. Historical records reveal how many of our predecessors have accepted, even commended, behavior we find barbaric. They have tolerated violence toward neighbors, extreme forms of punishment, fanaticism, slavery, the subjugation of women, hostility toward people who love members of their own sex, and any number of other practices condemned by later generations.[13] Recognizing how conduct we find abhorrent was once accepted without demur, we should expect our own moral codes to be infected by similar errors. Contemporary societies ought to wonder just where their own blind spots are. They should thus be open to the need not only for extension but also for revision.

I have spoken casually of societies and communities as having moral codes. A common form of characterization, to be sure, but one requiring more scrutiny than it typically receives. From a stratospheric perspective, it's sometimes useful to look down on the moral stance taken at a particular time in a particular place—twenty-first-century America, say—and to ask how it compares either with contemporaneous views held elsewhere or with

---

[12] For more on the significance of examples like these, see Chapter 3 of *Moral Progress*.

[13] For an illuminating discussion of some further examples, see Anthony Appiah, *The Honor Code* (New York: W. W. Norton, 2010).

160   THE MAIN ENTERPRISE OF THE WORLD

the moral ideas previously prevalent in the same place. Commentators look at the differences between attitudes in twenty-first-century Denmark and twenty-first-century China (say), or between the ways in which conceptions of morality have changed in England from the Victorian era to the present. Yet it is obviously an oversimplification to identify a single moral code in force across any sizeable community at any particular time. On some large issues, a social consensus may exist. In most, perhaps all, contemporary societies, a repudiation of slavery forms part of the moral code. To make that attribution is not to maintain that nobody continues to believe in the permissibility of slaveholding or to suppose that the practice has vanished entirely. Consensus is marked in two ways. First, through the character of public discourse, in which any proposal to reintroduce slavery would arouse massive indignation. Second, in a commitment that the wrongness of slavery is an important lesson, to be taught to young members of the society. The common moral code makes its presence felt in the limits on acceptable speech and in the ways all children are socialized.

Yet most contemporary societies are pluralistic, in the sense of allowing smaller communities within them to extend the common moral code in alternative ways. A full representation of the moral life of a society would show a tree-like structure. At the apex would be the broadest moral code, embodying everything belonging to the social consensus. Descending along the various branches, the codes operative within smaller and smaller subcommunities would articulate further the perspectives prevalent in the groups to which they belong. Sometimes differences simply reflect the relative salience of problems that arise in some locations, and are absent from others. Views about some environmental issues may be developed quite differently depending on where a community lives. Other types of variation depend on affiliation with a particular religious perspective, or with some specific way of reacting against religion. People who identify as Christians often share some moral views that separate them from Muslims, Jews, Hindus, or Buddhists. Within Christianity, as within the other major religions, there is further division into sects, each distinguished by its own list of approved duties and permissions. When non-religious people join humanist communities, they become bound together in a similar fashion. At the terminal nodes of the tree, the tips of the branches, are highly articulated codes, embodying the shared attitudes of a local community.

Children develop morally through a series of interactions, with the family, with members of the local community (particularly their peers), and through

MORAL DEVELOPMENT 161

their formal schooling. What goal exactly should this process achieve? Furthermore, how should the work of attaining it be divided up among the three spheres of interchange? Although these questions are rarely posed explicitly, they are implicitly contested. Answers to the former question divide along at least two dimensions. First, there is a choice of levels in the tree-like structure, the hierarchy of moral codes: how narrow, or how broad, should be the community whose values the growing child is to absorb? Second, a decision must be made about the extent of conformity: given a particular chosen moral code, how much of its set of principles and tenets must the well-educated child end up accepting? Two varieties of conservativism correspond to two species of liberalism. At the conservative poles, the chosen level is narrowest, the code of the local community, and the inculcation of belief is to be complete, comprising all pieces of received moral doctrine. At the liberal poles, the focus is on the most general moral code—perhaps even on a set of cosmopolitan principles, shared by all humanity; beyond these "universal moral truths," the emerging adults are encouraged to think for themselves.

Conservatives tend to overlook the importance of Dewey's point—that any set of commandments will prove incomplete—and to underappreciate the historical message of moral blindness. Yet even people who would bristle at any suggestion of their conservativism fall into a similar trap, and are thus led to make the same mistakes. The codes transmitted across the generations are reduced to collections of rules, or, possibly, sets of exemplary stories (parables?) intended to highlight some approved (or condemned) pattern of conduct. The aim is to set up in the properly developed individual a corpus of beliefs, centered on the principles and patterns, together with a strong disposition to act in accordance with those beliefs (a strong will, one capable of resisting temptations to deviate). If all sets of principles and patterns are incomplete, and if all moral codes are properly subject to revision, achieving that goal will not be enough. Moral education must also instill abilities to act correctly when the advice offered by the subject's existing beliefs is blank or unclear or ambiguous. It must also enable people, individually or collectively, to identify and correct the errors of the moral codes they have inherited.

Without serious thought about how that is to be done, discussions of moral development are incomplete—if not worthless.

162　THE MAIN ENTERPRISE OF THE WORLD

To make progress with the crucial questions it's useful to introduce a technical term for the psychological state moral education is supposed to instill. From their early socialization people come to have what I shall call a *moral practice*. The view just criticized adopts a two-component characterization of individual moral practices. Someone's moral practice is seen as consisting of a set of moral beliefs—propositions about the rightness or wrongness of particular classes of actions, say—together with a disposition to act. Given a particular context, the disposition will either yield an action according with the moral beliefs, or it will not. People whose tendencies to action lead to conduct concordant with the moral beliefs across a broader range of contexts (all contexts? the contexts they tend to encounter?) have a stronger will. If the range of concordant contexts is impressively large they have "admirable moral character." They are good people.

Parts of this view are perfectly sensible, but, as I have argued, it is overly simple.[14] For it overlooks the need for individual people and for their societies to make moral advances, either by resolving indeterminate cases or by remedying the mistakes of the past. Something needs to be added. But what?

There's an obvious suggestion. Once the vulnerability of individuals and societies to moral error is clearly in view, some standard of correctness or appropriateness has entered the picture. Some theorists will present this standard in the most straightforward way: claims about the rightness or wrongness of actions are *true*. Others will resist that language. They will opt instead for supposing morality to aim at the expression of proper emotions ("apt feelings"), or at being permanently justified. In whatever way the standard is understood, moral education will be taken to differ from instruction in table manners or other conventional niceties, in its introducing young people to precepts with a special status. What is taught is not simply what a community has agreed on. Rather, the favored precepts are candidates for the special status, hailed by the local society as the real thing. For moral practices to guide people properly throughout their lives they need skills enabling them to acquire new beliefs enjoying this status, going beyond what they have been explicitly taught. They must be able to extend the scope of the inherited code, as well as to diagnose any defects in the tradition.

If societies had arrived at a clear and definite consensus about how to arrive at the right moral attitudes, the history of morality would be very different. Many important insights have emerged slowly, from protracted struggles in

---

[14] For more detail about the notion of a moral practice, see Chapter 3 of *Moral Progress*.

which some of those who campaigned for reform have lost their lives. The route to understanding the wrongness of torture, of slavery, and of many forms of discrimination has been long and bloody. Nor can the disputes of today—debates about our obligations to future generations, about the extent to which inequalities can be justified, about our treatment of non-human animals (to name just three examples)—be dissolved by applying some agreed-on method for reaching moral knowledge. These failures show that any counsel offered to the young, any precise vision of the necessary additional skills and how they are inculcated, is bound to be incomplete. Nevertheless, drawing on the ways in which human beings have made moral progress, individually in addressing the new predicaments arising to challenge people during their lives, collectively in the course of human history, it might prove possible to prepare the next generation so that it can build on past achievements. Reflection on episodes in which past moral advances have been made—that is, on moral transitions for which there is broad consensus about their progressiveness—can reveal patterns of thought conducive to moral insight. Our descendants would benefit not just from beginning from the improved corpus of precepts a painful history has bequeathed to them, but also from learning methods of thinking through which the past advances have been achieved and which might be applied more self-consciously and less bloodily in the future.

The positive proposals for moral education offered below will emerge from applying this strategy. We can use the history of moral attitudes, both on the grand scale of social reform and on the smaller canvas of individual lives, as a laboratory for generating and testing hypotheses about moral methodology. To the extent we are able to discern methods that have previously been successful, moral practice need no longer be conceived in the usual narrow fashion. Incompleteness can be addressed and an avenue opened for thoughtful criticism by training young people to follow the kinds of psychological processes found to be successful in the past. Through instilling capacities for reflection of the valuable kinds, moral practice is extended and the routes to future moral advances become shorter and less painful.

Before I try to show how the recommended strategy might be implemented, it's useful to remedy an injustice in my suggestion that problems of incompleteness and hidden error have been ignored in traditional thought about moral development. Proposals for supplementing moral practice have been

164   THE MAIN ENTERPRISE OF THE WORLD

offered. The most culturally prominent of these have arisen when moral education has been viewed as a province of religion. Fundamental moral principles are conceived as the law set down by the deity. These are to be learned and followed. They are not revisable. Yet, in evaluating the moral powers of ordinary folk, religions often implicitly recognize the difficulties attending everyday application of the divine law. When lay people are perplexed about what to do, as is often the case, given the limitations of their understanding, two possibilities for recourse are open to them. If their predicament allows time for consultation, they may turn to those who are especially pious, people who understand the word of the deity (and the texts in which it is articulated) far better than they do. They may go to the priest, the imam, the rabbi, or the holy hermit for advice. When matters are urgent, and no appropriate human advisor is at hand, they are to apply directly to the source. Prayer is the answer.

Typically, praying is supposed to discharge a number of functions. Supplicants celebrate the splendor of the deity, they express their own subordination to the divine will, they find spiritual refreshment. In addition, they seek counsel, whether it be offered in terms of a message of moral insight or through the proper direction of heart and will. George Herbert meditates on the diverse meanings of the act of prayer, including these possibilities of guidance:

> The soul in paraphrase, heart in pilgrimage,
> The Christian plummet sounding heav'n and earth;

His poetic catalog concludes by emphasizing psychological change: "something understood."[15]

Even for those committed to a particular religion, reflection on the history of moral change should make the inadequacies of the proposal evident. With respect to major controversies, past and present, religious texts are (at best) ambiguous: not only *can* the devil cite scripture for his purpose,[16] but, historically, he often has. In the debate about the legitimacy of chattel slavery in North America, from 1700 on, both sides regularly appealed to the Bible to

---

[15] George Herbert, "Prayer," in *The Metaphysical Poets*, ed. Helen Gardner (Harmondsworth: Penguin, 1957), 124. "Prayer" should be compared with Herbert's more famous poem, "The Collar" (ibid., 135), and particularly with the lines in which the protagonist (an incipient rebel) questions the moral enterprise: "leave thy cold dispute/Of what is fit and not. Forsake thy cage,/ Thy rope of sands,/Which pettie thoughts have made, and made to thee/Good cable, to enforce and draw,/And be thy law." He is recalled by the voice of God: "Me thoughts I heard one calling, *Child!/* And I reply'd, *My Lord!*"

[16] Shakespeare, *Merchant of Venice*, Act I, Scene 3, 93.

buttress their assertions.[17] Perhaps it will be claimed that those now viewed as being on the wrong side of the issue failed to read the texts correctly or were defective in their efforts to seek guidance through prayer. If so, any attempt to co-opt religious resources in moral education will have to separate the sheep from the goats. Children will have to be taught skills in proper reading and proper prayer. Given the large class of apparently devout people who blundered so badly in the past, inculcating these abilities does not seem likely.

During the past few millennia, identifying moral correctness with some kind of divine law has been by far the most popular way to view the basis of morality. Given the identification, the proposal just reviewed makes excellent sense. When people are in moral doubt, they should ask the deity for direction. Or, perhaps, given their cognitive shortcomings, they should consult someone who is especially good at contacting and understanding this ultimate source. History reveals the radical unreliability of attempts to do so. Philosophers, usually sympathetic to Plato's suspicions about grounding morality in the divine will, have sometimes still taken the deity to be especially authoritative on moral matters. Nevertheless, they have typically been sensitive to the divergent opinions of those who claimed to be speaking on behalf of God. Much of the history of moral philosophy was forged in full awareness of the effects of schism. Hence philosophers have sought to provide more reliable counsel. Can they do better?

Philosophical ventures in trying to resolve moral disputes divide into two main types. One tradition contests Dewey's claim of incompleteness, contending that morality, properly understood, comprises a system of principles so comprehensive as to cover all cases.[18] More recently, some thinkers, discouraged about the prospects for discovering an all-encompassing moral theory, have embraced moral particularism.[19] They focus on cultivating habits of thought capable of resolving specific moral problems.[20]

---

[17] See Mason Lowance, ed., *Against Slavery: An Abolitionist Reader* (Harmondsworth: Penguin, 2000), 15–20. Both John Saffin and Cotton Mather defended slavery on religious grounds. The practice continued into the nineteenth century, for example in the speeches and writings of Jefferson Davis.

[18] This becomes fully explicit, for example, in Derek Parfit's *On What Matters* (Oxford: Clarendon Press, 2011), although it is tacitly present in any quest for a "supreme principle (or principles) of morality."

[19] A classic source is Jonathan Dancy, *Ethics without Principles* (Oxford: Clarendon Press, 2004).

[20] In some professional contexts, attempts to help practitioners make better moral decisions often view their task in these terms. Doctors, engineers, and business executives are to form improved

166 THE MAIN ENTERPRISE OF THE WORLD

A striking feature of the search for a complete moral system is its extraordinary ambition. When people think about moral life, they are often tempted to compare moral belief with scientific knowledge—usually to the disadvantage of morality. Moral judgments appear more mysterious, tentative, and open to dispute than judgments about those parts of the natural world amenable to successful scientific description. It is abundantly clear, however, that our knowledge of the cosmos is partial and incomplete, and, with respect to many aspects of nature, our ignorance is vast. Some scientists "dream" of a complete theory,[21] powerful enough to subsume all natural phenomena. The prospect is very distant, as even the most optimistic of them would concede. By contrast, the great moral systematizers claim to have done something analogous in the moral domain, making it available in the here and now. As we shall see later, the idea of any complete theory of the natural world is a delusion.[22] If those who advertise—or seek—a complete theory of the moral realm were aware of the point, they would probably reappraise their aspirations.

Since the late eighteenth century, the search for a complete system of morality has taken two major forms.[23] Jeremy Bentham pioneered a movement—utilitarianism—based upon a single overarching principle: people should always act so as to produce the largest balance of pleasure over pain. In the hands of his successors, from John Stuart Mill and Henry Sedgwick to Peter Singer, the central idea—to measure the rightness of actions according to the amount of good achieved by their consequences—has been developed in a large variety of ways.[24] Later philosophers have debated whether the measure should be applied to individual actions or to general rules for action, they have wondered how goodness and badness should be measured and how different kinds of goods can be represented on a common scale, and, most fundamentally, they have disagreed about what goodness is. Their

moral habits. It's hoped that their ethical training will not simply apply to single instances, but help them across the spectrum of circumstances they encounter in their professional lives. Thanks to Randy Curren for reminding me of this.

[21] See Steven Weinberg, *Dreams of a Final Theory* (New York: Vintage, 1992).

[22] See Chapter 7 below, 234–38.

[23] The two versions I shall consider, utilitarianism and Kantianism, were intended to capture insights of everyday morality. But the point of theorizing was to go further, to offer more general advice in situations for which ordinary moral thinking offered unclear advice—or none at all.

[24] From John Stuart Mill on, many consequentialists have characterized Bentham's identification of the good with pleasure and the absence of pain as far too simple. Depending on how a view enriches the concept of good, consequentialism can become very elastic. See Bernard Williams's contribution to J. J. C. Smart and Williams, *Utilitarianism: For and Against* (Cambridge, UK: Cambridge University Press, 1973), §2; §45 of *The Ethical Project* builds on Williams's analysis.

MORAL DEVELOPMENT   167

controversies, especially on the last score, are inevitably colored and modified by the circumstances in which moral conclusions are to be applied. Changes in human society, in human culture, and in technology affect the understanding of how to circumscribe the good. Even if the theorist adheres to Bentham's original conception, focusing on pleasure and the absence of pain, identifying what counts as pleasure or pain and how different kinds are to be compared and measured, depends on further decisions that must be made in light of an evolving set of situations. As our current debates make evident, *moral* decisions are required to make sense of the potential benefits and costs of immersing ourselves in life online. The concept of the good is not fixed in advance, ready to be plugged into some consequentialist theory. It must be worked out anew in the age of the internet.[25]

The major rival approach to the varieties of consequentialism descending from Bentham stems from Kant. In the original version, it attempts to ground morality in principles of practical reason, precepts available to a rational subject through pure reflection. The first formulation of Kant's Categorical Imperative presents a test we are to apply when faced with a morally challenging situation: we are to ask whether the maxim of our action (roughly: the way in which we characterize to ourselves what we are considering doing) could be a general principle applying to all rational beings. If it could, we are permitted to go ahead. If not, if there is a "contradiction" in our attempt to make the maxim fully general, then we should refrain.[26] Famously, Kant supplements his first formulation with two further versions of the Categorical Imperative, all claimed to be equivalent to one another. One of these announces the special status of human beings: they are always to be treated as ends and never as means. The third version (a formulation whose profile in subsequent history is significantly lower[27]) challenges people making decisions to think of themselves as "lawgivers in a kingdom of ends."

Given the complexity of Kant's ideas, it is unsurprising that they have subsequently been elaborated along a variety of lines. Some of his followers

[25] See, for example, Dean Cocking and Jeroen van der Hoeven, *Evil Online* (Oxford: Blackwell, 2018).

[26] Kant distinguishes two types of contradiction: one that lies in the maxim itself (there is an internal inconsistency) and the other in the attempt to will the maxim. A familiar concern about Kant's test focuses on the imprecision of his notion of contradiction.

[27] Its principal influence is on two recent "contractualist" proposals in moral theory, those of John Rawls (*A Theory of Justice*, and "Kantian Constructivism in Moral Theory," *Journal of Philosophy* 77 [1980]: 515–72) and T. M. Scanlon (*What We Owe to Each Other*, Cambridge MA: Harvard University Press, 1998). As will be apparent later, my own approach connects to the third version of the Categorical Imperative.

168   THE MAIN ENTERPRISE OF THE WORLD

have tried to develop the thought of testing principles by their potential for universal applicability (thus following the first formulation). Others have appealed to the conception of human beings as having intrinsic worth, viewing Kant's insight as the recognition of inalienable rights, shared by all members of our species. A different direction of development has taken the core of the view to lie in the idea of practical reason, and seen moral actions as those "we have most reason to do, all things considered."[28] Views of this latter type are sometimes elaborated by suggesting that reasons are best judged by considering ourselves as legislators among other legislators of equal worth, thus forging a link with the third version of the Categorical Imperative.

Even more strikingly than in the case of the consequentialist approaches proliferated since Bentham, these brief remarks are inadequate to the nuances and subtleties of the practice of moral philosophy in the Kantian tradition. A vast compendium of scholarly books and articles explores the promise and the difficulties of conceiving morality along these lines. For present purposes, the details are not necessary. For, as with consequentialism, any proposal to offer an encompassing system, applicable to all situations, founders on the need for further moral decisions in the light of new circumstances. How we apply the key concepts—whether of *universalization* or of *contradiction* or of *human worth* or of *practical rationality* or of *rights* or of *reasons*—cannot be fixed in advance. Attempts to detach these concepts from the circumstances of human life, to set them outside human history, either end in vagueness (thus depriving the supposedly universal system of its intended role in guidance) or gain precision through circumscribing and confining them to the kinds of contexts familiar to the would-be theorist. Just as a "universal system of the world" is a dream, so too for the moral sphere. The search for an all-encompassing moral theory shares the predicament often found in areas of natural science.[29] It is possible to be general and precise, but not accurate; or accurate and precise, but not general; or—and this is surely the usual fate of any sensitive moral theorist who is also ambitious—to be general and accurate, but not precise.

That diagnosis motivates a turn toward particularism—to seek principles at a lower level of generality, or even judgments about individual instances. According to particularists, some moral questions can be resolved without

---

[28] Adopted by Thomas Nagel, *The View from Nowhere*, New York: Oxford University Press, 1987, and by Scanlon, *What We Owe to Each Other*.

[29] Brilliantly presented in the opening chapter of Richard Levins, *Evolution in Changing Environments* (Princeton: Princeton University Press, 1968).

deriving answers from any overarching theory. How is this done? To the extent that methods for addressing moral conundrums could be specified, they might be integrated into education to generate skills potentially applicable throughout the course of a person's life, even in those circumstances where attempts to apply the prevalent moral code break down. Perhaps they could also be deployed to scrutinize the precepts of accepted morality, leading people, and ultimately societies, to detect errors and to engage in progressive reform. Hence, particularism holds out hope for finding the necessary supplement to moral practice narrowly conceived (that is, viewed as a corpus of precepts together with a disposition to follow them).

Contemporary versions of the approach are a mixture, offering a useful suggestion, typically distorted by a flawed picture of moral truth. The insight lies in an analogy with legal decision-making. Judges make decisions about newly arising cases by comparing situations, some of them actual, others imagined possibilities with various degrees of similarity to the circumstances of the case at hand. Analogies are deployed to extend precedents to the question to be resolved. Current reflections on moral problems often pursue a similar strategy. Thus, to take a well-known example, Judith Jarvis Thomson defends the permissibility of abortion by conducting a thought-experiment.[30] She imagines a protagonist who wakes up one morning to discover that she is attached to another person, a celebrated violinist, who will need to be plugged into her body for the next nine months. Would it be reasonable, she asks, to demand that the connection be removed? Thomson expects the answer to be "Yes," and she uses the analogy to justify women's decisions to terminate a pregnancy (in at least some instances).

Fantasies of this kind can stimulate the moral imagination, allowing people to view their situations from novel angles. Should the judgments they provoke be heralded as disclosing new moral truths (or judgments meeting whatever standard is taken as appropriate for morality to seek)? That is, in my view, a difficult question. Contemporary moral philosophy often assumes an optimistic answer. The processes through which respondents arrive at their answers are given an honorific title—the stories stimulate *intuitions*, typically conceived by analogy to everyday perceptions. Just as we acquire particular beliefs about the physical world by using our senses—perceiving the objects around us—so too these intuitions disclose features of the moral realm, the ground of moral truth (or guide us to apt feelings or justified beliefs). Of

---

[30] "A Defense of Abortion," *Philosophy and Public Affairs* 1 (1971): 47–66.

170   THE MAIN ENTERPRISE OF THE WORLD

course, in the perceptual case, a lot is now known about the ways in which sensory information is reliable in generating belief. By contrast, the character of "moral reality" (assuming that any such thing exists) is extremely cloudy, and the way in which our "intuitions" prompted by contrived stories might give us access to it is utterly mysterious. Why should we suppose the processes through which philosophers (and the students to whom they present their "puzzle cases") arrive at their conclusions are responsive in any way to a "reality" beyond the subjects who make the judgments? Why think of them as exposing appropriate feelings, or justifying us in our conclusions? Why suppose that anything more than antecedent predilections and prejudices are being expressed in what are mistakenly viewed as independent checks on the moral code in which those subjects are immersed? Why take these "intuitions" to be reliable sources of belief?

These questions are sharpened when, as all too often occurs, judgment of some kind is forced. In my own experience, many people, when told the stories from which the intended moral judgments are to be obtained, find themselves reluctant to commit themselves to any of the conclusions among which they are supposed to choose.[31] The fictions constructed are too abstract, too remote from everyday life, to inspire confidence about any reaction. You are told tales about a trolley, hurtling toward five unlucky people bound to the tracks.[32] Close at hand is a switch. Pulling it would enable you to divert the trolley to another track, to which only one unfortunate individual is tied. Or you are to imagine yourself standing on a high bridge, over the tracks. A fat man sits on the parapet. Were you to push him you could save the five, at the cost of his life. What are your intuitions about what you should do?[33]

[31] Classes in moral philosophy often present cases to undergraduates, and ask them for their responses (their "intuitions" about them). So long as the instructor takes pains to leave the expected answer open, students are—at least in my own experience—often unsure about what to say. They prefer to sit in uneasy silence.

[32] Stories of this kind are intended to play either of two functions. They can be told in hopes of illuminating situations in which, responding to very serious threats, an agent has the option to intervene and cause some damage (saving a woman's life by aborting the fetus she is carrying). Or they can be viewed as tests of general moral hypotheses or of whole moral theories.

[33] Harry Brighouse has suggested to me that these well-known examples can actually teach us something important. Rather than prompting any substantive moral judgments (you should flip the switch and divert the trolley, you shouldn't push the fat man), they should bring home the ways in which reactions to closely related scenarios can vary, thus emphasizing the importance of caution in drawing conclusions from the analogies we deploy. Although this hardly corresponds to the ways in which enthusiastic moral philosophers use their appeals to intuition, the recommendation to scrutinize initial impulses seems to me entirely correct. Our responses always need to be set in the context of a much more wide-ranging course of reflection. Chapter 8 will elaborate this point in the context of considering how some works of fiction can help us to see our customary practices in new ways.

MORAL DEVELOPMENT 171

Of course, if either of those situations were to confront you, you would seek some better option. Perhaps you would try to signal the driver of the trolley, or to liberate the victims in some other way. Maybe you would interpose your own body. Or appeal to the fat man: "Fat man," you might say, "let us leap together." Given the moral dispositions set up in you by your socialization, you would be dissatisfied by either of the options on which philosophers insist: pull the switch or don't; push the fat man, or let him be. Alternatives are ruled out by *fiat*. You know for certain that the driver cannot be prevented from smashing into the victim(s); you know for certain that you are too light to stop the trolley; you know for certain that the people cannot be freed; you know for certain that the fat man would fall if you pushed, and that he would block the trolley; you know for certain that appealing to his better nature would be useless.

People who hear this story, and take seriously the task of imagining what they would do in the situation described, find the limitations on their options hard to cope with. Real life just isn't like that. When we are in circumstances demanding quick decisions, we *never* know the kinds of things of which the schematic figures in the story are supposed to be aware. If you were standing beside the track, you *might* know that pulling a particular switch would divert the trolley. But if you saw the single person on the other track, you would probably try some different method. Perhaps you would flap your arms, dance up and down on the track, and scream at the top of your lungs. No small voice would whisper in your ear, telling you that behaving like that was doomed to fail. Nor, if you were standing on the bridge, would you be likely to think, "Well . . . I could always push the fat man . . . ."

Conscientious people who try to place themselves in the situation of the story must draw on whatever moral resources their past experience has supplied. The habits of thought they bring to the imagined decision are products of education within a particular culture, refined over the course of their lives. Whatever dispositions they have acquired are attuned to the kinds of situations they have experienced—and those experienced by generations of predecessors who have shaped the moral tradition they have inherited. When these people are required to pass judgment on a world so different from the one in which they live, a world in which options are artificially narrowed by introducing absurd certainties, their psychological machinery no longer functions smoothly. The gears don't mesh. The wheels spin idly. Hence comes the tentativeness many respondents feel, their reluctance to judge which of the narrow range of choices permitted them is morally correct. Of course,

172   THE MAIN ENTERPRISE OF THE WORLD

they can be browbeaten into determinate judgment, in a milder version of the coercion familiar from notorious psychological experiments.[34] But, when a philosopher compels some judgment on such remote and abstract cases, there is no reason to take it to be trustworthy.

My conclusion is not at odds with viewing fiction as sometimes useful in stimulating the moral imagination.[35] It is a plea for caution. Attempts to deploy "intuition" as a guide should always be attentive to the possibility of mismatch between the oversimplifications of the story and the psychological resources available to people who reflect on it. The analogy with perception ought to be taken seriously: with respect to complex matters, people have to be *trained* to observe properly.[36] Of course, it doesn't help that, in the case of moral "intuitions," philosophers are so reticent about the "moral reality" supposed to be fathomed (or the standard supposed to be met), and about the psychological mechanisms through which conclusions are generated.

Sometimes a well-told tale can bring clarification. We are in doubt about what to do in our current situation, and we recall a similar predicament we have experienced or remember a story (or a fable or a parable), and indecision is consequently resolved. Now we know what should be done. My diagnosis of what goes wrong in the problematic appeals to intuition helps us see what is happening when that occurs. The obvious ways of appealing to our moral practice left us blank. Given the stimulus of the analogy, however, moral resources that we hadn't thought of drawing on are put to work. Our moral code is apparently extended, through yielding a conclusion for a new context—and the expansion occurs through making explicit what was already implicitly present.

A similar point can be made on behalf of the general principles philosophers have proposed in their search for the grand system of moral truths. They can prove *locally* helpful, applicable to particular types of

---

[34] As participants in Stanley Milgram's famous experiment were commanded to follow the conditions laid down at the start. In recognizing the kinship, I am not, of course, supposing that any serious psychological damage is done to the undergraduates whose "intuitions" philosophers canvass. The verdicts of more seasoned respondents, already immersed in philosophical culture, are subject to a more familiar worry. They are likely to be infected by prior philosophical commitments.

[35] Indeed, I shall argue below (Chapter 8) for a Deweyan thesis: literary arts are valuable in facilitating moral discovery. But the fictions must engage in the right ways with the psychological dispositions people come to have. Between the messiness of the real-life situations people struggle to resolve and the abstract fantasies imposing unrealistic conditions and constraints—often in the worthy interest of drawing sharp lines—lies a class of fictions that simplify actual predicaments while enabling our psychological abilities to retain a grip on them. (For discussions on this point, I am indebted to Lorraine Daston.)

[36] See Lorraine Daston and Peter Galison, *Objectivity* (New York: Zone Books, 2007).

MORAL DEVELOPMENT 173

difficult decisions. Just as the demise of the idea of a complete theory of nature does not condemn the sciences to enumerating particulars, allowing for models developed at different levels of generality, so too, in moral practice considerations philosophers have hoped to count as universal precepts can serve as useful tools for handling specific classes of moral quandaries. Both in its traditional systematic form and in its turn to reliance on "intuition," moral philosophy has miscast its main achievements. They are tools, available for individuals and societies, as they attempt to advance the project of morality.

The world's religions have also contributed to the toolbox, most evidently in their stories of exemplary individuals, in their depictions of valuable lives, and in the parables through which they have tried to guide moral conduct. The challenge for moral education is to collect the tools and to help people make use of them. To address that challenge, we shall need to clarify the character of moral life, and to understand how it is advanced.

Discussions of morality all too often ignore the fact that it has a history. A long history. Moral life emerged in our species tens of thousands of years ago—probably between fifty thousand and one hundred thousand years before the present—as our remote ancestors began an unprecedented project. Each generation faces the task of continuing that project, attempting to make further progress in it by overcoming the moral problems of the age. The project has no *telos*. There is no final all-inclusive code of principles, engraved on stone tablets or embodied in some supposed non-natural realm of values. Morality is a thoroughly human endeavor, one that is never finished.

This picture of moral life views it as grounded in features of the human predicament. Specifically, *Homo sapiens* has evolved to be a particular type of social species, one living in groups mixed by age and sex. That kind of group life requires a psychological capacity, *responsiveness*, enabling us to recognize (at least sometimes) the wishes, plans, and intentions of our fellows, and to adjust our actions (at least sometimes) in ways those fellows and we find acceptable (even helpful). The capacity makes it possible for us to live together. Unfortunately, human responsiveness is not so well adapted to our form of social life that we can live together smoothly and easily. Over a long period— at least fifty thousand years, maybe as much as one hundred thousand years—our ancestors have improved the situation. They have expanded our responsiveness to others by introducing rules and principles commending

174   THE MAIN ENTERPRISE OF THE WORLD

patterns of behavior, a rich vocabulary for describing character and a vast array of myths and stories, systems of blaming and praising. All this is incorporated into the moral codes of different societies. The codes vary across time, and, to a far more limited extent, across the societies present at any given time. The moral project has transformed human life—and even what it means to be human. It has given birth to societies, institutions, and self-conceptions far beyond the conceptual horizons of the people who began it.

Societies make moral progress through overcoming the moral problems arising at a time. As with technology, efforts to solve one problem typically introduce derivative problems, spun off from the original problem that initiated the technological program. In this case, the *ur*-problem—our limited responsiveness—continues to emerge in new forms throughout the subsequent generations. Despite all our successes in fostering greater responsiveness to others, new situations still arise in which human beings fail to recognize or to support the aspirations of their fellows. With all the ramifications and complexities of our moral codes, evident already five thousand years ago, in the earliest written documents to have survived, the limitations of human responsiveness and the difficulties to which they give rise remain evident.

How are these recurrent problems, often new versions of the *ur*-problem, to be addressed? If we were to model the moral pioneers on the hunter-gatherers of today, whose way of life most resembles that of our Paleolithic ancestors, we would see them as sitting down together in moments of social calm—in Hume's "cool hour"[37]—exchanging their perspectives, and drawing on the information available to them to try to fashion a solution acceptable to all members of the band. They invented, and realized, the ideal of democratic deliberation. We should emulate them. Not because the ideal is theirs, but because limitations of responsiveness are best overcome by pooling perspectives and striving for a solution everyone affected by the problem can tolerate. Full representation and mutual engagement are the most promising ways of tackling this species of problem. Adequate solutions are more likely to be achieved if they are crafted in light of the best factual information at hand.

I offer a thesis about moral method. Societies should revise their moral codes through identifying the moral problems of the times and resolving

---

[37] David Hume, *A Treatise of Human Nature*, Part III, Book 1, Chapter 1.

MORAL DEVELOPMENT   175

them.[38] Both the work of identification, and the efforts to overcome the problems, should be undertaken by fashioning the best available approximation to the ideal of democratic deliberation. Deep democracy, committed to the ideal of democratic deliberation, and thus to mutual education and to solidarity, should underlie moral life, as it should be the ground of political life. It demands mutual enlightenment and attempts at mutual sympathy. In this sense, democracy is education.

So, I claim, we should imitate the pioneers, the hunter-gatherers who began the project of morality. Not simply because we should honor the ancestors, and not just because the method is well-suited to the *ur*-problem. In addition, the method they introduced, probably crudely and imperfectly, is supported by the subsequent history of moral life. When we look to the most obvious examples of episodes we can hail as moral advances, they are protracted, confused, messy, and vulnerable to historical contingency. The methodology I recommend would have streamlined the process.

Consider the three most obvious examples of society-wide moral progress during the past few centuries. The institution of slavery has been repudiated, opportunities for women have been substantially expanded, and (in my own lifetime) the persecution visited upon people who love members of their own sex has been, at least officially, condemned. Of course, even today, there are people in various places who take these developments to be regressive. Typically, their defenses of traditional attitudes rest on appealing to particular religious texts as morally authoritative.[39] In what follows, I shall assume their dissent to be mistaken. But the analysis I'll offer of these three episodes would, I believe, apply to any reasonable instance of moral progress the dissenters would be happy to accept.

The first point to make about the three cases concerns the contingency and mess of actual history.[40] The battle for abolition of slavery involved decades

[38] Perhaps the most obvious contemporary attempts to go in this direction have been attempts to develop ethical codes for some professions. Thus the Belmont Commission attempted to formulate a code for the treatment of experimental subjects. Although I view its work as having been broadly beneficial, the approach I recommend goes significantly further. It proposes to make the group of deliberators more inclusive than such commissions typically do. It is not content to stop with generalities that often prove difficult to apply in practice. Moreover, it is always concerned to engage with the variety of perspectives, neither terminating the process with flabby compromises nor resorting to voting before all avenues have been thoroughly explored. Hence I see ventures of this type as pointing the way, rather than reaching the goal.

[39] The next chapter will subject such claims to critical scrutiny.

[40] The themes of this paragraph and those that follow are developed further in my *Moral Progress*.

176   THE MAIN ENTERPRISE OF THE WORLD

of suffering and bloodshed. Many women, as well as some of their male supporters, sacrificed their homes, their careers, and even their lives in the struggle for freedom. Gays and lesbians were imprisoned, humiliated, and ostracized when they dared to speak up for their right to love as they chose. On the winding, bumpy road to abolishing slavery and to permitting women to take on broader roles in public life, many crucial incidents could easily have gone the other way. The fate of Oscar Wilde might well have been shared by those who fought back at the Stonewall bar.

A search for more reliable methods for making moral progress can begin by trying to understand what brought about the successful advance. In all three instances, minds were changed through making vivid aspects of the lives of others. Voices previously suppressed or ignored became heard for the first time. Slaves, dismissed as members of an inferior race, had been effectively silenced. Women's ability to speak on particular topics had been curtailed by appealing to unjustified assumptions about "female nature." People attracted to members of their own sex could participate in topics on a large number of issues, so long as they kept their sexual proclivities well concealed. Moral progress was fueled when people who had taken traditional ideas for granted came to enter and engage with the lives of others whom those ideas had confined and wounded.

In an over-optimistic moment, William James announces a corrective for philosophical reflections on morality. Philosophers, he thinks, have no great superiority in judging "the best universe in the concrete emergency"; they do know "somewhat better than most men what the question always is"; but their efforts at answering it can easily go astray; nevertheless, there is a check: the philosopher "only knows that if he makes a bad mistake the cries of the wounded will soon inform him of the fact."[41] James's insight lies in recognizing the importance of listening to the cries of the wounded. His optimism consists in assuming that the wounded always cry. All too often in human history, those whom later generations view as oppressed will adopt the image of themselves current in their society. Slaves accept their own inferiority; women acquiesce in the roles assigned to them; gays concede that they are sinful and depraved.[42] And, in our own times, people whose aspirations are consistently marginalized by their societies, whose plans and

---

[41] William James, "The Moral Philosopher and the Moral Life," in *The Will to Believe* (Cambridge MA: Harvard University Press, 1979), 158.

[42] These examples are often seen as instances of adaptive preferences: the oppressed people form preferences enabling them to get by under the conditions of oppression. For valuable discussions of

MORAL DEVELOPMENT 177

projects are given no chance of success, take the limits cramping their lives to be unfortunate by-products of a just system and see themselves as simply unlucky.

One species of false consciousness lies in not recognizing one's own wounds, and in a consequent failure to protest the customs, institutions, and individual people who inflict the wounds.[43] To varying degrees, my three examples are a mixture, in which some of the wounded cry, while many do not. The silence of the lambs is then used to discredit the voices raised in protest.[44] As the result of a slow, wasteful, and chancy process, the plight of the wounded finally becomes broadly recognized, and moral advance occurs. Deweyans, who hope to make moral progress more systematic and sure-footed than it has been, seek to identify a methodology for doing better. The obvious approach develops a two-part social procedure. First, set up a framework for hearing and resolving the complaints that are voiced— making sure that all citizens (and not only philosophers) hear the cries of the wounded. Second, add to that framework an institution designed to uncover the wounds concealed by false consciousness.

One obvious source of inspiration lies in the procedures of the law. Societies have set up channels through which individuals and groups may present their complaints, and for resolving those complaints. The results are surely imperfect. Yet they are surely better than when such procedures are absent, when "frontier justice" is the best that can be sought, when the strong are free to dominate, and when the human situation is of the types Hobbes and Locke feared.[45] Moreover, the importance of listening to one another emerges directly from my characterization of moral life. The *ur*-problem— to which morality is the inevitably partial solution—lies in ourselves, in the limitations of our responsiveness to our fellows. If that is the problem, moral

such preferences, see Jon Elster, *Sour Grapes* (Cambridge UK: Cambridge University Press, 1983); Amartya Sen, "Gender Inequality and Theories of Justice," in *Women, Culture and Development*, ed. Martha C. Nussbaum and Jonathan Glover (Oxford: Oxford University Press, 1995), 259–73, and Martha Nussbaum, *Women and Human Development* (Cambridge UK: Cambridge University Press, 2000), 111–66. I suspect that there are (rare) examples of the species of false consciousness with which I'm concerned here in which the distortions aren't readily understood as preferences and/or aren't adaptive; and that there are instances of adaptive preferences that don't belong to that species; nevertheless, there's broad overlap between the two concepts.

[43] In *Moral Progress*, I sometimes write as if this is the only—or the main—type of false consciousness. The remarks of my commentators, particularly those of Rahel Jaeggi, have convinced me that this is not right. My "Response to Commentaries" begins to correct the mistake.

[44] This is especially evident with respect to the campaign for women's rights. See Chapter 2 of *Moral Progress*.

[45] Thomas Hobbes, *Leviathan*, Chapter 13; John Locke, *Second Treatise of Government*, Chapter 3.

178   THE MAIN ENTERPRISE OF THE WORLD

method and moral inquiry should be guided by attempts to bring the confinement of other lives into clear light, and to generate sympathetic responses to the forms confinement takes. We need structures—and, as I'll propose later, a reform of education—to help us to listen better.

In the three cases I have hailed as examples of moral progress, the initial state is one in which practices that will later be condemned are regarded as completely acceptable. The first step in moral inquiry should be to identify problems. Ignoring false consciousness for the moment, let's focus on the actual complaints arising at a given time. Not all of these will be justified. Some people are habitual whiners (and others, probably far fewer, are overly stoical). Ideally, there might be a body set up to attend to *all* the pleas for relief. Since we lack world enough and time (not to mention other resources) for any such comprehensive review, the first task is to imitate the law and to separate the important cases from the trivial ones. The body should, for the time being, suspend judgment on whether each individual complaint is justified. It should focus on a simpler question: which of these pleas, if found to be justified and consequently addressed, would bring the largest amount of relief?

The task is to draw up a list of urgent *potential* problems, to be recognized as justified complaints or dismissed by a further investigation. The body constructs an agenda for subsequent moral inquiry. How should it proceed? In accordance with the themes advanced in this chapter and its predecessor, the answer is straightforward: through democratic deliberation. The participants should include representatives of as many subgroups within the society as can be managed, allowing for a diversity of perspectives. They should hear from the plaintiffs, and should gather whatever empirical information they need to evaluate the relief the proposed reform would be expected to bring. They should be scrupulous in avoiding judgments about whether any particular complaint is or is not justified. Only assessments of relative urgency are their concern.

At the next stage of the procedure, the complaints ranked as most significant are investigated by further deliberation.[46] With respect to each of the urgent potential problems, there will be an associated class of people affected by the situation generating the appeal for relief. This class of people, the *stakeholders*,

---

[46] How far the society will go down the ordered list will be fixed by considering assessments of potential relief, and, secondarily, by judgments about the use of societal resources. Even if significant amounts of time and human commitment were required to evaluate complaints for which the confinement of lives was judged to be severe—of the same order as in the case of major historical examples—further investigation for all of them would still be warranted.

MORAL DEVELOPMENT   179

are those whose lives would be significantly modified by any judgment about the need for reform. In deciding whether the appeal is justified, the body of deliberators must satisfy three (familiar!) conditions. First, it must contain representatives of each class of stakeholders, and must do so without giving priority to any particular class. (In a dispute about slavery, the deliberating body should not be composed of a disproportionately large representation of slaveholders— or, for that matter, of slaves.) Second, the deliberation should be conducted by using the best available factual information. Assertions at odds with current accepted knowledge are to be dismissed. Claims unsupported in the light of the available evidence are admissible as conjectures, but cannot be introduced as premises of allegedly sound arguments. Third, the discussion must meet the condition of *mutual engagement*. Each participant must be committed to aim at a conclusion all can tolerate.

The goal of these discussions is to bring the predicaments of all the people involved in the focal issue—the stakeholders—into clear view, so that all can be understood. On the basis of sharing the perspectives of all others, deliberators may agree in recognizing the need for modifying the *status quo*. In accordance with the idea of mutual engagement, they identify sympathetically with each party in turn, and discover in the process that the condition of some of the affected groups requires amelioration. The complaint is then treated as justified, recognized as proceeding from a genuine problem.

To solve the problem, deliberation must go further, seeking a modification all can accept (although, perhaps often, none of the discussants may rank it highest among the options considered.) As possible changes are explored, however, the composition of the deliberating body will likely require amending. New proposals may affect the lives of people not included among the initial stakeholders, and, when that occurs, people from these groups will need to be represented.[47] The newly arrived participants must operate within the frame of the earlier discussion: the status of the complaint as genuine cannot be revoked. Deliberation then aims at the strongest form of consensus attainable, attempting always to avoid an outcome viewed by one of the groups represented as intolerable.[48]

[47] Another possibility: some of the original stakeholders, people satisfied with the *status quo*, may be unaffected by any of the changes considered. When that occurs, their representatives should not take any further part in the deliberation. Winnowing in this way is, however, best postponed to a point at which a final list of options has been drawn up. Otherwise there is an obvious danger. After the representatives have left, difficulties in reaching agreement prompt an expansion of the set of potential changes, including some with impact on people no longer represented.

[48] See the discussions of types of consensus in the previous chapter, 145–47 above.

180 THE MAIN ENTERPRISE OF THE WORLD

Perhaps it is impossible to realize any close approximation to the ideal procedures just outlined. When perspectives on a question are nuanced, subject to fine-grained variation, representing all individual points of view would prove unworkable. Actual discussions must settle for lumping, representing groups within which there are diverse attitudes by a single discussant. Specifying what counts as available knowledge may itself be controversial, and settling the status of propositions relevant to the focal issue may require preliminary working through the evidence and consulting experts.[49] Although face-to-face exchanges are likely to improve prospects of mutual understanding—sharing an alien perspective is more common when that viewpoint is elaborated by an individual interlocutor than when it is attributed to a faceless group—it is reasonable to worry about the degree to which mutual engagement can be achieved. Here, as we shall see below, is an important role for education.

Nevertheless, the ideal conditions indicate a direction for *decreasing* the messiness, waste, and contingency of past episodes of moral change. They streamline the processes through which progress has been made. Instead of awaiting a moment at which hitherto powerless people are given a forum in which to register their complaints, those who see themselves as subjects of oppression are invited in to describe their plight. The change is analogous to one considered by Locke in his account of the origins of government.[50] A state in which something like clan warfare settles disputed questions is replaced by one where recourse to courts and independent adjudication becomes available. Whether or not the creation of an institutionalized system for facilitating moral progress removes the need for violent protest entirely, it is surely likely to decrease it.[51]

So far, a method for addressing the *voiced* complaints issuing from groups who see themselves as wrongly treated. Or, more exactly, a *provisional* method. Just as the suggestions about inquiry made by the pioneers in the history of the physical sciences—Bacon, Descartes, Galileo, and Newton, for example—were vague and often inconsistent with one another, so too, what I have offered is the beginning of an enterprise in which first, crude, ideas

---

[49] Here the practical difficulties connect to questions about reaching factual consensus, discussed in the previous chapter, 131 n.40, above.

[50] John Locke, *Second Treatise on Government*, Chapter 3. The reworking of this by Robert Nozick, in *Anarchy, State, and Utopia* (New York: Basic Books, 1974), Chapter 2, is also useful for understanding the analogy.

[51] For more on this issue, see *Moral Progress*, "Response to the Commentaries." The proposals for rethinking education offered below are intended to reinforce the point.

MORAL DEVELOPMENT 181

will (with luck and effort) be progressively refined. We should hope that our successors will be equipped with as rich an array of methods as contemporary scientists employ. Perhaps they will look back at the first gestures toward investigating moral method with a sympathetic smile, indulging the shortcomings of the early tentative steps.[52]

In any event, even the provisional method remains importantly incomplete. More is needed to tackle the problem of false consciousness. Moreover, without an extension to cope with that problem, actual efforts to implement the method outlined are likely to fail. For, as history reveals, when a substantial fraction of an oppressed group acquiesces in the *status quo*, those who raise their voices in protest are easily cast as troublemakers, deviants, or worse. How can a society find ways of exposing a moral wrong that very few people—in the limit, nobody—can yet feel?

Morality, as I understand it, derives primarily from the *ur*-problem of human beings' limited responsiveness to one another. Its initial focus is (was) on actions toward others. In the course of its evolution, the sphere of morality expands, as deeds affecting someone's future character fall within its purview. So-called self-regarding duties—requirements that people should be industrious or should maintain their bodily skills—emerged initially, I hypothesize, from their indirect connection to actions with consequences for other people. The young must work hard to acquire abilities of particular kinds so that they may become useful members of the band—and once they have those skills they should not neglect them. Human prehistory also saw another expansion. Besides considering how people should act, they also began to reflect on a broader question: What kind of person should I be?

The introduction of this question marks a shift from morality to ethical life.[53] It embeds the moral concern with action in a broader field, one centered on how people should live.[54] Broader because any adequate answer to

---

[52] For elaboration of the idea of methodology in any domain as an evolving achievement, see *Moral Progress* 31–33, 75–77.

[53] My distinction between morality and ethics follows the seminal work of Bernard Williams. See his *Ethics and the Limits of Philosophy* (London: Fontana, 1985). Williams sees ethics as historically prior and morality as a later narrowing of its proper scope. Since I take a longer view of the history of both, I see morality as coming first and ethics as arising (long before the ancient thinkers who are Williams's starting point) in an expansion of it.

[54] Thus ethics starts the line of reflection leading to the considerations about fulfillment discussed above in Chapter 3.

182 THE MAIN ENTERPRISE OF THE WORLD

the question of how to be must already endorse following the requirements on action morality prescribes.[55] As I have already suggested, for a large segment of human prehistory, questions of how to live were otiose. To the extent that anyone posed them, they would have been answered by reference to the agreed-on moral code and its requirements for action, and by recognizing the stringent constraints of survival from day to day. Alternative ways of living, according with morality but diverging from one another in their patterns of conduct, only became real options once particular kinds of development had occurred. Division of labor led to the articulation of alternative roles within the small band. It allowed repeated cooperation between particular people. That, in turn, fostered new emotions—affection, love—and consequently new relationships. Gradually, a wider spectrum of possibilities within the sphere of morality emerged. By the time of the earliest written records, different modes of life are clearly visible, apparent in the conceptions of enduring relationships and of alternative ways of making a living and of contributing to the community. The question, "How should I live?," acquires a sense, even if initially the obvious answer is, "In the manner suited to the circumstances of your birth."

For more than three millennia, however, some people (perhaps only a tiny minority) have been able to consider various lives as possible for themselves. They could aspire to govern, or to serve the deities, or to lead a revolt, or to dedicate themselves to conserving (or building on?) the wisdom acquired within their society. A larger number might make humbler, though no less significant decisions, about marriage or friendship, about the character of their family life. Life plans can be attributed to them. With those life plans come *ideals of the self*, conceptions of a life directed toward the goals the life plan makes central. In the ancient world, the distribution of such ideals is severely restricted. Many ideals are only deemed suitable for a strictly limited group. Enthusiasts for ancient ethical life should never forget that the supposedly highest ideals of the self are only suited to the well-born men of the *polis*.

---

[55] To see ethics as including moral requirements is not to take a stand on issues about explanatory priority. Even if morality is *historically* prior, it does not follow that deciding how to live should be constrained by some independently established body of moral norms. It is possible to hold—with Williams, Elizabeth Anscombe, Philippa Foot, and a host of their successors who have found inspiration in the ethical writings of ancient thinkers—that right actions are those a virtuous person would do, and thus that moral questions are resolved by first understanding the good life (a life of virtue).

MORAL DEVELOPMENT   183

The discussion may seem to have strayed from my official goal of tackling the problem of false consciousness. In light of my proposed history of ethical life, it's now relatively easy to specify a species of false consciousness, one recurring throughout human history.[56] From the ancient world to the present, societies have understood some ideals of the self to be restricted to particular groups of people. The practice didn't die with the passing of the *polis*. It flourished in the American colonies ("the Africans transported to the plantations are natural slaves"),[57] in Victorian England ("a woman should be the goddess of hearth and home"), and in many affluent societies in the late twentieth century ("marriage is a sacrament between a man and a woman"). Part of what occurred in each of my three historical instances of moral progress was an explicit cancellation of a prior restriction on ideals of the self. Prior to the advance, many of those debarred from the pertinent ideal would have accepted it as not apt for them. False consciousness of the type on which I focus occurs when individuals who have been arbitrarily excluded from an ideal of the self—often through the building of obstacles making it difficult, if not impossible, for any of them to adopt it and pursue it—acquiesce in the restrictions their society imposes.

How should moral inquiry be conducted to cope with problems of this sort? Divide the cases into two types, those in which some members of the society protest the restriction (while many others do not) and those in which everyone agrees in excluding the group from pursuing the ideal. When some of the wounded cry, and when a traditional judgment is invoked to marginalize them—to see them as "uppity" or "monstrous" or "depraved"—that judgment needs scrutiny. Hence the deliberations envisaged in my proposed methodology must be preceded by examining the grounds (if any) supposed to support the restriction. As the examples reveal, inquiry into what justifies excluding members of the relevant group will sometimes be inconclusive. Traditionalists will insist that particular activities are unsuited to those people, they are by nature incapable of undertaking them, or at least of doing them well; or, perhaps, the consequences of their engaging in them will divert them from their "proper roles" and thus cause great social harm. Ambitious reformers announce the equal ability of those they seek to liberate, and deny the supposed damage. Neither side can point to strong evidence in favor of its

[56] Although the diagnosis I shall offer is prompted by three specific cases involving adaptive preferences, I do not offer it as a general account of adaptive preferences and how to respond to them.
[57] Harriet Beecher Stowe brilliantly caricatures attitudes of this sort in her portrait of Marie St. Clare in *Uncle Tom's Cabin*.

184 · THE MAIN ENTERPRISE OF THE WORLD

position. Moderate reformers will suggest a middle way: let another "experiment of living" proceed.[58] Allow those who clamor for the opportunities currently denied to them to pursue the kinds of lives to which they aspire. When women express their wish to be educated as fully as their brothers are, when they demand access to the professions or the right to vote, set up a fair trial and deliberate again in light of the results. Given the conditions on deliberation imposed by moral method, discussants should be aware of the need to ensure a genuine expansion of opportunities. The people who aspire to break an established barrier should not enter under adverse conditions: when young people belonging to racial minorities make their way to the previously segregated university, the path should not be lined with angry faces shouting insults.[59]

Once a protest has already begun, moral inquiry already has a direction in which investigation of restrictive judgments about ideals of the self should go. In light of my reconstruction of the history of human moral life, our views concerning the aptness of specific ideals for particular groups are always likely to contain errors. False consciousness is always likely to be with us. Is it possible to eliminate our own blind spots, even in the extreme cases where *nobody* recognizes a restriction as arbitrary and unwarranted? Plainly, this is far more difficult than pursuing a question protesters have already raised. Devising perfect procedures for exposing all instances of this kind of ethical mistake is almost certainly impossible. Nonetheless, a society committed to streamlining moral progress—a *Deweyan* society—can institute procedures for making it more likely for us to appreciate some of the errors inherited unthinkingly from our traditions.

Central to Dewey's account of the growth of the individual (and of his view of the individual mind) is his insistence that education should not only prepare people to live within a society but also to change their society for the better.[60] The appropriate stance toward any moral code is to take it seriously while simultaneously honoring the need for revision. How is it possible for

---

[58] The phrase is Mill's—see OL. In *On the Subjection of Women*, Mill and Harriet Taylor argue against dogmatically opposing social experiments on the grounds that the outcomes are already known.

[59] There are important hard questions about the conduct of social experiments, especially concerning the tendency to abandon them prematurely. It is worth remembering a lesson from studies of the natural sciences: typically, it takes considerable time and adjustment to make a new experiment work. For a little more on these issues, see Chapter 2 of *Moral Progress*.

[60] This theme is common to discussions in *Democracy and Education* (MW 9) and *Experience and Nature* (LW 1). It is illuminating to read *Democracy and Education* in light of Chapters 6 and 7 of the later work.

MORAL DEVELOPMENT   185

people to engage thoroughly in investigations of how their moral practices might be modified, while simultaneously using existing moral attitudes in guiding their conduct?

An obvious proposal: through creating a protected space in which the traditions of a society are critically examined. Besides the deliberations prompted by actual complaints, a Deweyan society could set up an institution dedicated to continuous scrutiny of the ethical code (the moral code with its ethical extensions), including accepted judgments about restrictions on ideals of the self. A permanent deliberative body, representative of the variation in ethical opinion present in the society, meets regularly to consider places where the ethical tradition might need significant reform. Subject to the conditions imposed on ideal deliberation (inclusiveness, use of well-grounded information, mutual engagement), it establishes an agenda of topics for inquiry, and investigates them. In particular, it is directed toward examining ideals of the self and their social distribution. The people who pursue these inquiries occupy a new role, that of social critic. Outside the space in which they meet to discuss, they abide by the accepted code. Within it, no holds are barred—they are free to suspend judgment about any aspect of ethical life. When they reach agreement on some particular reform, their consensus remains provisional. It must then be ratified by bringing together a deliberative body as fully representative of the population as is feasible. Only after that body has endorsed the change is the proposal brought to the wider public.

Social critics are, in effect, professional plaintiffs, people who probe for wounds nobody has yet felt. They help spur advances in the moral code, but, until their suggestions acquire wide public backing, they, like others, conform to the tradition they seek to improve. The public institution should not be the only vehicle of moral change, however. As citizens live their daily lives, they too extend the moral ideas they were taught. Through their responses to difficult situations, as cultural transmission spreads successful responses to problems, they collectively contribute to progress in the moral project.

So we return to the individual whose moral practice needs a supplement to what was explicitly taught. How can people be equipped to cope with the problematic situations inevitably arising in their lives? My discussion has largely focused on *social* change. The method proposed for moral progress appeals to groups, assembled to identify and solve problems through joint deliberation. Where do the everyday challenges that beset all of us fit in?

186   THE MAIN ENTERPRISE OF THE WORLD

Individual moral agents need to decide what to do when the moral practice they have developed is inadequate in guiding them. They should also be able to play their part in the deliberations through which their society makes moral progress. Fortunately, the skills required to carry out one of these tasks are those required for the other. Moreover, they contribute to the formation of citizens, able to play their part in Deweyan democracy.

This happy concurrence is no coincidence. At the heart of the approach to shaping citizens adopted in the previous chapter is a conception of proper government as requiring us to address the same problem—the *ur*-problem posed by our limited responsiveness to one another—taken to lie at the center of moral life. Thus the educational proposals made at the close of Chapter 4 are defended from a new angle in my account of the moral project. Children need to learn to listen to one another and to make joint plans not only because those abilities are required for democracy, but also because they enhance responsiveness, and hence promote moral development. Moreover, the moral perspective invites us to go further, to cultivate capacities conducive both to political and to ethical life.

Moral agents should have a sense of when to suspend the operation of habits, when to stop and think. They should also have capacities—*sensitivities* as I shall call them—enabling them to pursue moral inquiry, when it is needed.[61] The basic sensitivity responds to circumstances, either allowing an agent to proceed on autopilot or to trigger reflection. At that point, further sensitivities come into play, as the agent considers whether the situation is genuinely problematic, and, if so, attempts to define the problem as precisely as possible. There follows an attempt at solution, guided by sensitivities that combine to yield an assessment of the options for action. Human behavior can go wrong in numerous ways, from an initial misfiring of the basic sensitivity to the faulty assessment of the circumstances to confusion or error about the character of the problem to a failure to solve it at all or to a misguided solution. Saints aside, all of us recognize many (if not all) of the possible deviations not only from observing our fellows but also from ruefully pondering the history of our own conduct. We have plunged ahead where we should not. We have sometimes paused to consider where we ought to have acted decisively. We have misunderstood the character of the situation, standing haplessly by in confusion while events around us went

---

[61] For more discussion of sensitivities, see Chapter 3 of *Moral Progress*.

MORAL DEVELOPMENT 187

awry. We have thought about our circumstances in the wrong way, missed the real problem, and made an inappropriate response as a result. We have seen the problem, but, wringing our hands, we have failed to find any course of action that would solve it. Or we have found what we took (incorrectly) to be a solution, and, by acting in accord with it, we have only made matters worse. Perhaps the Book of Common Prayer is not so far off the mark when it characterizes us as "miserable offenders" and urges us to acknowledge that "there is no health in us."[62]

How can people be equipped so as to do better, so that the number of occasions on which they go astray is reduced? Individuals don't have the opportunity to use the method I have outlined to govern the social pursuit of moral inquiry. None of us can snap our fingers, summoning up a representative body of deliberators to consider our situation and to generate the consensus view of how we should behave. We are on our own.

What we *can* do, however, is to attempt to simulate the kind of discussion that ideal body would have. We can try to view our predicament from different angles, imagining how the different people potentially affected by what we do would urge us to act. We can compare the current context with other situations, either by recalling occasions in our own past (or in the past of others) or by imagining cases we can envisage fully as realistic possibilities.[63] We can conceive some of the potential stakeholders as introducing principles in support of their position, and think of the likely ensuing dialogue. How far our reflections lead will naturally depend on the urgency of the situation. On some occasions, of course, any hesitation will clearly be problematic, and our moral inquiry must be sharply curtailed. At other times, even a relatively swift exploration of how our actions might bear on the lives of others, and how they would look at the various options we have, can convince us that a particular course would be acceptable to all.

Besides the basic sensitivity (allowing habitual behavior to proceed or stopping us in our tracks), each of us needs sensitivities enabling us to recognize the people on whom we might have an impact, to envisage how actions would look from their perspectives, to identify options for our conduct, to envisage how deliberation among all of us might proceed, and what might ultimately

---

[62] These phrases occur in the "General Confession" for both Morning Prayer and Evening Prayer.
[63] Here I draw on the earlier discussion about thought-experiments, recapitulating the requirement to make the imagined scenario sufficiently close to real life to allow for responsible judgment. See above, 170–73.

188 THE MAIN ENTERPRISE OF THE WORLD

prove tolerable to everyone. As I suggested earlier, the parables offered by religion and the thought-experiments constructed by philosophers can provide tools for exercising these sensitivities. So too, can the principles or rules supplied by secular and religious traditions alike. None of this apparatus will, all by itself, deliver an authoritative conclusion. But thinking about these resources as figuring in the discussion, as ways of elaborating perspectives and responding to the perspectives of other discussants, can offer aids to reflection. Attempts to employ the moral imagination can be helped by the kinds of conversations we are able to have, by explaining how we are conceptualizing a situation and inviting others to add their own perspectives. Sometimes, our friends can alert us to the ways in which we have been blind, or shortsighted, or unsympathetic in our efforts.

How might early education improve the sensitivities moral agents need? The kinds of activities recommended in Proposals 6–11 would surely be helpful. They can be supplemented by a direct attempt to foster an ability to identify stakeholders and to share their perspectives. Besides the usual presentation of principles and the telling of uplifting stories, moral training can benefit from exercises tuned to developing particular sensitivities. First, we need to instill a functional basic sensitivity, to help avoid the thoughtless recourse to habit and (probably to forestall a lesser danger) to promote decisiveness where it is needed.

12. *At some early stage of their elementary education, students should become acquainted with cases in which people blindly follow their habits when it is clearly wrong to do so. They should also become aware of examples of people who fail to be decisive enough. Once they have heard descriptions of these two types of moral mistakes, or actually encountered such mistakes in their own experience, they should participate in role-playing scenarios, designed to confront them with the two kinds of situations. As they grow, these exercises should become more complex and more difficult.*

They also need to understand how moral inquiry can properly be conducted and how it can go astray.

To this end, I suggest another combination of study and practice:

13. *Part of elementary education should include study of parts of the history of moral life, exploring how different groups made progressive changes*

MORAL DEVELOPMENT 189

and how they were sometimes blind to the need for change. Once children have learned about crucial aspects of the process of moral inquiry—the need for inclusion, the need to use the best available information, the need to engage with all the relevant perspectives–they should be challenged with role-playing exercises, in which their sensitivities should be appraised by teachers and other adult onlookers.[64] Their ability to identify the stakeholders, their capacity for understanding a variety of points of view, their power to imagine potential courses of action, and their comprehensiveness in working through the likely course of a deliberation will all be assessed. The aim will be (gently!) to help them understand their own weaknesses, and to try to overcome them.

As they grow and develop, people will be encouraged to reflect on the important moral decisions they have made, and to discuss them with others.

14. *From adolescence on, people should have opportunities to form groups devoted to discussion of the questions arising in their lives. Where possible, the groups should aim for diversity in backgrounds, and should change their composition regularly. It should go without saying that their deliberations ought to be conducted in the spirit of mutual engagement.*

The proposals just made are only a first attempt to outline how a serious understanding of moral methodology—recognized as applying to advances at the *social* level—might be translated first into procedures for the individual, and then into a reformed practice of moral education. Even if the analysis of (social) moral inquiry begun here were correct and complete, many complex issues would need to be resolved before implementing it in classrooms or in the contexts of everyday life.[65] And, as I have acknowledged, the envisaged moral methods are only the beginning of a process, in which, from relatively crude beginnings, a progressive sequence of more refined methods

---

[64] Schools might take a further step, using moral deliberations for running the daily life of the school (as, for example, A. S. Neill did at Summerhill). Students might develop their sensitivities further by joining in an attempt to create a "just school." Thanks to Randy Curren for this suggestion.

[65] Proposal 14 is particularly schematic. As Harry Brighouse has reminded me, the kinds of exercises I have in mind are hard enough to run profitably with undergraduates, let alone adolescents. Plainly, experimentation is required to identify useful techniques for focusing questions and prompting mutually engaged discussions. I'm inclined to think, however, that students who have been used to joint planning from their earliest days in school will have acquired habits capable of rendering classroom moral conversations more productive than they currently tend to be.

190 THE MAIN ENTERPRISE OF THE WORLD

might (with luck) emerge. Hence, the approach offered in this chapter should be seen as a schema, within which moral development and moral education should be rethought. It points in the direction of experiments, changes we might try, if we are serious about improving conduct—and, perhaps, putting an end to the long history of complaints about the degeneracy of the young.

6

A Role for Religion?

All around the world, the approach I have so far adopted would be viewed—often by virtually the entire population of a nation—as completely missing the point. Focusing on self-maintenance, on personal fulfillment, and on citizenship, I would be charged with overlooking the central goal of fostering the development of the young. Only in considering them as moral agents, have I begun to attend to the most serious task of education—and, in doing so, my treatment would appear wrongheaded, if not perverse. What does it profit the growing child to achieve the skills, knowledge, and traits of character with which the previous chapters have been concerned, and to lose the greatest benefits of all, benefits only gained by schooling in the true religion? Religion, so the view contends, should be central to education.

The wonderful secondary school I attended officially subscribed to that view, not only in its name but also in its preferred self-characterization: "the religious, royal, and ancient foundation of Christ's Hospital" put the Christian deity before monarch and country. Yet its more extensive motto—"Honour all men. Love the brotherhood. Fear God. Honour the King."—derived from the first epistle of Peter,[1] hints at the priority of human beings and of their relationships. The approach adopted in earlier chapters makes a more forthright claim for humanism. Does it allow any role at all for religion to play in the education of the young?

One popular version of a negative answer would fasten on an obvious point. When there is significant diversity of beliefs, no particular religion can be selected and taught in the schools. No matter what the religious traditions of the nation may have been, once a variety of believers (and non-believers) has arisen, selecting a specific corpus of doctrines and rites as privileged is bound to foster division and to diminish social cohesion. Religion does not belong to the public sphere. Particular groups advocating different faiths are

---

[1] 1 Peter 2:17. The text is that of the Authorized Version (the King James Bible). Today, the motto would surely be amended in favor of the more inclusive language (gender-neutral pronouns) of more recent translations. It is, however, chiseled into the stonework in various places.

The Main Enterprise of the World. Philip Kitcher, Oxford University Press. © Oxford University Press 2022.
DOI: 10.1093/oso/9780190928971.003.0007

192 THE MAIN ENTERPRISE OF THE WORLD

entitled to teach their children as they please, even to set up schools with alternative curricula so as to make their preferred religion central. They cannot require the public schools to conform to their wishes, whatever the pedigree of their religion and however relatively popular it may be. So long as the society contains people of other faiths, state-directed education should not play favorites.

A more strident critique hopes to go further. It aims at the eradication of religion not only from the public schools but also from society. Many contemporary atheists regard the religions of the world as different forms of noxious trash, to be disposed of as efficiently as possible.[2] Religious education is a form of indoctrination, a species of child abuse, in which the vulnerable young are tricked into believing absurdities, only escaping their plight after protracted struggles that leave emotional scars behind.[3]

Neither of these positions strikes me as correct. The hygiene pursued by the zealots is oblivious to the valuable effects religious belief brings to the lives of many devout people. The popular strategy of removing religion from the public sphere, and then leaving it a free hand, assigns a role—but the wrong one. This chapter will attempt to straighten out a confused discussion.

Current debates about religion in the Anglophone world are badly malformed. The most heated—and thus the most prominent—controversy centers on the credibility of religious doctrines. A small but vocal coterie of eloquent speakers and writers have assailed people they view as committed to absurd claims about reality. The New Atheists[4] treat their opponents as benighted literalists, naïve believers in entities as dubious as the Flying Spaghetti Monster. People sympathetic to religion fight back, accusing the militant atheists of mischaracterizing religion, seeing fundamentalists under every pew or prayer mat. Dogmatic literalism may infect some sects and some believers. But it is false advertising to present an attack on the most

---

[2] Among them is a friend, a philosopher whom I hold in high regard. In 2009, at one of the many celebrations of Darwin's bicentennial, we had breakfast together, engaging in a lively debate about how humanists should respond to religion. It concluded with a canonization: my friend anointed me as "the Pope of the I'm-an-atheist-but movement." He would surely regard this chapter as a (piece of) papal bull.

[3] See, for example, Richard Dawkins, *The God Delusion* (New York: Houghton Mifflin, 2006).

[4] Often identified as led by a quartet, the "Four Horsemen" as somebody has dubbed them: Richard Dawkins, Daniel Dennett, Sam Harris, and Christopher Hitchens.

A ROLE FOR RELIGION? 193

primitive form of religions as exposing the inadequacies of more sophisticated forms of faith.[5]

The New Atheists have a powerful riposte. In many societies, the loudest religious voices, those dominating the media and attracting the most (and most dedicated) followers, are the ones they target. New Atheists are unmoved by well-informed scholars who point out how literalist readings of texts are latecomers in the history of scriptural interpretation. What concerns them is the religion on sale *today*, with its poisonous offerings to the young and vulnerable. Their enthusiasm for science sometimes leads them to portray themselves as crusaders intent on liberating the Holy City of Opinion from the Tyranny of False Belief. When they write or speak in this mood, they are inclined to lament the plight of those who have been prevented from appreciating the Darwinian view of life on Earth. To be sure, those whose educations soft-pedal the topic of evolution—or "evil-you-shun"—have been deprived of something. Their loss is not, however, one of the great tragedies of our age.

The deeper, more compelling, motivation for assailing religion today lies in a second malformed debate. That controversy centers on the role precepts drawn from religious texts ought to play in society-wide discussions of ethics, law, and public policy. Eminent philosophers have defended excluding religious justifications from the public forum on the grounds that democratic exchanges require participants to rely on premises they can expect their interlocutors to endorse.[6] The space in which we reason together ought to aim at delivering arguments all can share. Appeals to religion serve as conversation-stoppers. They are points at which joint deliberation breaks down.

Many religious people must regard this apparently even-handed demarcation of a secular sphere as unsatisfactory. For, given their commitments, it gives priority to the value of a particular style of government, and

---

[5] For the most extensive elaboration and defense of this important point, see Karen Armstrong, *The Case for God* (New York: Knopf, 2009). Other important arguments have been offered by Elaine Pagels, *Beyond Belief* (New York: Vintage, 2003) and *Why Religion?* (New York: HarperCollins, 2018); and by Tim Crane, *The Meaning of Belief* (Cambridge, MA: Harvard University Press, 2017).

[6] The extensive literature on public reason descending from John Rawls's influential account in *Political Liberalism* (New York: Columbia University Press, 1993) has explored and debated this thesis. Besides Rawls's seminal work, other important sources are Jürgen Habermas, "Reconciliation through the Public Use of Reason: Remarks on John Rawls's Political Liberalism," *Journal of Philosophy* 92 (1995): 109–31 and *Between Facts and Norms* (Cambridge, MA: MIT Press, 1996); and Gerald Gaus, *The Tyranny of the Ideal* (Princeton: Princeton University Press, 2016). At the end of this chapter, I shall offer a direct comparison of my approach with the version of liberalism favored by Rawls.

194 THE MAIN ENTERPRISE OF THE WORLD

shortchanges the most fundamental values of all, those grounded in the transcendent order of the cosmos. Theists cannot view the requirements of democratic institutions as on a par with the demands of service to the deity (or deities). Human arrangements should not curtail or frustrate the will of God. On the other hand, while atheists, perhaps in milder mood, might support the democratic case for sequestering the public forum, they are unlikely to see it as presenting the heart of the matter. Religion should not enter public discussions because it will infect them with falsehoods, *harmful* falsehoods to boot.

The New Atheists are incorrect when they see all false beliefs as damaging, and issue their demands for intellectual hygiene.[7] Most people believe plenty of false statements, and only a small proportion of those mistaken judgments do genuine harm. The troublesome ones are those guiding morally significant action.[8] Believers in progressive forms of religion ought to sympathize with this conclusion. Unlike the strident critics, they would not view all the moral suggestions derived from religious texts as noxious and untrue. Nevertheless, just as more thoughtful religious people abandon literal interpretations of some doctrinal statements, their religious commitments also advance by recognizing the importance of independent standards for assessing the moral counsel of the scriptures. Consequently, when in matters of public debate religious doctrines are interpreted in ways apparently reasonable citizens protest as harmful, the authority of that reading of the precepts becomes questionable. Wherever there is a case for taking the application of scripture to be morally wrong, a progressive believer cannot simply declare that the scriptures settle the matter. Independent, secular moral debate is required.

The sophisticated believers I have in mind appreciate the priority of morality. They reject the bumper-sticker slogan: "The Bible says it. I believe it. And that settles it." Quite probably they would advocate a different approach to moral inquiry from the one proposed in the previous chapter. Yet they share common ground with the humanist. A scriptural precept can only be accepted if it passes the test of an independent moral evaluation.

---

[7] The view of false belief as an infectious agent, capable of sweeping through an entire society, was eloquently presented in William Clifford, *The Ethics of Belief* (1877; repr., Amherst, NY: Prometheus Books, 1999). Clifford's essay inspired James's "The Will to Believe."

[8] Including not only moral beliefs but also factual claims that, in combination with justified moral beliefs, can direct actions with appalling consequences. In this chapter, I shall only be concerned with unjustified moral beliefs.

A ROLE FOR RELIGION? 195

What should be said to the devout advocates who insist on the authority of their favored scriptures in moral matters?

Two points need to be made. First, even the staunchest champion of a particular religion has to recognize the variations in doctrine, including moral prescriptions for action, not only across different religions but also among rival interpretations of the same scriptures. Christians diverge on whether the readings from which they draw inspiration forbid abortion or castigate homosexual relationships. Muslims differ on the exact implications of the call to *jihad*.[9] Second, and more fundamentally, Kant identified the flaw in the foot-stamping, conversation-stopping of the bumper sticker slogan. He writes:

> [E]very example of [morality] that is presented to me must itself first be judged according to principles of morality, whether it is actually worthy to serve as an original example, i.e. as a model; but by no means can it furnish the concept of it at the outset. Even the Holy One of the Gospel must first be compared with our ideal of moral perfection before he is recognized as one.[10]

Whether or not you accept the details of Kant's distinctive approach to morality (with, for example, its talk of principles, concepts, and ideals), this passage presents a deep point, on which it's worth expanding.

Most Jews and Christians don't feel entitled to go around the world "smiting" groups of people with whom they are at odds, putting their male enemies to death, collecting their foreskins,[11] and recruiting the wives and daughters as concubines. Very few are troubled by the fact that the places in which they worship aren't in strict accordance with the detailed and exacting requirements laid down at excruciating length in the book of Numbers. Some Christians do think that their non-believing friends, even the ones whose conduct appears in other respects morally admirable, are bound for

---

[9] For example, Surah 2 ("The Cow") verse 216 of the Quran has given rise to extensive exegetical discussions.

[10] *Groundwork of the Metaphysics of Morals*, ed. and trans. Mary Gregor and Jens Timmerman (Cambridge, UK: Cambridge University Press, 2011) 45.

[11] James Joyce offers a witty reminder of some of the oddities ascribed to the Old Testament God when he has Buck Mulligan testify to the influence of religion on Irish life: "The islanders, Mulligan said to Haines casually, speak much of the collector of prepuces." *Ulysses*, Gabler ed. (New York: Vintage, 1986), 12 (Episode 1: 394–95).

196 THE MAIN ENTERPRISE OF THE WORLD

an afterlife of infinite and indescribable torment.[12] How many of them actually face up to the consequences of this belief?

In practice, then, the scriptures typically aren't treated, in all their parts, as morally authoritative. Devout people back away from certain parts of the moral framework presented by texts they take to be divinely inspired. They concede something to Kant's insight, using a *filter* to screen out those bits that violate their *independent* moral sensibilities. If they didn't filter, if they followed all the recommendations of writings they claim to be morally fundamental, their actions would be widely denounced as cruel and savage. But the commitment to morality as flowing from their religion is supposed to survive this selective attitude. Can it do so?

Let's proceed slowly. Consider, first, an attempt to evade the Kantian point, by focusing on non-moral properties of the deity who stands behind the religious writings. Imagine a theist who challenges the need to assess the scriptures on the basis of some independent, prior, moral standard. According to this theist, the deity (or deities) he worships is (are) immensely powerful and responsible for setting up the entire cosmos. Recognizing that extraordinary power, believers should do whatever the deity commands, simply because the deity commands it.

Anyone who reflects on the history of the twentieth century should be able to diagnose what is wrong with this line of reasoning. The commandants of camps in which masses of innocent people were brutalized and put to death—whether under the aegis of Nazism or Soviet Communism or East Asian attempts at social transformation—offered just the same line of defense. "We obeyed the leaders. They were powerful, they set up the system under which we operated, they saw further than we did. It was not our place to question." At the heart of Kant's insight is the repudiation of that final sentence. When ordered to commit atrocities, it *is* the subordinate's place to question, and to refuse to carry out the command.[13]

---

[12] Few readers of James Joyce's *A Portrait of the Artist as a Young Man* forget the sermons to which the young (and sinful) Stephen Dedalus is forced to listen (in Part 3 of the novel). As literary scholars have shown, the terrifying visions of hell derive from a seventeenth-century tract by the Jesuit Giovanni Pinamonti. In the nineteenth century it was translated into English as *Hell Opened to Christians, To Caution Them from Entering into It*. By adapting Pinamonti's horrific descriptions, Joyce shows convincingly how a sensitive boy might be driven to confess. (A seminal article in tracing the sources is J. R. Thrane, "Joyce's Sermon on Hell: Its Source and Backgrounds," *Modern Philology* 57 [1960]: 172–98; interestingly, Thrane's title embodies a memory slip occurring in many readers— the collapse of four sermons into one; that results, I suspect, from the power of the appalling vision.)

[13] As those who read about Stanley Milgram's famous experiment, in which subjects were ordered to administer what they took to be shocks to an apparently "incompetent learner," typically suppose that the commands should have been disobeyed. Indeed, that is the retrospective reaction of many of the subjects themselves, and the source of their subsequent psychological distress. Precisely because

A ROLE FOR RELIGION? 197

Most religious people understand that might doesn't make right. Hence they filter the scriptures. Nevertheless, some of them think of their scriptures as offering them guidance on moral matters where their independent moral standards don't deliver a decision. To be sure, the Bible contains some repugnant passages, but, allegedly, it can still be trusted in denying the permissibility of abortion or denouncing the sinfulness of same-sex love. Is that a legitimate attitude?

Devout people of this sort behave like a more thoughtful and sensitive commandant. Instead of always following the orders sent down from the supreme leader, our commandant sometimes demurs. If the prescription clearly violates his moral principles—as when he is asked to torture the people under his charge or to engage in mass executions—he refuses to go along. You can even imagine that he takes steps to ensure that his actions are concealed and that the intended victims are thus protected. In other instances, what he's asked to do rings no moral alarm bells. On some occasions, however, the order from on high is difficult to assess. He recognizes the seriousness of the consequences for the lives of some of those whom he controls. When he tries to think through the question, he has an inclination to resist, but he has to acknowledge the moral complexity of the situation. Finding it hard to decide, he eventually acquiesces in the order. After all, it comes from the leader.

That, too, is a moral error. For our commandant knows enough about the orders issued from on high to warrant a general skepticism about the moral authority of the leadership. Those who have commanded unspeakable actions in the past cannot serve as decisive voices in hard cases. Kant's point generalizes when it is combined with a well-known biblical text—"By their fruits, ye shall know them." However difficult it may be to work through some moral issues, the answer isn't to consult dubious authorities and to follow their counsel.

Consider, in this light, the religious believer who contends that abortion is murder, always and everywhere, or his fellow who defends the invariable sinfulness of same-sex love. Blanket bans are vulnerable to confrontation with extreme cases. To deny abortion to a twelve-year-old girl, raped by a close relative, when the pregnancy will inevitably result not only in the early and painful death of a child whose development is radically disrupted, but in the death (or serious incapacitation) of the girl herself, is, on the face of it, an

---

the judgment seems so evident, the experiment generates self-reproach and even trauma—so that it is rightly seen as morally problematic.

198 THE MAIN ENTERPRISE OF THE WORLD

exercise in gratuitous cruelty. (It would be hard to interpret it as imbued with a sense of the priority of the living—as being "Pro-Life.") To suppose that the deeply devoted love of two men or two women, committed to an enduring relationship that sustains the work they do in fostering many other human lives, is somehow an evil that must be rooted out, is, on the face of it, to focus on irrelevant aspects of human love; which anatomical parts make contact in the expression of love is, you might think, far less significant than the quality of the emotions that fuel the relationship. How, then, can the religious believer appeal to texts as morally decisive, when they are commonly read as contravening important values in human life in the cases at hand—abortion, homosexuality—and also contain other prescriptions that are morally repulsive? A scripture that not only announces but even delights in the extreme torments to be visited on those, however virtuous, who fail to acknowledge the deity is hardly a reliable guide on moral matters.[14] Especially when, as other parts of the text reveal, that deity is prepared to advocate wholesale murder and sexual slavery and also manifests an obsessive narcissism in stipulating the conditions under which he is properly to be worshipped.

Yet my analogy with the commandant is generous to the religious believer. Let's make it more realistic, by invoking a point made earlier about variations in moral perspectives among different religions and alternative interpretations of the same supposedly privileged texts. The regime our commandant serves is affected, at the highest level, by a power struggle—and the commandant knows this. The orders received come from different factions at different times. Because he sees himself as serving a particular faction, the commandant strives to identify the commands favored by that faction, and to carry them out (subject, of course, to eliminating those that violate his moral scruples). Perhaps because of the turmoil in the upper echelons of the regime, many of the directions he receives are cryptic and obscure. Furthermore, he knows from his interactions with other commandants who favor the same faction he does that some of these orders are interpreted in different ways. Finally, it's common knowledge that some camps are supervised

---

[14] A point forcefully made by David Lewis in an outline for a paper, left unwritten at his premature death. On the last occasion on which I had seen David, we discussed the projected paper at some length, and in consultation with David's widow, Stephanie Lewis, I completed a version of it as David Lewis, "Divine Evil," in *Philosophers without Gods*, ed. Louise Antony (New York: Oxford University Press, 2007), 231–42. I am sure that that version is inferior to what David would have written, but I hope it will be read as one philosopher's tribute to another, indeed to a much-admired mentor and friend.

A ROLE FOR RELIGION? 199

by people who support rival factions, so that there's considerable diversity in how camps are run and which orders are followed.

Under these circumstances, the idea of following orders from on high in the difficult cases is even more suspect. Not only does our commandant know that some of the commands issued by his preferred faction are morally repulsive. He should also wonder about his understanding of the commands, and about whether the faction to which he has committed himself is the morally right choice. What alternative does he have to offer to the recommendation that he use his own independent moral understanding in deciding what to do?

Suppose the commandant believes that there's a single extremely powerful leader behind the regime, who has removed himself from the scene (possibly to attend to other pressing business). The commandant aspires to be the faithful servant of this leader, administering the regime in ways that accord with the leader's design. His commitment to the faction he chooses expresses a conviction that this particular group of high-level subordinates attempts to carry out the plans framed by the supreme authority. Shouldn't he then view the clash of opinions and the obscurity of the commands as indicating a failure—a moral failure—in the foundation of the whole enterprise? Shouldn't he view the leader's absence and lack of clarity as indications either of serious limitations in power or else as dereliction of duty? To the extent that the regime is understood as wisely designed, isn't the confusion sown among those charged with carrying out the great plan itself a sign of the creator's moral turpitude?

Properly conducted moral and political deliberations can only be secular, only using premises that are not grounded in appeals to religious texts, because the texts in question and the cacophony of their discordant voices leave no option except to use our prior and independent moral convictions. Kant's insight cuts deep. Moreover, many religious people and religious sects have recognized the insight. They have seen how morality, as articulated by those who have concentrated on humanity and on the lives human beings live, overrides the appeal to scriptures, sometimes showing how passages need to be discarded, sometimes revealing how they are best understood. Embracing this kind of humanism is one mode of religious progress.

Or is it? The fundamentalists whose moral dogmatism appalls the New Atheists, inspiring them to their fierce denunciations, are unlikely to find a convincing rebuttal to the line of reasoning I have derived from Kant. Nevertheless, one religious tradition, commonly viewed as sophisticated and progressive, would view the argument as denying the core of the religious attitude. What humanists hail as religious progress is a dilution of true faith, a watered-down creed designed for the humanist palate. For this religious tradition, to subject God's word to secular moral scrutiny is to underrate the power and the glory of faith. Søren Kierkegaard's subtle attempt to uncover the psychological character of the "knight of faith" is the classic expression of a rejoinder to the Kantian argument.[15] Instead of conceding that divine commandments must be subordinated to the judgments of (human) morality, Kierkegaard identifies faith with the "teleological suspension of the ethical." Precisely because Abraham is prepared to obey the command to kill his beloved son, Isaac, and to do so recognizing the full horror and even the absurdity of that deed, he is the exemplary "knight of faith," the historical model of the religious believer. Considering alternative constellations of Abraham's psychological attitudes, ways of conceiving his situation so as to rationalize what he does and is prepared to do, Kierkegaard denies that any of the scenarios making Abraham comprehensible according to our ordinary lights will recognize his greatness. Conventional thought cannot understand him. He is willing to obey the command of God, a command he knows to be horrible and absurd. His willingness is the supreme expression of faith.

Kierkegaard's celebration of this extreme form of religious commitment faces an obvious objection. By killing Isaac, Abraham would have deprived his son—and indeed any number of the descendants God has promised him—the opportunity to make a similar profession of faith. If the total commitment to obeying the Almighty is so valuable, ought anyone deny it to others? It is not hard to see how the objection would be brushed aside. To pose such questions is to import into the consideration of faith our everyday moral perspectives, our concerns for the lives of other human beings for example. Precisely the point of the story of Abraham is to show how these ideas have been transcended. For any person, at any time, the commitment to God is overriding.

A more flat-footed question asks how far the suspension of the ethical should be permitted. Imagine a world populated by "knights of faith." Every day, devout people read their scriptures, finding what they take to be new

---

[15] Søren Kierkegaard, *Fear and Trembling*, trans. Howard Hong and Edna Hong, Vol. 6 of *Kierkegaard's Works* (Princeton: Princeton University Press, 1983).

illumination in their texts, often becoming convinced that the voice of their chosen deity is speaking directly to them. Inspired by the commands they take themselves to receive, they act, often flouting the precepts of human-centered morality to carry out atrocities. Infidels are persecuted and tortured in the interests of instructing them in the true faith. Great wars are begun with the aim of hastening the "end of days" when humanity shall be finally redeemed. Abraham has millions . . . hundreds of millions . . . billions of spiritual descendants. Each of them reaches that condition Kierkegaard so admires. Each is completely devoted to a preferred deity, willing to do anything the deity is taken to command. All of them act in full awareness of the horror and absurdity of what they do.

Of course, from any given religious perspective—that of nineteenth-century Danish protestant Christianity, for example—most of these people will be profoundly in error. The large majority of "knights of faith" will be following imaginary messages from a nonexistent being. Yet for the enthusiastic partisans of faith to condemn them on those grounds would be to repeat the error supposedly diagnosed in rebutting the charge directed at Abraham: he would deprive Isaac of a similar opportunity to show his dedication to God. To criticize those who, by your own lights, worship the wrong deity would import our everyday standards where they have been transcended. Commitment to a higher being, we should recall, is everything. Faith does the absurd because it is absurd.[16]

No distinctions can be drawn to separate the sheep from the goats. Partisans will inveigh against those they view as misguided, but, by hypothesis, the commitment leading them to their own stance, inspiring them to think of themselves and those akin to them as uniquely right, is exactly the same unfounded leap as that taken by those whom they condemn. Suspending the ethical may appear admirable when "knights of faith" are rare, and when the leap is directed to the correct place. In the murky world in which human beings live, casting off demands for evidence and "transcending" ethical life is an appalling disaster. It leads to a world in which the most ruthless and fanatical camp commandants are effectively given free rein.

Wilfred Owen probably never read Kierkegaard, but he saw the danger. His experience of trench warfare in Flanders led him to rewrite the Abraham story. "The Parable of the Old Man and the Young" begins after the command

---

[16] It is absurd to suppose that *all* of these devout fanatics are acting correctly—but is that also something each of them should believe?

202 THE MAIN ENTERPRISE OF THE WORLD

has been given, with Abraham and Isaac journeying to the mountain where the boy is to be killed. The boy asks where they are to find the animal for the sacrifice. His father does not reply.

> Then Abram bound the youth with belts and straps,
> and builded parapets and trenches there,
> And stretchèd forth the knife to slay his son.
> When lo! an angel called him out of heaven,
> Saying, Lay not thy hand upon the lad,
> Neither do anything to him. Behold,
> A ram, caught in a thicket by its horns;
> Offer the Ram of Pride instead of him.
> But the old man would not so, but slew his son,
> And half the seed of Europe, one by one.[17]

Owen's version exposes an everyday assumption lurking in the Genesis story: when the angel speaks, Abraham *recognizes* what is said as a new message from God, one that overrides the previous command. Yet why should Kierkegaard's knight of faith do that? Why not view this as a last temptation to lapse from honoring the divine command? Those who celebrate the absolute commitment of faith must explain why it is not *more* admirable to suspect messages promising relief, why the knight of faith should not be stalwart in resisting any suggestions that the terrible trial has now come to a happy end.

Moreover, Owen provides a rival psychological account that would-be knights of faith should confront and reckon with. What an agent sees as obeying the word of God, even though it inflicts pain and suffering, even though it is—when judged by everyday standards—cruel and savage, may express, in part or wholly, an underlying urge to violence. Owen's Abraham is implacable, in the grip of a desire to wound and kill, bequeathed to his descendants as they flounder in the mud of the Western Front.

In the end, then, appeals for the suspension of the ethical oppose the progress made by the major religions of the world as they have given priority to the demands of morality. If you cross the world full of "knights of faith" with that

---

[17] *The Poems of Wilfred Owen*, ed. Jon Stallworthy (London: Chatto and Windus, 1990).

A ROLE FOR RELIGION? 203

described in Owen's war poetry, the result is a magnified version of a condition humanity has repeatedly experienced. From the first millennium before the common era through the religious wars erupting ever since, "knights of faith" have jousted with one another, proliferating vast amounts of human misery along the way.

Ancient religions seem to have been tribal. Residues of tribalism remain in writings that endure in the canon, to become prime targets of subsequent filtering. Those early strands reveal how deities were once viewed as protective chieftains, interested in advancing the mundane struggles of some local group. When neighbors compete or fight, part of the point is to show that "our god is bigger than your god."

As a moral corollary of such attitudes, actions forbidden among members of the tribe are permitted, even encouraged, toward outsiders. Violence against other tribes doesn't simply erupt from disputes about land or over scarce resources. It expresses a determination to defend the honor and demonstrate the power of the divine protector. Local gods are *jealous* gods.[18] They disdain tolerance of those who worship rival deities. Attempts to eliminate people who favor "false gods" are entirely justified. Extreme sacrifices on behalf of the tribe are morally praiseworthy, in part because they show the extent of the heroes' devotion. Apparently they caress the ego of a giant narcissist.

The idea of a jealous god who requires his followers to extirpate unbelievers gives way, in stages, to more progressive conceptions.[19] In the initial state, there are no doubts about the reality of the rival gods. Earthly struggles among competing groups are projected into another sphere—into the sky, say—where mutually hostile patrons conduct their own quarrels. One line of development consists in modifying the view of religious alternatives. Instead

[18] See, for example, Exodus 20:5 and 34:14. As the former verse makes clear, the *descendants* of those who are unfaithful (going off to worship other gods) are to be punished "to the third and fourth generations."

[19] Here, and in what follows, I conceive religious progress in *social* terms. I focus on the changes in the practices prescribed by religious traditions, and offer a (rough) account of how some changes have been progressive. Of course, it is also possible to understand the religious progress made by individual people through their lifetimes. This is properly conceived in very different terms, as a deepening of the commitment to a particular deity (or deities). Devout people often view themselves as becoming *better* Muslims or Hindus, *better* servants of God, *better* at carrying out the divine purposes, and so forth. In these self-appraisals the framework of the religion (the socially prescribed practices) serve as a background, held constant, serving as the standard by which improvements are judged. Thus the forms of individual religious progress should not be confused with the social changes on which I concentrate. Thanks to Harry Brighouse for comments prompting me to clarify this point.

204   THE MAIN ENTERPRISE OF THE WORLD

of seeing rival devotions as directed toward different real beings, there's a single powerful deity, often envisaged as the creator. Religious disagreement consists in differing ideas about the attributes of this being. Nevertheless, jealousy endures. The deity demands acceptance of the correct doctrines and worship of the correct sort. Unbelievers fail on at least one count, and typically on both. Because their failures are so offensive to this jealous god, the faithful are still required to root out wrong views, wherever and whenever they can. The religious community continues to be an army, recruited to fight on behalf of the one true god.

A different form of religious progress retains the vision of many deities but mitigates the jealousies among them. The quarrels in the heavenly sphere are no longer so extreme. The gods are not always at odds, and they tolerate worshippers who divide their allegiances differently. If you most regularly participate in the ceremonies for Apollo, and I am more inclined to sacrifice to Athene or to Minerva, there's no necessary injunction for either of us to use violence in attempts to set the other straight. Of course, disputes between us, or between our cities, may break out for quite independent reasons, and the religious disagreement may then figure in our hostilities. But the lack of concordance in our religious allegiances doesn't drive us to resort to arms.

Ecumenical religion emerges in history when doctrinal advance offers the picture of a single transcendent regime. In the simplest version, there is only a single divinity, the deity who planned and created the cosmos. Other variants allow multiple heavenly beings, often (though not always) ordered hierarchically. The moral aspect of religious progress consists in abandoning the imperative to stamp out those who disagree. People seduced by other religions are still in error. Their views of the transcendent order and how to worship continue to be incorrect. Nevertheless, the devout are no longer required to breach standard moral boundaries in efforts to bring them to the truth. Attempts may be made to persuade them, to show them the correct path, but, if they persist in refusing, they cannot be treated in ways that would be prohibited in interactions among the faithful. In particular, they may not be killed or tortured or stripped of all they possess.

Can this attitude coexist with the vision of a jealous god to whom our reverence and service are due? The history of religion shows that it can. Ecumenical religion often supposes that the deity cares deeply about matters of doctrine, and, perhaps especially about the expression of doctrine in rites and rituals. Defenders of a particular style of ecumenical religion frequently insist on the correctness of their own views. They know how the deity (or deities) must be served, and those who differ with them are profoundly wrong. Despite those errors, it would be wrong to violate the independent requirements of morality in attempting to bring the misguided to the truth. The faithful are no longer god's army. He can handle the problem himself.

For, at this first stage of ecumenical religion, it is still seen as a problem. The deity still insists on proper recognition through doctrinal faith and correct worship. Indeed, the matter is so important that those who obstinately refuse to follow the true way may meet with terrible punishment. Moreover, although apparent commands to "smite" the unbelievers are not to be followed, the canonical religious texts are, in general, morally authoritative. Thus the first stage of ecumenical religion combines four attitudes. First, it takes the doctrines and observances of the religion to be uniquely correct. Second, it prohibits violence toward people with false doctrinal beliefs (and, correspondingly, erroneous ideas about religious service) even if the actions aim to chastise or to convert them. Third, it continues to view those with incorrect religious commitments as being in error sufficiently deep and important to deserve severe, perhaps infinite, divine punishment. Fourth, it retains part of the moral authority of the favored religious texts: except where they order us to engage in violence toward unbelievers, the scriptures provide moral guidance.

At this stage of ecumenical religion, believers engage in the filtering I considered earlier. Their acceptance of the second point leads them to disregard the apparent commands delivered by certain passages in their canonical religious texts. Nonetheless, they are prepared to employ the scriptures to settle difficult moral questions.

How do the categories introduced so far—tribal religion and first-stage ecumenical religion—apply to the world in which we live today? Ecumenical religion characterized by the fourfold commitment just noted is probably the most common form of religion found around the globe. It is a genuine advance over tribal religion. Unfortunately, however, tribal religion still survives, found in militant versions of Islam—and also in the persecution of Muslims by Buddhists, Hindus, Jews, and Christians. To eradicate tribal religion in favor of ecumenical religion, even the first stage of ecumenical religion, would be a welcome progressive step.

Yet this first stage of ecumenical religion is inherently unstable. Combining the four commitments is not easy, once they are made explicit and juxtaposed. For if we are sure that our religion captures the supremely important truth, if deviations from it are so offensive to the one true god, why should we

206 THE MAIN ENTERPRISE OF THE WORLD

bow to secular morality in our conduct toward unbelievers? Why shouldn't we act as God's soldiers, taking all possible means to bring them to the light? If they face eternal torment unless they amend their ways, aren't we deficient in our duty toward them if we fail to use all possible means in attempts at conversion? Cotton Mather saw the point, arguing that those who abstained from enslaving Africans, were morally derelict:

> The State of your *Negroes* in the World, must be low, and mean, and abject; a State of servitude. No *Great Things* in this World, can be done for them. Something then, let there be done towards their welfare in the *World to Come.* . . . *Every one of us shall give account of himself to God.*[20]

Moreover, the very fact that the deity is prepared to inflict such severe punishment on those whose only misdeed consists in harboring erroneous beliefs about him, or about how he is to be served, undercuts the practice of relying on canonical scriptures for moral guidance.

The second stage of ecumenical religion emerges when the moral instability of the first stage is recognized. Believers acknowledge Kant's deep insight about the priority of morality. They now appeal to moral principles and secular moral deliberation to resolve questions about how to act. Additionally, they revise their conception of the deity in light of their moral understandings. A god who visited eternal torment on unbelievers, however virtuous—indeed a god who was prepared to punish *anyone* on the scale typically envisaged—would be a monster.[21] No being who authored such infinite injustice—divine evil—deserves service or worship. The vindictive narcissist is replaced by a deity who is loving and merciful. Non-believers in our society are no longer semi-humans, so vile in the eyes of the deity that they must be eternally damned. They become fellow citizens, worthy of respect and love, God's and ours.

Second-stage ecumenical religion modifies some of the attitudes of the first stage. It retains the confidence of the first commitment: the doctrines and observances of the religion continue to be seen as uniquely correct. The second point is expanded: even when the scriptures appear to command them, breaches of morality are *never* justified. A new image of the deity

---

[20] *Against Slavery*, 19; see also John Saffin's reply to an early abolitionist tract—*Against Slavery*, 16 (Objection 2). Mather believes enslaving benighted "Negroes" to be the best way to show them the route to heaven. Hence acquiring slaves is not merely permissible, but a moral duty.

[21] Thus, they accept the argument of Lewis's "Divine Evil."

modifies the third commitment: those with false religious belief are in error, but they will (perhaps only belatedly) receive divine forgiveness. Finally, the role of religious texts in morality is revised: they can inspire moral proposals, but the credentials of those proposals must be assessed through independent (secular) moral inquiry. Second-stage ecumenical religion represents further religious progress.

How commonly does this form of advance occur? Second-stage ecumenical religion is probably not as frequent in human history, or even today, as its first-stage predecessor. Perhaps (a depressing thought) it may draw fewer adherents than the surviving versions of tribal religion. Even where religious groups work their way to a position embracing the revised versions of the first three commitments, they sometimes stop short of embracing the fourth; the full force of Kant's point is often missed.

If you believe, as I do, that the central threat posed by religion in the contemporary world lies in the tendency to subordinate moral and political debates to the supposed authority of religious doctrines, then you should draw an obvious conclusion. A transition in which many religious communities progressed to second-stage ecumenical religion would be a major step forward. The total eradication of religion is not required.

At the second stage, ecumenical religion breathes acceptance and tolerance toward people of different faiths—or of none. Because non-believers now count as morally excusable, the decision not to wage crusades against them is no longer an odd exception to a general policy of viewing them as mired in sin. Yet some instability remains. To the extent that the actions of non-believers can be regarded with equanimity, shouldn't the believer also wonder whether their *doctrines* should be firmly dismissed? The fault lines in second-stage ecumenical religion no longer run within the sphere of moral judgment, dividing the issue of violence in the name of god from other moral questions, but between the moral and the epistemic. Despite their errors, even about the most important aspects of the cosmos, those who have not turned to the true religion are accepted as people who exhibit the same moral range found among the devout. Many of them are good, and deserve divine forgiveness. Appreciating their moral parity, isn't it also appropriate to ask if their epistemic situation is as dire as it is taken to be?

Second-stage ecumenical religion faces serious questions about what distinguishes any particular set of doctrines as privileged.[22] As the

---

[22] A more detailed version of the argument presented in the following discussion is given in Chapter 1 of my *Life after Faith* (New Haven, CT: Yale University Press, 2014).

208   THE MAIN ENTERPRISE OF THE WORLD

second-stage ecumenical Christian considers members of other Christian sects, or Muslims or Jews, or Hindus or Buddhists, she is struck by the similarities between these people and the fellow members of her own congregation. Recognizing some of them as moral equals of her co-religionists, she also sees them as coming to their distinctive faiths by paths very similar to those traversed by her friends among the faithful. Many of them were born into a religious community whose doctrines were imbibed in childhood. Others switched their religious allegiance, finding another style of worship more suited to the attitudes their early socialization had instilled in them. Extending her historical perspective, she appreciates how the doctrines, rites, and ceremonies of all the major religions have evolved, how they have been reinterpreted in response to changing social and political environments. When she interacts with second-stage ecumenical worshippers of rival faiths, she understands how their perspective on her is equivalent to the attitude she takes toward them. She sees her religious commitments as privileged, and thus concludes that the others are mistaken. Each of them regards his own perspective as the correct one, and judges her to be in error. Since all have reached the second stage of ecumenical religion, they don't go on to draw invidious moral judgments. In the moral sphere, the declaration "I'm OK, you're OK" prevails. Why, then, the insistence on epistemic asymmetry? Whence comes the confidence that we have the central truth about the universe, and the rest of you are wrong?

The second stage of ecumenical religion comes under pressure to reconcile the doctrinal differences among religions. Investigations of the origins of religious texts and of the cultural evolution of religions intensify that pressure. Comparative studies reveal how individuals of different faiths come to their adult beliefs in very similar ways. It is hard to identify some distinctive form of experience or reasoning legitimizing a verdict that some particular religion—and it alone—is on the track of truth. Attention to the social and political factors that figure in reshaping religious commitments reinforces the point.[23]

When thoughtful people feel these pressures, the religion they endorse moves to a new stage. The first step is to seek common ground across sects and religions. "We may seem to disagree," the believer says, "but fundamentally we are in accord. We all worship the same God." Hence the idea that *some* of the world's devout people are privileged in having found doctrinal

---

[23] See Chapter 1 of *Life after Faith*.

A ROLE FOR RELIGION? 209

truth is modified or abandoned. No single religion is *uniquely* correct. All of them share "core doctrines," all recognize the most central and significant religious truths. To be sure, these truths are expressed rather differently among the world's major religions. Even though Jews, Christians, and Muslims worship a single deity, they tell different stories about him. Hindus apparently recognize many gods, and major strands in Buddhism admit none. To reconcile all these different perspectives, the idea of religious language as literal has to go. A new attitude emerges.

Religion is now seen as an attempt to recognize and to respond to an aspect of the universe of immense human significance. Human beings are limited. Our everyday ways of inquiring into nature, most highly developed in the various sciences, are quite inadequate to make sense of the reality toward which the world's religions gesture. That *transcendent* reality (to give it a name) eludes literal description. The great religious texts and the myths passed on in successive generations of many human communities provide, in their distinctive ways, some inklings of the transcendent. Through doing so they are able to enrich the lives of the people who ponder them and who come together in the rites and ceremonies out of which the scriptures and myths have grown[24] and in which they continue to be embedded.

Beyond the second stage of ecumenical religion lies a further progressive step. It culminates in what I have elsewhere called "refined religion."[25] This stage of religion embraces the following commitments. First, it regards none of the world's religions as uniquely correct. Second, it views all religions as (necessarily limited) attempts to gesture towards a transcendent. Religious texts must be seen as non-literal, containing stories, allegories, and metaphors for presenting what cannot be expressed in literal language. Third, the religious response to the transcendent provides a unique enrichment of human lives. Without it, human existence would be impoverished. Fourth, it denies that religious texts, even those that inspire the devout, can be used as reliable guides on moral questions. Moral standards have to be worked out independently. If religion has a connection to moral life, it consists in deepening the significance of moral precepts whose proper grounds lie elsewhere.

---

[24] Here, quite evidently, I draw on the seminal ideas of Emile Durkheim. See his *Elementary Forms of the Religious Life* (1912; repr., New York: Oxford University Press, 2001).
[25] *Life after Faith*, Chapter 3.

210   THE MAIN ENTERPRISE OF THE WORLD

Refined religion is thoroughly ecumenical, treating all religions on a par and emphasizing the importance of religion in human life. The moral insight, Kant's point, achieved at the second stage of ecumenical religion, is retained. Any monopoly on religious insight is rejected. The challenges of integrating the priority of secular morality with scriptural texts are solved by abandoning literalism. By giving vivid examples of moral worth, religious parables and precepts reinforce main features of morality. They can be helpful as reminders in moral deliberation, both at the social level and in the reflections of individuals, not because they offer evidence for principles unrecognized by secular inquiry, but because they bring home the force of independently grounded moral considerations.

Refined religion has been practiced in human history. Indeed, it is probably a popular position with scholars who have wrestled with the intellectual conundrums posed by their various faiths. Within the Christian tradition, Ralph Waldo Emerson, William James, Paul Tillich, John Robinson, and John Shelby Spong have all offered versions of it. Among Jews, Martin Buber provides a famous exposition. Yet, it must be conceded, refined religion is far from common in the contemporary world. If it were the only form of religion secular humanism could tolerate, the role assigned to religion in the societies humanists envisage and the educational practices they commend would be so slender as to trivialize conceding it. Many religious people would—reasonably—view the supposedly kindly secular humanist as a wolf in sheep's clothing, a New Atheist with a milder tone and a deceptively gentle smile.

Secular humanism, at least the form of it I espouse, is very close to refined religion. Perhaps the difference can be localized to a single word. My secular humanism specifically denies the thought of religion as *uniquely* enriching human lives. It concedes the possibility of religious enrichment. Even though there is no "transcendent," the non-literal language used to gesture toward some "higher" aspect of reality can—like other myths, allegories, stories, and poems, in my view—deepen human experience. Yet, secular humanism can be more sympathetic, appreciating the ways in which *many* less progressive forms of religion have promoted important human values. Religion has often reinforced moral commitments, and strengthened the social ties among people.[26] The supposed sayings of those who figure centrally in the world's religions—the Hebrew patriarchs and prophets, the Buddha, Krishna, Jesus,

---

[26] For a rich, and important, exposition and defense of this view, see Rabindranath Tagore, *The Religion of Man*.

A ROLE FOR RELIGION? 211

and Muhammad—have inspired believers to act well. Stories and parables have aided moral deliberation, even when they were viewed as more than valuable fictions. Rites and ceremonies have built communities, leading them to act together in morally important projects. Before all religions are cast aside, thrown away as noxious trash, it is well to acknowledge the good that they have sometimes done.

Of course, from a secular point of view, that good is compromised. It is outweighed by the damage widespread religious belief has often inflicted. The imbalance is most obvious with respect to tribal religion. However much the idea of serving "our" god may have motivated the faithful to act well, however strongly it has bound a community together, the fierce intolerance toward outsiders, often expressed in appalling violence, undercuts any claim it has to a role in contemporary societies. Moreover, if the crucial issue is that of preventing illicit incursions of religion into public morality, the pertinent humanist community should include all those who subscribe to the independence of moral deliberation, and exclude those who continue to take their preferred scriptures as morally authoritative. *Second-stage ecumenical religion marks the critical step.* Hence a guiding idea emerges for the social and educational reforms I envisage. Secular humanism aims to build an alliance not only with refined religion but also with religious practices that have reached the second ecumenical stage.[27]

15. *Educational practices should provide a role for religion, recognizing the values of forms of religion at or beyond the second ecumenical stage.*

Later in this chapter, I shall try to specify as precisely as possible what that role should be. (I hope that committed secularists will postpone dismissing Proposal 15 until that clarification comes.)

First, however, it is useful to reflect more extensively on the guiding thought just proposed. Why not opt for the simpler line of campaigning to eliminate *all* religions (with the possible exception of the tiny minority that advocate

---

[27] *Life after Faith* envisaged an alliance between secular humanists and defenders of progressive religion, people who seek a middle way between fundamentalist religion and fundamentalist atheism. There I concentrated on devotees of refined religion. I now believe I drew the borders too narrowly. The natural allies should include all those who recognize the Kantian insight, so that a significant group of religious believers is now added. This reflects my growing conviction that what matters is not doctrinal belief, but the ways in which moral decisions are made and conduct is guided.

212   THE MAIN ENTERPRISE OF THE WORLD

refined religion, a domesticated few who can hang around because they are rare and harmless)?

As I briefly noted above, many religions have discovered ways of building communities. Perhaps, at early stages, festivals and rites served to reinforce bonds among members of the same tribe. Later phases of the history of religions sometimes reveal institutionalized assemblies in which subtle forms of human relations are strengthened. Community is built along many dimensions. The faithful come together not only to celebrate and to worship, but to participate in joint projects, to provide mutual aid, to give consolation and comfort, to enrich the socialization of the young, and to explore questions that are central to human lives. Even the most fully developed secular movements fail to provide their adherents with the richness offered by the major religions, at their best. Secular humanists can learn from the many ways in which religions have sometimes enriched the lives of the faithful.

Part of that enrichment consists in providing spaces in which the deepest and most serious questions can be openly discussed, how people can consider what their lives amount to, and how they can find the straight way when it has been lost. Further, the proposal that religious commitments endow our experiences and our moral convictions with an extra depth, a thesis eloquently defended by William James and eloquently renewed by Charles Taylor, should be taken seriously.[28] Secular humanists face a double challenge, to build satisfying forms of community and to deepen our sense of ourselves and of our lives. Meeting that challenge without resorting to religious commitments, even in the sophisticated—"refined"!—forms favored by James and others like him, is not impossible. But there is much to be learned from approximately two millennia during which the world's major religions have carried out their various social experiments.

New Atheism dismisses much of that history. Relentlessly focusing on matters of doctrine, its well-intentioned champions write as if the worst that could happen to anyone is to lapse into false belief. Anything is better than being conned. Yet, as James's nemesis William Clifford saw more than a century ago, the real trouble with false belief isn't individual but social.[29] The danger is that false beliefs will damage the moral and political health of societies. Public discussion and public policy have to be insulated against religious dogmatism. Yet, like those whose opinions they deride, the New

---

[28] William James, "The Moral Philosopher and the Moral Life"; Charles Taylor, *A Secular Age* (Cambridge, MA: Harvard University Press, 2007).
[29] In "The Ethics of Belief."

A ROLE FOR RELIGION? 213

Atheists make individual opinion everything. Religious fundamentalists see unbelievers as justly punished, infinitely punished, by their deity; New Atheists view the lives of the devout as so diminished by their false beliefs that they would be better off discarding those beliefs, whatever their circumstances and whatever the ways in which religious observance enhances, or even transforms, their lives. The fundamentalist's crude image of a tribal deity, vindictive in his narcissism, is matched by the New Atheist's one-eyed conviction that believing the truth is the most important feature of a person's life.

Secular *humanism* sees the quality of human lives and the health of human societies as central. To be sure, lives are improved when people give up delusions and gain a clearer picture of reality—when enlightenment comes without any serious loss. Societies grow healthier when moral and political deliberations are freed from religious distortion. An attempt to foster these forms of progress should look at all aspects of human life. It should aim to entrench Kant's insight about the priority of secular morality, and to develop further the social practices and institutions that help individual people to live well. Humanists, whether atheists, agnostics, champions of refined religion or of stage-two ecumenical religion, can join together in this enterprise.

Religious progress is often conceived as a teleological affair. Most believers think of it as consisting in approximating the ideal form of the One True Religion.[30] Secular humanists easily adopt a parallel picture. They view religions as progressing toward a long-term goal, the achievement of a fixed secular humanism serving as the endpoint, with progress to be measured by the diminution of religious belief.[31] As religions progress, they will abandon literalism, become more ecumenical, eventually achieve refinement, and, ultimately, doctrine will wither away entirely. This teleological vision retains traces of New Atheist error. Secular humanists, even of milder dispensations, tend to see themselves as runners who have already finished an arduous race. As they stand behind the finish line, they are filled with sympathy for people they like and respect who are still heading toward the tape. They shout words of encouragement: "Come on! Keep going! You're so close!"

That attitude strikes me as too self-confident, too arrogant. A better—humbler—conception recognizes both religious traditions *and* their

---

[30] As I have pointed out above (n.19 on 203), many devout people would not characterize their *individual* progress in these terms. They would, however, think of the religious tradition to which they belong as making progress by approximating—or even attaining—final religious truth.

[31] In *Life after Faith*, I fell into this trap.

214 THE MAIN ENTERPRISE OF THE WORLD

secularist counterparts as permanently and inevitably incomplete. Progress consists in amending flaws and overcoming limits, where these are assessed against the most inclusive humanist standard. What matters is the improvement of people's lives. Instead of supposing some enduring perfect limit, toward which, as they become less benighted, the world's religions tend, we should see a co-evolutionary process. The alliance between all humanists, whether secular or religious, should be genuine and symmetrical. We can hope to learn from one another. Hence the valuable forms of religion, those making the transition to absorb Kant's insight, should have a role in society and in education.

What role, exactly? To answer the question, it is helpful to return to Mill. Lumping moral and religious traditions together, he proposes to acquaint students with the teachings of all the major systems.[32] The presentation should be ecumenical, for "it is not the teacher's business to take a side, and fight stoutly for some one against the rest."[33] Instead, each of the rivals has insights and defects: there is "not one from which there is not something to be learned by the votaries of others."[34] Indeed, he takes the "characteristic infirmity" of all religions and moral systems to lie in their "undervaluing" the "important truths" appreciated by their rivals.[35]

Mill's emphasis on studying religions comparatively is valuable, for it is likely to help in consolidating a religious stance at (or beyond) the second ecumenical stage. The context of his remarks (the Inaugural Address at St. Andrews) suggests a concern with university education. Why not earlier? Very likely, children will be introduced to their parents' favored form of religious practice before they start to attend school. It would be good for them, from the very beginning, to be aware of the merits of rival faiths—and of secular versions of humanism. An understanding of alternative religions would facilitate their interactions with those of their peers who have been brought up differently, and would especially contribute to the early exercises in joint deliberation central both to citizenship and moral development. Hence, I suggest:

[32] SMC 347. Among the religions, Mill mentions only Judaism and Christianity. This is an unwarranted restriction.
[33] Ibid.
[34] Ibid.
[35] Ibid.

A ROLE FOR RELIGION? 215

16. *From early in their formal education, children should be shown how their religious (or secular) attitudes have counterparts in the lives of others. They should learn about the values to which those attitudes contribute, and also about the oversights of the alternative stances.*

In proposing some focus on deficiencies in the various faiths (and in versions of secular humanism), I encourage early appreciation of such frameworks as evolving over time. Comparative study of religion should extend to understanding the ways in which scholars have shown scriptural canons and the texts they obtain to be *human* selections, often motivated by a wide variety of political and social considerations. The idea of any piece of scripture as the unadulterated word of a divine being should be exposed as false. In particular, the importance of Kant's insight that religious injunctions be appraised in light of prior moral standards should be central to this area of the curriculum from the earliest stages at which it can be introduced.

Religious education should provide a clear sense of the distinctive stages in the progress of religions. In particular, it ought to emphasize the divide between tribal religion and first stage ecumenical religion, on the one hand, and second stage ecumenical religion, refined religion, and secular humanism, on the other. Even though Mill is correct to oppose "fighting stoutly" for one religion against the rest, it *is* the teacher's business—in a healthy society—to defend the three most progressive frameworks against the two more primitive ones. Thus:

17. *Although it should not favor any particular broad progressive framework over its rivals, a primary aim of religious education is to recognize the defects of tribal and first-stage ecumenical religions. From childhood on, students ought to learn why these forms of belief are socially and morally dangerous.*

No doubt this proposal will arouse opposition, and even ire. It's worth considering the most obvious objections to it.

Many liberals are fiercely devoted to maintaining the right to think as one pleases. Mill's *On Liberty* is the culmination of a long struggle for tolerance, and it has—rightly—inspired subsequent attempts to safeguard the spaces within which people formulate and defend their opinions. Liberal society depends on a treaty of toleration.[36] Yet, as is abundantly clear, toleration

[36] See David Lewis, "Mill and Milquetoast."

216 THE MAIN ENTERPRISE OF THE WORLD

cannot be extended indefinitely. In particular, however committed a society may be to tolerance, it must defend itself against those who preach intolerance. Freedoms sometimes have to be limited in order to preserve other freedoms. We rightly curtail the right to speak when the speaker aims to cause social chaos or when the speech expresses hate toward particular types of people. Thus religions professing intolerance toward other members of society are justifiably subject to scrutiny.

But must the scrutiny result in an absolute ban? Or in indoctrinating the young to reject them? Can't the religions in question be safely corralled within some sphere? Should we return to a pre-Millian state in which tolerance is extended to some frameworks but not to others?[37] Yes, yes, no, and yes. There is no safe quarantine. Intolerant believers don't live double lives, carefully setting aside their attitudes when they step out of the circle of their friends and engage in public affairs. Given their beliefs, their sense of service to the deity as overriding, to do so, assuming it would be psychologically possible, would be a severe moral error. Yet, in a Deweyan democratic society, they are asked to participate in social and moral deliberation. The conditions of deliberation require them to engage with the perspectives of people whom they view as benighted and sinful. Their convictions always threaten attempts to resolve moral and social problems. They cannot become the citizens a democratic society needs.

A line must be drawn. Has it been drawn in the correct place? Followers of tribal religion, bent on extirpating all those who do not worship as they do, appear to be sufficiently close to the purveyors of hate speech to deserve the refusal of toleration. Those committed to first-stage ecumenical religion present a trickier case. After all, these people don't go around "smiting the infidels." Do they deserve the withholding of tolerance?

Central to the application of tolerance within a society are decisions about which forms of conduct are morally (and legally) intolerable. Making those decisions requires the proper pursuit of moral inquiry. If, as I have argued, moral inquiry demands our best efforts to engage with the perspectives of others, people whose religious beliefs subordinate such attempts to the deliverances of a supposedly privileged text are in conflict with the proper exercise of tolerance. Their incorrect acceptance of the authority of the

---

[37] As, for example, in Locke's *Letter on Toleration*, where tolerance is extended toward many forms of Christian faith, but not to Catholicism or to atheism. Locke's argument identifies some attitudes as socially or politically dangerous. I accept his criterion, but focus the ban to exclude practices opposed to tolerance itself. This results in a different division between the "safe" and the "dangerous."

A ROLE FOR RELIGION? 217

scriptures, the error they share with the commandants of my earlier scenarios, sets them in conflict with moral inquiry, and thus with the best decisions we can make about the limits of tolerance. They will thus systematically draw boundaries in the wrong places, permitting some actions that should be forbidden, and prohibiting others deserving permission. These abstract possibilities stand out in familiar examples: guided by scripture, the devout prolong the sufferings of the terminally sick, rail against the sins of homosexuals, and condemn women and families to death or destitution or misery by insisting on the continuation of unwanted pregnancies. Sometimes the effects of their actions are as devastating as those of the enthusiastic "smiters."

Finally, those who subscribe to first-stage ecumenical religion can retain almost all they desire by proceeding to the second stage. They can rejoin society through the simple step of embracing Kant's insight. What stands in the way? Presumably, devotion to a deity, a jealous god who insists on obedience to his commandments. Yet it is worth asking why we should honor the whims of any being—whether it be the *Führer* or an almighty creator—when they are at odds with the deliverances of our best attempt to work out what morality requires. Why should the first Christian commandment take precedence over the second? Why should inhumane actions be done to satisfy the precepts supposedly stemming from the deity? Any divine being worthy of our worship would sympathize with actions taken to foster the lives of human beings. To insist on destroying or damaging the lives of those agents who fail to deliver the right form of worship, simply because of the supposed defect, would be an expression of cosmic narcissism.[38] Narcissists, however powerful, do not deserve our adoration.

Splitting the status of different versions of the same religion, for the reasons just canvassed, has consequences for broader social issues.[39] Consistency requires extending the division between the two stages of ecumenical religion beyond the sphere of public education. If, as suggested, tribal religion and first-stage ecumenicism are in conflict with the tolerance democracy and morality require, the idea of private institutions devoted to celebrating

---

[38] A clear expression of that narcissism is the idea of divine punishment (even eternal and infinite punishment) for those who do not have the "right" beliefs. To condemn those whose lives are dedicated to self-sacrifice on behalf of their fellows, solely on the basis of their failure to subscribe to particular doctrines, is so monstrous a moral error as to justify opposing—rather than worshipping—any being willing to inflict such punishment.

[39] The ways on which my educational proposals have ramifications for wider social questions will be the central focus of Chapter 10.

218   THE MAIN ENTERPRISE OF THE WORLD

and transmitting those forms of faith should be scrutinized. Schools aligned with these types of religion cannot be tolerated. Nor can young people be "protected" from the standard forms of preparation provided by public education. Hence, a further proposal:

18. *All students should attend schools whose instruction accords with society-wide constraints, elaborated in democratic discussion—the basic principles of the public school curriculum.*[40] *Some forms of private education are permissible, but only when they neither contradict nor subvert the preparation for citizenship and for moral deliberation central to the public school curriculum. In particular, extending public education with schooling in a particular religion is allowable when and only when that religion adheres to the commitments of second-stage ecumenicism or of refined religion; schools set up to teach some secular framework must follow parallel commitments.*

Again, tolerance must be limited. The treaty of toleration cannot be extended to ventures designed to undermine it.

This chapter began by rejecting two alternative visions of the role of religion in society. The sweeping condemnation of the New Atheists overlooks the value some forms of religion can offer. In effect it treats all stages of religion as if they were the most primitive. Its great insight is to recognize the harm primitive types of religion can wreak within the public sphere. By contrast, the popular assignment of religion to a—supposedly safe— sphere misses (or underrates) that threat, while appreciating the positive contributions religion often makes to human lives. The remedy for both

---

[40] I assume that these basic principles will be applied in all schools receiving public funding. The aim of Proposal 18 is to close off the possibility of privately funded schools diverging from these principles. Education is seen as contributing to a collective mission, articulated in the kind of democratic discussion I have envisaged. Thus, if I am correct in thinking the role I envisage for religion, with the limits I've suggested, would emerge from the deliberations of a democratic society, all schools, even those set up by groups with particular interests, have a duty to honor the publicly justifiable goals, and not to attempt to subvert them.

Perhaps the most straightforward way (but surely not the only way) of implementing Proposal 18 is to set up a system in which all students attend schools funded entirely from the public treasury. Parents who want to add on to the public school curriculum—in any fashion—may arrange further instruction in whatever material they take to provide important supplements, but, in doing so, they must leave the guiding principles of the public school curriculum uncompromised. Their children should not receive the democratically decided approach on schooldays, only to be informed on the Sabbath that they should disregard this "indoctrination."

Thanks to Harry Brighouse for alerting me to the need to address this point, and for help in formulating it.

defects is to draw a different kind of distinction, aiming to separate religions whose commitments are socially dangerous from those for which the genuine values are not outweighed by the harms they cause. A truly progressive society can find a place for religion, and even continue to be informed by religion as it strives to make further advances. The religions in question, however, must themselves have progressed beyond the first ecumenical stage.

Are the proposals presented in this chapter too harsh? Do they impose undue burdens on religious believers? Do they conflict with fundamental principles of liberal democracy?[41] I shall close my discussion of religion by attempting to answer these natural and important questions.

The approach I've adopted draws a line separating two kinds of religion. Some are given a place within educational and political institutions; others are excluded. The boundary is defined by Kant's insight: ethical inquiry must assess the purported prescriptions offered by religious texts or teachings. To insist on that does not prevent a devout person from maintaining a particular moral claim, or from viewing it as the will of a preferred deity, or from taking some piece of scripture to offer ethical insights. What is ruled out is a practice of *grounding* a moral claim in an appeal to some writing or traditional teaching. So long as the devout are prepared to propose the lessons they draw from their religion to the further test of collective moral inquiry, and to abandon their original interpretation of their sources should such inquiry reject the moral counsel they claim to have derived, they are entirely free to worship their deity and to regard that being as good and as the author of the good.[42]

Many denominations of the world's major religions have already taken this step. All should be prepared to do so. After all, almost every sect has already begun to move in this direction by appreciating the need to filter. Thankfully, enthusiastic "smiters" of the heathen are less common than they once were. Moreover, religious people should be sensitive to the many erroneous ways in which their own supposedly authoritative doctrines have been understood in the past—and by the analogous ways in which rival religions

---

[41] Many thanks to Martha Nussbaum for posing these questions with great clarity and force.

[42] Their attitude should be: "My reading of my scriptures inclined me to believe *p*. I recognized, from the beginning, my responsibility to revise my tentative acceptance in light of moral inquiry. Now that moral inquiry has shown revision to be needed, I view my original interpretation as mistaken. The author of the good would not have willed the principle I took from my reading."

220   THE MAIN ENTERPRISE OF THE WORLD

have consulted other (non-authoritative) teachings and have frequently misinterpreted them. They should want to distinguish themselves from the commandants of my earlier discussion.

The proposals I have offered do not preclude education in any (second-stage) ecumenical religion. In addition to the schooling children receive in common with one another, they can be offered special instruction to acquaint them with religious practices and doctrines. They can be encouraged to look to what they have learned for guidance, as they face decisions about what to do. But they are to understand the fallibility of interpretations, and the need for moral evaluation of the inspiration they draw from religion. Scriptures may point them towards a valuable moral insight—even though their reading does not provide justification.[43]

These issues can, I think, be clarified further by comparing the approach adopted here with that offered by John Rawls.[44] Central to Rawls's political liberalism is the idea of reasonable pluralism:

[P]olitical liberalism supposes that there are many conflicting reasonable comprehensive doctrines with their conceptions of the good, each compatible with the full rationality of human persons, so far as that can be ascertained with the resources of a political conception of justice.[45]

From these different standpoints, the rival comprehensive doctrines are supposed to agree on a framework for the polity: "social unity" is "founded on an overlapping consensus on a political conception of justice."[46]

Rawls's account appears to be more indulgent than the one I have offered, allowing as "reasonable comprehensive doctrines" forms of religion my Kant-inspired boundary debars. Nevertheless, he too is in the exclusion

[43] To use a familiar distinction from the philosophy of science, religious teachings can play a role in the context of discovery, but not in the context of justification.

[44] Again, I thank Martha Nussbaum for suggesting that I might clarify and defend my approach by making an explicit comparison with Rawls.

[45] John Rawls, *Political Liberalism* (New York: Columbia University Press, 1993), 135. The (murky) last clause is articulated a little in a footnote: "The point here is that while some would want to claim that given the full resources of philosophical reason, there is but one reasonable conception of the good, that cannot be shown by the resources of a reasonable political conception of justice." The elaboration might raise concerns in two distinct ways: first, is there a clear and uncontroversial account of just what the "resources of a reasonable political conception of justice" are? Second, is it appropriate to divorce a weaker set of requirements of reason from reason *tout court*? Perhaps my own pluralism is more thoroughgoing than Rawls's? I see no grounds for supposing that "the full resources of philosophical reason" would reduce all the alternatives to one, and hypothesize that progress in working out conceptions of the good might generate a number of divergent traditions.

[46] Ibid., 145.

A ROLE FOR RELIGION? 221

business. The notion of a *reasonable* comprehensive doctrine does some work for him. In noting that "reasonable pluralism is not an unfortunate condition of human life," he distinguishes it from "pluralism as such," which would countenance "doctrines that are not only irrational but mad and aggressive."[47] I suspect that he would wish to exclude tribal religion on grounds of aggression.

The account offered in this chapter can also be seen as pluralist: I allow for alternative reasonable comprehensive doctrines with their individual conceptions of the good. My pluralism appears more miserly, Rawls's more generous. Yet it is important to recognize just where the difference in inclusiveness lies. Distinguish between the *substantial claims* of a conception of the good and the *epistemic basis* of those claims. Substantial claims are judgments about what kinds of states of affairs are good (or, perhaps, what actions are right, or what traits of character virtuous). The epistemic basis associated with a conception of the good specifies how the substantial claims are to be justified. Given any conception of the good Rawls would admit as reasonable, there is an alternative conception sharing exactly the same substantial claims, one that would be included within my boundary.[48] If Rawls's approach admits more forms of religion, it does so because he allows as reasonable those conceptions of the good with a specific epistemic basis: forms of religion that take appeals to scriptures and traditional teachings as constituting full and final justification. By contrast, I am prepared to admit only those conceptions of the good that will subject substantial claims derived from texts and teachings to the further scrutiny of moral inquiry.

So I am applying a more stringent test than Rawls, denying that comprehensive doctrines count as reasonable if they take a particular epistemological stance. That, I contend, is entirely appropriate. It is unreasonable to think moral inquiry can be overridden (or bypassed) through an appeal to religious texts and teachings. Does this contention violate the condition to which Rawls alludes in the footnote I have cited—that is, have I exceeded "the resources of a reasonable political conception of justice"? Given the vagueness of the latter notion, it is hard to be sure. I am confident, however, that I have not exploited the "full resources of philosophical reason." To suppose the unreliability of treating religious sources as not subject to further check

---

[47] Ibid., 144.

[48] Of course, by recognizing Kant's insight, a believer is committed to engaging in moral inquiry, and moral inquiry might reveal the need for revising certain substantial claims. Religious believers ought to welcome this.

222   THE MAIN ENTERPRISE OF THE WORLD

is, at this stage of human history, about as reasonable, in an everyday sense, as any widely accepted epistemological stance—that should be the judgment of informed common sense, not of recondite philosophy. The recorded past testifies to the variant ways in which all of the major world religions—*and many secular ideologies as well*—have gone grotesquely astray when they have tried to substitute supposedly authoritative texts for moral inquiry. For the epistemological stance I oppose conjoins two strong claims: "This text is authoritative on moral matters *and* our tradition provides a correct interpretation of it." Episode after episode from human history—and not just from the history of religion[49]—reveals that at least one of the conjuncts is false.

My difference with Rawls can be viewed from a different angle by focusing on the target of the overlapping consensus. Just as I want to endorse a pluralism of reasonable comprehensive doctrines, so too, I accept the idea of agreement on a common political framework. Rawls sees that as constituted by a shared "political conception of justice." I view it slightly differently, in terms of a shared *method* for working out together a progressively evolving conception of justice. To my mind, recognizing pluralism is important precisely because the diversity of comprehensive doctrines can play a valuable role in the process through which political life makes progress. Once again, I emphasize the Deweyan thought of a community as bound by a commitment to mutual engagement and mutual learning—democracy as education. For that to occur, moral inquiry cannot be abridged or circumvented by appeals to dubious authority. There cannot be "conversation stoppers." To be reasonable in the pertinent sense is, then, to be open to a kind of exchange that the epistemic bases I reject would prevent.

This aspect of the difference is crystallized in a disagreement over the notion of community. For Rawls, communities are bound together by agreement on "a comprehensive conception of the good."[50] Although some communities exhibit this feature, many do not. Indeed, if whole societies are thought of as potentially communities—as "Great Communities"—they are surely bound together on quite different dimensions.[51] To think of

[49] I have in mind appeals to secular texts that have inspired political ideologies and actions performed to entrench those ideologies. Soviet communism provides well-known examples.

[50] *Political Liberalism*, 146, n.13.

[51] The idea of a "Great Community" is introduced as a political aspiration in Dewey's *The Public and Its Problems*. As I have noted in previous chapters, there are many dimensions to communities, since people can be bound together by all sorts of common projects. In the case of political units (nations, for example), the appropriate shared interest is, I suggest, in working together to create institutions and policies that will contribute to the advancement of the lives of all. Hence agreement

A ROLE FOR RELIGION? 223

democracy as education is to recognize differences as potentially able to lead all citizens, conceiving themselves as committed to a common project, to cooperate in forging policies for advancing the understandings and the lives of all.[52] Epistemological restrictions are needed to facilitate that.

I conclude with direct answers to the questions I originally posed. Forbidding recourse to an unreliable epistemological practice, one that would interfere with democratic deliberation, is not imposing a harsh burden. It in no way restricts the substantial claims of particular religions—only the ways in which they can be publicly defended. The burdens imposed on religious believers are those required of all. Citizens are expected to engage in moral inquiry, and to do so in ways history has not revealed as thoroughly flawed. Pluralism is to be celebrated. Channeling it productively is a proper part of the celebration.[53]

on a method for that cooperative work is the crucial element in political community—and one that can be furthered by divergence among conceptions of the good.

[52] Martha Nussbaum has suggested to me that an earlier version of the proposals made in this chapter conflicted with the Establishment Clause of the US Constitution (and with analogous provisions adopted by other nations.) As I see it, there is a clear line of defense of the formulations adopted here against this charge. Restrictions on religions—or other comprehensive doctrines—are appropriate when they prevent practices threatening central features of political life. Faulty ideas about the grounds of contested moral doctrines can be injurious to democratic discussion, and, when the epistemological failures are made evident by history, invoking those ideas in attempts at justification ought to be debarred. Making epistemological progress should not be confused with establishing a religion or a form of secular ideology.

[53] Nobody who discusses these topics should fail to acknowledge the importance of Rawls's contributions to political philosophy. My own thinking has been greatly influenced by his seminal ideas, and, even in disagreement, I take his writings to be illuminating. Hence this brief attempt to use the contrast between us to respond to important concerns.

PART II

7
The Natural Sciences

Many of the most prominent issues in discussions of education have hardly surfaced in previous chapters. Little has been said about what should be taught or about how it should be taught. Emphasizing instead the place of formal education as part of a lifelong activity of growth, I have focused on three large aims for the individual—self-sustaining, participation in civic life, and self-fulfillment. The discussion could now continue with a radical proposal. Provided those aims are achieved, nothing else matters. Anything that works will do. Choose a curriculum and methods of teaching adapted to those ends.

Given the arguments of the preceding chapters, any such curriculum should be tailored to suit the development of individuals, in ways promoting their fruitful interactions with one another. Important implications follow. First, there are serious questions about how much of the curriculum should be shared. On the one hand, communication goes more easily when all parties can draw on a common body of knowledge and skills. On the other, for individuals to find their own paths and their distinctive forms of fulfillment, attention must be devoted to eliciting and developing their special propensities and talents. The dialogue between society and the individual-in-the-making should offer opportunities without imposing. In accordance with proposals of Chapter 2, for this to work, each classroom will need to contain many people who play the role of teacher.[1] Second, curricular matters ought not to be automatically subordinated to the forms of competition dominating the world for which young people are being prepared. Creating a citizenry—and a human population—containing a wide diversity of types can contribute to the health of societies and to the flourishing of their members. Children should not be funneled into those channels currently seen as promoting "productivity" as understood in economic terms: they are not interchangeable

---

[1] See Proposals 3 and 4 of Chapter 2, 73–74 above. The possibility that some pupils can learn from others ought not to be overlooked. Finnish schools have achieved considerable successes along these lines.

The Main Enterprise of the World. Philip Kitcher, Oxford University Press. © Oxford University Press 2022.
DOI: 10.1093/oso/9780190928971.003.0008

228 THE MAIN ENTERPRISE OF THE WORLD

cogs to be supplied to some socioeconomic machine. When the defects of the wider world are taken to constrain the curriculum and to demand relentless competition within the classroom, the correct response is to change the broader context, not to acquiesce in the prevailing deformities.[2]

The radical proposal reacts to the neglect of human values in contemporary educational policy. It rightly objects to the economic pressures subordinating the young to the felt need to maintain a nation's wealth and status, to the competition often introduced before children even begin their formal schooling, to the overscheduling of their lives aimed at providing them with passports to elite colleges and prestigious careers. Yet it also overreacts. Concerns about the educational damage done in a world dominated by competition and consumerism should not be confused with a brief for cultural and intellectual stagnation. To recognize the folly and the harm of blindly multiplying material goods beyond necessity ought not to be to overlook the importance of fostering progress in advancing our knowledge of the world in which we live and our power to modify it to promote worthy ends. Enhancing our ability to understand, to predict, and to control is important to the human project in which we all participate. A natural place to start understanding how those valuable ends might be achieved is with the subjects most frequently associated with positive contributions to human well-being and to human lives. That is, with the natural sciences.

In recent centuries the sciences have transformed human existence. Because they can give so much, they also make demands on educational policymaking. If the values celebrated in previous chapters are to be secured, extended, and refined, it is important to understand how the science curriculum and the associated methods of teaching would usefully be reshaped. What should young people learn in and about the sciences? How are they best taught? Those questions are the topic of the present chapter. Parallel issues concerning other important branches of human knowledge and culture—about the arts and the human sciences—will be pursued in the two subsequent chapters.

Before embarking on this enterprise, one important point should be made explicit. As Chapter 1 argued, curricular proposals often succumb to the problem of overload. In the store of educational goodies, it is easy to overconsume. I shall attempt to avoid overload in two ways. First, conceiving

---

[2] As noted in the previous chapter, working through the educational issues has consequences for social reform. See 218–19 above. Of course, the feasibility of alternative arrangements has to be considered—as they will be in Chapters 10 and 11.

education as a lifelong activity, with opportunities regularly available for extending previous studies or adding new ones, removes the pressure to cram everything in during some initial (twelve-year?) period. Second, while all students should share certain educational experiences in the school years of their youth, my emphasis on individual development encourages them to pursue their own selection of more specialized explorations. When the details of curricula are surveyed, what should be seen is a core general education and a luxuriant diversity of more specialized extensions.

———

The radical proposal would be entirely adequate for most of the societies in which members of our species have lived. Those societies needed to prepare their young members for survival, often in a hostile environment, for participation in the collective life of a community (typically quite small), and to fulfill themselves in some form of *communal hedonism*. As noted earlier,[3] throughout almost all of human history, the idea of the good life as one in which people make autonomous choices of their "central project" or "life plan" would be an insensitive joke. Under the circumstances in which the vast majority of people have lived, the best available response to Socrates' foundational question, "How to live?," would be to commit yourself to alleviating suffering and obtaining pleasure, not just for yourself but for your fellows. For the hunter-gatherers of the Paleolithic, for the peasants who lived under feudalism or other forms of serfdom, and for many marginalized people in the world today, the hedonist credo, so derided in the history of philosophy, is an entirely appropriate reaction to the hardships of the environment. Diminishing suffering, maintaining the life of the group, and celebrating together when you can probably constitutes the best form of life available.

Education in societies like these understandably consists in providing the skills needed for people to sustain themselves, and in imbuing them with the traditions binding the group together. Its task is to enable the replication of a culture, through producing new members who have absorbed that culture. Some educational theorists, Michael Oakeshott and R. S. Peters, for example, understand education in all societies, including affluent contemporary

---

[3] See Chapter 3 above, 99–101.

230   THE MAIN ENTERPRISE OF THE WORLD

democracies in just this way.[4] Their ideas are unknowingly echoed by conservative parents who protest the disruptive influences to which their children are subjected in classrooms where they are told about the history of life on Earth or about the conditions of the oppressed in the antebellum South.[5]

Why is simple preservation of a past tradition inadequate, however rich it may appear to its adherents? Because of our understanding of the historical process out of which the rich traditions of today have emerged. Grateful for what has been bequeathed to us, we also recognize the slow accumulation of resources—of scientific advances, of works of art, of social insights and their translation into institutional reform. Society and culture are seen as having progressed in some respects—and as potentially progressive in further ways, including some beyond our present imaginings. The function of formal education cannot merely be to enable the next generation to absorb our lore, as it now exists. It should also enable people, individually and cooperatively, to improve it.[6] In a democratic society, future progress will be, in part, a collective effort. It will be brought about through citizens' abilities to recognize some new policies as making progressive changes. Progress will also depend on exceptional individuals, people who are capable of taking on the role Newton assigned himself—of standing on the shoulders of giants and so seeing further than the predecessors.[7]

A truly ambitious educational program might seek conditions under which almost all students might be enabled to play this part, in some field or another. Almost certainly, that aim is too ambitious. Most human lives don't create or discover something "for the ages"; nor would they have gone much differently in this respect, no matter what system of education had been provided. Their more modest accomplishments do not condemn them as worthless. Value and meaning are almost always achieved through local

---

[4] Timothy Fuller, ed., *Michael Oakeshott on Education* (New Haven: Yale University Press, 1989); R. S. Peters, "Education as Initiation," in *Philosophical Analysis of Education*, ed. Reginald D. Achambault, 87–111 (New York: Humanities Press, 1965).

[5] As Chapter 6 argued, requests of this kind should not be honored unless there is a serious body of evidence raising doubts about the correctness of the claims to which parents object. In neither of the two examples is this the case. The supposed challenges to evolution have been widely discussed by many people. My own attempts to rebut them appear in *Abusing Science: The Case against Creationism* (Cambridge, MA: MIT Press, 1982) and *Living with Darwin* (New York: Oxford University Press, 2007).

[6] This is an important theme in Dewey's work. See for example *Democracy and Education* (MW 9), 97–105, and Chapter 6 of *Experience and Nature* (LW 1).

[7] Newton made his famous claim in a letter to Robert Hooke of February 5, 1675. The thought was not original with Newton, and had appeared in English in 1621 in Robert Burton's *Anatomy of Melancholy*. Apparently, it goes back at least as far as John of Salisbury (1159).

THE NATURAL SCIENCES   231

effects, through positive contributions to the lives of other people. Providing opportunities for self-fulfillment doesn't require turning every baby into an Einstein or a Picasso. The task is to educate all students to make thoughtful decisions about issues that will arise in their lifetimes, while also encouraging those with the taste and with the talent to make further advances in some domain of inquiry or of culture. Progress depends on good collective decisions, and thus on enabling as large a fraction of the citizens as possible to think through complex issues; and also on individual creativity, manifested in people who can extend the frontiers of their chosen domain.

Talk of creativity and individuality easily falls into a trap. There are some—a very few—who change the world in profound ways. Others—the herd[8]—are doomed to lives of bovine conformity, leaving no imprint in the world inhabited by their successors. Yet what passes as a stark dichotomy is actually a continuum. Given appropriate guidance and encouragement, almost any of us can discover areas within human life to which we can contribute and, indeed, to introduce our own distinctive modifications. Some do that through their work in a genre of art or through particular extensions of a field of learning. Although an artist's paintings never find a place in any museum, although a scientist's articles are no longer read, the brushwork on a canvas or the report of a particular experiment inspires others to change their own artistic or scientific practices; those modifications, typically combined with others of a similar size, ultimately issue in a far larger advance; thus, behind the achievements celebrated by later generations stand not only past giants but also a multitude of humbler folk, whose smaller effects, though untraceable, are real nonetheless. Similarly, the individual recipe or the particular way of tending a plant or the modified technique for mending a broken artefact or the special skill for calming a tense situation can have its impact on the cuisine or the horticulture or the practices of repair or the social lives of subsequent generations. How far and how long the ripples from what we do will extend is highly variable.[9] It is, however, a mistake to see creativity only where the reverberations are obvious in their size and in their persistence. In principle, almost anyone has the chance to participate in creating a better world. When each of us becomes directly involved in guiding the development of the young, that opportunity is magnified. Hence, my proposal

[8] Since Nietzsche offers the most emphatic version of a fundamental division within our species, it seems appropriate to borrow his language.
[9] I discuss the ways in which the "ripples" from our lives can give them meaning in Chapter 4 of *Life after Faith*.

232   THE MAIN ENTERPRISE OF THE WORLD

to include all adults in the work of education enlarges the space in which our individual contributions can come into play. What is most needed is for us to discover the domains and the directions in which our individuality is well exercised. Education should acquaint us with our own talents, so we can, in our turn, foster the lives of others who share them.[10]

Potentially, there is so much for children to explore. How can a system of formal education offer sufficient breadth and sufficient depth to all? How can those who might happily contribute to some particular area of inquiry or culture be helped to find their proper home? How can these two goals be pursued together, and pursued without disrupting the conditions for flourishing individual lives and for deep democracy? If cultural and intellectual stagnation is to be avoided, are our societies inevitably condemned to cutthroat competition and a harsh meritocracy? Must the values emphasized in earlier chapters inevitably be sacrificed?

The approach I have taken to curricular matters may appear strange. Instead of asking directly, "What are the important bits of science everyone should know?," I have begun further back. To see education through the framework of Part I is to view the task in terms of understanding how scientific education might bear on three goals: self-maintenance, citizenship and moral agency, and personal fulfillment. We might collapse all three into a single aim, and formulate the curricular question differently: How should science education help guide the young to making their own distinctive contributions to the human project? How can we be prepared to assist with further progress?

In what follows, I'll take up that question by considering scientific progress and how what are taken to be advances in the sciences bear on the quality of the lives of sentient beings (humans prominent among them) and the health of human societies. The discussion will begin with a critique of the most popular view of scientific progress, the idea of science as aimed at "the truth, the whole truth, and nothing but the truth" about nature. Instead, I suggest, science is inevitably selective, advancing through offering answers to significant questions, and sometimes by refining its ideas about what makes for significance. The second mode of progress must be understood, I claim, in terms of what the answers offer people. Some would emphasize the practical benefits

---

[10] See Chapter 2, 77.

THE NATURAL SCIENCES   233

we obtain; others (including many researchers) would declare the great value of understanding for its own sake.

Once the sciences are recognized as socially embedded, answerable to the needs of sentient beings and of human societies, specialized researchers are no longer the final authorities on matters of significance. Democratic deliberation should assess the proposed research agenda. Hence, among the goals for scientific education must be to equip citizens to participate in policy discussions where scientific matters, whether of application or of future inquiry, are at stake. Once we understand the character of scientific progress, it becomes clear why the science curriculum is important *for all*. Everyone needs to develop scientific literacy, both for enjoying the benefit of greater understanding and for functioning as a responsible citizen.

I shall separate the task of *general* science education, important for all, from the kind of curriculum required by those whose lives are going to make use of some scientific domain, whether as researchers or as people whose daily routines require a scientific background. The central aim of this chapter is to outline a program for general science education that will preserve the natural curiosity so evident in young children, and enable all to benefit from the new scientific knowledge amassed during their lifetimes. Distinguishing this program from the specialized training required—and enjoyed!—by some is aimed at eliminating (or at least diminishing) the alienation from science, so common in our age.

———

Talk of advances, sometimes spectacular and achieved by the great figures in history, sometimes much smaller (yet real!) and resulting from the efforts of a large number of contributors, is sometimes greeted with skepticism.[11] Many claims of progress are glib, rightly accused of ignoring the negative results of the change considered. Yet, if there is one domain in which talk of progress is relatively uncontroversial, it is surely natural science. It's hard to deny the spectacular progress of physics since the seventeenth century, of chemistry since the late eighteenth century, and of genetics since 1900. Even when scientific research is not viewed simply as the key to economic improvement— when the discussion moves beyond supporting science education because it's important to stay ahead in the economic competition—the sciences enjoy a special place in the curriculum because of the broad consensus about their

[11] See, for example, John Gray, *Seven Types of Atheism* (New York: Farrar, Straus & Giroux, 2018).

234   THE MAIN ENTERPRISE OF THE WORLD

progress. But what exactly should that place be? How should the sciences be taught? Answering those questions depends on gaining a clear view of what advances in the sciences are, and what they provide.

Many people think about scientific progress teleologically. Scientific exploration is directed toward a goal. The closer human beings come to that goal, the better off we are. Anyone who adopts this perspective faces an obvious question: what precisely is the goal? A popular, but incautious, answer identifies it as providing a complete and accurate account of nature in all its rich detail. We want the truth, the whole truth, and nothing but the truth.

Characterizing this goal precisely raises some tricky questions. Would it be enough to describe it in terms of human belief, or should we insist on beliefs properly supported by evidence (and thus counting as knowledge)? In either case, who are the fortunate subjects? (Is there a collection of specialists, each of whom knows different things about distinct aspects of nature, so that, collectively, they know everything? Or are some lucky people omniscient?) Happily, it isn't necessary to answer these questions to understand the difficulties with the postulated goal. The trouble lies with the idea of the collection of all truths. Presumably, this is the set of all true sentences (in some language—which language?) about nature. It's not hard to see that this set (assuming it exists) is infinite, indeed at least as large as the continuum. For, consider any performance of your favorite piece of music. That takes place in a particular space throughout a particular time. Regarded as a chunk of space-time, it contains continuum many space-time points. At each of those points, physical magnitudes (and chemical concentrations, and physiological variables and . . .) take on specific values. So there must be continuum many true sentences, each characterizing the value of some magnitude at some point. Further, there are all the two-place relations among those values, all the three-place relations among those values, and so forth. Besides that, we have to take into account all the relations among sets of values, all the relations among sets of sets of values, and so on. At the very least, the cardinality of the whole truth about nature must be at least as large as that of the continuum.[12]

---

[12] Possibly much greater, assuming that some of the truths describe relations among sets at indefinitely high levels of the set-theoretic hierarchy. The size of the collection can obviously be reduced by supposing the goal of science is only to arrive at all the truths directly about objects and their properties and relations. Given that reduction, it seems plausible to take the set of all the pertinent truths to have exactly the cardinality of the continuum.

THE NATURAL SCIENCES   235

Can we coherently talk of a *set* of all truths about nature? Or is the supposed totality too large to count as a set? Even when this initial worry is waived, other concerns arise. How much of the whole truth about nature could the entire human population, from our origins to our ultimate extinction ever believe (let alone know)? A pathetic fraction. For during the career of our species, the number of human beings will be finite. Each of us, let us suppose, can believe countably many truths, together with all their logical consequences. Any particular individual thus knows only a countable set of truths. What *Homo sapiens* collectively believes is the union of all these sets. That union is formed (whether the beliefs are all different or whether beliefs sometimes overlap) by pooling a finite number of sets. The finite union of countable sets is countable. Hence, the totality of human belief is a countable set. It is a pitiful approximation to a vastly larger collection, the whole truth about nature. The best we could do would be to achieve an infinitesimal part of the alleged goal.

Suppose we took that goal seriously. How could we best approximate it? By behaving very differently from the ways in which the natural sciences actually function. Apparently our best strategy for acquiring as much truth as possible would be to identify which instruments were most efficient for data collection. We could then send investigators to the optimal locations for gathering the data as fast as possible, and ask them to record their measurements at maximum speed. Perhaps it would also be a good idea to invest in a team of logicians and mathematicians to draw out consequences as quickly and efficiently as they could. The cumbersome, difficult, and time-consuming processes through which cutting-edge research makes its uncertain ways would be eliminated in favor of procedures designed to optimize the accumulation of truth.

A first—naïve—approach to teleological progress proves grossly deficient. A more promising relative lies ready to hand.[13] Newton's Preface to his *Principia* presents an image of the scientific achievement that has inspired thought about the sciences from his day to ours. The aim, he proposes, is to reconstruct nature's rulebook (and thus understand the wisdom of God in designing His creation):

I wish we could derive the rest of the phenomena of nature by the same kind of reasoning from mechanical principles; for I am induced by many reasons

---

[13] See Bas van Fraassen, *The Scientific Image* (Oxford: Clarendon Press, 1980), 6.

236 THE MAIN ENTERPRISE OF THE WORLD

to suspect that they may all depend upon certain forces by which the particles of bodies, by some causes hitherto unknown, are either mutually impelled towards each other, and cohere in regular figures, or are repelled and recede from each other; which forces being unknown, philosophers have hitherto attempted the search of nature in vain; but I hope the principles here laid down will afford some light either to this or some truer method of philosophy.[14]

A proper scientific theory consists of an axiomatic system, whose first principles are the fundamental laws of that branch of inquiry. Once they have arrived at the correct theory, scientists working within the field can apply it by adding particular specifications (initial and boundary conditions) to derive descriptions of particular phenomena. Although they cannot come to believe *all* the true statements in the pertinent domain (because, as already recognized, there are too many), they can obtain *any* of them that proves to be of interest.

Although some contemporary physicists (those who dream of final theories) continue to adopt Newton's vision, the subsequent course of the natural sciences belies the picture of a unified science capable of encompassing all features of the natural world. Two major sources of difficulty have emerged. One derives from the relations among different sciences. Even though more complex entities, those studied by chemists, biologists, earth scientists, psychologists, linguists, sociologists, economists, and anthropologists, are ultimately made up of physical constituents, that does not entail the possibility of generating all the truths of these various fields from some corpus of fundamental physical laws. In practice, the understanding of chemical reactions, including relatively simple ones, defies explicit computation from the quantum-theoretic dynamics of elementary particles. More significant, biological classifications cut across the structural lines drawn in chemistry. Functional concepts appear in biology at all levels. Although all genes are segments of nucleic acids (mostly DNA, but sometimes, as with retroviruses, RNA), no common structure distinguishes all and only those segments we count as genes.[15] (If there were a common structure, the task of moving from

---

[14] Isaac Newton, *Mathematical Principles of Natural Philosophy*, trans. Andrew Motte and Florian Cajori, 2 vols. (Berkeley: University of California Press, 1962), Vol. 1, xviii. Newton is the most influential source for the view, dismissed in Chapter 5 above, 166, of a "theory of everything." Here I offer the reasons (the promised reasons) for my earlier dismissal.

[15] For more detail concerning the material of this paragraph, see David Hull, *Philosophy of Biological Science* (Englewood Cliffs, NJ: Prentice-Hall, 1974), Chapter 1, and my "1953 and All That: A Tale of Two Sciences," *Philosophical Review* 93 (1984: 335–73).

sequence data to a catalog of genes would be far simpler than it has turned out to be!) Indeed, the most basic parts of molecular biology deploy functional notions that do not align with the structural specifications of biochemistry: the major players in gene replication and transcription—the molecules known as "polymerases," for example—are so classified because of what they *do*. From the perspective of biochemistry they are heterogeneous. No general specification of them is available. As a result, no bridge principle links biochemistry to molecular biology, and the envisaged route to deriving all of molecular biology from biochemistry is blocked.[16]

Of course, chemical theory continues to be a powerful resource in biology. Biologists gain numerous insights every day by isolating important molecules and using the understanding of their structure biochemistry provides. Biological language connects to the language of chemistry in innumerable *particular* linkages. What fails, however, is the system of *general* specifications hoped for in the Newtonian vision. Not only does it break down in those areas of biology apparently in closest contact with underlying chemical structures. Its absence is even more striking in those domains where biologists study organs, plants, animals, and animal populations. The idea of giving a specification of hearts or leaves or reptiles or predators or ecosystems in chemical terms—let alone fundamental physical terms—boggles the imagination.

Of course, the difficulties with the Newtonian dream become even more evident with the human sciences. Economists hope to arrive at generalizations about what will occur (under specified circumstances) when the money supply is increased. Quite obviously, however, no purely physical description will pick out all and only those things we treat as money.[17] Besides coins and notes, traditional exchange objects (like salt) and contemporary currencies (Bitcoin), almost anything could serve. Money is whatever is used to facilitate the exchange of goods. Its status depends on the attitudes of people, engaged in making trades at a particular time and place. Trying to understand how those exchanges are effected in terms of "fundamental physics" would not only fail to find any characterization of them. It would also obscure the important causal and explanatory structures behind what is going on.[18] To see just why inflation might occur, given an increase in the

---

[16] See Sylvia Culp and Philip Kitcher, "Theory Structure and Theory Change in Contemporary Molecular Biology," *British Journal for the Philosophy of Science* 40 (1989): 459–83.

[17] See Jerry Fodor, "Special Sciences," *Synthese* 28 (1974): 97–115.

[18] A point well made in Alan Garfinkel, *Forms of Explanation* (New Haven: Yale University Press, 1981); see also "1953 and All That."

238 THE MAIN ENTERPRISE OF THE WORLD

money supply, you don't need to track the dynamic trajectories of a vastly disparate collection of physical systems. What is required is to see how demand curves respond and how they affect prices.

The second problem for a complete unified science stems from the peculiarity of the case Newton (and those he has influenced) took (take) as paradigmatic. Gravitational theory is rightly admired for its unifying power. Its ability to explain and predict bodily motions depends on the dominance of a particular force. The motions of the heavenly bodies (or, at least, those on which Newton focused) are shielded: besides gravity, nothing else is relevant.[19] Most of the world is very different. All sorts of causal factors are in play, interacting in highly diverse combinations. So, as investigations turn to more intricate systems, as researchers consider organisms and brains and geological strata and changes in the atmosphere and in the oceans, attempts to arrive at simple unifying general laws are constantly frustrated.[20] Inquiry has to settle for models, well adapted to particular instances, but vulnerable to inaccuracy and error when they are extended beyond their original range. In many instances, as with the climate, investigators work with a family of models, mutually inconsistent but valuable if they are coordinated with careful judgment. During the past century, major scientific advances—in biology, in earth and atmospheric sciences, in neuroscience—have consisted in finding new ways to model some of the complex phenomena most relevant to human welfare. The moral of those efforts is clear. For much of the natural world, including parts of enormous importance and interest, it is possible to find models satisfying two out of three desiderata: you can achieve generality and accuracy, at the cost of precision; you can be general and precise at the cost of accuracy; or you can gain accuracy and precision, by sacrificing generality.[21] Two out of three is not bad—and, of course, with care and with experience, you can combine models with different packages of virtues. Contra Newton, however, you can't have all three virtues at once. We live in a "dappled world."[22]

---

[19] Thus, as Nancy Cartwright lucidly argues, the solar system is one of the rare "nomological machines" given in nature, rather than resulting from human intervention to shield a system and thus generate regular effects. See *The Dappled World* (Cambridge UK: Cambridge University Press, 1999).

[20] Argued at length in John Dupré, *The Disorder of Things* (Cambridge, MA: Harvard University Press, 1993); also in Cartwright, *The Dappled World*.

[21] See Richard Levins, *Evolution in Changing Environments* (Princeton NJ: Princeton University Press, 1968), Chapter 1.

[22] Cartwright borrows her title phrase from a famous poem, "Pied Beauty," by Gerard Manley Hopkins.

THE NATURAL SCIENCES   239

Because the Newtonian vision and the teleological account of progress it has inspired have been so influential, I have devoted some time to exposing its shortcomings. A clear understanding of how the natural sciences advance is a prerequisite for considering their role in the curriculum. As we'll see, rejecting common mythology about scientific progress has educational implications.

Scientific progress is best conceived non-teleologically, as "progress from" rather than as "progress to." Fields of science progress by finding answers to the problems they identify as important. Some truths are worth knowing. Most are not. During their training, researchers acquire a sense of the field they will enter, coming to recognize which questions are marked as significant by the community they are joining. When outsiders wonder why an investigator is pursuing a particular line of inquiry, the scientist will typically have a story to tell. An apparently esoteric question gains its importance from the potential contribution it would make to some larger enterprise. If that question can be answered, the answer can be used in tackling another problem—and, in its turn, solving that problem would pave the way for some even grander investigation. So it goes, until the explanation arrives at a question whose interest is expected to be obvious to anyone.

A molecular geneticist, for instance, may devote years to an attempt to understand how a particular region in the genome of an organism (a fruit fly, perhaps, or a nematode worm) affects particular features of the organism in question. Why is that inquiry worth the effort expended? Because answering the apparently specialized question might provide insight into how the organism develops, allowing understanding of how normal functioning can be disrupted, and perhaps ultimately shedding light on a human disease. When the geneticist is asked to justify her research, she may explain the projected sequence of steps leading from the experiments she is now engaged in to a final question or to a new possibility of intervention. At the end there will emerge an understanding of how organisms develop (something any curious person would want to fathom) or new cures or treatments for disease (something all people should welcome).

The spectacular advances of genetics in the past few decades consist in more refined views of the structures of genomes, together with analyses of particular molecular mechanisms (transcription, translation, replication, and the like), as well as all sorts of machines and techniques for going further.

240   THE MAIN ENTERPRISE OF THE WORLD

Many of the questions on the recent agenda could not have been posed half a century ago. What counts as scientifically significant evolves over time.

And sometimes the way in which a scientific community identifies significant questions appears to later generations as highly dubious. By 1925, genetics had advanced considerably beyond its state in 1900, when three researchers independently rediscovered "Mendel's Rules." But it was not all gain. Genetics had become entangled with eugenics. Questions about genes for "thalassophilia" (expressed in adolescent boys who ran away to sea) and for "hereditary feeble-mindedness" (causing problems so urgent as to require compulsory sterilization programs) ranked high on the scientific agenda.[23]

Everyday judgments about scientific progress defer to the scientific community, and its identification of the significant questions. Yet the marriage between genetics and eugenics serves as a sobering reminder. Scientific investigations are embedded in social practices. When evaluations of what is scientifically significant contravene the larger human good, even when they are indifferent to it, the verdict of progress becomes suspect. Some forms of biological research have created or intensified the threats felt by vulnerable groups of people—as when genetic speculations about the causes of crime and of antisocial behavior were used to refuse admission to refugees seeking asylum, and when the refusal returned those who sought sanctuary to die in the genocide prevailing in their homelands. Others simply ignore the plight of sufferers who are too poor to pay the prices set for the medicines they need—pharmaceutical companies sometimes devote their research laboratories to manufacturing cosmetic creams, instead of seeking efficient ways to produce drugs to save distant children from blindness or to curb the spread of devastating (but faraway) infections.[24]

My story has a moral. Scientific communities are not the ultimate authorities on assigning significance to research questions. The natural sciences are embedded in a broader society, and that society benefits—or suffers—from their efforts. Scientific progress cannot be an internal matter, achieved when research groups solve the problems *they* mark out as important. The natural sciences provide a collection of resources for contributing to human progress. Advances are most evident when the questions hailed as significant

---

[23] Excellent historical studies of the entanglement of genetics with eugenics are given in Daniel Kevles, *In the Name of Eugenics* (New York: Knopf, 1985); and in Stephen Jay Gould, *The Mismeasure of Man* (New York: Norton, 1981).

[24] I have discussed the general issue in *Science, Truth, and Democracy* (New York: Oxford University Press, 2001); James Flory and I consider the distribution of biomedical research in "Global Health and the Scientific Research Agenda," *Philosophy and Public Affairs* 32 (2004): 36–65.

are those to which societies and individual people would most like answers, when the questions are answered so as to meet the human needs, and when the answers are accessible to the people and the groups who want them.[25] Science is an institution, working in concert with other institutions, to further the human project. Unfortunately, as we shall see, the ensemble is not always harmonious.[26]

What exactly are the contributions yielded by the sciences? If you were to ask most non-scientists, they would point to the technological advances scientific investigations have made possible: new methods of agriculture, new materials, labor-saving devices, inventions enabling people to transcend geographical limits, and perhaps, above all, cures and treatments for diseases. Thoughtful people might well go further, recognizing the social value of new abilities to predict. Being able to recognize in advance where earthquakes are likely to occur or to know how the climate is changing is information worth having. Touting such practical gains raises two major questions. First, to what extent do the practical benefits descend from theoretical science, rather than from applied sciences and the trial-and-error methods of artisans? Second, are the benefits unalloyed, or do they come with important losses?

Contrary to popular belief, many of the great practical innovations introduced in human history have been achieved by people we wouldn't count as scientists (although they might be seen as precursors of contemporary researchers). From the flint-knappers deep in our human (and hominin) past to the pioneers of the Industrial Revolution and many of their nineteenth-century successors, a vast number of technological advances have been achieved without guidance from systematic theory. Only with the development of the chemical dye industry did there begin a deliberate practice of applying results originally developed to address "pure" questions. Yet, once applied science starts to become recognized as a source for technology, it tends to swamp the prior practice of inspired tinkering. High theory emerges in the twentieth century as the great vindication of Francis Bacon's characterization of knowledge as power. The two technological advances responsible for the largest contemporary changes in human life and human society— the rise of molecular medicine and of information technology—are rooted

---

[25] This vision of "well-ordered science" is proposed and defended in *Science, Truth, and Democracy*, and elaborated further in *Science in a Democratic Society* (Amherst, NY: Prometheus Books, 2011).

[26] Thus, for example, the ways in which particular developments in a science are then taken up and applied in unforeseen ways may cast doubt on the progressive character of the original developments. Thanks to Harvey Siegel for pressing me on this point. His example of the development of nuclear weapons is considered (among others) below.

242 THE MAIN ENTERPRISE OF THE WORLD

in theoretical investigations whose practical import could not initially have been foreseen.

But, as the second question recognizes, the end products of applying "pure science" are not always beneficial. It's useful to distinguish between the resources the sciences supply and the uses to which those resources are then put. Chemistry and biology have delivered possibilities for curing, treating, and palliating diseases. The new tools they offer can also be employed to create terrible weapons and to cause irreversible harm to the natural environment. When a science provides resources for addressing a major human problem, it's reasonable to view it as making progress. If, subsequently, those resources are used to cause great harm, social progress and progress in the human project may not be the result. When that happens, deformation in some other area of social life is to blame. Warmongering politicians commission terrible new weapons; greedy entrepreneurs use pesticides or manufactured organisms to devastate a region of the world. Overall human progress depends on harmonious cooperation among many institutions. Where institutional friction is found, the advances achieved in one domain may be decisively reversed by actions taken in another. And, of course, where dire misuse can be foreseen, delicate questions of scientific responsibility arise.[27]

The everyday view of the contributions of the sciences, when suitably hedged and qualified, is defensible. But scientific researchers, particularly theorists, prefer a different answer to questions about what the sciences deliver. In February 2016, I was returning from a morning run when I bumped into a friend, a theoretical physicist. He was obviously very excited. "You must listen at 10:15," he said, "they're going to announce the greatest discovery of our lifetime." Since we were both born before the discovery of the molecular structure of DNA, my friend exaggerated a little. But, in support of

---

[27] We might think of judgments of progress as sometimes made on the basis of assessments of responsibility. When a science is entangled with social goals (as when genetics and eugenics were intricately intertwined) or when the connection between the research and social interventions can be predicted (as with various kinds of questions about differences with respect to race or sex), modifications leading to human suffering cannot be seen as by-products of an innocent enterprise. The investigators are partly responsible for the consequences, and the science cannot be absolved as progressive. When, on the other hand, it would have been reasonable for researchers not to anticipate the applications that later generate bad outcomes, a genuinely progressive change within a science can be misused, and the institution out of which the misuse comes is at fault. Thus, in the case of developments in nuclear physics, or in chemistry, or biology, that are later deployed to produce dreadful weapons, the progressiveness of the original research can be ratified. The judgment of genuine progress is especially compelling when people within the field (even including some whose work is later adapted to the machinery of death) campaign strenuously against the application.

his sense of the magnitude of the LIGO achievement, the Nobel Committee soon awarded the prize in physics for the discovery of gravitational waves.

For people like my friend, the main gifts stemming from the sciences are not the smartphones and the pesticides, the robots, or even the antibiotics. They consist in increased understanding, available in principle to all. Science benefits humanity through offering a richer, deeper appreciation of the world, physical, organic, even human and social. The value is epistemic.

The two views, the *lay view* and the *official view*, as I'll call them, can obviously be combined. Different people will weigh the practical and the epistemic ends differently. To the extent that emphasis is placed on increased understanding, it will seem important to set up education in the sciences so all students have the opportunity to enjoy the richer perspectives science delivers. Those who stress the practical benefits flowing from scientific inquiry will want to ensure a sizeable cohort of promising investigators in the next generation. So, even without worrying about our decline as foreign scientists advance the productivity of rival nations, there are grounds for encouraging young people[28] to consider careers in science and technology. Reasons, too, to want to distribute "scientific literacy" to all, not only to equip future citizens to make informed judgments about policy proposals, but also to allow them to enjoy the benefits of deeper understanding of the world they inhabit.

<hr/>

How can these educational goals best be achieved? A short answer: by differentiating the curriculum pursued by the future scientists from that taken by the future laity.

Like the reaction to Sputnik before it, the STEM initiative already signaled a perceived failure of the *status quo*. Incentives were felt to be needed, precisely because of the mediocre performances of American students in mathematics and science, when compared to other relatively affluent countries. (Americans are just above the OECD average in science, and somewhat below in mathematics.) At many major American universities, graduate

---

[28] Although my remarks here are surely influenced by my appraisal of contemporary American education—it is, after all, the system I know best—I intend my diagnoses and suggestions to apply throughout the affluent world. Most, perhaps all, of my recommendations should be relevant to the practices of education in Europe, Canada, Australia, New Zealand, Japan, Korea, Singapore, India, China, and in some parts of South America. The range of their pertinence and promise will surely vary from context to context, often including more than the countries named here; it will, I hope, almost always contain all of them.

244   THE MAIN ENTERPRISE OF THE WORLD

programs in the sciences are dominated by foreign-born students, particularly by students from Asia. Why are American schools failing to deliver an abundance of home-grown talent? What has gone wrong? I offer a hypothesis, one lending itself to test. Particularly in high school, and perhaps even beyond, American science education is the victim of a well-intentioned attempt to teach for two different constituencies, each of which might do better in the absence of the other. Moreover, whether or not educational policymakers in other countries are concerned about student performance in the sciences on the basis of the same reasons and to the same degree, I believe that their schools face versions of the same problems and that the approach proposed below would benefit them.

Young children are often interested, even enthralled, by the first scientific materials they encounter. Beyond the fascination with dinosaurs and with basic parts of astronomy, they enjoy the kinds of hands-on inquiry Dewey recommended for the early grades.[29] If they retained their lively curiosity into adulthood, they would have a far stronger motivation to engage with the scientific issues confronting them as citizens. Along the way, however, the romance of science frequently fades, withered by years of tedious, often futile, attempts to solve toy problems in physics or to memorize long lists of chemical formulae. To be sure, professional scientists will need the discipline of puzzle-solving, as well as a firm grasp of intricate details. The laypeople of the future will not. The many high school students who protest the boredom they feel in science classes will quickly forget the techniques they once more-or-less painfully acquired. The arcane terminology will vanish. All that will remain is the strong sense of the sciences as difficult, dull, and beyond their capacities.

After a relatively short exposure to the disciplined work required even for the first steps of rigorous scientific study, many young people know already that this is not for them. Why not let them go? Not from science, but from that particular pathway, the route to be traversed by those for whom science will be central to their lives.[30] They need something different. As adult citizens, they should be equipped to assess evidence. They should have an ability

[29] *Democracy and Education*, 48–57.
[30] As we shall see, this includes a wide range of connections to the sciences. Some, probably a relatively small minority, will devote their lives to research in some scientific field. Others will use scientific findings, at various grades of technicality, in addressing practical problems. Yet others will need scientific training to pursue their careers, even though they will not consult scientific sources on an everyday basis. During the high school years, all these groups can be treated as one. Differences will start to emerge later as they are prepared for the particular routes they intend to pursue.

to read presentations of new scientific findings—a kind of scientific literacy. Above all, they should keep the curiosity, the sense of wonder they once had, before dull exercises drummed it out of them. Preserving that curiosity would give them motivation to keep up with the scientific developments of their times. Fortunately, the past decades have encouraged many talented researchers to write about their fields in lively and accessible ways. Among scientists, "popularizer" is no longer uttered with a sneer. Once children have learned whether or not they are suited to a scientific career—and providing that self-knowledge ought to be possible before the high school years—the task of educating the many who recognize themselves as non-scientists is to prepare avid science appreciators. To create readers for all the important future books about exciting new developments and their bearing on public issues. Societies should foster the co-evolution of increasingly large (and enthusiastic) populations eager to keep up with the latest discoveries about nature and presentations in a variety of media—books, articles, videos, films, podcasts, and all their future successors—capable of satisfying their curiosity. Precisely because the sciences often advance so rapidly, education in science should be a lifelong project.

Set on one side, for the moment, the question of how high school science education for non-scientists should proceed. How does the separation I recommend help with the problem with which this discussion began—how to correct the perceived weakness of American students' performances in the sciences? A conjecture: at the high school and the university levels, science classes are slower—and duller—than they need to be, because teachers must cope with a mixed body of students. Selecting those who take to the discipline of particular sciences, including some who are enthusiastic about more than one, allows the class to move faster and to proceed to more interesting and more challenging material. Having grown up in an educational system under which students with an aptitude for mathematics learned calculus at fifteen, and sometimes mastered the material of most American undergraduate mathematics and physics majors before they attended university, I have always wondered at the awe directed toward those who have studied a little calculus in high school. The malaise inspiring the STEM initiative is a consequence of forcing all American[31] children to study science as if they were destined for a scientific career, and of attaching leaden weights to the bodies of those who might otherwise soar. Making this separation must be attentive

---

[31] As usual, I use the example I know best, but I expect the point to apply to many affluent societies.

246   THE MAIN ENTERPRISE OF THE WORLD

to the generic problems of stereotyping and competition. When different tracks are set up within the educational system, it is all too easy to generate mistaken assumptions about their relative rank. The key to recognizing difference without creating a hierarchy lies in the celebration of individuality begun at the earliest stages of formal schooling.[32] Children who have become aware, from the beginning, of the mix of inclinations and propensities—the "diversity of gifts"—among their schoolmates, and who have been encouraged to *rejoice* in the variety, should view the partition in studying science as merely another expression of a commonplace phenomenon.[33]

Of course, allowing students to choose one track rather than another, say at age fifteen, has potential disadvantages. Later in this chapter, I shall try to respond to some obvious concerns. For the present, however, let's leave the students passionate about science to scamper ahead at their own pace, and return to those who don't want to run on that track. Their scientific education, one that should continue through the high school years and be further elaborated if they go on to university, aims to preserve their interest in science, to make them "scientifically literate," and to instill the critical abilities to understand when advertised new findings are supported by evidence and when they are not. How is that achieved if they are not required to solve the irritating toy problems or to memorize the long lists? Isn't general science education inevitably superficial?[34]

The charge, of course, is that "physics for poets" or "rocks for jocks" courses produce, at their best, dilettantes. A first riposte would note the well-documented failure of standard curricula to yield even that much. Unless there are alternatives capable of doing more than generating mass alienation from science, American education would probably be considerably improved by simply abandoning attempts to "broaden" those who realize, sometime during adolescence, that rigorous scientific work isn't for them. Let them spend their time on subjects with more appeal—on music, or art,

---

[32] As proposed in Chapter 2, above.

[33] Chapter 10 will focus more extensively on the general problem of reducing competition within the educational system. Distinguishing those who are "good at science" from those who find it alien and dull may well appear a particularly tough special case. The prestige of science, and of scientists, lends a halo to young people who are especially "good at it"—and, of course, generates a backlash condensed in the stereotype of the "nerd." The next chapters will question the unique importance of science as advancing the well-being of humanity, and thus will attempt to mitigate the difficulty.

[34] The discussion to follow has been heavily influenced by the discussions, carried out over two years, in a committee assembled to rethink the general science curriculum for Columbia College. That committee was chaired by Peter de Menocal and me. I am grateful to Peter for his many thoughtful suggestions, and also to the other members of the committee: most particularly to Marty Chalfie, Jenny Davidson, Don Hood, Greg Wawro, Gareth Williams, and Bill Zajc.

THE NATURAL SCIENCES   247

or literature, or social studies, or history. Perhaps at some later stage, a fraction of them, not irreversibly turned off by the drills of the lab or the problem set, may even recapture their early fascination with learning about the natural world.

The mention of history offers a first clue to how our educational system might do better.[35] History, when well taught, retains its popularity for a psychologically well-established reason. Human beings like stories. The history of science is rich in good stories. Some of them are thrillers: the source of a cholera epidemic is discovered at the Broad Street Pump; apparently chaotic strata and their index fossils are brought to order by recognizing a new epoch—the Devonian emerges from "the Great Devonian Controversy."[36] Professional historians of science—as well as journalists—have written, often brilliantly, about many of these episodes. American high school students don't need the methodological sophistication and they don't need the filigree. The stories should be rewritten to highlight three major features.[37] First, student readers should come to understand the main contours of different perspectives. They are expected to grasp the principal scientific concepts at the core of large debates, and to see how those concepts were developed differently by the participants. Second, they would be asked to work through the ways in which evidence was assembled, and to recognize how a consensus view emerged. They would begin to grasp, through immersion in particular examples, the concepts at the heart of the various sciences, thus acquiring scientific literacy; and they would gain skills in discerning how to weigh evidence across many different fields and contexts.

The third feature connects the debates of the past with the practices of the present. Typically, the episodes conclude with some ancestor of the framework now accepted. Once that is clearly in view, the students are asked how to go on. They find themselves in a historical context that resembles the

---

[35] The case for using the history (and philosophy) of science in science education has been developed, with admirable clarity and force, by Michael R. Matthews in a series of important publications, spanning several decades. Particularly significant are *Science Teaching: The Role of History and Philosophy of Science* (New York: Routledge, 1994) and the brilliant study of the history of investigations of pendulum motion, *Time for Science Education* (New York: Kluwer, 2000). The Columbia committee arrived at similar views without knowing Matthews's work in this area. I now see that work as exceptionally valuable in elaborating and implementing one part of the approach proposed here.

[36] See Sandra Hempel, *The Medical Detective* (London: Granta 2006); and Martin Rudwick, *The Great Devonian Controversy* (Chicago: University of Chicago Press, 1985).

[37] I owe this suggestion for introducing science to students by way of structured discussions of major discoveries (and, potentially, other scientific episodes) to Marty Chalfie. Marty constructed a brilliant template for studying Mendel's elaboration of ("Mendelian") genetics.

248   THE MAIN ENTERPRISE OF THE WORLD

happy explorations of their early years in elementary school, when they were asked to work together on a practical problem. A new task is assigned them. They are to try to understand how new questions could be generated, new experiments tried or new evidence sought, what possible lines for scientific progress have been opened up by the now-resolved controversy. The path on which they decide is then compared with the route taken historically, and as they move from past to present, they are invited to consider, and to debate, possibilities an actual scientific field may have overlooked. Eventually, they emerge at the current frontier, with an understanding not only of the language now used in the pertinent field, but with a clear picture of how it relates to a past history of solving problems.[38]

I hope the approach just described would prove valuable as well as enjoyable. But it would not be enough. Lively presentation and analysis of the development of various parts of science—offered in modules to lead students from relatively simple cases to more complex ones—should be supplemented by, probably interspersed with, units aimed at improving reasoning. Appraising evidence requires a capacity for logical thinking. Students need to understand the elements of formal logic, and to practice applying them to particular situations. They should learn to diagnose fallacious reasoning—and to see how it has sometimes stymied scientific discussion. A basic grasp of probability, as well as some sense of statistical concepts and their use in statistical testing, should follow in the later high school grades.

Does this supplementary material inevitably signal a return to aridity and alienation? Not necessarily. Skilled teachers have powerful allies—in the bookie, the card sharp, and the physician's assistant who calls to tell you the bad news. Elementary probabilistic concepts can be exemplified in games, and later adapted to life decisions about insurance and mortgages. My own students have never failed to see the point of Bayes' Theorem, once I confront them with an imaginary medical scenario in which they learn that they have tested positive for a rare—and horrible—disease.

Further types of study lighten the presentation of formal canons of reasoning. Gathering and using the evidence is often a matter of learning how to compare and measure things for which there are no previous standards.

---

[38] As I write (November 2020), the Covid-19 pandemic provides a superb opportunity for extending scientific literacy. Excerpts from John M. Barry's masterly study *The Great Influenza* (New York: Penguin, 2004) could be used to review some of the ways in which scientists and officials struggled to understand the "Spanish Influenza" of 1918–1919, and to trace the scientific route to our current picture of influenza epidemics. Questions about current practices could then be posed and explored. I strongly suspect that student interest would be guaranteed.

THE NATURAL SCIENCES 249

Once again, high school students can return to the open exploration of the early grades. Entering the classroom, they find on a table a collection of ape and hominin skulls.[39] They are challenged to devise measurement procedures for ranking the skulls as similar or different. On other occasions, they are confronted with an instrument, and asked to use it to answer a question. Or they must devise a new one to complete a particular task. Perhaps all students should experience James Thurber's famous bafflement on trying to see through a microscope,[40] and learn to move beyond it. Perhaps all of them should figure out how to weigh something too big to place on a scale, or to take the temperature of an object for which standard thermometers are inadequate.[41]

Finally, there should be room for more vivid stories, tales of heroism, duty, and scandal. No general science course would be complete without some immersion in the practices of the sciences. Students should learn about the official norms of everyday scientific conduct. They should recognize how and why those norms are sometimes hard to follow, and study cases in which researchers have violated them. But the history should be genuinely mixed, juxtaposing the rascals with those who have resisted temptation to cut corners, or with those who have even sacrificed their careers to insisting on proper procedures. General education in science ought to prevent acceptance of two myths—the myth of scientists as saints in lab coats, and the myth of a research mafia bent on achieving its own nefarious ends.

Success in this amalgam of ventures could be measured by the percentage of students able to make the case for anthropogenic climate change. Armed with the desired formal skills and with a conceptual grasp of the greenhouse effect, the eighteen-year-old ought to be able to reconstruct the logical structure of the reasoning behind the climatological consensus. She should also be able to see the grounds of skeptical doubt: Are the measurements reliable, have they been properly recorded and analyzed, can the official graphs be trusted, have all potential causal factors been considered?[42] She should recognize her own limitations, her inability to work through all the data for herself. But her understanding of the scientific community, like so many other

[39] This classroom exercise was devised by Katharine Allen, who served as a consultant to the Columbia committee (c.f. n.34 above). It was extremely successful.

[40] James Thurber, "University Days," in *My Life and Hard Times* (1933; repr., New York: HarperCollins, 1999).

[41] I owe this example to James Valentini.

[42] That is, she should be able to reconstruct for herself, the line of reasoning Evelyn Fox Keller and I present in *The Seasons Alter*, 3–20.

250 THE MAIN ENTERPRISE OF THE WORLD

communities an imperfect moral community, should lead her to dismiss conspiracy theories. She should mock the hypothesis of a hoax perpetrated by the Chinese.

My account of the natural sciences and of their progress explicitly recognizes two major types of contributions they make to the broader human project. One, celebrated in the lay view, focuses on the practical benefits derived from research, the vaccines and the medicines, the advance notice of danger, the devices that save lives or make them easier or that provide entertainment. The other, given greater importance by fans of the official view (like my physicist friend), emphasizes the increase in our understanding of nature; it sees the glory of the scientific enterprise as lying in recognizing how the universe began, in fathoming the minute structure of matter, in deciphering the genetic code, and things of that ilk.

A third contribution is also implicit in my characterization of scientific research, and in the suggestions for science education I have offered. The kinship between technology guided by theory and the practices of artisans and tinkerers, not only over millennia but for hundreds of thousands of years, lies in part in the development and accumulation of methods adaptable to an ever larger collection of problems. As investigators learn about nature, whether in arriving at the theories of "basic science" or in working out how to intervene to reshape part of the world, they learn more about how to learn. The scientific work of the past provides tools for thinking about today's questions. Scientific education ought to teach young people "how to think."[43]

Schools and universities (and the institutions that provide further training) ought to deliver to the world a heterogeneous collection of people equipped to do a number of things. Dividing them roughly for present purposes, we can distinguish three major groups. Some will press forward in "pure science," further expanding human comprehension of the most intriguing aspects of the natural world. Others will deliver or add to the practical gifts that research in the sciences facilitates. This second group, almost certainly considerably larger than the first, comprises all those who will go on to use and apply the products of science and technology in contexts that require some understanding of the bases on which such applications are properly made. Among them are people who will be expected not only to understand large amounts

[43] Here I concur with Dewey. See his *How to Think* (MW 6; revised edition LW 8).

of "basic science," but also to stay current as the relevant scientific domains make further progress. Doctors and engineers are obvious examples. Others need less. Technicians who work in laboratories, people who must use particular instruments to measure important variables (concentrations of dangerous substances, for instance), those charged with repairing or upgrading complicated devices, nurses and paramedics—all these need a scientific background on which they can draw in difficult circumstances, but one that is more focused on the particular tasks they perform. The most obvious suggestion is to propose that they and members of the first group should share a common education in secondary school.[44] (After all, while it may be evident quite early that some young people are not destined for a science-based career, predictions about which fifteen-year-olds will end up as researchers and which of them will not would only rarely be reliable.) The third group comprises the potential "consumers," those who follow with fascination the discoveries of their age. During secondary education, the track taken by the first two groups should diverge from the track chosen by the third. More fine-grained divisions come later, as those who intend to use the knowledge already achieved in some particular field to address concrete problems must acquire skills irrelevant to those of the "basic researcher."

All human beings are consumers of information provided by others—and we always have been. If things go well, production and consumption are in harmony. The sciences are directed toward questions whose answers would advance the projects of many people, either by helping them pursue their individual goals or by satisfying their curiosity. Instances of past and present discord are obvious. Most evident is the prevalence of indifference, even hostility, toward what the official view advertises as the principal achievement of the sciences. Alienated by the education they have received, many people all around the world are not thrilled by announcements of the discovery of gravitational waves or by news about genetic similarities between human beings and chimpanzees (and some, of course, regard the latter as a diabolical lie). When the sciences are defended for their transformation of human understanding, for the grandeur of the view of life and of the cosmos they

---

[44] This conclusion might need revision in the light of data from the classroom. There may be circumstances under which it would be valuable to divide the "serious science" part of the curriculum into more than one track, most obviously when there is a clear division of the student body according to the pace at which students can master material in some scientific domain. It is always worth remembering however that such divisions come with costs. By segmenting the community, they may make the tasks of instilling and maintaining egalitarian and democratic attitudes more difficult. For further discussion of the dangers of competition, see Chapter 10, below.

252   THE MAIN ENTERPRISE OF THE WORLD

provide, more than a whiff of elitism pervades the defense. To whom do the epistemic benefits come? Are they widely shared? If these are the grounds for holding the sciences in high esteem (and for the funding invested in them?), are scientific investigations any more valuable than the endeavors aimed at pushing back artistic frontiers, the cutting-edge avant-garde in art or music or film-making?

To improve the chances that scientific investigations will deliver important epistemic and practical benefits, an obvious strategy is to combine a reform of science education with programs explicitly focused on the relations between the research community and the society(ies) within which it is embedded. Recognizing the need for preserving curiosity about the natural world motivates my suggestion of providing a different track for the many students who come to see that a career in science is not for them. Yet the research agenda should also be subject to public scrutiny.[45] For the epistemic goods to be widely appreciated, an audience eager to learn of new insights about nature is not enough. Specialists easily slip into regarding their own research questions as sufficiently fascinating to enthrall any curious outsider. If they are wrong, the much-touted intellectual benefits will only be enjoyed by a small elite. Even more importantly, directing inquiry toward practical goals whose achievement would enhance the lives of privileged people, while leaving the problems of the poor untouched—as when pharmaceutical companies expend their resources on profitable cosmetics rather than on tackling diseases afflicting millions—should be checked. To come to terms with the social embedding of science entails an extension of democracy. Scientific research should fall within the scope of the forms of deliberation Deweyan democracy envisages.

We can thus recognize the diverse goals toward which science education ought to strive. For all, pure researchers, applied scientists, and specialized workers, for those whose daily work presupposes a scientific background and the general public alike, it should maintain and even increase curiosity about the natural world. By developing skills in recognizing and assessing evidence, it ought to improve the quality of debates on matters of policy, especially where they turn on controversial (or supposedly controversial) factual claims. The urgent need for improvements of that kind was strikingly apparent as I was writing this book. Many people, even many well-educated

---

[45] The ideas I sketch here are elaborated at much greater length in *Science, Truth, and Democracy* and in *Science in a Democratic Society*.

THE NATURAL SCIENCES   253

people, have difficulty in appreciating the magnitude of the threat posed to the human future by a warming planet. More surprisingly, in the midst of a pandemic, in which, besides a significant mortality rate, many of those afflicted suffered longer-term consequences from the disease, large segments of some populations (especially in the United States and the United Kingdom) ignored or dismissed scientific findings. Instilling a sense of the methods through which a large variety of problems have been overcome, an education focused on scientific literacy for all can help efforts to overcome the practical difficulties we face in our daily lives. Finally, by focusing on research as directed toward human and social goods, it should instill an awareness of the moral and social responsibilities of scientists. Popular images of science ought to go. Scientists are neither lofty geniuses, removed from the mundane world and dedicated to contemplation of pure truth; nor are they, as Francis Galton supposed, a secular priesthood; nor are they sinister conspirators, bent on manipulating the public to serve their own esoteric ends; nor are they versions of the anti-Christ, using their sophistries to shake the faith of the devout. Think of them instead as workers in a common human cause, honing and using their talents to provide practical and epistemic benefits—and, at their best, conscious of the role they play in the human project and determined to promote human well-being.

As in earlier chapters, I shall distill my approach to reforming education in the sciences as a series of proposals for experiments. (The general structure could plainly be tried out in many different ways, and it would be hard to predict which versions would best advance the specified goals.)

19. *At early stages in elementary education, introduce students to areas of science that young children find especially intriguing and/or initially puzzling.*
20. *Combine presentations and discussions of "fascinating science" with everyday practical problems in which groups of students are asked to figure out how to reach some goal (Dewey offers a number of promising examples, probably based on his experiences at the Chicago Lab School).*
21. *For students who are interested in pursuing rigorous science, combine a fast-paced specialized introduction to the areas they wish to explore, with an accelerated version of the general education science course. The specialized studies should start at the beginning of high school, and be*

254 THE MAIN ENTERPRISE OF THE WORLD

taught in small classes with individualized attention (perhaps ten stu-dents with two instructors).

22. *The general science course, taken by the non-scientists, should be di-vided into modules. Some modules should present cases from the devel-opment of the sciences. In each of these historically oriented modules, attention would be focused on (i) the central concepts of the scientific research under study; (ii) the way in which evidence was assembled to support findings, to solve apparent problems, and to resolve debates; and (iii) the route leading from the main scientific achievement studied to the present state of the field, emphasizing new questions and conceptual developments. Other modules would study formal logical, probabilistic, and statistical reasoning; the character of particular types of material evidence; and the social structure of scientific communities (with partic-ular attention to their norms). Classes should be small enough, and the student-teacher ratio low enough, to enable group projects with teacher facilitation.*

If the outlined program were sufficiently successful at remedying the per-ceived difficulties in high school scientific performance, a further educa-tional program could seek to extend it to the university level.

Plainly, these proposals are at odds with—and even diametrically op-posed to—the calls for rethinking science education now ringing loudly around the world. Many nations see their future success as depending on producing a cadre of researchers whose discoveries will bring national pros-perity. Leaders puzzle anxiously over the tables revealing how children and adolescents stack up against one another in mathematics and the natural sci-ences. Just as Sputnik inspired new programs for strengthening science ed-ucation in the West, so too do contemporary announcements of the latest state of the World Science League Table. Nor are the public reactions cover for more complex political motives. As I learned in the early 1990s, economic competition is the root of concern for the state of science education. After I had been invited by the Library of Congress to serve as a Fellow, with the assignment of assessing the promise of the Human Genome Project, I was sufficiently realistic to expect enthusiasts for the project not to be primarily moved by the rhetoric of huge advances in understanding our species. The corridors of power seemed unlikely to echo with talk of deciphering "the Code of Codes" and of reading "the Book of Life." As it transpired, I was nonetheless naïve. Instead of the anticipated emphasis on medical benefits,

THE NATURAL SCIENCES   255

primarily cures for major diseases,[46] the primary (often the sole) reason was presented bluntly: "We see biotechnology as our best bet for keeping up with the Japanese."

The idea of the national science as crucial to national prosperity is in obvious tension with an ideal of scientific research, one surprisingly well approximated in many domains of scientific practice. Many scientists view themselves as part of an international—panhuman—effort, and collaborate willingly and enthusiastically across borders. The flow of published information often makes it difficult for a technologically relevant new finding to become the "intellectual property" of the discoverers, or of their financial backers, or of their country. Jonas Salk famously expressed an ethos common to many (at least in an earlier age). When asked by an interviewer whether he planned to seek a patent on the polio vaccine, he replied, "You wouldn't patent the sun."

From the beginnings of socially organized modern science, cooperation among researchers has been viewed as central to the advancement of knowledge. Perhaps those who originally urged the open exchange of ideas would have lapsed from their lofty ideals if they had realized just how much wealth can be amassed in the pursuit of science. But the ideals still linger. The world we inhabit is a hybrid. Collaboration lives on, cheek by jowl with determination to use research for large economic profits—and thus keep the nation ahead of the competition.

It is an uncomfortable mixture. One, moreover, with consequences for education. All over the globe, building projects at universities increase the proportion of physical space devoted to science, and especially to the applied sciences. The relentless struggle among nations for scientific eminence (and, if possible, pre-eminence) distorts the development and narrows the horizons of hundreds of millions of young people. If the analysis and the arguments of this chapter have any merit, the disastrous character of emphasizing that kind of competition should be evident.[47]

---

[46] Of course, as commentators recognized (and pointed out) in advance, diagnostic improvements would precede treatments and cures.

[47] The next chapters will consider in more detail how competitive pressures have distorted education. The general problem of resisting competitive pressures will be taken up in Chapter 10.

8

The Arts

When school budgets are tight, administrators usually decide to cut back on "the frills." By that, they mean the arts. Classes in music and the visual arts disappear. Instruction in the "less important" languages, including the dead ones, is abandoned. In the remaining humanities classes, teachers are urged to concentrate on the basics. Less time for literature, more emphasis on functional literacy. Such attitudes are echoed at higher levels of educational policy. Governments decide to cut—or slash—the already meager budgets for the humanities and the arts. In the United States, scientists often bewail the reduction of funds to support research. Although the National Science Foundation and the National Institutes of Health may be pinched by policymakers apparently bereft of any sense of the value of research, the scorn directed at the National Endowment for the Humanities and the National Endowment for the Arts is far more intense. Those agencies are permanently threatened by the barbarians within the gates.

Why is there no analog of the STEM initiative? Why no public wringing of hands about the quality of American education in the arts and humanities? To be sure, international comparisons are more difficult in these areas, and data on relative performance harder to come by. Measures of reading skills show American students performing slightly above the average for affluent countries—occupying a similar level to their position in the science rankings.[1] Although the finding may have sparked the demand for focusing on functional literacy, the cry for reform is far more muted than in the scientific case. Students from Europe and from many parts of Asia are notably superior to Americans in their ability to speak foreign languages. Should that also be a source of concern?

One argument for marginalizing education in the arts (and the humanities) appeals to economics. Governments properly invest in educating citizens to contribute to national productivity. The sciences provide the keys to

[1] For the data on the PISA test for 2018, see https://www.oecd.org/pisa/publications/pisa-2018-results.htm.

The Main Enterprise of the World. Philip Kitcher, Oxford University Press. © Oxford University Press 2022.
DOI: 10.1093/oso/9780190928971.003.0009

future technological innovations, capable of preserving American economic strength.[2] The arts and humanities do not. Or, more exactly, to the extent that they do, the United States is already doing very nicely. Hollywood dominates the globe.

Even if you were to rest the case on adopting the economic frame, the complacent conclusion about the arts seems no more warranted than a parallel judgment about scientific innovation. American research laboratories, inside and outside our universities, lead the way in most scientific fields. STEM stems from anxiety about whether their lead *can be maintained*. Yet the economic frame is suspect, and not only for its subordination of the individual perspective to a narrow vision of the social good. The previous chapter adopted a broader view in presenting the case for reforming science education. It saw the sciences as advancing the human project. On the lay view, the contributions are the practical benefits from technology, conceived not as augmenting one nation's GDP but as improving human lives. The official view, by contrast, identified scientific progress in the enriched understanding of nature, available in principle to all.

We should take a parallel approach to the arts. Can they also be seen as advancing the human project? At first blush, there's an obvious disanalogy. Science is the parade case for progress. On the other hand, "everybody knows" that the arts (and the humanities) don't make progress. Yet we ought to press the point. *Is* this something that everybody—or anybody—*knows*?

The common judgment rests on familiar grounds. Consider English drama. A highly fertile period at the turn of the seventeenth century was followed by a far more impoverished time. Between 1580 and 1620, Ben Jonson, Christopher Marlowe, Thomas Kyd, Robert Greene, Francis Beaumont, John Fletcher, John Webster, George Peele, and others produced the works for which they are most famous. By contrast, the period 1620–1640 offers only two works to compare with the highlights of the previous forty years: *The Changeling*, by Thomas Middleton and William Rowley, and John Ford's *'Tis Pity She's a Whore*.[3] (Of course, I've cheated a bit, choosing the dates as I have,

---

[2] As in previous chapters, I shall sometimes draw on the example of the United States, the country whose educational practices I know best. But, as before, references to the American context serve as placeholders; my proposals are supposed to apply to any nation pursuing similar policies.

[3] Many thanks to Martha Nussbaum for correcting an incautious formulation I offered in an earlier draft.

258 THE MAIN ENTERPRISE OF THE WORLD

since the theaters were closed under Cromwell.) Another case of regress, this time from music. In 1905, Debussy composed *La Mer*, Schoenberg wrote his first string quartet, and Webern wrote his *Langsamer Satz* for string quartet. What does 2015 have to offer by way of comparison? Or, to take a more popular genre, can the past decade rival the offerings of the Beatles, the Stones, Bob Dylan, Joan Baez, and Simon and Garfunkel between 1964 and 1974?

When scrutinized, this line of reasoning is a cheat and a disappointment. It rests on assessing progress by comparing the works of art *produced* in different time periods. If that yardstick were applied to the sciences, it would subvert the cheery confidence in scientific progress. I chose my dates, 1905 and 2015, with malice aforethought. In 1905, Einstein produced four remarkable articles that transformed physics—one on the photoelectric effect, one on Brownian motion, one on mass-energy equivalence ($E=mc^2$), and the foundational paper on special relativity. The entire sum of what physicists did in 2015 doesn't rank with that (nor, despite the enthusiasm of my physicist friend, do the total achievements of 2016).

The approach to progress developed for the sciences offered a very different criterion. Socially embedded scientific progress consists in providing a set of resources for contributing to the human project. The physics of today doesn't lose the brilliant advances Einstein made in 1905. It builds on them. The resources available in 2020 include the earlier accomplishments and much more besides. Today, technology has a broader collection of tools for addressing practical problems (thus yielding the benefits celebrated in the lay view). Accumulation also offers an ever richer picture of nature, advancing human understanding (as the official view emphasizes).

Similar points can be made in the case of the arts. Fiction, poetry, drama, painting, sculpture, ceramics, architecture, film, dance, and music are, in the main, cumulative. We don't lose Sophocles and Shakespeare when we acquire Beckett, Ionesco, and Pinter. Adès doesn't make Verdi and Wagner irrelevant. To be sure, there are some losses. The buildings of previous centuries can only rarely be seen as parts of their original environments; many great performances, in dance and theater and music, have gone unrecorded. Moreover, as T. S. Eliot recognized, newer developments in the arts affect the reception of older works.[4] After reading the great modernist poets, Yeats, Pound, and Eliot himself, we may be unable to hear Tennyson as the

---

[4] T. S. Eliot, "Tradition and the Individual Talent" in *Selected Prose of T. S. Eliot*, ed. Frank Kermode (New York: Farrar, Straus & Giroux, 1975), 38–39.

THE ARTS 259

Victorians heard him. *Invisible Man* changes the resonances of passages in *Huckleberry Finn*. Nevertheless, the losses are small in comparison with the gains, as the body of artistic resources expands. A simple test: would the resources for your aesthetic experience be enhanced or diminished if any art form had stopped at some particular point in the past? Reflect on whatever art means the most to you. Imagine scenarios in which its further development ends a century ago, or two centuries ago. What, if anything, would you have gained? What would you have lost?

The parallel depends, of course, on claiming artworks as *resources*, capable of making contributions to human lives or to human societies. Evidently, any such contributions differ from those identified in the lay view of science: novels don't cure diseases and landscape paintings don't advance agriculture. The goods hailed in the official view provide more promising models. Champions of the epistemic value of the sciences are committed to thinking of individual lives as improved through gaining access to particular subjective states. Richard Dawkins offers a characteristically eloquent presentation of the theme, when he expresses sympathy with the predicaments of people who have not learned to see the organic world through a Darwinian lens.[5] And the close of Darwin's *Origin* already anticipates Dawkins's reaction— "There is grandeur in this view of life."[6]

When the official view is made explicit in this way, an obvious question arises. Are human lives enriched more through the episodes in which people acquire new scientific understanding or by their encounters with works of art? I have no systematic data to support an answer. But, after posing the question to a number of audiences, made up of undergraduates, graduate students, and faculty, a significant majority take their artistic experiences to be the more important ones. (Those who demur are usually professional scientists or scientists-in-training.) If my ramshackle evidence represents the human population, a subversive conclusion follows. The official view of scientific progress entails that the case for progress in the arts is stronger than that for progress in the sciences.

---

[5] See Richard Dawkins, *River out of Eden* (New York: Basic Books, 1995).
[6] Charles Darwin, *Origin of Species* (London: John Murray, 1859; facsimile repr., Harvard University Press), 490.

260 THE MAIN ENTERPRISE OF THE WORLD

Better, though, to be ecumenical. It's enough to concede the importance people ascribe to their aesthetic experiences. Yet we should probe. Do these subjective responses indicate anything significant? What exactly do the arts do for us?

Following Dewey, I'll distinguish three aspects of aesthetic experience.[7] First is the joy and uplift felt during our encounters with the works of art— or the parts of nature[8]—that move us most. What prompts these moments varies widely from person to person, and, I suspect, the psychological reactions, with their mixtures of awareness and emotion, are also highly diverse. They are united in a single category, *aesthetic experience*, primarily by a sense of intensity and vitality. On these occasions, we might say, we are most vividly aware, perhaps most vividly alive. Without them, human lives would not necessarily be drab or unpleasant. The high points of aesthetic experience grade imperceptibly into other occasions on which people are amused or absorbed or entertained. Nevertheless, simply in themselves, aesthetic experiences add something rich to human existence, something people are inclined to characterize as more than "mere pleasure."

Here, as so often, everyday enjoyments do not receive their due. Talk of aesthetic experience rightly acknowledges the most intense moments, the occasions on which we thrill to some aspect of the environment or become enraptured by an artistic work. Even those most enthusiastic about the impact of "high art" don't want to dwell forever on the heights. People for whom modernism represents the peak of the novel—who read and reread Proust and Mann and Musil and Woolf and Joyce—sometimes need the entertainment of lighter fiction, turning to detective stories or the writings of humorists. Devotees of serialism sometimes forsake Schoenberg and Webern to listen to popular songs or to go to musicals. Indeed, indulging in a variety of artistic experiences may enhance each of the occasions: when a music-hall song runs through your head, your appreciation of passages in *Ulysses* and *Finnegans Wake* may well be enriched.

To point to those possibilities of enhancement could be to attribute only a subordinate role to the occasions on which people "take a holiday" from their serious aesthetic lives. The worth of the detective story lies in its setting

---

[7] Here I draw not only from Dewey's *Art as Experience* (LW 10), but also from the closing chapter of *Experience and Nature* (LW 1) and from passages in *A Common Faith* (LW 9).

[8] Tagore devotes far more attention than Dewey does to the educational importance of aesthetic experiences of nature. See "To Students," "To Teachers," and "My School" (*A Tagore Reader*, 206–23). See also the comparison of Wordsworth with the modernist response that Tagore dislikes (ibid., 236).

THE ARTS   261

off the reading of the great novel—as if the evening spent with Ruth Rendell or Tana French were analogous to the exercises at the gym required of the climber who plans to scale the heights. That is a mistake. The philosophical distaste for hedonism dies hard. Sometimes the gripping or the amusing is not only just what we need, but also rewarding in itself. People find aesthetic satisfaction, and even joy and uplift, in different places. A mix of aesthetic experiences may suit us all. Different people savoring the same menu may grade the individual courses differently. Or simply not grade at all.

Aesthetic encounters are significant components of our lives. As we look back, we often treasure individual moments. We relive them with those who enjoyed them with us. "Don't you remember that wonderful performance of *Lucia*," we exclaim, "Sutherland's farewell to Covent Garden, with the young Pavarotti, beaming as if he were ready to sing the whole thing again, on the spot?" Joint returns to a past are exercises in communal hedonism, reviving shared pleasures. They indicate two further aspects of the experiences. First (a point that will occupy us later) we delight in sharing with others what has entranced (gripped, moved, amused) us. Second, besides their value in the moment, they resonate further in our lives, sometimes through the whole course of our subsequent existence.

The vital individual moment sometimes proves experientially transformative. It can leave its impress on future sensory experience, changing how the world is seen or heard or felt. An autumn walk in the woods becomes impregnated by the cadences of a lyric;[9] the surface of a New York apartment building suddenly shimmers as it is momentarily transformed into the front of Rouen cathedral.[10] Something in the air or in the scene around you reminds you of a song you sang long ago, one somehow suited to this moment and this mood. Past aesthetic experience reverberates in the present, making the world richer than it would otherwise have been.

Moreover, the sense of aptness can return you to a work you know and love. The present resonances provoke a thought: I must really go back and read/hear/see that again. Inspired by the idea you revisit the book or song or picture. Often, you find it changed, and, on occasion, you are disappointed.[11] Perhaps you are puzzled by the attraction it once held for you—it proves

---

[9] For example, famous poems by Keats and Rilke.

[10] As in Monet's famous series of pictures.

[11] Half a century ago I took *The Idiot* to be Dostoyevsky's masterpiece. On re-reading, it came to seem relatively clumsy by comparison with his three other major novels. *Demons* has held steady, while *Crime and Punishment* and *The Brothers Karamazov* have climbed even higher in my estimation. I suspect other re-readers find similar shifts.

262   THE MAIN ENTERPRISE OF THE WORLD

dull, unstimulating, and you set it aside. More significant are the times when the difference is thrilling, when you recognize new aspects of an old friend, when it comes to seem richer, deeper, even more fascinating than you had remembered. The works of art we treasure most are those that appear inexhaustible. As we grow, they show us new sides of themselves, appearing thenceforward on different occasions in our experiential lives, lending themselves to new contexts and to new emotions. Ever since I first read *Ulysses* as a teenager—finding it extraordinary, while acutely aware of the limitations of my comprehension—I have re-read it at roughly five-year intervals. It has never seemed to me the same. Different parts of the novel spring out to me with new vividness. Like other works I love deeply, *Ulysses* is a companion for a lifetime, often nudging me to appreciate some facet of my experience I would otherwise have overlooked. Part of my life is a conversation with Joyce's masterpieces.[12]

Hence the full value of an aesthetic encounter is not always limited to the moment. Aesthetic life flourishes in trans-temporal connections. Further, the sensory transformations wrought by them are sometimes accompanied by cognitive changes. Works of art can have epistemic significance. Not because they directly supply evidence for new premises from which we might now reason. Rather, through their ability to unsettle habitual ways of thinking.[13] Much of human thought begins from judgments acquired from the society in which we live, and sustained by the similar opinions of those with whom we interact. Ever since Descartes, epistemology has been inspired (or haunted?) by the thought of some ultimate grounding, the exposure of a foundation on which beliefs could safely rest. That is a myth.[14] Our epistemic lives always start in the middle, with a mix of judgments, concepts, and values we inherit with our mothers' milk. Scientists, mathematicians, philosophers, as well as

---

[12] Although my serious acquaintance with *Finnegans Wake* is more recent, it has come to play the same role as *Ulysses*.

[13] As Harvey Siegel reminded me, this point is brilliantly explored by Israel Scheffler in his essay "In Praise of the Cognitive Emotions"; see Scheffler, *In Praise of the Cognitive Emotions* (New York: Routledge, 2010), 3–17; the essay was originally published in 1977, in the *Teachers College Record*.

[14] The myth is best exposed in the pragmatist tradition, beginning with early papers of C. S. Peirce and developed by Dewey in *The Quest for Certainty* (LW 4). The insights of the tradition are encapsulated not only in the writings of W. V. Quine and Nelson Goodman, but also in the epigraph to Quine's *Word and Object* (Cambridge, MA: MIT Press, 1960). Quine cites a passage from Otto Neurath: "We are like sailors who must rebuild our ship on the open sea, without ever being able to set it into dry dock and reconstruct it from the best materials."

THE ARTS 263

all the rest of humanity, can only try to *improve* the mix, and to pass on some better version to their successors.

The quest for improvement is aided by the experiences that bring us up short. Those might occur in the laboratory—as with Röntgen's fluorescing screen or Fleming's odd-looking Petri dish.[15] Far more common, and sometimes equally profound in their impact on human lives, are the cognitive changes provoked by works of art.

Consider two straightforward examples from nineteenth-century fiction. Whether Abraham Lincoln actually characterized Harriet Beecher Stowe as the "little woman who wrote the book that made this great war," there's a point to the story.[16] The immediate reaction—counter-novels to defend the institution of slavery—testifies to fears about the impact of *Uncle Tom's Cabin*.[17] A modest conclusion: Stowe's book prompted at least some people, possibly a considerable number, to scrutinize their racial stereotypes and to take up the cause of abolitionism. Similarly, Dickens's novels sometimes changed—even changed radically—the opinions of his readers on social issues. *Bleak House* not only offers a sympathetic portrait of a young boy, Jo, the slum-dwelling crossing-sweeper. It also brilliantly weaves into the narratives the voices of bourgeois complacency, those who discuss slum clearance in Parliament, those who preach the glories of being "a human boy," those who can find nothing to do with Jo but tell him to "move on." Dickens rebukes them all in his obituary for Jo:

> Dead, your Majesty. Dead my lords and gentlemen. Dead, Right Reverends and Wrong Reverends of every order. Dead, men and women, born with Heavenly compassion in your hearts. And dying thus around us every day.[18]

---

[15] Röntgen was conducting an experiment using what he took to be a completely shielded glass tube; noticing that a screen in the room was illuminated, he began an inquiry that eventually led to the discovery of X-rays. Similarly, Fleming, returning to his laboratory after a holiday, found an oddity in one of the Petri dishes containing colonies of bacteria; on one side of the dish, the usual signs of bacteria were absent and a blob of mold was growing; further investigation led to the discovery of antibiotics.

[16] Lincoln is supposed to have said this when he met Harriet Beecher Stowe on Thanksgiving Day in 1862. For an illuminating account of the history of this "legend," see Daniel Vollaro, "Lincoln, Stowe, and the 'Little Woman/Great War' Story: The Making, and Breaking, of a Great American Anecdote," *Journal of the Abraham Lincoln Association* 30 (2009): 18–34.

[17] Between 1852 and 1860, more than twenty novels were published in attempts to rebut the account given in *Uncle Tom's Cabin*. One of the earliest (and most widely read) was Mary Henderson Eastman's *Aunt Phillis's Cabin; or Southern Life as It Is* (Philadelphia: Lippincott, 1852).

[18] *Bleak House*; this passage closes Chapter 47.

264 THE MAIN ENTERPRISE OF THE WORLD

Many Victorian readers found it hard to avoid hearing their own voices, complacent or uncomprehending, in the novel—and were led to wonder about the "Heavenly compassion" expressed in their own attitudes and conduct.

Stowe and Dickens modified the ways in which people think and reason in a very specific domain. Often, works of art will influence cognition more diffusely. A Renaissance portrait might incline you to look at your contemporaries with different eyes, initiating a process of reflections that culminates in displacing attitudes and concepts you have previously taken for granted. A Beethoven String Quartet or a protest song might inspire different meditations on the human condition and on the health of contemporary society. Your imagination moves in new directions, uncoupling some emotional reactions from previously envisaged scenarios, and yoking new feelings to judgments you have previously dismissed. In such cases the artwork produces its changes by way of a more-or-less systematic reviewing of past experience. Episodes once classified together are differentiated, and find new bedfellows. You learn a new perspective, a different language for describing familiar things. Many kinds of subsequent experiences feel the effects of the shift.

How exactly does this work? We come to our interactions with literature, paintings and sculpture, music in many genres, dance, theater, and film with minds already shaped in distinctive ways. As we read or look on or listen we bring to the exchange our own individual synthetic complexes,[19] mixes of beliefs, aspirations, emotions, and dispositions to develop all these in our own idiosyncratic fashion. The encounter triggers a change, rendering some synthetic complex unstable. We feel the need to stop and to ponder. How can we integrate our first understanding of the work with what we have thought or hoped for or felt? So we reflect, connecting the work to a variety of psychological attitudes, until we find a new equilibrium. Often the process is extensive, involving considerable casting about for how exactly change should occur—we may go back, again and again, to the work, testing and refining our tentative sense of what it says to us. Sometimes, though, the work is a lightning bolt. Reading Dickens or Stowe or Orwell or Toni Morrison, we can no longer believe what we previously accepted. Whether the process is slow or speedy, when we eventually settle down, we see ourselves as having learned something. The work has taught us to think or feel differently.

---

[19] I introduced this concept in *Deaths in Venice*; see 181–87. Although more detail is given there, the idea still needs psychological development.

THE ARTS   265

Skeptics worry about the use of cognitive language—"taught," "learned"—here. Works of art don't furnish scientific evidence. In stimulating emotions, they may sweep us away, leading us to conclusions for which we have no basis.[20] Admirable as it is when previously insensitive and well-to-do people come to feel concern for the plight of the urban poor, Dicken was no sociologist. The change of mind (and heart) is welcome, but to view it as an *epistemic* advance is to misunderstand what encounters with works of art can do.

Skeptics of this stripe overlook an important aspect of cognitive advances. Progress is sometimes not a matter of accepting new statements *couched in the same language*. The most striking forms of progress are those in which a class of situations is reconceptualized. Experience jars. We become convinced that something is amiss, and it must be fixed. Röntgen discovered X-rays and Fleming discovered antibiotics as a consequence of episodes that forced on them the inadequacy of their everyday assumptions. They too had to reshape synthetic complexes. Long processes of reflection and further interactions with the strange environments they had found led them to what we standardly judge to be new knowledge. Why not extend the same courtesy to the reader or viewer or listener? Changing your mind after an aesthetic encounter need not be a matter of being "swept away." You reflect, you read further, you talk to those you trust, you go back to the work, and you conclude by adopting some new beliefs, even modifying the ways in which you conceptualize your experiences. In scientific change, as in the modifications of belief artworks provoke, the epistemic burden may be carried by the inquiry to which the initial experience leads. Yet it would be hard to deny the importance of that initiating event: Röntgen's observation of the screen, Fleming's observation of the Petri dish. The work of art ought to receive analogous credit.

Although the case for cognitive contributions can be made across many fields and genres of the arts, it is most straightforward (and thus perhaps strongest) for literature, or, more generally, for works in which words play a prominent role. Drama, film, opera, fiction, and poetry all have the power to stir the imagination to novel explorations. Sometimes, as with Stowe and Dickens, Wilfred Owen and Bertolt Brecht, Wisława Szymborska and Toni Morrison, the ethical import of a play or poem or novel is almost unmissable. The work demands of its readers that they wrestle with particular moral questions, raised by vivid or puzzling or uncanny situations. Other

---

[20] Here I am grateful to Todd Jones.

266 THE MAIN ENTERPRISE OF THE WORLD

works, the plays of Sophocles, Shakespeare, and Ibsen, the poetry of Dante and Wordsworth and T. S. Eliot, the fiction of Dostoyevsky and Proust and Joyce, raise ethical questions across so wide a compass, that they can seem less "philosophical," precisely because they are less insistent in prodding their audience in a particular direction. The authors just mentioned draw us back to them, over the course of a lifetime, because of just that many-sided quality. People constantly return to particular works with new eyes and ears and minds, because they provide so much impetus to perspective-changing ethical thought. Dewey was right to identify the role played by the arts in human ethical progress:

> As empirical fact, however, the arts, those of converse and the literary arts which are the enhanced continuations of social converse, have been the means by which goods are brought home to human perception. The writings of moralists have been efficacious in this direction upon the whole not in their professed intent as theoretical doctrines, but in as far as they have genially participated in the arts of poetry, fiction, parable and drama.[21]

It's no accident that the works most human beings turn to for moral instruction, scriptures like the Bhagavad Gita and the Bible, are either centered on or full of vivid stories.

Immersion in the arts educates the emotions. Part of that education consists in refinement of the moral sentiments. Applying Dewey's insight to the problems of earlier chapters—How to prepare citizens? How to foster moral development?—suggests an obvious case for the import of the so-called frills. Deep democracy and moral growth depend on the expansion of sympathy. Without a prominent place for the arts, there will be too little stirring of the imagination, too little stretching of the emotional repertoire. Crowding out visual art, music, and especially literature, to make room for more chemistry or more economics, more "useful stuff," will produce an impoverished citizenry and diminished moral agents.

The power of literature (or art) to refine the moral sentiments should not be exaggerated.[22] Preliminary psychological studies do not provide convincing evidence for any *generic* increase in empathy. Across the board,

---

[21] *Experience and Nature*, LW 1, 322.
[22] The discussion of this paragraph is heavily indebted to conversations with Ellen Winner. Her book *How Art Works* (New York: Oxford University Press, 2019) is a groundbreaking exploration of central issues in the psychology of art.

readers don't appear to be more empathetic than their non-reading peers (at least as far as the relatively crude studies so far undertaken can disclose). The best version of the Deweyan hypothesis emphasizes *local* gains. With respect to a particular class of people or in connection with specific types of predicaments, some works prompt their readers to respond to the plight of others. Historical evidence shows the power of art to extend empathy in specific directions: witness the impact of Dickens and Stowe and Orwell and Morrison.

So far, however, my brief for the arts is too narrow, too dominated by the utilitarian thinking against which it reacts. My focus on the cognitive contributions of the arts has proceeded to greater lengths only because those benefits are often unrecognized or even denied. Recall the first two positive effects Dewey ascribes to aesthetic experiences: those episodes are especially vivid and they are broadly transformative. Cutting the alleged "frills" doesn't just weaken democracy. It also produces stunted people, people who live impoverished lives.

Education in the arts, I have claimed, contributes to two out of the three principal goals for fostering the developing person. When it is done well, it opens new avenues to fulfillment and instills habits of thought and feeling conducive to good citizenship and moral growth. Of course, for some people it offers a new career path. They will maintain themselves as artists of some style. However much we may be attracted by that possibility, it is not an option for most of us. In the contemporary world, those who can sustain themselves through their creative artistic work are rare. The majority will interact with the arts as consumers, rather than as producers.

The previous chapter recognized a dichotomy: between students who aspire to a career in the sciences and those who (with luck) retain their curiosity, follow the research achievements obtained in their lifetimes, becoming better able to form opinions on matters of policy. The dichotomy arises here too. Should it be addressed in parallel fashion?

Not completely. Although there may come a stage in children's development at which the few who are talented and passionate about some form of art are provided opportunities for undergoing the rigorous discipline of their chosen genre, some space for continuing to create should be preserved throughout formal schooling—and beyond. At bottom, the point is a corollary of my hypothesis about the power of aesthetic experience to transform

268 THE MAIN ENTERPRISE OF THE WORLD

lives. If most people, on reflection, conclude that their encounters with paintings or poetry or drama have been significant factors in their growth—more significant than their appreciation of any scientific perspective on the world—education ought to prepare the young to receive the benefits art can bring. If consumer choice and consumer satisfaction are improved by continued creative activity, in some chosen genre, people should be helped to explore and to improve their skills, throughout their lives.

As noted earlier, sharing our aesthetic lives with others is important. We recommend books and plays and films and exhibitions and concerts to our friends. When they respond enthusiastically to the works or events we have suggested, their pleasure heightens our own. Excited discussions may follow, leading all of us to discern even more—perhaps the popularity of book clubs testifies to their ability (when things go well) to provide opportunities for this to occur. Another reason for continuing art education is to build communities of these kinds.

So far, the bare sketch of a line of reasoning. Can it be elaborated in convincing detail? Let's begin with some commonplace facts.

Just as young children are curious about the natural world, so too they respond enthusiastically to the arts. They love songs, and pictures, and stories. And, of course, they can sit mesmerized while watching a film. Typically, they spontaneously go beyond passive consumption. They dance and sing, experiment with crayons, and make up tales of their own. None of the children I have known has ever had the chance to make a film, but most of them would have leapt at the opportunity.

Early schooling takes advantage of these widespread propensities. Young pupils are introduced to a wider range of media than were previously available. Classes in art and music allow them to paint, to model clay, to sing together, to dance together, and to try simple musical instruments.[23] As they learn to read and write, they are asked to construct stories and sometimes to write poems. Usually, however, the periods in the art studio or the music room are treated as ancillaries—as "frills"—valuable in providing time for

---

[23] As Martha Nussbaum emphasizes, both song and dance are major components of Tagore's pedagogy (see "Tagore, Dewey, and the Imminent Demise of Liberal Education," especially 56, 57). In the educational writings reprinted in *A Tagore Reader*, Tagore is concerned both with the cultivation of children's freedom (in relation to nature and to one another) and with the need for finding pathways along which that freedom can be expressed. The disciplines of singing and dancing are identified as major ways of achieving the right combination. To my mind, this is an important extension of Dewey's emphasis (shared completely by Tagore) on freedom of movement in the early school-years. If, as I have been told, Dewey was tone-deaf, his propensity to treat art in terms of the visual and to neglect the sonic may be responsible for the limitations of his brief for the importance of the arts.

THE ARTS 269

recreation and relaxation, from which children return refreshed to their "proper studies." As they grow, the time assigned to the arts dwindles, often vanishing entirely. Fostering creative production succumbs to overload.

In its own way, this style of presenting the arts and the attitudes underlying it are as contrary to the aims of education as the standard modes of teaching science. Although it may not alienate young people from the arts, treating music and visual art as peripheral, valuable only as diversions, fails to develop their creative talents or to deepen their sensitivity to works in the genres of most interest to them. When pupils are asked to "express themselves" through writing "poems," and when these exercises are seen primarily as tests of their skills in penmanship and grammar, the chances of acquiring any powers of discrimination are low. Some years ago, the distinguished critic Helen Vendler wrote a brilliantly scathing review of an anthology of "poetry" produced by children. The editor was much impressed by the authenticity of the pieces included, seeing them as expressions of individual voices. Vendler drew a different comparison: she invited her readers to imagine bringing violins into an ordinary classroom, handing them out to the children and asking them to play.[24]

A central insight of Whitehead's influential book *The Aims of Education* divides students' educational careers into periods during which nascent interests are aroused, maintained, and reinforced, and phases of rigorous discipline, capable of inculcating the skills required to develop those interests further.[25] One moral of the previous chapter can be stated in Whiteheadian terms. For many students, curiosity about the natural world cannot be sustained when they are subjected to the frustrations of the appropriate disciplinary regime; finding their own aptitudes inadequate to what they are asked to do, they become alienated and their curiosity withers. Education in the arts presents a contrary problem. Because the arts are dismissed as "frills," educators shy away from imposing any kind of discipline. Any sequence of words makes a poem—no sense of form, or rhythm, or assonance is needed to refine the "expression of the authentic voice." Singing and painting are

---

[24] The book reviewed was Bill Moyers, *The Language of Life* (New York: Doubleday, 1995). Vendler's review appeared in the *New York Times*, June 18, 1995. As I understand Vendler's point, the trouble lay not in asking the children to write (or not in offering them musical instruments) but in not following up so they could acquire serious capacities for self-expression. A similar point about poetry and the importance of form is made by Lewis Turco in *Poetry: An Introduction through Writing* (Reston, VA: Reston Publishing Company, 1973). See also Stephen Fry's witty—and informative— broadside *The Ode Less Travelled* (London: Penguin, 2006).

[25] A. N. Whitehead, *The Aims of Education* (New York: Free Press, 1929).

270 THE MAIN ENTERPRISE OF THE WORLD

occasionally subjected to slightly more stringent critique. But how many schools provide rigorous instruction in brushwork or drawing? How many set up exercises in ear training and in vocal production?

I offer an example from my own experience. For the better part of seventy years I have sung. My vocal life has been lived in various choirs, mostly focused on the staples of Western choral music, with periodic forays into solo singing. The serious training I have had has been sporadic (mainly from choir conductors, occasionally from professional singing teachers), but it has enabled me to develop further than I (or any of those who know me well) would have anticipated. By contrast, my childhood enjoyment of painting came to an end relatively early in my adolescence. Although my art teachers complimented me on some of my efforts, I was never taught to draw. *Faute de mieux*, I had to become a (low-budget) impressionist. Concluding that drawing was "something I was bad at," I abandoned attempts to paint differently.

Close to sixty years on, I hope to resume my long-interrupted career with the brush. When I confessed my aspirations—and my limitations to a friend—she rejected my self-diagnosis. "Anyone can learn to draw," she told me.[26] As I have discovered, she is at least partly correct. There are exercises through which the untalented (or those like me who think of themselves in this way) can improve their graphic abilities. Although I have a long way to go before my skills as a draughtsman are adequate to my painterly ambitions, the possibility of progress has become evident.

Even my rudimentary self-training (largely through reading books[27] and following the exercises they suggest) has brought unexpected benefits. First, I have gained a lively appreciation of and interest in the drawings of many artists. The mere awareness of techniques I am far from mastering yields an appreciation of what can be done with line and shading. Second, I view paintings differently, attending to details of which I had previously been unaware. Third, and most importantly, the world through which I move has become a richer, visually more exciting, place. It has taken me years to arrive at a banal truism, one known to every artist and art teacher: learning to draw and to paint is a matter of learning how to see.

[26] Thanks to Jennifer Worrall for the original conversation, and to Jane Emmerson and Orna Panfil for subsequent encouragement.
[27] Two particularly helpful books are Claire Watson Garcia, *Drawing for the Absolute and Utter Beginner* (New York: Watson-Guptill, 2003); and Betty Edwards, *Drawing on the Right Side of the Brain* (New York: Penguin, 2012).

THE ARTS 271

My staggering realization of the obvious is concordant with my lifelong experience with music. For anyone who has learned to sing or to play a musical instrument, hearing performances is enriched. Even without advanced theoretical knowledge, the amateur performer discerns the separate voices, recognizes harmonic shifts, senses structures that the untrained ear fails to detect. Of course, the effect is particularly striking with works the hearer has performed— or with works heard repeatedly. Some pieces of music are part of my life to the extent that they *inhabit* me. I am profoundly grateful for their presence.

Standard educational priorities deprive vast numbers of people of aesthetic possibilities, of experiences whose vitality and whose impact they cannot imagine. Since the arts are taken to be dispensable, useful for giving students a break, but of no further significance, any serious attempt to develop the eye or hand or ear[28] through a disciplined program of exercises (exercises bringing their own rewards) is foregone. Perhaps, here and there, a perceptive teacher tries to do more than "let the children express themselves." From the perspective of official policy, however, such ventures are unnecessary, irrelevant, and possibly subversive.

My case is so far incomplete. For it takes too narrow a view of creative work. Not all children will be inclined to develop their creativity within the spheres of painting and music and writing—by pursuing the "fine" arts. The forms of individual production to which they might gravitate, if given the chance would lie elsewhere, closer to the practices of everyday life. As Dewey reminded his readers, creativity and individual expression (without quotes) have sometimes permeated people's daily activities.[29] The contemporary world has divorced art from quotidian behavior. Art thus becomes alien, remote, something to be visited on special occasions in special places—if at all.

A significant number of people don't particularly want to paint or make music or write or act. Instead, they would prefer to work with clay or wood or metal, to sew or to cook, to lay out a garden or build a small structure. Many would probably enjoy learning to express themselves through dancing.[30]

---

[28] Or, in the case of dance, the whole body.

[29] This theme is presented forcefully in Chapter 1 of *Art as Experience*.

[30] As Martha Nussbaum pointed out to me, dance connects both to the arts and, because of the physical involvement of so much of the body, to athletic activities. The twin linkages may be useful in fostering the aesthetic interests of those young people for whom sports are the best part of school. (I am confident that one of my sons was not the only second-grader who, when asked what his favorite school period was, answered "recess.")

Recognizing this linkage provokes an obvious question: what is the place of physical education (and organized sports) within the framework I develop here? Since I am unsure about how to answer it, I have omitted any discussion of physical education from this book—although I acknowledge the

272   THE MAIN ENTERPRISE OF THE WORLD

Education in the arts should find a place for them. It should foster their creativity through an appropriately disciplined form of training. Here, once again, I emphasize attending to the propensities of the individual-in-the-making. Early in formal schooling, the wealth of possibilities should be presented. Careful attention to the proclivities of each child should guide attempts to steer them toward a form of creative production capable of generating a deep and abiding interest. As always, the presence of many adults in the schoolroom, sharing their own diverse enthusiasms, is crucial.

And education in the arts should continue through the adult years, offering not only opportunities to extend skills in areas of long-standing interest, but also to explore genres previously dismissed as unattractive but now seeming intriguing. Artistic growth is a matter for a lifetime.

———

Understanding the similarities and the differences between progress in the arts and progress in the sciences exposes an important problem. Both the sciences and the arts accumulate resources for enriching human lives. Once that point is appreciated, the need for educational reform becomes clear. Yet, there are further wrinkles that complicate decisions about how to do better.

The characteristics of the accumulation are different. In building on the efforts of earlier generations—in standing on the shoulders of the dead giants (and the less visible army of smaller precursors)—the sciences typically occlude the achievements of previous decades. No practicing chemist today needs to read Lavoisier's groundbreaking book; no astronomer need spend time looking through Galileo's telescope. To be sure, evolutionary biologists do still turn to Darwin's writings for inspiration, but this is a rare exception to the general rule. Because later developments almost always make studying the original sources irrelevant (except for the purposes of fostering scientific literacy—as in the proposed "General Science" curriculum),[31] specialized education in any individual scientific field can economize. Discard almost everything more than a decade or so old.

---

importance of the omission. One way to approach the question would be to take sports as forms of aesthetic expression. That thought has been pursued, with considerable eloquence and force, by Hans Ulrich Gumbrecht—see his *In Praise of Athletic Beauty* (Cambridge, MA: Harvard University Press, 2006).

[31] See the previous chapter, 245–53.

THE ARTS   273

Not so with the arts. Eliot was correct to remind us of how new works can modify perception of their predecessors. Rarely, however, do the favorites of past generations become completely worthless for later audiences. For people passionate about string quartets, Bartók and Schoenberg don't make Haydn and Beethoven irrelevant. Aficionados of musicals return to Jerome Kern, George Gershwin, Cole Porter, and Richard Rodgers. Even at the time of Mill's Inaugural Address, the collection of known works of art challenged educators to select—and their selections have produced versions of the canon whose special status is constantly debated. With the enormous expansion of the collection, with translations of literature from many languages, with appreciation of the visual and the performing arts from a large number of traditions, the task of selecting becomes even more onerous. So many genres, so many cultures, so many historical periods. How should the educational system choose among all the potential riches?

Answering the question is difficult because of a mundane fact. Tastes differ. What some people, perhaps especially people like Mill and me, hail as the most significant artistic accomplishments leave others, even a large majority of the human population, entirely cold. To take aesthetic experience seriously is to seek a selection of works capable of providing, for *all* of the young, access to episodes with the Deweyan virtues: moments of intense vitality, encounters that transform future experience, opportunities for new insights and the development of refined emotions. If you take all the varieties of art to be equally capable of delivering the goods, and each person to be individually inclined to a different range of modes and genres and periods, a democratic curriculum in the arts appears as an enormous monster, ready to devour all available time.

Educators confronted with that vision can, perhaps, be forgiven for insisting on a privileged canon. They believe, or at least give lip service to, the *Elitist Thesis*: A relatively small collection of works of art are the pinnacles of artistic achievement; presenting students with these, and these alone, provides all of them with access to experiences rich in the Deweyan virtues. What, then, to make of the vast numbers of people who are completely unmoved by the canonical works—people who would prefer to listen to reggae rather than Beethoven, to read fantasy literature instead of Victorian novels? To save the Elitist Thesis, you need to diagnose those people either as the victims of inadequate teaching or as suffering from some defect— insensitivity, indolence, or the like. Neither version of the diagnosis is compelling. Although many, perhaps most, American adults are uninterested in

274 THE MAIN ENTERPRISE OF THE WORLD

the arts, except as providing entertainment, some of those whom canonical works leave utterly cold display an extraordinary interest in and enthusiasm for art in other modes and genres, or from other times and places. Elitists must come to terms with the empirical facts: alternatives to the orthodox canon sometimes seem capable of delivering the goods, when the supposedly privileged works do not; and there appears to be a wide range of such alternatives.

At this point a different line of solution arises. Egalitarians advise educators not to worry. *All* the works of art, high or low, that turn people on yield the same opportunities. Education in the arts is extremely easy. So easy that art can safely be cut from the curriculum. Each person will find his way to the bits of culture he finds satisfying. All will end up enjoying the same sorts of experiences.

Adopting this style of egalitarianism depends on denying any special status to aesthetic experience (as well as ignoring the role creative production plays in deepening tastes). Nothing separates the experiences of the reader deeply moved by *Madame Bovary* from the person who folds the laundry while the TV shows *Days of Our Lives*, or divides the listener absorbed in the *St. Matthew Passion* from the subway rider plugged in to a casually chosen playlist. Champions of the importance of art should reject egalitarian flattening. Access to the vital, transforming moments varies across the course of an individual's life. Sometimes, when the sensitive reader or musically educated listener is tired or distracted, even the works she regards as richest fail to work their usual magic. For most of us, there are occasions on which undemanding entertainment is exactly what we need—times when a gripping TV thriller does more for us than the art films of our favorite director, when a Sudoku puzzle is preferable to Shakespeare, when pushpin is more appropriate than poetry. Observed *intra*personal variation rebuts double-barreled egalitarianism, with its refusal to differentiate either works or experiences.

Moderate egalitarians extend the point. Perhaps *inter*personal variation displays the same pattern. Some fortunate people find their way to works offering repeated experiences with the Deweyan virtues. Others never do.[32] For the less lucky people, encounters with artworks never give more than

---

[32] J. K. Rowling is often applauded for "getting kids hooked on reading." That commendation underrates her achievement. On the level of the individual sentences, Rowling is no great stylist. She is, however, absolutely masterly in her construction of a rich and complex fictional world. She not only prepares the way for children to explore other forms of fantasy literature, but, I conjecture, to appreciate the complexities of novels to which literary scholars devote their lives. We should all be grateful for her educational impact.

entertainment and transient pleasure. Aesthetic experience never figures in their lives. So far, apparently a kind of elitism. But the differentiation of experiences and of lives according to their aesthetic richness can be coupled with an appreciation of the many different modes of art capable of generating vital and transformative episodes.[33] The moderate egalitarian can deny the existence of any privileged canon, and call for reform of an educational system exclusively devoted to "high culture." I endorse that species of moderate egalitarianism. More exactly, I propose three conjectures:

A. Many American adults live lives almost completely bereft of aesthetic experiences (episodes rich in the Deweyan virtues).
B. Most (perhaps almost all) of these people would have been able to enjoy such experiences, if they had had a different education in the arts, perhaps one that took a much wider view of the arts (including, perhaps, possibilities of creative expression in activities like cooking and gardening). Unfortunately, the works presented to them during the course of their years in school (and possibly at university) were not suited to trigger their capacities for aesthetic experience.
C. For each person, there is a range of works capable of generating a life with many significant aesthetic experiences—call that collection of works the person's *favorites*. There are massive differences among the favorites of the American population, differences in types of art, styles, genres, cultures, and periods.

The egalitarian strain in this position surfaces in recognizing the potential for aesthetic experience in people who are badly served by current education in the arts, and in the recognition of a wide diversity of works as able to actualize that potential. The collection of all the works belonging to someone's favorites—the union of all the sets of favorites—is expected to be very large indeed. But not, I conjecture, to contain every work of art ever produced. Not by a long shot.

---

[33] J. M. Coetzee's essay, "What Is a Classic?," in *Stranger Shores* (New York: Penguin, 2001), 1–16, offers an alternative way of making the distinction Dewey celebrates. The works yielding rich aesthetic experiences are those counting as classics (in Coetzee's first sense)—they continue to "live." Moderate egalitarians will not suppose that some works live for (virtually) all while others live for (virtually) none, thus generating a division between the canonical and non-canonical. They view the sets of works that live for different people as diverse, possibly with no significant intersections. The search for the "true canon" thus becomes misguided. (Thanks to Natalia Rogach Alexander for referring me to Coetzee's essay.)

276 THE MAIN ENTERPRISE OF THE WORLD

Moderate egalitarianism parallels my earlier critique of education in the sciences. Just as many students are turned off science for life by the curriculum through which they suffer, so too for the arts. Hence arises a need for reform. Not only should art remain in the curriculum, but the works students encounter ought to be far more varied. Recognizing the great diversity among favorites raises again the specter of the art-monster, poised to consume a vast number of school hours. Improving science education turns out to be the easy case.

Before offering some suggestions about tackling this difficult problem, objections must be heard. Extreme egalitarians would challenge the phenomenological reports used to support claims of difference between aesthetic experience and "mere" entertainment. A blunt question: why take the glorification of "vital" or "transformative" or "illuminating" encounters with artworks to be anything more than self-deception, perhaps produced by cultural brainwashing? My answer begins with a concession. The variation in people's reactions to artworks deserves far more systematic study than it has so far received. Further psychological and sociological investigations might expose the evidential weakness of the qualitative differences to which champions of aesthetic experience point.

But differences there are. People passionate about painting or films or music or literature behave very differently from those who treat artworks as pleasant entertainment. Aficionados discuss their favorite works with others, they describe the effects those works have had on their own subsequent reflections, they return to the same works again and again and report discovering new inspiration in them, and the passion often glows in their animated accounts. Sometimes, they go to great lengths to learn more about the background of their favorites. These features contrast sharply with a prevailing tendency to treat other books or pictures or movies or songs as disposable goods, something apt for the moment but nothing to cherish.

How might the character of these apparent differences be better understood? Two lines of inquiry suggest themselves. The first would study the attitudes of those originally unmoved by the artistic education they received, but who later discover an art form they find truly exciting. Presumably these people have escaped any brainwashing by the art-educational establishment, and might be especially valuable on the felt differences between their earlier interactions with artworks and the later experiences with their newfound favorites. The second would explore the reactions of deeply religious people. They might be asked to compare their attitudes to the works of secular art

THE ARTS 277

they turn to for entertainment with their experiences of the stories of their scriptures, of the visual arts used to adorn their sites of worship, and with the music associated with their rituals. Do they feel a greater depth and import, when the art is set in a religious frame?

In advance of knowing what such inquiries (and other potential investigations) would show, I shall rest with a speculative thesis. Moderate egalitarianism is correct. The problem of education in the arts is thus a genuine one.

What can be done about it?

The first, and most important, task is to establish a bridgehead. During the very early school years, children should be introduced to a variety of arts. The initial search would be for works that excite them. At this stage it would be crucial not only to offer a diverse set of options, but also to observe the individual reactions. Thus, as Chapter 2 proposed, the classroom should contain a large number of adults—teachers, aides, parents, volunteers—all with their own aesthetic passions. Children explore alternative types of art, both as potential creators and as appreciators. Art forms, genres, and styles that leave them indifferent are temporarily removed from the choices offered to them. The adults who mentor them try to guide them to a small but diverse collection of arts—perhaps one type of literature, one species of performing art, one genre of visual art—that they find particularly fascinating.

The second stage allows them to explore their chosen art forms further. Now they no longer attend art class with their age peers, but find themselves among others who share their interests. The goal is to develop the skills required for creation, and the understanding needed for appreciation. Children are allowed to strike their individual balance between creation and appreciation. While they are encouraged to spend time on the techniques and styles they find most appealing, they are also urged to pursue aspects of the chosen form they initially find difficult or off-putting. Throughout, the extensive records kept by the mentors at the first stage are used to suggest directions of further development. Particularly when a child's original enthusiasm wanes, the early propensities offer clues about how to find an appropriate modification or even a substitute.

Once a bridgehead has been established, once a child has found a small cluster of arts she finds rewarding, education enters its third phase. Some of the time is now assigned to broadening from the bridgehead. Children

278   THE MAIN ENTERPRISE OF THE WORLD

are asked to return to art forms, genres, and styles they originally rejected, reappraising them in light of the skills and tastes they have since developed. Mentors guide them in discerning similarities between works they admire and others they find dull, or alien, or baffling. Teachers and aides who are passionate about the unattractive works point out how those works have qualities not possessed by the favorites. With a combination of individual attention, critical skill and (probably) a bit of luck, the child's artistic compass expands. New styles and genres are taken up in the fashion already exemplified at stage two. Here too, appreciation and creative work (expanding skills) must be pursued in tandem. So it continues through the school years.

And after as well. Adults, too, need opportunities to develop their tastes, to learn about styles of art they have not previously explored, even to develop creative skills in fields that are new for them. (As I have discovered in my belated efforts at drawing, it is never too late to learn.) School education ought to be embedded in a milieu containing cultural centers, spaces for further training and for exhibiting and sharing works of art. Those centers, freely available to all, would embody opportunities for mutual learning. Aesthetic exchange would be part of deep democracy.

Would it work? Nobody can know in advance. As before, I offer suggestions for educational experiments. The program just outlined could be developed in many alternative ways, but it would start with the well-documented interest young children show in different kinds of art. Integrating creative activities with occasions for appreciation, including explorations of the natural environment, can be used not only to build technical skills—learning to draw the contours of everyday objects or to sing simple melodies in tune—but also to indicate where a child's interests might lie. As Dewey famously advised, art should be part of everyday activities.[34] Aesthetic sense is developed as young students learn to arrange the objects in a small space, to design part of a flower bed, or to choose recorded music to accompany a short dramatic performance. With luck, the developed sense carries over into later life, and into the ways adults set up, maintain, and modify their environments.

As with the sciences, the most critical achievement would be preserving the curiosity and joy that typically accompany young children's artistic activities. So long as the time spent in dance or song or carving or play-acting or photography continues to be deeply satisfying, art can occupy a large part of the curriculum without short-changing other educational domains. Simply

[34] In *Democracy and Education*, and *Art as Experience*.

THE ARTS 279

expand the school day. If the extra hours are given over to activities the students enjoy, consumer resistance is less likely. Moreover, an elongated day would provide for all students the opportunities many professional couples currently purchase for their children.

———————

As with the earlier discussion of scientific education, I'll sum up the sketch of a program as a series of proposals for experimentation:

23. *During the early elementary school grades, offer students a wide range of alternatives in the arts (visual arts, performing arts, and literature). Introduce different genres and styles, as well as the arts of different cultures and periods. Mix creative work with opportunities for appreciation.*

24. *Provide serious individual attention to each child. During the time spent on art, the classroom should contain a large number of adults (possibly as many as one adult per child), with different aesthetic interests. Careful records of each student's interests and aptitudes should be kept, and periodically reviewed by the adults who mentor the child.*

25. *As a particular profile of interest and indifference emerges, offer opportunities for deeper exploration of areas, styles, or genres the child finds particularly attractive. At this stage, art education should no longer group children by age but by interest. Classrooms should contain students fascinated by some particular art form, with more advanced students encouraged to help those who are at earlier stages.*

26. *Punctuate the more specialized education with periods at which the children return to a common age group. During these times, they are asked to exchange their enthusiasms with one another, and also to explore genres and media they had previously rejected.*

27. *At all stages of aesthetic education, bring the creative and appreciative activities into everyday tasks and link them to the world beyond the school. Provide opportunities for projects, individual and collective, in which parts of the local environment are designed and subsequently modified. Use photography and film to show the variety of the natural world and of the human-made environment. Arrange excursions for older children to experience places that might inspire artistic projects.*

28. *Combine all this with opportunities for adults, throughout their lives, to develop their aesthetic sense and to acquire new creative skills. Establish*

280 THE MAIN ENTERPRISE OF THE WORLD

> *community centers dedicated to exhibiting, discussing, and teaching
> the arts. These centers could also support democratic decision-making
> about modification of the local environment.*

Overall, the experimental program demands much greater support for education in the arts. It takes seriously the idea of aesthetic experience, experience rich in the Deweyan virtues, as centrally important to human lives. It seeks to enrich the worlds in which each person lives. If it were to succeed, wouldn't that count as *real* progress?

9

Understanding Ourselves

The English language divides the educational spectrum into four parts. Between the natural sciences and the arts lie the social sciences (including economics, sociology, and political science) and the humanities (languages and literature, and philosophy). History and anthropology lack assured places, sometimes appearing in one subdivision, sometimes in the other. Psychology too finds no stable home, assigned either to the social or the natural sciences by different taxonomists. Other cultures simplify, and thus resolve the ambiguities. German, for example, separates the *Naturwissenschaften* from the *Geisteswissenschaften*—the natural sciences from studies dealing with mind and culture.[1] By doing so, it recognizes an important kinship. Whatever the differences among their methods, the sprawl of research areas between the arts and the natural sciences is concerned to advance our understanding of ourselves. These domains of inquiry aim to disclose significant aspects of human life and of human societies.

Enthusiasm for the achievements of the natural sciences, expressed in celebrations of their impressive progress, easily inspires impatience and disdain for more tentative forms of investigation. Respect can grow into worship, breeding a new religion: scientism. For the scientistic faithful, the intermediate zones are backward and primitive, dominated by superstition and pretense, offering ill-supported, misleading, and potentially dangerous "findings."[2] At best, they are temporary substitutes for the serious

---

[1] The great explorer of the differences between the two *Wissenschaften* is Wilhelm Dilthey. He makes much of the distinction, and considers the possibility of studying the methods of the *Geisteswissenschaften* in ways parallel to those philosophers have developed for the natural sciences. Perhaps because of the widespread neglect of his writings, this interesting possibility has rarely been taken seriously—although Dewey's interest in a general account of method in all areas of inquiry can be viewed as an independent step in the same direction. (I am grateful to Raine Daston for recommending a text in which Dilthey makes this important point with unusual succinctness.)

[2] A classic source of this approach appears in E. O. Wilson, *Sociobiology: The New Synthesis* (Cambridge, MA: Harvard University Press, 1975). It is echoed by Alexander Rosenberg, *The Atheist's Guide to Reality* (New York: W. W. Norton, 2013) and *How History Gets Things Wrong* (Cambridge, MA: MIT Press, 2018). Apparently (but only apparently) less harsh are some of Steven Pinker's writings; see "Science Is Not Your Enemy" (*The New Republic*, August 6, 2012; https://newrepublic.com/article/114127/science-not-enemy-humanities) and *Enlightenment Now* (New York: Penguin, 2018). In a later issue of *The New Republic*, Leon Wieseltier responded to Pinker in "Crimes against Humanities"; https://newrepublic.com/article/114548/leon-wieseltier-responds-steven-pinkers-scientism.

The Main Enterprise of the World. Philip Kitcher, Oxford University Press. © Oxford University Press 2022.
DOI: 10.1093/oso/9780190928971.003.0010

282 THE MAIN ENTERPRISE OF THE WORLD

investigation and genuine knowledge to be delivered once the relevant parts of real science—evolutionary psychology, neuropsychology, neuroeconomics, and the like—have come to the fruition they already promise. Perhaps, for the moment, some fragments of educational time should be allotted to social sciences and the humanities. Instruction should, however, always be accompanied by clear acknowledgment of their shortcomings. The evangelists of scientism loudly protest the idea of displaying the Ten Commandments in the classroom. Their scorn for the humanities and social sciences often suggests that they would prefer to substitute a different placard, one akin to the warnings governments use to discourage the purchase of some products: "Non-scientific subjects can be harmful to your mental hygiene and your psychological health."

Scientism is an overreaction to an unfortunate tardiness in the history of education. Long after the natural sciences had displayed their prowess, proficiency in classical studies remained the hallmark of the "educated man."[3] That requirement lapsed in the twentieth century. Today the prestige awarded to those capable of writing Greek hexameters appears quaint. Yet the rise of scientism, apparently tilting the scale in the opposite direction, often provokes counterattack. Already in the 1960s, prominent humanists were prepared to take up the cudgels. In my last undergraduate year in Cambridge, the university extended its support for the annual collegiate drama festival by recruiting eminent members of the faculty to give lunchtime talks on the plays to be performed. My own college dramatic society was rehearsing *The Imaginary Invalid*, and we invited the distinguished critic George Steiner to speak to us. His presentation was brilliant—and forthright. One claim he made has remained with me ever since: "Molière and Stendhal have taught us more about what it is to be human than all the psychologists there have ever been, combined."[4]

Steiner's dictum is an exaggeration—even if, in times when the humanities are suspect and the social sciences are viewed as poor relatives of their natural cousins, it is a necessary pushback against the evangelists of scientism. Psychology, pursued from a diversity of perspectives, has enlightened us about many aspects of human mental life and of human behavior,

---

[3] This was particularly evident in the evolution of the British university, where, until the mid-nineteenth-century, only mathematics was assigned a status remotely approximating that given to the study of classical languages and literature.

[4] I am not sure that these were Steiner's exact words, but I have no doubt that he made just this comparison.

UNDERSTANDING OURSELVES 283

sometimes through understanding the lives of other animals, often by controlled observations of human behavior. Laboratory studies have enlarged the understanding of perception, memory, emotional responses, decision-making, perspective-sharing, and other significant mental processes. These achievements do not displace the contributions of playwrights and novelists, nor are they superseded by them. Learning can, and should, come from all directions. Understanding human life, of the individual and of the group, is best advanced through the *interaction* of disciplines. Marking off particular areas of inquiry as barren—"Nothing there for me!"—is a foolish dogmatism, whether it serves as the proud credo of the scientistically devout or as the reprimand of a great literary critic.[5]

The fruitfulness of fostering interdisciplinary interaction should be a commonplace. *Of course*, the playwright and the art historian should learn from the natural sciences. Old-fashioned medicine and old-fashioned conceptions of the mind are easily forgiven in classic dramas—audiences indulge Elizabethan references to humors and vital spirits. Outdated scientific ideas would often (but not always) prove jarring in a modern play or film. On the other hand, successor notions, drawn from the contemporary sciences, can provide vivid material for writers and spectators alike.[6] Similarly, applications of physics and chemistry, to study the changes in appearance that pigments undergo, assist art historians (and, more directly, those who undertake restoration). *Equally*, the arrow of illumination can point in the opposite direction. Many of the advances in early modern science were prompted by new techniques of pictorial representation.[7] Copernican astronomy, as its originator confessed, was inspired by literary and philosophical views about the centrality of the sun.[8] Darwin famously gained the idea of natural selection by "reading Malthus on population" (for "enjoyment," it

[5] Steiner may well have been reacting in part to a famous lecture by one of his Cambridge predecessors, C. P. Snow. Snow's controversial "Two Cultures" quite reasonably worried about the asymmetry of accusing those who know nothing of literary classics of gross ignorance, while withholding the charge from people who are clueless about the Second Law of Thermodynamics. Snow's position is milder than the scientism that has since emerged, but, for reasons canvassed in the previous two chapters, I regard his conception of education in the sciences (and in the arts) as profoundly misguided. In "Two Forms of Blindness: On the Need for Both Cultures" (*Technology in Society*, 32, no. 1 [2010]: 40–48), I offer a more detailed assessment of Snow's lecture.

[6] As, for example, with Kazuo Ishiguro's *Never Let Me Go* (New York: Knopf, 2005).

[7] Pamela Smith, *The Body of the Artisan: Art and Experience in the Scientific Revolution* (Chicago: University of Chicago Press, 2004).

[8] A point forcefully made by Thomas Kuhn in *The Copernican Revolution* (Cambridge, MA: Harvard University Press, 1957). Kuhn quotes telling passages from the Preface to *De Revolutionibus*.

284 THE MAIN ENTERPRISE OF THE WORLD

was his evening reading!).[9] We should also recall his wistful regret about the loss of his literary taste, expressed in a conditional resolution: if he were to live his life over again, he would vow to "read a little poetry every day."[10]

Even more obviously, efforts to study human life, human society, human behavior, and human culture, however they may be undertaken, cannot afford to neglect the reflections offered by anthropologists, historians, literary critics, poets, and novelists. So I amend Steiner's dictum to envisage an interactive alliance among highly diverse domains of study. Our best attempt to understand ourselves should make use of all available resources, and the capacities required for full employment of them should be instilled in schooling the young.

The task of this chapter is to articulate this manifesto more precisely—to explain more clearly how the envisaged alliance might work.

———

One way of proceeding would be to emulate Mill: review in sequence the various disciplines, the branches of social science and the humanities, identify their "greatest hits," and then consider what parts of each are needed for a proper education (and, perhaps, at what stage they should be introduced). I shall not follow that route. Instead, I shall proceed in parallel to the course charted in the previous chapters, seeking to understand the ways in which this part of the curriculum might advance the large goals identified in Part I. The main divergence from the treatment of the natural sciences will stem from the potential for using different parts of the humanities and social sciences in concert with one another. Having pointed to a particular style of benefit—increase in self-understanding, for example—I'll consider how this diverse cluster of domains might contribute, and, in particular, how *interactions* among elements drawn from different disciplines might promote the envisaged goal.

---

[9] "In October 1838, that is, fifteen months after I had begun my systematic inquiry, I happened to read for amusement Malthus on *Population*, and being well prepared to appreciate the struggle for existence which everywhere goes on from long-continued observation of the habits of animals and plants, it at once struck me that under these circumstances favourable variations would tend to be preserved, and unfavourable ones to be destroyed. The results of this would be the formation of a new species. Here, then I had at last got a theory by which to work." Charles Darwin, *Autobiography*, originally written in 1876, first published in 1887 (New York: Norton, 1969).

[10] "[I]f I had to live my life again I would have made a rule to read some poetry and listen to some music at least once every week; for perhaps the parts of my brain now atrophied could thus have been kept active through use." Charles Darwin, *Autobiography*.

Earlier chapters have presented a vision of education as helping the young in three ways: providing them with the ability to maintain themselves, developing citizens and responsible moral agents, and fostering capacities for leading fulfilling lives. I shall begin with the last, postponing the benefits with respect to self-maintenance to the very end of this chapter.

A fulfilling life has been conceived as one in which the individual person arrives at a sense of self, expressed in an autonomous choice of life plan (or plans) that makes its (their) own distinctive contributions to the human project. Enhancing the self-understanding of the young is plainly relevant to their chances of choosing wisely. Moreover, understanding the diversity of human lives, the different circumstances in which people live and the (often narrow) range of opportunities available to them, promotes awareness of where and how an individual might contribute to the lives of others. From all sorts of angles, the *Geisteswissenschaften* help people fashion their ideals of themselves, guiding them to find worthwhile ends to pursue.

Autonomous choice of your way of life depends on a delicate dialogue between the growing individual and the ambient society. Social pressures can diminish autonomy by closing off attractive paths. Barriers can be constructed and obstacles introduced in two different ways. Societies can impose outright bans: women cannot have access to higher education—or even to any education at all; members of a particular caste (or ethnic group) may only pursue a limited number of occupations. Or, as is far more common in the contemporary world, they can couple *de jure* possibility to a *de facto* constraint: "Of course, any African American child can become a lawyer"—but, without jobs for the sole parent, without a place in which to live, and with access only to schools awash in drugs and crime, staffed by a rotating corps of disillusioned teachers, any real prospects for a legal career are dashed at the start.[11] Complacent political leaders preen themselves on the existence of "opportunities for all," overlooking the myriad ways in which the obstacles to taking advantage of the alleged "opportunities" crush the hopes and aspirations of the young.

The delicate dialogue goes awry in two distinct ways, limiting autonomy by closing off potential lines of development *and* by failing to provide the

---

[11] The American Bar Association's profile of the legal profession gives the figure of 5 percent for the percentage of African-American lawyers, less than half the percentage of African Americans in the US population. (The ABA takes this latter percentage to be 13.6; estimates vary, with 12–13 percent as a popular range.) For the ABA report, see https://www.americanbar.org/news/reporter_resources/profile-of-profession/.

286   THE MAIN ENTERPRISE OF THE WORLD

support needed to grow in attractive directions. The latter failure is most evident in the material conditions of existence. Homeless people, or people mired in poverty or trapped in neighborhoods overrun by gang violence, need food, clean water, clean air, medical care, and safe shelter. Beyond these necessities,[12] their children also require schools to which they can go without fear—schools that will offer them genuine chances of finding out where their talents lie and what kinds of life might prove fulfilling. In delivering those chances, the humanities and social sciences have an important role to play.

Formal education is central to the cultivation of positive freedom, of freedom *to* rather than freedom *from*.[13] Children should learn who they are and what kinds of people they might realistically become. Without resources to identify their distinctive talents and interests, or to understand what kinds of lives are available to them, their autonomy is diminished. The dialogue between growing individual and society is unhealthy, not because the voices of authority issue decrees forbidding a large range of options, but because those voices are virtually silent when it comes to positive suggestions. They supply no conceptual nourishment on which the developing imagination can fasten.

How exactly can the humanities supply what is lacking? Through making vivid the diverse possibilities for a human life. Literature, drama, film, and the visual arts can all stimulate the young imagination, revealing ways in which human beings might live, how they might prosper, and how their lives might prove miserable and empty. History ranges across time to add detailed portraits of parts of the actual past. Geography and ethnography are comparably expansive across space.

In the earliest years of schooling, children are rightly expected to acquire basic skills. They must learn how to read and write,[14] to add, subtract, and so forth. These capacities will be called on as they explore the rich possibilities of human existence. Yet, even at the start, they can be captivated by stories, vivid tales of the past, accounts of life in strange—and exotic—places. Long before they are able to probe the details of forms of life, to appreciate nuances

---

[12] The next chapter takes up the question of supplying the material necessities.

[13] As noted above, the Anglo-Saxon political tradition emphasizes Isaiah Berlin's "negative freedom" and tends to ignore its positive counterpart. The imbalance is especially evident in the United States, where a tradition of seeing government as required only to "keep other people out of your way" reinforces a faith in laissez-faire economics. In its extreme form, this culminates in magical thinking: just so long as they are allowed to tap their own resources, all children have the chance to succeed. The myth of Horatio Alger dies hard.

[14] Whether future children will need to spend hours practicing penmanship seems to me a tricky question. Perhaps the ability to write legibly might be a by-product of teaching the young how to draw?

UNDERSTANDING OURSELVES 287

of success and failure, of virtue and moral error, they can thrill to simple pictures, entranced by great heroes and heroines, appalled by villains—and recognize that the patterns of their familiar life are not the only possibilities.

Once reading skills have advanced sufficiently far, a more systematic evaluation of alternative modes of existence becomes possible. Geography and history classes can contain segments in which children learn the details of life in different contemporary places, at different times in the past of their own society, and in circumstances remote both in time and space. Some parts of their study should include arranging conditions enabling them to *feel* such alien forms of existence. By this, I don't intend the pallid exercises in which children bring to the classroom a motley of dishes allegedly representing those consumed by their forebears—and then sit down to a more-or-less palatable common meal. Rather, they should learn how to make the implements required to grow the crops, they should plant and tend them, prepare the food—and, if all goes well, share in a convivial final feast. Along the way, they should be asked to solve, individually and collectively, the problems that would have arisen for the community whose way of life they are exploring. Work of this type also allows for practice in applying mathematical skills and coping with the kinds of situations experimental scientists face daily.[15]

All this paves the way for deeper engagement with a small number of (diverse) forms of life during the last few years in secondary school. A possible strategy for organizing this: require each student to choose a particular place and period, to spend a significant part of the school year (perhaps all of it?) researching how people lived there and then, culminating in a detailed historico-ethnographic report and a presentation to fellow students. At each step of the way, students would have opportunities to consult with knowledgeable mentors (recall the importance of involving *many* adults in the classroom). They would be expected to read widely, and to treat some aspects of the alien culture in great detail.

The three phases envisaged in this program are intended to help students discover two things. Early training prepares them to enter deeply into lives very different from their own. As they choose to focus on groups of people, located at particular places and times, they discover what aspects of cultural life interest them most, and they are asked to understand the demands and constraints experienced by people very different from themselves. One

---

[15] Here I follow Dewey in deploying practical activities to integrate the curriculum. See *Democracy and Education* (MW 9).

288   THE MAIN ENTERPRISE OF THE WORLD

goal is to bring them to recognize their own proclivities, thus helping them to chart a satisfying direction for their own careers. Another is to expand their consciousness of human needs, their ability to see and feel from other perspectives.

As they grow, they should discover how to read a particular style of history, not that focused on the large affairs of states, on rulers and conquests and sweeping social reforms—that has a different place in the curriculum. Rather, they are asked to attend to the details of everyday life. Reading not only historical analyses, but also primary documents, they are expected to enter into the lives of others. Along the way, depending on their focal society, they may need to absorb, and apply, some parts of economics and sociology. To the extent their education succeeds, the skills they acquire are likely to prove valuable throughout their lives, as their pursuit of their favored projects leads them to actions with consequences for distant strangers. They will be prepared not to view those whom they affect remotely as faceless masses, and (with luck) they will be inspired to inquire and to reflect before implementing their plans. ·

So far, an interdisciplinary program whose contributory domains are primarily geography and history, as well as those parts of anthropology flowing naturally from their explorations. Other areas of social science—economics, sociology, political science, and psychology—may also put in appearances. As they proceed with the individual studies of their later school years, this program should also be in dialogue with central areas of the humanities. None of the special inquiries would be complete without attending to the literary and artistic traditions of the group studied. Thus in their classes in literature, music, and visual art, students should have opportunities to engage with the writings (or with the poems and stories passed on in oral traditions), the music, the paintings, sculptures, and architecture of the groups on which they have chosen to focus. Here, too, they will need guidance, benefiting from interactions with mentors who can help them in the work of interpretation.

For this to succeed, they must first be taught how to read, how to listen, and how to see. While the primary materials with which they engage are works of art, their ability to engage profitably with them will depend on historians and critics, specialists in understanding and analyzing literature or painting or song. The later studies of the secondary school (as I have envisaged them) can only succeed if there are people trained in the humanities who can enable their pupils to find in works of art what those works have to offer. Historians of art and music, like literary critics, are mediators, "liaison officers,"[16] revealing precious insights in works that would be misunderstood, or dismissed as incomprehensible, without their guidance. The art historian invites students to attend to the relation between two areas of a canvas. The architectural historian points to the curve of a cornice and its echo in the shape of windows. The musicologist plays a short figure on the piano, before accompanying a recording of an orchestral work with exaggerated gestures, inviting hearers to recognize the recurrence of that figure.[17] The literary critic points out the overtones and ambiguities of particular words in a lyric poem.

In the beginning, none of us knows how to do similar things for ourselves. We need instruction from people who have acquired the pertinent skills and who know how to convey them to others. Among the school staff there should be teachers who have so deep an understanding of particular genres as to make works of the pertinent types come alive for their students. Humanists, specifically historians and critics of literature, art, music, film, and drama, are needed at two levels. Researchers advance the interpretation of the nineteenth-century novel, or of science fiction, or of conceptual art, or of Renaissance sculpture, or of film noir, or of the Romantic song cycle, or of Greek tragedy, or of television docudramas, or. . . . Their achievements are registered in their own teaching (typically at universities) and in their critical writings. As they frame the work of interpreting their focal genre(s), they enable their students and readers to see how to go on. Armed with the skills acquired by steeping themselves in the research level, these students and readers form a cadre at a second level, one that makes direct contact with pupils in secondary schools (and, perhaps, at earlier educational stages). Humanists at this second level are, and should be, less specialized. They ought to range more broadly, over the visual arts of a number of periods or through the grand sweep of poetry in their native language, for example. The task for them is to instill in those they teach precursor capacities to those their own education has given them. From the first stages of adolescence (if not before),

[16] I borrow the phrase from Dewey, who characterizes philosophy as "a liaison officer, making reciprocally intelligible voices speaking provincial tongues." *Experience and Nature* (LW 1) 306.

[17] The examples I have chosen derive from memories of powerful lectures given by Michael Fried, Robert Harrist, Alfred Brendel, and Elaine Sissman. Thomas Mann clearly appreciated the role played by the mediating scholar. In his *Doctor Faustus*, the central protagonist, Adrian Leverkühn, learns much from the public lectures of his teacher, Wendell Kretzschmar—and Mann gives a vivid description of the exaggerated gestures and loud singing with which Kretzschmar accompanies the late Beethoven piano sonatas, thus conveying their structure.

290   THE MAIN ENTERPRISE OF THE WORLD

their pupils should have the chance to learn to read and see and hear, not in the elementary ways of the very young, but with attention to nuance and subtlety. The childhood passion inspired by Jo March may endure, but it is set within an understanding of the strengths and foibles of Elizabeth Bennett and Hester Prynne—perhaps even of Dorothea Brooke, Isabel Archer, and Mrs. Dalloway.

Because of the considerations raised in the previous chapter, specifically the need to recognize the different proclivities of young people and to cater to all of them (or, at least, as many as possible), schools don't just need *some* second-level humanists. A number of people, *with diverse tastes and interests*, should move through the secondary school classroom. Not all of them need to be trained teachers. The principal teachers of literature, music, and art should not only offer their own wide repertoire of genres, but also supplement and coordinate the visits of others who can introduce an even broader array of works of art. Using their own interpretive skills, they should seek ways of helping their students come alive to the features that excite the visitors who bring their distinctive enthusiasms. Advising pupils who are stirred to similar enthusiasms, they oversee their further development as interpreters, guiding them to suitable mentors and translating what those mentors convey into formulations apt for inculcating enhanced skills. Humanist teachers thus become liaison officers in two different senses: they mediate directly between some works of art and their students, and indirectly between those students and other potential liaison officers, whose fluency is inadequate to convey the messages they hope to offer.

Data on the performance of American students in mathematics and science are far better known than the gloomy statistics about the reading of American adults. One recent survey gives a figure of 27 percent for the population of adults who have not read any book (*or even a part of any book*) within the prior year.[18] Almost 50 percent of American adults had read at least part of *at most* three books in that period. In the "league table" of adult readers, the United States ranked an equal twenty-second (tied with Germany). Other figures show a decline in the amount of time spent per day in leisure reading, from the first decade of the twenty-first century to the second. How much of whatever reading occurs might contribute to self-understanding is anybody's guess. I have not been able to track down any statistics for reading

---

[18] Pew Survey 2019. This includes electronic media as well as print.

UNDERSTANDING OURSELVES   291

fiction—let alone for novels and short stories capable of stimulating reflection (rather than page-turners). Nevertheless, one trend has encouraged some educators.[19] Whereas in 2012, only 7 percent of American adults had read a poem in the previous year, the figure for 2017 was 11.7 percent.

Overall, it seems fair to conclude that American schools (and universities!) do not generate a swarm of avid readers, eager to garner the benefits I have attributed to engagement with literature.

Chapter 7 lamented the quenching of scientific curiosity. Equally, educators ought to worry about the quashing of interest in literature. Why do so many people abandon reading once their formal education (whether at school or at university) is completed? There are obvious potential explanations. Many of those who graduate from secondary schools, or even colleges, may always have found reading difficult. They may have struggled through the materials assigned to them, and felt relief when they no longer have to exercise basic skills they know to be incomplete and inadequate. Alternatively, the "golden age of television" could have inspired a turn to watching series (documentaries or dramas) offering occasions for reflection and promoting greater self-understanding. No available data support so hopeful a conclusion. For the past decade, the most popular television turns out to be sports events (particularly what Americans call "football");[20] previous decades showed clear preferences for comedy and drama series, some of them surely rewarding to watch and providing food for thought.[21] Whether popularity aligns with the verdicts of critics who hail television's "golden age" seems dubious.[22] A conjecture: the people who were gripped throughout all the seasons of *The Wire* and *Homeland* are also people who continue to read books.

The goal of making Americans great readers (and great observers and great listeners) again is educationally important. Achieving it surely demands a serious campaign to help all children become fluent readers by

---

[19] The survey, conducted by the National Endowment for the Arts, is reported at https://psmag.com/education/why-are-more-americans-reading-poetry-right-now.

[20] As the previous chapter noted, athletic events may be viewed as having aesthetic qualities (see 272 n.30). The case for that view might be accompanied by defending the idea of sports as promoting self-understanding—perhaps through revealing possibilities of cooperation and teamwork?

[21] For some data, see https://en.wikipedia.org/wiki/Top-rated_United_States_television_programs_by_season.

[22] But perhaps I am falling into a trap identified by Alexander Nehamas in his brilliant *Only a Promise of Happiness* (Princeton, NJ: Princeton University Press, 2007), snobbishly dismissing popular television shows (Nehamas's examples are *Frasier*, *Oz*, and *St. Elsewhere*). For insightful and eloquent defenses of the aesthetic worth and philosophical promise of television, see 47, 80, 93, and 128.

292 THE MAIN ENTERPRISE OF THE WORLD

the time of their adolescence. It also requires more. Literacy should be understood as a matter of degree—all of us, including the most adept readers, are inevitably imperfectly literate: there will *always* be some kinds of writing in our native language we find difficult, even impenetrable. Formal education, through the secondary school, ought to provide each pupil with a profile in reading ability sufficient to make accessible—indeed *pleasurably* accessible—a range of written texts capable of yielding the principal fruits of literacy. In particular, it should prepare them to read, with curiosity, interest, and joy, works able to prompt reflection and enhanced self-understanding. To achieve that goal (or some reasonable approximation to it), I suggest strengthening the connections between the two levels of humanists. Teachers of literature in secondary schools should have a passion for the genres they introduce to their pupils, combined with strong interpretive skills. They should be given the opportunities to refine those skills, and to extend them to other styles through periodic leaves that enable them to work with scholars engaged in humanistic research. Their schools should contain enough colleagues to form a community, regularly interacting with one another. The community would constantly be renewed by its contacts with research, in which the individual members can continue to develop and grow.

Parallel points apply to the visual arts and to music. Indeed, the *status quo* in these areas is almost certainly more dismal. Because education in the non-literary arts is so frequently curtailed, lopped off in times of budgetary shortage, visual and auditory literacy only attain more primitive levels. In these areas, the liaison officers are fewer, the time assigned to their mediatory work is minimal, and the range of material they might be expected to introduce far too extensive. Like their colleagues in literature, they need to enhance their own capacities for sensitive seeing and listening, to recognize their fundamental task as one in which similar skills are germinated and developed in their students, and to find vital ways of conveying what is required. Teachers of art and music should have the chance to learn from scholars, critics, and historians of art and music, who engage in research, and sometimes change the framework within which works of art are understood.

Very few young people are fortunate enough (as I once was) to listen to a critic as perceptive as George Steiner. All of them deserve, however, to be instructed by teachers who are imbued with Steiner's (overstated)

UNDERSTANDING OURSELVES   293

dictum, who recognize the importance of literature, music, and art for the growth of self-understanding, whose passion for a range of works is accompanied by mature interpretive skills, and who have techniques for instilling precursor capacities in their students. That is, to be sure, a lot to ask for. Yet it represents an important goal toward which education ought to strive.

Literature, art, and music provide access to possibilities for developing individuals, enabling them to try on unrealized alternatives for size. As my passing remark about identification with Jo March indicates, that is relatively straightforward in the case of literature. The impulse to emulate a fictional character, to be as free and strong as Jo or as brave and resourceful as Jim Hawkins, is only the simplest form of literary impact. More complex novels and plays inspire diagnostic reflections on one's own conduct. They led some of Dickens's readers to shudder as his characters mouthed unfeeling words echoing those readers' own utterances.[23] The more ambiguous figures delineated in "novels for adults" can provoke extended self-reflection: in the contrast between Dorothea Brooke's impulsive warmth and generosity of spirit and the caution of her more conventional sister, an attentive reader may find material for exploring either the narrowness of his own altruistic sentiments or his own lack of prudence.[24] Reading *Ulysses* or *Finnegans Wake* can reorient our understanding of virtues and vices, change our conception of the heroic, and provoke new ways of working through the successes and failures of our lives.[25]

Can visual art achieve similar effects? Can music? I believe so. Consider a well-known painting by the Renaissance master Domenico Ghirlandaio:

[23] See the brief discussion of the impact of *Bleak House* in the previous chapter, above, 213–15.
[24] Virginia Woolf famously described *Middlemarch* as a "magnificent book which with all its imperfections is one of the few English novels written for grown-up people." Woolf's estimate of the size of the class is, to my mind, uncharitable, although even with high standards for inclusion *Middlemarch* would surely count—as would several of Woolf's own novels. Some books ostensibly for children can also count as "novels for grown-ups." I would cite *Little Women, Treasure Island, Lord of the Rings*, and the later volumes of the Harry Potter series.
[25] I have elaborated and defended these themes in "Something Rich and Strange: Joyce's Perspectivism," in Philip Kitcher, ed., *Ulysses: Philosophical Perspectives* (New York: Oxford University Press, 2020, 207–51) and *Joyce's Kaleidoscope: An Invitation to "Finnegans Wake"* (New York: Oxford University Press, 2007).

Sometimes known as *An Old Man and His Grandson*, or *An Old Man with a Young Boy*, this portrait readily prompts reflections on the relations between age and youth, the possibility of deep bonds of affection across the generations, the ability to find beauty in what would otherwise be regarded as ugly and deformed; and even speculations: Does the old man's nose show the marks of syphilis? Have the raw passions of the past been overcome in the calm joy of this loving relationship? Has the physical disease brought the old man to wisdom and a cure for his previously disordered spirit? The more we scrutinize, guided by art historians and critics who can point out details we would otherwise have overlooked, the more our imaginings and reflections can be nourished.

Music most obviously achieves similar effects when it is allied to words, when the moods and emotions it arouses in listeners are given particular direction by a text. The great Romantic song cycles—of which Schubert's *Winterreise* is an outstanding example—continue to prompt deep and extensive thought, not because of the richness of the poetry, but because of the intensity generated by the composer's setting.[26] Yet, once our ears have focused

---

[26] Ian Bostridge's *Schubert's Winter Journey: Anatomy of an Obsession* (New York: Knopf, 2015) brilliantly articulates the reflections and emotions *Winterreise* has provoked in one of its most distinguished interpreters. It would be wrong to credit the impact to the poems: Wilhelm Müller's verse

UNDERSTANDING OURSELVES   295

a composer's musical idiom through direct linkage to a text (typically, but not always, poetry), we can extend and ramify those connections even when no words are present. Engagement with Wagner's vocal settings enables the hearer to interpret orchestral passages: the close of *Götterdämmerung* comes to be heard as partly affirmative, even in the context of a world-changing catastrophe.[27] Similarly, after the final movement of *Das Lied von der Erde* ("*Der Abschied*"—The Farewell) has inspired reflections on farewell—and on our own inevitable final farewell[28]—Mahler's Ninth Symphony (his next work, entirely orchestral and bereft of text) is readily heard as an extended goodbye, whose shifting moods can be traced in detail.

Literature, drama, film, art, and music can stimulate new ways of thinking and feeling, opening up possibilities for our lives, prompting us to revisit our own past conduct, supplying new goals and aspirations—and thus teaching us who we are, who we have been, and who we might hope to become. Yet so far, I have turned the gaze inward, considering how the conversations with ourselves, provoked by our well-instructed readings, seeings, and hearings, might redirect a purely personal and private search for fulfillment. That is to ignore the changes wrought in the ways we look outward. Can't refined capacities for reading and viewing and listening also broaden and deepen our sensitivities to the lives of others? Don't they also sometimes lead us to recognize possibilities to make our own distinctive contributions to a larger human world?

◆────◆

Indeed, they can and do. Education in the humanities not only makes us more self-aware, it also promotes our fulfillment through attuning us more closely to people whose welfare and whose aspirations we might affect. That

---

is workmanlike, but, taken on its own, eminently forgettable. The reaction listeners often have to performances of the cycle—continued mental attention to rhythms, themes, and harmonies, associated with meditations on the predicament of the vocal protagonist—derives from the musical richness. The specific emotions expressed in the score are *pointed* by the words, linked to particular episodes and moments hearers vicariously experience. Bostridge's book exemplifies some of this, and thus enriches the reader's experiences (since many listeners share Bostridge's obsession, returning to it again and again). For probing analysis of the expressive powers of musical works, see Christopher Peacocke, "The Distinctive Character of Aesthetic Experience," *British Journal of Aesthetics* 60 (2020): 183–97. I am much indebted to him for many enjoyable and illuminating discussions.

[27] Richard Schacht and I discuss this orchestral passage in our co-authored book on the *Ring* cycle. See our *Finding an Ending: Reflections on Wagner's Ring* (New York: Oxford University Press, 2004), Chapters 19-21.

[28] I discuss this movement in *Deaths in Venice*, 159–71.

296 THE MAIN ENTERPRISE OF THE WORLD

formulation, however, is still held by the inward gaze. Surely we should not clamor for humanistic education on the grounds that, through its opening our eyes to possibilities for aiding others, we may become fulfilled! Those whom we help should not be thought of as means to our own fulfillment.[29] Whatever private good our enhanced understanding of human existence may bring is a secondary matter. Rather, we should commend the well-schooled sensibilities for their power to make us better citizens and more highly developed moral agents. So we turn from the first broad aim of education (individual fulfillment) to a second cluster, preparation for citizenship and good conduct.

Democracy, I have argued, depends on the ability of citizens to deliberate together, with a commitment to finding an outcome with which all potentially affected parties can live. Mutual engagement of this form might be generated from prolonged encounters with people representing all the different perspectives. Through living and working among and with these people, citizens come to understand those points of view. Perspectives once alien, dismissed as the products of ignorance and selfishness, appear in a softer light. They become comprehensible reactions to a difficult situation. Although disagreement, even strong disagreement, may survive the transformation, the once-despised perspectives acquire human faces. The ensuing dialogue may begin in a different place. Reaching behind the opposed attitudes, people who disagree may attend to the underlying predicaments, identifying factors responsible for the conflict and seeking responses to those factors that might combine to resolve it. Thus, the sociologist Arlie Russell Hochschild immersed herself in the culture of a Louisiana bayou community, seeking to understand why its members were so adamantly opposed to environmental regulation.[30] As she discovered, their hostility was costly—their polluted waterways adversely affected their health. Through tracing their response to their anxieties about employment, coupled as they were to hopes for their children, she was able to enter into productive dialogue with people whose views were initially incomprehensible (if not to her, at least to many of her Berkeley colleagues).

Proposals 6–11, presented in Chapter 4, are first attempts to instill the capacities needed for thoughtful and sensitive engagement with alternative points of view. By no means can they exhaust the varieties in perspectives the

---

[29] Kant's Second Formulation of the Categorical Imperative is naturally adapted to this context.
[30] See her *Strangers in Their Own Land: Anger and Mourning on the American Right* (New York: The New Press, 2018).

schoolchildren will encounter during the course of their lives. The full range of deliberations arising for their society is unpredictable, and also too vast to introduce young people to all the specific occasions on which they may be required to listen and to comprehend the lives of others.[31] All education can provide is practice in the art of listening and planning together, hoping the particular examples through which children proceed fix dispositions they can continue to apply in whatever democratic contexts arise for them. The program suggested in Chapter 4 leads them through a sequence of situations of increasing complexity, aiming to inculcate generalizable habits of conversation.

Humanistic education can reinforce such habits, and even expand them. Coupled to the series of exercises in joint planning and decision-making, learning to interpret works of fiction (as well as to respond to visual art and to music) can induce skills for recognizing the perspectives and predicaments of others. Thus the way is prepared for deeper mutual engagement when citizens need to deliberate together. We should not, however, expect casual recommendations to read to work magic. Recall a point from the previous chapter: there is, as yet, no evidence to support the thesis that people who read fiction become more empathetic than their non-reading peers.[32] Historical cases suggest the power of *particular kinds* of fiction to generate greater understanding of and sympathy for people whose perspectives previously seemed alien, incomprehensible, or abhorrent.[33] On that basis, a carefully chosen set of readings, skillfully interpreted in the classroom, can provide students with the experience of entering the lives of others. Children who are initially inclined to condemn particular kinds of people or specific forms of behavior can be offered stories whose protagonists are relatively similar, and whose conditions of existence are explored in sympathetic detail. Their teacher poses imaginative questions about how they might have behaved in the circumstances of the story or whether they would have sided with other characters who refused to listen or provide aid. The aim of class discussion will not be to impose a final verdict, but rather to lead each child

---

[31] The point here is parallel to one made about the sciences and about preparation for informed decisions about policy proposals turning on delicate technical matters. See Chapter 4 above, 129–30.

[32] See Chapter 8, n.22, 266–67, above. No difference was found between subjects who had read a short passage of fiction just before being assessed for their empathetic responsiveness, and those who did not. Of course, there is no reason to think that the groups divided in this way separate regular readers from confirmed non-readers. Again, I am grateful to Ellen Winner for generous advice.

[33] See the discussion of the impact of Dickens, Stowe, Orwell, and Morrison in Chapter 8, 264–67, above.

298   THE MAIN ENTERPRISE OF THE WORLD

to greater understanding. Whatever the concluding judgment may be, children should come to see themselves as making it on a deeper understanding of the situation and of the thoughts and emotions of those whom they had been inclined to dismiss as beyond the pale. Exercises of this kind can be developed in many different ways, and experimental trials are needed to determine what approach and what kinds of materials are best suited to strengthen empathetic habits. Testing will reveal how best to do for schoolchildren what Dickens and Stowe did for their nineteenth-century publics.

More advanced students would be expected to develop subtler skills, using their understanding of the many-sidedness of complex fictional characters as a resource in political and moral discussions. Classes in literature (and other arts) serve as points of reference when students deliberate together. When a group seems to have reached an impasse, its members can be asked to recall previous successes in empathetic extension. Teachers remind them of occasions on which they entered into the perspective of a fictional protagonist. Returning to concrete instances of successful advances in understanding, the moments when an apparently alien way of life came to make greater sense, they are invited to seek similar illumination in the case at hand. Building on achievements made under circumstances where greater empathy came without cost—our attitudes toward fictitious people pose no moral or political demands—they are prompted to apply their interpretive skills in more taxing domains. The practice deliberations of the classroom take a consequential step toward the full responsibilities of the political citizen and the moral agent.

Nor, quite evidently, are the humanistic disciplines on which I have so far concentrated the only areas relevant to preparing good citizens. History is an obvious source. So too are geography and anthropology. All three subjects can expand the sense of human possibilities, presenting the challenges people have faced at different times and in different places and recording their diverse efforts to meet them. Students can find ample material to perplex and to repel them—thus provoking questions about how people could have been led to accept such puzzling and repulsive ways of life.

Although historical education has a place for dates, for the glorious deeds of national heroes, and for the pageantry imaginatively constructed to celebrate a society's past, these are not, in my view, central to its pedagogical importance. To be sure, if students are badly misinformed about chronology, they will be in a poor position to understand how important changes occurred. Lacking any appreciation of their country's triumphs (especially those without any connection to battlefields), their commitment to furthering its progress may become lukewarm. Above all, however, they need to recognize their own society with its distinctive institutions as one among many, to view their own nation, like other nations, as having sometimes succeeded and sometimes fallen short. They should have a sense of the grand sweep of human history, from the emergence of our species to the present. In reconstructing the period before the invention of writing (roughly six millennia ago), history must borrow from archeology and anthropology, to map the significant changes of the remote past: the evolution of language, the expansion of human societies in the late Paleolithic, the domestication of plants and animals, the growth of cities, and the crafting of a complex social and moral order, already recognizable in the oldest surviving documents. Within the framework these achievements have generated, they can start to understand the distinctive elaborations pursued by different societies, and how the institutions thus fashioned responded to the specific problems posed by a local environment.

Particularly important for the development of citizenship and moral agency is study of the principal episodes of moral and social change—for good, and for bad. Attention should be given to the construction of oppressive hierarchies, in the ancient world and in more recent times. Similarly, students should know how cruel practices were challenged and overthrown. Understanding the forms of slavery in Greece and Rome, in the Renaissance, and in the New World is a clear and obvious example, profoundly relevant for future American citizens. Because the resonances of the institution of chattel slavery continue to sound in the society to whose future they will contribute, American children need to understand why slaves were originally brought to the American colonies, why the practice of keeping slaves persisted and how it was defended, how it came to be opposed, the character of the debate over abolitionism, how social conditions for former slaves and their descendants evolved, and how the legacy of slavery affects differential life prospects in the United States today. Charting that social history is vastly more valuable than depicting the campaigns and battles of the American Civil War.[34] Similarly, following the course of the Second World War is far less crucial than understanding the circumstances facilitating Hitler's rise to power, exploring

---

[34] For a passionate, and deeply researched, study of the contrast between the United States and Germany in coming to terms (respectively) with the legacies of slavery and of the Holocaust, see Susan Neiman, *Learning from the Germans* (New York: Farrar, Straus & Giroux), 2019.

300   THE MAIN ENTERPRISE OF THE WORLD

how ordinary German citizens could support Nazism and its policies, recognizing how the Holocaust was planned and how it was executed.

In short, focusing on episodes of social change, especially those that are strikingly progressive or strikingly regressive, should be central to the history curriculum. Examples are legion: the emergence and decline of Greek democracy, the construction of a complex bureaucracy in imperial China, the spread of Christianity in the Roman Empire, the collapse of Rome, various examples of colonial genocide, resistance to colonial rule particularly in South Asia and Africa, opposition to autocracy and the development of democracy, the expansion of opportunities for women, shifts in attitudes toward same-sex love across the centuries and across societies, and many more. In studying these episodes, it is important to avoid the sanitized simplifications offered in many paeans to a whitewashed past. The historical events, and the historical actors should be shown, and discussed, warts and all.

Success in enlarging national history to cover all parts of the human world (however the local and global are balanced) must be based on geographical understanding. If, as suggested, history is far more than dates, geography is not simply about maps. Naturally, just as a student's chronology should be approximately accurate, so too her sense of the spatial relations among nations and societies ought to be roughly right. That sense is the basis for knowledge of the climatic and environmental conditions of people's ways of life. In turn, appreciating the specific opportunities and challenges posed by living in a particular place underlies consideration of the ways in which local conventions and institutions have developed. Geography, as it figures in the education of citizens, must borrow first from the earth and environmental sciences, from demography, and ultimately extend its reach into economics and anthropology.

Elementary education in geography provides the foundations, teaching the young the basic features of the globe, about climate and weather, natural resources, and the like. Secondary education builds on those foundations, introducing detailed understandings of the economic life of particular groups and taking up the contributions of the most distinguished ethnographies. Students should combine a broad understanding of the diversity of human social arrangements with a much deeper grasp of a small number of societies very different from their own. They are thus at least minimally prepared to come to terms with predicaments and perspectives potentially relevant to future political debates (where the interests of other nations are at stake), and also given opportunities to extend their empathy by comprehending the viewpoints of people with radically different customs and patterns of conduct. History and geography, as I have envisaged them, offer further opportunities (perhaps adding more detail) to the exercises in perspective sharing and identification with others provided by literature.

So far, my discussion of the potential roles the humanities and social sciences might play in fostering citizenship would appear to have overlooked their most obvious contributions. Isn't part of the task of formal education to acquaint young people with the institutions of the society in which they live? They need parts of political science to enable them to understand the workings of government (and to compare their own system with alternatives); they should know how economic transactions are carried out and how various kinds of interventions would affect prices, wages, and employment; and historical accounts can deepen their appreciation of the reasons leading their predecessors to construct the economic and political structures they inherit. Why focus on developing capacities for empathy, when the need for factual information is so evident?

The answer lies in the Deweyan approach to democracy proposed in Chapter 4. In his voluminous writings, Dewey insisted again and again that preparing students for democratic life required more than teaching them "the civics."[35] If democracy is to be a way of life, shot through and through with occasions of joint deliberation, future citizens must learn how to be adept discussants. They must become good listeners, able to enter and understand others' perspectives, skilled at mutual engagement.

Champions of Millian democracy who balk at the further Deweyan step may see matters differently.[36] For them, the crucial outcome of schooling is a generation of citizens able to assess the questions of policy arising in their lifetimes. If interests are to be aligned with voting preferences, the electorate will have to be equipped with cognitive skills enabling them to discern which policy proposals advance their most important goals. Especially in a world where authority is contested and where a variety of clashing sources portray

---

[35] This theme runs through Dewey's writings on education. Two particularly clear instances are found relatively early in his career: "The School as Social Centre" (MW 2, 80–93, particularly 82–83); and "Democracy in Education" (MW 3, 229–39).

[36] See Chapter 4, above 147–49. In my view, Mill would not see the "Millian" argument that follows as sufficient. Like Dewey, he recognizes the need to develop social sympathies.

302 THE MAIN ENTERPRISE OF THE WORLD

themselves as uniquely able to present reliable information, citizens will have to think through issues and arguments for themselves. To be sure, they will need more than "the civics" (as conventionally understood), but the extra material will draw heavily from social sciences, from economics, political science, sociology, and psychology, with (perhaps) a little history thrown in to leaven the mix. Most of the humanities offer very little (if anything) to this enterprise.

This "Millian" argument is partly correct. It recognizes the *incompleteness* of the Deweyan approach to preparing citizens, as I have so far developed it. Recall the conditions for democratic deliberation. The ideal points us toward making discussions as inclusive as possible, as well-informed as possible, and as mutually engaged as possible. Neither the cognitive nor the affective dimension can be neglected. To be sure, however concerned deliberators are to enter into one another's points of view and to understand them sympathetically, if they are factually misguided and clueless at reasoning, the conversation is unlikely to go well. Equally, if those who take part speak with the tongues of superhuman economists and angelic political theorists, and have not mutual engagement, their voices will be as sounding brass and tinkling cymbals. When orthodox authority is routinely rejected, productive joint inquiry can only begin when all the participants can trust others to engage with their own distinctive concerns.[37] Without the advance assurance that one's voice will be heard, that one's needs will be acknowledged and taken into account, the search for reliable information and for policies tolerable by all will not get off the ground.

Hence I have begun with the most elementary precondition for Deweyan democracy, the shaping of a citizenry committed to listening and seeking community. To start in this way is not to deny the "Millian" point, but to amplify it.[38] Assuming that the curriculum sketched in the previous section will achieve its purpose, we should ask how the knowledge and skills required for thinking through complex policy issues are to be transmitted.

When it turns to "social studies," contemporary schooling, not only in America but in other affluent democracies as well, overemphasizes the knowledge and underrepresents the skills. The mistake is akin to one already discerned in considering education in the natural sciences. Basic information about the features of the national political and economic systems is, of

---

[37] See Chapter 4, above 131, n.40. Again, I take Mill to appreciate the point.
[38] Thus I take Dewey to elaborate a conception of democratic discussion already latent in Mill.

UNDERSTANDING OURSELVES   303

course, necessary. Some of that can easily be introduced in elementary school and supplemented in the higher grades. The mass of information often inflicted on the young, occupying their memories in an indigestible lump for a few days, and then happily expelled once the test is over, dulls whatever curiosity they may once have had for fathoming how social systems work. Once they are clear about the basic structure of their own governance and their own economic life—and have points of reference in alternative efforts, some historical, some contemporary—the most important educational task is to provide them with resources to extend their grasp, filling in gaps and elaborating details, as information is needed to tackle the policy questions arising for them throughout their lives. Attempting to predict those issues, to identify the material future citizens will have to absorb in addressing them, and to force-feed it all at once, is as foolish and deadening as the comparable ventures in inculcating "scientific facts." What those future citizens need most are capacities for analyzing the evidence presented on behalf of political and economic proposals.

How should this be done? By adapting the approach adopted for natural sciences to their human counterparts. One significant lesson should be clearly and loudly presented as soon as social science is introduced into the curriculum, and repeated at frequent intervals to forestall any tendency to forget it. Because of the complexity of the phenomena they study, research into facets of human life is exceptionally difficult. In consequence, the conclusions drawn by economists, quantitative political scientists, and quantitative sociologists are typically provisional. More exactly, they are likely to hold for a range of instances that investigators don't know how to specify—and hence are vulnerable in applications to new contexts. Proper appreciation of these parts of social science depends on admiring the delineation of clear abstract structures (even while recognizing how those structures are often, perhaps always, modified and distorted in actual instances), and on welcoming the precise and accurate conclusions drawn about particular cases (even though the exact extent to which those conclusions can be generalized is as yet, and maybe always must be, unknown).

A second lesson, of comparable significance, points out constraints on human decision-making. Sometimes when people recognize their inability to predict whether an intervention they envisage would bring about the effect they hope for, the correct strategy is to seek more evidence. Often, however, the luxury of deferral is denied. Action is needed now. When that occurs, comparative assessments are required. In the best case, it would

304 THE MAIN ENTERPRISE OF THE WORLD

be possible to identify the relevant probabilities—What are the chances of the intervention's delivering each of a range of possible outcomes?—*and* to provide quantitative estimates of the costs and benefits of those outcomes. Standard cost-benefit analysis then computes the expected utility of the intervention, recommending the envisaged action just in case the calculated value is greater than the expected utility of doing nothing.[39] In many real-life instances, assigning numerical values to probabilities and quantifying costs and benefits is simply impossible. When this occurs, the comparative assessments have to be derived from qualitative judgments—and this, too, is something future citizens should recognize.[40]

As I have already suggested,[41] the standard mathematical curriculum should be revised to equip young people with the formal skills most relevant to their future lives. Some understanding of probability and statistics will be far more significant for their decision-making than most of the algebra, geometry, and trigonometry they are currently supposed to learn. To be sure, once a firm grasp of arithmetical operations is in hand, further mathematical development presupposes the ability to operate with symbols, and hence motivates including the most basic parts of algebra—the concept of a variable, algebraic equations, and techniques for solving them—in the mathematics curriculum.[42] Once these abilities are in place, the way is open to begin exploring the potentially fascinating and readily applicable fields of probability and statistics. Armed with probabilistic tools, students can then learn how to assess social scientific claims that bear on their health, on their wealth, and on their ability to realize their plans.

As in the case of the natural sciences, introducing formal methods for evaluating social scientific hypotheses should be combined with studying particular cases. The instances should be chosen to acquaint students with important concepts from the pertinent disciplines. With respect to

[39] The expected utility of the intervention is $\Sigma p_i u_i$ where the summation ranges over the outcomes, where p_i is the probability of the ith outcome, and u_i the quantitative value assigned to the ith outcome. There are many excellent introductions to cost-benefit analysis and formal decision theory. See for example, the early chapters of Martin Peterson, *An Introduction to Decision Theory* (Cambridge, UK: Cambridge University Press, 2009).

[40] Decision-making under risk (where numerical values can be assigned) contrasts with decision-making under uncertainty (where they cannot). For a penetrating investigation of the more difficult case of uncertainty, see Isaac Levi, *Hard Choices* (Cambridge UK: Cambridge University Press, 1986).

[41] See 130 and 248, above.

[42] A case for geometry can also be made, in that studying the most elementary parts of Euclidean geometry can instill the concept of proof. But, as in so many instances of scientific education, too much emphasis is placed on identifying those who are ingenious enough—and interested enough!—to discover tricky proofs of recherché theorems.

economics, for example, they might begin with simple models of markets, and then consider particular kinds of transactions in which those models turn out to be inapplicable.[43] Equally, they could be introduced to the ways in which economists (and other social scientists) analyze data through considering explanations of the rise in prison populations in the United States during recent decades.[44] Similarly, they might learn of the difficulties of sampling through considering the problems pollsters face.[45] Thomas Schelling's writings provide ample material for understanding the complexities of human interactions.[46]

There is, of course, a place to present larger perspectives on areas of social science, to outline the grand theories proposed—and interminably debated. Concentrating on those alone, however, easily generates an attitude likely to harden into scientism: The natural sciences make progress; the social sciences flounder around in mush. Hence, when parts of social science enter the curriculum—probably in the late years of secondary school—the principal emphasis should be on the real achievements, the local studies dedicated to collecting robust evidence and using the data to answer focused, but significant, questions. Thinking of economic life as entirely comprehensible in terms of the interactions of members of the species *Homo economicus*, or of social change as determined by class warfare under the material conditions of existence may be momentarily exhilarating, but a hangover will almost certainly follow. Better to study the methods of the various disciplines through their success with specific—fascinating—issues: Why are there so many more African Americans in US prisons than there used to be? Why has the crime rate dropped in many major cities? Why does segregation, by race, sex, and class persist? How do you conduct a survey to give reliable predictions of how people will vote? Why will hockey players only wear helmets if they are required to do so? Why is it difficult to set up a market in used cars? Focusing on the core of the social sciences, as they are practiced at

---

[43] George Akerlof's classic study of markets in used cars provides a useful illustration here. See his *An Economic Theorist's Book of Tales* (Cambridge, UK: Cambridge University Press, 1984).

[44] An imaginative teacher could present the alternative accounts offered by Michelle Alexander, *The New Jim Crow* (New York: The New Press, 2012); John Pfaff, *Locked In* (New York: Basic Books, 2017); and Brendan O'Flaherty and Rajiv Sethi, *Shadows of Doubt* (Cambridge, MA: Harvard University Press, 2019).

[45] Nate Silver, *The Signal and the Noise* (New York: Penguin, 2012), provides a number of fascinating examples.

[46] See, in particular, *Micromotives and Macrobehavior* (New York: W. W. Norton, 1978). The chapters on racial segregation and the use of hockey helmets are particularly valuable for presenting important ideas in a relatively simple form.

306 THE MAIN ENTERPRISE OF THE WORLD

their best, not only reveals interesting aspects of human behavior and human life, but also prepares young people to think through the matters of social policy (whatever they are) arising in their lifetimes. With luck, it may even encourage some of them to disobey one of Auden's famous commandments to students—inspiring them "to sit with statisticians" and "commit a social science."[47]

The same approach should apply to the *Geisteswissenschaft*, apparently moving back and forth across the no-man's-land separating the natural and social sciences, psychology. Secondary education might devote a class or two to the grand theories of human mental life, acquainting students with the central ideas of influential thinkers: Freud, William James, B. F. Skinner, Noam Chomsky.[48] The bulk of time ought to be devoted to some of the many rigorous experimental studies offering precise elucidations of particular facets of cognitive and emotional life. Citizens who have learned about the unreliability of eyewitness testimony, who appreciate the power of social contagion, who understand how people sometimes violate principles commonly taken to be requirements of rationality, who know something of the limits of their memories and their tendencies to confabulate, who recognize the power of authority to lead people to perform actions they would otherwise reject, and who are aware of stereotype threat—citizens acquainted with all these established aspects of our mental lives will be attentive to their own foibles, less insistent on overriding their fellows, more willing to resist pressures to "go along," and, in consequence, they will be superior deliberators and better citizens.[49] If the system-builders are to figure in the psychology classroom, their more general theories might best be illustrated by the observational and experimental studies most central to them. A presentation on Freud could describe some of his own interpretations of dreams, considering them in the light of more recent data; James's account of emotion could be supplemented

---

[47] W. H. Auden, "Under Which Lyre," originally delivered to the Harvard Chapter of Phi Beta Kappa in 1946. Available at: https://allpoetry.com/Under-Which-Lyre.

[48] Perhaps even mentioning the current enthusiasm for evolutionary psychology, as outlined by Steven Pinker, *How the Mind Works* (New York: W. W. Norton, 1997). For reasons given in my *Vaulting Ambition* (Cambridge, MA: MIT Press, 1985) and "Pop Sociobiology Reborn," co-authored with Leah Vickers and originally published in *Evolution, Gender, and Rape*, ed. Cheryl Travis (Cambridge, MA: MIT Press, 2003), attention to evolutionary psychology should be accompanied by a clear warning: *Caveat emptor*.

[49] In presenting the findings to which I have alluded, teachers can draw on the seminal studies and experiments of Elizabeth Loftus, Solomon Asch, Amos Tversky, Daniel Kahneman, Richard Nisbet, Gerd Gigerenzer, George Miller, Stanley Schachter, Stanley Milgram, Philip Zimbardo, George Akerlof, and Claude Steele. There are many lively and accessible presentations of this material, some by the investigators themselves.

with later findings about emotional responses; Skinner's behaviorism could be developed through his studies of conditioning and intermittent reinforcement; and Chomsky's computationalism is naturally explained through the work on the structure of languages that revealed him as one of the greatest scientists of the twentieth century.

To treat psychology as a domain in which large pictures of the human mind endlessly battle one another is to shortchange the discipline and to forgo an important educational opportunity. Turning to the clear successes, the careful studies exposing facets of mental life, offers citizens-in-the-making valuable information about themselves. Steiner's dictum needs to be balanced by recognizing how the great psychological experimenters have complemented Molière and Stendhal, offering insights of comparable significance. Studying some of those experiments teaches valuable lessons about how to extend psychological inquiry. With luck, those who learn the lessons will include some who are encouraged to enter the discipline and contribute to its further progress.

<hr/>

To round out the discussion of how the human sciences contribute to the education of citizens, two remaining topics deserve attention. So far, I have said nothing about the study of foreign languages, and the possible role learning a second (or third or . . .) language might play. Nor, in considering preparation for citizenship have I ventured into the related issue of fostering moral development. Much of the ground for attending to these questions has already been laid. Hence my treatment of them can be relatively brief.

Traditional defenses of the value of studying languages, specifically Latin and Greek, plainly do not rest on the advantages of being able to speak to people for whom these are their native tongues. Nor, in the past two or three centuries, has the ability to read and write fluently in Latin been a passport to an international world of letters or to the hierarchy of the Catholic church. More recent versions of the case for Classics, understood broadly as concerned not only with language and literature but as embracing history, art, social life, and culture, have pointed to the potential insights gleaned from being able to enter into different forms of human existence and to understand them (thanks to a long tradition of transmitting and interpreting a rich hoard of documents and artefacts) in considerable depth.[50] Unsurprisingly, champions of other languages, ancient and modern, have co-opted the

[50] In two of her books, *Cultivating Humanity: A Classical Defense of Reform in Liberal Education* (Cambridge MA: Harvard University Press, 1997), and *Not for Profit: Why Democracy Needs the*

308 THE MAIN ENTERPRISE OF THE WORLD

argument. They have urged the richness of the culture(s) of the language(s) on whose behalf they plead, denying the special status long attributed to Latin and Greek.[51] As a bonus, the defenders of modern languages add, young people who have gone far enough in their linguistic studies will be able to communicate easily with contemporaries reared in other societies, thus enriching their understanding of a different culture.

Anyone who has learned a foreign language, either early or (with more difficulty) later in life, can recognize the advertised value. Becoming fluent opens up conversations of broad range and satisfying depth, it unlocks a treasury of writings, and it expands the available menu for film and drama. Beyond the large features of an alien culture, details and subtleties too can be discerned and appreciated. Once immersed in that culture, the linguistically fluent have a perch from which to compare, and to reflect on features of their own society they would otherwise have taken for granted. Besides new possibilities of sympathetic identification, they gain new powers of critical scrutiny. Traveling into another culture really does broaden the mind.

Every society, even those whose native tongue serves as the world's *lingua franca*, will always need citizens who speak and read other languages. Given the interconnections among nations, and the importance of full mutual understanding in negotiations over complex policies, they cannot rely on others' agreeing to formulate everything in their supposedly universal idiom. Ideally, the language used by any other contemporary human group should be familiar to some of their citizens. Hence, it is wise for societies to identify a cohort of children who can contribute to national and international life by serving as channels of unperturbed communication.[52] If only because such people are needed, it is prudent to begin education in a second language—for all children—early in their schooling (at the time of their lives when acquisition of another language is easiest). Indeed, as studies of children who are reared in a bilingual environment show, there are clear benefits of learning two languages from the very beginning. The obvious moral of those studies: the earlier the better.[53]

Humanities (Princeton: Princeton University Press), Martha Nussbaum offers detailed arguments of the continued importance of Classical Languages and Literature.

[51] A point with which Nussbaum concurs.
[52] It is entirely possible that this role doesn't require any special talents, and that almost any child can play it, provided instruction in a second language begins early enough.
[53] The writings of Ellen Bialystok make a powerful case for early learning of a second language.

UNDERSTANDING OURSELVES 309

How far should foreign language instruction go? Should it aim at turning *all* young children into adults who are fluent in at least one language other than their own? Here, I suggest, policy should be guided by data on how children from non-English-speaking countries have reacted to being required to learn English. In Finland, for example, children are required to learn foreign languages (studying two foreign languages in secondary school is standard), and they begin their linguistic studies at nine. At that age, several options are allowed, but the overwhelming majority of Finns learn English as their first foreign language. Young people in Finland tend to agree, or strongly agree, that knowing English is necessary in a multicultural society.[54] Given the advantages of starting to learn a foreign language before age ten, it would seem wise to begin in the early grades of elementary school, so that some facility in speaking, hearing, reading and writing can be acquired before secondary education begins. Perhaps, at that stage, students who feel that attaining full fluency in the foreign tongue they have so far studied is unnecessary for them could be permitted either to begin a different language, or to drop linguistic study entirely in favor of pursuing something else. Here, as always, individual assessment and consultation with mentors would be important.

English speakers enjoy the luxury of speaking a language they can expect others to understand, and to be able to converse in. The privilege comes with a responsibility. Anglo-Saxons who conform to the cartoon version of the species—when their foreign interlocutor fails to comprehend what they have said, they repeat their remarks at higher volume—ought to understand the years of work required to indulge them. They should also recognize the costs of having to write in a second language, even for those whose English is fluent. Despite my own investment of considerable time in improving my German, it remains inferior to the English commanded by many of my German-speaking colleagues. When I sit in their offices, I am constantly struck—and ashamed—by the inevitable row of books devoted to reading and writing in English, visible among the many volumes of their special discipline. They typically estimate the extra time they need to publish in English to be between one or two weeks and a month—a significant addition in fast-moving areas of research. What right do I have to cut those corners?

---

[54] See Sirpa Leppännen et al., *National Survey on the English Language in Finland: Uses, Meanings, and Attitudes* (2011); available online at www.helsinki.fi>varieng>series>volumes>evarieng-vol5. The survey contains a wealth of interesting information; see, in particular, 22–24, and 81–83.

310   THE MAIN ENTERPRISE OF THE WORLD

Similarly, it is easy to underestimate the importance of being able to speak to fellow-citizens in their own first languages. One of our sons is a physician, whose Spanish is fluent. Many years ago, he rightly resisted the advice of his stuffy parents to study French or German as his (required) foreign language. Now, unlike those of his colleagues who speak no Spanish at all or only "medical Spanish," he can respond to the concerns of anxious patients and their families, people whose English is vastly inferior to their native Spanish. Instead of requiring them to voice their worries in words inadequate to express what they want to say, he can listen to the whole story, and, consequently, reassure, console, and advise.

Citizenship today requires us to reach out into other forms of life, both at home in our own multicultural democracies, and abroad in facing the problems confronting our species as a whole. Thus, we should encourage all young people to learn a second language, and, unless they have compelling reasons for stopping, to continue to fluency or to diversify their linguistic repertoire. The benefits are diverse. Particular gains will be more salient for some people than for others. Learning a language can help you communicate more readily with co-workers or with neighbors with whom you regularly interact. It can enable you to keep in touch with a society and culture of especial interest to you. It can provide a perspective on your own society, influencing your deliberations about important issues. It can open up aesthetic experiences you would not otherwise have enjoyed. It can increase your mastery of your own native language.[55] Or, through expanding your sympathies, it can make you a better citizen.

Because the benefits are diverse, study of languages at the secondary level is best designed for the emerging individual. As a clear profile of interests and aspirations starts to emerge, wise advisors can help students tailor their further linguistic study in ways likely to prove rewarding for them. Some of them, fascinated by history, or captivated by discerning linguistic structures,

---

[55] Famously, Winston Churchill's rhetorical style was shaped by his reading of Gibbon, and by his delight in the rhythms and periods of *The Decline and Fall of the Roman Empire*. Churchill was notoriously a mediocre pupil at Harrow. Since I share his taste for Gibbon, I once assigned a class of bright American undergraduates a selection of a few pages, as supplementary reading for a segment about the Roman Empire in a General Education course. To my astonishment, several of them, including students of high academic achievement, confessed to me their inability to understand the passages I had asked them to read. How had they been baffled by a text to which the (unbookish) Churchill had thrilled? None of them, as I discovered, had any significant fluency in any foreign language—and, not having been forced to recognize the syntactical features contemporary English has suppressed, Gibbon's complex sentences were beyond their powers of processing. However poor a Latin scholar he was, Churchill had made acquaintance with declensions and conjugations, with a variety of subordinate clauses, with moods and tenses. That acquaintance taught him English.

may opt to learn the complex languages of the past. Latin and Greek should no longer be mandatory—marks of the finished gentleman. Yet they, as well as other "dead" languages like Sanskrit, should be available to those who aspire to carry on the life of brilliant and illuminating scholarly traditions.

Given the connections drawn in earlier chapters between democratic citizenship and developed moral character, the importance of an interactive program in the human sciences for the fostering of moral agents should be obvious. A progressive society hopes to identify the moral errors embedded in its conventions and institutions and to correct them (to the greatest extent possible). The history of moral practice, around the globe, is a vivid reminder of the blindness of our predecessors. How could they *not* have seen the awfulness of sacrificing innocent young people to preserve the honor of the clan, how could they have condoned savage forms of male domination, tolerated slavery, inflicted cruel punishments and forms of torture, shamed and brutally murdered supposed social deviants? The frequency with which appalling things have been done, accepted as normal or even rewarded with praise, ought to undercut any confidence that *our* moral vision is acute, that *our* ability to hear "the cries of the wounded" is perfect, and *our* determination to bind up the wounds fully resolute.

Elsewhere, I have proposed a first methodology for pursuing moral inquiry so that our own likely blindness and deafness may partially be alleviated.[56] The Deweyan society I envisage sets up institutions through which those who suffer may make a case for moral change. Yet, as thoughtful critics have pointed out, those institutions will be staffed by actual people, human beings with their various imperfections and prejudices. Can one realistically imagine conversations among *actual people* serving as any close approximations to my three ideal conditions (inclusiveness, well-informedness, and mutual engagement), and thus having any serious chance of making progress more systematic and secure than the dismal history of moral practice shows it to have been?

I reply: the very fact of making public an ideal method for moral inquiry can make a difference to human conduct. Bringing representatives of different perspectives together, and asking them to deliberate under the aegis of employing the best available information and seeking an outcome all can

---

[56] See my *Moral Progress*.

312 THE MAIN ENTERPRISE OF THE WORLD

live with, surely will not magically dissolve all their prejudices, remove all tendencies for them to appeal to their customary beliefs, or turn them into perfectly sympathetic listeners. Yet it does place pressure on them to move in those directions. If a mediator sits in on their deliberations, that person may periodically remind them of the ideals or even chide them when their contributions are bereft of supportive evidence or demonstrably lacking in sympathy. (If the discussion lacks any moderator, other participants may remonstrate with them.) Even the constitutionally loud and exuberant tend to lower their voices in church.

In obvious ways, the institution I have recommended recapitulates the procedures of the law.[57] Imagine, with Locke, the introduction of a system of courts and judges and jury trials into a society used to settle disputes through clan warfare. Extend the story. When that system is originally proposed, the gloomy naysayers predict its failure to make any difference. "After all," they say, "those who preside over the court, who testify before it, and who serve on juries will be actual people, with all their prejudices, misinformation, and failures of sympathy. Why should we think the verdicts they reach will be any better than the trials of strength we have now?" The complaint underrates the power of explicit conventions and common knowledge of them to put people "on their best behavior." The history of legal procedures is, to be sure, littered with corrupt episodes—even some that provoke revulsion and disgust.[58] On the whole, however, witnesses testify sincerely, juries suspend at least some of their prejudices when they deliberate, and judges attempt to abide by the law. Because of a shared understanding of how the system is supposed to work, it comes closer to functioning in the intended fashion. Judges' verdicts will be reviewed, witnesses are liable to prosecution for perjury, and jurors who attempt to sway others in the direction of their evident biases are typically reprimanded by their fellows. The imperfect institutions of the law deliver just verdicts more regularly and reliably than the "frontier justice" they replaced, and their overall performance belies the predictions of my imagined naysayers.

---

[57] I introduced this comparison in *Moral Progress*; see 168. The present discussion attempts to make the analogy more explicit.

[58] That continues today, even in societies advertising themselves as democracies. As I write, a Turkish philanthropist, Osman Kavala, a man who has brought comfort, joy, and hope to the lives of thousands, sits in solitary confinement in Istanbul. Although outside courts and groups dedicated to human rights have protested his imprisonment, and although a Turkish court pronounced him not guilty of the accusations originally brought against him, he was not released but immediately re-arrested on new and trumped-up charges. His many friends and well-wishers fear that he is doomed to spend the rest of his life in prison.

UNDERSTANDING OURSELVES   313

Deweyans hoping to improve the prospects for moral progress can proceed at either of two levels. They can recommend institutions, to be implemented in a Deweyan society, so as to increase the chances of identifying the moral problems of the current state and of addressing them—even though the officials and participants in those institutions are unchanged. Moral progress is achieved through amending the structure of society, leaving the moral propensities of individual people unaltered. Or, Deweyans can attempt to improve the moral agents themselves. My proposals for moral progress begin at the social level. Given my understanding of the fundamental problem out of which morality arises, that is entirely appropriate. Morality, recall, is a social technology for amplifying our responsiveness to others. Nevertheless, although it starts at the social level, it doesn't need to end there. Why not proceed on both fronts?

The history of legal institutions shows how some advances can be made without significantly modifying moral character. Yet the imaginary pessimists have a point: wouldn't moral progress be more secure and sure-footed—*even more* secure and sure-footed—if those who participate in the Deweyan institution of moral inquiry (as I have envisaged it) were better able to distinguish well-founded conclusions from baseless speculations, if they were more inclined to undertake joint inquiry with people holding opposite views, and, above all, if they had greater talents for recognizing and sympathizing with the perspectives and predicaments of others. Previous chapters, and earlier parts of this chapter, have tried to outline a reformed curriculum aimed at achieving these results. In moving young people toward these ends it will not only prepare them to live more fulfilling lives and to become better citizens. It will also advance their moral development—and thereby further facilitate moral progress.[59]

If I am right, the proposals for reform deliver a fortunate bonus. But might other changes add to the good effects? Might there not be some studies specially directed toward refining individual moral capacities?

---

[59] Observant readers will recognize that I make an important assumption. It is in principle possible to improve a system in either of two distinct ways, even though pursuing both strategies at once leads to a worse outcome. (Imagine, for instance, two people who want to spend an evening together, who have opposed preferences about how to spend it, and who cannot communicate. If what matters most to both is togetherness, then they are better off if one is altruistic, going where the partner wants to go, and the other is selfish. If *both* decide to be altruistic, the result is the worst of all possibilities: neither achieves the preferred way of passing the evening, and they are separated.) I presuppose that conflicts don't arise, that there are no interactions and the gains are additive. Staffing better institutions with better people is superior both to staffing those institutions with unchanged people and staffing the old institutions with better people. The presupposition is plausible, but deserves testing.

314   THE MAIN ENTERPRISE OF THE WORLD

My own subject, philosophy, has not so far figured in my suggestions. Although it is often not available to students before they attend university (where it frequently attracts some extraordinarily talented undergraduates), there have been successful ventures in introducing it in secondary schools.[60] With respect to moral development, philosophy is pertinent in two ways. First, and most obviously, classical works of Western philosophy, from Plato to the present, explicitly discuss moral and ethical questions. Canonical texts (some much more readable than others) reflect on what should be done and how to live. Out of these works come suggested principles, susceptible of comparison both with one another and with the prescriptions of the world's religions. On my understanding of the moral project (and the more inclusive ethical project), none of these principles can stand as a conversation-stopping last word. They are, however, useful resources for the kinds of conversations out of which moral advances occur (the deliberations of the Deweyan society). If participants in actual versions of ideal moral conversations were thoroughly familiar with such principles, they could often deploy them in making evident the problematic character of the situation under consideration or indicate some line along which the group might seek a solution. As Chapter 5 already noted, they are tools, useful for some occasions.[61] Recognizing them as such is entirely concordant with abandoning the conception of them as all-purpose devices, suited to regulate all conduct.

Studying philosophy can, however, offer more than simply introducing young people to seminal ways of approaching moral questions. It can extend and fortify two kinds of skills to help in moral reflection. Chapter 5 recognized a technique for thinking through a decision, that of comparing the available options with those arising in a structurally similar situation, where the character of the alternatives might emerge with greater clarity. I warned against the possibility of simplifying too much—introducing constraints to detach the conditions of the probative story from reality, leaving our capacities for responding without any purchase, and thus blocking the route to

---

[60] The presence of philosophy in secondary education varies across countries. In France, for example, philosophy is not only part of the curriculum, but an examination in philosophy is part of the baccalaureate. Some British and American schools have introduced philosophy, usually as an optional subject. Some years ago, an enterprising group of Columbia graduate students (some from philosophy, some from the philosophy of education program at Teachers College) began an outreach initiative, taking philosophy into New York high schools, many of them where average academic performance was poor. The philosophy clubs they started, and the optional classes that followed, attracted a significant number of students. Preliminary studies showed considerable improvement, across all subjects, among those students who regularly attended philosophy events.

[61] See above, 156.

confident judgment.[62] That, I claimed, is the trouble with trolley problems and many analogous philosophical exercises. Real life is too messy; philosophical scenarios are too remote; novelists and dramatists often strike a happy balance. Combining philosophy with carefully chosen works of fiction, a teacher can instill valuable skills of imaginative construction, on which their pupils will be able to draw either as they deliberate with others, or in those moments when they must work things through for themselves.

Fostering philosophical imagination is one way of assisting individual moral advances. The second lies in an effect to which philosophers point with justified pride. Learning to address philosophical problems promotes habits of clear thinking. Philosophy students are taught to disambiguate questions, to sharpen initially vague concepts, to probe arguments, and to fathom hidden presuppositions. Beginning undergraduates are often confronted by questions with a long pedigree, the "classical problems of philosophy,"[63] and shown the many ways in which they have been reformulated and how lines of reasoning have been made explicit and so clarified. Similar pedagogical techniques can easily be employed in the secondary school, and perhaps even earlier. They can instill capacities for thinking better across the board, and, in particular in navigating the difficult terrain of our moral lives.

<hr />

From some traditional perspectives on education, these long discussions of how to help young people find their ways to fulfilling lives, how to fashion better citizens, and how to promote moral progress, at both the social and the individual level, may seem to miss the point. Education, it is frequently held, is about preparing children for "good jobs"; with luck, better jobs than those their parents could hope for. If a proposed curriculum fails to contribute to— perhaps even detracts from—this crucial endeavor, should it be dismissed as counterproductive? Whatever other virtues it may have, can they really override the importance of fostering a capacity for self-maintenance?

Before this concern can be addressed, it's crucial to ask a few questions. First, what kinds of workers will societies need in the coming decades? Second, to what extent do the *existing* curricula of elementary and secondary

---

[62] See Chapter 5, above, 170–72.

[63] Many philosophers would also take these problems to be intrinsically significant questions. Perhaps some of them are, but many, in my view, lack the importance often attributed to them. Nevertheless, they are exceptionally useful—like five-finger exercises for the aspiring pianist—in generating skills for clearer thinking.

316   THE MAIN ENTERPRISE OF THE WORLD

schools prepare the young for the positions through which they will earn their livelihoods? If I am correct in thinking of the future labor market as one in which most of the historically central work of production will be achieved through automation, with the frequency of service workers increasing as a result,[64] then a program focused on fostering individual fulfillment, and developing capacities for cooperating with others and for making thoughtful moral decisions, looks to be just what coming decades will need. The proposals of this chapter and its two predecessors are by no means at odds with the thought of a society, half of whose citizens make their main contributions through caring for others. Indeed, viewing *all* adults as giving significant time to bringing their distinctive perspectives and talents to educating the young reinforces suggestions to reform pre-university education along the lines outlined here.

Of course, societies will continue to require workers to grow the crops, make the artefacts and machines, maintain and run the armies of robots, write the software and continue developing new technologies, and so forth. Many of these jobs do not require any extensive training. Just as today's workers undertake them on the basis of whatever schooling they have had, so too in the future. These positions will continue to be open to anyone who has acquired the most basic forms of literacy and numeracy. Others are quite specialized in ways for which existing schools do not prepare. Plumbers and electricians, dental hygienists and beauticians, all have to acquire the techniques they need without any significant help from their years in the classroom. The only types of work potentially suffering interference from my reformed curriculum would appear to be those for which secondary school (and later university) provides a substantial basis, on which later specialized training can then build. Engineers, nurses, financial analysts, doctors, and veterinarians need a background in specific branches of knowledge before they take up the (often lengthy) apprenticeships enabling them to practice. Why think, however, of the proposed reforms as inimical to staffing these important lines of work? Restructuring *general* education along the lines proposed would allow young people whose proclivities lead them toward the relevant special studies to pursue them in at least the same depth. As I have already noted, permitting those who recognize that mathematics or chemistry is not for them to opt for a different type of science education might well accelerate the pace of classes in these areas. Those intrigued by algebra or fascinated by chemical reactions

[64] See Chapter 2 above, 68–72.

could scamper ahead, without having to wait for their reluctant, plodding friends to catch on. And, to repeat, the unwilling might retain a curiosity for science, inclining them, later in life, to be attracted by some different area of research, and even to participate in it.

From the very beginning of this book, the emphasis has been on attending carefully to individual talents and propensities. Attempts to make the dialogue between society and the growing person go as well as possible should make evident the full range of possibilities for a fulfilling and productive life. In adopting that aim, my proposed reforms pose a series of challenges for skeptics, concerned about some future absence of specialized workers, thoroughly trained in highly technical fields. Should we assume that future children will find those fields so unattractive as to need coercion or bribes to enter them? Why should the future distribution of scientific talent and interest be expected to be different from what is already observed—especially given a commitment to develop the talents of *all* children and to preserve their curiosity? Is it appropriate educational policy to force or entice the young to spend their lives in careers to which they feel themselves deeply unsuited? When schools are seen as places where students are carefully led to appreciate the various ways in which people in their society can make rewarding contributions, and thus to make a reflective choice about the line(s) along which they want their lives to develop—and when they are later provided with chances to revisit their initial decisions and to choose different directions—these challenges arise with even greater force. Especially when full educational attention is given across the entire society, when no segment of the young is short-changed, regarded as dispensable.

But in this last point I already trespass on themes of the chapters that follow, on the coordination of educational reform with broader social change.

Two kinds of suggestions have figured in the foregoing discussion. The general plan of coordinating the humanities and the social sciences to promote self-understanding has been illustrated by particular examples of what I intend. The status of the two levels is different. My principal aim has been to offer a framework, to be elaborated in accordance with the needs and interests of the particular groups of students. Hence, the illustrations should not be regarded as firm recommendations about how the framework *must* be articulated, but rather as indications of how that *could* be done. The

318   THE MAIN ENTERPRISE OF THE WORLD

following proposals are thus concerned with the framework, and not its detailed development:

29. *In elementary school, children should be introduced to basic features of history and geography. Historical study should include both world history and the past of their own nation. Geography should acquaint them with differences in conditions of life around the world. Emphasis ought to be placed throughout on understanding the lives of different groups of people.*

30. *The exercises in joint planning and cooperative decision-making, pursued in fostering capacities of empathy and good citizenship, should be integrated with some presentations drawn from the research of historians and ethnographers. In this part of the curriculum, some extended role-playing is likely to be helpful.*

31. *From the very beginning of elementary school through all the grades of secondary school, historical and social scientific studies of "experiments of living" should be combined with the interpretation of literature, so that the capacity for entering into the lives of others is developed not only for actual alternatives but for the possibilities envisaged by writers (and film-makers, dramatists, painters, and musicians).*

32. *In the later grades of secondary school, the literary-historical-geographical-anthropological cluster should be supplemented through presentations of main concepts of economics, sociology, political science, and psychology. This segment of the curriculum should instill an appreciation for the methods used by these disciplines, as well as the difficulties often arising in applying them and the kinds of debates to which their usage often gives rise.*

33. *Before they are ten years old, all children should begin study of a foreign language. Choice of the language or languages offered as possibilities for them should be determined by considering the children's interests, the ethnic character of the community, the foreseeable future of their interactions with people who speak other languages, as well as by the availability of teachers or assistants able to help them.*

34. *In the final year or two of secondary school, some consideration ought to be given to spending time introducing classic philosophical texts and methods of philosophical analysis and argumentation. When this is done, it should be with an aim to integrating philosophical reflection (and clear thinking) with the multidisciplinary studies directed toward*

improving self-understanding and the range of possibilities for human existence.

The last sentence stands for the guiding idea governing all six proposals. Study of the *Geisteswissenschaften* shows the individual disciplines in their interaction, with the end of imbuing habits of thought and feeling apt for promoting fulfillment, good citizenship, and moral development. No special steps are taken to prepare for self-maintenance—for if the three specified goals are attained, the fourth is expected to follow.

The three chapters of this part attempt to explain how formal, pre-university schooling, under the aegis of the values heralded in Part I, ought to go. The two chapters to follow in Part III take up two obvious questions. What social changes, within schools and in the wider environment, are needed if any such program is to succeed? Is this a pipe dream, impossible to realize or approximate, and incapable of offering any direction for educational progress?

Let us see.

PART III

10
Social Change

No school is an island. What goes on in the classroom is inevitably shaped by conditions in the ambient society. Obvious examples abound. When the children who enter are hungry, sleep-deprived, and have no opportunities to do the homework assigned them, they are unlikely to listen as attentively or to behave as cooperatively as their more fortunate peers. When the ratio of students to teachers is very high, the chances of individualized attention are diminished. When those who teach are ill-paid, and forced to take on additional work to support themselves and their families, the quality of the education they give is not likely to be improved by the extra hours of labor. When the buildings are dilapidated, the playgrounds poorly equipped and ill-maintained, and the surrounding streets dangerous, truancy and absenteeism are likely to rise.

These are only the *most* obvious ways in which large features of social policy impinge upon formal schooling. Nations that tolerate poverty and homelessness, that save money (for what?) by cutting the budget for teachers' pay, that slash taxes for well-to-do people or build prisons instead of refurbishing schools, can expect to cultivate a sizeable crop of young people for whom education has been a desolate waste of their childhood years. If indeed the money has been used to construct prisons, they will probably be well-filled. The connections between political decisions and their consequences are, in such instances, about as straightforward as social science ever gets.

Subtler linkages also deserve attention. A society's tolerance for prejudice toward particular types of people and the stereotypes dominating attitudes toward ethnic groups will spill over into the smaller society of the school, shaping the interactions among its pupils. Ideas about the differential worth of occupations will color children's perceptions of the importance of different subjects, affecting their views of one another. Often they will generate dismissive judgments. Those who are slow to read, or have difficulty with arithmetic, will be mocked as "stupid," "dumb," "moronic"—whatever their talents for tuneful singing or for growing plants or for constructing a scale model.

The Main Enterprise of the World. Philip Kitcher, Oxford University Press. © Oxford University Press 2022.
DOI: 10.1093/oso/9780190928971.003.0011

324 THE MAIN ENTERPRISE OF THE WORLD

Inegalitarian societies, lavishing rich rewards on the few—the "great contributors" to national wealth—while allowing a large majority to labor long hours for low wages exacerbate such effects. The relentless competition through which the glittering prizes are assigned is felt in muted form already in the early grades. Its intensity grows as ambition takes firmer hold, as the "stupid" fall away in greater numbers, as the hurdles become higher and the number of those remaining in the chase dwindles. Curriculum narrows, becoming centered on the "important subjects." Ideals of fulfillment or of good citizenship fade, bleached by the unforgiving glare of productivity. Some children resign themselves to lives of pursuing humdrum occupations, graced with a handful of mediocre material rewards. For the continuing competitors the whispering voices are ever more urgent: "There must be more money, there must be more money...."[1]

Although the lack of agreement between the educational ideals defended in Part I and the conditions of social life is far harsher and more extensive in some societies than in others, no nation has ever resolved all tensions of this kind. As already emphasized in earlier chapters, the most common way of responding is to allow existing social arrangements—and especially existing economic arrangements—to dictate the proper goals for education.[2] Previous discussions have attempted to turn this strategy on its head. Rather than view existing socioeconomic organization as a fixed constraint to which formal education must adapt, we should begin by deciding what education should achieve, and then ask how societies and their economic structures ought to be modified to help us move more easily toward our educational goals. By inverting the usual assumption about dependence, we focus on what is truly significant—preparation for human lives that are truly worth living. To make that turn is to take seriously Emerson's conception of "the main enterprise of the world."[3]

The voices of "realism" refuse to remain silent any longer. "What a preposterous idea! Utopian fantasies may captivate dilettantes. They are unworkable in an unyielding reality." Those rejoinders deserve to be taken seriously. Yet a commitment to any set of educational ideals should not immediately retreat when "realism" erupts to mock them. Announcing impossibility is

---

[1] Such societies resemble the child protagonist in D. H. Lawrence's short story "The Rocking Horse Winner," whose riding accelerates as these words sound with every greater frenzy in his ear. In consequence of these exertions, the child dies.

[2] See Chapter 2, above 51 ff.

[3] Or, more exactly, the interpretation I have given of that phrase.

not the same as demonstrating it. Investigation is required to discover the points of conflict between ideals and the current conditions of society, and to see what socioeconomic amendments might be necessary to allow the ideals to guide educational practice. Once a clear picture of what scheme of modification would resolve all discords has emerged, it will be possible to investigate whether that scheme can be implemented, yielding a viable new society in which the educational ideals are given full rein. This chapter is devoted to the first task: to seeking a picture of how a society concordant with my educational framework would differ from those we currently know. On that basis, the next (and final) chapter will inquire whether there are grounds to take societies corresponding to the picture to be impossible.

For the sake of clarity, I have oversimplified, representing the opposition as starker than it is. A second theme of previous chapters is my rejection of a teleological conception of ideals. As repeatedly noted,[4] ideals do not characterize some state we aspire to reach or even to approximate. People often make good use of inconsistent sets of ideals, working out their goals in light of the guidance those ideals, taken individually or in clusters, provide.[5] Ideals serve us as diagnostic tools, pointing to problems in our current state and offering directions in which to amend it. Thus the question whether society can be reconstructed to accord with educational ideals, while a good question to answer, is not the only one of interest. We should also seek to understand whether various ways of modifying our socioeconomic arrangements to overcome the problems disclosed by our diagnostic ideals might take us to an achievable and sustainable future, one that improved on the *status quo* (all things considered). Equipped with the picture this chapter attempts to present, we can ask if various ways of amending socioeconomic structures to fit, more or less approximately, with parts of it could yield stable advances on the way we live now.

[4] See Chapters 1 and 3 above, 44 and 92–93.

[5] Recall an example I used in the first chapter, n.84, 44, above. Imagine a homeowner, discontented with the appearance of her garden. She has various ideals: she would like an attractive display of flowers; she would like the beds to be easy to tend; she would like a continuous display, lasting for several months; she does not want to spend vast sums of money; particular combinations of colors appeal, others do not. She simply doesn't know how to prioritize or combine these ideals. But they provide direction for her horticulture. As she goes, she discovers changes that work, and changes that don't. Constantly adjusting, she eventually achieves a satisfying state, one she couldn't have envisaged in advance. She has made pragmatic progress. Whereas she doesn't have any desire for further change, she recognizes very clearly that her efforts might have gone in different directions and proved equally satisfactory.

326   THE MAIN ENTERPRISE OF THE WORLD

The shallowness of "realism" should now be apparent. Not only does it announce impossibilities without providing evidence—and without even specifying the kinds of unavailable changes it holds to be required to realize the idealists' dreams!—but it also fails to consider complex questions about myriad lines along which an educational idealist might hope for pragmatic progress. For the present, reflecting on how those complex questions might be addressed will be postponed (that is part of the work of the next chapter). Our task is to recognize clearly the directions in which my educational ideals point, when they are brought to bear as diagnostic tools on the societies we currently inhabit.

The list of conflicts between the healthy school and the ambient society, offered at the beginning of this chapter, provides a useful starting point. Although it is surely incomplete, it can serve to present a collection of precise questions. With respect to each discord, we can ask what would be needed to resolve it. In what follows, I shall proceed sequentially, examining the instances figuring on the list. It will be useful to start with the easiest, then move on to those requiring more radical changes.

Surely the simplest issues are those turning on budgetary allotments. These raise no questions about modifying fundamental features of the economic order. They accept the major features of the ways in which contemporary (market) economies run, proposing only a reassignment of funds from some (unspecified) area of the nation's budget, to be devoted instead to educational purposes. The simple way of remedying the problem of underpaid teachers is to increase their salaries. Equally straightforwardly, the difficulties posed by dilapidated, structurally unsound, and even toxic schools can be overcome by investing in repairs, rebuilding, and sometimes constructing new schools, located in different places. The latter option is necessary when some recurrent source of damage is likely to thwart attempts simply to refurbish the existing site. Thus a school liable to floods from a nearby river, full of industrial waste, or a school now located near a major highway (whose air quality threatens the health of those who attend it) should not be patched up. New facilities, in healthier locations, are needed.[6]

---

[6] Jonathan Kozol describes in wrenching detail an East St. Louis school, through whose premises toxic chemicals periodically flow. See his *Savage Inequalities* (New York: Broadway, 1991).

SOCIAL CHANGE   327

In many countries, the problems of underpaid teachers and shoddy (or dangerous) schools are severe enough to affect the education many children receive. The United States does not fare well in this regard, and, predictably, the victims typically come from poor families and belong to racial and ethnic minorities. Other countries do better. South Korea, Belgium, Israel, and Australia (to give examples from different parts of the world) all pay their teachers substantially more than American teachers receive.[7] Interestingly, Finland, often viewed as a leader in successful educational policy, does not stand out for its *economic* support of teachers. Although Finnish teachers have higher salaries than their American counterparts, Finland attracts the best and the brightest of college applicants to the teaching profession through the importance and prestige given to teaching.[8] As will become clear, this is a point to remember in considering possibilities of social change.

Not all of the most blatant issues on my initial list succumb to budgetary reallocation, however. Governments might clean up their overburdened, overcrowded, and decaying schools through investing in programs to attract more young people into the teaching profession, providing higher salaries, hiring teachers in greater numbers, and refurbishing school buildings. The result might be shiny new facilities, well equipped, staffed with enthusiastic, well-trained professionals, ready to engage with a manageable roomful of students. Nevertheless, the children might still face a menacing journey on the way to school, and even be vulnerable on the school site itself. Their families might still be homeless, or crammed into too small a space. Food might still be scarce, healthy meals a rarity. None of these problems allows a straightforward solution by simply changing funding priorities.

A subtler instance of the same phenomenon. Although the teacher-student ratio would obviously be lowered if more teachers were hired, taking that route to advance is only a part of my recommended reform. Even if the new teachers were superbly trained and among the most gifted members of the profession, the fully individualized program proposed above requires the presence of a large number of adults in the classroom, especially in the early grades. Parents are expected to spend time observing, guiding, and assisting the young, working not only with their own children but with their

[7] See the Brookings Institution's comparison of teacher salaries around the world: https://www. brookings.edu/blog/brown-center-chalkboard/2016/06/20/teacher-pay-around-the-world/.

[8] See the Brookings Report cited in the previous note, and also the NCEE assessment of the character of the teaching profession in Finland: http://ncee.org/what-we-do/center-on-international-education-benchmarking/top-performing-countries/finland-overview/finland-teacher-and-principal-quality/.

328 THE MAIN ENTERPRISE OF THE WORLD

children's peers. Other members of the community, from young adults to septuagenarians (or even older people?), are expected to bring their own distinctive enthusiasms, skills, and perspectives. Effectively, children pass through a sequence of transitory villages—with some continuity among them—in which they are raised. The time spent by the many people who guide them is taken away from other occupations, requiring changes in patterns of work. Modifying the distribution of effort during the workweek demands more than simply moving money from one pot into another. Thus an apparently budgetary matter becomes an issue involving more sweeping reforms. Restructuring labor is an issue I shall postpone to much later in this chapter.

Two issues, however, deserve immediate clarification. First, the proposal to recruit adults as aides in the classroom poses a danger of reintroducing or intensifying gender stereotypes. *This role must be filled equally by men and by women.* As the eruption of the Covid-19 pandemic has demonstrated, under current economic conditions, increasing parental participation in child care has led to greater inequalities between male and female partners in providing what is required.[9] Equalizing wages and salaries (both with respect to the sexes, and in general) would help to blunt the threat. So too would adjustments of work to enable more flexibility with respect to hours: "understudies" or teams of substitutes can be organized to step in for people who must respond to other calls on their time.[10] As we shall see, combatting all kinds of stereotypes will be important if the educational program I have envisaged is to be implemented. One result of the campaign should be a society-wide expectation that men will do their share: the husband who fails to participate in education would no longer be viewed as someone whose duties were too important for such trivial matters, but as a parasite—a drone.

A second and related point: teaching well is a complex skill, and, although there may be some "naturals," teachers need serious training. Can my proposal to bring more adults into the classroom really add educational value unless the "aides" are instructed in what is required of them? It is easy to envisage blundering newcomers doing more harm than good. Yet, I think the fear is overblown. Those without any classroom experience join a team.

---

[9] This is brilliantly documented in Claudia Goldin's 2020 Feldstein Lecture, "Journey across a Century of Women," https://www.nber.org/lecture/2020-martin-feldstein-lecture-journey-across-century-women. I am grateful to Dan O'Flaherty for calling my attention to this important and illuminating presentation.

[10] This possibility is discussed by Goldin in her Feldstein Lecture. She points out that it has already been implemented in some medical specialties.

SOCIAL CHANGE   329

They are guided by other adults who have already spent years acquiring skills in fostering children's development, by professionally trained aides, and by teachers, who can try to draw on the newcomers' strengths to enrich what is offered to the young. It is well to remember how first-time parents undergo on-the-job training. They may be helped by the advice of friends who can recall their own early problems, and suggest solutions. The broad involvement of adults in education, envisaged in previous chapters, makes the nurturing of *parents* (and of beginning classroom helpers) more systematic. We should think of the adult group of mentors as another democratic space in which mutual learning constantly occurs. Of course, if future data show potential benefits of training programs for adults in the classroom (that is—for all adults), then providing that would be a further step.

The previous point bears on a different cluster of challenges.[11] My conception of the classroom, particularly in elementary school, sees it as the well-tilled ground in which democracy germinates and takes root. If that is to occur, a high level of cooperation will be required—not only among the children but also among the adults who observe and who assist their progress. The degree to which those present work together would likely be significantly greater than that to which we are accustomed, when groups of unrelated strangers face a common problem. How is such cooperation to be established, and how is it to be maintained?

Introducing a cooperative atmosphere among the children is probably the easy part. Considerable attention has been given to designing games for teaching young children (three to five years old) to cooperate.[12] Harder problems start to emerge when playtime stops. Especially as children grow, as study requires more effort, as they are assessed and graded, as they compare their performances with those of others, as they compete for small marks of distinction, for prizes, for passage to an "advanced group," for being singled out as "gifted and talented," forms of solidarity and comradeship attained at earlier stages start to break down. Skillful teachers, vigilant in spotting incipient rivalries, can take steps to make comparisons more difficult—perhaps by celebrating a wide range of individual triumphs spread across many different

[11] As the discussion of 339–42 should make clear.
[12] Any internet search for "teaching cooperation in young children" will turn up a large number of suggestions.

330   THE MAIN ENTERPRISE OF THE WORLD

types of school activity. My proposed commitment to identifying the talents and interests of each child will surely help in this. But, as the structure of the larger world starts to loom, as different patches of light and shade are cast within the classroom, praise for achievements in "trivial" or "unimportant" domains will begin to sound hollow, unconsoling, even patronizing. Applauding the neatness of a thirteen-year-old's handwriting doesn't compensate for the spurts of correcting red disfiguring the essay.

How, then, to reconcile a program aimed at helping all students to find their own distinctive ways of contributing to their societies—and thus to fulfill themselves—with their inevitable growing realization of the very different values assigned by those societies to alternative types of contribution? Society's values are reflected in the variety of rewards bestowed on different jobs and professions—even in the language of "job," "career," and "profession" itself. Scales of compensation mark clear distinctions, as do observable features: differential command of resources and variant lifestyles. Yet, as the example of Finnish teachers should remind us, those are not the only ways in which social attitudes can lend allure to a particular style of social contribution.

If prevalent social attitudes remain unchanged, the students educated as I have recommended will experience an Orwellian moment of awakening. Like the inhabitants of *Animal Farm*, they will have been brought up to believe in the equality of all ways of advancing the lives of others and of the collective life of their societies. They will discover, in adolescence, if not before, that some of these equal possibilities are more equal than others. The illumination they receive may well provoke cynicism about a charade in which they now see themselves as having participated.

When the problem is formulated in this way, the solution is not hard to identify. If we expect the young to appreciate the value of all kinds of work, two large social changes must occur: first, occupations without social worth should be exposed for what they are; second, the contributions of those who do make positive differences to others' lives ought to be recognized and appreciated. As a corollary of the first change, useless lines of work should be expected to wither away and vanish; in accordance with the second, the basis for honoring those who contribute ought not to be the rarity of the associated talents or the difficulties of acquiring necessary skills, but the dedication brought to discharging the required tasks. For a large number of reasons (some of which will emerge below), rethinking education along the lines proposed entails a great diminution in the differences in rewards (financial compensation, social esteem, and the like) many societies currently tolerate. The Deweyan society must be far more egalitarian than most of those figuring in human history.[13] Meritocracy, to the extent it survives, is of a different species. Honoring all who play their part in advancing the common good, it distinguishes only in celebrating those whose devotion to their role—whatever it may be—leads them to outstanding effort in fulfilling it.

Talk of "useless labor" withering away deliberately provokes an anticipated reaction. Is the Deweyan society simply another dreary version of the well-known failures of twentieth-century egalitarianism, the supposed "workers' paradises" with their drab uniformity and dismal standards of living—as well, of course, as their corruption, surveillance, and suppression of freedoms?[14] No. It is, first and foremost, a place in which individuality is valued, where education is designed to promote individual fulfillment, and where that fulfillment is understood as a recognized personal contribution to the common good. True enough, the worker who delivers packages to people's homes and the conductor of the subway train are no longer seen as far inferior to the surgeon and the judge. No useful employment deserves the condescending label "menial work."

The examples of the delivery worker and the subway train conductor are particularly salient for me as I write these words: my home city, New York, is the "epicenter" of the current wave of the Covid-19 pandemic.[15] In consequence, people have revised their assessments of the value of some occupations. In a city under strict quarantine, many of whose residents are classed as "high risk," venturing out for necessary supplies has come to appear a perilous adventure, one to be avoided as much as possible. Those who deliver goods, whether the truck drivers or the cyclists (who often irritate and sometimes alarm unwary pedestrians), now promise deliverance, not mere delivery. The many "essential workers" from outer boroughs, who travel to their jobs on public transport, depend on the willingness of those who staff

---

[13] Dewey's own attitudes toward egalitarian approaches in politics become clear in many of his later writings. See, for example, Chapter 6 of *Individualism, Old and New* (LW 5, 90–98, especially 98), "The Underlying Philosophy of Education" (LW 8, 77–103, especially 83–86), and *Liberalism and Social Action* (LW 11, 5–65, especially 42–44, 53–56, 61–63.) In the text, I say "most" not "all" to recognize the ways in which social democracies, in particular those professing democratic socialism, have occasionally managed to reduce intra-societal inequality.

[14] Although I have attempted to respond to some concerns of this form here, and in the following chapter, I postpone a more general discussion of the danger of centralized coercion to Appendix 2. Thanks to Martha Nussbaum for alerting me to the fact that more needed to be said.

[15] This sentence was written in the spring of 2020. Sadly, the United States failed to learn the lesson, and other American cities and states would later vie for the distinction of being the principal site of infection.

332 THE MAIN ENTERPRISE OF THE WORLD

and maintain the trains and buses to show up daily, exposing themselves to infection. As is now clear, it is possible to become aware that you have previously underrated a particular line of work.

Yet there are surely some forms of employment that, when closely scrutinized, cannot be validated for their contributions to human lives. "Trinkets and baubles" are produced simply to allow those who can afford them to proclaim their high status.[16] Conspicuous consumption serves no useful purpose. Indeed, it reinforces the sense of inequality, incites envy, and weakens solidarity.[17] In its most pernicious forms, conspicuous consumption craves products lacking any worth independently of their serving to mark financial superiority. Demand for those products does not stem from any intrinsic value they may have. The product is designed and marketed to generate desires that would vanish in the absence of a social hierarchy in which purchasers hope to display their lofty place.[18] People who devote their lives to designing and producing such products, and to creating the seductive advertisements through which they come to be in demand, make no genuine contribution to the human good. Insofar as their work is central to their life project, they cannot be judged as finding fulfillment. The hired hands who participate in the work of production may well view the time they spend in the factory as unrewarding, merely a means to their central goals (supporting their families and seeking better lives for their children, for example). Unfolding the ways in which their work makes a difference to the lives of others, making its effects transparent, would not remove their sense of alienation but reinforce it. This labor—but, with luck, not their other-oriented lives—would be exposed as worthless.[19]

To appreciate this point is *not* to insist on directing all production toward satisfying basic needs, nor is it to commend requiring uniformity in appearance (for dress, architecture, cuisine, or any other area in which people express their genuine—and varying—tastes). Drawing such conclusions would

---

[16] The phrase is Adam Smith's; see WN 446–47. Book III of WN is devoted to explaining the collapse of the feudal system, and an important part of Smith's narrative ascribes the decreasing power of the landowning barons to their weakness for trinkets and baubles.

[17] The idea of conspicuous consumption was introduced by Thorstein Veblen in 1899 in his book *The Theory of the Leisure Class* (repr., New York: Dover, 2004). That book repays re-reading in our new gilded age.

[18] For the articulation of this concept, and for a critique of this form of consumption, see John Kenneth Galbraith, *The Affluent Society* (New York: Houghton Mifflin, 1958).

[19] For a vigorous critique of motivational research directed at creating consumer desires, see Vance Packard, *The Hidden Persuaders* (New York: McKay, 1957). Veblen, Packard, and Galbraith can be seen as allies in exposing the possibility of worthless labor in some forms of capitalism.

be entirely at odds with the individuality my educational proposals seek to foster. Resources, whether those of a particular person, a family, a local community, or a nation, should be assigned to advance as many of the chosen projects as possible—indeed, distributive policy should aim at promoting all. Chapter 8 celebrated the importance of aesthetic experiences in human lives.[20] Except in times of extreme scarcity—times at which all other goals must be sacrificed to the task of survival—forswearing all expenditures on satisfying individual aesthetic tastes would be a travesty of living well. Hence, while assembling closets full of the most costly brands of shoes (as a sign of one's wealth) is a pathology,[21] greatly decreasing the variance in the amounts of money commanded by people whose levels of wealth now differ grossly (and grotesquely) by no means entails the dreary conformity of the "workers' paradises." A far more egalitarian society can rejoice in individuals who express their tastes in dress and jewelry, or in tattoos, or in the design of their gardens, or in well-appointed kitchens, or in museum subscriptions, or in collections of books, or . . . . Some contemporary democracies have reduced inequality, while retaining an abundance of diversity in decoration and aesthetic life. Inferences to gloomy predictions for the Deweyan society require an extra premise. The further steps beyond the forms of egalitarianism manifested in social democracies (the Netherlands and the Nordic countries, for example) needed to yield a Deweyan society so disturb the underlying economy as to generate a permanent state of extreme scarcity (or worse). Arguments aimed at supporting this premise will occupy us in the next (and final) chapter.

The Deweyan society aims to expose and thus eliminate forms of labor whose *raisons d'être* lie (and lie only) in their ability to display socioeconomic status. In doing so it saves resources now assigned to some products—the marbled halls, aesthetically challenged gilded monstrosities, attractive only to status-seekers dreaming of dwelling in them. The Taj Mahal survives, Mar-a-Lago probably does not. With respect to the socially valuable occupations that remain, it offers public recognition of their worth, radically reducing the current inequalities in economic rewards. Redistributing resources in this way, it provides for all its members, assuring them shelter, food, clean water, clothing, medical care, free public education at all levels, and sufficient means

---

[20] See above, 260–66.
[21] The example stems from the well-known propensities of Imelda Marcos, former first lady of the Philippines.

334   THE MAIN ENTERPRISE OF THE WORLD

to allow people, young and old, to pursue and continue their educations.[22] That is a necessary basis for the democratic community to be created and developed in the school classrooms of the future.

———

Yet, if that community is to grow, more is required, both within the school and without. First, as I have already hinted, it will be important to modify the ways in which children—and workers—are assessed. Examinations, with their marks and grades, have traditionally played two roles. First, and currently more importantly, they allow for others—the school, later the society—to sort the candidates. Second, they provide information for those who are tested, showing them where their strengths and weaknesses are. The role of the former function is likely to be different, and the value of the latter is likely to be increased in a world where a wide variety of potential occupations are viewed with respect and where the variation in compensation is far less extreme.

Consider a happy fantasy about a young life. Entering school, a girl has only dim thoughts about "what she might like to be when she grows up." From a distance, a number of options appear attractive, and perhaps her ratings change quite rapidly during the first years of her school time. As she proceeds, she discovers her own profile of abilities. She does well in arithmetic and excels in music, but her progress in reading is relatively slow. When adults pose the "what do you want to be" question, her answers reflect her awareness of her talents and shortcomings. A future in journalism doesn't seem a good option, perhaps scientific work would suit her better, and maybe performing music would be the most exciting of all. Setting some possibilities, even possibilities once found exciting, on one side causes no acute pangs of disappointment, precipitates no crisis. Since her society recognizes the value of a wide range of occupations, she is happy to let her mentors guide her in the direction of her recognized talents. Eventually she takes up a post as an audiology technician, works hard at it, and enjoys a fulfilling career. As she ages, she has no regrets.

My protagonist is aided by whatever exercises are used for assessing her along the way. She learns important things about herself. Discovering what she would be good at, she is subject to no significant contrary pressures, to

---

[22] It thus favors the kinds of proposals made by such recent writers as Anthony Atkinson, in *Inequality*, and Philippe van Parijs and Yannick Vanderborght, in *Basic Income: A Radical Proposal for a Free Society and a Sane Economy* (Cambridge, MA: Harvard University Press, 2017).

strong winds blowing her toward a different course. In an obvious sense, her education enables her to become who she is.[23]

Compare her with the young people of the actual world. Early on in their schooling, many of them become aware of which jobs pay well (and which don't), which ones have high social prestige (and which ones are viewed as "inferior" or "menial").[24] Knowledge of these sorts inclines them to adopt a ranking of potential futures almost from the start. Not surprisingly, they—and their classmates—thus come to have relatively firm ideas about the "what do you want to be" question. Poor assessments in areas relevant to the goal on which they have set their hearts can then prove crushing, leading them to view themselves as failures. Or they may stimulate stubborn resistance, an urge to keep going along the path selected, come what may. Further lack of success, when it comes, augments the sense of failure. Perhaps a hard-won adequacy, achieved through clenched teeth, proves even worse. Finally slogging their way through to the chosen occupation, they spend a lifetime of struggle, always aware of their mediocrity. Other sides of their characters remain undeveloped. The talents they revealed in their early years—talents only suited to "unrewarding" occupations—go neglected. They have been blown off course. Their society has played a heavy-handed role in the formative dialogue, foisting a distorting identity upon them.

Moreover, the hierarchy of options poisons relations among peers. Students who remain in the chase become rivals as they strain toward the next rounds of winnowing. Those who drop out early may create and preserve forms of camaraderie, but they are also primed for viewing their peers, those meeting the criteria for "conventional success," with sour resentment. Perhaps they will develop a counterculture, offering a different hierarchy, prizing the ability to mock education and viewing "badness" as a badge of honor. Bringing members of these different groups together for democratic deliberation will not usually be profitable.

Rethinking education along the lines proposed above requires abandoning hierarchy. Multiplying hierarchies may be a natural strategy for consoling those in the lower tiers of the conventional pyramid. It does not, however, solve the problem. A Deweyan society must be predicated on viewing all contributions to the projects of others as important. It should not allow

---

[23] Once again, I echo Nietzsche. See the discussion of Chapter 3, 104–6.

[24] Often, of course, these divisions will coincide. Not always, though, as the example of the Finnish teachers reveals.

336 THE MAIN ENTERPRISE OF THE WORLD

large differences in prestige or rewards on the familiar grounds. Simply because a particular type of useful labor can be performed by many, while another demands rare abilities or lengthy training, does not justify dismissive attitudes toward the former and adulation of the latter. Human lives are interwoven, making the labor of the surgeon or the executive dependent on the efforts of those who deliver the packages and drive the trains. No school is an island. No human being is an island, either.

How much differentiation is tolerable? Specifying a precise limit of permissible variation, to be applied across the board, would be foolish. Yet, even in profoundly unequal societies, exact equality is not what the underprivileged need nor what they (and their allies) campaign for. Those who wish for better education for their children would be entirely satisfied if the facilities available to them were roughly comparable to the most sought-after schools. In many areas of life, even in matters of considerable significance, people are satisficers rather than optimizers. The outcome doesn't have to be identified as the best. It must be good enough.[25]

Delivery workers would probably not resent a situation in which surgeons received somewhat higher salaries than they did. They would understand the need to provide them with full support during their long training, and, once the training was completed, the reasonableness of making up any shortfall in earnings during medical apprenticeship. Perhaps they would even agree in offering more to people with highly developed skills who must make decisions on which human lives turn. *Precisely* equal salaries and *precisely* the same status are not required. At the other extreme, they would rightly reject allocation schemes offering themselves (and others in similar lines of work) only a modest wage, while providing surgeons with ten times that amount.[26] Where, between zero and nine, ought the differential to be set? Given my approach to settling political and moral issues, my answer should

---

[25] This is the insight behind Harry Frankfurt's critique of egalitarianism in *On Inequality* (Princeton, NJ: Princeton University Press, 2015). Frankfurt recognizes how providing people with enough answers to their wants and aspirations, making the further goal of equalizing unnecessary. Unfortunately, however, he is insufficiently attentive to a point frequently made in studies of inequality: what counts as enough depends on the societal distribution. When some of your co-citizens are vastly wealthier than you are, what would otherwise be an adequate reward will not be satisfactory. The aspirations you aim to satisfy are themselves partly determined by the possibilities taken to be available to others. For excellent expositions of this point, see Amartya Sen, *Inequality Reexamined* (Cambridge, MA: Harvard University Press, 1995); and Atkinson, *Inequality*.

[26] Salary.com sets the median salaries for people who drive delivery trucks at $42,300 per annum, and for surgeons at $393,000 a year. See: https://www.salary.com/research/salary/alternate/delivery-driver-salary and https://www.salary.com/research/salary/benchmark/surgeon-salary. I have rounded up slightly, so that the degree of inequality is somewhat increased.

be predictable. Collective bargaining ought to proceed under the guidance of my three constraints. All forms of work should be represented (this will obviously require lumping different occupations together—those assigned to the same group should be willing to accept the underlying principle of classification); deliberators should be given the best available information about the requirements and character of the types of labor; and they should seek a scheme of allocating resources all can accept.

The result should be a different form of meritocracy. It begins by honoring all the valuable species of work (and endeavors to eliminate any that are worthless or counterproductive). Whatever distinctions are made are approved by all. Within categories, merit is recognized and rewarded according to the care and diligence with which workers discharge the duties of their positions. But all are valued and supported in their quests to pursue their individual projects.

The aura of that meritocracy should descend upon the schools. However the developing citizens follow distinctive directions, leading them through their individually tailored curricula, the guiding principle will always be, from the early grades of elementary school until the end of their (first phase of)[27] formal education, to underscore the worth of the full range of socially necessary occupations. In any classroom, there may be children of quite different ages. Instead of using labels to separate the younger from the older—the "brilliant" from the "dim," the "geniuses" from the "morons"—the school will see all as acquiring capacities for serving the community in different ways, along lines of roughly equivalent value. It will rejoice in variety, welcoming a mixture of people with different predilections and propensities.

Assessments, grades, and examinations thus lose part of their significance. They no longer signal levels of inferiority and superiority. Their function reduces to one of conveying information to individual children and their mentors, showing the lines along which the psychological and physical traits so far developed might valuably be extended and refined. They tell the protagonist of my fantasy where her weaknesses lie, and point her to her strengths. No longer to be feared, they are lights directing her to strengthen where she is weak and to continue where she is most promising. Knowing that a worthwhile and well-supported future awaits her however the signals

---

[27] Recall my earlier proposal to allow opportunities for adults to return and to take up new kinds of study.

338   THE MAIN ENTERPRISE OF THE WORLD

flash, she can go forward in confidence. The need to measure herself against others disappears.

My case for a modified meritocracy rests on an obvious assumption. Is it reasonable to think of all children as having some special talent in whose development they may discover fulfillment?[28] Might not some children prove hopeless at everything?

The possibility cannot be excluded. Nevertheless, even in the absence of the empirical studies required to measure the frequency with which such instances occur, the wide variety of domains figuring in my approach to education militates against it. Besides all the subjects presently pursued in formal schooling, the proposed curriculum gives considerable emphasis to arts and crafts, to exercises in joint planning and deliberation, and to acquiring languages. The "hopeless cases" would not only struggle with the "three Rs"—they would also have to be unmusical, unartistic, terrible with their hands, poor gardeners, physically clumsy, with no talent for picking up new languages, and bereft of qualities of character valuable in democratic discussion. (Good listeners and students with "people skills" can distinguish themselves as mediators.) Along whatever lines the teachers and helpers of the early grades attempted to lead them, the path would quickly end in a cul-de-sac. Whether all of them would be classified under the "special needs" rubric used in existing schools, they would surely require extra attention and large amounts of individualized instruction. Techniques developed in helping children with disabilities (developmental disabilities, in particular) could also be deployed to promote fruitful and rewarding interactions with their peers.[29]

So far, I have mostly been concerned with fostering cooperation among the *children* within the classroom. Yet that space will also be a site at which adults come together—teachers, assistants, parents, visitors from the community—combining their talents, interests, and experiences in the enterprise of

---

[28] Interestingly, classical (and neoclassical) economics often makes a similar assumption about nations. Each country is taken to have a comparative advantage with respect to some mode of production. See, for example, WN 16–17, 485–88.

[29] The past decades have witnessed an upsurge of educational proposals for assisting children with special needs. An internet search reveals many suggestions, most of which would appear easier to implement under the education reforms sketched here. Although the evidence of effectiveness is hardly conclusive, it would seem valuable to continue along many of the lines currently pursued, and to increase the number and variety of the experiments.

SOCIAL CHANGE   339

building up human beings. From the viewpoint of growing good citizens, assembling a mono-racial, socioeconomically homogenous group is undesirable. On the other hand, if the assembly is a genuine mixture, multiracial, and running the gamut of the society's strata, are its members likely to work together harmoniously? To concur in their estimates of what individual children need? To agree on the content of what is presented or the style of the presentation?

Hence, it will be important to fashion a community—or communities—whose composition changes from year to year. During the time when their children are largely taught together in the same space, parents must take the time to discuss with one another, attempting to understand others' distinctive points of view. Ideally, this should become an opportunity for learning, as the exchange of ideas prompts all members of the parental group to recognize weaknesses in their own approaches to childrearing, and to find ways of improvement. While the primary responsibility remains within the nuclear family, some of the burdens of parenting can be lightened as children form social bonds and as individual parents can supervise—and guide—a cluster of schoolmates. Everybody benefits if Alex's mother knows she can trust Bella's father to look after him for the afternoon, especially if she recognizes what Alex will gain from time spent in Bella's and her father's company. And, of course, if the trust is reciprocated.

Collective childrearing of this kind already occurs, in rather different ways among groups of parents who live in prosperous suburbs and clusters of inner-city residents, many of them with family ties to one another.[30] My proposals institutionalize the practice through bringing parents together in their children's classrooms, and providing them with a far deeper understanding of the classmates' individual personalities. Nevertheless, so long as the social network forges stronger connections between children (and parents) whose cultures and economic status are highly similar, the educational value of exchanges will be limited. If Alex's home life is very much like Bella's, neither child's horizons are likely to be greatly expanded by visits to one another's houses or by joint excursions. Parents and children alike would grow through interactions with people very different from themselves, people whose lifestyles sometimes appeared strange and, although not dangerous, somewhat unsettling. Within the classroom and beyond, it is crucial

[30] The differences are documented by Annette Lareau, *Unequal Childhoods*.

340   THE MAIN ENTERPRISE OF THE WORLD

for children to come to know people exhibiting as much of the society's racial, cultural, and economic variation as possible.

For otherwise dangerous prejudices and stereotypes are likely to persist. Those pathologies do not appear to be present at the very beginning. Developmental studies suggest an absence of any significant preference for playmates of the same race among three- and four-year-old children.[31] In fact, the well-known intra-racial variation in the characteristics used as standard racial markers presents difficulties for young children in acquiring the concept of race.[32] Not only do they have to be carefully taught to regard some races as inferior. They also need significant practice before their use of racial vocabulary is fluent.

Probably the best way to drive harmful stereotypes out of a society is to magnify the confusion. Early in their lives, children should mingle with as many different age-mates from as many different categories as is possible. When your sample of X's includes a large number of individuals whose variety along multiple dimensions you have experienced and remembered, the temptation to form sweeping judgments, whether positive or negative, is undermined. The best antitoxins for the poisons of racial, ethnic, and cultural prejudice are to mix children in diverse groups from the start of their school-days, and to involve them in joint planning for activities they will share.

The melting pot works best, of course, when all the added ingredients are equally fresh. Once the Deweyan society has whittled away the socioeconomic inequalities so evident today, it will be far easier for young children to come together as equals. Banishing racial, ethnic, and cultural stereotypes will go more smoothly if the (marginalized) races, ethnic groups, and cultures are no longer correlated with economic disadvantages. The rough egalitarianism defended earlier is an important step toward overcoming

---

[31] See Kristin Shutts, Caroline K. Pemberton, and Elisabeth S. Spelke, "Children's Use of Social Categories in Thinking about People and Relationships," *Journal of Cognitive Development* 14 (2013): 35–62. Available online at https://www.ncbi.nlm.nih.gov/pmc/articles/PMC3640585/.

[32] For a study of phenotypic variation in traits often used to mark race, see J. H. Relethford, "Race and Global Patterns of Phenotypic Variation," *American Journal of Physical Anthropology* 139 (2009): 16–22. Available online at https://www.ncbi.nlm.nih.gov/pubmed/19226639. The difficulty this variation poses for young children was brought home to me when our elder son, then in kindergarten, made friends with two young boys each of whom had one African American parent. At some point in his schooling, he had been told that they were of "a different race." Puzzled by this, he asked us for an explanation. We suggested that the differences weren't important, that some people had darker skin than others. This immediately brought to his mind a former, much-loved caregiver, a woman of Italian heritage. During the summers she would develop a deep and lustrous tan, so that, when he saw her in the fall, her skin would be very dark—and his memory depicted her accurately as far darker than his friends. She was his first paradigm of "African Americans"!

SOCIAL CHANGE   341

prejudice. To escape the current situation requires beginning a virtuous spiral. Diminishing inequality decreases the supposed evidence for stereotypes, and the weakened stereotypes prompt more acceptance and more generous rewards, further reducing inequality, . . . and so it goes.

Initiating that spiral is crucial for creating my envisaged community of cooperating parents. Indeed, my earlier descriptions of it likely provoked either an amused smile or a sense of absurd fantasy. Contrast it with a more realistic vision. Imagine the parents of a kindergarten class assembling at the start of the school year. They look around, assessing the families from which their children's schoolmates will come. If the others are much like themselves, the auguries are good. Perceived familiarity breeds content. Signs of economic gaps—chasms?—especially when coupled to other socially salient differences, cause unease. If the mixed-race single mother, nervously hanging back, is obviously poor, probably unemployed, and possibly homeless, the professional couple will typically not hope for her child and their own to become bosom buddies. Or, if they do attempt to engage with her, the terms are likely to be patronizing and the overtures maladroit. For her part, as she compares her son's shabby state (even in his better clothes) with the shining new gear of the others, the single mother (she is, in fact, homeless) can only wonder how the boy will fit in. How, too, will she interact with people whose lives she can partly imagine (thanks to TV shows) but who probably have no conception of the difficulties she has faced and the problems besetting her life today? How can she hope to enter the classroom as an equal, or to raise her own voice in the parents' conversations?

In a Deweyan society, she no longer exists. Her counterpart receives economic support. She has a home in which to shelter and raise her family. On the school's opening day, her son doesn't look so very different from his classmates. She no longer takes the other parents to perceive her as a threat, someone whose child might befriend their own, luring his victim into a squalid and dangerous environment. True enough, she still has hesitations. Will these wealthier people bridle at her ideas about childrearing? Resolving to be open and unassertive, she discovers other parents who are no more confident than she. So the work of mutual learning begins, and, as the dialogues grow more relaxed, as the advice flows more easily and its helpful effects become more obvious, even the most self-assured recognize the benefits—and join in.

With a commitment to valuing all kinds of contributions, with a resolve to support all in meeting their material needs and pursuing their individual,

342 THE MAIN ENTERPRISE OF THE WORLD

socially directed, projects, the Deweyan society can overcome discrimination and eliminate stereotypes.[33] It can foster forms of cooperation in education to the advantage of children and parents alike.

I turn at last to the hardest cluster of issues, those raised by taking seriously education as a lifetime venture, and by allowing a variety of patterns for integrating extended periods of study with productive or service work. My approach to the problem of overload (with which this book began) has been to champion idiosyncratic emphases on different parts of a rich general curriculum,[34] while permitting people to return and fill in gaps of which their further experience has made them aware. The Deweyan society offers no standard trajectory. It does not insist on some particular age at which schooling must begin and then proceed continuously to the point at which formal education forever ceases. Lives are not divided into four discrete chunks: a short initial period, a longer interval through which schools (and maybe colleges and universities) assume a major role in guiding the development of the young, an even longer span of work, and a final return to leisure, whose length is determined by the point at which retirement begins and the inevitable termination. Nor are there standard times for leaving school—say at sixteen or eighteen, or, if higher education is pursued, at twenty-two or at the end of graduate studies. Perhaps the first phase of formal education will typically last a dozen years. After an initial period, from birth to the first exit from school, applying, in some small number of alternatives to all, the interspersing of work, study, and leisure is permitted to vary quite radically in accordance with individual propensities and aspirations.

This luxuriant diversity inspires an obvious criticism. I'll call it "the threat of chaos." Critics wonder how it can all be managed. How will the necessary work of society get done? How will public institutions, businesses, important services be able to plan? How will educational facilities identify what will be required in the coming year? How will supply and demand be coordinated? Visions of unpredictable surges of quittings and joinings popping up

---

[33] Besides the measures I have sketched, it can also draw on the diagnoses and remedies offered by psychological research. See in particular Claude Steele, *Whistling Vivaldi*.

[34] The overall plan for general education, presented in Part II, might be pursued in some depth across the board by lengthening the school day for those who choose not to specialize early, or by extending the length of time spent in formal education. Individual trajectories might differ not only in the particular disciplines given most attention, but also in their pace. Here too one size doesn't fit all.

SOCIAL CHANGE 343

haphazardly across the social landscape prompt the label I have attached to the problem. It will all be chaos.

Yet what I have envisaged only magnifies patterns already present in contemporary societies. Ambitious young workers take two years' leave to attend business schools, teachers at universities and at some secondary schools are allowed a year off to pursue research or to acquire new expertise, young couples expand their families and are given parental leave.[35] All these practices temporarily remove workers from their normal jobs, but employers have learned to manage the changes. One of the key tools for coping is advance notice. In some instances, it is not hard to predict what the future will bring. Prospective parents will almost invariably know of the change in schedules for more than six months. Even if they choose not to inform their employers, by the end of the second trimester the secret will almost certainly be out. Of course, even then, they may not have decided just how much leave they want and how the leave time is to be divided between them.

Would it be hard to scale up? There are obvious ways of extending procedures already in place. Universities draw up schedules, allowing their teaching faculty to request leaves at fixed intervals, and they ask those who are eligible in a given year to let them know well beforehand if they intend to take a year for research (or further study). That strategy is easily generalized. On joining the workforce, whatever the occupation, the newly employed negotiate with their supervisors the framework governing their future "educational leaves."[36] Beginning workers formulate their future plans, as they foresee them. National policy lays down rules requiring both parties to limit their demands. Although the worker can request a leave within the first three years, the employer has the right to refuse, and also the right to demand at least three years of total service if the request is granted. No employer can refuse a request for a six month leave after three years' service, or for a year's leave after five. Policy also sets the terms of compensation during leave,

---

[35] Policies for parental leave vary greatly around the world, both in terms of the length of time permitted (while the job is protected) and in the amount and schedule of compensation. Predictably, most European nations are far more generous in allowing long leaves and in paying parents while they are on leave. The United States fares poorly in these respects, and is less supportive than some Asian and African countries. It does, however, post an average score on gender equality (treating new mothers and new fathers similarly). See "How Parental Leave Differs around the World" (https://www.cloudpay.net/resources/how-parental-leave-differs-around-the-world) for a 2019 report; and, for a more detailed review, from 2008, the Center for Economic Policy Research report "Parental Leave Policies in 21 Different Countries", authored by Rebecca Ray, Janet C. Gornick, and John Schmitt (available at cepr.net).

[36] This framework would not apply to parental leaves. They would be completely independent of educational leaves, and handled as they are today in the most generous countries (e.g., Sweden).

344 THE MAIN ENTERPRISE OF THE WORLD

specifying how much support the leave-taker will receive from the employer and how much will be contributed from public funds.

My figures, and indeed the structure of the policy, are, of course, purely illustrative. It would run contrary to the approach to democracy taken throughout this book to announce the "correct policies" from some philosophical podium (or pulpit). Devising an appropriate general framework to allow individuals freedom in choosing how to divide their lives into periods of valuable labor and intervals of further personal development, while providing managers opportunities to plan for likely absences, is a matter for democratic deliberation. The numbers I have assigned simply expose *one* possibility. Between the poles—the complete authority of the employer, total spontaneity for the worker—there are many ways of allowing lifelong education without plunging the labor market into chaos.

A further point of the illustration: the suggested limits on the freedom of individual workers do not seem unduly burdensome. To be sure, they place a bound on complete spontaneity. That is, I claim, inevitable. Despite my admiration for Emerson, and for his celebration of individualism, I cannot follow him so far as to propose allowing workers to "shun" their employment when their "genius" calls them, and to "write upon the lintels of the doorpost, *Whim*."[37]

So far, my response to the threat of chaos only takes up the "macro"-challenge. I've addressed the potential difficulties posed by allowing workers to take long educational leaves (I have thought in terms of a whole year, but some aspirations might be fulfilled in a shorter time, while some might need longer to satisfy). Yet, as frequently noted, these workers will also be encouraged to spend portions of their time—their regular workweeks—helping with the upbuilding of human beings. Sometimes they will do that in the classrooms; on other occasions they will mentor young people who are developing interests congruent to their own. These activities will remove them from the workplace. Hence arises a micro-challenge. How is that to be managed, so that necessary work is done and chaos is averted?

Once again, it is possible to draw on existing patterns of behavior. As I write, a significant percentage of the American workforce has been forced (by a pandemic) to "shelter in place." Many people cannot go to their usual places of employment. Some of them, however, continue to work from home,

---

[37] See Emerson, "Self-Reliance," in *The Selected Writings of Ralph Waldo Emerson* (New York: Modern Library, 1992), 132–53; the quote occurs at 135.

SOCIAL CHANGE 345

and, since schools and day-care centers are closed, they have to combine fulfilling their employment duties with supervising and teaching their children. Recognizing the competing demands, reasonable employers settle for lower productivity.[38]

In a Deweyan society, many people would find themselves in just this predicament. To participate in the education of younger generations (not necessarily their own children and grandchildren), they would take time from what would count, by present-day standards, as a standard workweek. For some of them, simply adding on the extra hours would suit their overall life plans. Others would find that option unsatisfactory. They would prefer to shorten the work week. Instead of forty hours (say) they would engage for thirty, allowing ten hours to be spent on their educational contributions. Decisions of this sort do not have to be taken once and for all. Lives in which people choose one solution at some stages and the alternative at others are easily imaginable.

The Deweyan society might well introduce measures to combat discrimination against job candidates who prefer to work a lower number of hours per week (say, by not allowing candidates to disclose their preference until they have been hired). As a result, the productivity of an enterprise would be expected to vary with the distribution of the choices: when more of those employed opt to work for the standard number of hours (performing their educational activities in their leisure time), productivity goes up. If it is essential to generate a certain level of goods or services in some domain—as, for example, when feeding the nation requires cultivating a particular amount of a crop—those who organize labor in that domain (farmers, agricultural producers, in the case just chosen) will have to hire more people. When all the workers choose to labor for thirty hours rather than for forty, extra hands will need to be hired, perhaps as many as one third of the original workforce.[39]

Where will these additional workers come from? Will enough be available? These are natural ways to reframe the chaos challenge. Two points made earlier underlie my response. The first, presented in this chapter, commits the Deweyan society to identifying and eliminating those forms of labor wasted on products and services whose only attraction lies in their

[38] Despite this, as noted above, the extra burden has fallen disproportionately on mothers. See the reference to Claudia Goldin in n.9, 328.
[39] If all the new hires prefer to work for forty hours, one quarter of the original workforce will have to be added; if all of them choose thirty hours, the need will be for one third of the original workforce. When some choose one way and the rest choose the other, the ratio will be intermediate between one quarter and one third.

346   THE MAIN ENTERPRISE OF THE WORLD

ability to serve as marks of status.[40] Any society able to generate enough to sustain itself—where that entails fostering and supporting the projects of its individual members—even when a significant amount of labor is directed toward worthless ends, will have a surplus of workers when those forms of work disappear. Because those workers aren't needed to sustain the society, their employment can free up time for those who choose a shorter work-week. More fundamentally, Chapter 2 already developed an account of the future labor market on the explicit assumption of increasing automation.[41] As more and more segments of production become automated, labor will be freed for service work, specifically in increasing the quality of care and nurturing offered to the sick, the elderly, and the young. Instead of conceiving automation as a threat, I proposed to recast it as an opportunity. Rather than making workers redundant, turning them into drones (of the organismic sort), it enables societies to spread valuable labor more evenly, allowing anyone who so wishes to participate in the rewarding work of education.

Continuing with my numerical example (and it is *only* an example), suppose that automation replaces one quarter of the occupations that used to be required to sustain the society. For simplicity's sake, assume that all occupations are equally productive, and that the labor involved in maintaining and supervising the robots can be neglected.[42] Even without considering contributions from eliminating worthless lines of work, that amount of automation suffices to allow an across-the-board reduction of the work week from forty hours to thirty.

At very least, the analyses I have sketched demonstrate the possibility of taking some steps—possibly large steps—toward meeting the threat of chaos. The Deweyan society is not doomed to collapse, either because the flows of activity it favors cannot be managed or because labor is no longer available to discharge all the tasks involved in sustaining it. One final twist is worth adding, however. It would probably assist the task of matching willing

---

[40] For further discussion of how this distinction is to be drawn, see Appendix 2.

[41] See above, 52 ff.

[42] The second assumption is justifiable on the grounds that supervisors and maintenance workers are typically only a tiny fraction of the population of workers displaced. Hence the true productivity of the amount of labor released from automation will be very close to that given in the simplified model. The first assumption is required to guard against the possibility that the productivity in the domains into which automation is introduced is significantly lower than the average productivity across the labor spectrum. In fact, the simplifying assumption of equal productivity across occupations can be replaced by the weaker supposition that the average productivity of the automated sectors (collectively) is no less than the average productivity across all forms of work.

candidates to positions for which they are already qualified, or for which they would gladly be trained, if there were a central clearinghouse to which people currently lacking employment or eager for a change of occupation could submit full dossiers. These dossiers might include details of their education (so far); assessments from teachers, mentors, and employers; statements of interest; and whatever personal details these job-seekers wished to provide. In the age of big data, it is not hard to envisage how this might be developed in diverse ways, channeling the flows of labor to help enterprises find the staff they need and workers discover job opportunities fitting their plans and projects.

Addressing the threat of chaos, as I have done, meets some challenges, while exposing the deepest form of skepticism. Readers with a background in economics, even a relatively limited one, will have observed a feature of my discussion of productivity. The task of managing labor was framed in terms of *showing how productivity sufficient to meet a particular set of needs* can be maintained. To do that, skeptics will suggest, is not enough. Healthy economies must *grow*. The trouble with Deweyan societies lies in their undercutting incentives for growth. When everyone is supported, aided in finding individual life plans and provided with enough resources to pursue them successfully, the pressure to strive harder is relaxed. The productivity of the society does not increase, or does not increase as rapidly as that of its non-Deweyan (pre-Deweyan) competitors. The straightforward worry: a stagnant Deweyan society will, sooner or later, face severe economic disadvantages in exchanging products with other societies, and will then decline until it becomes unsustainable. The subtler concern: even if a Deweyan society might prove sustainable, if it could once be reached, any steps toward it in a non-Deweyan (pre-Deweyan) world will inevitably experience competitive disadvantages and thus be punished.

<hr />

These skeptical questions are serious, and the final chapter will attempt to respond to them, as well as to some derivative issues they generate. Before doing so, it is worth presenting the promised general picture of the Deweyan society, to make clear just what it requires and thus what resources are available to soothe skeptical anxieties.

The rethinking of education envisaged in the first two parts of this book requires a society with special features. Specifically, this society, the Deweyan society, satisfies the following conditions:

348   THE MAIN ENTERPRISE OF THE WORLD

D1. The society is committed to valuing all kinds of labor generating products or services of all kinds, except for those existing solely as marks of status. All those contributing to the well-being of others receive esteem in roughly equal measures.

D2. The material compensation afforded all valuable forms of labor lies within a range. The ratio of the highest level allowed to the lowest level allowed is fixed through democratic deliberation. Democratic deliberation involving representatives of all valuable occupations also sets the full scale of wages and salaries.

D3. The society funds preschool programs, schools, colleges, universities, institutes of further adult education, and other educational facilities, open to all and without charge to all, designed and maintained to guide each individual to a potentially rewarding life plan. Large inequalities in the abilities of different facilities of the same type to deliver this are not tolerated. Resources are supplied to bring lower levels of performance up to the higher level.

D4. The society is committed to eradicating stereotypes based on race, gender, ethnicity, and culture. To this end it fully supports programs enabling young people to meet, and to deliberate with, peers who differ from them in all these respects. It seeks to introduce them to the full range of variation present in the society, and as much of the variation in the human population as can be arranged.

D5. Workers are encouraged to take periodic leaves to renew their education, and to pursue new educational interests. All adults are expected to participate in the education of the next generation. If they choose to devote some of the standard workweek to teaching, assisting, or mentoring, they are permitted to do so. The framework within which the individual work schedules are negotiated is settled through democratic deliberation.

D6. Non-working adults are supported at the lowest level of the allowable range. They are counseled to prepare and deposit their dossiers in the central clearinghouse. The same help is available to those who hope to switch their line of work.

D7. Any tendencies to reintroduce hierarchies of status for different occupations, and thus interfere with the educational mission of fostering individual development, are strenuously resisted.

SOCIAL CHANGE 349

Several of these conditions (e.g., D1, D4, D5, and D7) do not explicitly introduce economic features of Deweyan societies. They do, however, have economic implications. D1 presupposes D2. D4 presupposes D3. All four presuppose a commitment to support all adults, and that commitment is further articulated by D6. Together, I take D2, D3, and D6 to be sufficient to meet the economic requirements for the four "social" conditions. A society fulfilling D2, D3, and D6 might fail to be fully Deweyan, but the failure would not be due to *economic* features.

Hence, the hard skeptical questions can be focused precisely. Would a society satisfying D2, D3, and D6 inevitably suffer economic collapse? Would taking steps in the directions marked out by D2, D3, and D6 be so economically problematic that, to sustain itself, the society would have to retreat?

Affirmative answers to these questions are the basis for dismissing the proposed rethinking of education as utopian.

11

Utopia?

The book often seen as the founding document of subsequent economic theory,[1] Adam Smith's *Wealth of Nations*, begins with the division of labor. Almost one thousand pages before recognizing the potentially mind-numbing effects of confining workers to interminable repetition of simple tasks,[2] Smith celebrates the division of labor for one great success: increased productivity. In the famous example of the pin factory, he illustrates a striking effect: ten men, each of whom pursues a single specialized activity, make 48,000 pins in a day; without the division of labor, one man, working alone and thus having to carry out all the operations himself "could not . . . have made twenty, perhaps not one pin in a day."[3]

Why is this cause for celebration? Who could possibly want all those pins? Smith disarms the questions by inviting his readers to expand the horizon of their vision. Instead of looking locally—at the worker and his family, at the town, at the county, or even at the nation—we should think globally. Although it would have been possible beforehand to supply our own wants, or the local demand, without the greater productivity, generating a surplus is useful. Having that surplus, we can supply others, receiving in return goods they can produce more easily than we can. Indeed, the more we can make, in any branch of industry where the accidents of geography and history favor us with a competitive edge, the wealthier we shall become, our surpluses enabling us to command the labor of others. Workers, too, will benefit—at least economically. Given the drive to produce, as much labor as possible must be harnessed—production lines must be filled to maximum capacity. Demand for workers grows, and, as it outpaces the supply, different industrial sectors

---

[1] Historians trace some of the ideas Smith synthesizes back to the ancient world. His book drew heavily on intellectual currents in England, France, and Scotland during the century before its publication in 1776. In particular, Smith drew on Sir William Petty's explorations of "political arithmetic," on the work of the French thinkers François Quesnay and Anne Robert Jacques Turgot, and on the writings of his immediate Scottish predecessors, Frances Hutcheson and David Hume. The principal achievement of WN lies in its extraordinary power to systematize a wealth of researches that had previously been disconnected—and thus limited.

[2] See Chapter 2 above, 55–57.

[3] WN 5.

The Main Enterprise of the World. Philip Kitcher, Oxford University Press. © Oxford University Press 2022.
DOI: 10.1093/oso/9780190928971.003.0012

will have to compete for workers.[4] In consequence, wages will rise. That is "the liberal reward of labor."[5]

This dynamic—produce, produce, produce—might reach a stage at which it was bounded, when the command to keep producing lapsed. Yet Smith, like Marx after him, views its unlimited extension as part of the intrinsic logic of capitalism. Ironically, the younger Smith had acknowledged other valued aspects of human existence. Once, he had hailed the consciousness of being loved as the apogee of human happiness, and rhapsodized about the tranquility of the roadside beggar, free from the rigors felt by those whom fortune "has visited with ambition."[6] Yet his later work, the book for which he is best known, never takes seriously the possibility of declaring, at some point, that enough is enough. Profits must always be reinvested. Capital always seeks further returns. Apparently the "innate propensity to truck and barter" always proves dominant in decision-making.[7]

Why should this be? If time is money, why can't individuals—and, more significantly, societies—decide to take the revenues, gleaned from advances in the power to produce, in leisure hours rather than in greater wealth? A technological advance enables me (or us) to do today in four hours what took eight hours yesterday. What forces me (us) to expend eight hours' effort, thus producing twice as much, rather than enjoying four hours to pursue other ends? Would it be disastrous to seek less than the full amount of economic rewards now available and enjoy a bit more leisure time (working, say, for six hours, and taking two hours off)? An underlying assumption appears to have entered: once you start along the road to greater production, you can't stop. Apparently the logic of capitalism is orthogenesis.

"Orthogenesis" is a term from late nineteenth-century discussions of Darwin's account of evolution under natural selection (an account often compared with the laissez-faire economics descending from Smith). Critics pointed out puzzling features of some complex structures found in the animal kingdom—the large antlers of the Irish elk and the peacock's elaborate tail, for example. On the Darwinian account, the structures would have emerged

[4] WN 78–79. Here too the division of labor plays a role. Since the production process is split into tasks for which any of a large population of workers can quickly be trained, the workers become interchangeable, easily moved from one job to another and even to different branches of industry.

[5] WN 84.

[6] Adam Smith, *The Theory of Moral Sentiments* (Cambridge, UK: Cambridge University Press, 2002), 50, 132, 211–16.

[7] WN 302, 309; Marx gives the formulation in terms of the rapacity with which capital demands reinvestment of profits: *Capital*, Vol. I, 254.

352 THE MAIN ENTERPRISE OF THE WORLD

from an incremental process in which successively larger versions displaced their smaller precursors. Could natural selection have fueled the process? Quite plausibly, during the earlier stages. Apparently, however, the structures eventually became physical handicaps, so that, before reaching their present size, natural selection would have told *against* any further increases. Unable to see how to solve the problem, some of Darwin's champions posited an extra factor driving evolution, a hitherto unrecognized causal force. Once natural selection has started in a particular direction, the trend must be continued even after its later manifestations are opposed by natural selection. Natural selection starts a line of directed change, and, once that trend is under way, natural selection is powerless to stop it. That's orthogenesis.

Orthodox versions of contemporary Darwinism have no truck with this alleged force. They offer various explanations for the puzzling phenomena. Sometimes competitive advantages are invoked to offset the handicap; sometimes the trait is seen as a signal, valuable in attracting mates.[8] A mysterious supplement to the acknowledged drivers of evolutionary change is not needed.

All over the world, people scan newspapers, tune in to television news, and visit internet sites to gain information about their nation's growth. They have been taught to be happy when the news is good, when GDP takes a leap—and, correspondingly, dismayed when growth is sluggish or nonexistent. Why do we make a fetish of the figures? Do we still believe in a supposed imperative of capitalism: grow or die? Is economics committed to its own version of orthogenesis?

Growth matters to economists because it reflects the state of the business cycle. When the rate of growth slackens, or, worse, drops precipitously, that signals a potential recession in the offing. Action may have to be taken to guard against looming unemployment. *Given the economic and social arrangements as they currently stand*, there are sound reasons for measuring economic growth at regular intervals, and using the findings to adjust policy. Whether people should obsess about growth under different circumstances, in a Deweyan society fully committed to a distribution of resources to all its citizens, one that deploys automation to liberate people for the pursuit of what matters most to them, and that emphasizes (and values) employment through care, nurture, and education, is an entirely different matter. Why

---

[8] For various styles of explanation, see Stephen Jay Gould, *Ontogeny and Phylogeny* (Cambridge, MA: Harvard University Press, 1977); Richard Dawkins, *The Selfish Gene* (Oxford: Oxford University Press, 1976); and Richard Prum, *The Evolution of Beauty* (New York: Penguin Random House, 2018).

UTOPIA? 353

exactly would the Deweyan society fear a fall in the rate of growth, or even a state in which productivity was static? If economic orthogenesis doesn't yield the answer to that question, what exactly does?

The economically inspired skeptic about the possibility of Deweyan society speaks: "Just as neo-Darwinians can now explain the perplexities inspiring the desperate invocation of an evolutionary drive to continue trends, so contemporary economics understands why continued growth is essential to the health of *any* society. The flawed accounts of the early political economists—like Smith and Marx—have been replaced by serious explanations." If that is so, it must be possible to show why, when societies allow their production to remain static (or even shrink), principles governing individual and collective behavior will entail reverses, and sometimes disastrous consequences. Can that be done? How exactly does the demonstration go?

Let's focus the question. Imagine a society, of whatever size you like, equipped with the ability to meet current needs.[9] That is: the society can produce enough to supply, for all of its members, enough to sustain what each of them would endorse as a fulfilling life. At a particular stage in its history, the society votes unanimously to limit future effort to a level allowing for the total supply of everything needed, together with an "insurance surplus," intended to buffer against catastrophes. If technological changes bring further growth in productivity, that would be welcome,[10] but increased GDP is not mandatory. Why should we think this impossible? Why does the society have to emulate Lewis Carroll's Red Queen and keep running just to stay in place?

It's easy to think of several ways in which the policy might go awry. First, the population of the society might grow, increasing the number of young people—not yet ready to add their exertions to production—and requiring more goods than can be generated, given the agreed-upon workload. Here the individual needs don't change, but the population expands to outrun supply; the number of available workers is insufficient to deliver the full complement of resources to all the intended recipients, unless the workers toil for longer than was stipulated. Second, the set of resources required for

[9] A later discussion will respond to the concern that no society can ever reach this state. See below, 364–70, 386–87.

[10] Advocates for the Deweyan society aren't *opposed* to growth. They think of it as something it's nice to have so long as pursuing it doesn't interfere with the social conditions required for the Deweyan society to thrive. What's problematic is fetishism: insisting on economic growth at cost to more important things.

354 THE MAIN ENTERPRISE OF THE WORLD

a fulfilling life might become larger, exceeding what the population could generate without violating the bounds set on hours of labor. In this case, the population size stays constant, but successive generations of the society become more demanding. Third, the first and second scenarios might occur in combination—there's an expanding population of ever more needy individuals. Fourth, the society might not be able to insulate itself from what other societies do. Although, *given current conditions*, it is self-sufficient, its capacity for generating what it needs depends on its ability to import particular kinds of things (raw materials, for example, may be needed for its production lines). As things stand, it produces enough to trade with other societies, thus acquiring the crucial imports. If, however, the economies of those trading partners continue to grow, the prices it can set for its exports may fall sufficiently far to render it incapable of buying everything it requires. In a world with a global economy, you have to keep up with the neighbors.

As we shall see, the fourth scenario (already bruited at the end of the previous chapter) presents the most crucial challenge. Beginning with the first three, however, is useful in exposing conditions the hypothetical society must satisfy. Furthermore, considering those challenges forces us to separate styles of economic explanation, differentiating those appealing only to economic motives from others recognizing a broader array of aspirations and goals. These preliminary clarifications help present the fourth challenge more precisely than it has been formulated so far.

Before proceeding further, I want to set on one side an easy way of trying to dismiss all the scenarios. Each of them indicates a way in which trouble *might* arise for the envisaged society. But possibilities, you might reply, are cheap. All of us, throughout our lives, have to take risks. We never have absolute guarantees that our "best-laid schemes" won't "gang aft agley."[11] To be sure, my imagined society should recognize these possibilities. Why can't it proceed with its eyes open, hoping for the best?

Because no responsible agent, or responsible collective body, should take any such step without trying to estimate the magnitude of the risk. If there are genuine threats to the sustainability of societies seeking to move in a Deweyan direction, they might be sufficiently likely or sufficiently severe to undo everything it has achieved.[12] Although the current state might be

---

[11] Robert Burns, "To a Mouse."

[12] Likely threats of moderate severity should give would-be Deweyans pause—as should catastrophic consequences with very low probability. A responsible analysis should seek to assess the expected utility of the action envisaged. Assuming, of course, that probabilities can be estimated and utility scales constructed.

UTOPIA?   355

highly unsatisfactory, with few opportunities for fulfilling lives and a pale surrogate for democracy, the attempted remedy might so reduce the material conditions of existence that people's aspirations would become limited to a struggle for survival and democratic institutions would collapse entirely. Alternatively, the probability of a serious economic depression, with corresponding reductions in public services (including education), could be too high to justify the gamble. Hence, these scenarios should be considered more carefully.

What suffices today might not be enough in the future. The first three challenges elaborate ways in which shortfalls could come about. The most obvious of these is population growth. To resort to a hackneyed comparison, whether a pie is large enough to feed a group of people depends both on the size of the pie and the size of the group. Societies content with zero growth tolerate futures in which the pie does not become bigger. If they also allow the population to expand, placing no limits on its size, there are significant chances of a future in which the eaters are too numerous to receive adequate slices.

The statement of the problem indicates the obvious solution. Steps toward a Deweyan society should be coupled with policies to limit population growth. The simplest proposal would require the society's members only to reproduce at the level of population replacement.[13] A more sensitive policy would attune the counseling[14] given to citizens to patterns of growth and of population movement. In periods of economic growth, and when the net gain from migration (the rate of immigration minus the rate of emigration) is either negative or negligibly positive, a norm of two children per couple might be relaxed. If the economy were to contract, the advice to restrict families to two children might be announced more firmly. One small part of Deweyan education should focus on responsible parenting, and on the importance of not compromising the prospects of children whose birthright is the chance to lead fulfilling lives.

---

[13] To specify this in detail depends on the expected human lifespan. If people live longer, the number of those alive at a given time will go up. Thus reproductive rates have to be coordinated with the age distribution.

[14] I assume the policy to be a norm, not a law. Young people learn what their society expects of them in their family planning, but they are not punished by the state if they violate expectations.

356   THE MAIN ENTERPRISE OF THE WORLD

To speak of a "birthright" is to invite an obvious retort: What of the right of couples to have as many children as they choose? I reply: There is no such right. In a world where the resources human beings require are restricted, so that they *could not* suffice to sustain (let alone offer fulfillment to) a significantly larger human population, every couple has the responsibility to consider how their offspring are to be provided for. Nor, when wealth is distributed so unequally— and frequently so unjustly—is it possible for the rich to declare that *they* can support a large number of children and thus may *rightfully* proliferate. To add a further deprivation to the lives of the poor, denying them the right to any children, would be callous and cruel. (Indeed, the tendency to blame poor people for "over-reproduction" displays a monstrous lack of sympathy with their predicaments. To be sure, they may not reflect deeply on the lack of opportunities for their children. Yet, when societies treat their poorer citizens as marginal, even disposable, they should not piously denounce attempts to snatch a little love and comfort in one of the few places where the poor can find it.) Specifying the bounds of responsible reproduction is not a matter for individuals but a collective decision. The aggregate of resources in a society—its level of productivity—fixes the maximal size of its population. Once that is determined, the limit for the reproduction of individuals follows: each person is treated equally. It is, if you like, another case of dividing a pie.

The talk of rights and responsibilities of the previous paragraph needs to be understood in the terms of Chapter 5.[15] No single person has authority to declare what counts as a right and what does not. My discussion therefore rests on a conjecture: if any society deliberated on the question of reproduction and its potential restrictions, attempting to implement as far as possible the conditions on ideal conversation (inclusiveness, informedness, and mutual engagement), it would arrive at judgments supporting my claims. Children are owed the opportunity to lead fulfilling lives. No parent can rightfully claim greater license to reproduce than any other. The total reproduction of a group is properly bounded by the number of people for whom its aggregate resources provide opportunities for fulfilling lives. So far as I know, the experiment has not been tried: no representative body approximating the conditions has devoted itself to the topic. I expect (and hope!) that a trial would support my conjecture.[16] If it did not, and if no alternative

---

[15] Or in accord with the approach of *The Ethical Project* and *Moral Progress*.

[16] The principal objections to restrictions on reproduction—or at least the objections expressed in public debates—invoke the authority of religious texts. They thus fall foul of the arguments of Chapter 6. See above, 195–99.

UTOPIA? 357

response could be found, the first scenario would issue a serious challenge to the Deweyan program.

Besides the obvious—and often-expressed—concern about restrictions on population growth, a more theoretical worry arises. However you fix the limit on the population, it appears possible to add further lives, while only causing a small diminution in the quality of each one. A common illustration: start from a world in which everyone leads a life of great fulfillment; compare that with a world in which more people live, with their lives going almost as well—the only difference being that each person suffers one more day of headache; the latter world has seemed (at least to many philosophers) an improvement on the first; now keep going in the same fashion; you are led to a "Repugnant Conclusion," that the best of all worlds is one in which vast numbers of people live lives that are barely worth living.[17]

Many people who are used to numerical rankings of outcomes (as is standard in cost-benefit analysis, and other consequentialist ventures) view the quality of human lives as measurable on one numerical dimension. Any position committed to a one-dimensional ranking and satisfying the Archimedean axiom will fall victim to this argument.[18] The difficulty derives from not recognizing an important feature of the concept *quality of life*. A fulfilling life remains fulfilling when small burdens are successively added—unless or until those burdens make it impossible for the subject of the life to pursue the projects out of which fulfillment flows. In a certain sense, two people whose lives are exactly the same, with the exception of one containing a single additional headache, differ in quality. The quality of the headache sufferer's life is slightly less than that of the less headachy life. This difference is entirely trivial compared with the gulf between fulfilled and unfulfilled lives. From a formal point of view, quality of life is two-dimensional with a primary division into fulfilled and unfulfilled lives (or possibly a larger number of discrete categories). Once quality has been assessed on that prior dimension, lives can then be compared on the continuous dimension—assessed for the prevalence of headaches, for example. The formal puzzle is solved by appreciating a crucial point: Discreteness is the better part of value.

---

[17] The problem was formulated by Derek Parfit in the final part of his *Reasons and Persons* (Oxford: Clarendon Press, 1984) To my mind, this part of his book is Parfit's crowning philosophical achievement.

[18] The Archimedean Axiom states that, for any two positive numbers x, y, there is a positive integer N such that $Nx > y$. In "Parfit's Puzzle," *Noûs* 34 (2000): 550–77, I show how a one-dimensional ranking satisfying the Archimedean Axiom makes the puzzle insoluble.

358   THE MAIN ENTERPRISE OF THE WORLD

Turn now to the second scenario. Here, it's supposed, the inadequacy of the pie results from an increase in the demands of consumers. Bigger slices are needed to satisfy larger appetites. In a changed environment, people come to pursue projects requiring more support than they previously received. Two important questions must be answered if the challenge is to become precisely focused. First, what kinds of changes might bring about the new demands? Second, how do they displace, or render unsatisfying, the kinds of projects previously found fulfilling?

The most obvious answer to the first question points to advances in the goods produced. The Deweyan society, content with low (or zero) growth, continues to supply its citizens with outmoded products. Other contemporaneous societies increase their productivity, developing new forms of technology, and generating improved versions of old goods—or even new and more pleasing substitutes for them. As members of the Deweyan society become aware of the possibilities, they become increasingly dissatisfied with the options available to them. They want to share in the new bounty.[19]

Sometimes this reaction can be dismissed as mere consumerism, and, in consequence, the larger appetite is unwarranted. The latest, snazziest stuff isn't needed to pursue people's central goals. The second question should be posed—and answered by recognizing the case as one in which old approaches are still available and continue to satisfy justifiable aspirations. Reaching a particular end is important for someone's life plan. The person is still able to attain it, using the traditional means. Adding a requirement to achieve it in a specific, expensive, way is to confuse what is important with what is secondary.

Not all examples of the scenario are so easily set aside. For new technologies can overcome long-standing obstacles to the pursuit of central goals. For generations, people who wished for some kinds of regular connection with one another may have had to settle for infrequent contact, always achieved with long delays and significant uncertainties. Developments in communications technology can dissolve all the difficulties. Wouldn't we suppose a person's discontent with having to continue the old unsatisfactory methods to be entirely justifiable, in a world where the counterparts in other, richer, societies have the ability to accomplish what has always been wanted?

---

[19] This accords with a point made in the previous chapter (see n.25, 336 above). What counts as enough depends on the distribution of goods and opportunities. Here I apply it to the transnational context.

UTOPIA? 359

Consider an historical example of a long and frustrating separation. Like Charles Darwin, Thomas Henry Huxley sailed around the world on one of the Royal Navy's ships (HMS *Rattlesnake*). In Australia, he met a young woman—Henrietta Anne Heathorn. They fell in love, and became engaged. In May 1850, the *Rattlesnake* left Sydney and "Huxley was not to see his future wife again for five years more, when he was at length in a position to bid her come and join him."[20] The young couple devised ingenious schemes for keeping each other informed of their thoughts, feelings, and the events around them, but their communication was always slow and vulnerable to the vagaries of shipping.

Imagine, then, being in this predicament (or one very like it), and learning of a new technology, developed in another society, enabling people to talk to one another—even see one another—at any terrestrial distance. The iPhone has arrived. Unfortunately, the new devices are very expensive—more expensive than members of your society can afford, given the support they receive (support that previously seemed entirely adequate). Moreover, even if you were to sacrifice and save, equipping you and your partner with iPhones, the infrastructure in the regions you both inhabit cannot support instant communication. There are no cell phone towers or satellites. Because its economy hasn't grown, your society can't remedy the situation. In this new environment, what used to be sufficient to meet your needs is so no longer.

Scenarios like this escape the consumerism of many ways of elaborating the second challenge. When increased productivity generates goods that don't facilitate people's life projects—things they might like to possess but can forgo without sacrificing anything of central importance to them, the challenge can be shrugged off. Societies unconcerned with economic growth *über alles* can continue to support fulfilling lives for their members. The communications example strikes home because it connects so directly to a commonly felt central aspiration: relations with loved ones are often at the heart of human concerns, so that the limited ability to connect, in a world where others communicate with ease, is felt as a severe shortcoming and a loss. The tantalizing prospect of doing as the more fortunate communicators do causes dissatisfaction—reasonable discontent—with the cumbersome arrangements through which important relationships used to be sustained.

[20] Leonard Huxley, ed., *The Life and Letters of T. H. Huxley* (1903; repr., Cambridge, UK: Cambridge University Press, 2012) 49.

360 THE MAIN ENTERPRISE OF THE WORLD

Does this reveal the deficiencies of neglecting economic growth? Does it furnish the supposed impossibility proof? I don't believe so. Five kinds of considerations suggest a happier ending for the story.

1. *The costs of the mania for growth.* So far, the narrative only takes stock of a single aspect of life for members of the Deweyan society. It neither examines their lives as a whole, nor compares them with those of their apparently fortunate counterparts in the other society. As they reflect further, the Deweyan citizens come to see how there are costs to the emphasis on growth. To be sure, their counterparts can engage far more easily with distant friends (and even multiply their stock of distant "friends"). But their society restricts the scope and depth of human relations. Their opportunities to watch and shape the growth of the young are limited. Many of them work long hours for mediocre rewards in occupations whose significance is hard to fathom. Educational renewal is largely absent. From the Deweyan perspective, the opportunity for easier communication potentially allows human relations to be deepened and sustained, but so many features of the alien society cramp and cheapen those relations, that the bargain made by their counterparts comes to seem a bad one. Reaching this conclusions, the Deweyans reconcile themselves to their cumbersome ways of communicating with distant loved ones. They see it as a price to be paid for enjoying many significant benefits of their society.[21]

2. *Quid pro quo?* The story makes assumptions about the conditions under which innovation is likely to develop. Why should technological innovation be more likely to develop in the growth-oriented society? To be sure, economic gains *might* be reinvested in fostering research. That has occurred at times in recent history—most evidently in the more Deweyan America of the immediate postwar period. Equally, it seems, a society making education its central priority might produce a crop of imaginative innovators, especially if it were at pains to conserve and nourish curiosity and a fascination with inquiry into natural phenomena. All the funds lavished on laboratories and other research

---

[21] There are obvious affinities between this response and the reaction of some late Victorians to industrial production. The writings of both William Morris and John Ruskin eloquently articulate the sense of loss felt when efficiency is prized over artistry. Their ideas and arguments can, I believe, be stripped of their off-putting features: the hothouse Romanticism and the suggestions of elitism (present despite Morris's explicit commitments to socialism). Showing that, however, would be tangential to my main purposes here.

facilities have to be complemented by finding people with the skills to make good use of the equipment provided for them. In desperation, a society feeling a lack of home-grown talent can dragoon the young into careers it sees as "national priorities," or it can try to import, but it is far from clear why this approach would be superior to one of rethinking education along Deweyan lines. Indeed, several contemporary societies have combined egalitarianism with technological success.[22] Of course, if the Deweyan society can hold its own in producing innovations, it can try to exchange the goods generated by its own breakthroughs with those created elsewhere. That might occur in a piecemeal way, according to the usual practices of trucking and bartering. Or, in a more rational, more cooperative world, there could be a commitment to sharing, one making beneficial technological advances—those capable of facilitating fulfilling human projects—the common property of humankind.

3. *Technological imitation.* My tale also ignores another real possibility. Once new technologies start to circulate, revealing their attractions, it is rarely possible to confine them to the society originally producing them. Even without armies of industrial spies, scientists and engineers from other nations can obtain the products, analyze them, and try to rebuild their own versions (although, of course, their efforts are sometimes aided if moles have been planted in the right places). Supposing the Deweyan society to be permanently deprived of iPhones was always an implausible feature of the narrative (one I disguised, by treating the iPhone merely as an illustrative example). Not only are there American alternatives (Android), but Finland (Nokia), Japan (Sony), and South Korea (Samsung) have all produced rival versions. Perhaps the Deweyan society would not have been able to produce an equivalent capable of succeeding in global competition. That, however, is not the point. For Deweyan citizens to be doomed to lives of smartphonelessness requires denying the possibility of shifting resources from making now-outdated devices to designing and manufacturing a product able to deliver the main communication functions of the iPhone. The probability of the Deweyan society being unable to do that appears very low.

---

[22] Sweden and Finland are prominent examples.

362 THE MAIN ENTERPRISE OF THE WORLD

4. *Expanding markets.* One of the central themes of classical and neo-classical economics, from Adam Smith to today, takes entrepreneurs as constantly attempting to expand the market for their products. Hence, once the non-Deweyan world is flooded with devices for speedy and efficient communication, manufacturers will have incentives to design new varieties (equipped with exciting new functions). Very likely they will spot the possibility of offering small rebates to people who return the older outmoded models. These can then be refurbished, and sold at reduced prices to consumers who cannot afford to pay the going rate. They find it profitable to help poorer societies introduce the infrastructure needed, thus opening up the market for their products. Just as the technology has actually spread into developing countries, it makes its way into the Deweyan society too.[23]

5. *Facing catastrophes.* Deweyan societies have to be pragmatic as well as pragmatist. History teaches them a familiar lesson. From time to time, a society will face unusual threats and will have to take unusual measures to avoid a catastrophe. When such perils arise, ordinary practices are suspended. Citizens band together to save the situation, adjusting their conduct to the needs of the time. So, although a Deweyan society permits a shorter workweek, allowing its members to make their educational contributions (and to take their educational leaves) without also requiring them to expend forty hours in productive labor, more may sometimes be asked of them. The norm of nurturing the young remains in force. Now it must be honored while also devoting more than the usual time to a collective effort to meet the challenge. Nor is this necessarily at the cost of fulfillment. Many groups of people whose everyday lives have been disrupted by their participation in resisting a major threat have later described this period as the most rewarding and meaningful part of their lives: Londoners' testimony of their experience of the Blitz is a well-known example. In the same way, when lack of the ability to introduce a new technology, widely available elsewhere, comes to be seen as an important society-wide problem, the Deweyan society can demand special efforts from its citizens. Without sacrificing

---

[23] For interesting statistics about the spread of cellphones around the world, see the Pew Research Center's report "Smartphone Usage Is Growing Rapidly around the World but Not Always Equally," https://www.pewresearch.org/global/2019/02/05/digital-connectivity-growing-rapidly-in-emerging-economies/.

UTOPIA? 363

its fundamental commitments, the society temporarily sets aside some of its regular practices to overcome a recognized deficiency.

What do my five responses show? Not merely how five happier endings might come about. Sometimes, when ironclad arguments are hard to find, people wave their hands in the direction of several less conclusive lines of reasoning, in the hopes of constructing a vaguely convincing case. These five suggestions give us more. *Each* of them has a high probability, in the absence of the others, of remedying the problem. Hence, the probability that *none* of them will occur is extremely low (that probability is the product of five very small numbers). To the extent that my guiding example represents the second challenge, the risks for the Deweyan society are truly tiny.

In the end, though, the devil lies in the details. The challenge presents itself as a *general* exposition of a crucial difficulty for Deweyan societies. The five responses rebut that claim. As we might have expected (recall a conclusion about social science drawn in Chapter 9), this part of macroeconomic theory is unlikely to yield models with three desirable properties: precision, accuracy, and generality.[24] An overly general claim of impossibility has been refuted. That doesn't rule out the possibility of a more cautious macroeconomic argument, disclosing some narrower (related) challenge. As yet, however, nothing has been done to indicate that the narrower challenge succeeds.

Does the third challenge offer a candidate? No. Here, the first two challenges team up together. The Deweyan society is envisaged as growing too large and becoming filled with ever more demanding citizens. The size of the pie remains the same, while it must serve a greater number of people, each of them with increased appetites. Trouble would arise if there were amplifying interactions between the two members of the team. That is not so, however. The challenges act independently, and their effect is merely additive. Solving the first difficulty and solving the second difficulty yields a full solution to the third. So long as a policy restricting population growth is in force, and so long as the problem of new needs can be addressed in the manner just outlined, the third challenge will be met.

---

[24] See above, 305–6.

364 THE MAIN ENTERPRISE OF THE WORLD

We come now to the fourth—and most difficult—challenge. Here, the emphasis is on interactions among societies.[25] A single Deweyan society in an otherwise non-Deweyan world will, so it is claimed, inevitably lose the ability to sustain the economic underpinnings required for its educational and social policies. If all the world were Deweyan, it might, perhaps, remain so indefinitely. The project of this book is not utopian in one sense—if there were a magic wand to transform all societies according to the proposals offered in previous chapters, the result would not inevitably collapse but might sail on into a happy future. It suffers from a different lapse into utopianism. Efforts to rebuild societies in Deweyan directions would be snuffed out. You just can't get there from here.[26]

If a Deweyan society were entirely self-sufficient, never needing to import goods from others, there might be no problem.[27] Moreover, if there were a cluster of Deweyan societies, able to trade with one another and thus satisfy the needs of each member, perhaps all would be well. Hence, strictly speaking, it is not necessary to leap to the complete Deweyan world—if the revised socioeconomic system spreads far enough, it can be sustained. For the moment, however, let's assume Deweyanism starts small. A single society, dependent on trade with others, makes a partial Deweyan turn. Specifically, it adjusts

---

[25] To appreciate this as the most serious challenge accords, I think, with the most sophisticated understanding of economic growth. The models of growth offered by Robert Solow, *Growth Theory: An Exposition* (New York: Oxford University Press, 1970), and the many economic theorists influenced by his seminal work, recognize how differences among societies affect the patterns of growth and convergence to a steady state. Growth theory is, of course, concerned with a different set of questions from those I address here. It holds fixed a competitive economic framework and asks what will occur when different economic factors are considered and the distribution of parameters varies. I ask how a change in economic institutions, designed to foster particular social goals, will fare in a global economy of the standard type. Although I take the informal discussion of the text to be clear and adequate to present purposes, it would be interesting to explore whether it can be developed more formally within the framework of growth theory.

[26] The trouble is familiar from the dynamics of evolving systems. There are well-known cases in which a population would reach a stable state if a particular allele became prevalent. When, however, the allele is rare, selection tells against it. Some human populations contain an allele (the C allele) with two desirable properties: individuals bearing the C allele are resistant to malaria; people with two copies (CC homozygotes) do not suffer from sickle-cell disease. If all of us were CC, we should all have these welcome traits, and neither of the two more common alleles (the normal A-allele and the S-allele responsible—in double dose—for sickle-cell anemia) would be able to invade. Unfortunately, when the C allele is rare, it occurs mostly in heterozygotes—people who are AC or CS. These individuals are at a selective disadvantage. Thus natural selection drives the C allele out of the population. (More details about this case are given in my *Living with Darwin*, 106–8.)

[27] My cautious formulation, signaled by my use of "might" rather than "would," acknowledges the possibility of further versions of the problem that do not stem from trade among societies. International trade is the source of the most obvious difficulty, and I have thus chosen to focus on it. If there are other variants of the interaction problem, I conjecture that analogs of my proposed countermeasures would address them.

the conditions of labor, allowing citizens to opt for a shorter workweek, in which they devote the hours saved to nurturing the next generation and (secondarily) to their own further development. Productivity is maintained at a level sufficient to produce the resources required for supporting individual projects and the social institutions undergirding them. Increased automation allows for this. But the society equalizes salaries (along the lines suggested in the previous chapter) and relaxes competition. In so doing, it allows for economic growth—even welcomes it when it occurs—but does not subordinate its social goals to a demand for as much increase in productivity as possible. At times of decline (economic contraction), it takes steps to return overall production to the desired level. It willingly accepts zero growth, and, when production goes up, the possibility of obtaining a larger expansion at cost to its socio-educational commitments does not trouble it.

All around it, however, are societies, some of them its trading partners, giving higher priority to economic growth. These societies need not be completely cutthroat. They do, however, tolerate more extensive inequalities and more intense competition than their Deweyan counterpart. Will their productivity inevitably increase at a faster rate? Or, more precisely, we may differentiate two alternative questions. (1) If, during a particular period, production in the Deweyan society increases by X and the least value of added production in the other societies is Y, will X always be less than Y? (2) If, during a particular period, production in the Deweyan society increases by X, and the median of the production increases in the other societies is Z, will X always be less than Z?

Plainly, an affirmative answer to (2) is more likely than an answer to (1). The challenge can be formulated, however, without supposing the answer to either question to be "Yes." Inevitability isn't the issue—high probability is bad enough. All the challenger needs to launch the argument is a relatively weak assumption:

(P) If, during a particular period, production in the Deweyan society increases by X and the median of the production increases in the other societies is Z, then, with high probability, X is less than Z.

Here, "high probability" will be understood to indicate a probability significantly above 0.5. If the difference between the probability and 0.5 is small, the pressures against the Deweyan society will be weak and the process of its decline accordingly slow. That would allow for other factors to intervene and

366   THE MAIN ENTERPRISE OF THE WORLD

reverse the decline. Perceiving the social advantages of the Deweyan society, other societies might follow its lead!

In the initial state, the Deweyan society sustains itself through producing some of the goods and services it needs, acquiring some goods and services from trading partners, and providing other goods and services to trading partners (the two sets of partners not necessarily containing the same members). For simplicity, suppose the society doesn't borrow: it does not run deficits but pays as it goes.[28] It does, however, have a fund to buffer fluctuations and to deal with unpredictable emergencies.[29] Further idealizing, imagine trade not to go on continuously but to happen in discrete stages. On January 1 of each year, societies exchange the goods and services they offer and need. Initially, the Deweyan society sits at the median productivity among its trading partners. Hence, in year zero, the most likely outcome will balance the books. Its level of productivity will enable it to provide at competitive prices to those who seek the goods and services it offers, and to buy what it needs without drawing on the buffer fund. In the original situation, all goes well.

On New Year's Day of year one, the societies will come to the market, with the prices attached to goods and services modified in light of the growth they have experienced in the intervening year. Years will be characterized from the perspective of the Deweyan society. *Fat* years are those in which productivity in the Deweyan society has increased relative to that of its trading partners: (using the symbols in (P)) in a fat year, X is greater than Z. *Lean* years are those in which the Deweyan society's increase in productivity is relatively low: X is less than Z. Principle (P) takes lean years to be significantly more likely than fat years.

What happens in a lean year? That depends on a large number of details. Again, the challenge can be focused by introducing simplifying assumptions. Suppose, for any economic sector—any particular line of goods and services—there are exactly two suppliers and exactly two potential buyers. When the Deweyan society offers its goods and services, the prices it can set will more likely be those demanded by its competitor. For the productivity

---

[28] For actual societies, this would be an unrealistic assumption. On the other hand, under the imagined conditions, it is easy to conceive a situation—either at the beginning of the period envisaged or as the flagging growth of the Deweyan economy becomes evident—in which other societies become unwilling to extend credit.

[29] See 353.

of the competitor is probably higher than its own, and, as a result, the competitor can offer each item at a lower price. On the other hand, the prices Deweyans must pay for the goods and services they seek will only fall below the median in one case out of four—when the productivity of both suppliers is above the median. Under these circumstances, the balance of trade will be unfavorable, and, if the society is to "pay as it goes," it will have to draw on the buffer fund to meet its needs.

Conversely, in a fat year, the Deweyan society will be able to replenish the buffer fund. Simplifying again, and supposing the gains and losses to be equivalent in size, the state of the buffer fund will wax and wane. However, Principle (P) tells us to expect more lean years than fat years. Hence the downward shifts will predominate. The buffer fund will dwindle over time until it is depleted—like a frog attempting to escape from a well, who ascends two feet during the day and falls back three feet at night, and who eventually sinks to the bottom. Once the fund is depleted, the Deweyan society will no longer be able to pay its way, and thus no longer able to sustain itself.

This line of reasoning simplifies in many different ways, some of which I have explicitly noted. As just presented, it cheerfully ignores considerations about the ways in which various outcomes might be distributed, collapsing them by taking averages. Let's assume these shortcuts would be vindicated by a more careful formal treatment. On the face of it, then, unless the Deweyan society is self-sufficient, or part of a self-sufficient cluster of similar societies, it is highly likely to be short-lived, unable to sustain the economic preconditions for the social goals it pursues.

Besides the statistical simplifications, the challenge idealizes in ways common to many ambitious enterprises in economic modeling. Attention to some of these abstractions enables us to see how the challenge may be blunted.

Focus first on Principle (P). This principle retreats from overstatement, recognizing how Deweyan societies might outproduce their neighbors. It resorts to claiming that, across the entire class of Deweyan societies, the chances of reaching the level of productivity of competitors are low. To frame the issue in that way is to attribute an odd lack of agency to those who design and guide the elaboration of the Deweyan program. It is as if the decision to rethink education and society in the proposed fashion were to choose a ticket in a lottery. Deweyan societies pick from one urn, non-Deweyan societies from a different urn. Since the productivity values on the latter tickets are,

368 THE MAIN ENTERPRISE OF THE WORLD

on average, greater than those on the former tickets, the Deweyan is likely to lose in the comparison game.

Consider a different way of framing the problem. Deweyan societies attempt to craft the best available implementation of their socio-educational program. Assume the policies they devise are thoughtful responses to their situation. Suppose those who shape policy for their competitors are equally thoughtful. Will the productivity in the Deweyan society always be less than the median productivity of the competitors? Will that disadvantage occur with high probability?

There's an obvious reason for giving affirmative answers: the average workweek in the Deweyan society is shorter than that among its competitors. (In the illustrative example of the previous chapter, all non-Deweyans worked forty hours a week; Deweyans chose a number of hours between thirty and forty.) If the societies are of similar sizes, the number of work hours per week among the non-Deweyans will exceed that among the Deweyans. Is there any feature of the Deweyan society allowing it to make up for that deficit? You might think not. "Anything Deweyans can do, non-Deweyans can imitate." Not so. The Deweyan society differs in two relevant respects: in its educational program and in its relative egalitarianism.

Those features are expected to contribute to Deweyan productivity in three distinct ways. The emphasis given to individual development guides people to occupations for which they feel themselves suited (and that promote their fulfillment). Knowing themselves to be recognized and honored for their contributions to their society, they are likely to work more conscientiously than their non-Deweyan counterparts. Second, the same individual attention, together with the flexible curriculum through which it is elaborated, will tend to produce people who can express their originality and creativity in their chosen line of work. Consequently, the level of innovation in the Deweyan society will probably be higher. Third, because all members of the Deweyan society are adequately supported, there are no "throwaway children." Young people have adequate food and shelter, they do not come to school hungry and exhausted, and they are helped to learn from their earliest years. Literacy levels, numerical abilities, and other skills are likely to be higher on average. The more skilled workforce will probably prove more productive than a non-Deweyan counterpart.

Are these effects large enough to balance the deficit caused by the reduction of the average workweek? Until the experiment has been tried, nobody knows the answer. Nonetheless, current statistics on productivity around the world reveal an interesting trend. Productivity does not correlate well with the length of the workweek. Some countries with short workweeks have greater productivity than those in which workers devote more hours to their jobs. Workers in Luxembourg and Norway, for example, work 1,512 and 1,424 hours a year (respectively)—considerably less than the 1,781 hours of the American worker.[30] Nevertheless, the average worker in Luxembourg contributed more to GDP per week ($2,709) than the American counterpart ($2,295). Norwegian workers provided $2,219 per week, somewhat less than those in the United States; but, with just one more hour added to their twenty-nine-hour workweek, they would deliver $2,301, putting them slightly ahead.[31]

The data just cited do not decide the question. It is one thing to compare two very different countries—one large and multiethnic and the other small and relatively homogenous—and quite another to ask whether a particular set of socioeconomic reforms, carried out in a particular society, would increase or decrease that society's productivity. The numbers do reveal, however, a potential flaw in Principle (P) and its relatives. Greater egalitarianism combined with a shorter workweek need not be accompanied by lower productivity.

A second form of idealization lies in the apparently simple inference from increased productivity to advantage in the marketplace. To be sure, if you are able to make goods similar to those I manufacture, and if you are able to do so at lower cost, you will be able to sell them at lower prices, thus attracting more buyers. If, on the other hand, I can differentiate my product, equipping it with qualities consumers value, matters are not so straightforward. They may prefer my more expensive goods over yours.

The fact is thoroughly familiar. It underlies the success of Swiss watches, German cars and precision tools, Belgian beer and chocolate, Korean and Japanese electronics, Persian carpets, Scandinavian furniture, and a host of other sought-after goods. Banal though it is, it brings a moral for the present discussion. Fortunes in trade don't depend on overall productivity, but

---

[30] Data from Wikipedia entry on "Working time" (drawn from OECD statistics): https://en.wikipedia.org/wiki/Working_time#European_countries.

[31] Data from a *Time* magazine report "These Are the Most Productive Countries in the World," citing OECD statistics: https://time.com/4621185/worker-productivity-countries/. I have multiplied the GDP/hour (given in US dollars) by the figure given for the workweek. The number of hours given in the OECD chart for the Norwegian workweek is 27.3; the discrepancy between that and the many standard references to a twenty-nine-hour workweek in Norway stems from the fact that Norwegians work forty-nine weeks per year (with three weeks' paid leave).

370 THE MAIN ENTERPRISE OF THE WORLD

on the ability to maintain an advantage in a particular sector of production, by offering goods with features others find it hard to emulate. That sector then serves as the domain in which a society trades, using the returns to meet its own needs for imported goods. Here again, the egalitarianism and educational policies of the Deweyan society can help. Through fostering the individual development of all children, by encouraging diversity in the expression of talent, the Deweyan society expands the range of sectors in which it might deliver reliable and attractive goods attuned to people's needs and wants. It can thus aspire to defeat the competition, not by lowering prices but through making rival products appear second-rate.

The two considerations just raised *blunt* the fourth challenge. Supposedly, societies implementing a Deweyan socio-educational program—or going too far in that direction—are doomed to lowered productivity, disadvantages in trade, and consequent decline and collapse. The supposition has not been decisively refuted. Rather, the verdict must be "not proven." Some considerations support the dismal thesis. Others provide grounds for hope. Declarations of how the clash will go, predictions about which ones will predominate, are overambitious and unwarranted. Nor should this state of affairs surprise anyone. It is a familiar feature of large-scale macro-economics. The complexities of actual situations elude accurate modeling. To discover whether a Deweyan society would succumb to the fourth challenge, or, more exactly, just how far it is possible to go in a Deweyan direction while maintaining a stable society, we shall just have to try it and see.

I shall return to this theme—the importance of cautious pragmatic experimentation—later. Before doing so, however, three tasks need attention. First, I shall explore a strategy for undercutting the fourth challenge entirely. After that, two further doubts about the viability of Deweyan societies must be addressed. The way will then be prepared for assessing whether the approach of previous chapters is a realistic option, or a utopian fantasy.

——◆——

To view trade, specifically trade with more productive societies, as posing a threat to the sustainability of the Deweyan program presupposes the necessity of exchanging goods with others. If the Deweyan society were self-sufficient, the difficulty would vanish. A pan-human commitment to the socio-educational reforms proposed here would create a single society concerned to meet the needs of all its members. Indeed, if Deweyanism spread sufficiently broadly, across a cluster of societies with diverse capacities for production, the need of trade with outsiders would be obviated. The fourth challenge would dissolve.

Two objections naturally arise. First, utopian thinking re-emerges in supposing that any significant fraction of the human population (let alone the entire species) could generate everything the socio-educational program requires. Even if the GDP of a single affluent nation were enough to support the program—temporarily, before competition and trade undermine it—it is fantasy to imagine that occurring across all the developed countries, let alone the entire world. Second, recent history reveals a clear trend away from larger unions. Local discontents provoke movements to leave long-standing economic associations (witness Brexit); nationalist voices decry globalism and cosmopolitanism. Proposing further ventures in large-scale international cooperation is, to say the least, unfashionable. These points need to be addressed. I shall begin with the second.

Underlying the suspicion of cooperative associations are two entirely reasonable worries. If the cooperation is halfhearted, superimposed on an economic system in which competition dominates, those who feel their standards of living slipping blame (sometimes correctly) the rules imposed from some distant central body.[32] Their hands are tied, and they suffer a competitive disadvantage in consequence. Better, then, to withdraw from the union, unlock the fetters, and take their economic lives into their own hands again. Here, I suggest, socioeconomic integration hasn't gone far enough.

The second concern is cultural rather than economic. Participation in a larger association is taken to threaten local values and local traditions. Smaller communities are submerged in a huge melting pot. They are forced to tolerate customs and perspectives they find perplexing, alien, sometimes even offensive. Their own cherished ideals and standards are, they feel, mocked and dishonored. Often their reaction is nostalgia for a prettified past, encapsulated in rosy visions of a return (an impossible return).[33] Here too, the problem derives from halfhearted pursuit of a worthy goal. The

[32] This, I believe, is the source of much discontent with the European Union. Several recent studies have diagnosed the failure to match political integration with economic integration as the root cause of dissatisfaction. See, for example, Vivien A. Schmidt, "The Eurozone's Crisis of Democratic Legitimacy: Can the EU Rebuild Public Trust and Support for Economic Integration?," available at http://ec.europa.eu/economy_finance/publications/eedp/dp015_en.htm.

[33] These two considerations, the desire of economically disadvantaged people to reassert local control and nostalgia for the period "when their country was great," are prominent in the thinking of those who supported Brexit. They also apply, I believe, to the movement to "make America great again" and to other nationalist and separatist campaigns.

372   THE MAIN ENTERPRISE OF THE WORLD

broadening of democracy across national boundaries is too shallow to prove satisfying.

Unions framed by commitment to the Deweyan program would avoid both of these deficiencies. Because Deweyan societies are founded on support for all citizens, because they provide for the individualized development of each person in each community, they are designed to attend to cases in which some groups start to feel left behind. The heart of their translation of morality into political life is a set of institutions for uncovering and responding to complaints. They listen to the cries of those who feel wounded, they inspect the source of trouble and treat the wounds before they fester. Similarly, they seek to shape citizens able to participate in deep democracy. From children's early years, they are taught to work together with others who have very different attitudes and perspectives, to learn how to engage, how to sympathize, how to understand. Within the constraints of a moral framework, constantly scrutinized and refined in inclusive, informed, and mutually responsive deliberations, they respect differences, not attempting to eradicate what others hold dear, but rejoicing in a luxuriant cultural ecosystem. As far as guiding *ideas* are concerned, the suggested socioeconomic reforms respond directly and precisely to the motives of those who oppose international democracy and pan-human cooperation.

"But now the fantasy has only been shifted to a different place! These institutions will be set up, maintained, revised, managed and staffed by human beings—and what is supposed to solve problems in theory will not translate into practice." The riposte is predictable, and it has a point. From Plato on, anyone who ponders the problems of social and political theory has to worry about how whatever designs emerge will be implemented. Will the defects in human character ruin everything? Cynics take failure to be inevitable. If they are thorough in their thinking, they may even abandon ventures in reflecting on the social, economic, political, and educational orders. Given the inevitably dismal outcomes, there is little point in worrying about reform or redesign. I read the riposte differently, not as recommending a knowing quietism, but as a challenge. How can the institutions proposed in a plan for social change best be protected against the danger of decay? How can a society best guard against the flaws of the guardians? Like any society, the Deweyan society must exercise constant vigilance, reflecting on how these questions apply in its current state, and on what should be done to blunt the envisaged threats. These are practical questions, and how they are addressed will depend on details of the state in which the society finds itself.

UTOPIA? 373

In our pre-Deweyan days, a would-be reformer must face a different practical question. Given contemporary suspicions of international cooperation, how can people be motivated to take seriously the prospect of socio-educational reform cutting across national boundaries? The answer is the usual one: sticks and carrots. Previous chapters have attempted to grow a sumptuous crop of carrots, offering an attractive picture of what life in a Deweyan society might be like. On the specific issue of large-scale cooperation, however, it's necessary to turn to the sticks. Heavy sticks lie at hand, ready to be wielded.

In the contemporary world, human societies are thoroughly causally interconnected. As a result, isolationism in economics has become impossible. None of the developing countries can carry on its production independently of others. Supply lines radiate out, linking nations in a vast web. Setbacks in one region of the world reverberate in the economic life of many distant nations. Bound together in this way, financial health in one place depends on maintaining similar health elsewhere, even in societies with whom political relations are often tense.

What applies in the financial sphere pertains also to physical health. As I write, the Covid-19 pandemic is sweeping across the globe. Millions are falling ill, and tens of thousands are dying. The grim disease ought to teach many nations many lessons. Prominent among them is the crucial importance of international cooperation with respect to outbreaks of infectious disease. By this I don't simply mean such obvious measures as the free flow of biomedical information (especially that relating to the development of tests, treatments, and vaccines) without regard to considerations of personal or corporate or national profit. Nor should it stop with the provision of necessary materials (particularly drugs and vaccines) to societies unable to develop them for themselves or to pay high prices. Although such strategies would limit the spread of disease to the benefit of all, cooperation should venture beyond mitigation to prevent future eruptions of vectors from developing into a full-blown pandemic (or an epidemic). Under a system encouraging nations to protect their economic status by concealing their early detection of a new virus (or bacterium), delay in reporting can easily be the crucial factor allowing infection to spread. If societies were bound by cooperative ties, requiring them to come to others' medical assistance, immediately, when such circumstances arise—rather than using the occasion for economic jockeying—internationally agreed-on steps could be taken to nip incipient pandemics in the bud.

374 THE MAIN ENTERPRISE OF THE WORLD

There is every reason to believe that the future will bring such pandemics with increasing frequency.[34] On our warming planet, the ecological relations among organisms are changing, providing opportunities for a disease vector adapted to one species to invade another. Climate change is likely to promote leaps of this kind, and even to allow the evolution of new—and dangerous—microorganisms.[35] Meeting the coming challenges to human health will demand, even force, increased cooperation among all nations.

So too will the general problem of coping with a warmer world. Unless nations work together far more cooperatively than they have previously done, our descendants will inherit a harsh environment, subject to cascades of what we view as catastrophic events. The problems they will confront are likely to make any discussions of educational policy, of fulfillment, and even of balancing labor against leisure seem academic exercises. A minimal strategy for limiting emissions, and thus avoiding producing an environment whose perils will strain the resources of future generations, requires countries to enter into agreements with one another, restraining themselves from activities promoting their immediate (myopic) economic interests. The Nobel Prize–winning economist William Nordhaus has proposed the existence of "climate clubs," groups of nations committed to limiting production and trade, so that targets for reducing the emission of greenhouse gases can be reached and maintained.[36] Although his proposals for international cooperation are by no means as ambitious as those recommended by other writers on climate change, climate clubs take exactly the form of my imagined compacts binding different Deweyan societies into a harmonious cluster.

If all goes well, if our species finally takes the climate problem with the seriousness it deserves, the steps we shall have to take will oppose the trend to withdraw from international unions. Attracted by the prospect of a world

[34] The case for this claim was eloquently made by Laurie Garrett in her prophetic book, *The Coming Plague* (New York: Farrar, Straus & Giroux, 1994).

[35] In *The Seasons Alter*, Evelyn Fox Keller and I laid greater emphasis on these possibilities than is customary in discussions of climate change. (Perhaps that is the consequence of our having spent considerable time thinking about issues in evolutionary biology.) Some readers suggested to us that incorporating an episode in which changed ecological relations give rise to a new disease in our opening apocalyptic scenario was something of an exaggeration. In light of the outbreak of Covid-19, at least one of them has undergone a change of mind.

[36] For Nordhaus's seminal article see "Climate Clubs: Overcoming Free-Riding in International Climate Policy," *American Economic Review* 105, no. 4 (2015): 1339–70. Nordhaus's earlier (and highly accessible) account of economic issues surrounding climate change is given in *The Climate Casino* (New Haven: Yale University Press, 2013). In *The Seasons Alter*, Evelyn Fox Keller and I extend some of Nordhaus's ideas (see Chapter 4), and argue that even further types of international cooperation are required (Chapters 5 and 6).

in which our descendants are all supported in ways promoting fulfilling lives, some people may overcome their reluctance to large-scale cooperative associations. For those who do not find that an irresistible carrot, I offer the (connected) threats of coming plagues and catastrophes induced by climate change. Although we have so far ignored them, they should be very big sticks.

I turn now to the other line of objection posed against the idea of the complete (or largely complete) Deweyan world. Is it possible for total human production to generate all the resources required to support a pan-human society, whose social, economic, and educational arrangements accorded with the proposals offered above?

Let's begin with a simpler question. Imagine an affluent society, the United States, for example. Could its productive activity and its budgetary priorities be reorganized to fund adequate economic support for all, and to introduce and maintain the suggested educational and social reforms? The answer is relatively easy. Since a vast amount of American productive activity is wasted, directed toward goods and services making negligible contributions to the value of human lives—and sometimes even subtracting from them—there is ample room for reassignment.

To repeat, reforming along Deweyan lines attempts to reduce, and if possible eliminate, labor spent on products whose sole *raison d'être* lies in their serving as marks of status. (As I have emphasized, this is not to wage war on objects providing genuine aesthetic satisfaction.) Public buildings ought to be well designed to serve their functions *and* serve as sources of delight both to those who enter them and those who view them from afar. Private dwellings should be on a sensible scale, not overgrown, sprawling monstrosities ("McMansions"), intended to announce wealth.[37] Brand-name clothing and personal ornaments often add nothing to the aesthetic value of far less expensive versions, except, of course, the advertisement of the wearers' affluence.

By far the principal source of waste, however, is the American military budget. Solving the problem of paying for new school facilities, for increasing teachers' pay, for hiring many more educators and aides—in short, for funding the central features of the Deweyan educational program—requires no more than thinking along the lines announced in thousands of wistful

---

[37] The site *McMansion Hell* shows some amusing examples: https://mcmansionhell.com/.

376 THE MAIN ENTERPRISE OF THE WORLD

placards and bumper stickers. We can all look forward to the day when education is well supported, and the armed forces have to hold bake sales to replenish their store of expensive toys.

To be sure, countries need ways of defending themselves against aggression, and a nation with a long history of serving as "the defender of the free world" must spend more than most. Yet expenditures ought to be congruent with the character of the threat. How large a nuclear arsenal is required for purposes of deterrence? (As another famous bumper sticker once reminded people, "One nuclear bomb can ruin your whole day.") How many costly warships, aircraft carriers, fighter jets, and other "conventional weapons" are needed to meet the actual challenges to the "free world"? How many troops, bases, training centers, and the like? Should defensive funding nowadays be oriented toward detection and to devices for combating terrorism (including cyberterrorism)?

The pressure to bloat military spending can be relieved by fostering cooperation, developing enforceable agreements to limit the production and spread of weapons. As has often been pointed out, two trends reduce the frequency of hostilities: increasing democratization and ever thicker and more entangled economic relations among nations.[38] To the extent that different societies must band together to address threats to our entire species— pandemics, global heating—the thick web of connections may eventually allow international democracy to succeed in a metamorphosis. Outbreaks of violence will be viewed as a problem for *policing*, and the job taken over by a transnational body.

Even before that state is reached, however, there are ample reasons to think reductions in defense spending by affluent nations (particularly the United States) can easily provide what is required to support the specifically educational part of the Deweyan program. As the previous chapter argued, for that program to attain its goals, wider social changes are required. Gross inequalities in income and wealth must be significantly reduced, and support provided for all citizens. Here too the problem is straightforwardly solved. Distinguished thinkers (as well as progressive politicians) have recognized the possibility of generating revenues for raising the living standards of the

---

[38] The idea that democratic governments are less likely to make war descends from Immanuel Kant's *Perpetual Peace*. For a recent empirical defense, see Håvard Hegre, "Democracy and Armed Conflict," *Journal of Peace Research* 51 (2014): 159–72. Hegre's review article also emphasizes the significance of economic relations.

poor by increasing taxes on the rich.[39] Indeed, they have pointed out how the proposed redistribution does no more than return tax codes to forms they took during times of great prosperity and productivity.[40]

So the answer to the specific question about the United States—and almost certainly about other affluent nations—is a clear "Yes." Nor are there any good reasons for supposing the redistribution of budgets and of wealth would detract from the ability to engage in other necessary projects, organizing a project to ward off potential pandemics or to limit the threat of climate change. When the horizon of attention expands, however, when we ask whether current total worldwide productivity would suffice to support a global Deweyan society, any assessment must be far less confident. At least three complicating factors come into play.

1. The need for many of the world's nations to develop, and to do so without contributing further to the emissions fueling global heating.
2. The need to resettle a significant fraction of the human population (almost all of it in developing countries). More than a billion human beings currently live in regions likely to become uninhabitable within the next few decades.[41]
3. The need to curb the rapid growth of the human population.

The costs of meeting these needs can only be met by the world's affluent societies. With respect to the third, the solution is clear: invest in education—particularly female education—throughout those regions where population increases are above replacement levels.[42] In principle, what is required for

---

[39] See Anthony Atkinson, *Inequality*, and Philippe van Parijs and Yannick Vanderborght, *Basic Income*. Suggestions along these lines were central to Elizabeth Warren's announced plans for tax reform, offered during her campaign for nomination as the Democratic Party's presidential candidate for 2020. Although Warren's campaign was not successful, polls show that her "billionaire's tax" proposal is extremely popular with American citizens.

[40] In *The Economists' Hour: False Prophets, Free Markets, and the Fracture of Society* (New York: Little Brown, 2019), Binyamin Appelbaum shows how the lowering of top tax rates (pioneered under Ronald Reagan, and a staple of Republican economic policy ever since) failed to promote growth. See Chapter 4.

[41] See *The Guardian*, May 5, 2020; https://www.theguardian.com/environment/2020/may/05/one-billion-people-will-live-in-insufferable-heat-within-50-years-study.

[42] A seminal article is Amartya Sen, "Gender Equity and the Population Problem," *International Journal of Health Services* 31 (2001): 469–74. More recent analyses of empirical data have largely confirmed Sen's original conclusions. See, for example, Homi Kharas, "Climate Change, Fertility, and Girls' Education," at https://www.brookings.edu/blog/future-development/2016/02/16/climate-change-fertility-and-girls-education/. The graphs provide compelling evidence of the trend to reduced family size when girls receive more education.

378   THE MAIN ENTERPRISE OF THE WORLD

the first is also evident: provide technologies of production based on renewable sources of energy (particularly solar power and wind). For the second problem, as recent migration crises and intense opposition to immigration have made all too clear, we have very little clue.

Even to arrive at responsible *conjectures* about the costs of addressing all three of these needs would take another book (and more research than I have yet done). Thus the only answer available to the global question—Could worldwide Deweyanism be introduced and sustained in our current situation?—must be "We don't know." Here, as on other occasions in life, the human family faces consequential decisions without possessing reliable information for ranking the options.

What, then, should be done to move forward? The surplus productivity of the affluent countries might not extend to cover everything required to introduce and sustain a worldwide society exemplifying the Deweyan program proposed in previous chapters, as well as allowing for serious efforts to address the three needs just listed. Under those circumstances, the surplus would have to be divided into different budgets, designated for making a Deweyan transition in the affluent world as well as coping with the three problems. How that division should be made is a matter for global democratic discussion. I recommend, however, at least giving some consideration to beginning the project of the Deweyan society. My recommendation rests on three grounds. First, to redistribute income and wealth in affluent nations would not reduce the resources available for addressing the three needs below what could have been redirected to those needs if no readjustments in the affluent world had been made. Second, it is useful to explore possibilities for implementing the Deweyan program. We may expect to learn from early experiments. Third, and perhaps most importantly, even at times of grave challenges, it is valuable to be able to see human life as guided by inspiring ideals. No generation is likely to dedicate itself thoroughly to difficult tasks if it recognizes its activities as grim efforts to hang on. Human motivations ought not to be completely dominated by sticks. There should also be some carrots.

———

I shall return below to the points just briefly made, and to some pragmatic ideas about elaborating them. Before doing so, however, one final version of the charge of utopianism should be considered and evaluated. Since the late 1970s, predominantly in the United States and the United Kingdom but to

UTOPIA? 379

a lesser extent in other affluent democracies, suspicion of "planned economies" and of "government regulation" has grown. The unfavorable reputation of "state interference" is accompanied by paeans to the wonders of the "free market."[43] Because the socio-educational program presented in earlier chapters plainly requires directed redistribution of resources and institutions to manage the economy in various ways, it will obviously seem suspect. "Your proposals," I shall be told, "are recipes for inefficiency, mismanagement, and waste." Or possibly worse.

Wholesale distrust of centralized planning and of state intervention is impossible. Celebrations of the "free market" rest on a myth. We might as well sing hymns to the unicorn or offer sacrifices to the tooth fairy. That these points are not universally appreciated is a scandal. In the twentieth century, decades before worship of the "free market" became a fetish, Karl Polanyi offered a powerful exposé.[44] Yet some of the essential arguments are far older, presented in the book worshipers often cite as scripture. Already in *The Wealth of Nations*, Adam Smith undermines the idea of the completely free market.

Perhaps the devout should be forgiven. *The Wealth of Nations* is lengthy (like the Bible), and in both instances reading the whole takes more time than even the faithful can devote. Moreover, Smith's exploration of the preconditions for a market economy comes in the very last part, Book V—although it does amount to roughly a third of the whole. For markets to work, Smith argues, there has to be a public body providing a system of justice, protecting the security of producers and consumers, constructing and maintaining ways in which suppliers and buyers can be brought into contact with one another—and even, as we have seen, reflecting on how those who labor to make the goods are to be educated.[45] Finally, he turns to the question of how this central body—the government—will acquire the resources to discharge the tasks assigned to it. Here, perhaps to the consternation of people who take themselves to be obeying his commandments, he is not so much interested in railing against the evils of levying taxes. Rather than

[43] In *The Economists' Hour*, Binyamin Appelbaum provides an informative account of this trend, of how starkly it differs from previous policymaking, and of how the common plaudits are often at odds with the evidence.

[44] Karl Polanyi, *The Great Transformation* (1944; paperback ed., Boston: Beacon, 1957). Even after the emergence of market theology, more judicious theorists assimilated Polanyi's insights. See, for example, Charles Lindblom, *The Market System* (New Haven: Yale University Press, 2001).

[45] See Chapter 2 above, 54–57.

380 THE MAIN ENTERPRISE OF THE WORLD

viewing taxation as theft, he seeks to understand how tax rates can be set fairly and how taxes can efficiently and justly be collected.

The basic points are crushingly obvious. Nobody is going to devote hours, days, weeks, or even years to producing something if there are serious possibilities of outsiders (marauders, pirates, gangs of thieves) breaking in and making off with the goods. Nobody will come to the trading place unless they are confident that what they bring will not be snatched from them. The trading place will be empty without means for producers and consumers to reach it: Smith envisages roads and canals; we could add railways, highways and delivery trucks, advertisements and internet connections. Finally, many exchanges in the eighteenth-century world—and even more today—will depend on the ability of consumers to read and to do arithmetic. Sometimes, people need to scrutinize the advertisements and the fine print. Sometimes they have to calculate to determine what should go into their basket of goods.

"Very well," the free marketeer may reply, "but some of these background conditions may be set in place by free markets. We can privatize—allow private security agencies, private prisons, private railroads, and private schools to emerge from the rigors of competition in a free market, and thus be superior to anything a flabby (or duplicitous) government would provide." True enough. Nevertheless, the envisaged markets yielding these goods and services will require to solve their own versions of the protection problem, the connection problem, and the training problem. Some background system will be needed to guarantee the security of those who interact in the trades, to bring those who produce into contact with aspiring consumers, to ensure the participants are prepared to make informed decisions in their trading. The marketeer is involved in a regress. You can't have free markets all the way down (or should it be "all the way up"?). What can (and does) emerge is a multilevel system, where markets sometimes offer alternatives to goods and services provided by public bodies, and in which every market is dependent on some form of governmental support and regulation. The result actually multiplies the sites of state intervention. Thus, there are public and private educational institutions (schools and universities), and, at a different level, an agency to regulate public and private institutions alike.

Fundamentalist market theology, often encapsulated in political slogans, is incoherent. Yet it is unfair to treat all those who sing the praises of the free market as fundamentalists (and I have been unfair.) The serious position in the vicinity consists in a commitment to impose no more conditions on the market than those required for it to work its magic. Sophisticated champions

UTOPIA? 381

of free markets hope to *minimize* the amount of regulation. But what exactly counts as "minimization" here? There's no obvious way to count rules: any system of rules, however numerous in its initial formulation, can be collapsed into a single rule by conjoining all the original directives. More importantly, does minimization involve descending (or ascending?) in the hierarchy of markets envisaged in the previous paragraph, introducing regulation at the most fundamental (abstract?) level possible? Here, marketology divides into sects, and it is far from evident what would count as orthodoxy.

Yet *why* exactly should the idea of a market subject only to minimal conditions appear attractive? There are, I suggest, a number of popular reasons, none of them convincing. First, and perhaps most influential, is the collapse of a collection of regimes, all of which were commonly associated with determined egalitarianism and central management of the economy—the Soviet Union and its satellites. No one should doubt the existence of vast defects, economic and political, in those regimes, but it is foolish to take them either as representing theoretical Marxism or as the only alternative to a minimal free market economy. To appreciate the latter point (more relevant for my, non-Marxist, purposes), it's only necessary to look to nations that have imposed further conditions on markets, typically in the intent of equalizing wealth and providing a range of services for all their citizens—countries committed to what may go under the banner either of social democracy or of market socialism. As we shall see later, the important question to raise about these economic approaches is not whether they are the most efficient or the most competitive. It concerns the quality of the lives they offer their citizens.

A far more sophisticated defense of minimal intervention derives from the argument of a brilliant defender of free markets (and free societies), Friedrich Hayek. In "The Use of Knowledge in Society," Hayek addressed the problem of constructing and maintaining a "rational economic order."[46] Central planners, he reasoned, will always have difficulties in directing resources because the information they require is widely dispersed. Their decisions about investing resources in various places will always be handicapped by lack of knowledge about what is needed where. The phenomenon was well illustrated by Soviet exercises in planning, with notorious shortages (often accompanied by surpluses in different regions of the country). Markets, on the other hand, aggregate information. Entrepreneurs will be motivated to produce what is required in places where it is currently scarce, where they

---

[46] *American Economic Review* 35 (1945): 519–30.

382   THE MAIN ENTERPRISE OF THE WORLD

can demand higher prices than could be set in locations where supply is good. Central planners have to operate by guesswork, and frequently bungle. Markets deliver the goods.

Of course, Hayek's argument depends on assuming some things about the flow of information. No channels lead from all potential sites to the central planning agency. Some channels connect places currently in need to particular entrepreneurs, who are then able to seize the opportunity presented to them. Perhaps there mustn't be too many such channels, allowing too many entrepreneurs to swing into action—and thus engage in competition that will diminish the anticipated profits. The argument also works best in cases where the time lag between registering the opportunity and generating the product is not too large. Otherwise, by the time the goods are ready to deliver, the demand may have passed: perhaps the population has had to migrate elsewhere, or it has changed its tastes, or (sadly) succumbed. From the perspective of 1945, however, Hayek quite reasonably believed that benign conditions would arise with sufficient frequency to support his main thesis. Markets can make efficient use of information; central planners cannot.

Today, however, matters look very different. Public agencies have all sorts of ways of acquiring all sorts of information. Many people are more inclined to worry about the extent of what is known about them than to pity the poor bureaucrats deprived of the insights needed for making good decisions. Technological change has facilitated gathering data, aggregating it, and analyzing it. Indeed, the political leaders free marketeers admire, as well as those they dislike, run their campaigns by discovering what voters of various types want. Successful central planning abounds.

Ironically, however, the vicissitudes of information flow sometimes disrupt markets. One of the triumphs of mathematical economics is a result proved by two Nobel laureates, Kenneth Arrow and Gérard Debreu—and perhaps appreciation of the Arrow-Debreu theorem provides the most sophisticated reason for enthusiasm about markets. Arrow and Debreu demonstrated that, under apparently minimal conditions, a market economy will attain an equilibrium state in which aggregate supply and aggregate demand match.[47] Despite this reassuring result, there are well-known instances in which markets fail. One important type of failure stems from asymmetries in access to information. A classic presentation of the phenomenon is given by

---

[47] The proof of the Arrow-Debreu theorem involves some advanced mathematics. The most accessible presentation I know is in Hal Varian, *Microeconomic Analysis* (New York: W. W. Norton, 1978).

UTOPIA? 383

George Akerlof's analysis of the used-car market.[48] According to some eminent economists, market failure is pervasive.[49]

Consider a case very like Akerlof's (one overlapping my own experience). Our family is moving to the city in which you live, and you have put up your house for sale. It is attractive, in a neighborhood we like, and the advertised price is affordable. Should we buy it? That depends. We know that you know where the bodies are buried (metaphorically, if not literally), and that we do not. The roof is extensive and complex, the climate is continental, with severe extremes. For all we know, it leaks badly, and there are gaps and holes, welcoming bats who will fly around at night and terrify the children. If we only had some assurance that you are not hiding serious defects, we would plunge ahead with the purchase. But we don't.[50] The transaction breaks down. So it goes with other buyers and other sellers. Renters and hoteliers thrive. Houses and apartments don't change hands.

Under circumstances like these, regulation prevents market failure. Sellers must certify that they have disclosed any defects known to them, and, if their failure to do so is later revealed, buyers can obtain legal redress and compensation. Knowing that in advance, buyers have the assurances required to ward off market failure. A minimally regulated market is significantly inferior to one in which "the state interferes."

Why, then, are the tributes to the free market (more exactly: to the minimally regulated market) so loud and so frequent? Because minimal regulation is "efficient." "Efficient" here is a technical term, not a vague gesture in the direction of all virtues. Economists who think market failure is rare take minimal regulation to be the default ideal. For, given two markets subject to different levels of external constraint, the one less regulated will set lower

---

[48] Given in Chapter 1 of *An Economic Theorist's Book of Tales* (Cambridge, UK: Cambridge University Press, 1984). In 2001, Akerlof, together with Michael Spence and Joseph Stiglitz, was awarded the Nobel Prize in Economics (officially the prize is "in memory of Alfred Nobel" since Nobel himself didn't institute a prize in economics). Had a fourth person been permitted to share the prize, a likely candidate would have been Michael Rothschild, whose collaboration with Stiglitz (Michael Rothschild and Joseph Stiglitz, "Equilibrium in Competitive Insurance Markets: An Essay on the Economics of Imperfect Information," *Quarterly Journal of Economics* 90 [1976]: 629–49) is one of the classic studies of asymmetric information and market failure. I am grateful to Mike for many illuminating discussions of economic issues, and for more than thirty years of warm friendship.

[49] At the inaugural meeting of the "Society for Progress," held in 2015 in London, the brilliant and indefatigable Kenneth Arrow surprised all of us when he announced, "It's Akerlof everywhere."

[50] In the spring of 1986, we moved to Minneapolis and bought a house. It turned out to have just the features described—although, with a fair bit of vigilance, we managed to prevent any of the bats in our attic colony from frightening the children. Fortunately, a local ordinance required sellers to declare that there were no known defects they were concealing, and, after the problems had become evident, we were able to recover from the former owners the (considerable) costs of re-roofing.

384   THE MAIN ENTERPRISE OF THE WORLD

prices. Adding regulation imposes costs. The extra costs are unnecessary, they constitute waste—that is, inefficiency.

Suppose the controversial assumption—market failure is rare—to be granted. What follows? That minimal regulation allows consumers to buy more cheaply than they otherwise would. Surely, when other things are equal, that is a good thing. But are they equal? As is becoming ever more evident, an economic system subject to the relentless insistence on minimizing regulation generates innumerable undesirable consequences—environmental decay, lack of protection for workers and consumers, grotesque inequalities in wealth, perpetuation of poverty and deprivation.[51] When this is appreciated, the tribute of "efficiency" marks a decision to treat one kind of desirable effect as dominating all others. "Let people buy as cheaply–and thus as much—as possible!" The praise of the free market is exposed for what it is: Consumerism writ large.

Throughout this book, I have resisted this perverse distortion of human aspirations and of human lives.[52] To be fobbed off with the prospect of toys when communities suffer and when individuals are blocked from fulfilling lives is—to use the neutral language of economics—a bad bargain. Nor have economists failed to note the point. In his Nobel lecture, "The Theory and Practice of Market Design,"[53] Alvin Roth reiterates the advice the Cheshire Cat once gave Alice: the direction in which you ought to go is the one leading to the place you hope to reach.[54] We should design markets—imposing constraints and regulations—so that they will generate the consequences we hope for. In thinking about design, of course, it's worth thinking about the entire spectrum of effects, taking into account all the valuable ends we wish to promote and all the predicaments we would like to avoid. A corollary: What

[51] As Angus Deaton emphasizes in his important book, *The Great Escape* (Princeton: Princeton University Press, 2013), it is entirely correct for economists to celebrate the ways in which market economies have raised overall standards of living, so long as they acknowledge the severe negative consequences they have inflicted on those who have been "left behind." Together with Anne Case, Deaton has taken the argument further in *Deaths of Despair and the Future of Capitalism* (Princeton, NJ: Princeton University Press, 2020). Other voices in harmony with those of Case and Deaton include Thomas Piketty, *Capital* (Cambridge, MA: Harvard University Press, 2013), and Emmanuel Saez and Gabriel Zucman, *The Triumph of Injustice* (New York: W. W. Norton, 2019). Again, Anthony Atkinson's *Inequality* should also be included here.

[52] Deaton's *Great Escape* is admirably clear on differentiating economic benefits from other dimensions of well-being.

[53] The lecture is freely available at https://www.nobelprize.org/prizes/economic-sciences/2012/roth/lecture/.

[54] Lewis Carroll, *Alice in Wonderland*, Chapter 6.

UTOPIA?   385

economists hail as "efficiency" might well be part of what we consider—but it is madness to think of it as the *summum bonum*, or as the whole.

Although he presents the idea of market design clearly and eloquently, Roth was hardly the first economist to recognize its significance. In the heyday of classical political economy, the point was made—with equal clarity and eloquence—by a thinker we have met before: John Stuart Mill.

This book began with Mill (in his guise as rector of St. Andrews), and it is fitting for him to make a (triumphant) return as it nears its close. During his lifetime no fewer than seven editions of his *Principles of Political Economy* appeared, and this book had a wide influence. Yet it contained two major challenges to orthodox thinking. First, Mill devoted an entire part ("book") to questions of the distribution of wealth, rather than supposing, as most of his predecessors did, that distribution should simply be left to the market. Viewing that as intolerable, Mill argued for attempting to assure all young people of adequate economic support, and to bring this about by limiting the amount any single individual could inherit.[55] Second, instead of fearing a state in which the economy ceases to grow, he welcomed it.[56]

Malthus's writings on population had alerted early nineteenth-century economists to an apparent problem (already implicit, as Mill pointed out in Smith's *Wealth of Nations*). Can economies grow forever? Malthus was commonly read as arguing for a dismal conclusion: growth must inevitably terminate in a condition where it comes to a halt—the dreaded "stationary state." Given the virtues traditionally ascribed to growth, the Malthusian threat provoked the best economic minds of the age to pursue two lines of inquiry. Can the stationary state be avoided? If not, how can it be postponed as long as possible?

Mill argued that the supposedly dismal conclusion was correct, but, in contrast to his many contemporaries who had arrived at a similar judgment, that the stationary state would allow the development of happy and fulfilling forms of life. He confessed his repugnance at the cutthroat competition

[55] PPE 218–26 (Book II, chapter ii, §§ 3–4). Mill's focus on distribution should come as a shock to all the many people who take him to be a card-carrying aggregative utilitarian. Mill's thought is doomed to be oversimplified by interpreters who read *Utilitarianism* without considering his large corpus of other writings. In "Mill's Consequentialism," in *The Routledge Companion to Nineteenth Century Thought*, ed. Dean Moyar, 633–57 (London: Routledge, 2010), I try to correct common misreadings of Mill's ethical stance.

[56] PPE Book IV, chapter vi, especially §2, 753–57.

386 THE MAIN ENTERPRISE OF THE WORLD

already visible in the early stages of industrial capitalism, at the "struggling to get on," at the neglect of important values in the pursuit of profit. Once a nation had advanced far enough economically, the relentless treading on one another can cease—the stationary state, he claims, "would be, on the whole, a very considerable improvement on our present condition."[57]

To support his provocative evaluation, Mill proposed a remedy of the state of his society, as he found it: "what is economically needed is a better distribution."[58] Trimming the wealth of entrepreneurs enables all people to receive adequate support. Rejecting the insistence on maximizing productivity allows advances in technology to do what they should always have done: abridge the working day, and open up time for human development. Mill anticipates Roth's point. Markets should be designed (or redesigned) to generate socially and individually valuable states. Moreover, in assessing what is valuable, the philosophical economist should focus on what really matters.

Although he urges his readers to support moving to the stationary state more rapidly than is necessary, Mill does not provide any detailed blueprint. He offers suggestions—the proposal to limit inheritance is one of them. Without a fully elaborated plan for the transition to the kind of society he takes to be an advance upon his own, he is, of course, vulnerable to the charge of Utopianism. "Give us the specifics!" commands the critic, "Show us how this wonderful world can come into being!" Mill cannot fulfill that order.

Neither can I. This book has attempted to adumbrate similar ideals, treating them from the perspective of fostering human development, both individual and social. The present chapter has, I hope, rebutted attempts to show the impossibility of the Deweyan society, or even efforts aimed at disclosing the improbability of sustaining a society of that kind. It has not offered a roadmap or a detailed guide for preserving the destination once we reach it.

For that task *is* impossible. The human sciences are not ready—and probably never will be—to tackle problems of that scale and complexity. What practical implications, then, do my proposals—or Mill's—have?

To answer that question, it is worth turning to one of Mill's successors, a thinker who greatly admired him. Nearly a quarter of a century after Mill's death, William James published *Pragmatism*, a series of lectures outlining a new philosophical movement. He dedicated the volume to "[t]he memory

---

[57] PPE 754.
[58] PPE 755.

UTOPIA? 387

of John Stuart Mill from whom I first learned the pragmatic openness of mind and whom my fancy likes to picture as our leader were he alive today."[59] Themes in pragmatism had already been sounded in James's earlier writings. In particular, the idea of a pragmatic strategy for working toward goals, when it is impossible to specify an advance route, figures in the concluding paragraph of his most famous essay, "The Will to Believe."[60] There, James borrows an image from the British jurist Fitzjames Stephen. Stephen compares the human predicament to that of people stranded on a mountain pass in a blinding snowstorm. Although they only are given momentary perceptions of possible ways to safety, they must choose the most promising, for, to stand still will soon bring death by hypothermia.

Vary the image to a more familiar situation. People who enjoy hiking in the woods sometimes lose their way, and as dusk descends must find their way out. Intensify the problem, by supposing the locale to be home to dangerous nocturnal animals. What to do?

The answer is obvious: look for glimmers of light between the trees; follow potential trails leading toward them. Promising leads may peter out. In that case, it will be necessary to adjust. The predicament would be less grave if it were shared by a group of friends, allowing different possibilities to be explored, especially if the whole band could then join together to pursue the most likely option.

Lacking a detailed map to lead us to a Deweyan society, we should opt for the approach taken by any sensible group of hikers. Look for the glimmers of light—changes taking us in Deweyan directions. Try to implement them, and see what works. Develop further the approaches holding the most promise. Keep adjusting, and keep going.

It is not guaranteed to succeed, or to yield constant progress. Yet, through experimentation and cooperation, we may hope to advance. For those who share Mill's, Dewey's, and my own discontents with the way we live now, who protest the idea that material prosperity, unevenly shared, at cost to human fulfillment, is the best we can do, Stephen and James offer sound advice. Try, and see how far you can get.

---

[59] James, *Pragmatism* (Cambridge, MA: Harvard University Press, 1975), 3.
[60] *The Will to Believe* (Cambridge, MA: Harvard University Press, 1979), 13–33. "The Will to Believe" is probably the most influential article ever written by an American philosopher. The image from Stephen occurs at 33.

388   THE MAIN ENTERPRISE OF THE WORLD

A final association and a final image. Mill is not principally known today for the works of his I have cited: the Inaugural Address at St. Andrews and the *Principles of Political Economy*. His fame rests on his defense of a (revisionary) utilitarianism and, above all, for *On Liberty*.[61] Nor is his great predecessor in defending freedom of the press, John Milton, best known for *Areopagitica*. Milton is primarily the author of the great English-language epic—the purportedly Christian poem *Paradise Lost*.

From the eighteenth century on, critics have suspected Milton's orthodoxy. Blake and Shelley famously took Milton to be "of the devil's party," and the tradition thrives in the twentieth and twenty-first centuries.[62] With some reason. *Paradise Lost* opens with a long sentence defining the poet's aim—"to justify the ways of God to man." Who needed the justification? Surely Milton himself, the devoted servant of a Commonwealth, dedicated to the pure worship of the Almighty, at a time when that regime had been replaced by a corrupt monarchy, when he himself had been imprisoned and released only out of compassion for his growing blindness. When Milton brings the deity onstage, God preens himself on his omniscience and righteousness. Predicting the Fall, with all its consequences for humanity, he asks (in the style of many political leaders ever since)

> . . . whose fault?
> Whose but his own? Ingrate, he had of me
> All he could have; I made him just and right
> Sufficient to have stood, though free to fall.[63]

When the Almighty speaks like that, he would seem to need justification.

Yet those who settle for Satan as the hero overlook Milton's humanism. The great figure in his drama is Adam, the man prepared to give up Eden for the feckless Eve.[64] The grandeur of the human venture is made evident in the poem's closing lines:

---

[61] In some quarters he is also notorious for insensitive remarks about the unreadiness of some societies (about whose history and culture he appears ignorant) for democratic self-government. These ideas erupt occasionally in *On Liberty* and are more prominent in *Considerations on Representative Government*.

[62] See, for example, William Empson's brilliant *Milton's God* (London: Chatto & Windus), 1961.

[63] *Paradise Lost*, Book III, 96–100.

[64] There's no way of glossing over Milton's asymmetric treatment of the sexes, or his misogyny. The tone is set early, and doesn't vary: "He for God only, she for God in him" (Book IV, 299).

UTOPIA? 389

> Some natural tears they dropped, but wiped them soon
> The world was all before them, where to choose
> Their place of rest, and providence their guide.
> They, hand in hand, with wandering steps and slow
> Through Eden took their solitary way.[65]

The vision Milton leaves to his readers is of a human project, begun in a world made newly harsh and challenging, directed—through uncertain steps—toward fashioning lives aspiring to fulfillment. It is a project pursued together to transform the conditions of our existence, to make new kinds of societies and new and more rewarding forms of human existence. We may dismantle the theological framework, and still retain the sense of grandeur.

As Emerson did: the main enterprise of the world, for splendor, for extent, is the upbuilding of a human being.[66]

---

[65] Book XII, 645–49.

[66] Again I amend Emerson's formulation to avoid suggestions of sexual asymmetry. Emerson does not share Milton's misogyny, but he does not anticipate contemporary sensitivities about gendered nouns either.

Appendix 1

Chapter 3 understands fulfilling lives as satisfying three conditions: they pursue a project (or projects) that are freely chosen; those projects are successful, that is they achieve enough of their central goals; and they contribute to the lives of others. As I have acknowledged, the potential targets of our efforts include not only members of our own species, but all sentient beings. Yet, throughout most of my discussions, the emphasis is on the positive effects on human lives. Is this approach too narrow? Might a life prove fulfilling through its contributions to something other than human lives?

Although I would answer both questions affirmatively, I contend that such fulfillment is sufficiently rare to make my practice a reasonable idealization. The aim of this brief Appendix is to explain and defend the contention.

In a world rife with cruelty and mistreatment of non-human animals, people who protest what is casually and callously done may find fulfillment in the changes they bring about. If zoos become more humane, or if protocols for experiments become attuned to avoiding the distortion of animal lives, or if the rearing of animals for food is abandoned (or at least tempered by some vestige of humanity), the significance of the reformers' lives may be understood—*in part*—as stemming from the relief of animal suffering. I say "in part," because the reforms occur via the enlightenment brought to some contemporaries: the people who run the zoos, who supervise animal experimentation—and all those who consume the products of factory farming. Also because the protesters live in a human social world, and how completely their lives are fulfilled depends on the impact they have on the people with whom they directly interact.

In some instances, however, this direct involvement with the human world is diminished. The most obvious option is to consider people whose lifetimes are devoted to tending particular non-human animals. Jane Goodall, for example, has surely enjoyed a wonderfully fulfilling life, although much of it has been spent in the company of the chimpanzees of Gombe. Nobody who studies her work can fail to be moved by her dedication to the individual chimps whom she describes so vividly (and with such affection).[1] She has enriched the lives of these animals, not only in the obvious material ways but also through the relationships she has developed with them.

Goodall's achievement is, however, many-sided. She has, one might say, fulfilled herself many times over. Primatologists, as well as many other scholars from different fields, have had their lives permanently altered by her insights into chimpanzee behavior and social life. She has taught the world an immense amount. She has worked hard to ensure that Gombe will be maintained as a preserve for the chimpanzees, and that future generations will be able to carry on the interactions she pioneered. She has been a remarkable mentor to many younger investigators. The understanding of chimpanzee social life she has helped to give us has not only informed and delighted readers and viewers of nature documentaries—the sensitivities she has cultivated in them have also affected the ways in which animals are treated in zoos and animal parks around the world.

---

[1] See *The Chimpanzees of Gombe* (Cambridge, MA: Harvard University Press, 1986).

392   APPENDIX 1

In consequence, whether or not the differences she has made to the quality of non-human lives are taken into account, the *human* contributions already tilt the scales heavily toward fulfillment. And so it is generally. Those who spend many hours a week tending animals—the shepherds, the breeders, the veterinarians, the devoted pet owners—typically affect the lives of other people, both in their everyday relations to other human beings and through the care they provide for their non-human charges. The conscientious dog breeder seeks out future owners for the pups, people who can be trusted to care for the growing dog—and in doing so she both secures the animal's welfare and enriches the lives of a family. It is difficult to detach the non-human impact from the contributions made to human lives; also not to suspect that the latter may greatly outweigh the former.

To find a clear case in which fulfillment must be attributed to non-human contributions alone, it's necessary to disrupt the usual relations between the life's subject and other people. One way in which this might occur is to imagine an extreme version of Temple Grandin, a person who becomes deeply concerned for the welfare of animals, while avoiding all human relationships. Our protagonist formulates explicitly a life project, to make the treatment of domesticated animals more humane, and she cares nothing for the further consequences on human lives. Her advocacy succeeds in areas where her proposed reforms don't have damaging effects on people, and there are sufficiently many of these to generate many successes in attaining her ends.

Even here, however, there are disturbing factors. Unlike the actual Grandin, the fictional version is completely indifferent to human well-being. The proposals she makes never take human impact into account. She is equally committed to reforms that also improve human lives and to those that would be devastating for some people. The moral and legal framework of her society provides the necessary restraint, permitting her reforms to go ahead only when they satisfy a condition to which she is completely oblivious. Given this lack of moral sensitivity, I suggest, her project is flawed, and her life cannot count as fulfilled.

If this is correct, we need a subject who would be sensitive to the well-being of other people—and who thus would contribute to their lives—if there were opportunities to do so. In short, the protagonist has to be somehow detached from human society, with the ability to interact only with non-human animals. We need Robinson Crusoe (before Friday enters his life).

A revised Romulus or Siegfried won't do. You might imagine a boy, born in the wilderness, to a mother who dies giving birth, suckled by wolves or bears, permanently dwelling with the beasts and helping them in all sorts of ways. A life of this kind might be fulfilled in the limited way of children with severe cognitive or emotional developmental disruptions.[2] Without acquiring language, however, and without the developed self-consciousness for which language is a prerequisite, it is hard to make sense of a project for Romulus or Siegfried. It is reasonable to see his life as going better than it would under alternative conditions—if, for example, he lived in conflict with the animals around him—but it is hardly a fulfilled human life.

Hence the circumstances must allow for our subject to develop normally through childhood and adolescence, becoming able to speak, to reflect, to become self-aware, and so forth. Society is needed at the early stages of life. Then, in young adulthood, before the protagonist has done much to contribute to the lives of other people, human social

---

[2] See above, 91–92.

APPENDIX 1   393

connections have to be severed. In his new isolation, the only projects available to him are those benefiting non-human animals. Shipwrecked on a desert island, or cut off from the rest of the human population after some environmental catastrophe, our hero resolves to do whatever he can to aid and protect the beasts around him. He brings water to those too feeble to go to the waterhole, removes thorns from paws, mends the broken wings of birds, and so on. For fifty years he ministers to the animals. Finally, when he has grown weak, a band of explorers discovers him. His failing powers prevent him from conveying much to them about how he has spent his life—but, with their aid, he is given a painless and peaceful death.

A life fulfilled? I'm inclined to think so. Throughout his solitary years our Robinson may sometimes have doubts about the worth of the way in which he spends his time. Probably he will regret the critical event that separated him from the human world, the youthful plans that never came to fruition. Nevertheless, he can console himself with the reflection that he has made the best use of the limited circumstances forced upon him. He has built a community in the non-human world, of which he has been the mainstay. He has done much good. And how could he have done better?

Can the case be extended? Is it necessary for Robinson to interact with animals? Would it be enough for him to preserve the environment? Or to tend plants? Cultivate his garden?

Once again, it's crucial to exclude potential impact on other human lives. We rightly honor those who spend years exploring parts of the natural world, whether they map it or preserve it. The John Muirs find fulfillment because they enrich the lives of those who come after them, the hikers, climbers, and campers who are enraptured by the time spent in the mountains—and, sometimes, improve the lives of animals indigenous to the regions the pioneers have explored. Unlike the sentient animals, mountains, lakes, and trees do not have any point of view.[3] Our actions bring neither good nor harm *to them*. In carelessly tossing our trash, or scrawling graffiti on a rock, we do not cause inanimate nature to suffer. Our actions count as damage done only because they deprive other human beings of joys they might otherwise have had, or because they ruin the environments of the native animals. Our debt is not to our planet but to our fellows (our fellow creatures).[4]

If there were no sentient animals, and no possibility for another person ever to enter Robinson's domain, he might still cultivate the plants and tend the local environment. That would pass the time, and provide him some aesthetic satisfaction. His doings would be less pathological than those of an obsessive grass-counter, but they would lack connection to the lives of others. Robinson's life would then be unfulfilled.

I conclude: it is possible to live a fulfilling human life solely through a project that contributes to the lives of non-human—sentient—animals. But the circumstances under which that can occur are sufficiently rare to make the account offered in Chapter 3 a useful idealization.

---

[3] Several authors have written eloquently on the importance of having a point of view when considering whether various kinds of entities have intrinsic moral significance. The point was originally made by Tom Regan in *The Case for Animal Rights* (Berkeley: University of California Press, 1983), and it is powerfully renewed and developed in Christine Korsgaard's *Fellow Creatures* (New York: Oxford University Press, 2018).

[4] For more on this theme, see my essay "What Do We Owe Our Planet?," *Los Angeles Review of Books*, https://lareviewofbooks.org/article/what-do-we-owe-our-planet/.

Appendix 2

Although Part III's vision of the Deweyan society (and of the measures required to sustain it) relies on the operation of markets, it proposes to direct them toward attaining desirable social ends through appropriately designed regulations. In doing so, it will surely spark fears that the envisaged interventions are coercive. I hope to allay such concerns.

Consider two cases. First, as I have noted, future conditions may demand limiting population growth. Indeed, a time at which the human population has to be held constant (or decreased) appears almost inevitable. Hence, I have imagined policies directed toward reproduction at replacement levels, most obviously by limiting families to two children. Second, my suggestions for re-evaluation of forms of work distinguish socially valuable labor from efforts expended on generating goods and services whose only value lies in their ability to advertise status. Here, some central authority would have to identify the line of demarcation, declaring which types are validated and which seen as socially disruptive waste.

Both instances provoke a natural reaction. These measures are intrusions into the sphere of personal decisions. What public body has the authority to tell people the limits there should be on the size of their families? Who has the right to decide which kinds of products and services are genuinely valuable, appealing to the aesthetic tastes of those who seek them, and which are simply serving as status symbols? For all my protestations, doesn't the Deweyan society head off in the direction of the Politburo and of the drab uniformity of Soviet-style culture? (We might recall the protests directed at China's former policy restricting couples to a single child.)

I begin with a point derived from Mill. In his economic writings and in *On Liberty*, Mill insists on the *distribution* of freedoms. The freedom properly enjoyed by any individual is limited by that individual's constriction of the like liberties of others. When one couple's decision to have more children would demand a larger share of the available resources, thereby restricting the ability of others to nurture the (fewer) children they have, the distribution insisted on by the greedy ought to be debarred. Perhaps room can be left for voluntary agreements. A Deweyan society might allow a market in which some "trade" all or part of their "propagation allowance" to others who provide what is accepted as adequate compensation. But the Deweyan society will require that any such exchanges not be coercive. For that, the equalities on which Chapter 10 insists must be firmly in place.

The status-seekers can be debarred by a similar rationale. They violate the underlying principles of the Deweyan society in two distinct ways. First, they siphon off labor that might have been deployed to serve the public good. In doing so, they subtract from what is available to support the institutions through which the society advances its ends, thus weakening the system through which opportunities are provided for all. Recall how the distinction between types of labor was motivated. Funding for public goods depends on reallocating resources, and eliminating particular types of waste is an instrument for doing that. When wastage is tolerated, important institutions may be under-supported and, consequently, valuable goals forfeited. Second, and more obviously, status-seeking entrenches or reintroduces the forms of hierarchy Deweyan societies resist.

Well and good. These Millian points demonstrate the need for decisions to ensure the fair distribution of opportunities. Those who worry about governmental coercion are

396 APPENDIX 2

likely, however, to remain unsatisfied. Haunted by their visions of "central planning" and its evils, they will suggest that any public body will draw lines in the wrong places, imposing unjustified limits on individual freedom. They might agree in the importance of preventing the freedoms of some from curtailing the liberties of others, while denying the ability of public institutions to distinguish the cases in which dangers arise from those that are socially harmless. They will prefer the rough and tumble of interactions among citizens to any delineation handed down from on high.

Yet this, I believe, is to present a false choice. The core of my approach to democracy (and to morality) in Chapters 4 and 5 is a special type of deliberation among citizens. Policies emerge from procedures in which representatives of all the stakeholders, equipped with the best available information, attempt to engage with the lives and perspectives of all the others. Those who question a limit on family size come together to discuss with those who worry about the consequences for their lives (and those of their children) if the population grows and strains the institutions on which prospects for fulfilling lives depend. People who find aesthetic value in goods others see as merely announcing higher status must deliberate together with others who cannot detect any difference between the desired products and things available at far lesser cost.

It would be folly to pretend that these conversations will be easy—or to claim that efforts of this kind will always reach good answers. Throughout this book, I have taken a more modest stance. At whatever scale, with respect to social policies or moral questions, this is the best we can do. Objectors who fear "governmental coercion," even seeing it as a kind of dictatorship, overlook the everyday forms of constriction and constraint generated by the rough and tumble of *laissez-faire*. They are guilty of a form of pretense: just leave people alone, and the proper distribution of freedoms will emerge. History reveals again and again the effects of that policy. Inequalities of wealth and power produce situations in which certain "freedoms" celebrated by some are completely denied to others. Formally, they may be granted—but the masses are clearly aware of their absence.

No sure-fire method exists for guaranteeing the absence of coercion. What is important is to recognize the different faces of coercion. Sometimes it comes with the grim scowl of a governmental authority. At others, it wears the carefree—and careless—expression of the wealthy or the powerful, whose profligacy curtails the lives of the less fortunate.

Democratic deliberation, under the best approximation we can find to the conditions on which I have insisted, looks like the most promising way to go forward, attempting to chart a non-coercive route between coercive alternatives. The endeavor may fail. In my view, the chances of success are increased in a Deweyan society, one whose citizens are educated in the ways I have outlined here. Moreover, even as it recognizes failure, a society using the methods I have recommended, may find its way to something better. To a society, and a form of human life, we cannot yet envisage.

This book is, after all, an essay in pragmatism....

Bibliography

Acemoglu, Daron, and Pascual Restrepo. "Artificial Intelligence, Automation, and Work." NBER Working Paper 24196.

Akerlof, George. *An Economic Theorist's Book of Tales*. Cambridge, UK: Cambridge University Press, 1984.

Alexander, Michelle. *The New Jim Crow*. New York: The New Press, 2012.

Appelbaum, Binyamin. *The Economists' Hour: False Prophets, Free Markets, and the Fracture of Society*. New York: Little Brown, 2019.

Appiah, Kwame Anthony. *The Honor Code*. New York: Norton, 2010.

Appiah, Kwame Anthony. *The Lies That Bind*. New York: W. W. Norton, 2018.

Armstrong, Karen. *The Case for God*. New York: Knopf, 2009.

Atkinson, Anthony. *Inequality*. Cambridge, MA: Harvard University Press, 2015.

Autor, David, and Philip Kitcher. "As You Like It: Work, Life, and Satisfaction." Chapter 8 in *Capitalism beyond Mutuality*, edited by Subramanian Rangan, 139–60. New York: Oxford University Press, 2018.

Bächtiger, Andre, John S. Dryzek, Jane Mansbridge, and Mark Warren, eds. *The Oxford Handbook of Deliberative Democracy*. New York: Oxford University Press, 2018.

Barry, John M. *The Great Influenza*. New York: Penguin, 2004.

Bentham, Jeremy. *Introduction to the Principles of Morals and Legislation*. London: Methuen, 1980. First published 1780.

Boehm, Christoph. *Hierarchy in the Forest*. Cambridge, MA: Harvard University Press, 1999.

Bostridge, Ian. *Schubert's Winter Journey: Anatomy of an Obsession*. New York: Knopf, 2015.

Briggs, Jean. *Never in Anger*. Cambridge, MA: Harvard University Press, 1971.

Brighouse, Harry. *On Education*. Abingdon: Routledge, 2006.

Brighouse, Harry, Helen F. Ladd, Susanna Loeb, and Adam Swift. *Educational Goods*. Chicago: University of Chicago Press, 2018.

Budge, E. A. W., ed. *The Egyptian Book of the Dead*. New York: Dover, 1967.

Callan, Eamonn. *Creating Citizens*. Oxford: Oxford University Press, 1997.

Cartwright, Nancy. *The Dappled World*. Cambridge, UK: Cambridge University Press, 1999.

Case, Anne, and Angus Deaton. *Deaths of Despair and the Future of Capitalism*. Princeton, NJ: Princeton University Press, 2020.

Clifford, William. *The Ethics of Belief*. Amherst NY: Prometheus Books, 1999. First published 1877.

Cocking, Dean, and Jeroen van der Hoeven. *Evil Online*. Oxford: Blackwell, 2018.

Coetzee, J. M. "What Is a Classic?" In *Stranger Shores*, 1–16. New York: Penguin, 2001.

Craig, Edward. *Knowledge and the State of Nature*. Oxford: Clarendon Press, 1990.

Crane, Tim. *The Meaning of Belief*. Cambridge, MA: Harvard University Press, 2017.

Culp, Sylvia, and Philip Kitcher, "Theory Structure and Theory Change in Contemporary Molecular Biology." *British Journal for the Philosophy of Science* 40 (1989): 459–83.

398 BIBLIOGRAPHY

Curren, Randall. "Peters Redux: The Motivational Power of Inherently Valuable Learning." *Journal of Philosophy of Education* 54 (2020): 731–43.

Curren, Randall. "Children of the Broken Heartlands." *Social Theory and Practice*, forthcoming.

Dahl, Robert. *On Democracy*. New Haven: Yale University Press, 1998.

Dancy, Jonathan. *Ethics without Principles*. Oxford: Clarendon Press, 2004.

Darwin, Charles. *Autobiography*. New York: Norton, 1969. Written 1876, first published 1887.

Darwin, Charles. *Origin of Species*. Cambridge, MA: Harvard University Press, 1964. First published 1859.

Daston, Lorraine, and Peter Galison. *Objectivity*. New York: Zone Books, 2007.

Dawkins, Richard. *The God Delusion*. New York: Houghton Mifflin, 2006.

Dawkins, Richard. *River out of Eden*. New York: Basic Books, 1995.

Deaton, Angus. *The Great Escape*. Princeton, NJ: Princeton University Press, 2013.

Delbanco, Andrew. *College: What It Is, Was, and Should Be*. Princeton, NJ: Princeton University Press, 2012.

Dewey, John. *Art as Experience*. LW 10.

Dewey, John. *A Common Faith*. LW 9.

Dewey, John. *Democracy and Education*. MW 9.

Dewey, John. "Democracy in Education." MW 3, 229–39.

Dewey, John. *Experience and Nature*. LW 1.

Dewey, John. *How to Think*. MW 6; rev. ed. LW 8.

Dewey, John. *Human Nature and Conduct*. MW 14.

Dewey, John. *Individualism, Old and New*. LW 5, 90–98.

Dewey, John. *Liberalism and Social Action*. LW 11, 5–65.

Dewey, John. "The School as Social Centre." MW 2, 80–93.

Dewey, John. "The Underlying Philosophy of Education." LW 8, 77–103.

Du Bois, W. E. B. "Education and Work." In *The Education of Black People*. New York: Monthly Review Press, 2001.

Du Bois, W. E. B. *The Souls of Black Folk*. Norton Critical Edition. New York: W. W. Norton, 1999.

Dupré, John. *The Disorder of Things*. Cambridge, MA: Harvard University Press, 1993.

Durkheim, Émile. *Elementary Forms of the Religious Life*. Oxford World's Classics. New York: Oxford University Press, 2001. First published 1912.

Eby, Frederick, and Charles Flinn Arrowood. *The History and Philosophy of Education, Ancient and Medieval*. New York: Prentice-Hall, 1940.

Edwards, Betty. *Drawing on the Right Side of the Brain*. New York: Penguin, 2012.

Eliot, T. S. "Tradition and the Individual Talent." In *Selected Prose of T. S. Eliot*, edited by Frank Kermode, 38–39. New York: Farrar, Straus & Giroux, 1975.

Elster, Jon. *Sour Grapes*. Cambridge, UK: Cambridge University Press, 1983.

Emerson, Ralph Waldo. "Self-Reliance." In *The Selected Writings of Ralph Waldo Emerson*, 132–53. New York: Modern Library, 1992.

Emerson, Ralph Waldo. *The Complete Writings of Ralph Waldo Emerson*. New York: W. M. Wise, 1913.

Empson, William. *Milton's God*. London: Chatto & Windus, 1961.

Engels, Friedrich. *The Condition of the Working Class in England*. Oxford World's Classics. Oxford: Oxford University Press, 2009.

Ennis, Robert, and David Hitchcock. "Critical Thinking." In Stanford Encyclopedia of Philosophy. Available online at https://plato.stanford.edu/entries/critical-thinking/.

Feinberg, Joel. "The Child's Right to an Open Future." In *Philosophy of Education*, edited by Randall Curren, 112–23. Oxford: Blackwell, 2007.

Feller, Avi, et al. "Compared to What?: Variation in the Impact of Early Child Education by Alternative Care Type." *Annals of Applied Statistics* 10 (2016): 1245–85.

Firth, Raymond. *We the Tikopia*. Boston: Beacon, 1961.

Flory, James, and Philip Kitcher. "Global Health and the Scientific Research Agenda." *Philosophy and Public Affairs* 32 (2004): 36–65.

Fodor, Jerry. "Special Sciences." *Synthese* 28 (1974): 97–115.

Frankfurt, Harry. *On Inequality*. Princeton, NJ: Princeton University Press, 2015.

Frey, C. B., and M. A. Osborne. "The Future of Employment: How susceptible Are Jobs to Computerisation?" Available online at https://scholar.google.com/scholar?hl=en&as_sdt=0%2C33&q=frey+osborne+2013&btnG=.

Fry, Stephen. *The Ode Less Travelled*. London: Penguin, 2006.

Galbraith, John Kenneth. *The Affluent Society*. New York: Houghton Mifflin, 1958.

Garfinkel, Alan. *Forms of Explanation*. New Haven: Yale University Press, 1981.

Garrett, Laurie. *The Coming Plague*. New York: Farrar, Straus & Giroux, 1994.

Gaus, Gerald. *The Tyranny of the Ideal*. Princeton, NJ: Princeton University Press, 2016.

Goldin, Claudia. "Journey Across a Century of Women." 2020 Feldstein Lecture, available online at https://www.nber.org/lecture/2020-martin-feldstein-lecture-journey-across-century-women.

Goldman, Alvin. *Knowledge in a Social World*. New York: Oxford University Press, 1999.

Goodall, Jane. *The Chimpanzees of Gombe*. Cambridge, MA: Harvard University Press, 1986.

Gopnik, Alison. *The Gardener and the Carpenter*. New York: Farrar, Straus & Giroux. 2016.

Gopnik, Alison, Andrew Meltzhoff, and Patricia Kuhl. *The Scientist in the Crib*. New York: William Morrow, 1999.

Gould, Stephen Jay. *The Mismeasure of Man*. New York: W. W. Norton, 1981.

Gould, Stephen Jay. *Ontogeny and Phylogeny*. Cambridge, MA: Harvard University Press, 1977.

Graham, Patricia Albjerg. *Schooling America: How the Public Schools Meet the Nation's Changing Needs*. New York: Oxford University Press, 2005.

Gray, John. *Seven Types of Atheism*. New York: Farrar, Straus & Giroux, 2018.

Gruen, Lori. *Ethics and Animals*. New York: Cambridge University Press, 2011.

Gumbrecht, Hans Ulrich. *In Praise of Athletic Beauty*. Cambridge, MA: Harvard University Press, 2006.

Gutmann, Amy, and Dennis Thompson. *Democracy and Disagreement*. Cambridge, MA: Harvard University Press, 1998.

Gutting, Gary. *Michel Foucault's Archeology of Scientific Reason*. Cambridge, UK: Cambridge University Press, 1989.

Habermas, Jürgen. *Between Facts and Norms*. Cambridge, MA: MIT Press, 1996.

Habermas, Jürgen. "Reconciliation through the Public Use of Reason: Remarks on John Rawls's Political Liberalism." *Journal of Philosophy* 92 (1995): 109–31.

Harris, Paul. *Trusting What You're Told: How Children Learn from Others*. Cambridge, MA: Harvard University Press, 2012.

Harris, Paul. *The Work of the Imagination*. Oxford: Blackwell, 2000.

400 BIBLIOGRAPHY

Hayek, Friedrich. "The Use of Knowledge in Society." *American Economic Review* 35 (1945): 519–30.

Heckman, James J., and Ganesh Karapakula. "Intergenerational and Intragenerational Externalities of the Perry Preschool Project." NBER Working Paper No. 25889. Available online at https://www.nber.org/papers/w25889.

Hegre, Håvard. "Democracy and Armed Conflict." *Journal of Peace Research* 51 (2014): 159–72.

Hempel, Sandra. *The Medical Detective.* London: Granta 2006.

Hobbes, Thomas. *Leviathan.* London: Penguin, 2017.

Hochschild, Arlie Russell. *Strangers in Their Own Land: Anger and Mourning on the American Right.* New York: The New Press, 2018.

Hodder, Ian. "Çatal Hüyük: The Leopard Changes Its Spots. A Summary of Recent Work." *Anatolian Studies* 64 (2014): 1–22.

Hull, David. *Philosophy of Biological Science.* Englewood Cliffs, NJ: Prentice-Hall, 1974.

Hume, David. *A Treatise of Human Nature.* Edited by L. A. Selby-Bigge. Oxford: Clarendon Press, 1888.

Huxley, Leonard, ed. *The Life and Letters of T. H.Huxley.* Cambridge, UK: Cambridge University Press, 2012. First published 1903.

Jacoby, Susan. *The Age of American Unreason in a Culture of Lies.* 2nd ed. New York: Vintage, 2018.

Jaeggi, Rahel. *Alienation.* New York: Columbia University Press, 2014.

James, William. "The Moral Philosopher and the Moral Life." In *The Will to Believe*, 141–62. Cambridge, MA: Harvard University Press, 1979.

Joyce, James. *A Portrait of the Artist as a Young Man.* New York: W. W. Norton, 2007.

Joyce, James. *Ulysses.* Edited by Hans Walter Gabler. New York: Vintage, 1986.

Kahan, Dan M. "Climate-Science Communication and the Measurement Problem." *Political Psychology* 36 (2015): S1, 1–43.

Kant, Immanuel. *Groundwork of the Metaphysics of Morals.* Edited and translated by Mary Gregor and Jens Timmerman. Cambridge, UK: Cambridge University Press, 2011.

Kant, Immanuel. *Toward Perpetual Peace.* Cambridge, UK: Cambridge University Press, 1996.

Kevles, Daniel. *In the Name of Eugenics.* New York: Knopf, 1985.

Kharas, Homi. "Climate Change, Fertility, and Girls' Education." Available online at https://www.brookings.edu/blog/future-development/2016/02/16/climate-change-fertility-and-girls-education/.

Kierkegaard, Søren. *Fear and Trembling.* Vol. 6 of *Kierkegaard's Works*, translated by Howard Hong and Edna Hong. Princeton, NJ: Princeton University Press, 1983.

Kitcher, Philip. "1953 and All That: A Tale of Two Sciences." *Philosophical Review* 93 (1984): 335–73.

Kitcher, Philip. *Abusing Science: The Case against Creationism.* Cambridge, MA: MIT Press, 1982.

Kitcher, Philip. "Battling the Undead: How (and How Not) to Resist Genetic Determinism." In *Thinking about Evolution: Historical, Philosophical and Political Perspectives*, edited by Rama Singh, Costas Krimbas, Diane Paul, and John Beatty, 396–414. New York: Cambridge University Press, 2001.

Kitcher, Philip. *Deaths in Venice: The Cases of Gustav von Aschenbach.* New York: Columbia University Press, 2013.

BIBLIOGRAPHY 401

Kitcher, Philip. "Education, Democracy, and Capitalism." Chapter 17 in *The Oxford Handbook of Philosophy of Education*, edited by Harvey Siegel, 300–18. New York: Oxford University Press, 2009.

Kitcher, Philip *The Ethical Project*. Cambridge, MA: Harvard University Press, 2011.

Kitcher, Philip. "Experimental Animals." *Philosophy and Public Affairs* 43 (2015): 287–311.

Kitcher, Philip. "Governing Darwin's World." In *Animals: Historical Perspectives*, edited by Peter Adamson and G. Faye Edwards, 269–92. New York: Oxford University Press, 2018.

Kitcher, Philip. *Homo Quaerens: Progress, Truth, and Values*. In preparation.

Kitcher, Philip. *Joyce's Kaleidoscope: An Invitation to "Finnegans Wake."* New York: Oxford University Press, 2007.

Kitcher, Philip. *Life after Faith: The Case for Secular Humanism*. New Haven: Yale University Press, 2016.

Kitcher, Philip. *Living with Darwin*. New York: Oxford University Press, 2007.

Kitcher, Philip. "Mill, Education, and the Good Life." In *John Stuart Mill and the Art of Living*, edited by Ben Eggleston, Dale Miller, and David Weinstein, 192–211. New York: Oxford University Press, 2011.

Kitcher, Philip. "Mill's Consequentialism." In *The Routledge Companion to Nineteenth-Century Thought*, edited by Dean Moyar, 633–57. London: Routledge, 2010.

Kitcher, Philip. *Moral Progress*. New York: Oxford University Press, 2021.

Kitcher, Philip. "On Progress." In *Performance and Progress*, edited by Subramanian Rangan, 115–33. Oxford: Oxford University Press, 2015.

Kitcher, Philip. "Parfit's Puzzle." *Noûs* 34 (2000): 550–77.

Kitcher, Philip. *Science in a Democratic Society*. Amherst, NY: Prometheus Books, 2011.

Kitcher, Philip. *Science, Truth, and Democracy*. New York: Oxford University Press, 2001.

Kitcher, Philip. "Social Progress." *Social Philosophy and Policy* 34, no. 2 (2017): 46–65.

Kitcher, Philip. "Something Rich and Strange: Joyce's Perspectivism." In *Ulysses: Philosophical Perspectives*, edited by Philip Kitcher, 207–51. New York: Oxford University Press, 2020.

Kitcher, Philip. "Two Forms of Blindness: On the Need for Both Cultures." *Technology in Society* 32, no. 1 (2010): 40–48.

Kitcher, Philip. *Vaulting Ambition: Sociobiology and the Quest for Human Nature*. Cambridge, MA: MIT Press, 1985.

Kitcher, Philip. "What Do We Owe Our Planet?" *Los Angeles Review of Books*, 2018. Available online at https://lareviewofbooks.org/article/what-do-we-owe-our-planet/.

Kitcher, Philip, and Evelyn Fox Keller. *The Seasons Alter: How to Save Our Planet in Six Acts*. New York: Norton/Liveright, 2017.

Kitcher, Philip, and Richard Schacht. *Finding an Ending: Reflections on Wagner's Ring*. New York: Oxford University Press, 2004.

Korsgaard, Christine. *Fellow Creatures*. New York: Oxford University Press, 2018.

Kozol, Jonathan. *Savage Inequalities*. New York: Crown, 1991.

Kozol, Jonathan. *The Shame of the Nation*. New York: Crown, 2005.

Kuhn, T. S. *The Copernican Revolution*. Cambridge, MA: Harvard University Press, 1957.

Lareau, Annette. *Unequal Childhoods*. Berkeley: University of California Press, 2011.

Lee, Richard. *The !Kung San*. Cambridge, UK: Cambridge University Press, 1979.

Leppännen, Sirpa, et al. *National Survey on the English Language in Finland: Uses, Meanings, and Attitudes*, 2011. Available online at www.helsinki.fi>varieng>series>v olumes>evarieng-vol5.

402 BIBLIOGRAPHY

Levi, Isaac. *Hard Choices*. Cambridge, UK: Cambridge University Press, 1986.

Levins, Richard. *Evolution in Changing Environments*. Princeton, NJ: Princeton University Press, 1968.

Levinson, Meira. *No Citizen Left Behind*. Cambridge, MA: Harvard University Press, 2014.

Levitsky, Steven, and Daniel Ziblatt. *How Democracies Die*. New York: Penguin, 2018.

Lewis, David. "Divine Evil." In *Philosophers without Gods*, edited by Louise Antony, 231–42. New York: Oxford University Press, 2007.

Lewis, David. "Mill and Milquetoast." *Australasian Journal of Philosophy* 67 (1989: 152–71.

Lindblom, Charles E. *The Market System*. New Haven: Yale University Press, 2001.

Lippmann, Walter. *The Phantom Public*. London: Routledge, 2017. First published 1927.

Locke, John. *A Letter Concerning Toleration*. Indianapolis: Hackett, 1983.

Locke, John. *Second Treatise of Government*. Indianapolis: Hackett, 1980.

Lowance, Mason, ed. *Against Slavery: An Abolitionist Reader*. Harmondsworth: Penguin, 2000.

Marx, Karl. *Capital*. Vol. 1. New York: Vintage, 1977.

Marx, Karl. *The Economic and Philosophic Manuscripts of 1844*. Edited by Dirk Struik. New York: International Publishers, 1964.

Matthews, Michael R. *Science Teaching: The Role of History and Philosophy of Science*. New York: Routledge, 1994.

Matthews, Michael R. *Time for Science Education*. New York: Kluwer, 2000.

Mayhew, Katherine Camp, and Anna Camp Edwards. *The Dewey School: The Laboratory School of the University of Chicago, 1896–1903*. New York: Appleton, 1936.

McBrearty, Sally, and Andrea Brooks. "The Revolution That Wasn't: A New Interpretation of the Evolution of Modern Human Behavior." *Journal of Human Evolution* 39 (2000): 453–563.

McKinsey & Co. https://www.mckinsey.com/featured-insights/future-of-work/jobs-lost-jobs-gained-what-the-future-of-work-will-mean-for-jobs-skills-and-wages.

Mill, John Stuart. *Autobiography*. In *Collected Works of John Stuart Mill*, 1:1–290. Indianapolis: Liberty Fund: 2006. Selected from the University of Toronto's edition of the full set of *Mill's Works*.

Mill, John Stuart. "Bentham." In *Collected Works of John Stuart Mill*, 10:75–115. Indianapolis: Liberty Fund, 2006. Selected from the University of Toronto's edition of the full set of *Mill's Works*.

Mill, John Stuart. "Civilization—Signs of the Times." In *John Stuart Mill: Literary Essays*, edited by Edward Alexander, 109–30. Indianapolis: Bobbs-Merrill, 1967.

Mill, John Stuart. "Coleridge." In *Collected Works of John Stuart Mill*, 10:119–63. Indianapolis: Liberty Fund, 2006. Selected from the University of Toronto's edition of the full set of *Mill's Works*.

Mill, John Stuart. *Considerations on Representative Government*. In OL.

Mill, John Stuart. "On Genius." In *John Stuart Mill: Literary Essays*, edited by Edward Alexander, 31–46. Indianapolis: Bobbs-Merrill, 1967.

Mill, John Stuart. *A System of Logic*. Vol. 8 of *Collected Works of John Stuart Mill*. Indianapolis: Liberty Fund, 2006. Selected from the University of Toronto's edition of the full set of *Mill's Works*.

Mill, John Stuart, and Harriet Taylor. *On the Subjection of Women*. In OL.

Milton, John. *Areopagitica*. In *Milton's Prose: A Selection*. Oxford World's Classics. Oxford: Oxford University Press, 1963.

Mössner, Nicola, and Philip Kitcher. "Knowledge, Democracy, and the Internet." *Minerva* 55 (2017): 1–24.

BIBLIOGRAPHY 403

Müller, Jan-Werner. *What Is Populism?* Philadelphia: University of Pennsylvania Press, 2016.

Nagel, Thomas. *The View from Nowhere*. New York: Oxford University Press, 1986.

Nehamas, Alexander. *Only a Promise of Happiness*. Princeton, NJ: Princeton University Press, 2007.

Neill, A. S. *Summerhill School: A New View of Childhood*. Rev. ed. New York: St. Martin's, 1992.

Neiman, Susan. *Learning from the Germans*. New York: Farrar, Straus & Giroux, 2019.

Newman, J. H. *The Idea of a University*. New Haven: Yale University Press, 1996.

Newton, Isaac. *Mathematical Principles of Natural Philosophy*. Translated by Andrew Motte and Florian Cajori. 2 vols. Berkeley: University of California Press, 1962.

Nietzsche, Friedrich. *Beyond Good and Evil*. Cambridge, UK: Cambridge University Press, 2001.

Nietzsche, Friedrich. *The Gay Science*. Cambridge, UK: Cambridge University Press, 2001.

Nietzsche, Friedrich. *On the Genealogy of Morality*. Cambridge, UK: Cambridge University Press, 2017.

Nietzsche, Friedrich. *Untimely Meditations*. Cambridge, UK: Cambridge University Press, 1997.

Nordhaus, William. *The Climate Casino*. New Haven: Yale University Press, 2013.

Nordhaus, William. "Climate Clubs: Overcoming Free-Riding in International Climate Policy." *American Economic Review* 105, no. 4 (2015): 1339–70.

Nozick, Robert. *Anarchy, State, and Utopia*. New York: Basic Books, 1974.

Nussbaum, Martha C. *Creating Capabilities*. Cambridge, MA: Harvard University Press, 2011.

Nussbaum, Martha C. *Cultivating Humanity*. Cambridge, MA: Harvard University Press, 1997.

Nussbaum, Martha C. *Not for Profit*. Princeton, NJ: Princeton University Press, 2011.

Nussbaum, Martha C. *Political Emotions*. Cambridge, MA: Harvard University Press, 2013.

Nussbaum, Martha C. "Tagore, Dewey, and the Imminent Demise of Liberal Education." In *The Oxford Handbook of Philosophy of Education*, edited by Harvey Siegel, 52–64. New York: Oxford University Press, 2009.

Nussbaum, Martha C. *Women and Human Development*. Cambridge, UK: Cambridge University Press, 2000.

Nussbaum, Martha C., and Amartya Sen, eds. *The Quality of Life*. Oxford: Oxford University Press, 1993.

O'Flaherty, Brendan, and Rajiv Sethi. *Shadows of Doubt*. Cambridge, MA: Harvard University Press, 2019.

Oakeshott, Michael. *Michael Oakeshott on Education*. Edited by Timothy Fuller. New Haven: Yale University Press, 1989.

Oreskes, Naomi, and Erik Conway. *Merchants of Doubt*. New York: Bloomsbury, 2010.

Orwell, George. *The Road to Wigan Pier*. New York: Houghton Mifflin, 1958.

Packard, Vance. *The Hidden Persuaders*, New York: McKay, 1957.

Pagels, Elaine. *Beyond Belief*, New York: Vintage, 2003.

Pagels, Elaine. *Why Religion?* New York: HarperCollins, 2018.

Parfit, Derek. *On What Matters*. 2 vols. Oxford: Clarendon Press, 2011.

Parfit, Derek. *Reasons and Persons*. Oxford: Clarendon Press, 1984.

404 BIBLIOGRAPHY

Peacocke, Christopher. "The Distinctive Character of Aesthetic Experience." *British Journal of Aesthetics* 60 (2020): 183–97.

Peters, R. S. "Education as Initiation." In *Philosophical Analysis of Education*, edited by Reginald D. Achambault, 87–111. New York: Humanities Press, 1965.

Petersen, Sandra, et al. "The Use of Robotic Pets in Dementia Care." Available online at https://www.ncbi.nlm.nih.gov/pmc/articles/PMC5181659/.

Peterson, Martin. *An Introduction to Decision Theory.* Cambridge, UK: Cambridge University Press, 2009.

Pfaff, John. *Locked In.* New York: Basic Books, 2017.

Piketty, Thomas. *Capital.* Cambridge, MA: Harvard University Press, 2013.

Pinker, Steven. *The Better Angels of Our Nature.* New York: Viking, 2011.

Pinker, Steven. *Enlightenment Now.* New York: Viking, 2018.

Pinker, Steven. *How the Mind Works.* New York: W. W. Norton, 1997.

Pinker, Steven. "Science Is Not Your Enemy." *The New Republic*, August 6, 2012. Available online at https://newrepublic.com/article/114127/science-not-enemy-humanities.

Plato. *Euthyphro.* In *Complete Works*, edited by John Cooper, 1–16. Indianapolis: Hackett, 1997.

Polanyi, Karl. *The Great Transformation.* Boston: Beacon, 2001.

Pritchard, James B. *Ancient Near-Eastern Texts.* Princeton, NJ: Princeton University Press, 1969.

Proctor, Robert, and Linda Schiebinger, eds. *Agnotology: The Making and Unmaking of Ignorance.* Stanford, CA: Stanford University Press, 2008.

Proctor, Robert N. *Cancer Wars: How Politics Shapes What We Know and Don't Know about Cancer.* New York: Basic Books, 1995.

Prum, Richard. *The Evolution of Beauty.* New York: Penguin Random House, 2018.

Putnam, Robert. *Bowling Alone.* New York: Simon & Schuster, 2000.

Putnam, Robert. *Our Kids.* New York: Simon & Schuster, 2015.

Quine, W. V. O. *Word and Object.* Cambridge, MA: MIT Press, 1960.

Ravitch, Diana. *The Death and Life of the Great American School System.* Rev. and expanded ed. New York: Basic Books, 2016.

Rawls, John. "Kantian Constructivism in Moral Theory." *Journal of Philosophy* 77 (1980): 515–72.

Rawls, John. *Political Liberalism.* New York: Columbia University Press, 1993.

Rawls, John. *A Theory of Justice.* Rev. ed. Cambridge, MA: Harvard University Press 1999.

Ray, Rebecca, Janet C. Gornick, and John Schmitt. "Parental Leave Policies in 21 Different Countries." Center for Economic Policy Research report. Available online at cepr.net.

Regan, Tom. *The Case for Animal Rights.* 2nd ed., rev. Berkeley: University of California Press, 2004.

Relethford, J. H. "Race and Global Patterns of Phenotypic Variation." *American Journal of Physical Anthropology* 139 (2009: 16–22. Available online at https://www.ncbi.nlm.nih.gov/pubmed/19226639.

Renfrew, Colin, and Stephen Shennan. *Ranking, Resource, and Exchange.* Cambridge UK: Cambridge University Press, 1982.

Rosenberg, Alexander. *The Atheist's Guide to Reality.* New York: W. W. Norton, 2013.

Rosenberg, Alexander. *How History Gets Things Wrong.* Cambridge, MA: MIT Press, 2018.

Rothschild, Michael, and Joseph Stiglitz. "Equilibrium in Competitive Insurance Markets: An Essay on the Economics of Imperfect Information." *Quarterly Journal of Economics* 90 (1976): 629–49.

BIBLIOGRAPHY   405

Rudwick, Martin. *The Great Devonian Controversy*. Chicago: University of Chicago Press, 1985.

Runciman, David. *How Democracy Ends*. London: Profile Books, 2018.

Sachs, Jeffrey. *The Age of Sustainable Development*. New York: Columbia University Press, 2015.

Saez, Emmanuel, and Gabriel Zucman. *The Triumph of Injustice*. New York: W. W. Norton, 2019.

Scanlon, T. M. *What We Owe to Each Other*. Cambridge, MA: Harvard University Press, 1998.

Scheffler, Israel. *In Praise of the Cognitive Emotions*. New York: Routledge, 2010.

Schelling, Thomas. *Micromotives and Macrobehavior*. New York: W. W. Norton, 1978.

Schmidt, Vivien A. "The Eurozone's Crisis of Democratic Legitimacy: Can the EU Rebuild Public Trust and Support for Economic Integration?" Available online at http://ec.europa.eu/economy_finance/publications/eedp/dp015_en.htm.

Schopenhauer, Arthur. *The World as Will and Representation*. Cambridge, UK: Cambridge University Press, 2014

Sen, Amartya. "Gender Equity and the Population Problem." *International Journal of Health Services* 31 (2001): 469–74.

Sen, Amartya. "Gender Inequality and Theories of Justice." In *Women, Culture and Development*, edited by Martha C. Nussbaum and Jonathan Glover, 259–73. Oxford: Oxford University Press, 1995.

Sen, Amartya. *Inequality Reexamined*. Cambridge, MA: Harvard University Press, 1995.

Shostak, Marjorie. *Nisa*. Cambridge, MA: Harvard University Press, 1981.

Shutts, Kristin, Caroline K. Pemberton, and Elisabeth S. Spelke. "Children's Use of Social Categories in Thinking about People and Relationships." *Journal of Cognitive Development* 14 (2013): 35–62. Available online at https://www.ncbi.nlm.nih.gov/pmc/articles/PMC3640585/.

Siegel, Harvey. *Educating Reason*. London: Routledge, 1988.

Siegel, Harvey. "'Radical' Pedagogy Requires 'Conservative' Epistemology." *Journal of Philosophy of Education* 29 (1995): 33–46.

Silver, Nate. *The Signal and the Noise*. New York: Penguin, 2012.

Singer, Peter. *Animal Liberation*. New York: Random House, 1975.

Smart, J. J. C., and Williams, Bernard. *Utilitarianism: For and Against*. Cambridge UK: Cambridge University Press, 1973.

Smith, Adam. *The Theory of Moral Sentiments*. Indianapolis: Liberty Fund, 1984.

Smith, Pamela. *The Body of the Artisan: Art and Experience in the Scientific Revolution*. Chicago: University of Chicago Press, 2004.

Snow, C. P. *The Two Cultures*. Cambridge, UK: Cambridge University Press, 2001. First published 1959.

Soler, Meritxell Valenti, et al. "Social Robots in Aging Dementia." *Frontiers in Aging Neuroscience* 7 (2015) . Available online at https://www.ncbi.nlm.nih.gov/pmc/articles/PMC4558428/.

Solow, Robert. *Growth Theory: An Exposition*. New York: Oxford University Press, 1970.

Steele, Claude. *Whistling Vivaldi*. New York: W. W. Norton, 2010.

Tagore, Rabindranath. *The Religion of Man*. Mansfield Center, CT: Martino Publishing, 2013. First published 1931.

Tagore, Rahindranath. *A Tagore Reader*. Edited by Amiya Chakravarty. New York: Macmillan, 1961.

406 BIBLIOGRAPHY

Taylor, Charles. *A Secular Age*. Cambridge, MA: Harvard University Press, 2007.

Thomson, Judith Jarvis. "A Defense of Abortion." *Philosophy and Public Affairs* 1 (1971): 47–66.

Thrane, J. R. "Joyce's Sermon on Hell: Its Source and Backgrounds." *Modern Philology* 57 (1960): 172–98.

Thurber, James. "University Days." In *My Life and Hard Times*. New York: HarperCollins, 1999.

Tocqueville, Alexis de. *Democracy in America*. New York: Library of America, 2004.

Tolstoy, Leo. *The Death of Ivan Ilyich* New York: Vintage, 2012.

Turco, Lewis. *Poetry: An Introduction through Writing*. Reston, VA: Reston Publishing Company, 1973.

Twenge, Jean. "The Evidence for Generation Me and against Generation We." *Emerging Adulthood* 1 (2013): 11–16.

Twenge, Jean. *Generation Me*. Rev. ed. New York: Simon & Schuster, 2014.

van Fraassen, Bas *The Scientific Image*. Oxford: Clarendon Press, 1980.

van Parijs, Philippe, and Yannick Vanderborght. *Basic Income: A Radical Proposal for a Free Society and a Sane Economy*. Cambridge, MA: Harvard University Press, 2017.

Varian, Hal. *Microeconomic Analysis*. New York: W. W. Norton, 1978.

Veblen, Thorstein. *The Theory of the Leisure Class*. New York: Dover, 2004. First published 1899.

Vickers, A. Leah, and Philip Kitcher. "Pop Sociobiology Reborn." In *Evolution, Gender, and Rape*, edited by Cheryl Travis, 139–68. Cambridge, MA: MIT Press, 2003.

Vollaro, Daniel. "Lincoln, Stowe, and the 'Little Woman/Great War' Story: The Making, and Breaking, of a Great American Anecdote." *Journal of the Abraham Lincoln Association* 30 (2009): 18–34.

Watson Garcia, Claire. *Drawing for the Absolute and Utter Beginner*. New York: Watson-Guptill, 2003.

Weinberg, Steven. *Dreams of a Final Theory*. New York: Vintage, 1992.

White, John. *The Aims of Education Restated*. London: Routledge and Kegan Paul, 1982.

Whitehead, A. N. *The Aims of Education*. New York: Free Press, 1929.

Williams, Bernard. *Ethics and the Limits of Philosophy*. London: Fontana, 1985.

Williams, Bernard. "Persons, Character, and Morality." In *Moral Luck*, 1–19. Cambridge UK: Cambridge University Press, 1981.

Wilson, E. O. *Sociobiology: The New Synthesis*. Cambridge, MA: Harvard University Press, 1975.

Winner, Ellen. *How Art Works*. New York: Oxford University Press, 2019.

Wittgenstein, Ludwig. *Philosophical Investigations*. 4th ed., rev. Oxford: Wiley-Blackwell, 2009.

Wolf, Susan. *Meaning in Life and Why It Matters*. Princeton, NJ: Princeton University Press, 2010.

Yi, Chin-Yun, ed. *The Psychological Well-Being of East Asian Youth*. Vol. 2. Dordrecht: Springer, 2013.

Index

A Nation at Risk 31
Acemoglu, Daron 68nn40, 41
Adès, Thomas 258
Aesthetic experience 259–61, 267, 273–76, 270
Agnotology 129n35
Akerlof, George 305n43, 306n49, 383
Alexander, Michelle 305n44
Alexander, Natalia Rogach 72n52, 101n38, 104n48, 110n67, 275n33
Algebra 130, 304, 316
Alienation 47, 58, 75, 104, 105n52, 233, 246, 248, 332
Allen, Katharine 249n39
Allen, Woody 91n22
Altruism 112, 138, 293, 313n59
American Bar Association 285n11
Anscombe, Elizabeth 182n55
Anthropology 15, 65, 94, 151, 236, 281, 284, 288, 298, 299, 300, 318, 340n32
Appelbaum, Binyamin 377n40
Appiah, Kwame Anthony 19n2, 159n13
Architecture 258, 288, 332
Aristotle 35, 93n25
Armstrong, Karen 193n5
Arrow, Kenneth 382, 383n49
Arrow-Debreu Theorem 382
Arrowood, Charles Flinn 33n52
Art, 13–15, 59, 230–31, 246, 252, 258–59, 260, 262, 307
Arts,
    as increasing empathy 266–67
    cognitive functions of 14, 172n35, 262–67
    contributions of 13, 14, 15, 25, 65, 258–67, 283n5, 285, 289, 292, 298, 338
    creative work in 14, 230–31, 267 ff.
    history of 14, 283, 289–95, 307
    marginalization of 256–57
    progress in 13, 228, 252, 258–59
    role in education 13, 76, 267–80
Astronomy 24, 244, 283

Atheism 10, 211n27, 212, 216n37
Atkinson, Anthony 73n53, 334n22, 336n25, 377n39, 384n51
Auden, W.H. 306
Augustine 89
Automation 5, 52, 68, 73, 316, 346, 352, 365. *See also* Robots, CARESSES, PARO
Autonomy condition 39, 102, 110
Autonomy 6, 7, 29n42, 40n76, 41, 45, 69, 77, 84, 93–94, 97, 100, 101–102, 103–108, 110–13, 139, 140, 147, 229, 285–86,
Autor, David 68n41, 70n47

Bacon, Francis 180, 241
Baez, Joan 258
Barry, John M. 248n38
Basic training 32, 36, 51, 53, 55, 76
Beatles 258
Beaumont, Francis 257
Beckett, Samuel 258
Belmont Commission 175n38
Bentham, Jeremy 25n26, 85, 166, 167, 168
Berlin, Isaiah 286n13
Bernstein, Jay 102n42
Bernstein, Richard 102n42
Bialystok, Ellen 308n53
Biology 14, 61, 64, 104n49, 129, 236, 237, 238, 242, 374n35
Blake, William 388
Boehm, Christoph 33n52
Bostridge, Ian 294–95n26
Brendel, Alfred 289n17
Brexit 120n15, 371
Briggs, Jean 141n60
Brighouse, Harry 19n2, 29, 38n65, 40n76, 51n2, 61n32, 69n43, 79, 94n28, 102n40, 108n61, 170n33, 189n65, 203n19, 218n40,
Brooks, Andrea 33n54,
Buber, Martin 210
Burton, Robert 230n7

408 INDEX

Callan, Eamonn 29, 121n20, 128n32
Canon *See* Taste, variation in
CARESSES 70n44
Cartwright, Nancy 238nn19, 20, 22
Case, Anne 384n51
Chalfie, Martin 246n34, 247n37
Chemistry 24, 233, 236, 237, 242, 266, 283, 316
Chomsky, Noam 306, 307
Christ's Hospital 42, 191
Churchill, Winston 118, 310n55,
Citizens United v. FEC 119n14
Citizenship 4, 5, 7–10, 15, 16, 30, 41, 43,
    61, 68, 74, 123, 191, 214, 218, 232,
    267, 296, 299, 301, 307, 310, 311, 318,
    319, 324
Classical studies 23, 35, 151, 282, 307,
    308n50
    Latin 23, 24, 55, 56, 307–308, 310n55, 311
    Greek 23, 24n7, 25, 60, 84, 282, 289, 300,
        307, 308, 311
Clifford, William 194n7, 212
Climate change 8, 13, 118nn8–9, 122, 129,
    130–34, 143, 145, 152, 238, 241, 249,
    300, 374–75, 377
Cocking, Dean 167
Coetzee, J.M. 275n33
Coleridge, Samuel Taylor 25n26
Community condition 39, 102, 108, 110,
    112, 147
Computer science 61
Consensus, varieties of 90n21, 144–46
Conspicuous consumption 332
Consumer culture 79, 82. *See also*
    consumerism
Consumerism 228, 358–59, 384
Conway, Erik 132n42
Cooking 100, 275
Cooperation, international 371, 373, 374
Coordination, global 3. *See also*
    Cooperation, international
Craig, Edward 128n33
Crane, Tim 193n5
Cromwell, Oliver 50, 258
Cronkite, Walter 124, 128
Culp, Sylvia 237n16
Curren, Randall 19n2, 26n28, 34n60,
    41n78, 51n2, 57n52, 59n29, 66n38,
    79n2, 108n61, 120n18, 166n20,
    189n64

Curriculum 4, 10, 13, 16, 24–25, 35, 43,
    53–55, 61, 65–66, 76, 78, 108n62, 130,
    215, 218, 227–28, 233, 239, 243, 246n34,
    251n44, 272–78, 284, 287n15, 288, 300,
    302–305, 313, 314n60, 315–16, 318,
    324, 338, 342, 368

Dahl, Robert 119n13
Dance 14, 258, 264, 268, 271, 278
Dancy, Jonathan 165n19
Darwin, Charles 86, 87, 104n49, 259n6,
    283, 284nn9, 10, 359
Daston, Lorraine 172nn35, 36, 281n1
Davidson, Jenny 246n34
Davis, Jefferson 165n17
Dawkins, Richard 192nn3, 4, 259, 352n8
De Menocal, Peter 246n34
Deaton, Angus 81n5, 384n51
Debreu, Gérard 382
Debussy, Claude 258
Delbanco, Andrew 29, 61n32
Deliberation, democratic 8, 9, 118, 121,
    142n65, 143, 144, 145, 147, 151, 152,
    174, 175, 178, 179, 187, 193, 206, 214,
    216, 223, 233, 252, 301, 302, 335, 338,
    344, 348, 396
    Conditions on 8, 9, 143, 145, 184, 185, 302
    Inclusiveness in 8, 9, 143, 185, 302
    Informedness of 8, 9, 143, 144, 185, 302
    Mutual engagement in 8, 9, 143, 185, 302
Deliberative democracy 121n20, 123,
    141, 142n65. *See also* Deliberation,
    democratic
Democracy, global 8, 118, 134, 145, 152,
    372, 376, 377
Democracy, levels of 7, 8, 121
Democracy, polarization in 8, 118
Democracy, scales of 7, 8, 121, 122, 140,
    145, 152
Dennett, Daniel 192
Dewey, John 7, 8, 19, 25n23, 28n 37, 29n43,
    32n51, 38n64, 40, 46, 58, 59, 68, 73, 83,
    86, 89, 90, 93, 96n30, 102–104, 105n53,
    117, 118, 122n21, 134, 135, 141, 142,
    143n66, 147, 148, 158, 161, 165, 184,
    222n51, 230n6, 244, 250n43, 253, 260,
    262n14, 266, 267, 268n23, 271, 275n33,
    278, 281n1, 287n15, 289n16, 301,
    302n38, 331n13

INDEX   409

Deweyan democracy 8, 121, 123, 131, 134, 142, 149, 186, 252, 302
Deweyan society 17–19, 184, 185, 311, 313, 314, 331, 333, 335, 340, 341, 342, 345, 347, 352, 353, 355, 358, 360–68, 370, 372, 373, 377, 378, 386, 387, 395–96
   Principal features of 347–49
Dickens, Charles 263–65, 267, 293, 297n33
Dickinson, Emily 82, 114, 115n74
Dilthey, Wilhelm 281n1
Division of Labor 28n37, 34, 36, 53, 55, 56, 60, 182, 350, 351n4
Dostoyevsky, Fyodor 266
Drama 14, 257, 258, 265, 266, 268, 286, 289, 291, 295, 308
Du Bois, W.E.B. 28, 49, 61n32,
Dupré, John 238n20
Durkheim, Emile 209n24
Dylan, Bob 258

Earl of Shaftesbury 153
Eastman, Mary Henderson 263n17
Eby, Frederick 33n52
Economic competition 4, 16, 60, 64, 68, 72n52, 79, 81, 123, 227, 228, 232, 233, 254, 255, 361, 365, 370, 371, 380, 382, 385
Economic constraints 5, 6, 19, 24, 384
Economic efficiency 52, 58, 61, 62n36, 64, 360n21, 379, 384–85
Economic growth 18, 374, 352–53, 355, 358–60, 364n25, 365–66, 377n40, 385
Economics 15, 51, 61, 256, 266, 281, 286n13, 288, 300, 302, 305, 318, 338n28, 347, 351–53, 362, 370, 373, 382, 383n48, 384
Education as lifelong 17, 37, 152, 227, 229, 245, 271, 344
   Different patterns in 342 ff.
Education, aims of 4, 5, 9, 12, 26, 27, 31, 36, 37, 40, 44, 45, 46n87, 227, 269
Education, constraints on 2, 5–6, 19, 24
Education, experiments in 5, 48, 76n58, 149, 190, 253, 278, 338n29
Education, history of 2–4, 30, 32–33, 36, 37, 48, 155
Education, prehistory of 1–2, 32, 34
Educational leave 17, 292, 343–44, 348, 362
Edwards, Betty 270n27

Egalitarianism 14, 95, 101n37, 274, 275–77, 331, 333, 336n25, 340, 361, 368, 369, 370, 381
   Moderate 14, 275–77,
   Trans-temporal 95, 101n37
Einstein, Albert 231, 258
Eliot, T.S. 258, 266, 273
Elster, Jon 177n42
Emerson, Ralph Waldo 20, 74, 210, 344, 389
Emmerson, Jane 270n2
Empson, William 388n62
Engels, Friedrich 72n49
Ennis, Robert 124n27
Ethnography 286, 287, 300, 318
Eugenics 240, 242n27
European Union, dissatisfactions with 371n32
Evolution 1, 5, 30, 33, 34n60, 35, 36, 43, 46, 54n8, 63, 88, 95, 96, 168n29, 193, 208, 230n5, 238n21, 245, 282, 299, 351–52, 374
Evolutionary constraints 2, 36
Experts, trust in 120, 125, 130, 131, 132, 180

Family size 377n42, 396
Feinberg, Joel 106n56
Female education 377
   See also Population growth, Family size
Film 14, 252, 258, 264, 265, 268, 279, 283, 286, 289, 295, 308, 318
Findlay, Ronald 62n36
Firth, Raymond 33n52
Fletcher, John 257
Flory, James 240n24
Fodor, Jerry 237n17
Foot, Philippa 182n55
Ford, John 257
Foreign languages 16, 151, 256, 307–10, 318
Foucault, Michel 32n50
Frankfurt, Harry 336n25
Fraternity See Solidarity
Free market 19, 28n37, 53, 123, 128, 305, 377n40, 379–86, 395–96
Free speech 8, 199n14, 125–26
Freedom 7, 30, 38, 84, 93, 119, 120, 125, 126n30, 127, 136, 137, 138, 139, 141, 148, 176, 268n23, 286, 344, 388, 395–96
   Negative freedom 148, 286n13
   Positive freedom 148, 286

410 INDEX

French, Tana 261
Freud, Sigmund 306
Frey, C.B. 67n39
Fried, Michael 289n17
Fry, Stephen 269
Fulfillment 4, 5, 6, 7, 9–10, 15, 16–17, 38,
    40–41, 44, 52, 68, 74, 75, 77, 78, 81–115,
    122, 140, 147, 149, 157, 181n54, 191,
    227, 231, 232, 267, 295–96, 316, 319,
    324, 331, 332, 338, 356, 357, 362, 368,
    374, 387, 389, 391–93
Fundamentalism
    Market 380
    Religious, 10, 192, 199, 213

Galbraith, John Kenneth 332nn18, 19
Galileo 180, 272
Galison, Peter 172n36
Galton, Francis 253
Garcia, Claire Watson 270n27
Gardening 275
Garfinkel, Alan 237n18
Garrett, Laurie 374n34
Gaus, Gerald 193n6
Gauss, Christian 139
Gebert, Konstanty 136n53
Geisteswissenschaften 281, 285, 319
Genetics 233, 239–40, 242n27, 247n37
Geography 15, 151, 286–88, 298, 300–301, 318
Geometry 28n37, 55, 56, 130, 304
Gibbon, Edward 310n55
Gilligan, Carol 158n10
Globalization 5. *See also* Global warming;
    Democracy, global; Economic
    competition
Global warming 3, 132–34, 135n49, 376,
    377. *See also* Climate change
Glover, Jonathan 177n42
Goldin, Claudia 328nn9, 10
Goldman, Alvin 128n33
Goodall, Jane 391
Goodman, Nelson 262n14
Gopnik, Alison 105n55
Gould, Stephen Jay 105n54, 240n23, 352n8
Gove, Michael 120n15
Graham, Patricia Albjerg 31nn47, 49,
    154n5
Grandin, Temple 392

Gray, John 233n11
Gray, Thomas (*Elegy in a Country
    Churchyard*) 50
Greene, Robert 257
Growth theory 364n25
Gruen, Lori 85n11
Gumbrecht, Hans Ulrich 272n30
Gutmann, Amy 121n20
Gutting, Gary 32n50

Habermas, Jürgen 121n20, 193n6
Haidt, Jonathan 158n10
Happiness 27, 33, 91, 99–100, 114, 351
Harris, Paul 48n91, 128
Harris, Sam 192n4
Harrist, Robert 289n17
Hayek, Friedrich 381–82
Heathorn, Henrietta Anne 359
Heckman, James J. 48n91, 75n57
Hedonism 39n70, 91, 99, 100, 101, 229, 261
    Communal 39n70, 100–101, 229, 261
Hegre, Håvard 376n38
Hempel, Sandra 247n36
Hierarchy 95, 161, 246, 307, 332, 335, 381,
    395
History
    Contingency in 37, 42, 48, 350
    Of American schools 4, 30–32
    Of moral life 9, 89, 95, 111, 140, 141,
        153–56, 158–59, 162–65, 168, 173–
        181, 183–85, 193, 196, 204, 207, 210,
        212, 222, 229, 288, 298–301, 311
    Role in the curriculum 16, 23n6, 24,
        65–66, 151, 188, 230, 247–48, 249,
        281, 286, 287, 302, 307, 318
    See also Education, history of;
        Education, prehistory of
Hitchcock, David 125n27
Hitchens, Christopher 192n4
Hobbes, Thomas 177
Hochschild, Arlie Russell 296
Hodder, Ian 33n55
Honneth, Axel 102n42
Hood, Don 246n34
Hooke, Robert 230n7
Hull, David 236n15
Humanism 10, 40, 83, 89, 90, 160, 191,
    192n2, 194, 199, 200, 210–15, 388

INDEX 411

Humanities, role in education of 15–16, 23, 29, 42, 246, 256–57, 281–319 *passim*.
See also Foreign Languages; History; Literature; Philosophy
Hume, David 174, 350n1
Hutcheson, Francis 350n1
Huxley, Aldous 91n22
Huxley, Thomas Henry 359

Ideals, in education 30, 43, 46, 74, 76n59, 324, 325–26
Ideals of the self 157, 182–85, 285, 324
Ideals, role of 44–46, 48, 92, 143, 325–26
Individualism 41n78, 106, 344
Individuality 4, 6, 7, 9, 15, 20, 26–27, 30, 34, 38–43, 47, 52, 68, 83, 84, 90, 93–95, 102–10, 113, 139–40, 147, 180, 184, 227, 229, 231–32, 246, 251, 264, 271, 272, 277–79, 285–86, 296, 309–10, 313, 315–17, 329, 331, 333, 337, 341–42, 347–48, 365, 368, 370
Inequality 133, 159, 331–36, 341, 377n39, 384n51
Information sources, troubles of 122–29, 142, 251, 302–303
Integration, racial 30, 31, 43, 184, 305n46, 327, 339–40, 371
Ionesco, Eugene 258
Ishiguro, Kazuo 283n6

Jacoby, Susan 118n11
Jaeggi, Rahel 102n42, 105n52, 177n43
James, William 134n48, 176, 210, 212, 306, 386–87
John of Salisbury 230n7
Jones, Todd 265n20
Jonson, Ben 257
Joyce, James 96–97, 109–10, 195n11, 196n12, 260, 262, 266, 293n25
Jurisprudence 24, 303

Kahan, Dan M. 133n47, 135n49
Kant, Immanuel 10, 11, 38, 99, 167–68, 195–99, 200, 206, 207, 210, 213–15, 217, 219, 220, 296n29, 376n38
Kant's insight 11, 195–99, 206, 207, 210, 213–15, 217, 219, 221n48

Karapakula, Ganesh 48n91, 75n57
Kavala, Osman 312n58
Keller, Evelyn Fox 118nn8, 9, 249n42, 374nn35, 36
Kevles, Daniel 240n23
Kharas, Homi 377n42
Kierkegaard, Søren 200–201
Kohlberg, Lawrence 158n10
Korsgaard, Christine 85n11, 393n3
Kozol, Jonathan 79n2, 326n6
Kuhl, Patricia 105n55
Kuhn, T.S. 283n8
Kyd, Thomas 257

Ladd, Helen F. 29n42, 94n28
Lareau, Annette, 48n91, 80n4, 148n70, 339n30
Lawrence, D.H. 324n1
Lee, Richard 33n52
Lepännen, Sirpa 309n54
Levi, Isaac 304n40
Levins, Richard 168n29, 238n21
Levinson, Meira 19n2, 28, 79n2, 90n21, 101n39, 107n60, 108nn61, 62, 117n5
Levitsky, Steven 118n11, 120n18
Lewis, David 137n54, 198n14, 215n36
Lewis, Stephanie 198n14
Liberal education 23, 27, 28n37, 52, 61, 64–65, 307
Liberal tradition 6, 38, 39–40, 77, 93–103. See also Autonomy; Life plan
Life plan 6, 7, 45, 83–84, 97, 104, 108, 182, 229, 285, 348, 358
Lincoln, Abraham 263
Lippmann, Walter 122n21, 130n37
Literacy 13, 15, 34, 54, 233, 243, 245, 247, 248n38, 253, 256, 272, 292, 316, 368
Literary criticism 284, 288, 289
Literature 14, 23nn5, 6, 59, 65–66, 247, 256, 264–66, 273, 274n32, 276, 277, 279, 282n3, 286, 288–93, 295, 298, 301, 307, 308n50, 318
Locke, John 177, 180, 312
Loeb, Susanna 29n42, 94n28
Logic 24, 130, 248

Mahler, Gustav 295
Malthus, Thomas 283, 284n9, 385

412 INDEX

Mann, Thomas 109, 110, 260, 289n17
Marlowe, Christopher 257
Marx, Karl 28n37, 57–58, 59, 72n49, 73, 75, 351, 353
Mathematics 24, 42, 45, 53, 62, 130, 243, 245, 254, 282n3, 290, 304, 316, 382n47
Mather, Cotton 165n17, 206
Matthews, Michael R. 247n35
McBrearty, Sally 33n54
McCutcheon v. FEC 119n14
McKinsey 67n39
McMansions 375
Meaning, in human lives 38, 74, 91, 99, 102, 230, 231n9
  Religious perspective on 89–90, 99
Mechanics 28n37, 55, 56
Meltzhoff, Andrew 105n55
Mendel, Gregor 240, 247n37
Meritocracy 232, 331, 337, 338
Methodological guidelines 36, 37, 77
Middleton, Thomas 257
Milgram, Stanley 172n34, 196n13, 306n49
Military spending 375–76
Mill, John Stuart 4, 6, 8, 19, 23–26, 27, 33n53, 35, 37, 38, 39–40, 44, 46, 50, 61n32, 79, 93, 95n29, 99, 101n37, 102, 106n58, 108, 126, 128n32, 136, 157, 166, 184n58, 214, 215, 273, 284, 301n36, 302nn37, 38, 385–87, 388, 395
  Inaugural address 4, 23–26, 35, 37, 38, 39–40, 41, 44, 46, 48, 79, 81, 130, 151, 154, 214, 273, 284, 385, 388
  On political economy 385–87
Millian arena 126–28, 131–32
Millian democracy 127, 129, 131, 134–36, 140, 147–49, 301
Milton, John 125–26, 388–89
Mind, development of 56–57, 59, 103–105, 184
Molecular biology 61, 129, 237, 139, 241, 242
Molière 282, 307
Monet, Claude 261n10
Moody-Adams, Michele 145n67
Moral code 155–62, 169, 170, 172, 173, 182, 184, 185
Moral deliberation *see* Moral practice

Moral development, role of education in 9, 10, 15, 106, 153–61, 186–90, 214, 266, 307, 313–14, 318–19
Moral intuition 156, 168–72
Moral practice 162–63, 169, 172, 173, 186
Moral progress 9, 85, 157, 163, 174–81, 183–86, 313, 315
Morality,
  As grounded in religion 154, 164–65, 195–99
  Consequentialism 166–68
  In prehistory 173–75
  Kantian 167–68
  Priority of 195–96, 199, 205–207
  Ur-problem of 174–75, 177, 181, 186
Morris, William 360n21
Morrison, Toni 264, 265, 267, 297n33
Mössner, Nicola 120n17,
Moyers, Bill 269n24
Muir, John 393
Müller, Jan-Werner 121n19
Müller, Wilhelm 294n26
Music, history of 14, 246, 256, 258, 266, 288, 289–93,
Musil, Robert 260

Nagel, Thomas 168n28
Natural sciences 12–13, 15, 46n87, 129, 184n59, 227–55
Natural sciences, and understanding of nature 14, 242–43, 250
Natural sciences, contributions to technology of 14, 61, 241–43
Natural sciences, general education in 13, 243–50
Natural sciences, progress in 13, 232–39, 240, 248, 257–59
Natural selection 86–88, 283, 351–52, 364n26
Naturwissenschaften 281
Nehamas, Alexander 291
Neill, A.S. 29, 149n71, 189n64
Neimann, Susan 299n34
Neurath, Otto 262n14
Newman, John Henry 27–28, 31, 61n32,
Newton, Isaac 13, 42, 180, 230, 236n14, 238
Nietzsche, Friedrich 32n50, 104, 106, 107n59, 110n67, 115n74, 231n8, 335n23, 94n28, 102n40,

INDEX 413

Nordhaus, William 374
Nozick, Robert 91n22, 180n50
Nussbaum, Martha C. 29, 38n65, 51n2,
61n32, 86n15, 117nn5, 7, 141n62,
177n42, 219n41, 220n44, 223n52,
257n3, 268n23, 271n30, 308nn50, 51,
331n14

O'Flaherty, Dan 43n81, 68n40, 114n71,
305n44, 328n9
Oakeshott, Michael 29, 32, 37n63, 229,
230n4
Oreskes, Naomi 132n42
Orthogenesis
In economics 351–53
In biological evolution 351–52
Orwell, George 72n50, 119n14, 264, 267,
297n33, 330
Osborne, M.A. 67n39
Overload 3–5, 10, 26–37, 41, 46, 79, 124,
228, 269, 342
Owen, Wilfred 201–202, 265

Packard, Vance 332n19
Pagels, Elaine 193n5
Pandemics 248n38, 253, 328, 331, 344,
373–74, 376–77
Panfil, Orna 270n26
Parfit, Derek 165n18, 357nn17, 18
PARO 70
Pater, Walter 96n31
Peaceable Kingdom Thinking 86–87
Peacocke, Christopher 295n26
Peele, George 257
Pemberton, Caroline K. 240n31
Peter the Hermit 153
Peters, R.S. 229, 230n4
Petersen, Sandra 70n45
Peterson, Martin 304n39
Petty, William 350n1
Pew survey research 74–75, 290n18,
362n23
Pfaff, John 305n44
Philosophy 6, 16, 23n6, 24, 25, 26, 38, 46,
47, 66, 103n47, 155, 157, 165, 169,
170n31, 173, 222, 249, 281, 289n16,
314–15
Of education 2, 46, 51n2, 108n61, 247n35

Physics 24, 233, 237, 242n27, 243, 244,
245, 246, 258, 283
Piketty, Thomas 384n51
Pinamonti, Giovanni 196n12
Pinker, Steven 81n5, 306n48
Pinter, Harold 258
Plato 10, 26–27, 28n36, 51n3, 79, 139, 154,
314, 372
Pluralism 221–23
Polanyi, Karl 54n5, 379
Political liberalism 193n6, 220–23. See also
Rawls, John
Political theory 15, 372
Population growth 355–57
Pound, Ezra 258
Poverty 16, 81, 124, 133, 286,
323, 384
Pragmatism 46, 48, 142, 387
Pritchard, James B. 34n56
Probability 130, 248, 304, 355, 361, 363,
365, 368
Proctor, Robert 129n35
Productivity,
Supposed economic importance of 18,
19, 42, 68, 69, 227, 243, 256, 324, 345,
346n42, 347, 350, 353, 356, 358, 359,
377–78, 385–86
International comparisons of 243, 347,
365–70
Professional training 23, 35, 79,
166n20, 244
Progress, 6
Pragmatic 44, 46, 48, 107n60, 112–13,
143n66, 214, 239–42, 258–59, 325n5,
326, 387
Social 38, 42, 44, 45, 47, 74, 92, 109n64,
203n19, 228–32, 240–42, 250, 272,
280, 300, 315, 387
Teleological 48, 92n23, 173, 213,
234–39,
Proust, Marcel 260, 266
Prum, Richard 352n8
Psychology 15, 24, 281, 282, 288, 302,
306–307, 318
Putnam, Robert 148

Quesnay, François 350n1
Quine, W.V. 262n14

414 INDEX

Ravitch, Diane 31n48
Rawls, John 38, 39, 121n20, 167n27,
    193n6, 220–23
Reading levels, international statistics
    290–91
Regan, Tom 85n11, 393n3
Relethford, J.H. 340n32
Religion 10–11, 154, 160, 164, 188,
    191–223, 281
    Ecumenical 11, 89–90, 204–11, 213–19,
    220
    Refined 11, 209–13, 215, 218, 228,
    Role in education 10, 214–19
    Tribal 11, 203, 205, 207, 211, 213, 215,
    216, 217, 221
Rendell, Ruth 261
Renfrew, Colin 33n54
Restrepo, Pascual 68n40
Rilke, Rainer Maria 261n9
Robots 5, 67–70, 73, 243, 316, 346. *See also*
    CARESSES, PARO
Robinson, John 210
Rolling Stones 258
Rosenberg, Alexander 281n2
Roth, Alvin 384, 385
Rothschild, Michael 383n48
Rousseau, Jean-Jacques 27
Rowley, William 257
Rowling, J.K. 274n32, 293n24
Rudwick, Martin 247n36
Runciman, David 118n11
Ruskin, John 360n21

Sachs, Jeffrey 133n45
Saez, Emmanuel 384n51
Saffin, John 165n17
Salk, Jonas 255
Same-sex love, increasing acceptance of 9,
    157, 197, 300
Sanskrit 311
Scanlon, T.M. 167n27, 168n28
Schacht, Richard 295n27
Scheffler, Israel 51n2, 262n13
Schelling, Thomas 305
Schiebinger, Londa 129n35
Schoenberg, Arnold 258
Schools
    American, history of 4, 30

Failures of 51, 79, 323–27
Origins of 3, 34
Schopenhauer, Arthur 115n74
Schubert, Franz 294
Science
    Benefits of 14, 232, 240–43, 253
    Lay view of 241–42, 243, 250, 251,
    254–55, 257, 258
    Official view of 242–43, 250, 251, 257
Scientism 281–82, 283n5, 305
Sculpture 258, 264, 289
Sedgwick, Henry 166
Self-understanding 15, 16, 110, 111, 284–85,
    290, 291n20, 293, 317, 319
Sen, Amartya 94n28, 177n42, 336n25,
    377n42
Sentient beings 20, 83, 85–89, 232, 233,
    391–93
Seoul National University 42
Service work 5, 16, 52, 68–75, 316, 342, 346
    Stigma of 52, 70–73, 75, 346
Sethi, Rajiv 305n44
Sewing 15, 275
Shelley, Percy Bysshe 388
Shennan, Stephen 33n54
Shostak, Marjorie 33n52
Shutts, Kristin 340n31
Siegel, Harvey 19n2, 46n87, 51n2, 103n44,
    109n63, 124n27, 241n26, 262n13
Significant questions 232, 240, 305,
    315n63
Simon and Garfunkel 258
Singer, Peter 85n11, 166
Sissman, Elaine 289n17,
Skinner, B.F. 306
Slavery, abolition of 9, 157, 159–60, 163,
    164–65, 175–76, 179, 206n20, 263,
    299, 311
Smith, Adam 5, 28n37, 51, 53–63, 66, 73,
    114, 137, 350–51, 353, 362, 379–80
Smith, Pamela 283n7
Smith's Principle 51–52, 55, 58–61, 64, 67,
    73, 78, 81
Snow, C.P. 283n5
Social change 6, 17, 36, 45, 72, 76n59, 77,
    107n60, 114n70, 157, 185, 203n19,
    299–300, 305, 317, 319, 323–49, 372,
    376. *See also* Progress, social

INDEX 415

Social sciences 15–16, 42, 130n36, 281–82, 284, 286, 288, 301, 302, 303, 305–306, 317, 323, 363
Sociology 15, 66, 281, 288, 302, 318
Socrates 6, 27, 90, 110
Socratic question 6, 38, 84, 90–96, 101, 110, 111, 113, 229
  Liberal approach to 38–39, 93–96, 99–102
Soler, Meritxell Valenti 70n45
Solidarity 136–37, 139–41, 144, 175, 329, 332
Solow, Robert 364n25
Sophocles 258, 266
South Korean university entrance exam 42–43
Special needs, responses to 338
Spelke, Elizabeth S. 340n31
Spence, Michael 383n48
Spong, John Shelby 210
Stationary state 19, 385–86
Steele, Claude 306n49, 342n33
Steiner, George 282, 283n5, 292
STEM program 45, 51, 56, 243, 245, 256, 257
Stendhal 282, 307
Stephen, Fitzjames 134n48, 387
Stereotypes 16, 17, 107n60, 114n70, 246n33, 263, 306, 323, 328, 340–42, 348
Stiglitz, Joseph 383n48
Stonewall bar 176
Stowe, Harriet Beecher 183n57, 263–65, 267, 297n33, 298
Success condition 39, 102, 110, 112
Sustar, Predrag 127n31
Swift, Adam 29n42, 94n28

Tagore, Rabindranath 19, 141, 210n26, 260n8, 268n23
Taste, variation in 14, 107, 273–74, 275, 277–90
  Egalitarianism 274, 276
  Elitism 274–75
  Moderate Egalitarianism 274–77
Taylor, Charles 212
Teachers, pay of 5, 16, 70, 75, 79, 323, 326–27, 330, 335n24, 375
Television 101n39, 123–24, 289, 291
Tennyson, Alfred 258
Thompson, Dennis 121n20

Thomson, Judith Jarvis 169
Thrane, J.R. 196n12
Thunberg, Greta 132
Thurber, James 249
Tillich, Paul 210
Tocqueville, Alexis de 116, 117, 118, 121, 134–36
Tolstoy, Leo 115n74
Town meetings 116–17, 141, 142, 350
Turco, Lewis 269n24
Turgot, Anne Robert Jacques 350n1

Unemployment 18, 52, 124, 352
Unified science 236–39
Universities, history of 3, 35, 54, 57, 66
Useless labor 17, 53, 62n36, 330–31

Valentini, James 249n41
Van der Hoeven, Jeroen 167
Van Fraassen, Bas 235n13
Van Parijs, Philippe 334n22, 377n39
Vanderborght, Yannick 334n22, 377n29
Varian, Hal 382n47
Veblen, Thorsten 332nn17, 19
Vendler, Helen 269
Verdi, Giuseppe 258
Vickers, A. Leah 306n48
Visual art 14, 256, 266, 268n23, 269, 270, 273, 277, 279, 286, 288, 289, 292, 293, 297
Von Humboldt, Wilhelm 38
Voting 7–8, 119, 123, 125, 142, 145, 148, 175n38, 301
  Condorcet, ranked choice 119
  Tyranny of 122, 135–37

Wagner, Richard 109, 110
Warren, Elizabeth 377n39
Washington, Booker T. 50–51
Wawro, Gregory 246n34
Waypoint Robotics 70
Webern, Anton 258
Webster, John 257
Weinberg, Steven 166n21
White, John 27n33
Whitehead, A.N 27n33, 269n25
Wilde, Oscar 101n39, 176

416 INDEX

Williams, Bernard 38, 166n24, 181n53, 182n55
Williams, Gareth 246n34
Wilson, E.O. 281n2
Winner, Ellen 266n22, 297n32
Wolf, Susan 38, 102n41
Women's opportunities, expansion of 9, 41, 101, 107, 157, 175, 176, 183–84, 300
Woolf, Virginia 260, 293n24
Wordsworth, William 25, 83n9, 260n8, 266

Work 4, 5, 17, 30, 51, 52, 55, 57, 59, 61–78, 79, 81, 251–52, 316, 323, 328, 331–32, 334, 336–37, 342, 344, 345, 346, 348
Working time 345–46, 348, 368–69
Worrall, Jennifer 270n26

Yeats, W.B. 258
Yi, Chin-Yun 43n83

Zajc, William 246n34
Ziblatt, Daniel 118n11, 120n18
Zucman, Gabriel 384n51